Commercial Property and Multiple-Lines Underwriting

Commercial Property and Multiple-Lines Underwriting

E.P. HOLLINGSWORTH, CPCU, ARM
Vice President
Frank B. Hall & Co. Inc.

J.J. LAUNIE, Ph.D., CPCU
Professor of Finance and Insurance
California State University, Northridge

Second Edition • 1984

INSURANCE INSTITUTE OF AMERICA
Providence and Sugartown Roads, Malvern, Pennsylvania 19355

Preface

This text completes the four-volume series used in the Associate in Underwriting (AIU) Program. The first chapter presents an overview of the subject matter together with a consideration of property valuation. The second chapter contains an analysis of the characteristics, chemistry, and physics of fire, the dominant peril for property and fixed locations. This is followed by four chapters which consider the COPE factors of fire underwriting—Construction, Occupancy, Protection, and Exposures. Chapter 7 also deals with coverage as an underwriting variable. Chapter 8 covers indirect property loss exposures and underwriting. This is followed by a chapter on pricing. The next two chapters cover inland and ocean marine. Chapter 12 covers crime insurance. The final chapter contains a discussion of package policy underwriting and a capstone case study.

Each manuscript chapter for the first edition was reviewed by a group of insurance educators and practitioners. The authors deeply appreciate the critical reviews submitted by the following persons: Jack Adee, Ocean Marine Manager, Fireman's Fund Insurance Companies; Robert N. Barnes, CPCU, ARM, Director Commerical Property Underwriting, Employers Casualty Company; Edward B. Black, CPCU, Retired; Richard F. Blizzard, Secretary, Manager, Insurance Company of North America; Maurice R. Boulais, P.E., Senior Engineering Officer, Allendale Mutual Insurance Company; John M. Bowdish, CPCU, Commercial Lines Underwriter, Kemper Insurance Group; Howard Buckley, Senior Specialist, Marine (Retired), Crum & Forster Insurance Companies; Clarence Costa, CPCU, Assistant Manager, Fireman's Fund Insurance Companies; Walter J. Cowan, Manager Commerical Fire and Inland Marine, Commerical Union Assurance Companies; Garret S. Ditmars, CPCU, Senior Vice President, Inamar Ltd.; James T. Dunn, Commercial Inland Marine Underwriting Officer, Kemper Insurance Companies; John H. Ellen, CPCU, ARM, Proprietor, Insurance and Risk Management Services; John J. Ficeli, CPCU, ARM, Vice President, RMS, Inc.; W. D. Glass, CPCU, Vice President, Trinity Universal Insurance Company; Byron F. Goodloe, Commercial Inland Marine Specialist, Kemper Insurance Companies; Russell Hawkes, Commercial Lines Manager, Fireman's Fund Insurance Companies; George H. Kasbohm, CPCU, ARM, Vice President, Underwriting, Kemper Insurance Group; Tony Lane, Senior Product Manager, Insurance Company of North America; Malcolm H. Leggett, Senior Vice President, Commercial Union Assurance Companies; Harold R. Marsh, CPCU, Facultative Property Director, Allstate Insurance Company; Thomas M. Patton, Bond Underwriting Officer, Kemper Insurance Companies; Thomas A. Pine, CPCU, Account Manager, The Graham Company; David Rechner, Senior Commercial Underwriter, Allstate Insurance Company; Werner Reiners, Manager—Fidelity/Crime, Commercial Union Assurance Companies; Richard F. Rohan, Assistant Vice President of Loss Control, Crum & Forster Insurance Companies; Barry D. Smith, Ph.D., CPCU, CLU, FLMI, The Wharton School of Business, University of Pennsylvania; Leland T. Stowe, CPCU, ARM, Vice President, Alexander & Alexander of Texas, Inc.; Robert J. Throckmorton, Bond Director, Allstate Insurance Company; William N. Weld, CPCU, ARM, Vice President, Frank B. Hall & Co. Inc.; Homer O. White, Jr., CPCU, Secretary (Retired), Insurance Company of North America; George L. Yeager, Senior Vice President—Underwriting, Commercial Property, Crum & Forster Insurance Companies.

J. J. Launie would like to acknowledge an intellectual debt to James D. Ellett, CPCU, James D. Ellett Insurance Agency, Reno, Nevada, who introduced him to the mysteries of fire underwriting more years ago than either of them would care to remember. J. J. Launie would also like to acknowledge the kind assistance of Martha Curtis of NFPA, Quincy, Massachusetts, in gathering data for several exhibits.

This text would not have been possible except for the efforts of the staff of the Insurance Institute of America. The authors accept full responsibility for any errors which remain. The reader is urged to contact the authors with suggestions which will help make the next edition an even more valuable resource for the property underwriter.

E. P. Hollingsworth
J. J. Launie

Contributing Authors

The Insurance Institute of America and the authors acknowledge, with deep appreciation, the help of the following contributing authors whose manuscripts, written in their areas of expertise, served as the basis of the first edition of this book:

Steven M. Burns
Vice President Commercial Lines
American Association of Insurance Services

Walter E. Frasier, Jr., CPCU
Resident Secretary
Fireman's Fund Insurance Companies

Jerry Gallogly, CPCU
Vice President—Underwriting Administration
American States Insurance Companies

Bob A. Hedges, Ph.D., CPCU, CLU
Professor of Insurance and Risk
Temple University

Keith Kenway, CPCU, ARM
Casualty Manager
Reliance Specialty Lines

Malcolm H. Leggett
Senior Vice President
Commercial Union Assurance Companies

Harold R. Marsh, CPCU
Facultative Property Director
Allstate Insurance Company

Milton M. Nachbar, P.E., CPCU
Property Underwriting Director
Allstate Insurance Company

Dennis A. Stimeling, CPCU
Assistant Vice President
CIGNA Companies

William J. Taylor, CPCU
Special Risks Underwriter
Kemper Insurance Group

Table of Contents

Chapter 1—Introduction to Commercial Property Underwriting... 1

Historical Development ~ *Conflagrations; Additional Perils*

Commercial Property and Commercial Liability Underwriting Compared ~ *First Party Versus Third Party; Dynamics of Historical Development and Underwriting; Insurable Interest; Claims Settlement; Measures of Loss Severity; Loss Development Pricing Comparisons*

Determination of Value ~ *Actual Cash Value (ACV); Replacement Cost Valuation; Valued Policies*

Appraising Values Exposed to Loss ~ *Rules of Thumb; National Indexes; Appraisals; Special Valuation Problems*

Summary

Chapter 2—Analyzing Loss Potential from Fire............ 39

Introduction

Sources of Ignition ~ *Heating Devices; Cooking Equipment; Welding and Cutting; Mobile Heat Generators; Hot Liquids; Electrical Wiring and Equipment; Friction Static Electricity; Spontaneous Ignition; Chemical Reactions; Other Sources*

Fuels ~ *Flammability or Combustibility; Products of Combustion; Buildings as Fuel; Housekeeping; Common Fuels for Heat and Power*

Oxygen for Fires ~ *Atmospheric Oxygen; Oxidants*

Fire Spread and Extent ~ *Heat Spread; Flame Spread; Likely Damage*

Arson ~ *The Problem; Solution Efforts*

Analysis of Ownership and Management ~ *Financial Analysis for Hazard Evaluation*

Summary

Chapter 3—Analyzing Loss Potential from Other Major Perils 81

Introduction

Explosion ~ *Confined Spaces Other Than Pressure Vessels; Pressure Vessels*

Sprinkler Leakage and Water Damage ~ *Sprinkler Leakage; Water Damage; Factors Affecting Sprinkler Leakage and Water Damage Losses*

Riot and Civil Commotion ~ *Definitions; Incidence of Riot and Civil Commotion; The Urban Riots and Their Influence on Insurance*

Vandalism or Malicious Mischief ~ *Incidence; Dealing with the Vandalism Exposure*

Earthquake and Other Earth Movement ~ *Earthquake; Other Earth Movement*

Flood ~ *Flood and the Private Sector; The Scope of the Flood Problem; Flood Causes; Flood Incidence; Determining Flood Exposures; Flood Protection*

Windstorm and Hail ~ *Hurricanes; Storm Surge and Heavy Rainfall; Tornadoes; Hail*

Collapse ~ *Collapse; Principal Causes of Collapse Loss*

Catastrophe Underwriting ~ *Reinsurance Considerations; Development of a Sample Catastrophe Control Plan*

Summary

Chapter 4—Construction **131**

COPE ~ *Construction; Occupancy, Protection, and Exposures*

Fire Resistance and Flame Spread ~ *Fire Resistance; Flame Spread*

Building Construction Classifications ~ *Frame; Joisted Masonry; Noncombustible; Masonry Noncombustible; Modified Fire Resistive; Fire Resistive; Mixed Construction*

Construction Design ~ *High-Rise Buildings; Fire Divisions; Building Openings*

Construction Materials ~ *Insulation; Roofing; Other Factors*

Age ~ *Age and Perils*

Sources of Construction Information ~ *Applications; Rate Cards and Manuals; Bureau Reports; Inspection Reports and Diagrams; Local Building Codes*

Builders' Risk ~ *Course of Construction Coverage; Perils Insured Against; Builders' Risk and Probable Maximum Loss; Builders' Risk Selection Decisions*

Summary

Chapter 5—Occupancy **171**

Introduction

The Rating of Occupancy Hazards ~ *The Basic Occupancy Charge; Combustibility; Susceptibility; Additional Classifications of Contents*

Common and Special Hazards

Occupancy Hazards Grouped by Major Categories ~ *Habitational; Offices; Institutions; Mercantile Occupancies; Service Occupancies; Manufacturing and Wholesale Distribution*

Hazards of Representative Occupancy Classes ~ *Restaurant; Bowling Alleys; Commercial Printing; Grain Elevators*

Summary

Chapter 6—Protection 203

Introduction ~ *Elements of Fire Protection*

Public Protection Systems ~ *Rating of a Municipality's Fire Defense; Other Public Protection Services*

Private Fire Prevention Systems ~ *Major Elements of Private Fire Prevention; Commercial Fire Loss Control Programs*

Private Fire Detection Systems ~ *Control of Loss Severity; Watch Service Systems; Automatic Systems*

Private Extinguishment Systems ~ *Portable Fire Extinguishers; Standpipe and Hose Systems; Automatic Sprinkler Systems; Fire Brigades; Extinguishment Systems as a Hazard*

Protection as a Variable in Underwriting Decisions ~ *Effect on Premium; Effect on a Book of Business*

Summary

Chapter 7—External Exposures and Coverages 247

Analyzing External Exposures ~ *Introduction; Major Considerations; Factors Influencing the Severity of Exposures; Control of External Exposures*

Analyzing Insurance Contracts as a Variable in Underwriting Decisions ~ *Modifying Coverage; Warranties; Insurable Interests; Assignment; Duties of the Insured; Mortgagee Clause; Term*

Insurance to Value ~ *Valuation Clauses; Extensions of Coverage; Other Extensions of Coverage; Fluctuating Values at Risk; Replacement Cost Coverage*

Summary

Chapter 8—Underwriting Commercial Indirect
Property Losses 271

Introduction ~ *Indirect Loss Exposures; Indirect Loss Coverages; Business Interruption or Extra Expense?*

Business Interruption ~ *Gross Earnings Form; Valued or Per Diem Forms*

Extra Expense ~ *Coverage; Determination of the Amount of Insurance; Rating Extra Expense; Underwriting Considerations; Contingent Extra Expense; Combined Business Interruption and Extra Expense*

Other Indirect Loss Coverages ~ *Consequential Loss; Rental Value; Leasehold Interest; Tuition Fees Insurance; Demolition Costs; Contingent Liability from Operation of Building Laws; and Increased Cost of Construction Forms*

Summary

Chapter 9—Pricing... 317

Introduction

Fire Insurance Rates ~ *Class Rating; Specific (Schedule) Rating; Other Components of the Rate; Deductibles; Underwriting Factors Not Included in the Rates*

Fire Insurance Rate Review ~ *Experience Period; Statistical Period; Expenses; Large Losses; Credibility; Trending; Statewide Rate Adjustment; Class Relativities*

Rate Making for Extended Coverage Perils ~ *Experience Period; Catastrophe Evaluation*

Effect of Rate on Underwriting ~ *Understanding the Rate; Appropriateness of the Rate*

Summary

Chapter 10—Underwriting Commercial Inland Marine Insurance..................................... 351

The Definition of Marine Insurance ~ *The Importance of the Nation-Wide Definition*

Filed and Nonfiled Classes

Inland Marine Policy Terms and Conditions ~ *Valuation; Limitations on Partial Losses; Permissive and Restrictive Clauses Common to Inland Marine Policies*

Underwriting Inland Marine Coverages ~ *Property in Transit; Transportation Insurance; Instrumentalities of Transportation and Communication; Scheduled and Blanket Equipment Floaters; Bailees' Customers Policies; Block Policies; Miscellaneous Inland Marine Coverages; Manuscript Policies*

Summary

Chapter 11—Underwriting Commercial Ocean Marine Insurance 393

Introduction ~ *Multiple Perils Coverage; Valued Policy*

Underwriting Variables—Commercial Hulls ~ *The American Hull Insurance Syndicate (AHIS); The Water Quality Insurance Syndicate (WQIS); Coverage; Commercial Hull Hazards and Exposures*

Underwriting Variables—Protection and Indemnity (P&I) ~ *Coverage; Analysis of Protection and Indemnity Hazards and Exposures*

Underwriting Variables—Ocean Cargo ~ *Insurable Interest; Methods of Payment; Ocean Carrier's Liability; Types of Coverage; Coverage Provisions of the Open Ocean Cargo Policy; Underwriting Ocean Cargo Policies; Ocean Cargo Loss Control*

Summary

Chapter 12—Underwriting Commercial Crime Insurance 437

Introduction ~ *Definitions in Commercial Crime Insurance*

The Construction of Crime Policies

Conditions and Terms of Coverage ~ *Perils Insured Against; Limits of Liability; Deductibles; Warranties; Pricing and Loss Control*

Underwriting Decision-Making for Crime Insurance ~ *Assessing Crime Loss Potential; Types of Private Protection; Moral and Morale Hazard; Adverse Selection; Crime Underwriting Options*

Fidelity ~ *Fidelity Underwriting; Fidelity Loss Control*

Computer Crime ~ *Computer Security Considerations*

Summary

Chapter 13—Underwriting Other Property Lines and Package Policies...................................... 469

Introduction

Underwriting Specialty Property Lines ~ *Boiler and Machinery Insurance; Glass Insurance; Difference in Conditions; Crop Hail Insurance; Rain Insurance*

Underwriting Package Policies ~ *Kinds of Package Policies; Underwriting Considerations*

Underwriting Large Commercial Property Risks

Narragansett Manufacturing Co., Inc. Case Study ~ *Gathering Data and the Preliminary Commitment; Analyzing the Submission; Calculation of Exposure*

Summary

Bibliography... 539

Index... 543

CHAPTER 1

Introduction to Commercial Property Underwriting

It has been said that "insurance is the handmaiden of industry." In fact, commerce throughout the world is heavily dependent on insurance. Bankers and most other creditors seldom make loans on ventures without insisting on insurance protection from floods, fires, and other disasters that can and do occasionally befall factories, machines, trucks, raw materials, warehouses, and finished merchandise. Nor are the commercial venturers, the owners themselves, eager to have their goods and possessions subject to such losses in the absence of insurance protection. Without insurance, then, it is probably accurate to say, there would be no commerce.

On the other hand, without property there would be no insurance, not even general liability or workers' compensation insurance. Property, strictly construed, is the right of use and includes all manner of tangible objects and goods such as land, buildings, minerals, furniture, equipment, space, and so on. A person's or business firm's good name, while intangible, also is property. And through the centuries *all* these items of property, whether tangible or intangible, have had value to people. Frequently the value is objective, measured in terms of money. Even a firm's good name, or rather its goodwill, has found a place on balance sheets.

Those having title, ownership, or the right of use, therefore, have valuable assets. In the absence of assets, there is nothing to lose. Surely a person with no property has no need for fire insurance; and clearly the right to sue a person with no property through negligence or statutory law does not profit a third-party claimant.

The many forms of property and the limitless ways they can be destroyed or their value severely diminished naturally give rise to more

1

types of property risks and insurance than any one book could hope to cover. It is the intention here, rather, to present an approach to analyzing property exposures to loss and to suggest specific and general ways in which an underwriter can *evaluate and provide coverage for*, property submissions.

HISTORICAL DEVELOPMENT

Conflagrations

Fire dominates property insurance (and for that reason will dominate this text). Today, as yesterday, it can rage unchecked for weeks sweeping forests, towns, and even cities from view. The Great Fire of London, in 1666, began in the King's bake house and went on to destroy 13,000 buildings and blacken an area of over 500 acres of concentrated housing. Yet a dentist named Nicholas Barbon is credited with initiating and forcing the City Fathers to enact a building code requiring more stone and brick construction at the expense of wood as a result thereof. He further is credited with organizing the Fire Office, said by many to be the first insurer to issue policies on buildings against loss by fire.

The Great Chicago Fire of 1871 destroyed *insured* property valued at $100,225,780, written by 202 insurance companies. Again, as a result, building codes were enacted to minimize the use of wood. In many states the disaster resulted in legislation attempting to enforce the solvency of insurance companies, since many had been unable to meet their Chicago obligations. Cities across the nation tightened fire prevention ordinances and increased investments in fire departments—both in equipment and in more and better trained fire fighters.

While insurance companies were still reeling from the Chicago conflagration, the Boston fire of November 1872 destroyed property valued at approximately $75 million, two-thirds of which was insured. From that came an understanding of how concentrations of wood-shingled mansard roofs can aid and abet fire and of the folly of underwriters exposing their companies' assets to liquidation through concentrated, disproportionate writings in a single geographic area.

The huge fire of 1904 in Baltimore led, eventually, to national standardization of much fire fighting equipment—especially hose couplings and hydrant stems. For underwriters, the report of that fire from the National Fire Protection Association emphasized that the term "fireproof" was a misnomer for any kind of building and that it was to be discarded in favor of "fire resistive." This new and more accurate term has withstood the test of time.

The San Francisco disaster of 1906 is most often remembered as "the great earthquake." However, the major cause of loss actually was the fire that ensued from snapped and torn gas lines. Fire fighting was hampered by a lack of water and diminished pressure due to ruptured lines. The city burned for at least three days. From this came a recognition that this particular proximate cause of fire could render practically useless all the technology available for treating it. Furthermore, most insurers had written heavily in the city believing that they provided no coverage for earthquake losses. In fact, earthquake damage, per se, was comparatively slight. The earthquake was estimated by several competent on-site observers to have contributed, in the aggregate, to no more than 10 percent of the entire loss.[1]

In summary, conflagrations have had the following effects:

1. Extensive fires such as those enumerated above have had a cumulative effect on the technologies society has been willing to finance for loss prevention and reduction. After each conflagration, the energy, the will to change, and the necessary capital were found, although for varying periods of sustained interest.

2. Each successive disaster reinforced previously known facts and knowledge concerning the dynamics of fire out of control.
   - Attempts by society to control loss severity (the magnitude of an event) have included increasingly sophisticated building construction standards; better public water supplies; ordinances mandating larger clear spaces separating structures; better trained and equipped fire departments; improved fire alarm communication systems; increased standardization of fire protection equipment; and increased individual awareness of roles to be played in evacuations, the use of portable extinguishers, and the functions of automatic sprinkler and detection systems.
   - Loss prevention (action to avoid the occurrence of fire) has received emphasis by way of the introduction and periodic upgrading of electrical wiring codes, plumbing, and space heating systems, subjecting the manufacturing of electrical appliances and tools to standards of performance and external quality control checks, and again building construction standards.

3. The magnitude of insured losses and the effect of concentrated writings by a single insurer led insurers to limit their writings in one geographic area through underwriting guidelines or reinsurance.

When studying this text, remember the most primary and essential tenet of underwriting: a property insurance policy *insures people, covers property,* and *insures against perils.* The underwriter is always confronted first and foremost with the variable of human behavior. This includes not only that of the insured, but of society in general. Fire safety is not always the dominant consideration in determining the location and design of structures. Economics and the presence of other perils are important influences. While frame dwellings are inferior to masonry with respect to the peril of fire, they are far superior with respect to earthquake. Thus, a scarcity of land could lead to the building of frame dwellings directly in the path of brush fires which occur with almost predictable frequency. Cities have grown up directly over known active earthquake faults. Entire communities and even cities are constructed at low land elevations on the shores of rivers and oceans within known hurricane paths and known flood plains. Gigantic high-rise buildings are created sometimes with known fire resistive deficiencies, limited and insufficient means of exit, and with clearly inadequate standpipes, sprinklers, and water supplies.

Additional Perils

One effect the huge fires had on insurance companies was a conservatism that may appear somewhat curious today. For example, for several centuries underwriters would undertake only the peril of fire when insuring buildings and their contents. In contrast, marine underwriters were, at the time of the Great Fire of London, already writing broad forms of coverage that were virtually "all-risks."

Marine and fire underwriters both cover property, but marine underwriters, it would seem, have historically been more willing to respond to a client's loss exposure needs. Fire underwriters, on the other hand, have historically offered the public only what they, the underwriters, deemed necessary—or *prudent.* Yet, conflagrations had caused the bankruptcy of literally thousands of insurers, and the managements of the surviving companies rightfully felt and strongly believed in their moral obligation to their insureds to remain solvent. Thus, they were reluctant to undertake the writing of additional perils. (This is in sharp contrast with the rapid growth and expansion of liability insurance, which originated essentially in the late nineteenth century.)

The principle of diversification, recognized at least as early as the turn of the century, was to take two more decades before it reached maturity. It was in the 1920s that the extended coverage endorsement was born.

Coverage against tornadoes had been added via a clause attached to a fire policy as early as 1882 in the Midwest. The coverage innovation enjoyed almost immediate sales success, but the companies' inability to price it adequately was graphically illustrated by the tornado which struck St. Louis and East St. Louis in 1896. The losses severely depleted reserves of many companies writing in that area.

In later years experiments in providing coverage against riots, explosion, and windstorms other than tornadoes were proving expensive ventures in meeting the public's needs against such contingencies. The companies were facing the problem of *adverse selection.* For example, the rural insureds correctly perceived no need for riot insurance while congested metropolitan district property owners saw the coverage as a necessary protection. The premiums from this relatively small group who desired the coverage were not enough to offset the severe losses given an occurrence of this rare event. Similarly, East Coast property owners saw the need for windstorm coverage against hurricanes while inland property owners were less susceptible. The solution to the problem of adverse selection was to package several perils—i.e., each peril was mandatory—and the appeal of one or two such perils among all those offered provided it with a broad market. The contribution of many to a fund for the unfortunate few, the very basis of insurance, was thus broadened as a concept.

Broad form packages of perils, in addition to extended coverage, were a natural extension of this concept. Thus, collapse of a building, falling objects, water damage, and so on could be offered on a sound financial basis as long as each was included in a mandatory package with the others. This concept led eventually to the issuance of "all-risks" (although "all perils" would probably be a better description) property contracts. Only a couple of decades ago, an "all-risks" policy covering either buildings or contents was rare, and now due to court decisions the term "all-risks" may again disappear from insurance policies (although intended coverage may not change).

Innovation by fire underwriters moved fairly rapidly. Following the passage of the McCarran-Ferguson Act in 1945, there was a period of fundamental change in insurance regulation. Therefore, by 1950, legislation existed in almost every state permitting fire insurance companies to write policies including liability insurance and liability companies to write fire insurance. Thus, homeowners policies were made available, as was a single auto policy covering collision damage (heretofore a fire insurance company product) and liability coverage (a liability company product).

But multiple-lines underwriting is clearly a compounding of the underwriter's task. The underwriter is forced to view submissions from property points of view *and* from liability points of view. There is still disagreement as to whether a single underwriter can do both expertly.

COMMERCIAL PROPERTY
AND COMMERCIAL LIABILITY UNDERWRITING
COMPARED

First Party Versus Third Party

In property insurance, the underwriter provides insurance directly for the benefit of the insured. The owner of a building, by virtue of that asset, is exposed to the chance of its loss. The contract between the underwriter and the insured is a direct relationship. If the event insured against does occur, the insurer's response generally is to that owner alone and to no other party (recognizing that a mortgagee may have "ownership" in part of the property). Liability insurance, on the other hand, is direct protection for the named insured, but the payment of losses is *on behalf of* the insured to some third party who has suffered the actual loss because of the failure of the insured to act as the "prudent person."

Dynamics of Historical Development and Underwriting

As noted, property insurance has existed in very much its essential forms for several centuries. Despite the current era of technological explosion, the property exposed to loss, whether an existing masonry structure built decades ago or a communications satellite to be sent into space, is subject to primarily the same possible forms of damage. That is, both can catch fire and burn, be demolished by explosion, or be ravaged by collision.

Liability, however, is a relatively new social phenomenon. It is true that concepts of injury and recompense for accountable injurious performance or neglect have existed at least since the times of the Mesopotamian king, Hammurabi—some 4,500 years ago, but as an exposure to loss by the mass of persons, it has had significant growth after the turn of the current century. Furthermore, standards for measuring culpable neglect, injurious performance, and strict liability are continuously undergoing extensive judicial revision. The liability underwriter usually issues the contract for a one-year term; the damages society may decree as due and payable for an action or failure to act by an insured can vary by arithmetic, perhaps even geometric progression, even in that brief time period.

The property underwriter operates in a relatively stable environment. The incidence of insurable events is generally predictable, and variations in the costs of losses can be calculated fairly accurately at inception and moderated during the policy term primarily with inflation indexing. While new technologies may present new exposures and new ways of handling these exposures, the basic job of the underwriter has not greatly changed. Whether the exposure is damage by water from a burst faucet or a burst pipe in a solar heating system, the underwriter's job is still to underwrite against water damage.

In contrast the liability underwriter operates within a maelstrom. The dynamics of socio-legal changes are the working environment, and prediction of the trends and extent of change is extremely complex. Insurers are being held liable today for coverage under policies issued twenty, thirty, and forty years ago. No underwriters in the 1940s could have predicted the size of the asbestos problem today. Yet, those underwriters were underwriting (and pricing) coverages for which claims are being filed and paid in the 1980s.

Insurable Interest

Recovery under a property insurance contract is limited by the extent of the insured's interest. Insurable interests may be acquired by ownership, lien, or business relationship. The *principle of indemnity* which holds that a person's recovery should be limited to an amount sufficient to restore him or her to the status held prior to the loss is a property insurance concept. Contracts written on a replacement cost basis which provide "new for old" usually require that the insured actually replace the property, mitigating the inherent moral hazard.

Liability insurance, as stated earlier, responds on behalf of an insured. Thus, the liability underwriter is not concerned so much with the property interest of the insured but with the legality of a claim against the insured. In turn, a third-party claimant can attempt to improve his or her lot with a successful lawsuit, which may or may not include punitive damages, for literally millions of dollars beyond the actual sustained loss.

Claims Settlement

The property underwriter contemplates paying losses directly to the insured. Both parties desire to see a rapid and fair settlement of the loss.

The property claims adjuster primarily sees to it that:

- an insurable interest exists for the named insured,
- the damaged item is a covered object,
- the peril causing the loss is established and was insured against,
- the value of the covered item is determinable in dollars,

- the policy limits are sufficient, and
- coinsurance and other insurance-to-value clauses have been complied with.[2]

Liability is based on a duty owed some third party who is not a party to the insurance contract. A payment on behalf of an insured is predicated on a discovery of the insured's liability. Thus an insured may have indeed played some role in an event resulting in bodily injury to or property damage of some third party, but policy response requires that an insured's role in that event be established under law as an accountable one before a judgment will be paid.

The liability underwriter is thus faced with unknown amounts of losses. A negligently severed foot has a value to the interested parties, but the actual amount to be paid can depend on the third party's age, occupation, and the circumstances of the incident. A property underwriter has somewhat less difficulty in establishing the value of a building, a ship, or an article of merchandise.

Measures of Loss Severity

In liability insurance, the limit of liability is merely the maximum the underwriter must pay to a *third party* on behalf of the insured once the liability of the insured has been clearly established. But the costs in defending the insured are not contractually limited and, indeed, have frequently exceeded the limit of liability as a result of lengthy investigation, initial court proceedings, and appellate litigation. The liability underwriter issuing a policy for $100,000 bodily injury occurrence limits has no way of saying the probable maximum loss will be 25, 50, or 100 percent of that amount. Even *after* a covered accident has occurred, the underwriter must await not just the claims adjuster's valuation of that accident, but also the negotiative or litigious processes of several parties.

Property underwriters generally view the magnitude of potential loss through the following concepts:

1. amount subject (maximum possible loss),
2. probable maximum loss (PML), and
3. limit of liability.

Amount Subject   The amount subject, sometimes referred to as the *maximum possible loss*, is the total value that is exposed to loss by any one insured peril or at any one location. The amount subject may be different for the insured and the insured if all of the insured's property is not covered by one insurance company. Amount subject also differs by peril. For example, the amount subject for the peril of fire is determined on the basis of fire divisions. A *fire division* is defined as "a portion of a building which is so protected from other portions that a fire will be restricted from one to another."[3] Since such protection is usually accomplished by the means of fire walls and parapets, a building without these fire walls will constitute one fire division. However, a single building could consist of any number of separate fire divisions. In general, an underwriter will have a separate amount subject for each fire division. That is, if the insured happens to own two buildings which are two separate fire divisions, there would be two amount subjects—the first being the total value of the first building and the second being the total value of the second building.

When there are several buildings under one ownership, analysis of the buildings' height, construction, occupancy, and the clear space between the buildings is required to determine whether or not the buildings are "subject" to one another. It could be that technically the two buildings are so close that they constitute one fire division and the value of both buildings combined would be the amount subject. Other reasons for including more than one building in an amount subject would be deficiencies in construction or openings in the buildings. If the buildings are close enough that they are subject to the insured's building but are owned by other persons, they are considered part of the external exposure hazard which is discussed in a later chapter.

As mentioned above, amount subject will vary by peril. Even though the insured may own several buildings which are each a separate fire division and each has its own amount subject for the peril of fire, it is likely that all of the buildings would be included in the amount subject for the perils of earthquake or windstorm. An underwriter must always keep this in mind when determining amount subject and when considering the reinsurance arrangements which his or her company has. Although the discussion here and in the above paragraph has referred to the values of the buildings only, if the insurer covers the contents, these values must be included in the determination of amount subject.

Probable Maximum Loss The probable maximum loss (PML) is the largest loss that the underwriter considers likely to occur based on experience and judgment. Thus, the figure derived might be different for two different underwriters or two different insurers. The PML for underwriters with the same insurer should be close since most insurers give their underwriters specific guidelines on how to determine PML. This concept is usually applied only to fire and explosion. One approach that one underwriter has used is to consider that the first line of defense against fire fails. That is, the sprinkler system malfunctions or the fire department is summoned late. Next, the second line of defense against fire is considered to function properly. The damage caused by a fire of this magnitude is considered to be the probable maximum loss. However, note that this is only one person's definition and there is not total agreement on an exact definition of PML with regard to the first defense failing and the second line of defense working. Most persons agree only that the definition varies and that it is based on experience and judgment. In the case of a single frame structure, the probable maximum loss may well be the entire structure, which in this case would be the same as the amount subject.

Limit of Liability   In any event, the property underwriter has a known maximum loss from the very inception of the policy—the limit of liability. Only in rare instances is this amount exceeded in payments to insureds and even then the additional amounts are usually insignificant.

The concepts of amount subject, probable maximum loss, and limits of liability have significant and practical applications in property underwriting decisions. These concepts relate directly to one of the two major areas in *every* underwriter's decisions—*severity*. In other words, fundamental to the property *and* liability underwriter's decision-making process are these questions: How likely is a loss (i.e., its probability)? Given a loss, what will be its magnitude (i.e., its severity)? Severity will dictate such things as reinsurance or sharing of the line with another insurer.

Loss Development

A liability loss can result in months and even years of delay before final settlement, and only at final settlement will the full costs to the underwriter be known. For example, a seven-year-old girl was injured in a home accident. A surgeon is alleged to have been culpably negligent in the resulting corrective operation. The parents sued the surgeon, on her behalf, for malpractice. A court recently awarded the girl a sizable sum; she was thirteen at the time of the award. In addition, the court reminded the surgeon that under applicable state law the child had twelve months after reaching her majority (eighteen years of age) to reopen the complaint against the surgeon, since the current settlement was not binding on a party (a child) who, at law, was deemed unable to reach a binding settlement. In this case, the malpractice underwriter made the underwriting decision some six years prior to the preliminary judgment (which was subsequently paid) against the insured, and faces six more years of waiting before it is known whether this settlement is final. Conceivably, the eighteen-year-old victim can then institute suit that will take *another* six years or more to litigate.

The problem of loss development delay does not plague the property underwriter as it does the liability underwriter. Direct physical damage generally is reported promptly to the insurer as required in the policy; the adjuster determines the validity of coverage; the value of the property at the time of loss is calculated; and after deduction for deductibles, other insurance, coinsurance, and so on, a settlement is made. Rarely are independent appraisers and disinterested umpires required to step in and participate in the settlement of disputes on the amount of insurance or the amount of loss. Rarer still are cases requiring court adjudication.

For losses in the indirect damage area, such as business interruption losses, the settlement is more complicated and, perhaps, somewhat more prone to litigation, but still losses tend to be settled well within one year from the date of loss.

The ramifications of loss development delay include uncertainty of loss over a long period of time and uncertainty over pricing today's submission for uncertain loss payments in the future. Since property losses are settled more quickly than liability losses, the effects of loss development delay are of less concern for property underwriters than for liability underwriters.

Pricing Comparisons

For many risks, one individual fire insurance rate is promulgated for the building and another for its contents. The rate is variable from risk to risk depending upon construction, occupancy, protection, and exposures. These four factors, producing the acronym COPE, are common to almost every property underwriting decision. The role COPE plays in determining potential loss has been shown, e.g., in PML. The individual fire rate similarly weighs these factors via a detailed inspection, giving credit for some factors and debits for others. Hence, each of two masonry office buildings of similar design, size, and configuration and located only a block or two from each other can have different rates. The process is called *specific* or *schedule rating*. The experience of the class, all such masonry office buildings, may require an adjustment factor of a credit or debit if the absence or prevalence of fires so dictates.

Class rating is now used for certain small commercial fire risks. This class rating plan developed by the Insurance Services Office (ISO) eliminates the need to individually rate the smaller commercial risks, providing an important cost savings. (The plan is described in more detail in Chapter 9.) This approach is close to that found in many liability lines where specific or schedule rating is much less common.

In liability insurance most rates are developed by class. Automobile liability, general liability, and workers' compensation rates, for example, are primarily class or manual rated. Individual risk experience and individual risk characteristics may modify the base class rate. Generally, the class fire rate is a given for the underwriter. It is promulgated by a rating bureau and also adjusted for experience by that bureau. Liability underwriters themselves often calculate experience and individual risk characteristic variations after classifying and applying the manual rate. One underwriter has summarized the pricing comparison, saying property insurance is predominantly specific rating based on individual characteristics with a later modification due to class, whereas liability insurance is predominantly class rating with a later modification for individual characteristics.

On the other hand, the use of independent filings which permit the scheduling of credits and the use of experience modification plans and premium dispersion credits on larger commercial property risks provide a degree of pricing flexibility for the property underwriter. The difference is one of degree—while commercial property underwriters have some pricing flexibility, it is not as pervasive as is the case in commercial liability.

DETERMINATION OF VALUE

Measures of value have a direct effect on property underwriting results and underwriting processes. They determine the bases on which premiums are calculated, the amounts of insurance required and needed, the manner by which losses are adjusted, the amounts paid, and the dollar amount to be used with restrictive policy clauses such as coinsurance and pro rata distribution.

Actual Cash Value (ACV)

It has been a long established and accepted principle of property insurance that "actual cash value" is the replacement cost (new) of property less accumulated physical depreciation and obsolescence at the time of loss. While there have been numerous court cases contesting this definition over the years, in most instances the courts have found the definition worthy of continued usage. Individual cases demanding other settlements usually have had unusual mitigating circumstances that prove the exception rather than the rule.

In the Jefferson case the California Supreme Court interpreted the actual cash value clause to mean fair market value.[4] The case involved a building which had sustained approximately $25,000 damage. The replacement cost minus depreciation was determined to be $170,000 while the fair market value was only $65,000 due to obsolescence. Since the amount of insurance was $45,000 with a 70 percent coinsurance clause, the replacement cost minus depreciation figure would have resulted in a substantial coinsurance penalty. Since the court ruled that the fair market value figure was appropriate, the coinsurance penalty was relatively insignificant. The accepted legal definition of fair market value according to a different case is "the amount which in all probability would be arrived at by fair negotiations between an owner willing to sell and a purchaser desiring to buy."[5]

Obsolescence, as mentioned in the Jefferson case can be defined as the reduction in value caused by the loss of economic use. Generally one thinks of obsolescence as a result of something being outdated, old-fashioned, i.e., something that has been superseded by a newer model that includes modern styling or a more sophisticated technology. Clothing is a property item subject to wide swings of fashion. Yesterday's fashion rage becomes today's rag on the market. The seventy-five-year-old, stream-fed water driven saw mill is not economically viable today, given vast technological improvements and so on. Buildings with outdated heating systems, lack of air conditioning, no enclosed elevators, or inefficient factory machinery are probably obsolete.

The underwriter must be alert to submissions where unusual circumstances may cause problems with actual cash value settlements such as the following:

1. Vacant property, especially where vacancy has been prolonged, indicates possibilities of building obsolescence.
2. Buildings of unusual design and/or configuration often hint at unusual economic use value.
3. Old buildings also are frequently, but clearly not necessarily, verging on obsolescence.

When circumstances arise where an obsolete building is being insured, the policy should be endorsed (if the applicable regulations permit it) to clarify the mutual understanding between underwriter and insured as to value.

Singularly significant in the definition of ACV is the valuation's applicability *at the time of loss* as opposed to the inception date or writing of the insurance. The underlying concept is the principle of indemnity; depreciation must be calculated as of the time of the loss rather than at some prior date in order to avoid an insured profiting from the loss.

The concept of depreciation is the source of much confusion in the determination of actual cash value. The term does not refer to accounting depreciation in which the original cost is written off over the life of the asset utilizing either a straight-line or accelerated formula. Rather, *depreciation* in an insurance context refers to the decrease in the actual value of the building or item of equipment relative to its new counterpart. In determining the extent of depreciation, the normal useful life of the asset must be determined. Assume that a commercial building has a composition roof with a normal useful life of twenty years. Ten years after the roof is installed it is destroyed by fire. Since a new roof would also have a twenty-year life, and since it is impossible to construct a ten-year-old roof, the loss adjustment must be on the basis of the actual cash value which is the replacement cost less the depreciation which in this case is the erosion of ten years or half of the roof's useful life. (Depreciation is not always straight line, but will be used here for simplicity's sake.) If the roof were replaced by the insurance company with no deduction for depreciation, the insured would be better off after the loss since the need to replace the roof would have been moved ten years further into the future. This new roof would most likely also enhance the value of the property. Property insurance adjusters frequently refer to this effect as "betterment."

Using the example of the ten-year-old roof with an expected total life of twenty years, the replacement cost may have appreciated over a decade due to inflated costs of materials and labor. That is, a roof with an original cost of $4,500 is, at today's prices, replaceable at, perhaps, $9,000—a doubling of the original cost. After consideration of the depreciation of one-half of the useful life, the actual cash value of the loss would be $4,500. While this figure happens to coincide exactly with original cost, it also marks a proper reduction from current replacement value.

Not all insured property depreciates, however. Recently manufactured items of stock, raw materials used in the manufacturing process, and merchandise held for sale more often than not would have an actual cash value equal to the current undepreciated full cost to the owner. This presumes no loss of value through deterioration or obsolescence.

Replacement Cost Valuation

The principle of indemnity is primarily one of equity within the insurance mechanism. Nevertheless, there are circumstances where settling property losses strictly on actual cash value can mean a real hardship for an insured. If an insured's building through general wear and tear suffers depreciation, the deduction of that depreciation at settlement nonetheless leaves the insured less than whole. Not to take depreciation certainly would provide that insured a betterment, but the taking of depreciation presents a real economic loss to the owner.

This realistic and legitimate risk to an insured has been long recognized, and solutions have existed for upwards of two decades. The original solution was the depreciation endorsement that paid the additional depreciated amount or the difference between ACV and full replacement cost.

Today, replacement cost coverage for real property (buildings) is in common usage. It reflects a coverage that marine hull underwriters have long provided their insureds, i.e., loss settlement on a "new for old" basis.

The underwriter must take care in the providing of this coverage. The absence of depreciation in loss settlements presents a potential moral hazard. Building owners sometimes find themselves with obsolete buildings or buildings located in areas with severe economic decay. In such circumstances, the potential replacement cost recovery may exceed fair market value. Also, caution is required because the coverage provided varies in some jurisdictions and with some independent filings. The safeguards thus found in some forms may not be present in others. Common safeguards consist of the following contractual stipulations:

1. Only actual cash value is paid at the time of loss. The difference between ACV and the replacement cost, the amount of depreciation, is recovered only after the actual replacement of the destroyed property has been made. This practically precludes an owner from "selling" the destroyed building to the insurer.
2. Rebuilding must occur on the same site as the originally insured item. This obviously prohibits an owner from moving from an undesirable location at the full expense of the insurer.

Valued Policies

Several states have valued policy laws affecting insurance on real property. These laws, which date back as far as 1874, stipulate that if the structure is totally destroyed by a peril specified in the law, the policy limit must be paid. These generally do not change underwriting actions but reinforce the need of the underwriter to maintain accurate amounts of insurance to value.

APPRAISING VALUES EXPOSED TO LOSS

The underwriter must consider for each submission the following questions regarding the values exposed to loss:

1. Does the underwriting guide provide the capacity to assume all or only a portion of this risk?
2. Will facultative reinsurance be required?
3. Will this risk require submission for approval by higher underwriting management?
4. Are the values exposed to loss reasonably related to the amounts of insurance requested?
5. What are the actual values exposed to loss?

It is not incidental that questions 1 through 4 can be answered accurately only when the answer to question 5 is known. That question is vital to any property insurance underwriting decision.

The property underwriter has several tools which can be used to verify values submitted by an insured. Briefly, these tools are:

- Local costing figures that can be used as "rules of thumb" to compare against values found in applications for insurance.
- National data from key business operating ratio indexes that provide a yardstick to either deduce approximate values or to compare against requested policy limits.
- Appraisals of real and personal property by businesses specializing in such work or by the loss control department from the underwriter's own company. It should be noted, however, that property valuations, performed by insurance company inspectors, usually are only for real property.
- Finally the underwriter, generally as a last resort, can obtain information which is at least marginally useful from a summary of financial records furnished by the insured.

The literature on valuation emphasizes real as opposed to personal property values. While most real property that an underwriter is confronted with consists of buildings, extensive values of real property are not always highly visible or are frequently ignored. For example, buildings invariably have extensive foundations, plumbing, and other appurtenances located underground. In addition, roadways, fences, signs, and light and electrical utility poles also constitute real property. Machinery may also be considered real property, especially in factories.

For each submission the underwriter must determine the following:

1. What types of property in addition to the structure does the submission intend to cover?
2. Does the requested form include this property within the definition of covered property?
3. Do the requested values represent actual cash value or replacement cost of the property?

Personal property values invariably constitute a major exposure to loss. For example, the stock within a warehouse may well exceed the value of the warehouse itself several times over. Fortunately, values of finished goods or raw materials are usually more easily determined than real property values. When the values are difficult to resolve, an outside appraisal is almost always required. Rules of thumb, national indexes, and financial records, in such cases, may mislead even experienced underwriters.

Rules of Thumb

Most people frequently use benchmarks. For example, the speed of the car being driven and the distance between the car ahead and the car being driven, measured in roughly calculated car lengths, tell a driver whether he or she should drop back a bit. Rules of thumb for valuations play essentially the same role for the underwriter—they are benchmarks or rough yardsticks to tell whether a requested amount of insurance is roughly in line with the "conventional wisdom."

Underwriters who are consciously on the lookout for data to use as rules of thumb can, over even a short period of time, acquire a great amount of useful information. For example, a leading business newspaper estimated that smaller (one- to three-story) suburban and rural motels had an unfurnished unit cost of approximately $40,000. With that item of information, a suburban motel submission consisting of three ten-year-old, one-story buildings with an office, small restaurant, and sixty-five units requesting a real property limit of $525,000, would be suspect. Even when the office and restaurant are ignored, the implied unit cost is only $8,077 ($525,000 ÷ 65). Immediately, then, the policy limit alone should cause the underwriter to be cautious; the units alone, when valued at $40,000 per unit, as suggested by the newspaper article, would indicate values approaching $2,600,000. The valuation discrepancy should be resolved before any further effort is made on this submission. Clearly, the published figure may be only a national average; it ignores local cost variations, it does not indicate the type of construction, and it ignores the significant cost factor of quality of construction. In addition, it is possible that the author of the newspaper article got one person's estimate and that estimate may be totally inaccurate. If the figure did appear accurate, the underwriter here could quickly calibrate the $40,000 unit cost with the local environment by:

1. having his or her company's loss control department verify or adjust the national figure or produce its own benchmark costs for motels; and

2. calling a building contractor and requesting him or her to roughly estimate unit costs for the underwriter.

As a last resort, the underwriter can insist that an appraisal be made as a condition of policy issuance.

One insurance company publishes building cost benchmarks for each of its branch offices. When rates vary beyond a 10 percent standard (after allowance for coinsurance), the underwriter must either have his or her supervisor approve the requested limit or proceed with an appraisal before the risk can be accepted or rated. This company's rules of thumb include (1) square foot costs by construction type for local apartment houses, small shopping centers and independent retail stores, motels, churches, schools, and libraries; and (2) monthly unit or square foot rental costs for income coverage (business interruption insurance) for local apartment houses, retail stores, motels, and office buildings.

National Indexes

Standard and Poor's, Dun & Bradstreet, and other financial reporting firms provide compendiums and summaries of industry data which are useful to the property underwriter. These provide a rough guideline and will indicate if a submission contains values which are at variance with normal industry practice. One of these compendiums is Dun & Bradstreet's *Cost of Doing Business*, with separate issues for corporations and for partnerships and proprietorships. Exhibit 1-1 indicates the cost of doing business for certain industries. Each ratio represents a percentage of the gross income that is used in a particular business category for the captioned items.

For example, note that the wholesalers of alcoholic beverages spend approximately 78 percent of total income on the beverages that they sell. Assume that a wholesale liquor dealer's producer submits a business interruption proposal including net receipts of $2 million and $1.1 million for cost of merchandise sold, producing a gross earnings amount of $900,000 ($2 million less $1.1 million). For a 50 percent coinsurance form, the limit of liability must then be not less than $450,000. Further assume that $450,000 is the limit of liability requested for a 50 percent coinsurance form.

The industry ratio indicates that the limit of liability may be overstated. The average liquor dealer spends 78.22 percent of its net receipts for the merchandise that it sells. This dealer appears to be spending only 55 percent. Expected gross earnings for this firm would be $435,600 (net receipts of $2 million less cost of goods sold of

Exhibit 1-1
Cost of Doing Business — Corporations*

Industry	Total Number of Returns Filed	Cost of Goods Sold %	Gross Margin %	Selected Operating Expenses								
				Compensation of Officers %	Rent Paid on Business Property %	Repairs %	Bad Debts %	Interest Paid %	Taxes Paid† %	Amortization Depreciation Depletion %	Advertising %	Pension and Other Employee Benefit Plans %
All Industries	2,082,200	71.70	28.30	1.90	1.34	0.78	0.41	4.01	2.76	2.97	0.91	1.50
General Building Contractors and Operative Builders	78,115	86.79	13.21	2.67	0.41	0.34	0.19	1.64	1.52	1.27	0.27	0.55
General Merchandise Stores (Retail)	9,322	64.79	35.21	0.43	2.69	0.50	0.37	1.48	2.44	1.47	2.59	0.87
Food Stores (Retail)	31,370	78.08	21.92	0.60	1.49	0.49	0.05	0.32	1.25	0.96	1.00	0.81
Apparel and Accessory Stores (Retail)	38,497	59.41	40.59	3.33	6.02	0.36	0.25	0.71	2.23	1.15	2.26	0.60
Furniture and Home Furnishings Stores (Retail)	33,410	64.45	35.55	4.14	3.11	0.40	0.52	1.04	2.09	0.91	3.37	0.52
Farm-Product Raw Materials (Wholesale)	9,076	94.36	5.64	0.36	0.19	0.25	0.06	0.66	0.32	0.58	0.09	0.14
Hardware, Plumbing and Heating Equipment (Wholesale)	10,357	76.72	23.28	3.00	0.92	0.20	0.34	0.76	1.33	0.62	0.30	0.83
Alcoholic Beverages (Wholesale)	4,042	78.22	21.78	1.40	0.56	0.23	0.11	0.43	5.42	0.59	0.52	0.58

†Excludes federal income taxes.

*Adapted with permission from *Cost of Doing Business — Corporations* (New York: Dun & Bradstreet, Inc., 1982).

$1,564,400 [$2 million $\times$ .7822]). A 50 percent coinsurance form would then require a limit of $217,800. The discrepancy should be resolved.

Further uses of indexes include calculating an estimated figure for rental value once net receipts are known and for bad debts within the accounts receivable. (The producer also can do presales call research on whether pensions and health insurance are potential, valuable sales to be made.)

All major financial reporting services provide data on businesses indicating the industry average for the major financial ratios such as the current ratio and the net profit on net sales ratio. Financial reports can be obtained giving these values for individual insureds or the underwriter can obtain an income statement and balance sheet from the insured and calculate these ratios directly. Analysis of these ratios is covered in Chapter 10 of *Principles of Property and Liability Underwriting*, the AIU 61 text and briefly in *Commercial Liability Underwriting*, the AIU 63 text. Review of this material will indicate how financial analysis can aid in evaluating commercial property values.

Appraisals

There are a number of companies providing insurance appraisals including Marshall and Stevens and American Appraisal Associates, Inc. Appraisals can be performed on either real or personal property. The E.H. Boeckh Co., a Division of American Appraisal Associates, Inc. uses a technique employing three approaches to building appraisal: (1) the component method, (2) the model method, and (3) the general estimate method. These will be briefly reviewed here to indicate one company's methods of appraisals. Other companies have similar methods.

The Component Method   In this system a structure is analyzed component by component and current local building costs are calculated for each. The components include:

- living/working area,
- excavation,
- basement and flooring,
- basement walls and/or foundations,
- exterior walls,
- windows,
- interior partitions and finish,
- floor construction,
- floor finish,
- ceiling,

- roof,
- heating and air conditioning,
- electrical systems,
- essential fixtures, including plumbing and sewerage,
- other built-in fixtures, and so on.

The structure's components, once costed, are added together to provide an accurate total dollar cost as of the date of the appraisal.

The component system requires localized, up-to-date building costs for each possible type and quality of building component and, furthermore, requires a user who has an excellent knowledge of architecture as well as construction technology and operations. An appraiser using this system must refer to existing detailed plans and engineering and construction specifications whenever available.

The Model Method The model method is an adaptation of the component method. Individual components are used to reconstruct models of the more common structures that an appraiser might encounter. The model is then used as the basis of comparison for the building being appraised. When the carefully established procedures for using models is followed, a relatively high degree of accuracy in the appraisal is achieved.

There are occasions when the model does not fit the subject building, that is, when one or more components in the structure differ from the ones used to develop the model. In such cases, adjustments can be made by substituting component data that exist separately as a result of previous component studies.

The model method is systematically compared with the subject structure by a review of (1) basic construction data, (2) foundation structure, (3) perimeter, (4) living/working area, and (5) ground area (terrain and site location).

The General Estimate Method As its name suggests, the general estimate method provides a means of rapidly calculating approximate total building costs by using floor area (total square feet) and multiplying it by a building cost factor derived from a similar structure. To this are added additional costs for special features which may exist, such as elevators, air conditioners, automatic sprinkler systems, and so on. The general estimate method is similar to the square foot rules of thumb mentioned earlier.

Any appraisal system must maintain current data with appropriate modifications for geographic variations in costs. For example, one company's building cost appraisers are supplied bimonthly publications of such data. In addition, through update indexes, they are also able to trend building costs for over 200 cities throughout the United States

Exhibit 1-2
A Depreciation Grading Chart*

Grade	Amount of Depreciation
Excellent	0–5%
Good	5–15%
Fair—Good	15–25%
Fair	25–35%
Poor	35–50%
Dilapidated	50–100%

*Reprinted with permission of E.H. Boeckh Co., a Division of American Appraisal Associates Inc., Milwaukee, WI.

and Canada. Trending of building costs in various areas is useful to a building owner for calculating the effects of escalation clauses in construction contracts, but it is also useful for calculating a building's probable replacement cost several months into the future.

Generally, appraisals would be unnecessary if an insured could provide an accurate original building cost, because, as shown, an appraisal often starts by deriving an original cost and bringing it up-to-date by indexing it to today's building costs. When an insured has original cost data for a relatively recently built structure, formal appraisals usually are unnecessary. But, for older buildings, original costs frequently cannot be ascertained, may be inapplicable due to today's building technology, and often are inaccurate because they do not include subsequent modernizations and additions that have been added.

A Depreciation Grading Chart Appraisal systems derive a structure's 100 percent replacement cost. Given the replacement cost figure for a building, its actual cash value can be determined by using a grading chart such as that shown in Exhibit 1-2.

The gradings in Exhibit 1-2 are defined as follows:

- Excellent—structurally sound, with only slight deterioration, such as minor damage to surface finishes, caulked or pointed joints, and minor chipping of concrete and masonry surfaces.

- Good—structurally sound, with moderate deterioration confined to minor elements and damage deeper than surface finishes, such as minor roof erosion, minor damage to screens, windows, shades, piping, and small plastered surfaces.

- Fair-Good—structurally sound, but deterioration extends to both major and minor items, involving replacement rather than repair, such as parts of boilers, elevators, motors, pumps, and large areas of floor and wall surfaces.
- Fair—some structural faults exist of minor nature, with considerable deterioration throughout, such as settlement cracks, floor sags from overloading, extensive erosion of roofing, corrosion of the entire piping system, and deterioration of door and window sashes and frames.
- Poor—numerous structural faults and extensive deterioration, including excessive settling, moisture penetration, rusting, rotting, with a dire need for complete rewiring, repiping, and replacement of mechanical fixtures.
- Dilapidated—extensive structural faults and extensive deterioration, where complete replacement of components and materials is required.

Use of the Depreciation Grading Chart The depreciation grading chart is applied to the replacement cost as noted in the following example:

1. An appraisal establishes the structure's replacement cost at $1,685,000.
2. An inspection reveals:
   a. The normal economic life of this building is forty years. The building is, at the inspection date, eight years old. Thus, if the building has received expected maintenance and repairs, physical depreciation should be very slight or negligible.
   b. Observed depreciation, in fact, reveals:
      (1) rotting wood joists in the basement,
      (2) a rusting oil burner,
      (3) water stains on ceilings and upper floors,
      (4) broken window sash and window panes,
      (5) vertical cracks in exterior masonry walls, and
      (6) rusting plumbing pipes with several hasty emergency repairs still waiting for more careful and thorough repair.
3. An evaluation of the inspection report suggests the building falls into the "poor" category. A "poor" grading for an eight-year-old building illustrates that its expected life has, via negligent maintenance, been reduced drastically. Depreciation of perhaps 40 percent is warranted.

4. Depreciation:

$$\$1,685,000 \times \text{grading} = \$1,685,000 \times 0.40$$

$$= \$674,000 \text{ depreciation}$$

5. Actual Cash Value:

$$\text{Replacement cost} - \text{depreciation} = \$1,685,000 - \$674,000$$

$$= \$1,011,000 \text{ Actual Cash Value}$$

In this illustration, severe depreciation indicates more than the actual cash value; it strongly hints that the owner is either under financial stress and thus is unable to maintain the structure properly *or* the owner has deliberately withheld maintenance. Withholding maintenance, in turn, suggests extreme carelessness, possible obsolescence, or a neighborhood deterioration making the building an unattractive asset to the owner (possibly the owner even sees it as a liability). In any event, it would appear to be a suspect risk for insurance. Through the valuation process, the underwriter has learned much more about the insured property than its value.

A Modified Technique Due to the elaborate nature of the industry-wide valuation sources, some companies have found it expedient to create their own building valuation guides. The following is an example of a building value approximator which uses the basic principles of the Boeckh model method. After obtaining an adequate description of the building to be insured, the underwriter follows an eight step method to determine the actual cash value or replacement cost of the building. This is shown in Exhibit 1-3.

This example illustrates the process of evaluating a building taking a hypothetical submission through the eight steps of the technique. A sample of the cost estimating form is given in Exhibit 1-4.

The submission is made on the form given in Exhibit 1-4, providing all the information required for Step 1. Next, the underwriter refers to the occupancy/building type cross reference, an excerpt of which is given in Exhibit 1-5. This is Step 2. The occupancy/building type cross reference refers the underwriter to schedules M-5 and M-7. Since the building described in schedule M-7 is a multi-occupancy shopping center, the model in schedule M-5 most clearly describes the Gourmet Galley. Schedule M-5 is shown in Exhibit 1-6. Note that the description

Exhibit 1-3
Building Value Approximator*

Steps

1. Inspect building and determine

   Occupancy
   Number of stories
   Construction or wall type
   Basic specifications
   If building has a basement
   Physical condition and age

2. Determine building type and approximator schedule

   Refer to the Occupancy/Building Type Cross-Reference (Exhibit 1-5)

3. Determine ground floor area

   Note dimensions
   Calculate

4. Determine base building cost

   On the selected building type schedule, locate the appropriate construction or wall type; then select the building basic rate across from
   the calculated ground floor area. If that calculated ground area is
   between two of those listed, interpolate as described below.
     Add or deduct for adjustments shown at the bottom of each page.
   If the building is a multi-story structure, other than primary one
   listed, multiply by the proper multi-story factor listed under the
   building title.
     Multiply building rate times ground floor area.

5. Determine total other costs

   Select basement basic rate.
   Add or deduct for adjustments to determine basement rate.
   Multiply basement rate times area to determine basement cost.
   Add miscellaneous improvements and additions costs to base-
   ment cost to determine total other costs.

6. Determine total building cost

   Add step 4 and 5 results.

7. Apply the proper location multiplier to step 6 result to determine the
   100 percent replacement cost.

8. Depreciate step 7 result according to the normal depreciation
   guideline (or from other independent analysis) to determine actual
   cash value.

---

*Adapted with permission of E.H. Boeckh Co., a Division of American Appraisal
Associates Inc., Milwaukee, WI.

Exhibit 1-4
Commercial Cost Estimating Form*

COMMERCIAL COST ESTIMATING FORM

Policy No. 00006-7/8

Name
Gourmet Galley Supermarket

Property location
111 First St, Malvern, PA 19355

Mailing address
111 First Street

Prepared by
IIA Agency

Date
2/12/X4

List approximator building type and Table	Ground floor area (sq. ft.)	Construction or wall type selected	List adjustments included on model page	Number of stories above ground	Basement
Supermarket one story M-5	15,000	Masonry	None	One	☒ Yes sq. ft. 15,000 ☐ No

Explain any special building characteristics not listed in the approximator

Miscellaneous improvements and additions: ☐ elevators ☐ balconies ☐ fireplaces ☐ carport ☐ outbuildings ☐ other

For depreciation: Building age 10 years. Condition: ☐ excellent ☒ good ☐ average

Notes & sketches
Basic construction:
Masonry, windows 15% of exterior wall

foundation
Reinforced concrete

walls
Wood

structural floor
Ceramic tile

roof
Wood

Exhibit 1-5
Occupancy/Building Type Cross Reference*

Type	Schedule
Service, gas station	Ps-4
Shoe sales	M-2, M-3, M-4, M-7
Shoe repair	M-2, M-3, M-4, M-7
Shopping center	M-7
Supermarket	M-5, M-7
Tailor	M-2, M-3, M-4, M-7
Television sales and repair	M-2, M-3, M-4, M-6, M-7, M-11, M-12
Tire, battery, automotive accessories	M-2, M-3, M-4, M-6, M-7, M-11, M-12
Toy store	M-2, M-3, M-4, M-6, M-7, M-11, M-12
Travel agency	M-2, M-3, M-4, M-6, M-7, O-2, O-3
Warehouse	Ind-2, Ind-3, M-11, M-12
Watch repair	M-2, M-3, M-4, M-7
Women's clothing	M-2, M-3, M-4, M-7

*Reprinted with permission of E.H. Boeckh Co., a Division of American Appraisal Associates, Inc., Milwaukee, WI.

of the supermarket in schedule M-5 very closely resembles the Gourmet Galley in its basic specifications. The ground floor area of 15,000 square feet is provided in the commercial cost estimating form, Exhibit 1-4, and thus Step 3 is completed.

In Step 4 the basic building rate per square foot is determined, based on the ground floor area and the construction type. No additions or deductions are required since the building is air conditioned and we are not informed of any alarm or sprinkler system.

Because the ground floor area is between the 12,000 and 16,000 square feet categories shown in schedule M-5, it is necessary to interpolate in order to obtain the correct building rate. Interpolation is done as follows:

- Calculate the difference between the actual building ground floor area and the smaller area of those it is between.
- Divide that difference by the difference of the two listed areas it falls between.
- Multiply that result by the difference between the base rates for the listed areas used above.
- Subtract that result from the larger of the listed base rates.[6]

Exhibit 1-6
Building Type Schedule (M-5)*

Basic Specifications
Foundation: reinforced concrete   Framing: load supporting walls, posts and beams   Slab on Ground: reinforced concrete   Floor Finish: ceramic tile, vinyl tile and unfinished areas   Windows: 15% of exterior wall area   Plumbing: standard complement for type of occupancy
Heating and Air Conditioning: year-round central air conditioning   Electrical: commercial lighting fixtures   Fire Protection: none
Misc.: none

Ground Floor Area Sq. Ft.	Construction Types								Add for Unfinished Basement	
	Frame		Masonry		Noncombustible		Fire-resistive			
	Rate Per Sq. Ft.	Total $	Rate Per Sq. Ft.	Total $	Rate Per Sq. Ft.	Total $	Rate Per Sq. Ft.	Total $	Rate Per Sq. Ft.	Total $
5000	22.55	112,750	28.15	140,750	28.35	141,750	30.55	152,750	14.83	74,150
6000	22.05	132,300	27.15	162,900	27.35	164,100	29.59	177,540	14.41	86,460
8000	21.37	170,960	25.80	206,400	26.00	208,000	28.30	226,400	13.82	110,560
12000	20.53	246,360	24.16	289,920	24.36	292,320	26.73	320,760	13.11	157,320
16000	20.05	320,800	23.18	370,880	23.38	374,080	25.80	412,800	12.68	202,880
20000	19.71	394,200	22.51	450,200	22.71	424,200	25.16	503,200	12.39	247,800
25000	19.41	485,250	21.92	548,000	22.12	553,000	24.60	615,000	12.14	303,500
30000	19.18	575,400	21.47	644,100	21.67	650,100	24.17	725,100	11.94	358,200

Adjustments
Additions: For manual or automatic alarm system and storage area sprinklers, add $.38 per sq. ft.
Deductions: If building does not have central air conditioning, deduct $2.80 per sq. ft.

*Reprinted with permission of E.H. Boeckh Co., a Division of American Appraisal Associates, Inc., Milwaukee, WI.

Therefore:

15,000 sq.ft.	16,000	$24.16	$24.16
-12,000 sq.ft.	-12,000	- 23.18	- 0.74
3,000 sq.ft. ÷	4,000 = 0.75 ×	0.98 = 0.74	$23.42 (interpolated building rate)

Multiplying the building rate times the ground floor area gives the base building cost.

$$\$23.42 \times 15,000 \ = \ \$351,300 \text{ (base building cost)}$$

The same method of interpolation would be followed in determining the basement rate in Step 5. No miscellaneous improvements and addition costs are specified on the commercial cost estimating form, and therefore the basement rate is:

$$\$13.11 - \$12.68 \ = \ \$0.43 \times 0.75 \ = \ \$0.32$$

$$\$13.11 - \$0.32 \ = \ \$12.79 \times 15,000 \text{ sq. ft.} \ = \ \$191,850 \text{ (base basement cost)}$$

Step 6 would be:

$$\$351,300 \text{ (base building cost)} \ + \ \$191,850 \text{ (basement cost)} \ = \ \$543,150 \text{ (total cost)}$$

Next the underwriter refers to the location multiplier, which is determined by the first three digits of the zip code. The location multiplier represents adjustments in building costs which vary from location to location. Since the rate of inflation in building costs varies by geographic area, these location multipliers are updated frequently, usually every six months. An excerpt from a location multiplier table might be:

Pennsylvania

Zip Code	Multiplier
189-190	1.12
191-193	1.04
194-195	1.09

The 100 percent replacement cost value is determined by multiplying the total cost of building and basement by the location multiplier:

$$\$543,150 \times 1.04 \ = \ \$564,876 \text{ (100 percent replacement cost of building)}$$

This completes Step 7. If this particular building were to be written on an actual cash value basis, the depreciation amount would have to be subtracted from the 100 percent replacement cost.

Exhibit 1-7
Normal Depreciation Guideline Tables*

Rating	Years								
	0-2	3-5	10	15	20	25	30	35	40
Wood Frame or Masonry									
(E)	0%	3%	8%						
(G)	1	4	12	18%	25%	30%	36%	42%	47%
(A)	2	5	16	22	29	35	41	47	52

* Reprinted with permission of E.H. Boeckh Co., a Division of American Appraisal Associates, Inc., Milwaukee, WI.

The depreciation amount is based on construction, age, and condition of the building. Use of these tables requires rating of the condition of the building together with a determination of its age. All this information is available on the submission. The depreciation amounts are expressed as a percentage of replacement cost of the original building construction and originally installed mechanical equipment. The following definitions are utilized to evaluate the condition of the building. Exhibit 1-7 (which is an expanded version of a table such as that in Exhibit 1-2) uses these ratings to help in determining the depreciation.

Excellent (E) Building is in perfect condition; no evidence of deterioration.
Good (G) Minor deterioration visible.
Average (A) Normal wear and tear apparent.

In the Gourmet Galley example, the proper depreciation amount for a ten-year-old building in good condition would be 12 percent, so the actual cash value of the building (given depreciation of 12% × $564,876 or $67,785) would be:

$$\$564,876 - \$67,785 = \$497,091$$

Two things should be remembered in this value determination. First, any significant deviations from the standard model should be kept in mind when determining the building value. Adjustments, therefore, may be necessary in the standard amounts provided in the tables. Second, the resulting building amount, whether on a replacement cost or actual cash value basis, represents the 100 percent value of the building.

What to Do with the Calculated Value A building value calculated in the above manner is only an estimate. Buildings with unique or unusual features could have values considerably different from those determined by the above process. Oftentimes use of a building evaluation manual or a professional appraisal may be necessary if the particular building deviates too much from the model.

Even when the underwriter has arrived at a reasonable value for a particular building, there can be practical problems in insuring the building. The insured or producer may not want to insure to 100 percent of the value, or may totally disagree with the underwriter's estimate of the value.

From a practical standpoint, whenever a discrepancy exists between the value calculated by the underwriter and the amount of insurance requested, the underwriter should try to resolve the discrepancy. If a mistake was not made in the valuation, or no new information is offered to justify a lower value, the underwriter should alert the producer and/or the insured to the consequences of underinsurance. Generally, underwriters will accept an insurance amount that is 80 percent or more of the total value. If the insurance amount is less than 80 percent, the underwriter may reduce the coinsurance percentage, change from an agreed amount to a coinsurance basis, change from a replacement cost basis to actual cash value, obtain agreement from the producer to increase the values at the next renewal, or decline the risk.

Naturally, in order to determine accurate values, the underwriter must obtain accurate information from the application or inspection report. This would include precise measurements of the ground floor, the wall heights, the sizes of fire divisions, and a description of floors different in area from the ground floor.

There can be wide discrepancies between the value of the building as calculated by the underwriter and the producer's value. This often occurs with old buildings or buildings in economically declining neighborhoods. Insisting on 100 percent insurance to value would create a moral hazard; yet writing the building at a greatly reduced value would result in inadequate premium.

The answer to this problem lies in the underwriter's evaluation of the hazards. If the low market value is due to inadequate wiring, heating, or maintenance or the area has a high crime, arson, or vandalism rate, the building would probably not be acceptable at any insurance value. On the other hand, if the building is well maintained and not subject to extreme extended coverage hazards, the underwriter should find an acceptable method for insuring the property.

Special Valuation Problems

Inflation The economy is often subject to severe inflation. The early eighties saw record double-digit inflation; yet 1982 and 1983 saw

Exhibit 1-8
Inflation Adjustments

Automatic Quarterly Limit Increase	3-Year Effect on Limits	Annual Premium Increase	3-Year Premium Increase
+1.0%	+11.0%	+1.5%	5.0%
+1.5%	+16.5%	+2.25%	7.5%
+2.0%	+22.0%	+3.0%	10.0%

that reduced to single digits. In such a dynamic climate, appreciation must be considered as well as depreciation. Besides recalculating values periodically and requesting higher insurance amounts on renewal, underwriters have devised a few other methods of attempting to maintain insurance to value during inflationary periods.

Recognizing in periods of double-digit inflation that substantial annual increases in insurance amounts may create opposition from the insured and the producer and still not provide adequate insurance during the policy period, the inflation guard endorsement was introduced.

This *inflation guard endorsement* automatically increases the amount of insurance by a predetermined percentage. Some companies offer a range of percentage increases and permit the insured to select the most appropriate. Most forms increase the insurance amount each quarter, but other forms are available. While the percentage of increase also varies by insurance company, 1 percent, 1.5 percent, and 2 percent are common. (It must be realized that even a 2 percent quarterly increase does not keep up with double-digit inflation.) Since the amount of insurance is increased quarterly, the inflation guard endorsement also provides for an increase in premium to cover the increased insurance amount. Exhibit 1-8 illustrates a typical inflation guard program.

If an insured with a $100,000 building with a three-year policy chose a quarterly automatic increase of 1.5 percent by means of the inflation guard endorsement, the insured would have the following amounts of insurance:

Initial amount	$100,000
End of:	
first quarter	101,500
second quarter	103,000

Exhibit 1-9
Equipment Value Updaters as of December 19X6

	19X0	19X1	6/X2	12/X2	6/X3	12/X3	6/X4	12/X4	6/X5	12/X5	6/X6	12/X6
Average	1.56	1.50	1.47	1.44	1.49	1.39	1.26	1.12	1.09	1.08	1.04	1.00
Apartment	1.39	1.37	1.34	1.32	1.30	1.27	1.18	1.12	1.09	1.08	1.03	1.00
Bakery	1.56	1.50	1.46	1.44	1.42	1.39	1.27	1.13	1.09	1.08	1.03	1.00
Banking	1.51	1.47	1.44	1.41	1.38	1.35	1.23	1.11	1.08	1.07	1.03	1.00
Bottling	1.57	1.53	1.48	1.45	1.43	1.40	1.26	1.12	1.09	1.07	1.03	1.00
Church	1.45	1.42	1.40	1.37	1.34	1.31	1.20	1.12	1.10	1.08	1.03	1.00
Contractors Equipment	1.62	1.57	1.52	1.51	1.47	1.44	1.32	1.15	1.09	1.07	1.03	1.00
Dwelling	1.39	1.36	1.34	1.32	1.29	1.27	1.19	1.12	1.09	1.07	1.03	1.00
Electrical Equipment Manufacturing	1.54	1.50	1.47	1.44	1.42	1.39	1.26	1.12	1.09	1.07	1.04	1.00
Garage	1.55	1.49	1.44	1.42	1.40	1.37	1.25	1.12	1.08	1.06	1.03	1.00
Hotel	1.47	1.43	1.40	1.38	1.35	1.32	1.22	1.11	1.09	1.07	1.03	1.00
Laundry and Cleaning	1.56	1.51	1.48	1.45	1.42	1.40	1.26	1.11	1.08	1.07	1.03	1.00
Metalworking	1.60	1.55	1.51	1.48	1.45	1.42	1.28	1.13	1.09	1.07	1.03	1.00
Office	1.49	1.46	1.42	1.39	1.37	1.33	1.22	1.11	1.08	1.06	1.02	1.00
Printing	1.56	1.50	1.47	1.44	1.42	1.39	1.23	1.12	1.09	1.08	1.03	1.00
Restaurant	1.50	1.47	1.44	1.42	1.40	1.37	1.24	1.12	1.09	1.08	1.03	1.00
Schools	1.51	1.47	1.44	1.41	1.38	1.35	1.22	1.11	1.09	1.07	1.03	1.00
Store	1.50	1.46	1.43	1.40	1.38	1.34	1.21	1.12	1.10	1.08	1.03	1.00
Theatre	1.52	1.48	1.44	1.41	1.39	1.35	1.23	1.11	1.09	1.07	1.03	1.00
Warehousing	1.50	1.45	1.41	1.40	1.37	1.36	1.23	1.15	1.12	1.10	1.04	1.00
Woodworking	1.50	1.45	1.43	1.40	1.38	1.36	1.23	1.14	1.11	1.09	1.04	1.00

third quarter   104,500
fourth quarter   106,000

At the end of the first year, the premium would increase 2.25 percent but the amount of insurance would increase $6,000, or 6 percent. At the end of the three-year period, the amount of insurance would be $116,500 at a cost of 7.5 percent of the original premium.

The inflation guard endorsement does not affect the coinsurance requirements, but it does affect the application of the coinsurance formula. Assuming the insured meets the coinsurance requirements at the inception of the program, the *insurance carried* and *insurance required* values of the formula will automatically increase each quarter.

Underwriters encourage the use of the inflation guard endorsement during periods of inflation. But, it is still very important to establish the proper building value at policy inception; otherwise the automatic increases will continually lag behind the true value. Increasing by the inflation rate a value which began 20 percent too low does not solve the original inadequacy problem (with regard to both value and underwriting). If the building is properly underwritten and valued initially, the likelihood of an overinsurance situation developing is diminished.

Furniture, Fixtures, and Equipment   Since the inflation guard endorsement applies only to buildings, the underwriter must specifically request increases in furniture, fixtures, and equipment at each renewal. Guides providing replacement cost multipliers by type of industry have been compiled to aid the underwriter in establishing proper values for equipment. Exhibit 1-9 is an example of such a guide.

It can be determined by using Exhibit 1-9 that if a restaurant owner installed $50,000 of equipment in 19X0, it would cost $75,000 to replace the equipment in December of 19X6.

Depreciation of Furniture, Fixtures, and Equipment.   For policies written on an actual cash value basis, it is possible to determine the actual cash value for equipment and fixtures by applying a depreciation factor to the replacement cost determined above. An example of depreciation factors is shown in Exhibit 1-10.

Since this restaurant's equipment would have depreciated 50 percent in six years, the current actual cash value would be $37,500. The term "effective age" is an Internal Revenue Service term which means the actual age of the equipment minus the age which has been removed due to restoration, refinishing, or reconstruction. Since these depreciation factors have been based on the IRS averages for industry groups, the percentages may be overstated. The underwriter should be

Exhibit 1-10
Depreciation Guidelines

	Industry Groups—Depreciation			
Effective Age	I	II	III	IV
1	15	8	6	5
2	31	16	13	10
3	50	24	20	15
4		33	27	21
5		42	34	27
6		50	42	32
7			50	38
8				45
9				50
10				

I—Construction Equipment
II—Apartments, Banking, Garage, Hotel, Laundry and Dry Cleaning, Office, Printing, Restaurant, School, Stores, Warehousing
III—Bakery, Bottling, Cannery, Church, Dairy, Electrical Equipment Manufacturing, Metalworking
IV—Textile

cognizant of this possibility when determining the actual cash value of equipment using this technique.

SUMMARY

Fire is the predominant peril in property insurance. The history of property insurance is punctuated with major conflagrations which have greatly influenced property insurance underwriting. As fire insurance evolved, additional perils were added, first with the extended coverage endorsement, then with a gradual extension to "all-risks." Recovery under a property insurance policy is limited by the extent of the insured's insurable interest, following the principle of indemnity. When written on a replacement cost basis, the contracts usually require the insured to replace the structure, reducing moral hazard.

There are three principal measures of loss severity used in property insurance. These are:

1. amount subject (maximum possible loss),
2. probable maximum loss, and
3. limit of liability.

An essential part of property insurance underwriting is the proper determination of value. The definition and determination of the actual cash value of insured property is crucial. Actual cash value has been defined as replacement cost (new) less accumulated physical depreciation and obsolescence at the time of loss. In a number of states, valued policy laws require that the amount of insurance be paid on total losses without reference to the actual cash value of the insured property. This underlies the need for accurate and current appraisals of commercial property. Certain rules of thumb and reference to national business indexes can provide a rough approximation of property values. For a more accurate determination it is necessary to utilize a more formal appraisal technique.

Three of the appraisal methods currently being employed are:

1. the component method,
2. the model method, and
3. the general estimate method.

Appraisals provide the replacement cost of the structure. In order to arrive at actual cash value, depreciation must be determined. Most techniques arrive at this by consideration of the age and condition of the building.

During some periods, inflation presents a serious problem in determination of accurate current values. The inflation guard endorsement is one method for keeping the insured values of buildings current. When determining the current value of furniture, fixtures, and equipment, it is necessary to first determine the current replacement cost. This can be done by reference to tables indicating the appreciation for certain classes of equipment. The actual cash value of this type of property is then determined by calculation of the applicable amount of depreciation.

Chapter Notes

1. Robert Considine, *Man Against Fire* (New York: Doubleday and Co., 1955). See also John V. Morris, *Fires and Firefighters* (Boston: Little, Brown & Co., 1955).
2. P. B. Reed and P. I. Thomas, *Adjustment of Property Losses* (New York: McGraw-Hill Book Co., 1969), p. 1.
3. Robert B. Holtom, *Commercial Fire Underwriting* (Cincinnati: The National Underwriter Company, 1969), p. 21.
4. Jefferson Insurance Company of New York v. Superior Court of Alameda County, 1970 Commerce Clearing House (Fire and Casualty) 658.
5. Butler v. Aetna Insurance Co., 256 N.W. 214.
6. Based on a publication by E.H. Boeckh Co., A Division of American Appraisal Associates, Inc.

CHAPTER 2

Analyzing Loss Potential from Fire

INTRODUCTION

Fire is extremely rapid oxidation. At normal temperatures oxidation of most materials takes place slowly (e.g., rusting of iron, deterioration of natural rubber). Heat speeds up the process. With enough heat, oxidation takes place so rapidly it produces more heat—heat that is visible as a glow or flame. It is then called *fire* or *combustion*. Combustion is the process of self-catalyzed reactions producing heat involving either a condensed fuel phase (glow), a gas phase (flame), or both. Fire therefore requires the availability of oxygen and with most materials some source of heat beyond ordinary atmospheric temperatures to speed up the oxidation process to a self-sustaining level. There also must be something to be oxidized, something to burn. This combustion process may be viewed as a complex chain reaction. Certain chemical compounds used as extinguishing agents interrupt this chain reaction. Therefore, to start and sustain a fire, there are four necessary ingredients: heat, oxygen, fuel, and a chain reaction.

For many years the literature has referred to the triangle of fire, based on the components of air, fuel, and heat. Recent research has identified the role of a fourth component, an uninhibited chain reaction as part of the process. The four components of fire may be viewed as the fire tetrahedron. A tetrahedron is a three-sided pyramid with a base. Each of the four planes of the tetrahedron touches the others, illustrating the relationship between these components. If any one of these planes were removed, the fire would be extinguished. The fire tetrahedron is shown in Exhibit 2-1.

Exhibit 2-1
The Fire Tetrahedron*

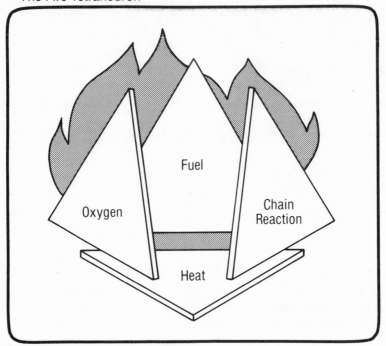

*Reprinted with permission from *Judging the Fire Risk*, 4th ed. (Chicago: Alliance of American Insurers, 1981), p.1.

Once oxidation has reached the fire or self-sustaining level, it produces its own heat. The heat produced can, and often does, cause the rapid oxidation in still more material so that material also flames or glows and the fire spreads. Thus, analysis for possibility as to spread of fire means investigation of the possibility that heat from an original fire will reach additional material—more fuel—causing it also to burn, with creation of still more heat, in a self-perpetuating chain reaction.

Fires deliberately kindled and properly confined are called *friendly*. But when they appear in or spread to places not intended, their character changes to *hostile*. Hostile fires are the subject of fire insurance and their possibility and potential must be estimated in advance by underwriters. In what follows, the word "fire" will refer to hostile fires except when the context makes another meaning clear.

SOURCES OF IGNITION

Analysis of fire loss possibility begins with identification of both present and possible sources of ignition.

Ignition sources may be *fixed* or *mobile.* The hazards associated with fixed sources, such as furnaces and incinerators, are subject to more complete identification and measurement than those associated with mobile sources. Mobile sources include cutting and welding torches used in maintenance and repair of buildings and equipment.

A distinction may be made with respect to heat sources between those in which the *heat itself is wanted* and those in which *it is unwanted.* Equipment installed for the specific purpose of generating heat, such as furnaces, kilns, forges, and driers, is usually readily recognizable as a heat source. Equipment which produces heat as an unwanted by-product is sometimes overlooked. All electrical equipment and wiring have heat potential, although in most instances the heat is undesirable. Wherever there is motion—in motors, shafts, skids, and a host of equipment types—there is friction, and friction produces heat. Overheated bearings and sparks from surfaces pulled across each other have caused serious fires. Friction also produces electricity which sometimes builds up in the atmosphere as static electricity providing sparks that set off a fire or an explosion.

Heating Devices

Nearly all buildings have some heat in the form of *space heating* that keeps the building's interior at an acceptable temperature. Furnaces and other equipment for providing that heat are a potential source of fire. The hazard centers in the burners or heating elements of the equipment. The equipment itself and the pipes, ducts, and flues leading from it also get hot. The pipes and flues that conduct combustion wastes to the outside, such as smokepipes or chimney flues, get extremely hot. The piping and ducts that spread heat throughout the interior of the building typically operate at temperatures that present less hazard; however, under some circumstances they can cause fires.

Cooking Equipment

Cooking equipment uses heat that can cause hostile fires and has flues and vents that can get hot. Properly designed, installed, and maintained heating and cooking equipment does not cause hostile fires. Underwriters' Laboratories, Inc., and other agencies test and certify

Exhibit 2-2
Structure Fires by Fire Ignition Sequence-1980*

Origin	Estimated Number	Estimated Loss (000 omitted)
Heating	179,852	$ 571,643
Cooking	123,595	202,802
Incendiary, suspicious	152,652	1,216,574
Smoking	79,904	243,007
Electrical distribution	74,553	492,176
Appliances	55,062	176,354
Children playing	47,909	113,027
Other equipment	58,498	342,864
Exposures	30,771	273,187
Natural (Lightning, sun, etc.)	17,221	122,355
Open-flame	51,010	202,482
Other-flame	16,364	70,634
Unknown	95,807	1,123,723
Total	983,198†	5,150,828

†Total may not equal sum of column due to rounding

*Adapted from *Fires in the United States*, 3rd ed. 1980, Federal Emergency Management Agency, Washington, D.C., 1982, Appendix, Table 35, page 36; Table 38, page 39. Based on 1980 National Fire Information Reporting System data.

types of equipment for safety in designated uses. The National Fire Protection Association (NFPA), other associations, and governmental bodies issue specifications and recommendations for the installation and maintenance of heating and cooking equipment.

Exhibit 2-2 indicates fire losses for 1980 by *fire ignition sequence.* Fire ignition sequence includes the identification of three factors—a heat source, fuel, and an event (i.e., human action, or natural act that combines the heat source and fuel to cause a fire). Note that heating and cooking equipment were involved in an estimated 303,447 fires resulting in approximately $774 million in damage.

Unfortunately, equipment is not always properly installed and managed. One thing that can go wrong is to change types of fuel— from natural to artificial gas, for example, or from No. 2 to No. 4 fuel oil. NFPA warns:

The specific gas or gases with which an appliance may be used is marked on the appliance. Although such appliances may be converted in the field to any one of the marked gases, the conversion may require some interchange of parts and may involve some element of hazard unless carefully done by experienced, qualified personnel.[1]

The same warning holds for other types of fuel.

Another type of error is to install or allow the presence of something that interferes with the flow of air into a combustion chamber. A frequent form of improper installation is failure to create adequate clear space between a heating unit and combustible portions of the building such as floors, framing, or partitions. Failure to maintain adequate clearance between chimneys or flues and combustible structural parts is also a significant cause of fires. In addition, soot inside the flue can catch fire. This is particularly a problem in cooking situations where vapors from foods and cooking oils are carried into the vent and leave greasy deposits there. Also, hot ashes and coals removed from the furnace are sometimes brought near or mixed with combustible items, including combustible containers.

Welding and Cutting

This is often referred to as "hot work." Welding and cutting equipment has been a significant source of fire loss when measured in dollars. The hazard needs to be divided between production and other uses of torches. Production welding is essentially a "fixed location" problem. The area of the exposure is known and can be arranged and protected accordingly. The more severe hazard lies in the mobile exposures—in the taking of cutting and welding torches to various locations for use in construction, installation, or repair on an ad hoc or temporary basis. Unless specific, thorough care is taken, such locations may *not* be properly arranged nor protected against flames, heat, and sparks from welding and cutting torches.

Mobile Heat Generators

Mobile heat generators of all kinds present fire hazards. An important class is that of portable heaters, including salamanders, that can be placed too close to easily flammable materials, where they can be knocked over, or where their flames and coals can be whipped up and spread by winds. Salamanders are miscellaneous portable heating devices, particularly used on construction jobs or other unheated locations. Often a salamander is fabricated from a metal drum with holes punched in it for draft, with wood scrap and other construction waste materials used as fuel. These present a severe spark hazard, and since they are not chimney connected, carbon monoxide poisoning is an additional hazard. Hazardous gas- and oil-fired salamanders, not tested and listed by recognized agencies, are also used.

Hot Liquids

Molten metals require special consideration as a source of heat to start or spread fires. The special problem arises with the escape of the metal from its container or intended channels. Such escape can be caused by container collapse or by inadvertent opening of an outlet at the wrong time. Once escaped, molten metal obviously is an intense fire hazard. Some other industrial liquids are circulated at temperatures hot enough to cause fires. These range from steam, particularly when superheated, to some isomer mixtures with boiling points of 750° F or more. Hot liquids thus can act as an extension of a heat source, spreading its influence over a wider area.

Electrical Wiring and Equipment

Exhibit 2-2 shows that electrical wiring and equipment is a particularly severe fire source. In 1980 electrical sources accounted for 17.6 percent of all nonincendiary fires of known origin and they accounted for 23.8 percent of the dollar loss in such fires. Most of the contribution was from wiring and its connections—10.1 percent of the frequency and 17.5 percent of the severity. The National Fire Protection Association reports that most electrical fires can be categorized as due to worn out or tired electrical equipment, improper use of approved equipment, defective installation, or an accidental occurrence.[2] It is clear that the care and reliability of management are major factors in fire loss prevention or lack thereof.

Friction

Friction is another source of heat that can cause fires. All types of equipment with rapidly moving parts present friction problems. Normally these are controlled by lubrication and by limits on operating conditions. Failure of lubrication or overloaded operation will cause increased heat and in the presence of easily combustible material, a fire can be started. Sparks are sometimes thrown by sliding equipment across hard surfaces. Friction and sparks may occur from dropping of tools or from tramp metal. Overall, this is a relatively small source except in dusty atmospheres or the presence of readily flammable vapors.

Static Electricity

Processes that produce friction also produce static electricity. Where conditions include both buildup of static electricity and explosive or flammable atmosphere or vapors, as in grain elevators, there is a major fire and explosion hazard requiring control.

Spontaneous Ignition

Some materials are subject to spontaneous ignition. Best known are oily rags and wastes. But some natural materials and chemicals used in industrial processes have similar capacity. Among these are coal, charcoal, some agricultural products such as alfalfa, corn and fish meals, and linseed and fish oils. Some explosives can be detonated by concussion, a "spontaneous ignition" in that it requires no external source of heat.

Chemical Reactions

Some chemical reactions generate enough heat to start fires. Often these reactions are essential to particular industrial processes. The heat itself is just a concomitant hazard.

In addition, there are many potent chemicals that produce high heat when misused or when certain kinds of accidents occur. Thus, sulfuric acid creates heat explosively on contact with water. Of course identification of all the chemicals and combinations that can produce dangerous heat is beyond the scope of this text. Commercial insurance underwriting departments must have available and use technical source materials. Examples include National Fire Protection Association publications No. 49, "Hazardous Chemicals Data," and No. 491M, "Manual of Hazardous Chemical Reactions."

Other Sources

Natural Causes   A dramatic source of heat for fires is lightning. Its overall importance is reflected in Exhibit 2-2, which shows natural causes to be a source in 2.3 percent of the known nonincendiary fires in 1980 and 4.4 percent of the dollar losses from such fires. Lightning is usually subject to control by a properly designed and maintained lightning arrester system. Other natural causes include fires resulting from unintentional focusing of the sun's rays on combustible material.

Smoking and Matches   A more important source is smoking and matches. Exhibit 2-2 shows that 10.9 percent of nonincendiary fires with known causes has come from "smoking related" sources. Fortunately these fires have severity a little less than average; they have contributed only 8.6 percent of total dollar loss. Their relative importance varies with the amount of personal and public exposure in an occupancy.

Control of loss by smoking and matches has two principal parts: prohibition in areas not designed for safety of smoking materials, and proper design and attendance of equipment such as ashtrays and butt and waste cans in areas where smoking is allowed. Control of smoking areas because of possible health hazard may also reduce fire loss depending on care taken with the areas into which smoking is concentrated. Management attitude, procedures, and practices constitute the essential ingredient in the control of the smoking hazard.

Exposure Fires   When fire spreads from one building to another, the source of ignition for the second building is said to be an *exposure fire*. The likelihood of loss from an exposure fire depends on many factors, including the probability of fire in an exposing building, the distance between the buildings, the combustibility of each of the buildings, weather and climate, and the protection provided the second building. This is covered in more detail in a later chapter.

The first step in analysis of exposure as a source of ignition is identification of the structures that are close enough to present a possible hazard. How close is "close enough" depends on the nature of the buildings, the climate, and the protection provided. Two fire resistive buildings with blank facing walls (no openings) of equal height in an area with good public fire protection present little exposure hazard to each other. Two frame buildings with many doors and windows, one many feet taller than the other, and no public fire protection require a great deal of clear space. The occupancies must also be considered.

The possible intensity and duration of a fire in the exposing building is a major factor in evaluating the exposure hazard. The NFPA states that the intensity and duration of a fully developed fire depends on the quantity of combustible materials available (*fuel load*), their burning rates (*flame spread*), and the air available for combustion.[3] The fuel load (sometimes referred to as *fire load*) is the expected maximum amount of combustible material in a given fire area. In a normal building, this consists of the combustible structural elements and the combustible contents contained within a single fire area. Fuel load is usually expressed as weight of combustible material per square foot of fire area. It is, in essence, a measure of the maximum heat that would be released if all the combustibles in a given area were to burn. The greater the probable and possible intensity of fire in the exposing building, the greater the clear space needed to prevent exposure fires.

Flame spread, as the term implies, is a measure of how quickly a flame will spread when a material or finish is ignited. Generally, the flame spread is a rating between zero and 100, where the higher numbers mean the fire or flame will spread more quickly.

Additional factors that affect spread of fire are as follows.[4]

1. In the exposing building:
   - type of construction of exterior walls and roof
   - building width, height
   - openings in exposing wall (if wall itself could resist fire)
   - fuel characteristics of interior, including the finish
   - size and shape of relevant rooms
   - ventilation characteristics of the burning room

2. In the exposed building:
   - type of construction of exterior walls and roof
   - size and orientation of exposed surface
   - openings in exposed wall and their protection
   - exposure of interior to heat and flying brands
   - fuel characteristics of interior
   - height relative to exposing building

3. Site and protection features:
   - clear distance between buildings
   - shielding by interposed noncombustible buildings
   - wind (direction and velocity), air temperature, and humidity
   - effectiveness of fire fighting
   - accessibility for fire fighting operation

The NFPA gives recommended minimum separation for prevention of spread of fires. The distances range from five feet more than 0.36 times the width or height of the exposing building, whichever is the smaller dimension, to five feet more than 13.15 times that dimension.[5] Exposure hazards are reflected in fire insurance rating schedules, but the distances at which these schedules produce no charge for an exposure are often less than the distances considered safe by the NFPA. Historical reasons for caution include a fire in a group of brick, wood-joisted buildings that spread across an 80-foot street to the upper stories of a taller, fire resistive building, and one that spread 100 feet upwind across a river.[6]

Incendiarism The number of fires caused by incendiarism is an estimate, in many cases reflecting the investigators' conclusions as to probable causes. Often there is not a full investigation; other times the evidence has been destroyed in the fire. Therefore, it is assumed that the actual number of fires of incendiary origin is greater than the reported number. The reported number in 1980 (Exhibit 2-2) was 17.2 percent of those with assigned causes; dollar losses came to 30.2 percent of the losses in fires with assigned causes. Experts suspect additional contribution from the "unknown cause" group actually raises those ratios. The NFPA figures for 1970 were 7.7 percent of the fires and 16.7 percent of the loss dollars. The increase came partly because more active and thorough investigation did a better job of identifying incendiary and suspicious cases. But experts believe some of the increase was also real, associated partly with harder times for many businesses and partly with better technology and organization among arsonists. Another factor has been some revival of incendiarism as a terrorist or social agitation tactic.

Underwriters need to divide incendiarism into two categories: incendiarism *against* the insured, and incendiarism *by* the insured or the insured's agents. Like other crime exposures, incendiarism against the insured is an insurable exposure in the absence of unusual intensity of hazard. Common motives for such incendiarism are (1) to cover other crimes, usually burglary or employee dishonesty, (2) revenge, usually by employees or former employees, and (3) vandalism.

With respect to conflicts with employees, two general categories exist: problems with disgruntled individuals and problems with cohesive groups. The former cases are often not discoverable by the underwriter. And when specific information *is* received, the underwriter should remember verbal threats are easy to make and seldom carried out. Labor problems with cohesive groups include those involving employees who are members of an established legitimate union, those involving attempts to unionize a nonunion plant, and other cases.

FUELS

The contributions that different fuel materials make toward fire loss come from their flammability or combustibility and from the by-products of combustion. *Combustible* is used to refer to a material or structure that can burn. *Flammable* refers to material that ignites very easily, burns intensely, or has a rapid rate of flame spread.

Flammability or Combustibility

Hydrogen burns more readily than carbon monoxide, gasoline

more readily than paraffin oil, wood more readily than steel. Fuel oil shot through a burner nozzle burns more readily than fuel oil in a storage tank; wood splinters burn more readily than the logs from which the splinters came. What characteristics of materials increase or decrease their likelihood of supporting a fire as fuel?

Vaporization   In general, solid and liquid materials do not burn; only vapors from them are combustible. That is, for fire to destroy a solid or liquid, the materials must first be vaporized. Materials that remain solid or liquid at ordinary temperatures must be heated until they give off combustible vapors. These then can be burned, producing more heat that creates more vapors to burn. Thus it is not really the combustible liquid, for example, that burns when exposed to a source of ignition under proper conditions, but the vapor from the evaporization of that liquid.

The amount of external heat required to produce flammable vaporization depends on the chemical nature of the substance and its physical arrangement. Among the key elements are the ease and rapidity of vaporization of the material and how much of the vapor there must be in the air before the mixture will spread flame.

Liquids.   By standard tests, flash points have been established for many liquids. The *lower flash point* in air is the lowest temperature at which the substance produces enough vapor to create a vapor-air mixture that will propagate flame at standard atmospheric pressure.

The flash point for 100 octane gasoline is about − 36° F. For No. 2 fuel it is about 100° F. Thus, at usual atmospheric temperatures, gasoline gives off vapors that once ignited will spread flame; No. 2 fuel oil does not. This is what makes gasoline more hazardous than fuel oil.

Gasoline is generally more hazardous than fuel oil despite the fact that a temperature of about 850° F is required to ignite the gasoline vapor mix, while only about 490° F is required to ignite a vapor mix from No. 2 fuel oil. Gasoline vapors are always present where gasoline is and need only to spread to a rather hot surface, spark, or flame to flash flame throughout the vaporized area. At usual atmospheric temperatures fuel oil usually does not produce enough vapor to spread flame although it can do so when exposed on extremely hot days.

Burnable liquids may be divided into class I, *flammable* and class II, *combustible*. In general, class I contains liquids with flash points below 100° F, and liquids with higher flash points belong in class II. There are also subdivisions for each class.[7]

Underwriters' Laboratories, Inc., uses a classification system based on the scale shown in Exhibit 2-3.[8]

Solids and Gases.   Solids, too, must give off vapors before they can be burned. The process is complex with many variables affecting it,

Exhibit 2-3
Relative Flammability of Liquids*

Flammable Liquids	Index Numbers (U.L. Standard)
Ether class	100
Gasoline class	90-100
Alcohol (ethyl) class	60-70
Kerosene class	30-40
Paraffin oil class	10-20

*Adapted with permission from Gordon P. McKinnon, ed., *Fire Protection Handbook*, 15th ed. (Quincy, MA: National Fire Protection Association, 1981), p.4-27.

but the main elements are these. First, heat is required to produce combustible vapors and to ignite them, and their burning produces more heat. If the original heat source plus the burning vapors produce enough total heat in temperature and duration, the solid itself becomes hot enough to continue burning even after the original ignition source is removed.

Flammable vapors are produced at temperatures lower than their ignition point. Therefore, a smoldering fire may produce a great deal of vapor that later bursts suddenly into flame when sufficient heat from the fire or some other ignition source finally reaches it. Some surface finishes, such as varnishes and waxes, are highly volatile. Therefore, fire is spread over a large area rapidly, even though the finished material, such as wood or wallboard, is not itself initially involved. Occasionally flame even spreads across polished masonry by combustion of waxes or other surface finishing materials. Normally, however, spread of flame across combustible solids is much slower than spread across flammable liquids because vaporization of solids commonly takes longer.

Flammable and combustible gases are themselves in vapor form, of course, so flame spreads rapidly through them, once ignition temperature has been reached.

Shape of Material A major factor affecting the heating of a solid is its shape. When flame is applied to the surface of a log, some of that heat is dissipated away from the heated point to other parts of the log—to elsewhere on its surface and to its interior. If the external heat source is soon removed, parts of the log will have been warmed but none will be hot enough to keep the fire going. But when a splinter is subjected to external flame, little total energy is required to heat the whole piece up to flame-sustaining temperature. Thus, small particles are much more flammable than large pieces: steel wool burns rather readily; nails, let alone structural beams, do not. When the particles are small enough and numerous, like the grain dust in a grain elevator, they can all be vaporized and consumed so rapidly as to be explosive.

Products of Combustion

The products of combustion include heat, water, solid particles, and gases. In complete combustion of organic materials, carbon dioxide is the principal gas product. However, combustion is seldom complete, especially in hostile fires, so carbon monoxide and other toxic gases are also produced. Particular fuels such as those containing sulfur, nitrogen, petroleum products, and chlorine give off such toxic gases as hydrogen sulfide, ammonia, acrolein, and phosgene. While a fire is burning, the solid particles it produces tend to be suspended in, and to move with, water vapor in the heated air. They are seen as smoke. The various products affect the amount of fire loss as follows.

Heat Some burning materials give off more heat than others— for example, burning a pound of asphalt gives off about twice as much heat as burning a pound of paper. The heat released by burning a material is known as its *calorific value*. Obviously, a material with high calorific value can cause more damage than the same amount of material with less calorific value. Also, hotter fires are usually harder to put out.

Gases and Smoke Toxic gases and smoke threaten injury to people, and smoke obscures visibility. These results affect fire loss because they hamper the action of fire fighters. Therefore, materials that give off more toxic fumes or dense smoke when burned tend to produce larger losses than do other materials. Examples of such materials include polyvinylchloride, urethane, acrylics, ammonium nitrate, wool, animal fats, and rubber.

Buildings as Fuel

Fuels for hostile fires occur as parts of buildings and as contents. They also occur outside of buildings, but commercial fire insurance underwriting is seldom concerned with these except as a possible cause of exposure fires. Buildings are discussed in Chapter 4 and their contents in Chapter 5.

Housekeeping

Every type of occupancy involves waste and trash. There are three parts of the exposure: uncollected litter, storage, and disposal.

Uncollected Litter Waste and trash in the form of uncollected litter can make a significant contribution to spread of fire. Particularly hazardous common types include oily or greasy items, paper and packing materials, small pieces of all kinds of combustibles, and discarded smoking materials.

In machining and many other industrial operations, lubricants must be widely used, so wastes and litter are often oily. Many janitorial cleaning functions involve oily substances or take place where oil or grease is present and so oily items such as rags and sweepings are produced. Accumulation of greasy soot in vents and flues, particularly over cooking stoves, has been mentioned earlier as a significant hazard.

The most common form of waste and litter is paper, which is especially combustible in litter form. Packing materials from incoming items are a major source of waste materials in stores and similar types of risks. Such materials tend to be concentrated in limited areas. Piled up loosely or haphazardly, they are ideal fuels for the growth and spread of fire.

As noted before, finely divided particles are especially combustible and sometimes highly explosive. A variety of operations produce large quantities of combustible lint or dust. Some of these collect on surfaces where they are less combustible than when suspended in air. The difference is due to the relationship with ambient oxygen. Wherever they are, lint and dust from organic or other combustible materials are hazardous as fuels for fire.

Somewhat larger particles of combustible litter are also hazardous, such as wood chips and metal shavings (usually oily). Another form of hazardous particles consists of soot in chimneys. As noted earlier, even apart from the special problem of oil wastes from cooking, simply burning fuel causes buildup of soot. Soft coal and wood create considerably more buildup than other fuels.

Storage Most commercial and institutional occupancies involve some storage of wastes. This means concentration of the material in a limited space. Depending on the material and the nature of the storage, such concentration and confinement may increase or decrease the hazard. Paper and cardboard, neatly stacked and enclosed, resists total burning better than the same quantity of material piled haphazardly and loosely. On the other hand, oily materials left undisturbed in a confined space may produce spontaneous ignition.

One problem with some storage is that different materials are mixed together with deleterious interaction. Common examples include putting unextinguished cigarettes in general trash bins and mixing oily wastes with quantities of dry combustibles.

Trash and waste storage should be in adequate and appropriate noncombustible containers. Apart from small quantities such as one wastebasket size, the storage should be well separated by adequate space or noncombustible barriers from all other exposures, especially sources of heat. Especially hazardous materials such as combustible metal shavings or powders and flammable liquids should be kept isolated from other waste.

Disposal When ultimate disposal of waste is on the premises, special precautions need to be taken. Disposal by incineration means creation of another heat source. Sparks and products of incomplete combustion are a common problem from burning of wastes. These are controlled by proper design and operation of the incinerator.

Mixtures of wastes present special problems. Common items such as aerosol cans and mercury batteries explode when burned. Some industrial wastes give off seriously toxic gases when burned; others produce extremely high temperatures or explode; some react violently with other materials that may be found in trash.

Removal and disposal of lint and dust require cleaning both of air and of surfaces. The process itself can cause fires if not properly done. The first step is removal by suction while operations are going on. What remains should be periodically vacuumed. In dust laden atmospheres, dust-ignition-proof motors are necessary. A complete cleaning by a specialized professional may occasionally be required.

Chimneys, too, should be cleaned periodically. The NFPA suggests annual cleaning where soft coal or wood are regularly used.

Common Fuels for Heat and Power

Fuels used in producing heat and power can also be fuel for hostile fires. Indeed, much of the hazard in heating and power equipment is that fuel and an ignition source must be brought together. The fuels may also be ignited by other sources.

In the past, there commonly was a problem with fuel being fed into the furnace but not ignited because of human error or failure of the pilot light. Later, ignition was inadvertently supplied and the accumulated fuel set off an explosion or large blaze. Automatic safety controls have greatly reduced the number of such events, but they can still occur. Automatic and human supervision are the antidotes.

Explosion from gas line leaks occur several times a year in the United States. Some leaks are very difficult to notice. Changes in line pressure can be a clue, but they are not always noticeable with small leaks. Marking of gases with an odor allows human detection. Under some industrial uses of gas, automatic detection is appropriate.

Liquefied petroleum gas (LP gas or LPG) is used as fuel in many places because of its power and portability, but it is highly flammable and powerfully explosive. A major cause of trouble is defects in the line between the bottle or tank containing the LP gas and the gas-using appliance. A container exposed to fire may fail, releasing its contents to the fire, frequently with catastrophic results. Since propane and butane are gases at normal temperatures, they are contained under pressure to keep them in liquid form. As a safety measure, containers have over-pressure relief devices. When these operate they relieve flammable vapor. If the vapor in a proper air mix reaches a source of ignition, fire will spread. Because of the hazards, bottles and tanks of liquefied petroleum gas, butane, or propane should not be kept indoors.

Fuel oils are less hazardous than fuel gases. As previously noted, the flash points of fuel oils are above usual atmospheric temperatures. The most serious hazards are associated with cleaning or removal of storage tanks that have been used. When unignited fuel oil accumulates from leakage or from malfunction of a burner and is subsequently ignited, it almost always burns poorly, emitting dense smoke. The smoke damage then greatly exceeds damage from heat and flame.

Coal presents much less hazard than oil or gas. Stored coal can burn, of course, but to flame continuously, it requires a steady through draft, essentially impossible in a coal pile. Coal, except high grade anthracite, is subject to spontaneous ignition, but the probability is very low and loss rarely extends to property other than the coal itself. The principal prevention is to limit the size of piles to no more than fifty tons.

Coal dust in general, and pulverized coal in particular, is more flammable than solid coal. With the right combinations of air and heat these forms are explosive. Equipment that uses pulverized coal must be designed to control and contain explosions. Dust from any use of coal requires control measures as described earlier for flammable and explosive dusts and lints.

OXYGEN FOR FIRES

Atmospheric Oxygen

The vast majority of hostile fires get their oxygen from the atmosphere. About 20 percent of earth's air is oxygen. However, the mixture of that oxygen and flammable or combustible vapor must be of appropriate proportions, or combustion will not take place. This physical law is illustrated by effects of different carburetor mixes in an automobile engine. When the mix is too *rich* with too much gasoline relative to air, the engine is "flooded" and dies. When the mixture is too "lean" with too little gasoline relative to air, the engine is "starved," and also dies.

The mixes of vapor and air that are combustible vary with the fuel. Vapors from gasoline burn when they constitute between 1.4 percent and 7.6 percent of the vapor and air mix. For natural gas the limits vary from 3.8 percent to 17 percent. This range is called the *explosive* or *flammable range*. The 1.4 percent is the *lower flammability limit* and the 7.6 percent is the *upper flammability limit*. The figures for solids are not generally known. Nonetheless, for a flame to be self-sustaining, there must be neither too little oxygen (too high of a vapor concentration) nor too little fuel (too low of a vapor concentration). A change in temperature will also change the range. Generally, when the temperature is increased, the range widens. A drop in temperature could possibly make the previously flammable liquid nonflammable for the conditions at hand.

Airflow in Fires When the amount of flammable vapor in a vapor-air mix is near the upper or lower flammable limits, combustion is slower and cooler than with concentrations in the middle of the range. In fire situations, being near the lower limit produces *smoldering*. The smoldering produces heat that causes increased production of flammable vapor, enriching the vapor-air mix; then the flame burns more brightly. However, if there is insufficient airflow, the available oxygen in the air is eventually used up, and the vapor-air mix gets too rich. Flaming dies down, and smoke reappears.

But air is heated by the fire, and heated air rises. It is replaced by fresh, cooler air, which brings more oxygen to the fire. This makes the mix leaner again, reviving the flame. In a strongly burning fire, the process is all in balance. Heat from the fire keeps creating more of the flammable combination—vapors plus oxygen from flowing air. As stated earlier, as the total temperature rises, the limits on flammable mixture move further apart—the higher limit goes up, the lower limit goes down. With a continuing supply of fuel and no interference, the heat keeps building. At the extreme, many solids are vaporized almost instantly, and the draft becomes a *fire storm* in which the speed of air movement reaches hurricane level. Fire storms occurred from bombings of some cities in World War II, and have happened occasionally in nonwar conflagrations.

Low Level of Oxygen As noted, low oxygen fires have imperfect combustion, with dense smoke. Also, carbon monoxide and, depending on the burning materials, other toxic gases are produced. Meanwhile, the fire continues to smolder, creating heat. Even if flames finally are starved out, the materials remain hot for some time. Then some additional event may happen: the slow burning fire may break through a window, partition, wall, or roof, allowing air to flow. If the breakthrough is above the fire, hot air flows out, cooling the area above the fire and lowering air pressure in the fire area. Unless the lower area is airtight, replacement air is forced in, bringing new oxygen. Wherever materials and surfaces have been heated enough to produce flammable vapors, flaming breaks out in the presence of this fresh oxygen. If the initial breakthrough is below the fire, air pressure in the area containing the fire may prevent the entry of fresh air.

The described process indicates why an entire enclosed space may suddenly burst into flame upon the opening of a door or other *venting*. This may happen with the opening of the door of a closet or enclosed storage area in which fire has been smoldering, or spontaneous heating taking place. But in larger areas, the principal initial effect of venting is removal of accumulated heat above the fire, slowing fire spread. The term venting is often used to describe the planned and systematic removal of smoke, heat, and fire gases from a burning building. It is also used to describe any one of a number of other methods of allowing the smoke and gases to purposely escape to aid fire fighting efforts and reduce damage.[9]

This process is complicated by the fact that many new buildings have been constructed without windows to save energy. Windows in some older buildings have been sealed with masonry for security purposes. The result is often an uncontrolled venting through the roof. The windowless structure will also be plunged into darkness if the power fails during a fire, imperiling the occupants and hindering fire suppression efforts.[10] The problem is illustrated in Exhibit 2-4.

Oxygen Rich Atmospheres Science teachers sometimes illustrate the effects of oxygen by dipping a glowing stick into a jar containing pure oxygen. The stick immediately bursts into flame. Some hot metals can be made to flame with extra oxygen. Such events represent the usual fire effects of oxygen enrichment—lower ignition temperature, more rapid spread of flame, and greater heat.

Oxygen enriched atmospheres are found in hospitals in operating rooms, oxygen tents, and incubators; in welding and cutting torch operations and some industrial processes; in underwater tunneling and caisson work; and may develop around oxygen processing, storage, or transport.

Exhibit 2-4
Fire in a Windowless Building*

*Photo by Paul Martin.

Oxidants

Some few materials can burn without oxygen from air; they can obtain oxygen from other sources. Burning magnesium, for example, can extract oxygen from water. Organic peroxides are self-oxidizing; oxygen for combustion or explosion can come from within. They are widely used in the plastics industry, in flour milling, and in chemical and drug manufacture.

A variety of chemicals, not themselves combustible, can provide oxygen for combustion of other materials. These include nitrates and nitrites, inorganic peroxides such as hydrogen peroxide, chlorates and chlorites, and permanganates. Some of these chemicals are explosive, and most of them provide such rapid oxidation to organic materials that the result is explosive.

FIRE SPREAD AND EXTENT

The elements required for the existence and spread of fires have been described separately. A remaining question is the extent to which they all will interact in a given setting and the sizes of fire they will produce.

Heat Spread

The outer limit of a fire loss is set by the fuel it may reach. How far can it go before it runs out of fuel? That limit is determined by how far the heat can reach beyond material already burning to additional material. Heat spreads by *conduction, convection,* and *radiation.*

Conduction Conduction is defined as heat transferred from one body to another through *physical contact.*[11] When the bowl of a silver spoon is placed in hot liquid, the handle soon becomes very hot. That is spread of heat by conduction. When there is a fire on one side of a solid wall, eventually the other side heats up—very slowly in the case of bricks, faster in the case of wood, and much faster still in the case of steel. In practice, part of the difference in speed is due to the relative thickness of the usual walls of brick (thickest), wood (thinner), and steel (thinnest). Heat is conducted over shorter distances faster than over longer ones. But another important difference among the three walls is the nature of the materials: steel conducts heat more rapidly than wood, and wood more rapidly than brick.

An important practical example of these differences appears in the encasement of flue gases. A thin metal smoke pipe transmits much heat to the outside and is hazardous to nearby combustible materials. A brick chimney conveys heat to the outside so slowly that heat is ordinarily dissipated as fast as it arrives at the outside surface.

All materials conduct heat. The question is how much and how fast. One general rule is that solids are better conductors than gases. With a given material, the total amount of heat transferred depends on the size of cross section of the material. A steel bar two inches in diameter conducts more heat than a steel nail does.

Insulating material conducts heat more slowly. The best insulating materials use the principles that have been mentioned by employing a low conductivity solid material in fine particle or fiber form with spaces between filled by air. And best installation allows air movement to carry away the heat that penetrates to the far side of the insulation. Obviously the amount of fuel that will be fired directly by conduction is the amount in contact with the conducting material.

Convection Convection is defined as heat *circulated* by a liquid or gas *circulating medium.*[12] Heated materials commonly expand. When heated material is free to move, as in fluids (gases and liquids), it tends to rise. The place left by the rising warm material is filled by cooler material. Thus, the upper portion of a heated room or a heated pool heats up more rapidly than the lower portion. The flow is subject to alteration by currents operating on the fluid, such as by wind in the air.

Some of the significance of convection in fires has already been discussed. Another is the well-known fact that material above a fire is generally more likely to be burned than material in other directions. One practical result is that high stacking of materials promotes fire spread; so does construction that includes tall shafts. The practical limit of fuel that will be fired directly by convection is the fuel that can be reached by airflow from the existing fire.

Radiation Radiation is defined as heat transferred in the form of *waves* passing through material or space.[13] One who comes near a fire feels heat directly. That heat is one part of the general class of energy waves. Other parts include radio waves and light. Energy waves move out in all directions from their source at about 186,000 miles per second, the speed of light. This form of transfer of heat is radiation.

Radiated heat is subject to little absorption by air. It is stopped by any opaque substance. What stops light stops heat waves. Of course, the stopping material receives the heat and absorbs some of it. The rate of absorption depends on the size and intensity of the original source, distance from that source, and physical nature and color of the absorbing body. In general, black materials absorb the most radiant heat; white, the least. The amount absorbed varies inversely with the distance. And the amount varies directly with the fourth power of the absolute temperature of the source; thus an increase in heat at the source is greatly magnified by the increase in radiated heat energy. An increase in area of the source also is greatly magnified by the increase in radiation, but the relationship cannot be so simply stated.

Flame Spread

While all heat spread is conduction, convection, and radiation, more is needed for practical explanation of differences in fire spread. From a practical view, two different kinds of fire spread processes are visible.

One is the fire that develops slowly, through an initial smoldering stage. This type was generally described earlier in the subsection on "airflow in fires." The second kind spreads suddenly, with a bang or a whoosh; one moment there is no visible fire, the next a large area is in flames.

Flash Flaming Sudden spread of flame over a considerable area can result from several different kinds of circumstances. In a few cases, the cause is sudden introduction of extra oxygen into a heated area. More frequently the cause is one of the two following conditions.

In some cases, flammable materials such as dust, gases, or vapors from volatile liquids are spread through an area until some portion of them reaches, or is reached by, a source of ignition. Then heat and flame spread throughout the whole mass almost simultaneously.

Another form of rapid spread is called *flashover*. It consists of sudden flaming of a large portion of the upper level in a space containing a limited hostile fire. Current theory is that flashover is caused as follows: radiated heat reflected back from ceiling and upper walls heats the contents of the area. When the general temperature level is sufficiently raised, there is simultaneous ignition of most combustibles.[14]

Factors in length of time to flashover include heat reflectivity of ceiling and upper walls; their distance from the heat source and from the materials to be heated; and the heat absorption and combustibility of the latter materials. Among the relevant combustibility features is the relative homogeneity of the materials; if they have widely differing combustibility, they will not flash into flame simultaneously. Note also that adequate venting, by removing heat from the area, prevents flashover.

At the extreme, flash flaming becomes combustion explosion of the deflagration type, as will be discussed in Chapter 3; there is no fixed boundary line.

Other Uncontrolled Spread in an Undivided Area Commonly, spread of flame, especially in the early stages of a fire in any area, is at less than a "flash" rate. Particularly in ordinary combustibles, spread depends heavily on airflow behavior.

When a fire starts, air heated by radiation from the open flames and by conduction from materials already heated, moves up, carrying heat with it. Also in the rising hot air are any incompletely consumed vapors from the original burning materials. If the accumulating hot air and vapors are not cleared, eventually the vapor concentration may reach flammable concentration and/or a flashover may occur. Even without these, if the originating fire is not put out and does not run out of immediate available combustibles, the general area continues to get hotter (primarily from convection and radiation), until all is burning.

Still assuming fire fighting has not been effective, further spread depends on barriers to radiation and convection and limits to conduction.

Contained Fire. Consider first an area totally enclosed by adequate fire resistive walls, that is, by walls capable of resisting all the heat that can be generated by all the combustibles within. Typically, there will be places, such as windows or some part of the roof, where the accumulated heat can break through to the outside and set up an air draft—hot air out at the top, and fresh air in below, the *stack effect.* Then the whole process operates just like a wood or coal stove until the fuel is gone.

The interior of the masonry walls is strongly heated. But "adequate fire resistance" means that the walls (1) conduct heat away to the outside rapidly enough to keep their masonry content from overheating and collapsing, but (2) not so rapidly that the heat that reaches the outside cannot there be transferred to the air by radiation and carried away by convection or other cause of air circulation rapidly enough to keep the wall material from being destroyed. Requirement (2) is normally satisfied in any fire resistive wall simply by exposure to open air. However, all combustible material inside the walls including combustible building materials will be consumed, or essentially so. Whatever is not consumed will be damaged by heat and by the effects of roof and floor collapse. This may bring some of the walls down, too.

This example applies also to any undivided area in a fully fire resistive structure. However, whether there will be serious damage to structural components will depend on their respective fire resistance compared to the heat output (i.e., the intensity and duration of the fire). That heat output will depend on the nature of the area's contents, as discussed later. Commonly, the walls of a fire resistive structure will remain intact.

Total Fire in a Single Area. Suppose the walls in the case just described lack adequate fire resistance. Either they cannot conduct heat to the outside rapidly enough to keep their interior surface from burning, such as frame construction, or the heat conducted to the outside cannot be taken away rapidly enough by the outside air, such as light metal walls. The walls are consumed or collapse. In the case of exposed metal pillars and trusses, heat expands them unevenly, even softens them; they bend out of shape, commonly collapsing. "Unprotected lightweight [structural steel] sections, such as those found in trusses and open web joints, can collapse after 5 or 10 min[utes] of exposure."[15]

Horizontal Spread to Another Area   Consider again a fire area surrounded by fire resistive walls. Transmission of heat through the walls to an adjacent area is uncommon but possible. Fires have spread through as much as two feet of solid concrete.[16] Such conduction requires a very long, continuous exposure, however, and is generally relevant only to regular sources of heat such as furnaces, not to hostile fires. Still, adequate cooling on the exterior of walls, by convection or other air movement, or by water from fire fighters or sprinklers, does matter. If combustibles abut the far side of the wall, or air cannot flow, under the worst of conditions flames can occur in the adjacent area.

Fire Resistive Division.   The significant hazard for spread of fire to an adjacent area comes from openings in the wall. These can range from small spaces around communicating piping, ductwork, or conduit, to open archways. Fire can spread through an opening by convection or radiation. Openings higher than the fire invite spread by convection. However, if a strong airflow is established elsewhere—as by adequate venting in the roof, or burning of a large hole in the roof—*small* openings in the side walls will not carry out much hot air until the original area is well involved in flame. In a fully involved area, air pressure will be on the order of three times normal. Such pressure will push hot air through every available exit not needed for inflowing air.

Radiation may come directly from the hostile fire, or by reflection from various surfaces. Either way, very small holes allow little heat transfer. Window and door openings are another matter.

Control of horizontal spread therefore requires protection of openings in dividing walls. Standard forms of protection include approved forms of fire doors, window shutters, and, where these cannot be used, as where certain types of conveyors penetrate a wall, special sprinklers. Automatic protection is preferred in all of these. The NFPA Fire Doors and Windows Standard contains recommendations for proper installations. Still, it is always possible for protection devices to be inoperative, as when fire doors are blocked open.

Frame and Metal Partitions.   Now consider walls that are not fire resistive. Even frame construction gives some protection. For example, a dividing wall of two-by-four-inch studs with three-eighths-inch gypsum wallboard on each side has a twenty-five-minute fire resistance rating. The same studs with five-eighths-inch Type X gypsum wallboard have a rating of one hour.[17] Simple metal partitions have no rating, but hollow metal partitions with mineral board or plaster surfaces have ratings of as high as two hours, which, for an interior partition, is adequate for rating as "fire resistive" in many situations.

It is useless to give openings any greater fire resistance than their surrounding walls, but at least as much is important for life safety. A door that holds fire back for even five minutes can make the difference between safe exit and serious injury or death for people.

Glass Windows. Glass windows not only transmit radiated heat, but also break and fall out when exposed to high temperature, thus facilitating convection. This may provide direct or indirect communication between one area and another. The first would occur with loss of a window in a door in the dividing wall or partition. The second would occur when an exterior window exposes an exterior wall, particularly one with an opening in it, of the other area. This case may involve an open window. Wired glass in metal sash in a closed window is minimum useful protection.

Ductwork. Ductwork that penetrates any wall—e.g., ventilating ducts or ducts for conduit—represents an opening also. Ventilating ducts, being specifically designed for the movement of air, are a special problem. At minimum, forced air movement through ducts needs to be turned off. In addition to this, automatic dampers are required in all but the smallest ducts to stop flow of heat from fire in one area to another area.

Electrical and Equipment Lines. Heat may be conducted by various equipment lines that go through walls, especially lines made of metal. Disturbances in electrical equipment sometimes cause overheating or sparking elsewhere in the electrical system. This can cause spread of fire. Two counteractions are shutdown of electrical supply when fire occurs and proper circuit breaking.

Up and Around. A significant mode of horizontal spread of fire is up and around and, sometimes, down and around. For example, multiple units of frame or ordinary construction sometimes have common attics; that is, dividing partitions do not extend between highest interior ceiling and the building roof. Occasionally a similar condition exists below the floor. Usually this occurs only when the division is made some time after the building has been constructed. Where such conditions exist, the entire collection of units is best considered as a single area for spread of fire rather than as several units.

Fire Walls. In any type of construction, a fire that breaks through a combustible roof over one area may spread to the roof of another area. Therefore, full division requires the dividing wall to extend through and beyond the roof, except where the roof deck is fire resistive. Similarly, with combustible exterior walls, the division should extend out to the sides beyond those walls. And, of course, the division should extend down to the lowest basement floor. A fire resistive division that meets these requirements and has no openings, or all openings protected by approved equipment, is called a fire wall. In

Exhibit 2-5
Inadequate Fire Walls*

The remains of a collapsed fire wall and a fire wall opening can be seen following the fire that totally destroyed the K Mart Distribution Center. Note that there is no evidence of a fire door protecting the opening. This wall separated Quadrants B and C.

*Reprinted with permission from *Fire Journal* (May 1983), p.74.

buildings not themselves fire resistive, a further requirement for fire walls is that they be self-supporting; that is, capable of standing even when the building on either side collapses. Some less extensive divisions are called *fire partitions.*

The failure of interior fire walls was a contributing factor in the $100 million K-Mart warehouse fire. This 1,200,000 square foot building was divided into quadrants by fire walls. These walls were inadequately tied to the structure and contained inadequately protected openings.[18] The openings and the collapsed fire wall are shown in Exhibit 2-5.

Vertical Spread to Another Floor Two conditions make vertical spread, from floor to floor, significantly more likely than horizontal spread: (1) heat rises; and (2) in multistory buildings, between-story divisions have to be pierced for access such as stairs, elevators, escalators, wires, pipes, and ducts. Where there is a break in the barrier between the fire area and the area above it, the rising hot vapor and air will find it.

Designed Openings. Stack effect is increased by distance between the levels. Therefore, tall open shafts such as chimneys, stairwells, and elevator shafts and high-rise lobbies and theatrical stages increase the air movement that feeds and spreads fire. While open shafts are the most conducive to stack effect, any design that allows heated, expanded air from a fire to push upward, with replacement by cooler air from below, promotes combustion.

Standard design for personnel as well as property safety includes stairwells and elevator shafts surrounded by fire resistant barriers. The arrangement should include self-closing doors for the stairs. Escalators present a design problem. While they can be separately enclosed, automatic sprinklers or shutters are preferred by most building owners.

Other openings required for movement of things between floors, such as chutes, also require fire resistive enclosure. Openings for service lines such as wiring and plumbing should be tightly fire-stopped. Fire-stopping is also required around ducts; in addition, movement of air through their interior is also a hazard and needs to be controlled as was described in the horizontal fire spread section.

Floor Separations. By consuming the ceilings and floors that divide stories, fires can create their own openings. Clearly, a fire in frame or ordinary construction has this potential. However, in most multistory buildings of such construction, unprotected stairs and other openings will lead the fire upwards before ceiling/floor dividers are burned through.

Likely Damage

So far, spread of fire has been discussed without reference to counteractive efforts, such as sprinklers and fire fighting. Essentially, what has been under consideration has been the amount subject. Now it is time to consider the effects of counteraction, and other factors affecting probable maximum loss.

Alarms, sprinklers, fire fighting, and related subjects are discussed at length in Chapter 6, but some points must be noted for the present discussion. Whether a fire will be stopped short of destruction of all the amount subject commonly depends on the efficacy of counteraction: the operation of sprinklers or portable extinguishers and the speed of notice to, and subsequent arrival of, trained and equipped fire fighters. How much is likely to be damaged, supposing some ordinary "reasonably likely" delay in response? The answer depends on the fuel in the initial area, the size and shape of the area, and the duration of the fire. The relationship has not been reduced to mathematical calculation. Only tendencies and relativities can be given.

Fuel Fuels can contribute to the damage done by a fire in a given area two ways. First, as mentioned, the fuel load refers to the quantity of the materials in the area measured by weight per square foot. Second, fuels will differ in the amount of heat produced per pound when burned. This is referred to as the *calorific* or *fuel* value.

In any given occupancy, there will usually be a mixture of items with differing calorific values, and estimation of fuel or calorific value, item by item, is difficult or impossible. Therefore, fire protection engineers and underwriters both use averages according to the nature of the occupancy. One set of classifications, from NFPA, is as follows.[19] Note that building as well as occupancy combustibility is recognized.

Slight

    Well-arranged office, metal furniture, noncombustible building.

    Welding areas containing slight combustibles.

    Noncombustible power house.

    Noncombustible buildings, slight amount of combustible occupancy.

Moderate

    Cotton and waste paper storage (baled) and well-arranged, noncombustible building.

    Paper-making processes, noncombustible building.

    Noncombustible institutional buildings with combustible occupancy.

Moderately Severe

    Well-arranged combustible storage, e.g., wooden, patterns, noncombustible buildings.

    Machine shop having noncombustible floors.

Severe

    Manufacturing areas, combustible products, noncombustible building.

    Congested combustible storage areas, noncombustible building.

Maximum Severity

    Flammable liquids.

    Woodworking areas.

Office, combustible furniture and buildings.

Paper working, printing, etc.

Furniture manufacturing and finishing.

Machine shop having combustible floors.

Size and Shape of Area   Distance from the fire to the ceiling is the first important factor. When rising hot air reaches the ceiling, it spreads out. If the area is small, the heat buildup is rapid. In a large area, the depth of hot gases below the ceiling is thinner. If there is no venting and the fire continues, the buildup will ignite materials sooner in a smaller area than in a larger one, and sooner with a lower ceiling than with a higher. Of course, venting through or near a high ceiling means increased stack effect, which improves combustion. Larger areas also mean more fire and more heat when they do catch fire. With higher ceilings and larger open areas, fires tend to develop more slowly, but, once well developed, generally do more damage. Exceptions depend on occurrence of flashover.

Duration of Fire.   The most important single factor in estimation of probable fire damage is duration of the fire, that is, how long before it is put out. Most fires, fortunately, are put out before they burn out. Therefore, the most likely loss is only a fraction of the value exposed in the initial fire area. Maximum probable loss assumes worse circumstances. One benchmark is that, in ordinary construction, the total value within a set of masonry walls is the "maximum probable loss." One way of looking at maximum probable loss in other construction is that it is the amount that would be lost in a fire of duration similar to that of total loss in ordinary construction.

ARSON

The Problem

Arson presents a persistent and serious problem for the property underwriter. Despite the concerted efforts of police and fire officials, arson fires continue to take a heavy toll in both property damage and lives.

Incendiary and suspicious fires destroyed over $1.5 billion in property and caused 910 civilian deaths in 1982. Frequency is also a problem in arson as these categories were involved in 129,000 structure fires in that same period. This is shown in Exhibit 2-6.

Many persons believe insurance is found to be the leading cause of arson. However, vandalism is a much more prevalent reason. This is shown in Exhibit 2-7. This exhibit indicates that underwriting emphasis

Exhibit 2-6
Estimates of 1982 United States Fires, Deaths, and Direct Property Loss for Incendiary and Suspicious Fires in Structures*

Type of Fire	Number of Fires		Number of Civilian Deaths		Direct Property Loss[1]	
	Estimate	Percent Change from 1981	Estimate	Percent Change from 1981	Estimate	Percent Change from 1981
Structure fires of incendiary origin	77,500	-11.9[2]	720	+29.7	$1,088,000,000	-4.7
Structure fires of suspicious origin	51,500	-22.6[2]	190	-28.3	$516,000,000	0.0
Total structure fires of incendiary or suspicious origin	129,000	-16.5[2]	910	+11.0	$1,604,000,000	-3.3

The estimates are based on data reported to the NFPA by fire departments that responded to the 1982 National Fire Experience Survey.

[1] Includes overall direct property loss (loss to contents, structure, a vehicle, machinery, vegetation, or anything else involved in a fire), and does not include indirect losses, e.g., business interruption or temporary shelter costs; no adjustment was made for inflation in the year-to-year comparison.

[2] Change was statistically significant at the 0.01 level.

*Reprinted with permission from Michael J. Karter, Jr., "Fire Loss in the United States During 1982," *Fire Journal* (September 1983), p.54.

Exhibit 2-7
What Motivates an Arsonist*

Arson Motive	Residential		Commercial	
	Percent of Arson Fires	Percent of Total Arson Costs	Percent of Arson Fires	Percent of Total Arson Costs
Arson Fraud	14%	22%	12%	8%
Vandalism	53	40	49	61
Revenge	12	12	11	6
Concealment	6	8	8	6
Pyromania	3	3	3	5
Other	13	15	16	16

Figures are for voluntary market coverage only. No breakdown by motive for FAIR Plan fire losses was available. Source: All-Industry Research Advisory Council (AIRAC).

*Adapted with permission from "Arson: What it Costs, Who's to Blame," *Journal of American Insurance* (Summer 1982), p.14.

on arson fraud on behalf of the insured may be misplaced. Fraud accounts for only 12 percent of the commercial arson fires and 8 percent of the dollar loss to commercial structures from this cause. While analysis of the ownership and management of a commercial risk remains of vital importance in an effort to discern the existence of moral hazard, this is not enough. The vulnerability of a particular structure to arson from the motives comprising the other 88 percent of the frequency appears to be more significant. This may be overlooked.

Credit reports may indicate the presence of labor strife or industry conflicts that could give rise to revenge arson fires. The other two largest categories of motives are vandalism and concealment of other crimes, which together account for 57 percent of the commercial arson frequency and 67 percent of the commercial dollar losses.

The vulnerability of a structure to vandalism and burglary is determined by a number of factors, including location, type of structure, police protection, and adequacy of private protection systems. Even if crime insurance coverages are not provided, complete fire underwriting review should include consideration of vulnerability to burglary losses. Concealment fires usually are started to conceal a burglary. Even if vandalism or malicious mischief are not insured perils, the prominence of the vandalism motive in arson fires means that this hazard should be evaluated carefully for all commercial insureds.

Solution Efforts

The current federal government effort to combat arson stems from congressional hearings in 1977 and 1978. A Federal Arson Task Force was created coordinating the efforts of fourteen federal agencies. These agencies, including the Department of Justice, the FBI, and the Federal Emergency Management Agency (FEMA) have developed a National Arson Strategy.[20] On behalf of the task force, FEMA at the end of fiscal year 1982 submitted *A Report to Congress, The National Anti-Arson Strategy—Its Progress and Status.* This report noted that while progress had been made, the United States has more arson fires than any other industrialized nation. The task force found the problem to persist in rural as well as urban areas.

Among the factors cited in the report as contributing to this problem, one is of particular significance to the property underwriter.

> Limited availability of credit and an unstable housing market can turn a desperate property owner to arson. These factors can result in arson when:
>
> Costs of maintaining a building exceed the income obtainable from the building;
>
> Economic conditions and poor maintenance cause a decline in the market value of the property; and
>
> Poorly conceived housing assistance programs inadvertently become incentives for arson. For example, fire code enforcement programs that are not coupled with rehabilitation assistance for owners may cause undue hardship on people already in financial trouble.[21]

Within the insurance industry, the Insurance Committee for Arson Control is working on this difficult problem. This committee works in a number of areas, including:

1. Education and training for local fire and police officials in arson control techniques.
2. Increasing public awareness of the problem.
3. Coordination of public and private sector efforts to reduce arson.
4. Making recommendations for legislative and regulatory measures to assist in the anti-arson battle.

An example of the legislative efforts of this committee is the Insurance Model Arson Reporting Immunity Law. A similar law was adopted by Ohio in 1976. As of April 1981, forty-three states have passed some form of arson reporting immunity legislation. A summary of the arson reporting immunity laws is shown in Exhibit 2-8.

Other current legislative concerns of the Insurance Committee for Arson Control include anti-arson applications and inspections, amendments to unfair claims settlement practices legislation, and model arson penal laws.[22]

ANALYSIS OF OWNERSHIP AND MANAGEMENT

An analysis of the condition of ownership reflects the manner in which the operation manages its resources just as a physical inspection reflects the manner in which physical hazards are controlled. This evaluation of the nonphysical aspect of property underwriting is equally important because managerial errors are ultimately as costly to insurance companies as are physical hazards. The consequences for enterprises which take on more work than they can handle could be (1) a rush to meet deadlines, (2) outgrowth of the physical plant, (3) hiring of lower calibre and possibly temporary employees, (4) pushing old equipment beyond its capacity, and (5) eliminating maintenance and replacement schedules. The same applies to enterprises which enter unfamiliar fields, show little growth, or are in a highly competitive industry. Eventually, business problems show themselves in financial results.

A Dun & Bradstreet study underlines the relationship between fire losses and financial condition. Using their San Francisco data base, Dun & Bradstreet made a search of all mercantile fires reported during a six-month period through the records of the San Francisco City and County Fire Department. The results of this survey revealed the following:

1. 6.4 percent of damaging fires had a high (favorable) rating;
2. 17.0 percent had good ratings; and
3. 76.6 percent had either fair, limited, or listed but not rated ratings.

Dun & Bradstreet asked the question: "Can we not conclude that this [third group] is where the dangerous and questionable risks are located?"[23]

To analyze and understand the financial condition of a business, the underwriter goes through three stages. Stage one involves analyzing the history of the business—its track record and its ability to establish confidence by operating successfully. Most cases will go no further than this stage.

Stage two is entered when certain unanswered questions remain. In this stage the underwriter seeks to find out what the operation's creditors and suppliers think of this business. Usually, the underwriter reviews a credit statement, credit interchange report, or direct com-

Exhibit 2-8
Arson Reporting-Immunity Laws (September, 1980*

			Civil Immunity	Criminal Immunity	Agencies Get Information	Companies Initiate Contact	Companies Get Information	Notice to One Agency	Authorities Testify	Agencies Share Information
			1	2	3	4	5	6	7	8
ALABAMA	1979	SB359	X	X	X	X	—	X	X	—
ALASKA	1980	SB303	X	X	X	X	X	X	—	X
ARIZONA	1979	HB2014	X	X	X	X	—	X	X	X
ARKANSAS	—									
CALIFORNIA	1978	SB1386	X	X	X	X	—	X	—	X
COLORADO	1979	SB30	X^F	X	X	—	X	X	X
CONNECTICUT	1977,9	SB385	X	X	X	X	X	—	X	—
DELAWARE	1980	SB251	X	X	X	X	X	X	X	X
FLORIDA	1978	SB754	X	X	X	X	—	X	X	X
GEORGIA	1977	HB257	X	X	X	X	—	X	X	X
HAWAII	1979	HB988	X	X	X	X	X	X	X	—
IDAHO	—									
	1980	SB1994								
ILLINOIS	1977	HB2220	X	X	X	X	3*	—	X	—
INDIANA	1979	HB1940	X	X	X	X	X	X	—	X
IOWA	1979	SF339	X	X	X	X	X	—	X	X
KANSAS	1979	HB2134	X	—	X	X	X	X	X	X
KENTUCKY	1980	HB106	X	X	X	X	X	X	X	X
LOUISIANA	1978	SB419	X	X	X	X	—	X	X	—
MAINE	1977	HB959	X	X	—	—	—	—	—	—
MARYLAND	1978	HB370	X	X	X	X	—	—	—	—
MASSACHUSETTS	1978	HB5914	X	X	X	X	X	X	X	X
MICHIGAN	1978	SB1264	X	X	X	X	—	X	X	—
MINNESOTA	1979	HF1324	X	X	X	X	—	X	—	X
MISSISSIPPI	—									
MISSOURI	—									
MONTANA	1979	SB148	X	—	X	X	—	X	X	X
NEBRASKA	1979	LB301	X	X	X	X	X	X	X	X

State	Year	Bill								
NEVADA	—									
NEW HAMPSHIRE	1979	HB742	X	X	X	X	X	X	X	—
NEW JERSEY	—									
NEW MEXICO	1979	SB216	X	X	X	X	X	X	—	X
	1980	AB0319								
NEW YORK	1977	SB4393	X	X	X	X	3*	X	X	—
NORTH CAROLINA	1977	SB408	X	X	X	X	—	X	X	—
NORTH DAKOTA	1979	HB1500	X	X	X	2*	X	X	—	—
	1980	SB298								
OHIO	1976	SB452	X	X	X	X	X	X	X	—
OKLAHOMA	1979	HB1031	X	X	X	X	3*	X	X	X
OREGON	—									
PENNSYLVANIA	1980	HB1106	X	X	X	X	X	X	—	X
		HB7445								
RHODE ISLAND	1978,9	HB6208	X	X	X	X	X	X	X	X
SOUTH CAROLINA	—									
SOUTH DAKOTA	1979	HB1104	X	X	X	X	X	X	X	X
TENNESSEE	1979	SB43	X	X	X	X	—	—	X	—
TEXAS	1977	SB1260	X	X	X	—	—	—	X	—
UTAH	1979	HB260	X	X	X	X	—	X	—	—
VERMONT	—									
VIRGINIA	1979	HB1243	X	X	X	X	X	X	—	X
WASHINGTON	1979	SB2727	X	X	X	X	X	X	X	X
WEST VIRGINIA	1978	SB365	X^F	X	X	—	X	X	—	
WISCONSIN	1978	SB317	X	X	X	2*	X	—	—	—
WYOMING										

X^F grants limited immunity but does not use the terms criminal or civil

2* does not require insurance companies to report suspicious claims but states that they may report

3* provides that insurance companies may ask agencies for information but does not specifically state that release of the information by the agencies is mandatory

*Adapted with permission from *Current Arson Issues*, Insurance Committee for Arson Control, Chicago, 1981.

ments from bankers and suppliers. The third stage requires analysis of the financial statements. (This is covered in more detail in AIU 61.)[24]

Key indicators of potential financial weakness include:

1. New or young venture in its first five years of operation.
2. The risk is one in a line with a high failure rate (see Exhibit 2-9).
3. Management has less than three years experience.
4. The business has been at present location less than three years.

Financial Analysis for Hazard Evaluation

Much has been said so far about physical hazards. However, calculations based on the data in Exhibit 2-2 show that average severity of nonincendiary fires with known causes, in 1980, was $3,825. Average severity of incendiary fires was $7,970. Average severity of fires with unknown causes including an unknown amount of undetected arson, was a tremendous $11,729. Not all of even the incendiary cases were arson by insureds, but that constituted an important element. How is existence of moral hazard to be recognized?

Mentioned before was the history of the insured. Discussion of the sources for, and content of, such information is presented in various places in the IIA Associate in Underwriting texts. The student is referred to the AIU 61 text for the financial ratios. This section mentions those ratios that are helpful in assessing the potential moral hazard that could result in arson.

Two additional areas of concern are (1) those relating to the insured's property and its possible obsolescence or deterioration and (2) those relating to the insured's cash flow.

Property

Inventory. The sign of obsolescence in inventory is that it does not sell. When it does not sell, it generally piles up. The primary index of such dead portions of inventory is the ratio of sales or of cost of goods sold to inventory. Naturally, with obsolescent inventory, this ratio is almost always lower than usual.

Of course, the low sales-to-inventory ratio can be due just to low sales without presence of useless inventory. Particularly sensitive to the problem is the ratio of inventory to total current assets. A quick ratio (current ratio which does not include inventory in the determination of current assets) that is very low when the current ratio is not, or quick ratio normal while the current ratio is high, is another indication. Of course, certain key business ratios for the concern being underwritten are usually compared to the same ratios for firms doing business in the same field or to the same ratios of the firm from previous years.

Exhibit 2-9

Failures in Specific Retail and Manufacturing Lines (Rate per 10,000 Operating Concerns—1981)*

Retail Lines

Lines of Business	Failure Rate
Infants' and children's wear	114
Furniture and furnishings	84
Dry goods and general merchandise	78
Sporting goods	78
Lumber and building materials	64
Women's ready-to-wear	61
Men's wear	57
Appliances, radio and TV	56
Cameras and photographic supplies	46
Auto parts and accessories	46
Shoes	42
Books and stationery	40
Bakeries	39
Eating and drinking places	37
Hardware	37
Automobiles	34
Gifts	33
Toys and hobby crafts	26
Jewelry	24
Women's accessories	23
Groceries, meats and produce	21
Drugs	20
Department stores	16

Manufacturing Industries

Lines of Business	Failure Rate
Furniture	173
Transportation equipment	120
Textiles	91
Electrical machinery	73
Apparel	72
Rubber and fabricated plastic products	64
Leather and shoes	61
Printing and publishing	59
Lumber	58
Metals, primary and fabricated	57
Machinery, except electrical	51
Stone, clay and glass	46
Food	45
Paper	40
Chemicals and drugs	39

*Adapted with permission from *The 1981 Dun & Bradstreet Business Failure Record* (New York: Dun & Bradstreet, 1983).

Fixed Assets. Economic conditions may produce obsolescence or induce physical deterioration in fixed assets also.

OBSOLESCENCE. Suppose a business has had declining sales, but also appropriately declining inventory, or a declining service business, that has little or no inventory—say, a restaurant—how might these use their fire insurer as a savior? Only the fixed assets are available. Fixed assets standing in place are worth what they earn. Removed, there may be little or no market value for them, and buildings cannot generally be removed.

Such a situation presents a real problem for the underwriter. Not every business person in difficulty "sells" his or her property to the insurer; indeed, most do not. But some do, and those few are expensive. The character of the insured is crucial.

DETERIORATION. Sometimes an owner deliberately lets a property become run-down. One classic type of case is that of rent control. Within a wide range of building quality, the landlord collects the same regulated amount of rent whether he or she maintains the quality of the building, improves it, or lets it deteriorate. Even if he or she can get a rent increase by making improvements, the increase must be approved by the rent control office—after the fact, and subject to arguments and delays. And the increase sometimes is less than the return from investing the same money elsewhere. Conversely, when the property deteriorates, the tenants then must obtain the rent decrease through the regulatory process, with all its delays, and the amount when granted often comes to less than can be earned by placing the maintenance money in other investments. Overall, the property becomes worth less and less, and the only way to get the owner's money out may be a "sale" to the insurer. This temptation is in addition to the increased physical hazards of the poorly maintained property, and associated moral hazards from the tenants.

Rent control is not the only cause of such circumstances. Whenever poor maintenance and physical deterioration of property do not directly affect revenue obtained from it, or affect revenue less than proportionately, it is more profitable to let the property deteriorate.

Sometimes a deliberate decision to let property deteriorate reflects not so much profit maximization as loss minimization. When net income is low or negative, expenses will be cut. First choices go to those expenses that do not immediately affect income. Among these are some of the expenses for maintenance and protection. An historical example has been the sad history of railroad roadbed maintenance, or the lack thereof. Given a deteriorating financial situation in an insured organization previously known to have been acceptable, a recheck on management of housekeeping and maintenance practices could be wise.

Total Assets. The efficacy of the total mix of business assets is reflected in the ratio of net profit to total assets. Unfortunately, this ratio is sometimes heavily affected by the way fixed assets are evaluated under generally accepted accounting principles (GAAP). When there is a mix of assets of different ages, with some new and some old, the situation is not so bad. But having mostly new or mostly old affects the computed ratio considerably, so that it does not give the needed information. Mostly old, depreciated (accounting-wise) equipment may give a high rate, which may be misleading.

The best way to consider the productive value of fixed assets is observation. Are they well maintained and functional? Are they obsolescent, compared to others in the industry? Will they need replacement or major repairs shortly? If the answers are, respectively, "Yes," "No," and "No," and other ratios (such as sales-to-inventory and profit margin-on-sales) are satisfactory, the fixed assets should be considered to have adequate value for present purposes of the business. Note that this does not necessarily give the fair insurable value of the assets, only their functional worth.

In other words, for financial analysis of a going concern, the approach to evaluation of fixed assets is essentially negative: physical deterioration or technical obsolescence indicates low value; otherwise, they are assumed to be properly valued.

Another concern is the *capacity utilization rate.* A business slowdown may result in an excessive amount of fixed assets. Underutilized or closed-down plants may present severe problems to the property underwriter.

Cash Flow   Declines in cash flow put pressure on management to reduce outlays. Postponable expenditures are postponed. As noted, these commonly include some expenditures on maintenance and protection. They may also include payment of insurance premiums.

Depreciation and Replacement.   Depreciation is a subtraction from income but not from cash flow. Replacement expenditures are a subtraction from cash flow but not from income. In a stable economy and stable organization, the two figures would balance. Each year, a certain portion of the total fixed asset value would be used up, and each year that same value would be spent on new replacements—leaving the total fixed asset value unchanged. But neither economies nor organizations are stable. In particular, economies have for some time been subject to rapid inflation, making replacement equipment cost more than the assets it replaces. This difference creates a cash flow problem. The problem is of interest to underwriters because it can cause increased reliance on old, obsolete, possibly defective, equipment. And, later on, when the old items *have* to be replaced, there may be a cash crisis.

Receivables. Sales and revenue produce cash flow only to the extent that cash is received. When sales go up $100,000 while receivables go up by $60,000, only $40,000 is added to cash flow. But the costs and expenses incurred to make the added $100,000 in sales often have to be paid now. This, too, can create a cash flow problem, although if sales and receivables have gone up at the same rate, no serious effect should appear. Difficulty can appear when for some reason, such as a general economic slowdown, receivables go up without any increase in sales. Note that such a *lengthening of receivables* (as it is called) is a drag on cash flow even if the new increased amount comes to no more than the industry average. While the increase is occurring, cash flow is decreased.

The standard method for determining whether the collection period on receivables is lengthening is to compare sales-to-receivables ratios from consecutive balance sheets. Occasionally an increase in this ratio will occur because the ratio of credit sales to total sales is increasing, rather than because collection rate is slower. The increse is still a drain on cash flow. And, as with any other alteration in usual ratios, the reasons for the change are of interest. For example, an increase in proportion of sales on credit rather than for cash may indicate an attempt to "buy" business by easing credit terms—a change that may lead to later difficulty with collections.

Payables. When debt comes due, cash is required. Although good managers plan ahead so that cash is on hand when debts are due, plans cannot always be implemented. Debts due, with no cash to pay them, have always been a motive for crime, especially commercial crime.

Cash flow problems may be alleviated by more borrowing, that is, by increases in payables. This postpones the need for cash. But the new liabilities must be paid later, so increases in debt must be evaluated against future ability to pay.

One frequent cause of an increase in short-term debt is inability to make payments because of a cash shortage. When debt grows more rapidly than sales, net income, or assets, problems can arise. For an insurance underwriter, such growth normally is in the nature of a "weather advisory" or "storm watch," rather than an immediate "storm warning." Checks should be made occasionally for further changes in the insured's finances or operations. Notice should particularly be taken when an unusually large amount of debt is coming due. However, most sources will not give debt maturity dates beyond dividing them into "current"—i.e., within one year—and "long-term." When the current figure jumps suddenly, a large cash need is at hand.

Dividends. Dividends and other withdrawals by owners take cash. Besides that effect on cash flow, unusually large withdrawals often signal some major change in the owners' interests, financial conditions, or relationships to the business. Major withdrawals should be investigated.

SUMMARY[25]

Fire is extremely rapid oxidation. It requires the availability of oxygen, some source of heat, fuel, and a chain reaction. When fire gets out of control it is a hostile fire. Heat sources include space heating and cooking, welding and cutting, other commercial equipment, and hot liquids. Unintended heat occurs with electrical wiring and equipment, friction, static electricity, spontaneous ignition, and chemical reactions.

Other heat sources include lightning, smoking and matches, exposure fires, and arson. Arson has increased greatly in recent years and is a major source of property damage. The flammability and combustibility of the fuels have a great influence upon the extent and intensity of fires. The vaporization rate of liquids, solids, and gases is an important variable. The shape of material is also important. Iron filings will burn while iron bars are relatively incombustible. The products of combustion include heat, gases, and smoke.

Another important variable is the amount of oxygen available at the fire site. In the extreme case a fire storm may develop in which the fire creates its own wind. The heat from a fire spreads by conduction, convection, and radiation. Flame spread varies from relatively low speed to flash flaming. The likely damage caused by a fire is a function of the amount and type of fuel, the size and shape of the fire area, and the duration of the fire.

Two general types of financial results should commonly be investigated: any unusual key ratios and all significant trends.

The key ratios and trends are those that indicate the usefulness (looking at both economic and physical obsolescence and depreciation) of property, and those that show adequacy of and changes in cash flow.

Chapter Notes

1. *Fire Protection Handbook*, 15th ed. (Quincy, MA: National Fire Protection Association, 1981), p. 7-41.
2. *Fire Protection Handbook*, p. 7-6.
3. *Fire Protection Handbook*, p. 5-88.
4. *Fire Protection Handbook*, pp. 5-18, 5-19.
5. *Fire Protection Handbook*, p. 5-20.
6. *Fire Protection Handbook*, pp. 5-16, 5-19.
7. *Fire Protection Handbook*, p. 4-27. An additional characteristic required for class I is related to the liquid's "vapor pressure." Liquids with high vapor pressure (greater than 40 psi absolute at 100°F) are not class I.
8. *Fire Protection Handbook*, p. 4-27.
9. See *Fire Protection Handbook*, Section 5, Chapters 9 and 10.
10. Robert T. Burns, "Windowless Buildings," *Firehouse* (September 1983), pp. 56, 58, and 160.
11. *Judging the Fire Risk*, 4th ed. (Chicago: Alliance of American Insurers, 1981), p. 1.
12. *Judging the Fire Risk*, p. 1.
13. *Judging the Fire Risk*, p. 1.
14. *Fire Protection Handbook*, p. 5-48.
15. *Fire Protection Handbook*, p. 5-80.
16. *Fire Protection Handbook*, p. 3-9.
17. *Fire Protection Handbook*, p. 5-78.
18. Richard Best, "Fire Walls that Failed: The K-Mart Corporation Distribution Center Fire," *Fire Journal* (May 1983), pp. 74, 83, and 86.
19. *Fire Protection Handbook*, p. 5-92.
20. Herman M. Weisman, "The National Anti-Arson Strategy: Its Progress and Status," *Fire Journal* (May 1983), pp. 48, 49, and 145.
21. Herman M. Weisman, p. 45.
22. See *Current Arson Issues* (Chicago: Insurance Committee for Arson Control, 1981).
23. Dun & Bradstreet circular to subscribers, "Fire Loss Study with Respect to Credit Ratings," 1970.
24. See J. J. Launie, J. Finley Lee, and Norman A. Baglini, *Principles of Property and Liability Underwriting*, 2nd ed. (Malvern, PA: Insurance Institute of America, 1977), Chapter 10.
25. As evidenced by the Chapter Notes, much of this chapter is based on NFPA's *Fire Protection Handbook*. While underwriters do not make use of this publication to the extent that loss control persons do, every underwriter should be aware of the book and generally familiar with the type of information it contains.

CHAPTER 3

Analyzing Loss Potential from Other Major Perils

INTRODUCTION

The property underwriter of today must analyze a great variety of insured perils in a society growing ever more complex and more concentrated in diminishing livable space. Although this text primarily will emphasize the fire peril, the "other" major perils covered under property policies cannot be ignored and will sometimes make unacceptable what otherwise would be an acceptable risk.

Early in this century, property insurance policies covered only the perils of fire and lightning, plus "removal," or relocation of the property endangered by these perils. In 1925 an additional hazards supplemental contract, intended for endorsement to the standard fire policy, was introduced. As discussed earlier, this was followed by the extended coverage endorsement, which after some experimentation has become the uniform method of providing coverage for the majority of the additional perils. As the need arose, special endorsements to cover specific perils such as vandalism or malicious mischief, earthquake, or sprinkler leakage were added. Thus, over time, a series of forms and endorsements have been developed to provide coverage for those specified or named perils. With modifications, these forms are in use today, and the named peril approach is still the most commonly used.

A simultaneous development in providing needed additional coverage has led to the "all-risks" contracts. There are a number of different property insurance contracts written on an "all-risks" basis, including the difference in conditions (DIC) policy. The purpose of these policies is to provide coverage for "all-risks" of loss except those specifically excluded. The "all-risks" approach was heavily influenced in the early part of the century by the rapid growth of inland marine coverages. In its early stages, inland marine was unhampered by insurance regulation, and marine insurers provided broad "all-risks" coverage—a competitive tool the fire insurers could not use. This competition was checked by the adoption of the Nation-Wide Marine Definition in 1933. However, by then the "all-risks" concept was firmly established and still plays a significant role in today's insurance contracts. The term "all-risks" may be abandoned soon due to the concurrent causation doctrine, described later. The concept and coverage intent will probably remain, however.

Although the "all-risks" form presents some unique problems, the majority of the additional perils covered are common to both the named peril and "all-risks" ("all-perils") approach and are the subject of this chapter.

EXPLOSION

An explosion occurs when pressure within a confined space exerts force exceeding the strength of the enclosing material; the resultant sudden failure of the enclosure allows the extremely rapid expansion of gases into the atmosphere. This is in contrast to an *implosion*, which is a violent inward collapse.

Confined Spaces Other Than Pressure Vessels

Flammable dust, vapor, mist, or gas, when mixed with air under the right conditions, can ignite and burn with sufficient speed to generate high pressure in a confined space resulting in an explosion. These confined spaces could include a compartment, a room, or even a building. Explosions resulting from such chemical reactions (i.e., burning) can be divided into two major types:

1. *Deflagration.* This is a rapid burning in which the reaction moves through the material by conduction, radiation, and convection at a speed slower than sound.
2. *Detonation.* This is rapid burning which produces a shock wave. A detonation moves through the material at a speed faster than sound and the reaction is propagated by heat compression caused by the shock wave.

While both types of reactions can produce large pressure rises and great destruction, detonations are about twice as severe as deflagrations. Detonations can be produced from gases, dust, and from decomposition of certain unstable materials including high explosives. Deflagration can be produced from gases, dusts, mists, and low explosives such as black powder.

Sources of Explosion—Other than Pressure Vessels Flammable liquids produce vapors at their surface which can burn. If the vapors mix with air in the correct proportion, the burning becomes very rapid and difficult to control. Most flammable vapors which are not controlled tend to sink to the floor and run toward low spots. This is common to most flammable vapors, as they usually are heavier than air. Usual spots for these vapors to gather are basements, furnace pits, switching equipment shafts, and so forth. In these spots, the vapors can concentrate until a burning mixture is reached. Ignition can be caused by the spark of a closing electrical switch or a furnace start-up. The mixture of vapors and air may burn and flash back to the source or it may explode. If flammable vapors saturate an atmosphere or if temperature and humidity conditions are proper, the vapor may condense into a mist. Flammable mists can also deflagrate causing an explosion.

Gases transmitted through pipes may leak through poorly maintained connections, joints, and valves. Gases escaping between walls can concentrate and reach a burnable mixture. If contained sufficiently, the result will be an explosion.

The preceding chapter described how every flammable vapor or gas has a ratio of the vapor or gas to air which must be achieved before it will burn. Actually this ratio is a range. The lower limit is the least gas- or vapor-to-air ratio at which it will burn; the higher limit is the greatest gas- or vapor-to-air ratio at which it will burn. These are the *limits of flammability.* The lower is the *lean limit;* the upper, the *rich limit.* These limits are changed by pressure and temperature. The vapors and gases which collect and concentrate because of a leak or an uncontrolled process must reach and stay between the lean and rich limits if a deflagration is to occur.

Most finely divided combustible materials are dangerous. When combustible dust is suspended in air and ignited the result can be a severe explosion. Whether a dust cloud will ignite depends upon the size of the particles, the concentration of particles, the amount of oxygen, and the strength of the source of ignition. Dust explosions usually occur in series—a small deflagration with just enough strength to knock dust from beams or to rupture dust collectors may be followed by a major, secondary explosion generated by the new, large dust cloud stirred by the primary deflagration.

The smaller the size of the particles in a dust cloud, the easier the cloud is to ignite. The rate of pressure rise during a deflagration is similarly affected. The smaller the particle, the greater the rate of pressure rise. As is the case with vapor and gas, a certain range of dust concentration is required before an explosion can occur. The measure of this value varies with the size of the particles and the strength of the ignition source. Wetting the dust particles increases the ignition temperature but cannot be considered as an effective method of explosion prevention. The moisture does not increase the temperature enough to overcome the energy by the deflagration. Turbulence in a dust cloud, caused by mixing oxygen with the dust, increases the violence of the explosion. Dust clouds are commonly produced by coal mining, sorting, and processing; grain grinding, milling, and storage; plastic grinding; and grinding of certain metals.

Prevention The primary and most effective method of explosion prevention is to replace the explosive material with one which is less explosive or noncombustible. Needless to say, this is not always possible or economically feasible. It is then necessary to keep flammable concentrations of materials and oxygen from gathering. Numerous standards have been written by insurance and fire prevention groups. The basic thrust of these is to contain gases, exclude oxygen, reduce or vent vapors, and reduce dusts. The details of these preventive procedures can be found in the appropriate National Fire Prevention Association (NFPA) pamphlet.

An important method for preventing an explosion is the use of an *inert gas* (a gas that is normally chemically inactive, especially in not burning or supporting combustion). Inert gas prevents the concentration of a flammable vapor and oxygen mixture by substituting the inert gas for oxygen. Inert gas can be used in storage applications, repair operations (as on flammable liquid storage tanks), and in processing operations. While this preventive method is effective, it has limited applications as the inert gas may foul the substance being protected or interfere with personnel working in the area.

Another important method is the removal of the ignition source. Sealed electrical equipment, "explosion proof," keeps the possible explosive gases away from potential spark sources. Explosion-proof electrical equipment has been designed for many applications. Electrical equipment can also be kept away from flammable vapors by purging the enclosure with clear air or inert gas. In such a system, air or inert gas under pressure is forced into the electrical equipment container. This air under pressure forces a flow of gas away from the container and forces flammable vapors out of the equipment chamber. Thus, the air around the equipment remains nonflammable.

Deflagrations occur when a preventive measure fails. Explosion suppression devices are now available to stop the deflagration before sufficient pressure develops to cause an explosion. The suppression systems are for use in relatively closed containers.

Suppression systems have a pressure or radiation detector. These operate on a very slight change in pressure or radiation. High sensitivity is vital, since the time lag between ignition and the development of destructive pressures is brief. For example, the detector may operate within about thirty to thirty-five milliseconds of ignition. The detector, in turn, releases a suppressant which stops the deflagration. The choice of the suppressant depends upon the material likely to explode. The suppressant terminates the deflagration before pressure causes the explosion. Because the suppressant device requires the deflagration to start and pressures to build up to some degree before being fully suppressed, the enclosure must be strong enough to withstand a pressure of at least three pounds per square inch.

Suppression systems are applicable to grinding plants, storage tanks, coal pulverizing, feed and grain processing, chemical reactors, plastic grinding, and in the transportation of various explosive materials.

Damage Control The failure of preventive and control mechanisms does happen. To prevent severe structural damage in areas where explosions are anticipated in spite of all other efforts, *explosion vents* are sometimes used. The purpose of an explosion vent is to relieve pressures built up by a deflagration or detonation. Vents are simply doors, panels, or diaphragms which are easily blown open by an explosive pressure. By design they swing or burst open permitting the release of expanding gases and thus saving the rest of the structure from damage. The design, size, location, and number of vents must be tailored to the specific situation. It is important to realize that vents can often save buildings from damage of *minor explosions* but rarely can they effectively release the pressure of a major detonation. The explosion and destruction of a dozen buildings at a New York fireworks factory in 1983 is a good example of the limited capability of many explosion damage control devices.

There are several other damage control devices of varying effectiveness. Isolation, if possible, is probably one of the most effective against damage to other property. If the explosive operations, equipment, and so on, are isolated, they can do little damage to other buildings. Such isolation must be proper in relation to the security of the explosion hazard.

The construction used for the building, walls, and so on is also important. Roofs may be built to blow away, leaving walls, it is hoped, intact. Construction can also direct the force of the explosion away from susceptible and/or nearby buildings or operations. Finally, some form of retaining barrier may prevent an explosion from seriously damaging nearby property. As with construction, such barriers can direct the force of the explosion but can also prevent it from damaging other nearby property.

The underwriting of the peril of explosion requires attention to detail and awareness of the various causes and effects. In most manufacturing and processing plants, the explosion hazards are recognized and protected. It is the part-time or marginal operation which often fails to recognize or is unable to sustain the cost of controlling its explosion hazard. The rash of grain elevator explosions in late 1977 and early 1978, however, illustrates that property and human life conservation requires vigorous and continuous attention even when the operations are large, sophisticated, and financially successful concerns.

Pressure Vessels

The elevation of pressure within a pressure vessel beyond its strength, through uncontrolled external application of heat or uncontrolled delivery or release of contents by external mechanical devices, may result in explosion.

Sources of Explosion—Pressure Vessels Pressure vessels are found in homes, processing and manufacturing operations, service businesses, and even offices which may have boilers for heat or pressure tanks for circulating water.

Vessels can fail when pressure builds up over safe limits. This can occur when a process gets out of hand, developing pressures more rapidly than expected. It can happen in a boiler when the heat source continues to operate after operating temperatures and pressures have been achieved; frequently the fault lies in the automatic switching device. It can also happen when insufficient water is in the vessel due to faulty intake valves.

Explosion of pressure vessels may also result from the weakening of the vessel walls. Age, corrosion, and heat can lead to a vessel's being unable to operate at its design specifications. During a hostile fire, the heat generated by combustibles around the vessel can cause the metal to weaken, while simultaneously increasing the likelihood of explosion.

Flammable gases are often stored in tanks under pressure. If these gases escape from their containers, they can mix with air and burn or explode just as vapors or liquids do. The fact that gases are often stored under pressure means that the pressure inside the tank varies according to temperature. As the temperature rises, such as in a building fire, pressures may reach the container's failure point. The heat from the fire may also cause the container to weaken. The dual results can produce a pressure explosion, releasing the flammable gas into the fire and causing a second deflagration explosion.

If the content of a vessel is a combustible liquid or gas, the rupture of a vessel by internal pressure forces a spray of the combustible onto the surrounding fire. The result is a second explosion. This is called a *Boiling Liquid—Expanding Vapor Explosion,* also known by its acronym "BLEVE." A BLEVE produces large fire balls and tremendous force. This type of explosion is most common to fires involving plants using compressed gases or liquefied petroleum gas.

Prevention Pressure vessels, by design, can withstand certain anticipated pressures. To prevent pressures beyond those anticipated from building up, safety relief valves are used. These are set to release pressure which exceeds normal operating pressure, but which is less than the maximum pressure the vessel is designed to withstand. Normal operations should not cause the relief valve to operate and therefore they may remain shut for years. In the absence of a sound maintenance program, such long periods of not operating may lead to corrosion which renders them frozen in place and inoperative. This situation, combined with a pressure buildup, leads to an explosion of the vessel. The ubiquity of pressure vessels caused the development of not only insurance to indemnify for losses but also a companion inspection service to prevent losses. Insureds depend heavily on automatic controls to monitor these operations, and frequent, periodic inspections of all systems by competent engineers are necessary.

Damage Control Damage by the explosion of pressure vessels can be extremely severe. A major explosion can send a pressure vessel in rocket fashion through walls, floors, or roofs of buildings. In some instances, it may be practical to separate pressure vessels from other areas by sturdy walls which can absorb the force of a minor explosion. Also, where feasible, power plants should be in separate structures (isolation). Normally, the best damage control is prevention.

Incidence Explosions, whether from reactions or pressure vessel failure, are infrequent severe occurrences which must be anticipated. Most buildings suffer only one major explosion, so a clean, explosion-free record is to be expected. Any other pattern should be questioned. Modern technology has provided the means of preventing, suppressing, and controlling explosions and explosion damage. It is a real peril to property and not to be ignored, but a peril which can be controlled.

SPRINKLER LEAKAGE AND WATER DAMAGE

Sprinkler Leakage

Sprinkler leakage coverage provides protection against the accidental discharge of an automatic sprinkler system. A sprinkler system is defined as including the pipes, sprinkler heads, valves, and fittings as well as storage tanks, hydrants, and hose outlets feeding or fed by an automatic sprinkler system.

The modern automatic sprinkler system can be traced back to 1878, and since then it has been continuously improved and perfected. Today's system is rugged and reliable, but like any other mechanical device, a sprinkler system must receive a certain amount of attention. With proper care and maintenance the chance of accidental discharge is quite small. Sprinkler systems are covered in detail in Chapter 6.

Damage to the sprinkler system itself from fire, extended coverage perils, or vandalism or malicious mischief is covered as part of the building. Therefore, the valuation of the sprinkler system should be included when setting amounts of building insurance.

Causes of Sprinkler Leakage Although sprinkler leakage losses are infrequent, they do occur. In the vast majority of cases, however, the causes can be successfully controlled if fully understood and appreciated.

One of the most common causes of accidental discharge is freezing. Since most systems that are subject to below freezing temperatures are designed as either dry systems or wet systems with antifreeze loops in low temperature areas, freezing is usually the result of accidental heating failure. Until recently, heating failures have usually been caused by breakdown of the heating unit itself or temporary interruption of power. It is possible that the recent shortages of adequate energy in those portions of the country subject to very cold weather may increase the amount of heating failures, which in turn may elevate the number of losses caused by freezing.

Mechanical injury is another cause of sprinkler leakage. Material handling by forklift trucks presents the most common mechanical injury exposure. Warehouses using forklifts should have guards on each sprinkler head, and pipes and *risers* (the vertical piping connecting the water supply and the horizontal feed mains) should also be protected. Forklift operators must be trained and frequently warned of the hazard they constitute when careless. Risks in areas subject to earthquake should have sprinkler systems installed to earthquake specifications. Stock should be piled in such a fashion that, should it overturn, it cannot damage any portion of the sprinkler system.

Improper installation and maintenance can lead to accidental discharge. The piping should be frequently checked and regularly maintained. Hangers and supports should be kept in good condition and pipes should never be used to support stock, ladders, or other material. Proper clearance should be provided where pipes pass through walls and foundations so minor settling does not put undue strain on the pipe network.

Overheating due to high ceiling temperatures is also a cause of loss. A variety of sprinkler heads are available, each designed to operate at different ceiling temperatures. Heads can overheat if they are subject to sudden unexpected high temperatures caused by such things as the failure of ventilating systems or cooling systems. Frequently, overheating can be a slow process. Heads may be exposed to temperatures sufficiently high to cause gradual weakening in the heat responsive element within the sprinkler head, eventually causing the head to operate. Overheating often occurs when a new operation is introduced into a manufacturing process or a new tenant occupies a building and heads are not changed to meet the new occupancy requirements.

Heads exposed to an industrial operation which creates a corrosive atmosphere can weaken over time and then suddenly fail. In such cases, heads should be protected with a coating of lead, rubber, wax, or similar corrosive-resistant material. Care must be taken to be sure the corrosive-resistant material used will not delay the action of the heat responsive element or in any way interfere with the free release of the head's operating parts when the sprinkler is intended to operate.

Water Damage

Water damage insurance covers direct loss caused by accidental discharge, leakage, or overflow of water or steam from plumbing and heating systems, tanks, industrial and domestic appliances, and refrigerating and air conditioning systems. It also covers rain or snow admitted directly into the building through defective roofs or windows, or through open windows. The coverage is not widely sold separately but it is a covered peril in many forms currently in use.

The proper maintenance of the building and its plumbing, heating, and air conditioning systems is a major underwriting consideration. A problem may arise when the insured is a tenant and the building is owned by another; maintenance may be beyond the insured's control or interest. Selection against the insurer is an ever-present danger, as those most in need of the coverage may be the least insurable.

Causes of Water Damage Loss Leakage from plumbing, heating, and cooling systems is most frequently due to lack of maintenance and attention. Older pipes, particularly those made of cast iron, can corrode and fittings and joints can become loose over time. Internal obstructions in drains caused by foreign matter can cause backup and overflow. As with sprinkler systems, freezing can cause joints to leak and pipes to burst. Cooling towers and storage tanks, usually located on the roof, must be regularly checked and maintained, since leakage can involve large quantities of water and can damage each succeeding floor in turn. Roof storage tanks usually are fitted with electric heating elements which are thermostatically controlled. When the thermostat failed to operate on the sprinkler tank of a Philadelphia theater in 1972, extensive damage resulted from a bursting of frozen pipes: the stage floor was ruined, a $30,000 curtain was irreparably stained, costumes for a current production were destroyed, and a loss of revenue was sustained from a four-day closing. A subsequent inspection revealed that the heater and its thermostat had not been checked for more than a decade. Hot water tanks and their connecting fittings and pipes must also receive regular attention. A simple but severe exposure causing frequent loss stems from persons leaving faucets open in public or private washrooms.

Building maintenance is also important. Roof surfaces must be in good repair and roof drains must be kept free of debris. Sloping roofs in colder climates may require special protection as ice may build up along the eaves. This can prevent rain or melting snow from running off properly, causing water to back up under the roof surface and resulting in damage to both building and contents. Broken windows must be replaced at once and poorly fitting window frames should be corrected.

The underwriter must also be concerned about the local town or city water supply and sewage systems. In some older cities there still exist wooden water lines and early cast iron piping over 150 years old. A burst line in the street can be undetected for a length of time sufficient to allow substantial erosion and eventual leakage into basement storage areas of nearby businesses.

Factors Affecting Sprinkler Leakage and Water Damage Losses

Multistory buildings which sustain either sprinkler leakage or water damage on upper floors can suffer damage not only on the floor of origin but on all lower floors as well. Floor construction and floor openings, such as stairwells, conduits, and pipe chases are important considerations. Concrete floors, particularly if provided with adequate scuppers (an opening in the wall of a building to permit water to drain off a floor or flat roof) and floor drains, are superior to wooden floors. Contents in basements, which are at the lowest level and below grade, are particularly vulnerable. Basements used for stock storage should be provided with adequate sumps and, if necessary, sump pumps.

The susceptibility of contents to damage by water is of prime importance in evaluating loss potential from both sprinkler leakage and water damage. Food, clothing, drugs, electrical equipment, paper goods, and similar items are highly susceptible to water damage. Generally, the damageability of contents is self-evident but, if in doubt, the classification table of the ISO Commercial Lines Manual can be a valuable guide. Damageability is classified as slight, medium, and high, and reference to the damageability rating can often aid underwriters in their evaluation. Rates are based on these divisions as well as consideration of the type of floors (e.g., concrete) and building height.

Stock storage methods are also important. Stock stored directly on the floor is particularly subject to damage. Stock in cardboard containers is highly vulnerable to loss when stored directly on the floor. Through capillary action substantial amounts of water can be absorbed into the lower boxes causing them to lose their shape and permitting the piles to overturn. Wherever possible stock should be stored on skids or pallets, in bins, or on racks. In any event, stock storage in basements should be avoided unless adequate drainage facilities exist. Consideration must also be given to proper stockpiling so that sprinklers may operate properly in the event of fire. Guard and automatic alarm services are desirable for sprinklered risks to reduce leakage damage. These are described in Chapter 6.

RIOT AND CIVIL COMMOTION

As with other property perils, the perils of riot and civil commotion are not defined in the policy itself. Property policies do contain a war clause which excludes insurrection, including governmental action in combating or subduing an insurrection. Since insurrection is undefined as well, some confusion can exist as to what is covered and what is not. Without policy definitions, the statutes and court interpretations of the various states must be relied on for a definitive determination of coverage. These statutes and interpretations vary from state to state but are generally similar. The recent "fighting" in Beirut has led to at least one court case in trying to determine whether or not a "war" exists. The dividing lines between the terms are not clear.

Definitions

Riot Riot is commonly understood to be an assembly of individuals who act together unlawfully with force or violence against the person or property of another, or commit an unlawful act in a violent or tumultuous manner to the terror or disturbance of others. The number of people necessary to constitute a riot depends on the state in question. Most states follow the English common-law requirement of at least three. In some states two people can be deemed to have caused a riot and in one state twelve armed or thirty unarmed persons must be involved.

There are several court cases which have established what unlawful, violent acts are *not* considered riots. Damage done quietly and by stealth is not riot. Damage done at night with no disturbance or tumult has been held to be vandalism or malicious mischief rather than riot.

Civil Commotion Civil commotion is even more difficult to define. The most common definition describes it as an uprising among a large number of people which occasions a serious prolonged disturbance; an infraction of civil order not attaining the status of war or an armed rebellion. The difference between riot and civil commotion seems principally one of degree. As few as two people are necessary for a riot. A large mass of people are required for a civil commotion.

Insurrection Insurrection has a reasonably precise definition which hinges on its motivation. Insurrection is the use of armed force against the government to achieve public ends, which cannot be achieved peacefully, by usurping governmental authority. To quote one State Court, "To constitute an insurrection . . . there must have been a movement accompanied by action specifically intended to overthrow the constituted government and to take possession of the inherent powers thereof."[1] Thus, with no planned objective clearly thought out in advance, and no organized leadership who intend to seize the powers of government, an insurrection cannot take place.

Incidence of Riot and Civil Commotion

The history of the United States is checkered with major riots. Perhaps the first riot of prominence occurred in Boston on 5 March 1770. A group of people provoked the sentries standing guard at the Boston Customs House, and the sentries fired into the crowd, killing five people. This incident is remembered as the Boston Massacre. Historically, riot and civil commotion have frequently occurred in the context of labor disputes. The framers of the riot and civil commotion coverage language were clearly conscious of this connection when they specifically included the words "riot attending a strike." The great railway strikes of 1877, the Haymarket Square riots in Chicago in 1886, and the Carnegie Steel lockout in Homestead, Pennsylvania, in 1892, were all major civil disorders, equal in their time to the impact of the urban riots of the mid-1960s. With the acceptance of the labor movement and the federally sanctioned collective bargaining process, major strike-associated riot has now all but disappeared and destruction has been limited to sporadic and relatively slight cases of property damage.

The Urban Riots and Their Influence on Insurance

The urban riots of the mid-1960s caused major property damage in many American cities. Commencing with the Watts riot in Los Angeles, city after city experienced civil disorders. In addition to the Los Angeles riot, major civil disorders occurred in Newark and Detroit and lesser riots occurred in such cities as Hartford and Cincinnati. In just a few years, over 150 cities experienced urban rioting. Rioting has more recently occurred in Miami in the early eighties.

As a shocked and perplexed nation began to debate the underlying causes of these urban civil disorders, President Johnson in 1967 appointed the National Advisory Commission on Civil Disorders to investigate their origins and make recommendations to prevent or contain them in the future. To examine the associated insurance problems, the commission in turn appointed the National Advisory Panel on Insurance in Riot-Affected Areas. This panel has since been known as the Hughes Panel because it was chaired by then Governor Richard J. Hughes of New Jersey.

In its basic findings, the Hughes Panel noted a "serious lack of property insurance in our nation's cities." Two specific conclusions were stressed in the panel's final report. First, insurance is a necessity for the security and safety of property owners. Second, insurance is essential if urban areas are to be revitalized. The report also stated that insurers are legitimately interested in profits and in maintaining their financial stability, and therefore seek to avoid high risks. It also concluded that federal measures should be taken to alleviate the problem but as support rather than replacement of the existing insurance mechanism.

As a result of the Hughes Panel's report, the Urban Property Protection and Reinsurance Act of 1968 was passed into law as part of the Housing and Urban Development Act of 1968. The act made available federal riot reinsurance in those states which, as a prerequisite, had established plans to which insurers must belong for the purpose of providing the insurance needed in urban areas. These are called Fair Access to Insurance Requirements (FAIR) Plans. Insurers were only able to purchase the federal riot reinsurance in those states where a FAIR Plan existed and such plan was in conformity with federal statute.

As of January 1984, FAIR Plans had been established in twenty-six states, Puerto Rico, and the District of Columbia. With three exceptions (Indiana, Iowa, and Kansas) an insurer, to be able to write property insurance in the state, must belong to the FAIR Plan. Participation is based on each insurer's share of property writings in the state. There are many variations among the state plans which are too numerous to mention here.

About half of the states with FAIR Plans have failed to comply with a 1978 amendment requiring that the FAIR Plan rates for standard insureds be no higher than rates in the voluntary market for standard insureds. Thus, the plans of these states no longer meet the federal requirements for an "approved" plan. This fact, combined with the fact that only eight companies were reinsured as of the fall of 1983, led Congress to discontinue offering the riot reinsurance coverage. The coverage for those eight companies continued until the fall of 1984 at which time the program ended, but no new riot reinsurance coverage was accepted after Congress terminated the program.

The establishment of FAIR Plans, and indeed the entire subject of involuntary plans which have proliferated in recent years, has raised issues and problems far beyond the scope of this chapter. However, the peril of riot and civil commotion and the problems associated with it during the turbulent 1960s have played a major role in the development of such programs.

VANDALISM OR MALICIOUS MISCHIEF

Vandalism protection provides coverage for the deliberate, willful damage or destruction of the insured property. Historically, malicious mischief was included in the coverage to avoid a narrow, dictionary definition of vandalism, now archaic, which limited vandalism to the destruction of things of beauty or art.

Because damage must be deliberate and willful, a certain level of intelligence is required on the part of the perpetrator. Vandalism cannot occur without an awareness of wrongdoing by the party committing the act. For this reason damage caused by children has at times been determined not to be vandalism by the courts, as the damage done was not intended and could not be foreseen by the child. Generally, the courts consider a child's act to be vandalism if the child is capable of understanding its consequences, even if the specific intent to cause injury was lacking.

Incidence

The principal perpetrators of vandalism loss have traditionally been children and young adults. As is true of crimes like burglary and auto theft, 75 to 80 percent of all vandalism is committed by persons under twenty-five years of age. Therefore, those risks which are associated with children often have a history of vandalism. Schools, churches, parks, sports fields, playgrounds, and youth centers typically fall into this category. Since childhood vandalism is often the act of a group rather than a single individual, those areas with a high child population are also likely to be exposed. Thus, on the average, urban locations are likely to be more exposed than rural ones. Areas of high unemployment among young people can also be expected to have a higher incidence of vandalism.

Willful and deliberate destruction can also be the consequence of labor disputes and poor labor relations. Vandalism has often been committed during wildcat strikes. It can also be directed at plants employing nonunion labor, particularly when plants of a similar type are out on strike. Individual acts of sabotage by discontented workers can also occur. The acceptance of the labor movement and the collective bargaining process has diminished incidence from this cause somewhat. However, labor-associated vandalism can still occur to almost any individual risk and particularly within those industries with a history of worker hostility and militancy.

Historically, college campuses have frequently suffered vandalism damage. During the 1960s, colleges were the focal point for the dissatisfaction of young people over the draft, the Vietnam conflict, social injustice, and similar causes for protests. Such destructive acts have receded in recent years, but the possibility exists that they may flare up again in the future.

As violent protest has become a more popular means of public expression among some groups, a new form of vandalism exposure now confronts the underwriter. These groups are willing to use destruction as a means of drawing public attention to themselves. In addition, as terrorist bombings in the Middle East have shown, people are willing to die for the causes in which they believe, making prevention even more difficult. As a result, risks never before considered to be vandalism-prone have become potential problems. Such risks as the headquarters of multinational corporations, oil companies, offices of foreign airlines, government buildings in Washington, D.C., and even the homes of public and private officials have been the target for acts of vandalism.

This kind of vandalism sometimes seems to be almost impossible to predict. Dealing with this exposure is very complex and beyond the scope of this text.

Dealing with the Vandalism Exposure

Those risks subject to a frequent but relatively predictable level of vandalism loss can normally be dealt with through the use of deductibles. Schools, youth centers, and other risks specifically child oriented fall into this category because they are characterized by a frequency of relatively small losses. The vandalism problem of such risks can often be overcome by using a larger deductible, either on a per occurrence or an annual aggregate basis. Deductibles will not solve the entire problem. While they will eliminate many of the smaller losses for the insurer, these frequent small losses will often precede a more severe loss. One method which can be used by schools to curb vandalism losses both in frequency and severity is the volunteer patrol of the schools by the parent-teacher organization, teachers, students, and other groups connected with the schools. The presence of anyone on the school premises is a very effective deterrent to vandalism. Lighting of the buildings, entrances, and surrounding area can also reduce vandalism. Vandals do not want to be identified. Conversely, some persons believe that all lighting does, especially in remote areas, is give vandals another target (the light) and let them see their other targets more clearly.

Central station intrusion alarms have also proven to be an effective deterrent. Such alarms can be quite sophisticated. They can protect not only the building itself, but the perimeter of the outside yard as well. Central station guard service is also a strong deterrent to vandalism. Perhaps the best level of protection can be achieved through a combination of electronic intrusion alarms and guard service.

EARTHQUAKE AND OTHER EARTH MOVEMENT

Earthquake

The earthquake hazard presents the underwriter with a particularly difficult problem. Although great scientific advances have been made in understanding earthquakes and their causes, neither their frequency nor severity can be predicted accurately. Further, coverage is usually purchased only in those areas subject to earthquakes. Not only must insurance companies strive to avoid the natural adverse selection inherent in this situation, but also they must control their total earthquake writings so that their assets are protected from catastrophic loss.

Coverage for earthquake-related damage has recently been broadened by the doctrine of *concurrent causation* which has been upheld in the California courts. Essentially, this doctrine says that if damage is caused concurrently by two perils, one excluded and the other covered, the damage will be covered. Thus many insurers who covered the collapse peril but excluded earthquake damage were held liable for damage to buildings which collapsed due to an earthquake. Most insurers are presently (late 1983) trying to endorse all policies to specifically exclude such an interpretation of coverage in the future. This is an example of how liberal court rulings affect more than just liability insurance and stands as a reminder to the underwriter to be aware of such possibilities in the future.

Earthquake underwriting requires the assistance of many specialists. Underwriters must depend on the work of geologists, seismologists, engineers, soil specialists, and others. In addition to the magnitude of the shock itself, underwriting analysis of earthquake potential rests on four points: the distance of the site from the earthquake epicenter, the soil conditions, design and construction techniques, and materials.

Earthquake Causes   Within the last fifteen years, the *tectonic plate theory* has been widely accepted as the explanation for a number of worldwide geological phenomena, earthquakes and volcanic eruptions among them. Briefly, the theory postulates that the earth's outer shell consists of about eight large and over a dozen small semi-rigid interlocking plates. These plates fit together closely and are subject to forces from within the earth which cause them to move relative to one another. The average speed of this movement is extremely slow, usually about one-quarter inch per year, although movement along the San Andreas Fault is estimated to average between two and three inches a year. Due to the friction between the rough edges of the plate, movement is not always smooth. Often pressure has to be built up to overcome the friction present. When the accumulated strain is great enough it is released with a sudden jerk—an earthquake.

The earthquake belts of the world follow the edges of the plates forming the earth's surface. The type of earthquake activity in a particular area depends on how the plates are moving. Two plates can be moving away from each other, moving toward each other with one plate forced up over the other, or sliding past each other. The San Andreas Fault is of the third type, caused by the lateral movement of the Pacific Plate and the American Plate. Earthquakes are more frequent at the junction of two plates, but they can also occur across the width of the plates themselves.

Areas of Earthquake Activity in the United States   Although most earthquakes in the United States occur on the West Coast from Alaska to California, no area of the country is entirely free of earthquakes. In fact, while 90 percent of all United States earthquakes occur in California and western Nevada, the strongest earthquake in the country occurred in New Madrid, Missouri, in 1811.

The United States Office of Science and Technology has designated the seismic risk for each area of the country as indicated in Exhibit 3-1. Zone 0 represents areas where earthquake risk is almost nonexistent. Zone 1 is exposed to minor damage from earthquakes of Modified Mercalli Scales V and VI described in the next section. Zone 2 is exposed to moderate damage. Earthquakes up to Modified Mercalli VII have been recorded. Zone 3 represents areas of significant damage potential, where intensities of VIII and greater have been experienced. The concentration of writings of earthquake coverage in these areas must be monitored by insurers to avoid potential catastrophe problems. It should be remembered that at the time this study was done, exact seismological information was available for less than seventy years. The most common source of data is reports from eyewitnesses, which may be unreliable.

Earthquake Measurement   Earthquake measurement is commonly expressed in either *magnitude* (the Richter Scale) or *intensity* (Modified Mercalli Scale of 1931).

The Richter Scale measures the total energy released. It is intended as a totally objective, scientifically calculated rating. Magnitude is calculated from the wave amplitude of an earthquake as recorded by seismographs. The scale progresses logarithmically, which means each unit on the scale measures energy ten times greater than the energy of the previous unit. Thus, a magnitude 6 on the Richter Scale is ten times greater than a magnitude 5, a hundred times greater than a magnitude 4 and a thousand times greater than a 3. The scale has no ceiling, but 8.9 seems to be the largest magnitude of any known earthquake. The Richter Scale is merely a scientific means of measuring the energy released. It does not take into consideration location, depth, or soil conditions. Thus, the Richter Scale does not actually give an indication of the physical damage sustained to buildings and injury incurred by populations.

The Modified Mercalli Scale of 1931 measures intensity, or the degree of damage caused by an earthquake to people, structures, and the earth's surface. Thus, this scale would be of more use to the property underwriter since it gives an indication of the damage and

Exhibit 3-1
Seismic Risk by Geographic Area*

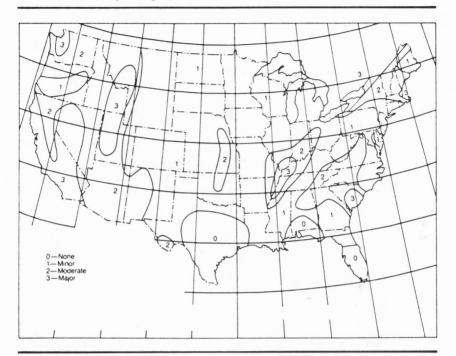

0—None
1—Minor
2—Moderate
3—Major

*Reprinted from National Oceanic and Atmospheric Administration and National Ocean Survey, *Seismic Risk Studies in the United States* (Washington: U.S. Department of Commerce).

destruction actually caused. The intensity grading is established by human observation and is subject to the inherent weaknesses of such an imprecise system. The scale's wording and some of its imagery is broad and in places vague, but as almost all earthquake sites are now inspected by engineers, geologists, seismologists, and other specialists, the Modified Mercalli Scale can be quite accurate. This scale has a more universal use than the Richter Scale. It has been used since inception by the U.S. government and is the commonly used scale on a worldwide basis. The Modified Mercalli Scale is shown in Exhibit 3-2.

Because the Richter and Modified Mercalli scales measure different things, direct comparisons between them are difficult. However, these differences can be illustrated by an example. Assume two earthquakes in different areas of the country occur with the same severity; the total energy released by each is identical. One occurs in a large city and the other in an area totally unpopulated. On the Richter Scale each would measure the same. On the Modified Mercalli Scale the one affecting the

Exhibit 3-2
The Modified Mercalli Scale

I. Not felt except by a very few under especially favorable circumstances.

II. Felt only by a few persons at rest, especially on upper floors of buildings. Delicately suspended objects may swing.

III. Felt quite noticeably indoors, especially on upper floors of buildings, but many people do not recognize it as an earthquake. Standing motor cars may rock slihtly. Vibration like passing truck. Duration estimated.

IV. During the day felt indoors by many, outdoors by few. At night some awakened. Dishes, windows, doors disturbed; walls make creaking sound. Sensation like heavy truck striking building. Standing motor cars rocked noticeably.

V. Felt by nearly everyone; many awakened. Some dishes, windows, etc., broken; a few instances of cracked plaster; unstable objects overturned. Disturbances of trees, poles, and other tall objects sometimes noticed. Pendulum clocks may stop.

VI. Felt by all; many frightened and run outdoors. Some heavy furniture moved; a few instances of fallen plaster or damaged chimneys. Damage slight.

VII. Everybody runs outdoors. Damage negligible in buildings of good design and construction; slight to moderate in well-built ordinary structures; considerable in poorly built or badly designed structures; some chimneys broken. Noticed by persons driving motor cars.

VII. Damage slight in specially designed structures; considerable in ordinary substantial buildings, with partial collapse; great in poorly built structures. Panel walls thrown out of frame structures. Fall of chimneys, factory stacks, columns, monuments, walls. Heavy furniture overturned. Sand and mud ejected in small amounts. Changes in well water. Disturbs persons driving motor cars.

IX. Damage considerable in specially designed structures; well designed frame structures thrown out of plumb; great in substantial buildings, with partial collapse. Buildings shifted off foundations. Ground cracked conspicuously. Underground pipes broken.

X. Some well built, wooden structures destroyed; most masonry and frame structures destroyed with foundations; ground badly cracked. Rails bent. Landslides considerable from river banks and steep slopes. Shifted sand and mud. Water splashed over banks.

XI. Few, if any, (masonry) structures remain standing. Bridges destroyed. Broad fissures in ground. Underground pipelines completely out of service. Earth slumps and land slips in soft ground. Rails bent greatly.

XII. Damage total. Waves seen on ground surfaces. Lines of sight and level distorted. Objects thrown upward into the air.

Exhibit 3-3
Focus and Epicenter of an Earthquake*

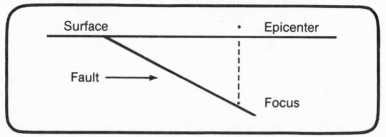

*Adapted with permission from a diagram appearing in the article,
"Earthquake Faults and Underwriting Faults," by Karl V. Steinbrugge
and Vincent R. Bush in the Property and Casualty Edition of *Western
Underwriter*, October 1956

large city would measure considerably higher than the one in the unpopulated area. Thus, an underwriter could gain more information of interest from the Modified Mercalli Scale.

Focus and Epicenter The point of origin of an earthquake is called the *focus* and is that point within the fault where slippage begins to occur. As movement proceeds along the fault surface, energy is released and radiates outward from the focus in seismic waves. The focus can occur at various depths beneath the surface. Most destructive earthquakes have shallow foci (within about twenty-five miles of the surface). The closer to the surface, the greater the ground motion. Pacific coast earthquakes are generally of the shallow type.

The *epicenter* is the point on the earth's surface directly above the focus. The fault plane frequently does not run perpendicular to the surface but at an angle. Therefore the epicenter of an earthquake in many cases may not be located within the fault line, as shown in Exhibit 3-3.

Generally, the closer the structures in question are to the epicenter, the greater the damage expected. However, no hard and fast rules exist as to how far away can be considered "safe," as soil conditions, building design, and construction materials play a large role. A well-constructed building with foundations on bedrock may better withstand an earthquake at a distance of one or two miles from the epicenter than a similar building on poor soil ten miles away. Furthermore, high-rise buildings present additional complications because they are sensitive to a different kind of seismic wave than are shorter buildings. Because the amplitude of these waves remains larger for greater distances, it is actually possible for such a building to sustain a higher loss as much as 120 miles from the epicenter than it would in the epicenter's immediate proximity.

Soil Conditions The ability of a structure to withstand an earthquake is heavily dependent on the soil on which it is built. Earthquakes produce vibrations in the earth mass which oscillate outward as seismic waves. When deep in bedrock these waves travel at small amplitudes, as the bedrock itself is able to withstand their force. However, in the more loosely consolidated soil the wave motion becomes magnified and more damaging. Two similar structures, one on bedrock and the other on soft soil, will each react differently to an earthquake, and generally greater damage will occur in the latter. Since bedrock can successfully withstand seismic waves, a building with its foundation firmly anchored to bedrock should sustain a minimum of structural damage. However, if the building is built over or adjacent to an active fault, even this will have little effect in preventing damage.

In most areas soil covers the bedrock from a depth of a few feet to a few hundred feet. In many cases it is not economically feasible to extend foundations to the bedrock and the building is built on the soil itself. The ability of soil to withstand seismic activity varies. *Consolidated soil* of long standing (measured in thousands of years) such as limestone and some clay, will stand up better than *unconsolidated soil* such as sand, gravel, or silt. These unconsolidated soils are particularly hazardous as is filled land, common in many large cities. Waterlogged soil, that is, soil with a high water table, is also dangerous. Such unconsolidated soil is subject to *liquefaction* during an earthquake; it becomes so unstable it acts as a liquid.

Building Design Nonseismic building construction is influenced principally by the vertical loads the building must bear. The loads include the weight of the building itself and its proposed contents. An earthquake, however, causes horizontal stresses which the weight-bearing walls and columns have not been designed to withstand. Walls, which are designed only to withstand the weight of the upper floors and roof, actually move out from under them, causing collapse. Mortar between bricks is not strong enough to hold walls together without some type of reinforcing; therefore, walls are shaken apart. Earthquake-resistant buildings are designed so the structure as a whole will resist the forces of earth movement. The most common method is to build a rigid structure with walls, columns, and pillars tied in securely to floors and roofs by horizontal, vertical, and cross members carried through to the foundations.

Because soil conditions play such an important role in earthquake loss, particular attention must be paid to a building's foundation. Not only is the size and weight of the building a consideration, but the soil condition itself. This is particularly important for buildings over three stories in height. If bedrock is close to the surface, the foundation should extend to it. Where this is not possible, the foundation must be built so as to allow the whole structure to move as a single unit when subjected to earthquake forces.

Construction.

FRAME. Frame construction of one or two stories has adequate earthquake-resistant properties when properly constructed. The framing should be securely bolted to the foundation and the walls should be firmly braced either by diagonal braces or by plywood sheathing. Frame structures generally "absorb" a good deal of shock or vibration. Damage may be sustained to chimneys and plate glass windows and plaster and stucco may crack; however, structural damage should be slight.

MASONRY. Ordinary brick buildings have a poor history as earthquake risks. Such buildings have no structural supports. The walls bear the weight of the roof without benefit of reinforcing. Many older buildings have been built with lime or lime-sand mortar which has a poor bonding quality and does not stand up well to the lateral forces of an earthquake. Modern mortars made from a combination of Portland cement, lime, and sandy aggregates provide better bonding, but without reinforcing, even walls with this type of mortar are highly susceptible to collapse.

Hollow concrete block and hollow tile buildings are similar in many respects to ordinary brick. If the cells within the blocks are filled solidly with tamped mortar and vertical reinforcing rods are provided every two to four feet, buildings of this construction can be quite effective if otherwise properly designed and constructed. However, hollow concrete block laid up with mortar only, and without reinforcing of any kind, is even more susceptible to earthquake than ordinary brick construction.

CONCRETE. Potentially, monolithic concrete structures have the greatest ability to stand up to earthquake forces. However, even these buildings can fail if improperly designed or improperly built. A well designed concrete structure should suffer only minimal damage.

Structures of precast concrete have not performed well in earthquakes due principally to lack of proper anchoring between the various precast elements. "Tilt-up" construction, in which wall sections are precast at the job site on the building's floor slab and then tilted-up and anchored to poured-in-place concrete columns, have not responded well for much the same reason.

HIGH-RISE BUILDINGS. High-rise structures of twenty-five or more stories are relatively recent in those areas subject to high earthquake incidence. Both steel frame and reinforced concrete frame construction have been used, although nearly all buildings in the twenty-five-story-plus range have been of steel frame construction. Because they are relatively new, there is a limited amount of experience with tall buildings in strong earthquakes, but the experience available is encouraging. Studies have shown that the properties of tall buildings are such that no special hazards arise simply because of height. Earthquake experience has demonstrated that well designed and constructed buildings, including tall buildings, can successfully withstand strong earthquake forces.

Other Physical Features. In addition to the foregoing, the following features should also be considered.[2]

- *Shape.* L-shaped and T-shaped buildings and other irregular forms are disadvantageous unless the wings are structurally separated or unless unusual design features have been incorporated. Long, thin buildings may be poor if the bracing is of the rigid, box type.
- *Area.* A large-area structure, such as a one-story warehouse with wood roof and concrete walls, may have a roof deck too flexible for the relatively rigid exterior concrete walls.
- *Wall Material.* Reinforced unit masonry, such as brick and hollow concrete block, requires a high degree of workmanship, which is difficult to obtain unless carefully supervised. While workmanship is also a factor for reinforced concrete construction, experience has shown that it is not as critical as for the unit masonry. Unreinforced masonry is always suspect.
- *Ornamentation.* Marble and most other veneers on walls of a flexible building may be readily loosened or damaged.
- *Partitions.* Plywood partitions and plastered partitions are easier to repair than hollow clay tile. Obviously, the number of partitions is a factor.
- *Previous Earthquake Damage.* Buildings not adequately repaired in one earthquake may be severely damaged in the next shock.
- *Exposure-Overhanging Walls.* A higher adjoining building may lose its brick parapet, and the force from this falling mass may destroy an adjoining, highly earthquake-resistant structure.
- *Exposure-Pounding.* Two adjoining structures will vibrate differently during an earthquake and may pound together. This pounding may cause extensive damage.
- *Deductibles.* Earthquake is truly a peril with catastrophic potential. Successful underwriting requires proper use of

deductibles. The property owner should retain through the use of deductibles those losses where damage is minor, such as cracked plaster and broken glass. These small claims should not place a severe financial burden on the property owner. The cumulative effect of thousands of individual losses of even moderate amounts can otherwise cause losses of such magnitude that earthquake capacity, already limited, would be even further reduced.

All standard earthquake insurance is generally written with a 5 percent deductible with the deductible applying to the limits of insurance and not to the amount of the loss. Buildings of an inferior type of construction require a 10 to 15 percent deductible. The dwelling classification is written with a 2 percent deductible. The maximum property deductible may be increased to 40 percent under tariff rules.

Other Earth Movement

While earthquakes are the principal source of loss by earth movement, loss can also be sustained from landslide, mud slide, and subsidence.

Landslide Landslides frequently occur as a result of seismic activity. Unconsolidated soil is particularly susceptible to landslides. These soils are by nature unstable and certain shale material can slide on an incline as little as five degrees from the horizontal. Landslides also can occur when cliffs along the seacoast become undermined through the action of waves.

Mud Slides Mud slides are a form of landslide and they are particularly common in southern California. After a major brush fire, large portions of California hillsides and mountainsides are left bare of vegetation. With nothing to restrain the soil, heavy rains can wash large quantities of wet soil down these hillsides, causing considerable devastation to structures below. Slag heaps around mine sites can cause a similar problem in other parts of the country.

Subsidence Subsidence can be caused by the tectonic mechanism through both the gradual creep along a fault or by an earthquake itself. It can also be caused by the extraction of minerals or water from the earth. Human-caused subsidence of this type has occurred around coal fields, salt mines, oil fields, and gas fields. In such areas, the great weight of the overburden is borne in part by the minerals themselves. As they are extracted, the surface weight is too great for the remaining material to support without reconsolidation. Many areas of the country are subject to subsidence and the underwriter must be aware of those in his or her territory.

Volcanoes In the first edition of this text, no mention was made of the danger of loss due to volcanic eruption since there were no known active volcanoes in the continential U.S. However, Mount St. Helens alerted underwriters convincingly that the possibility of property damage from volcanic eruption does exist in the continental U.S. and should be considered even for thought-to-be extinct volcanoes. A concentration of writings near any of these should be avoided.

FLOOD

Flood is one of the oldest perils known to man and it would seem likely that it would be one of the first to be addressed by the private insurance mechanism. Yet to this day flood has not been widely written by the private sector. In fact, the passage of the National Flood Insurance Act of 1968, which in turn led to the National Flood Insurance Association, was the first large-scale involvement of private insurers with this peril. After the demise of the National Flood Insurance Association on 31 December 1977, it appeared that insurers would once again revert to a position of minimal involvement with the flood peril, since it was largely written by the federal government. However, after being handled by the federal government with administrative and operational assistance from private businesses (EDP Federal Corporation and Computer Science Corporation), the government in October 1983 began to encourage private insurer involvement again through its Write Your Own (WYO) Program. Essentially, private insurers would write flood coverage in conjunction with their other policies but the government would bear the risk and reimburse insurers for their expenses.

Flood and the Private Sector

The flood peril has traditionally been thought to pose some insoluble problems for the private market. First, insurers were unable to achieve an adequate spread of risk to allow the law of large numbers to work successfully. Unlike fire and most other perils, proper spread of risk is not easily attained. To a large degree property is either subject to flood or it is not, with the result that only those located in areas subject to floods are interested in purchasing coverage.

Second, as coverage is attractive only to those with a significant probability of loss, actuarially sound rates must be so high as to be generally unaffordable. Several private insurers offered flood coverage following the floods caused by the New England hurricane of 1944. Because of the cost, very few policies were sold and after a few years of no losses, they were allowed to lapse.

A third problem has been of a social nature. Responsible people within both the insurance industry and the federal government have been concerned that a readily available market for flood insurance would lead to unwise land use, as those previously inhibited from building in known flood plains would no longer be restrained from doing so. This fear was apparently well founded. The National Flood Insurance Act initially contained stringent land use control provisions, but as time went on they were weakened because of political pressure.

However, there is again pressure to tighten such restrictions and some tightening has been accomplished. It was soon realized that people were building in flood areas contrary to the program's intent, and oddly enough, because of the program. Whereas lenders previously were unwilling to make funds available for such projects since flood coverage was unavailable, the flood program made such coverage available and thus the loans were made and buildings were built. In some geographic areas, this has now been legislatively prohibited.

The Scope of the Flood Problem

Although it is estimated that the federal government alone has invested over $9 billion in flood protection and control measures since 1936, flood is still one of the most destructive perils. Furthermore, in spite of the massive outlays of public monies in flood control projects, damage has increased steadily. Flood damage in the United States is estimated to be between $1.5 and $2 billion annually. About 50 million acres of the United States are regularly subject to flooding. The government estimates there to be 8 million potential insureds in flood zones, and only about 2 million of these have purchased coverage.

Damage from flood can be more severe than most people imagine. Along with the obvious water damage, there is also damage from mud and debris carried by the flood waters. It is not uncommon for a foot or more of muddy sediment to be left after a flood. Containers of fuel oil, acids, and other corrosive and toxic substances may be breached, causing contamination (e.g., Times Beach, Missouri). Graves may be opened, sewage may be spread over wide areas, and public water supplies polluted, causing serious health hazards.

The erosion caused by flooding can be substantial, and the erosion caused by repeated flooding of the same site can be enormous. As soil is eroded away in each flood, the flood basin grows deeper and deeper, subjecting it to even greater flood damage in the future. This problem is compounded as population increases. As rural areas are built up and paved, there is less ground area available for water to soak into. In the last fifty years, literally millions of square miles of land in flood plain areas have been paved. The water which would otherwise be soaked up must go somewhere. Since it cannot be absorbed, it builds up in streets and basements, runs off into secondary basin areas not previously subject to flooding, or flows back into rivers increasing their volume. Because of these problems, flood heights at a given site may increase over time. As a result, flood control measures which were at one time adequate may no longer be sufficient to control flooding, and areas which were considered safe may now be exposed.

Flood Causes

Flood is defined in the October 1983 edition of the standard flood insurance policy as:

A. A general and temporary condition of partial or complete inundation of normally dry land areas from:
1. The overflow of inland or tidal waters.
2. The unusual and rapid accumulation or runoff or surface waters from any source.
3. Mudslides (i.e., mudflows) which are proximately caused by flooding as defined in subparagraph A-2, above and are akin to a river of liquid and flowing mud on the surfaces of normally dry land areas, as when earth is carried by a current of water and deposited along the path of the current.

B. The collapse or subsidence of land along the shore of a lake or other body of water as a result of erosion or undermining caused by waves or currents of water exceeding the cyclical levels which result in flooding as defined in A-1 above.

Floods are caused by numerous weather-related events. *Simple floods* occur when the rise in a river stage is directly caused by excessive rainfall over the drainage basin upstream without any other contributory factors. *Tidal floods* result primarily from excessively high tides, driven by high winds, which back up into portions of rivers along seacoasts. Wind-driven high tides can also inundate portions of the seacoast itself.

Wind floods occur on streams discharging into a large body of water with a long free sweep exposed to wind. A strong wind blowing steadily for some length of time may raise the water level considerably, causing backwater effects in the rivers. *Backwater floods* are caused by a rise in the water level of a river at some point downstream which in turn causes the water surface in the river to rise for some distance upstream.

Accidental floods result from such things as dam failure upstream or improper operation of flood control devices. *Ice jam floods* are caused by the accumulation of ice chunks in a river as the ice breaks up during a thaw. The resulting ice dam will cause backwater upstream and if broken suddenly, can cause flooding downstream.

Snow-melt floods occur on many rivers when the normal spring floods are intensified by melting snow cover over the watershed area. *Debris floods* can result as the flood stage is increased by debris lodging against bridge piers and other obstructions.[3]

Flood Incidence

As is true when dealing with all natural catastrophies in the United States, accurate flood records do not go back in time more than 100 years or so. This, at first glance, seems an adequate period to determine flood incidence in a given area. However, a comparison with the Nile River of Egypt provides a somewhat different perspective. Because of its long association with a highly developed civilization, the Nile has been subject to discerning observation far longer than any other river in the world. Partial flood information goes back to between 3000 and 3500 B.C. and reasonably complete records exist in every year from A.D. 622 onward.

When discussing flood incidence, floods are often described on the basis of their frequency of reoccurrence. Thus, floods are described by terms such as a 10-year flood or a 100-year flood, meaning in each case a flood of such magnitude is likely to occur once in 10 years or once in 100 years, respectively. This does *not* mean that floods occur evenly spaced over 10-year, 100-year, or other time intervals. They can and do occur more frequently, sometimes in close succession. At the opposite extreme, a century or more can go by without a flood. However, on the average, over a period of time, perhaps as long as 1,000 years, there would be 100 10-year floods and 10 100-year floods. Because the history of flood incidence in the United States covers so short a period, each new flood may challenge the previously established grading as the new flood itself becomes part of the record. Thus, the lack of a sufficient flood history makes flood incidence difficult to ascertain.

Determining Flood Exposures

A considerable amount of flood information can be obtained. Since 1927 the U.S. Army Corps of Engineers has been heavily involved with the flood problem. The Corps can provide considerable information on areas subject to flooding and the flood control projects which have been devised to control flooding. The maps prepared by the Corps are particularly useful.

Under the National Flood Insurance Program, those communities containing areas susceptible to flooding must be identified. The identification process includes the creation of a *flood hazard boundary map*, used to determine whether individual properties are within or outside of a flood-prone area. Since a flood-prone area under the act means a land area adjoining a river, stream, watercourse, ocean, bay, or lake which is likely to be flooded, flood hazard boundary maps exist for a vast number of communities. A portion of a flood hazard boundary map is shown in Exhibit 3-4.

As soon as possible after a community becomes eligible for national flood insurance, the Federal Insurance Administration initiates detailed topographic and hydrologic (water distribution) studies. These studies develop information about the base flood elevations within the community that on average have a 100-year flood potential. From this and related studies, a *flood insurance rate map (FIRM)* is prepared. These maps provide flood information in greater detail than the flood hazard boundary maps.[4]

Flood Protection

While avoidance remains the most effective loss control option for floods, insureds located in flood-prone areas can take steps to reduce damage should flood occur. Walls can be strengthened to reduce the possibility of collapse, and window and door openings can be protected with flood shields. The building site can be protected by dikes of adequate height. Tanks and equipment can be anchored to resist flotation and lateral movement. Contingency plans can be created to move automobiles and mobile equipment out of the area and to move high valued contents to upper floors should a flood threaten. Backup systems can be provided for power, and pumps can be installed in basements and other low-lying areas. In short, the underwriter must examine the flood peril on the same individual risk basis by which other perils are approached. The fact that a risk is exposed to flooding does not in itself make a risk uninsurable for the peril of flood any more than a risk exposed to fire makes it uninsurable for fire.

WINDSTORM AND HAIL

Windstorm is one of the most destructive of all natural events. Every area of the United States, and indeed the world, has known winds of destructive force. The sandstorms of the Southwest, the northeasters of New England, the tornadoes of the Midwest and Southeast, and the hurricanes of the Gulf and Atlantic states all affect

Exhibit 3-4
Flood Insurance Rate Map Effective October 15, 1981—Township of
Willistown, Chester County, Pennsylvania*

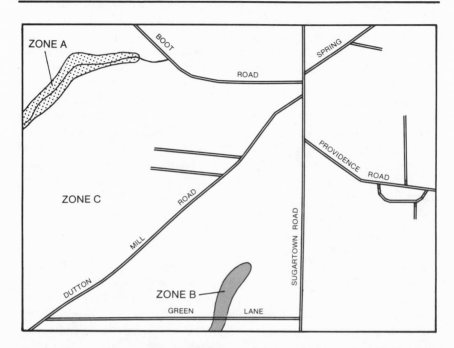

A Areas of 100-year flood; base flood elevations and flood hazard factors
   not determined.
B Areas between limits of the 100-year flood and 500-year flood; or certain
   areas subject to 100-year flooding with average depths less than one (1)
   foot or where the contributing drainage area is less than one square
   mile; or areas protected by levees from the base flood. (Medium
   shading)
C Areas of minimal flooding. (No shading)

*Adapted from Federal Emergency Management Agency, Federal Insurance
Administration.

our lives, at times cataclysmically. Of these storms, hurricanes and
tornadoes are the most damaging and occur on a regular basis.
Destructive hailstorms are a by-product of violent thunderstorms and
have also caused serious losses to the areas affected.

Hurricanes

Few natural events exceed the hurricane's potential for loss to life or property. One such storm killed an estimated 300,000 people in the Bay of Bengal in 1970. Hurricane Betsy, which struck New Orleans in 1965, caused *insured* losses of $715 million. In today's terms the insured losses caused by Betsy would approach $2.26 billion. In 1979, Hurricane Frederic hit the Gulf Coast (including Mobile) and caused $752.5 million in insured losses. In 1983, Alicia hit southeast Texas and caused an estimated $675.5 million in property damage. Adjusted for inflation, Betsy would still remain the most costly, however, in terms of insured damage.

Hurricanes are the product of a combination of atmospheric conditions, water temperatures, prevailing trade winds, and pressure systems. Their development is heavily influenced by the Bermuda High, a semi-permanent zone of high pressure which serves as a buffer between the temperate Northern Hemisphere and the tropical climate of the Southern Hemisphere. The hurricane season normally stretches from June to November in the Northern Hemisphere.

Hurricane Characteristics Hurricanes are cyclonic storms— massive wind systems circulating at high speeds in a counter-clockwise direction (in the Northern Hemisphere) about a center of relative calm called the "eye." The eye is usually 10 to 15 miles in diameter. The total storm size is usually 50 to 100 miles in diameter, although larger storms can reach a diameter of nearly 200 miles. Generally, the greatest damage comes from winds closest to the eye. Furthermore, those winds in the front-right quadrant (the northeast quadrant in storms moving north) are usually the highest.

Hurricanes are spawned in the warm waters of the Atlantic and as a general rule follow a roughly parabolic path with a tendency to reach into northern latitudes. They build up and maintain high wind speeds over warm ocean water (which in a real sense acts as fuel for the hurricane) and diminish in strength over cold ocean water. An average hurricane lasts nine days and covers a track 3,000 miles long.

Once hurricanes pass over land, they rapidly begin to lose intensity. Without the ocean to feed them, their intensity cannot be sustained and the land itself causes a friction effect which further reduces the wind speeds.

Hurricane Measurement The *Beaufort Scale*, a recognized worldwide grading of the observable effects of wind velocities, defines a hurricane as force 12 or higher, with wind speeds in excess of seventy-three miles per hour. The scale was originally zero to twelve, but was revised to seventeen divisions. The scale is shown in Exhibit 3-5. It should be noted that the exact point in wind speed where a storm becomes a hurricane will vary but somewhere in the seventy-three to seventy-five miles per hour range is most frequently used.

Exhibit 3-5
Beaufort Scale*

Beaufort Number	Name	Miles Per Hour	Description
0	Calm	Less than 1	Calm; smoke rises vertically
1	Light air	1—3	Direction of wind shown by smoke but not by wind vanes
2	Light breeze	4—7	Wind felt on face; leaves rustle; ordinary vane moved by wind
3	Gentle breeze	8—12	Leaves and small twigs in constant motion; wind extends light flag
4	Moderate breeze	13—18	Raises dust and loose paper; small branches are moved
5	Fresh breeze	19—24	Small trees in leaf begin to sway; crested wavelets form on inland waters
6	Strong breeze	25—31	Large branches in motion; telegraph wires whistle; umbrellas used with difficulty
7	Moderate gale	32—38	Whole trees in motion; inconvenience in walking against wind
8	Fresh gale	39—46	Breaks twigs off trees; generally impedes progress
9	Strong gale	47—54	Slight structural damage occurs; chimney pots and slates removed
10	Whole gale	55—63	Trees uprooted; considerable structural damage occurs
11	Storm	64—72	Very rarely experienced; accompanied by widespread damage
12	Hurricane	73—82	Devastation occurs
13	Hurricane	83—92	Devastation occurs
14	Hurricane	93—103	Devastation occurs
15	Hurricane	104—114	Devastation occurs
16	Hurricane	115—125	Devastation occurs
17	Hurricane	126—136	Devastation occurs

The *Saffir/Simpson Scale* (developed by Herbert Saffir, Consulting Engineer, and Robert H. Simpson, Past Director of the National Hurricane Center) is used by the National Weather Service to further classify hurricanes and provide a continuing assessment of the potential wind damage from a hurricane in progress. Saffir/Simpson Scale gradients range from 1 to 5. Scale 1 begins with hurricanes in which maximum sustained wind speeds are at least seventy-four miles per hour or will produce a storm surge of tidal waters four to five feet above normal. Scale 5 applies to those in which maximum sustained winds are 155 miles per hour or more. The National Weather Service emphasizes that the scale numbers are not forecasts, but are based on observed conditions at a given time. They represent an estimate of what a hurricane would do to a coastal area if it were to strike without change in size or strength. However, the underwriter will find the scale useful in assessing potential hurricane damage. The complete scale is shown in Exhibit 3-6.

Hurricane Paths When viewed over a number of years, hurricane tracks exhibit a certain uniformity. However, when looked at individually, each storm evidences its own peculiarities. Thus, it is a hopeless task to try to construct reasonably accurate paths which hurricanes of one type or another can be expected to follow. It is possible to construct hypothetical paths in severely exposed areas based on historical patterns. In general, storms moving northward from the Atlantic Ocean toward the United States mainland can be expected to take one of two separate paths before reaching Florida. One path leads into the Gulf of Mexico and the other along the East Coast from Florida northward. Even this is only a generality, since hurricanes have been known to move into the Gulf and then turn eastward, pass over Florida, and proceed up the East Coast. Conversely, storms have also started up the East Coast, reversed their course, and crossed over Florida and into the Gulf.

Hurricanes can impact the coastline in one of two ways. A *penetrating storm* occurs when the hurricane track strikes the coastline at approximately a right angle and moves directly inland. A *raking storm* occurs when the track parallels the coast. Due to the shape of the coastline, hurricanes can begin as raking storms and end as penetrating ones.

A penetrating hurricane, once the eye is over land, decreases in intensity very quickly. The ocean itself is no longer available to provide fuel and the friction produced by the land mass acts to slow the storm even further. By the time Hurricane Betsy had penetrated only 185 miles, wind speeds had dropped to below hurricane force. Destruction from a penetrating storm can be intense, but such destruction is

Exhibit 3-6
Saffir/Simpson Hurricane Scale*

Scale No.	Wind (MPH)	Surge (Feet)	Damage
1	74—95	4—5	Damage primarily to shrubbery, trees, foliage, and unanchored mobile homes. No real damage to other structures. Some damage to poorly constructed signs. And/or; low-lying coastal roads inundated, minor pier damage, some small craft in exposed anchorage torn from moorings.
2	96—110	6—8	Considerable damage to shrubbery and tree foliage, some trees blown down, major damage to exposed mobile homes. Extensive damage to poorly constructed signs. Some damage to roofing materials of buildings. And/or; coastal roads and low-lying escape routes inland cut by rising water 2 to 4 hours before arrival of hurricane center; considerable damage to piers; marinas flooded; small craft in unprotected anchorages torn from moorings; evacuation of some shoreline residences and low-lying areas required.
3	111—130	9—12	Foliage torn from trees, large trees blown down. Practically all poorly constructed signs blown down. Some damage to roofing materials of buildings, some window and door damage. Some structural damage to small buildings. Mobile homes destroyed. And/or; serious flooding at coast and many smaller structures near coast destroyed; larger structures near coast damaged by battering waves and floating debris; low-lying escape routes inland cut by rising water 3 to 5 hours before hurricane center arrives. Flat terrain 5 feet or less above sea level flooded inland 8 miles or more. Evacuation of low-lying residences within several blocks of shoreline possibly required.
4	131—155	13—18	Shrubs and trees blown down, all signs down. Extensive damage to roofing materials, windows and doors. Complete failure of roofs on many small residences. Complete destruction of mobile homes. And/or: flat terrain 10 feet or less above sea level flooded inland as far as 6 miles; major damage to lower floors of structures near shore due to flooding and battering by waves and floating debris; low-lying escape routes inland cut by rising water 3 to 5 hours before hurricane center arrives; major erosion of beaches; massive evacuation of all residences within 500 yards of shore possibly required, and all single-story residences on low ground within 2 miles of shore.
5	Over 155	Over 18	Shrubs and trees blown down, considerable damage to roofs of buildings; all signs down. Very severe and extensive damage to windows and doors. Complete failure of roofs on many residences and industrial buildings. Extensive shattering of glass in windows and doors. Some complete building failures. Small buildings overturned or blown away. Complete destruction of mobile homes. And/or; major damage to lower floors of all structures less than 15 feet above sea level within 500 yards of shore, low-lying escape routes inland cut by rising water 3 to 5 hours before hurricane center arrives; massive evacuation of residential areas on low ground within 5 to 10 miles of shore probably required.

*Adapted from Paul J. Herbert and Glen Taylor, "Hurricane Experience Levels of Coastal County Populations—Texas to Maine" (Washington: U.S. Department of Commerce, National Oceanic and Atmospheric Administration, National Weather Service).

usually limited to a relatively small area no wider than the storm itself (usually 50 to 100 miles) and no deeper than the distance required to reduce wind speeds to a safe level. The area of damage becomes narrower and narrower around the eye as it moves inland.

A raking storm moving parallel to the coast can maintain its intensity for a relatively long time. To do so, however, its eye must be over the ocean and remain far enough away from the coast itself. Because of the irregular shape of the coastline, it is almost impossible for a storm to continue indefinitely on a course parallel to the coast, without either passing inland or turning out to sea eventually. The maximum length of coastline that could be involved at full hurricane force is considered to be no more than 300 miles. However, considerable devastation can occur before such a storm passes inland and blows itself out or turns out to sea.

The Florida peninsula presents a unique problem. Penetrating storms crossing Florida may not reduce much in intensity. The peninsula is only about 140 miles wide and its topography is relatively flat and friction free. Further, when the eye passes over water again, particularly the warm waters of the Gulf, the storm can regenerate and strike the coastline at another point with renewed vigor.

Construction Considerations As high winds blow against a building, positive pressure is exerted on the windward side while the other sides experience a partial vacuum. The amount of negative pressure created by the vacuum will normally be no greater than the positive pressure of the wind itself. However, in irregularly shaped structures and buildings with large areas, the negative pressure of the vacuum may be twice as great as the positive pressure of the wind. Since the total wind force acting on the building is the sum of the positive and negative forces, it is important that buildings be designed with both forces in mind.

Roofs with a slope of more than thirty degrees will also have an area of positive pressure on the windward slope and a partial vacuum on the leeward slope. The forces acting on the roof in these circumstances can be quite similar to the forces acting on an airplane wing; lift is created which can jeopardize the roof surface and in extreme cases the roof itself. Overhanging eaves can provide pockets in which considerable pressure can be built up. Such projections should be avoided where possible or designed to resist the forces to which they may be subjected. Roof coverings of all types are susceptible to wind damage from both the direct wind force and the partial vacuum created on the lee side of sloping roofs. The greatest damage occurs when these coverings are not installed to the manufacturer's specifications and shortcut construction methods are employed.

Flying debris or the force of the wind itself frequently will break a window on the windward side of a structure exposing the interior to the full force of the wind. Much of the damage in downtown Houston from Hurricane Alicia was not from windows not being built to withstand hurricane force winds, but from such windows being shattered by flying debris. The interior not only can be exposed to wind-driven rain, but the wind also can exert positive pressure within the structure. This pressure, in combination with the external suction pressure, may lift off the roof or cause a lee wall to fail and collapse outward. Underwriters should check for "hurricane shutters" on buildings with much window exposure such as apartments facing the ocean. Such shutters are not feasible in modern high-rise glass office buildings. In such cases, the underwriter may want to consider the thickness of the glass and perhaps whether coverage should be provided at all.

Buildings of all kinds of construction—wood and steel frame, hollow concrete block, reinforced concrete, and others—are subject to damage from hurricane, but the extent of damage is governed by the quality of the local building code and the care taken during construction to meet the code. Those states most exposed to hurricanes have adopted rigid building codes which apply to construction in coastal areas. These codes are designed to minimize the damaging effects of hurricane winds. Care should be taken to ascertain that buildings insured are designed and constructed to meet these code requirements.

Hurricane Incidence About eight hurricanes a year are spawned in the Atlantic Ocean. Some of these will come ashore in the continental United States, somewhere between Texas and Maine. Such a statement, however, does not reflect the cyclical nature of these storms. Hurricanes do not occur with predictable regularity. In some years numerous hurricanes occur and in others none. In the period 1958 to 1982, the number of hurricanes reaching the continental U.S. ranged from zero to four per year. In this twenty-five year period, there were 32 hurricanes causing 848 deaths. There is some evidence that hurricane frequency is influenced by a twenty-year cycle, but such evidence is somewhat inconclusive. Furthermore, because a single hurricane can involve more than one state, often with varying effects in each state it touches, predicting hurricane frequencies, particularly on a state-by-state basis, is difficult.

Storm Surge and Heavy Rainfall

Storm surge is a combination of the much greater than normal high tides and the thunderous effect of tons of water contained in the huge waves that break against the shore and move inland flooding low ground. Structures built near or on the waterfront are particularly susceptible to damage caused by storm surge. Not only can they be flooded, but also they can be subjected to the direct pounding of the waves and their foundations can be exposed to the undermining and eroding effect of the wave action. Buildings further inland can also be flooded. Mean water levels may increase to eighteen feet or more. Since much of the densely populated portions of both the Atlantic and Gulf Coasts are no more than ten feet above sea level, storm surge can flood areas considerable distances inland. Waves and currents can erode beaches and highways. Damage to shipping in confined harbors can be extreme. Public water supplies can be contaminated by the brackish, dirty flood waters, causing a health hazard.

The typical hurricane brings six to twelve inches of rainfall to the area it crosses. The damage from the floods produced by such heavy rains often exceeds the loss caused by wind alone. Wind damage is usually contained within a relatively narrow area near the coast but rain can continue to fall long after wind speeds have diminished to below hurricane force. Thus, as the storm blows out it still drops substantial amounts of rain throughout the length of its track, frequently causing severe damage far inland. Hurricane Diane in 1955 caused little damage as it moved ashore, but long after its hurricane winds had subsided it brought floods to Pennsylvania, New York, and New England—floods that killed 200 people and caused damage estimated at $700 million. Hurricane Agnes barely reached hurricane force in 1972 but the rains it brought devastated the Appalachian area, particularly in Pennsylvania, causing losses from flooding estimated at $2.1 billion.

Tornadoes

Although much smaller in size than hurricanes, tornadoes are capable of causing almost as much damage. In fact, tornado winds are considerably higher, usually 200 miles per hour or more.

Tornado formation requires the presence of layers of air with contrasting characteristics of temperature, moisture, density, and wind flow. Although many theories exist as to how tornadoes are formed, no precise understanding of the process exists. The two most prevalent theories postulate that tornadoes are either the result of thermally induced rotary wind circulation, or the result of converging rotary winds. Neither is a truly satisfactory explanation. It is now felt that tornadoes are produced by the combined effects of thermal and mechanical forces.

Tornado Characteristics   Tornadoes are intense local storms of short duration. They consist of winds rotating at very high speeds, usually in a counter-clockwise (in the Northern Hemisphere) direction. The winds rotate around a *vortex*, a hollow cavity in which a partial vacuum is produced. As condensation occurs around the vortex, a pale cloud appears which defines the familiar funnel shape. As the storm comes into contact with the ground, dust and debris are drawn into the circulating system of air which causes the funnel to darken.

Tornadoes are formed several thousand feet in the air. Because they usually depend on warm, humid, unsettled weather for their formation, they are often spawned by thunderstorms and, in coastal states, hurricanes as well. In the case of thunderstorms, tornadoes usually appear as an extension of the storm cloud itself and stretch downward toward the ground. Some never reach the surface; others touch and rise again. As the thunderstorm moves, tornadoes may form at intervals along its path, travel a few miles, and dissipate.

On the average, tornado paths are only a quarter of a mile wide and seldom more than 16 miles long. They average a forward speed of 40 miles per hour. However, as is always the case when describing natural phenomena, there are exceptions. Tornadoes have been known to cause destruction along paths as much as 1 mile wide and over 300 miles long. Forward wind speeds have been clocked at up to 70 miles per hour.

Tornado Damage   The destructive power of a tornado is awesome. Damage is caused both by the high velocity of the winds circulating around the vortex and by the partial vacuum within the vortex. As the vortex passes over a building it subjects it to both high winds and to a sudden reduction in atmospheric pressure. The near vacuum in the vortex creates overpressure within the building, causing it literally to explode. Even in the most substantial buildings, windows shatter and roof coverings can be lifted and blown away. In less substantial buildings, walls can collapse or topple outward and entire roofs can be lifted. Heavy objects such as cars and farm machinery can be raised and carried for considerable distances. The combined effects of wind and vacuum produce near total destruction as a tornado progresses through a populated area, and with the destruction can come loss of life. Since the late 1950s, the tornado death toll in the U.S. has averaged 86 per year. On Palm Sunday, 11 April 1965, thirty-seven tornadoes in the Midwest caused 271 deaths and injured more than 5,000 people.

Tornado Incidence   Tornadoes occur all over the world but nowhere with more frequency than they do in the United States. No part of the country is immune from tornadoes; they have occurred in all fifty states. However, no area is more favorable for their formation than the great plains of the Midwest and Southwest.

Tornadoes can occur at any time of the year, although April, May, and June are the peak months. Over the years, tornado incidence follows a more or less regular pattern. In January and February the area of maximum frequency is in the Gulf states, in March and April it shifts to the southeast Atlantic states, in May it moves to the southern plains and, in June, northward to the northern plains and Great Lakes states as far east as western New York. After June, tornado incidence begins to diminish and it reaches its lowest point in December.

Tornado incidence during the period 1978 through 1982 is shown in Exhibit 3-7. In reviewing this information, the very randomness of tornado strikes must be kept in mind. Because they are so local in nature, the mathematical chance that a given location will be struck by a tornado in any one year is quite small. However, nature defies such easy categorization and there are many exceptions. Oklahoma City has been struck twenty-six times since 1892. Codell, Kansas, was struck in 1916, 1917, and 1918—and each time on May 20. Other such cases abound. However, due to their randomness, the property underwriting principle of spread and dispersion is one of the most reliable tools in dealing with the tornado exposure.

Hail

There are three general classifications of hail: *graupel* or *soft hail*, *small hail*, and *true hail*. Neither soft hail nor small hail is large enough to be very destructive. Thus, the underwriter's principal concern is with true hail.

True hail falls almost exclusively during violent thunderstorms. Two theories exist to explain hail formation. The first postulates that raindrops within a thunderstorm freeze as they fall towards the earth. As they drop through the moist atmosphere within the storm cloud, they pick up a coating of additional snow or frost and grow larger. The incipient hailstones are then caught in an updraft and blown upward through the storm. They ultimately begin to fall again, picking up additional moisture and growing even larger. Such alternate trips up and down through the storm cloud can occur until the hailstones are too large to be lifted upward by the updraft and fall to the earth. The second theory assumes that hailstones form in one continuous drop. Their fall may be slowed by the updraft, and at times they may remain stationary, but the stone grows continuously larger as moisture continues to freeze around it. In either case, hail results. Hailstones over five inches in diameter and weighing over one and one half pounds have been known to occur.

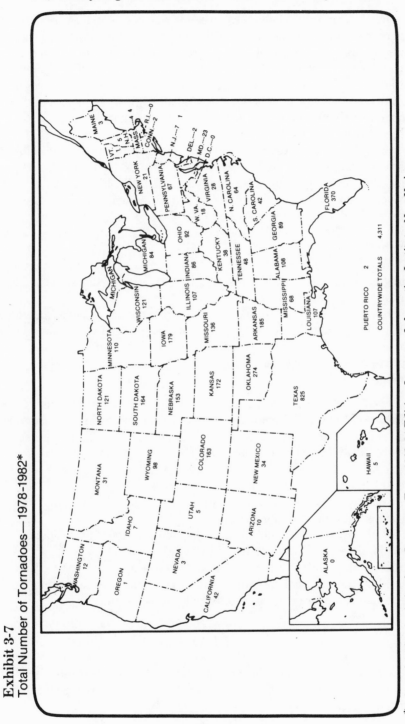

Exhibit 3-7
Total Number of Tornadoes—1978-1982*

*Adapted with permission from *Insurance Facts*, 1983-84 Edition, Insurance Information Institute, New York.

Hail Damage Hailstones are not always round. A variety of shapes can occur. Some may be like pyramids with flattened bases, while others may be completely irregular. Some may be covered with spikes from a quarter of an inch to almost an inch long. The shape can materially influence the amount of damage done. Glass is a regular casualty of hailstorms. Windows and sliding glass doors in buildings are frequently broken as are auto windows. Greenhouses are obviously subject to severe damage.

Shingles and roll roofing can be extensively damaged, especially if the roof pitch is slight. Asbestos shingles fare better than other types since they overlap each other and are generally laid on roofs of a steeper pitch. Roofs of tin and iron can withstand hail to a marked degree if laid over heavy boards or plywood sheeting. Aluminum roofs, being of a softer material, are likely to be dented and, in severe cases, punctured.

Wooden siding can be stripped of paint and in some cases the siding can even be split. Metal siding is particularly vulnerable to both denting and puncturing.

Hailstones of three to five inches in diameter have been known to kill small animals. In some unusual cases horses and cattle have been blinded or killed. The most prevalent damage is to growing crops. It is estimated that nearly 80 percent of all hail losses are from crop damage.

Hail Incidence No area of the United States is free from hailstorms. True hailstorms are similar to tornadoes in that they are spawned by thunderstorms and they follow a similar kind of seasonal pattern. They begin in January and February in the Gulf states and reach their peak frequency in practically all the remainder of the country in June. This cycle is an important one from the standpoint of crop damage, as the season of greatest frequency in many states coincides with the growing season.

Hail damage does not follow the same pattern of incidence as tornado damage. Many states which are relatively low in tornado incidence are relatively high in hail incidence and vice versa. This is caused by the fact that tornadoes and hailstorms, while springing from the same source, are caused by different natural events.

COLLAPSE

Collapse can result in heavy losses. While the frequency of building collapse is not high, the severity of this peril requires careful underwriting.

Collapse Coverage

Collapse coverage on commercial structures and their contents is usually written through an "all-risks" contract, particularly difference in conditions (DIC) policies. Specific coverage for damage caused by weight of ice, snow, or sleet is a form of collapse coverage provided by some named perils endorsements such as the SMP optional perils endorsement—MP-123. Even when provided as part of an "all-risks" contract, collapse coverage is subject to limitations. Loss by settling, shrinkage, or expansion of foundations, walls, floors, or ceilings is generally excluded as is loss by inherent vice, latent defect, wet or dry rot, termites, and other insects. Earthquake, subsidence, and earth movement are also normally excluded unless specifically added.

Principal Causes of Collapse Loss

The weight of ice, snow, or sleet is perhaps the most common cause of collapse. Roofs spanning large areas designed with few internal supports are particularly subject to collapse from greater than anticipated snow loads. Such structures as auditoriums, exhibition halls, and sports coliseums fall into this category, as to a lesser extent do schools, supermarkets, discount stores, and pole barns. The collapse of the Hartford Civic Center is an example of the collapse of such a large, yet new, structure. Snow can accumulate from heavy snowfalls and block roof drains. Roof drains can also be blocked by debris or be purposely clogged by vandals. Melting snow, unable to drain off, may accumulate at low points on flat roofs. This effect, called *ponding*, can concentrate additional weight in a relatively small area of an already overloaded roof, causing collapse. A heavy rain can be absorbed by snow accumulations already present, creating a weight load far in excess of the load the structure was designed to withstand.

Buildings can also collapse because of error, omission, or deficiency in design, specifications, or materials. Such coverage is provided in "all-risks" policies unless specifically excluded. Collapse from the weight of ice, snow, or sleet, of course, can often be traced to errors in design or construction. However, collapse coverage written as part of an "all-risks" policy is obviously far broader than that provided merely by coverage for ice, snow, or sleet. Buildings have been known to collapse for no apparent reason and upon investigation the cause is often traced to design or construction defect. Buildings in the course of construction can be particularly vulnerable to collapse, as can buildings that have been or are in the process of being extensively remodeled. Collapse in connection with earthquakes was mentioned earlier.

Because of the ever rising costs of building materials and labor, buildings are sometimes constructed to minimum code requirements with no margin for safety. New architectural designs are made possible by new building methods and materials. These new designs, as well as the new materials and methods, may not have been adequately tested over time with respect to collapse.

The "all-risks" approach to collapse may provide coverage for unusual losses which cannot be anticipated. Buildings have collapsed because their foundations were weakened by nearby excavation for the erection of a new adjoining building. Smaller structures built with light materials may be subject to collapse from sonic boom. Lift trucks can collide with a structure's internal supports causing collapse. These losses and others like them are difficult to foresee. Because of the broad scope of coverage, particular attention must be paid to the risk's physical characteristics. A qualified examination of construction materials and techniques, foundations, soil conditions, terrain, subsidence potential, and similar factors must be considered. Even with this information, underwriters must approach collapse coverage cautiously.

CATASTROPHE UNDERWRITING

From this discussion of the various property perils with which an insurance company must successfully cope, it should be evident that senior underwriting management is faced with a formidable task. Some perils, such as those associated with an individual risk, can and most appropriately should be underwritten by the local field office underwriter. Working within established company guidelines and authorities, and assisted by the company's loss control staff or outside services, the local underwriter is considered by most companies to be the most capable of committing the company's assets to individual risks, and by proper selection producing an underwriting profit on the book of business thus written. However, some of the perils insured against are such that many risks can be simultaneously exposed to the same catastrophic event. The aggregation of the losses sustained on each individual risk can be so large as to threaten the insurer's financial well-being. Moreover, the geographic areas exposed to such events may be so wide that more than one branch or regional office is involved, making control even more difficult.

Within its responsibility for formulation of broad underwriting policy, senior underwriting management has as one of its prime responsibilities the protection of the company's financial structure. This includes the creation and management of programs to contain the total of individual losses from the same event within acceptable levels. Therefore, the home office in most companies establishes a program to contain loss from catastrophic events within predetermined levels and looks to the field office underwriter to control liabilities in such a way that the program's objectives are met.

Reinsurance Considerations

Most companies consider their reinsurance arrangements to be an integral part of their catastrophe programs. Coverage for shock loss from fire, explosion, riot and civil commotion, windstorm, earthquake and following fire, and similar perils, is normally part of every company's reinsurance treaty. Without such protection, liability on both individual risks, and the aggregation of such risks subject to the same peril, would have to be suppressed to the net amount that could be lost without undue financial strain. This limitation has a crippling effect on capacity. Above this level of protection many insurers purchase reinsurance to specifically cover catastrophic loss. Such reinsurance is most often placed on an excess of loss basis. The insurance company assumes a certain amount of loss as a retention, with losses above the retention being covered by the catastrophe treaty.

Some companies may rely solely on their reinsurance treaties for protection without any underlying controls. Others may control specific perils to be sure that the principle of spread and dispersion is adhered to and liabilities are not clustered in a harmful way. A common example of such a control is the localizing program many companies use to keep track of fire liability at a single location, such as within a single city block or a group of city blocks; the main thrust of such a program being to control the amount subject to a single event, such as windstorm, hurricane, or conflagration.

Catastrophes are by their very nature infrequent and unpredictable. For those insurers who depend solely on their reinsurance arrangements to protect them from catastrophic loss, there is always the danger that such protection will prove to be inadequate when the event occurs. There is also the question of the financial ability of reinsurers to respond in the event of a massive catastrophe. Finally, there is also the question of availability and cost of future reinsurance should the reinsurer be responsible for an extrememly large loss arising from a concentration of writings. Thus, many companies choose to limit their concentrations of liability and total amount exposed to certain catastrophe perils. Most commonly such catastrophe control plans deal with exposure to hurricane and earthquake losses, although individual insurers may feel the need to devise other programs to meet their specific needs.

Development of a Sample Catastrophe Control Plan

When creating a program to control catastrophe exposure, most insurers first determine how much they are willing to lose in any one event. This is a financial decision to be made by senior management. It is usually based on an evaluation of loss effect on surplus or effect on earnings per share. After it has been determined, it becomes the responsibility of underwriting management to devise a program to contain losses within the figure nominated. The decision on the "willing-to-lose" figure is so closely allied with the basic decision on the type and amount of reinsurance protection to be purchased that they are often made in conjunction with each other. In many cases the willing-to-lose figure is reflected by the net or retention the company has elected to accept under its catastrophe reinsurance treaties. When arriving at this figure, such reinsurance considerations as basic cost, the number of times the treaty can be reinstated in any one year, the cost for such reinstatements, the depth to which the treaty may be penetrated, and similar topics must be examined. The willing-to-lose figure is usually set at some point that permits anticipated loss to penetrate the catastrophe treaty, but contains losses within the treaty to a point that provides a contingency reserve for errors in judgment and unknown or unforeseen events.

The company must also determine those geographic areas deemed subject to a particular catastrophe peril. For hurricanes such an area might be the Gulf and South Atlantic states; for earthquake it might be California, western Nevada, and Alaska. Whatever the selection, the purpose is to identify those broad geographic areas in which a catastrophe may strike. Such areas will usually be so large as to preclude the possibility that a single event could simultaneously involve all insureds within the boundaries chosen. Thus, these areas must be broken down into smaller geographic zones which reflect the estimated maximum extent of a catastrophe loss. Such zones might be an aggregation of a group of coastal counties in a state for hurricanes or areas adjacent to a known fault for earthquakes. The determination of these zones requires considerable judgment. It is impossible to predict the path of a hurricane or the epicenter of an earthquake. Thus, it cannot be expected that catastrophes of either type will occur in such a way that loss is contained within the zone boundaries chosen. The purpose of the zones is to force spread and dispersion and to establish the maximum concentrations of liabilities to which the company will be subjected in each. Thus, once the boundaries are determined, a cap or upper limit is established for each zone.

Establishing such a limit in turn requires considerable judgment. Since under even the worst of circumstances it is unlikely that each structure in a given zone will be totally destroyed, an estimation of the probable maximum loss that can be sustained in each must first be made. This is a difficult task in itself and requires a subjective analysis of such things as past catastrophe experience, historical average loss per unit (commercial and personal), upgraded for inflation, population concentration, building codes, predominant construction types, terrain, soil conditions, and so on.

Once the zones and the maximum amount to be exposed in each have been determined, a monitoring system must be devised to measure the company's liabilities in each zone against the maximums chosen. Most insurers depend on their EDP system as the most convenient method of recording liability. The most common approach is to use county codes or postal ZIP Codes since these are already available, although other methods may be used. By compiling statistics periodically as to the liability and number of risks written in each zone, the program can be successfully monitored.

This simplified example of a catastrophe control plan illustrates the complexity of the underwriting function for "other" major perils. Underwriting some perils goes far beyond the potential consequences to an individual risk. Underwriting management must deal also with the exposure represented by the aggregation of the individual risks exposed to the same peril. There is no standard method available to deal with such a problem. Many approaches may be used of which the above example is but one. In all cases, however, there is little concrete information available and one must rely on subjective judgment.

SUMMARY

Underwriting changes in response to the needs and demands of society. As society grows more complex, the kinds of insurance required increase, and the underwriter faces a greater array of perils which must be understood. Property insurance today covers a spectrum of perils and coverages undreamed of in the early part of this century.

Like fire insurance, some of these perils have a direct relationship to the physical characteristics of each risk and the kind of operation the insured conducts. Explosion, sprinkler leakage and water damage are such perils. The proper analysis of these perils depends on a clear understanding of the properties of the individual risk in question.

Other perils arise from the societal aspects of each risk. Exposure to these perils depends not as much on the operations conducted, as on the influences of those persons whose daily lives bring them in regular contact with the risk. The attitudes of those persons who live near, work at, attend, or otherwise interact with the risk become the governing feature for those perils such as vandalism, riot, and civil commotion.

Yet another group of perils involves the risk's relationship to natural forces. These natural forces are outside human control, and often can be neither accurately predicted nor prevented. Earthquake, flood, windstorm, and hail are in this category. Underwriters must concern themselves not only with the risk's ability to withstand these natural forces, but also with the aggregation of loss which can occur over a wide area from events of catastrophic proportion.

Chapter Notes

1. Home Insurance Company of New York v. Davila, CA 1954, 212 F2d 731.
2. The following section on physical features is based on material prepared by the National Board of Fire Underwriters and the Pacific Fire Rating Bureau.
3. Material in this and the two preceding paragraphs taken from *Studies of Floods and Flood Damage 1952-1955* published by the American Insurance Association, New York.
4. Both the flood hazard boundary map and the flood insurance rate map can be obtained from either the community itself or from the Regional Office of the Federal Insurance Administration or by writing the National Flood Insurance Program, P.O. Box 34604, Bethesda, MD 20817.

CHAPTER 4

Construction

COPE

Commercial property underwriting requires analysis of the physical, moral, and morale hazards of any particular risk. The physical hazards may be divided into four categories—*construction, occupancy, protection* and *exposures*—or COPE. Each of these categories requires individual analysis. The moral and morale hazards of a particular risk are determined by analysis of the character and financial stability of the owners and tenants of the property under consideration.

This chapter deals with the first of the COPE categories of physical hazards—construction. When dealing with property at a fixed location, such as a structure, the fire peril is usually the major consideration. Other perils such as windstorm, hail, collapse, flood, and earthquake have a varying impact on the underwriting decision, ranging from minor considerations in some instances to major in others. In some cases these perils are more important than fire in determining the acceptability of the risk.

Construction

When considering construction, the underwriter is concerned with far more than the basic construction classification. Concern is also directed toward how various structural features will contribute to the spread or containment of fire and withstand the effects of other insured perils. In analyzing a commercial property submission or renewal, the underwriter should consider the following questions:

1. What is going to happen to the building if a fire should occur? In other words, what is the *susceptibility* of the building to damage by the fire itself?
2. What is the susceptibility to damage by heat? Any type of building may be destroyed by extensive exposure to heat.
3. What is the susceptibility to damage by smoke and products of combustion, such as toxic and corrosive gases? Smoke and other products of combustion are major by-products of fire and often cause extensive damage. If a particular building is exposed to extensive smoke, what will be the result? Will a new coat of paint suffice or will the entire building interior have to be refinished?
4. When considering water damage from fire extinguishment the same points used in reference to smoke should be considered— vertical and horizontal openings, damageability of ceilings and building service machinery such as elevator motors, and heating and cooling equipment.
5. In addition, the building's susceptibility to damage from the perils of wind, hail, explosion, collapse, and so on should also be analyzed. In some geographic areas, the probable loss from one of the allied perils may be much higher than from fire.

The importance of construction as an underwriting factor cannot be overemphasized. Many of the other facets of underwriting a risk are at least partially dependent on construction.

Since the fire rate for a given risk is dependent primarily upon the building's construction, the construction directly affects the premium generated for that risk. The construction of a risk also has a bearing on the severity of exposure from a neighboring risk. The distance needed to eliminate exposure decreases as the fire resistance rating of the exposed wall is increased. This is very important when establishing the amount subject of a given risk. In addition, the probable maximum loss (PML) of any risk is influenced to a large degree by construction. Is the building frame, masonry, noncombustible, or fire resistive? What are the dimensions of the building in terms of height and square footage? How many fire divisions are there? Are there fire walls, division walls, and fire doors? How many stories are there? All these questions and more must be answered correctly if an underwriter is to establish an accurate PML for a given risk. Finally, the underwriter's line guide and authorization are partially based on construction.

As part of the judgment of whether a risk is acceptable or not, the underwriter must analyze the severity of the loss that might occur. Frame or masonry structures will add combustibles to a fire, while noncombustible, masonry noncombustible, or fire resistive structures will not. Fire resistive structures and structures with proper fire walls and vertical fire divisions may limit the spread of fire, reducing damage.

Occupancy, Protection, and Exposures

The effect of the physical hazards inherent in occupancy, protection, and exposure are considered in the following chapters. Chapter 5 considers occupancy hazards, including those common to virtually all commercial risks and those that are unique to certain industries or classifications. Chapter 6 analyzes public and private protection, including analysis of the municipal grading system. Chapter 7 concludes the analysis of physical hazards with consideration of internal and external exposures.

FIRE RESISTANCE AND FLAME SPREAD

In determining the appropriate classification for a particular structure, the *fire resistance* of the materials utilized in construction is frequently analyzed. In the interior of buildings, the *flame spread* of the interior materials or finish is important.

Fire Resistance

Materials are classified as to their fire resistance capabilities according to the Standard Methods of Fire Tests of Building Construction and Materials, NFPA Standard Number 251. In this standard, structural elements are exposed to a standard exposing fire. The minimum sizes for test specimens are:

- columns   9 feet
- beams and girders   12 feet
- partitions and walls   100 square feet
- floors and roofs   180 square feet[1]

These specimens are exposed to a reproducible standard fire following a time-temperature curve shown in Exhibit 4-1. The load bearing structural elements are loaded with the prescribed superimposed weight for the assembly being tested. The unit passes the test as long as it successfully resists its superimposed load and, in the case of partitions, walls, floors, and roofs, resists the passage of fire. Most tests are conducted at Underwriters' Laboratories, Inc.

Fire protection systems or assemblies are rated in terms of hours, such as one-hour or two-hour, depending on the time that the tested unit survived. There is some confusion about these ratings. Two-hour

Exhibit 4-1
Time-Temperature Curve—Standard Fire*

Minutes After Start of Test	Temperature[†]
5	1,000°F
30	1,550°F
60	1,700°F
120	1,850°F
180	1,925°F
240	2,000°F
480	2,300°F
	75°F per hour thereafter

[†]The temperatures listed above are temperatures of the exposing fire, and also represent increments of increase over the ambient temperature in the furnace at the start of the test.

*Adapted with permission from Francis L. Brannigan, *Building Construction for the Fire Service* (Boston: National Fire Protection Association, 1971), p. 191.

fire resistance does not mean that the building survived a two-hour fire unscathed. The fire damage might be quite severe, even with short exposure. The rating refers to structural integrity, not degree of damage. What the test means is:

> ... if the building reacts to the fire in the same manner as did the specimens for that particular type of construction in the test furnace, and if the fire load does not exceed the test fire load, and if the duration of the fire does not exceed the time span of survival specified for the components involved, then the structure should survive the fire.[2]

Flame Spread

The flame spread of materials is determined by use of the twenty-five-foot Steiner Tunnel Test. A standard gas fire is applied at one end of the tunnel and observations are made.

For comparison purposes, similar tests are also conducted on a piece of one-quarter-inch asbestos cement board and one piece of red oak flooring. The readings obtained from these materials are arbitrarily classified as 0 and 100 respectively. Similarly, the smoke developed and fuel contributed are measured.[3] Therefore, building members and interior finishes can be compared to these standards. A set of gradings *A* through *C* as well as a numerical rating are also used. The letter

Exhibit 4-2
Flame Spread Ratings*

Classification	Flame Spread Range
A	0—25
B	26—75
C	76—200

*Reprinted with permission from *Fire Protection Handbook*, 15th ed. (Quincy, MA: National Fire Protection Association, 1982), p. 5-50.

grade is often used in referring to exit codes and interior finish classifications. While some variations are found, the treatment of interior finish in NFPA 101, Life Safety Code is typical. This is given in Exhibit 4-2.

BUILDING CONSTRUCTION CLASSIFICATIONS

For the peril of fire, the Insurance Services Office divides building construction into six classifications (which will be the basis for this section):

Construction Class #1—frame,
Construction Class #2—joisted masonry,
Construction Class #3—noncombustible,
Construction Class #4—masonry noncombustible,
Construction Class #5—modified fire resistive, and
Construction Class #6—fire resistive.[4]

The classes are often referred to by the numbers listed. These divisions are based on three essential factors:

1. the materials used for the bearing portions of the exterior walls;
2. the materials used in the roof and floors of the building, especially the supports for the roof and floor; and
3. the fire resistance rating of the materials used in the building construction.

Frame

In wood frame construction, the exterior walls, floors and roof surfaces, and their supports are constructed of wood or other combustible material. This type of construction differs from ordinary

Exhibit 4-3
Example of Wood Frame Platform Construction*

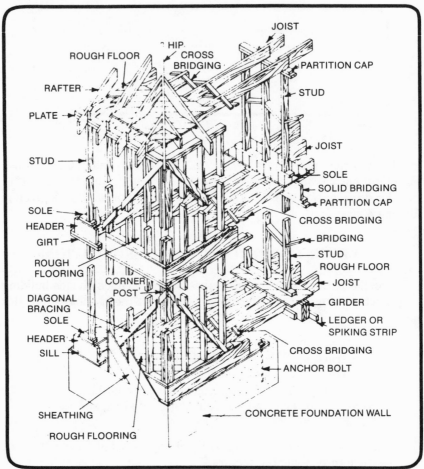

*Reprinted with permission from *Fire Protection Handbook*, 15th ed. (Quincy, MA: National Fire Protection Association, 1981), p. 5-31.

construction only with respect to the exterior wall surfaces. These are combustible in frame and noncombustible in ordinary construction. An example of frame construction is shown in Exhibit 4-3.

While most building codes make no differentiation between protected and unprotected frame buildings, they may require certain *fire-stop* devices. A fire-stop is an element of construction inserted in a concealed space, either a wall or roof area, that will prevent the passage of flame from one point to another. By containment of fire within the area of origin, the fire-stop will aid in early detection and possible extinguishment.

While frame construction is certainly of a lesser desirability than fire resistive or masonry noncombustible, certain occupancies may be acceptable within this construction type, such as occupancies of a low combustible nature or ones bearing a high level of protection. The basic frame members can be protected against both the vertical and horizontal spread of fire. In addition, the inherent problem of external surfaces being of a combustible nature and thus subjected to exposure fires can also be alleviated by such things as an external sprinkler system.

When discussing frame construction, it should be remembered that materials other than wood may be used in the building without changing the construction classification. Various composition boards may be used in place of wood and many other exterior wall covering materials may be used. Some of these are:

1. Brick or stone veneer, consisting of a single thickness of brick or stone (two to six inches thick) over a wood-framed structure, and dependent upon bonding to the wood structure for stability. This gives a building the appearance of standard brick or stone construction, but is not in any way equivalent. It does provide some degree of protection against external exposure such as from grass or brush fires.
2. Metal-clad or asbestos-clad construction consists of a sheet metal (steel or aluminum) covering fastened to the wooden structure or cement asbestos shingles or corrugated cement asbestos sheets over wood siding. While the covering may prevent ignition of the wood by small flames, it has relatively little value in protection against exposure fires. This type of construction is most commonly found in diners.
3. Stucco, consisting of cement plaster on lath over wood frame construction, has a slight degree of fire resistance depending upon the type of lath used and the thickness of the plaster.
4. Concrete block walls of unknown fire resistance are also classified as frame buildings from an insurance viewpoint. In fact, any building which cannot be classifed properly due to lack of information must be tentatively called a frame building.

Frame construction is found generally throughout this country, particularly in areas where other building materials, such as clay bricks, are unavailable or expensive. The northwest and the south central areas of the country contain a number of large frame buildings for these reasons. In addition, because of the earthquake hazard, many smaller frame structures are found throughout California. A frame structure that will give or bend with the tremors produced by an earthquake is a more desirable risk for that peril than one of masonry construction. However, the converse exists in the Southeast, where the hurricane hazard is of great concern.

Joisted Masonry

Joisted masonry construction has exterior walls of brick, adobe, concrete, gypsum block, stone, tile, or similar materials with combustible floors and roofs. This class consists of two commonly referred to subclassifications.

Ordinary Construction Ordinary construction is defined as exterior bearing walls of a noncombustible nature having a minimum of a one-hour fire resistance rating with combustible floors, roofs, and interior surfaces. Ordinary construction is also referred to as "brick," "wood joisted," or "brick joisted." An example of ordinary construction is shown in Exhibit 4-4.

This construction has all of the inherent hazards, due to both horizontal and vertical fire spread, of a combustible or frame structure. Therefore, fire-stops are just as important in the horizontal and vertical areas in ordinary construction as in frame.

Ordinary constructed buildings are found most in the major metropolitan areas in the northern states. They are infrequently over three stories high, since by definition the exterior walls must be bearing walls. The great majority of these were built prior to World War II. Thus, the underwriter is presented with a potential problem of age and deterioration. The derivation of proper insurance to value also frequently presents a difficulty. While an ordinary building is less desirable in an area subject to earthquakes, it has proven to be adequate in areas subject to hurricane-force winds.

Mill Construction The underwriter, on occasion, may be presented with a risk that can be classified as heavy timber or mill construction. This is sometimes referred to as "slow burning construction." This additional classification exists where (1) there is a minimum of two-hour fire resistance rating on the bearing walls; (2) the wood columns are not less than eight inches thick in any direction; (3) the wood beams, supports, and ties are not less than six inches in width or ten inches in depth; and (4) the floors are of "tongue and groove planks" not less than three inches thick with a one-inch overlay and the roof decks on heavy timbers with at least a two-inch thickness.

While heavy timber or mill construction is a subclass within the broader joisted masonry class, this may lead to some confusion. A major characteristic of the mill constructed building is the *absence* of

Exhibit 4-4
Ordinary Construction*

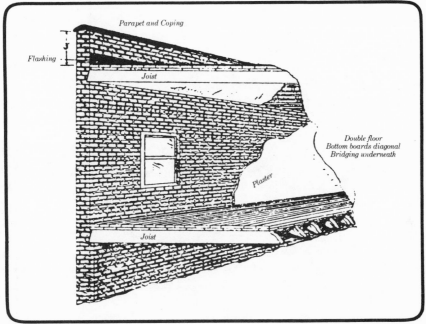

*Reprinted with permission from Charles C. Dominge and Walter O. Lincoln, *Building Construction as Applied to Fire Insurance*, 4th ed. (Philadelphia: Chilton Co., 1949), p. 32.

floor joists and their attendant air spaces and voids. Mill construction is shown in Exhibit 4-5.

Mill construction has two important characteristics from an underwriting standpoint:

1. The heavy floors, built without concealed spaces, constitute a fire-stop retarding the spread of flames.
2. The heavy timbers of the beams and columns give the building great structural strength, reducing the likelihood of collapse.

A structure of this type would be very expensive to construct today, though it nonetheless would stand a severe fire test. These mill buildings are often found in the northeast. Many of them were constructed during and immediately after the Civil War.

On occasion, a mill type building with laminated beams will be found in the western states. A risk of this type is usually a relatively new building and if truly of mill construction it is highly acceptable for most occupancies, such as a shopping center, church, or winery. However, many times these buildings will be of an unusual nature with

Exhibit 4-5
Heavy Timber Mill Construction*

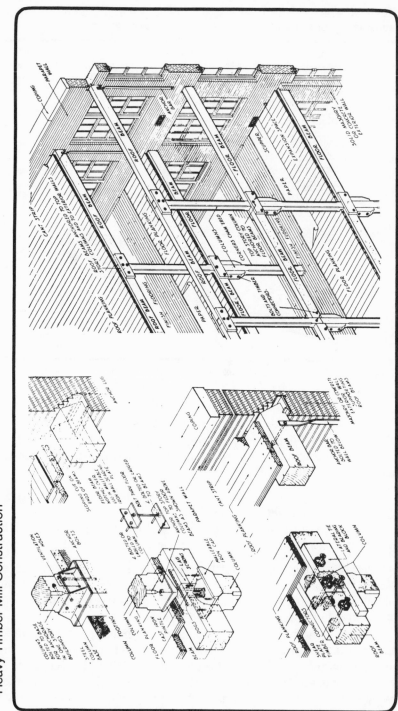

*Reprinted with permission from *Fire Protection Handbook*, 15th ed. (Quincy, MA: National Fire Protection Association, 1981), pp. 5-25, 5-26.

unique architectural design and configuration where repair and replacement cost coverage may present problems in reconstruction.

Noncombustible

This class includes buildings with exterior walls, floors, and roof of noncombustible materials supported by noncombustible supports such as metal, asbestos, and gypsum. These buildings are usually made of metal but the metal is unprotected and hence not fire resistive.

Masonry Noncombustible

This class includes buildings with exterior walls of masonry with noncombustible or slow burning floors and roof. A *slow burning floor or roof* is defined as having a flame spread rating of twenty-five or less. The main benefit of noncombustible construction, as opposed to either joisted masonry or frame construction, is that it will not aid in the spread of fire. On occasion the integrity of a noncombustible structure will be violated through the use of materials such as asphalt or felt vapor barriers on noncombustible roof deckings. A large loss in 1953 in Livonia, Michigan, of a noncombustible building occupied by a metal-working risk was attributed to this problem. The heat of the occupancy fire began to melt the asphalt roof surface, causing a near distillation process. During the fire, combustibles were generated which in turn were consumed by the spreading fire, causing a chain effect which ultimately totally destroyed the building.

The typical noncombustible building has a masonry nonbearing wall surface, a cement floor, some type of metal deck roof, and unprotected steel webbing supported by unprotected columns and roof members. The underwriter will usually encounter light to moderately severe fuel loads in these risks and must be very careful in selection due to the potential of collapse. However, risks of this type have withstood major windstorms and earthquakes with little or no damage. Low initial cost and low maintenance coupled with the ability to withstand these perils have made this type of construction extremely popular.

Most structures of this type are not provided with interior fire-stops in the form of fire walls. Thus, the horizontal spread of fire may present an additional hazard.

Modified Fire Resistive

This class includes buildings with exterior walls, floors, and roof constructed of masonry or fire resistive materials but with a fire resistance rating of between one and two hours. Fire resistive is described in the next section.

Fire Resistive

This class includes buildings constructed of any combination of the following materials:

1. Exterior walls or exterior structural frame
- Solid masonry, including reinforced concrete
- Hollow masonry not less than twelve inches in thickness
- Hollow masonry less than twelve inches, but not less than eight inches in thickness, with a listed fire resistance rating of not less than two hours
- Assemblies with a fire resistance rating of not less than two hours

2. Floors and roof
- Monolithic floors and roof of reinforced concrete with slabs not less than four inches in thickness
- Construction known as "Joist Systems" with slabs supported by concrete joists spaced not more than thirty-six inches on centers with a slab thickness of not less than two and three-quarters inches
- Floor and roof assemblies with a fire resistance rating of not less than two hours

3. Structural metal supports
- Horizontal and vertical load-bearing protected metal supports (including horizontal pre-stressed or post-tensioned concrete units) with a fire resistance rating of not less than two hours.[5]

From an underwriting standpoint this is the best construction. These buildings have walls, floors, columns, and roofs constructed of a noncombustible material. The materials either have a fire resistance rating in excess of two hours or they are protected through the use of a noncombustible covering such as plaster or gypsum, to obtain such a rating. "Fire resistive construction" is a general term which encompasses buildings with ratings between two and four hours. In terms of structural integrity, this is a wide range.

Virtually all types of occupancy classes may be found in fire resistive buildings. Most high-rise office and apartment buildings are constructed to these standards. Other important fire resistive occupancies include heavy manufacturing plants where large structural supports for machinery are required and warehouses with high fuel loads.

Mixed Construction

Many times the underwriter encounters buildings that do not fit exactly into any single construction type. The architectural design may have been an attempt at mixing building types or additions and changes may have been made by owners over the years. Depending upon the existence of proper fire divisions, the decisions dealing with possible and probable losses can be made separately for each division. In the absence of proper divisions, such decisions must weigh the relative values of the different types to arrive at a single decision for the entire entity. This also applies to any decision regarding the risk's overall desirability. The relative size of each type of construction is important.

This may be determined on a percentage basis by dividing the square footage of each type of construction by the total square footage of the entire building.

CONSTRUCTION DESIGN

In addition to basic construction of a building, its design characteristics greatly affect the risk's overall desirability. For example, a one-story risk of 50,000 square feet could have dimensions of 100 feet by 500 feet or could be 1,000 feet long and only 50 feet wide. The shape and size of the structure will greatly influence the ease with which fires can be controlled and extinguished.

High-Rise Buildings

The height of a structure also bears on the general desirability of a risk. Again, a 50,000 square foot building could be one, two, three, or four stories high. If the sum total of the floor area was 50,000 square feet, the exterior dimensions would be modified greatly; for example, a four-story square building would have walls 112 feet long. The underwriter is again presented with the problem of attempting to evaluate the design of the structure in terms of that structure's ability to confine fire, the capabilities of the exterior fire fighting force especially in view of the structure's design (e.g., short, windowless buildings), and the nature of the occupancy.

In recent years structures have been built that are beyond the capabilities of municipal fire protection. Buildings such as the Sears Tower, the twin towers of the World Trade Center (for which a decision was made recently to retrofit with a sprinkler system), or the Canadian National Tower in Toronto, Canada, which rise in excess of 1,000 feet above street level, present unique problems. Usually a municipal fire department is not capable of handling a fire from the exterior of a property in excess of 100 feet. A building 100 feet tall would have eight or nine floors. The underwriter must accept that the fire department cannot be of much assistance from the exterior of the premises in a modern high rise.

In a high rise, the fire department would have to attack the fire from inside. This may result in a time delay in fire fighting response. Therefore, an underwriter should pay particular attention to the fire resistive characteristics of the structure and the presence or lack of approved horizontal and vertical barriers that would confine the fire to its area of origin and the internal protection such as sprinklers and standpipes and hoses. For example, a high rise with heating and air conditioning ducts that penetrate vertical and horizontal barriers can aid in the spread of fire unless equipped with automatic shutoffs.

Structures of such great height require control of heavy combustible loads. The occupancy should not contain high fire hazards as a result of the tenants' operations or high fuel loads due to storage. Normally, high-rise structures are office occupancies and these are usually light hazard exposures. However, most offices have storage areas, duplicating areas, and data processing equipment. All of these contain a high level of combustibility. Therefore, the potential for a severe fire might exist in what are normally light hazard areas.

High rises sometimes have restaurants or bars located on the upper floors to take advantage of attractive views. In this location, restaurants are a hazardous occupancy. Without adequate control or private protection, they constitute a significant concern to the underwriter.

Coupled with these factors are the characteristics of a fire at an extended elevation. As soon as a fire occurs, the windows are normally vented. This limits the buildup of toxic gases. But while the wind at the street level may be minimal, it is oftentimes very severe fifty or more floors above the ground.

In addition, the underwriter should be concerned with life safety. A structure of 100 stories in height might have as many as 25,000 occupants. If a severe fire occurs on the fiftieth floor, on the average over 12,000 people may be located above the fire and therefore subjected to potential injury from flame, smoke, and gas. Often in fire resistive buildings, the occupants are instructed to go to a certain area and wait for further instructions from the appropriate authorities. Again, emphasis on integrity of the structure is important since these persons may not be able to pass through the fire area unless the structure is equipped with high level evacuation facilities. Life safety is important to the fire underwriter not only out of concern for the occupants, but also because firefighters arriving at the scene of the fire will concentrate on rescuing the occupants before turning to fighting the fire. Such a delay could turn what otherwise would have been a small loss into a major loss.

Fire Divisions

A different type of problem may be found in large horizontal structures. Structures with a total horizontal area approaching 1 million square feet are becoming more common. While the solution to many high-rise structure fire problems is vertical integrity, a corresponding solution for large horizontal areas is *fire divisions*.

As noted earlier, a fire division restricts the spread of fire. For insurance rating a fire division must meet specific requirements. Generally, the buildings must be separated by two independent walls or one continuous masonry party wall, both subject to a number of specific further requirements, such as thickness, communications, and so on.

Fire walls are essential to fire divisions. A fire wall is generally a wall erected to prevent the spread of fire. It should be able to "withstand the effects of the severest fire that may be expected to occur in the building and must provide a complete barrier to the spread of fire."[6] Such partitions must be relatively fire resistive or very slow-burning. They must not stop short of the ceiling or floor; nor must they interfere with the safe exit of the building occupants. A stream of superheated gas may pour through a one-inch opening like a blow torch. Generally, a wall must be at least eight inches of masonry material to be classified as a fire wall. The adequacy of fire walls is determined by the combustibility of the contents of the building. What is adequate for a school building may not be adequate to prevent fire spread in a heavy industrial plant, such as a paper mill. In a fire resistive building, all interior walls which extend from floor to ceiling should be of sufficient fire resistive quality to be called fire walls.

In a masonry or frame building, a fire wall must extend beyond the roof line in order to be effective. Since fire can spread via the roof in such buildings, these fire wall extensions, or *parapets*, must extend at least twenty-four inches above the normal roof line.

Frequently, industrial firms adopt automated production techniques to increase production and lower unit cost. Automation is best adapted to processes with uninterrupted horizontal production lines. Therefore fire loss control often conflicts with commercial economies of scale. While loss control considerations may suggest the introduction of horizontal cutoffs, these may interfere with efficient production.

The underwriter must take into consideration the occupancy and its fuel load in determining what is an acceptable fire division. A 100,000 square foot structure occupied by a steel warehouse presents

Exhibit 4-6
Curtain Boards and Roof Vents*

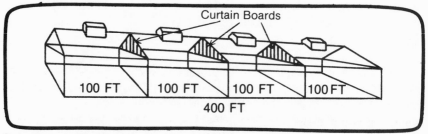

*Adapted with permission from *Fire Protection Handbook*, 15th ed. (Quincy, MA: National Fire Protection Association, 1981), p. 5-106.

few problems. However, a flammable liquid storage area in excess of 5,000 square feet is a severe problem.

In addition, the underwriter should suggest the segregation of occupancies in order to prevent consequential losses. The segregation of the finished goods warehouse from the production facilities and the raw material warehouse could prevent a major business interruption loss and possibly reduce the size of the direct loss. Again, the risk manager or plant owner has a conflict between production efficiency and exposure to loss.

The underwriter can also rely on *curtain boards* which are illustrated in Exhibit 4-6. These are partial fire walls, which when installed in concert with roof vents, will concentrate the hot smoke and gases in the area of origin, aiding the exterior venting of the property and simplifying the task of fire suppression.

Building Openings

The construction type may appear to be excellent and appropriate for the intended occupancy. However, during the construction process, the subcontractors, such as electricians, heating contractors, and air conditioning contractors, may have installed equipment throughout the structure. This equipment is designed to pass heat, electrical energy, or air conditioning throughout the premises. It is possible that vertical and horizontal fire-stops may have been violated by these subcontractors.

A loss involving a high-rise structure near completion occurred in New York City. The structural members of this building were of a noncombustible nature and originally had been adequately protected to afford a minimum of a two-hour fire rating. This protection was diminished by installation work by subcontractors. The effect was to lay bare the structural steel members. The completion of the structure did not include resurfacing these structural members with a protective coating. A subsequent fire weakened the steel to the point where it had to be removed before the structure could be occupied. While the damage to these members was minimal and their original cost was not inordinate, the replacement of major building supports within a structure nearing completion resulted in a multimillion dollar loss.

In addition to the other ducts and passageways that might be present within a structure, buildings are often equipped with door openings between fire divisions and floor openings for stairs between floors. In addition, elevators, dumbwaiters, conveyor belts, and air and light shafts are often present. All of these violate the basic integrity of a fire division. Some of these openings in certain rare instances cannot be protected, although most can be corrected with approved fire doors. Fire doors are usually rated according to their fire resistive hourly rating, such as a three-hour fire door. To be most effective, a fire door in a fire wall should be capable of withstanding the same fire as the wall itself. Generally, the protection used for openings in fire-rated walls has less resistance than is provided by the wall to firespread.

A vertical opening is corrected only when it is wholly segregated into a separate fire division. Therefore, elevators and stair wells, when properly constructed, constitute a building within a building. The theory is that the fire must pass horizontally from one floor through a barrier and into the stairwell, up the stairwell, and through a second barrier door.

Fire doors are "approved" when they meet design specifications of the National Fire Protection Association. Manufacturers of fire doors have their products tested by Underwriters' Laboratories, Inc., or the Factory Mutuals. An approved door is granted a seal which is usually placed on its edge indicating its rating.

Fire doors, as mentioned, are rated, according to hourly ratings, but an alphabetic designation (or a combination of the two) is also used. For example, fire doors can be rated in descending order of fire resistance, A through E. (Class A have a three-hour rating; Class E have a forty-five-minute rating.) These ratings measure the door's ability to prevent passage of heat, smoke, and other products of combustion. The rating may vary depending upon the occupancy and the location of the door within the building.

An approved fire door obviously is useless if propped open. Therefore each door must be automatically self-closing and unob-structed. Doors that must be left open to permit efficient industrial operations are fitted with fusable links that permit automatic self-closing when heat activated.

CONSTRUCTION MATERIALS

The interior finish of a structure has a definite effect on the overall desirability of a risk. For example, assume that a structure is of superior fire resistive construction, with all building members rated at four hours' fire resistance, with a light hazard occupancy such as an apartment or office. However, it might have an interior finish of a highly combustible nature with hazardous characteristics. The characteristics of interior finishes which are most relevant to fire problems include their ability to:

1. spread fire,
2. contribute fuel to the fire, and
3. develop smoke and noxious gases when burning.

Any of these three characteristics has an effect on the overall property loss potential as well as affecting the safety of the occupants. In the past ten years there have been several disastrous fires in Korea and in South America where there was little structural physical damage but severe loss of life as the result of highly combustible interior finishes. The MGM Hotel fire in Las Vegas also involved highly combustible decor and caused loss of life as well as physical damage to the structure.

Relatively noncombustible interior finishes include wall coverings such as plaster, gypsum, and wall board. Combustible interior finishes include wood or plywood, fiber ceiling tiles, and plastic wall coverings. Surface coatings such as certain paints, varnishes, and wallpapers when added to other combustible finishes could contribute significantly to the fuel load. Even the adhesives used in floor or ceiling tile can add substantially to a building's capacity to sustain or fuel a fire.

The interior finish hazard begins with its installation through the use of electrical equipment, torches, or other flame producing devices. During the course of construction, interior finishes can contribute materially to potential fire. Once the finish is installed, a small fire can involve this interior finish in a flash over. Even a small fire involving a highly combustible interior finish can generate highly toxic gases that can be distributed quickly throughout the building. The MGM fire involved heavy loss of life due to toxic fumes and smoke.

More recently fire underwriters have learned that a high level of interior combustibility can generate a fire that will literally climb the outside of a building, moving from one floor to the other, even when the vertical openings within the interior of the structure are well protected. While the structure itself may be of fire resistive construction and the occupancy of low combustibility, the interior finish must also be examined to determine the building's actual combustibility. The combustibility of interior finishes can be measured analytically, using flame spread tests.

Insulation

Just as the interior finish of a structure has a great effect on the structure's combustibility, insulation may also add problems. While a common form of insulation is glass fiber, it is, unfortunately, usually bound by a combustible membrane. Insulation material also can include combustible substances such as wood chips formed into fiber board or recycled paper. Insulation is used not only for heat conservation but as a sound barrier. Therefore, combustible insulation can be found in the interior walls of otherwise highly fire resistive buildings.

Whether the insulation is installed for the conservation of heat or the suppression of sound, the underwriter should attempt to determine its flame spread, fuel contribution, or smoke contribution characteristics. If this information is unavailable, the material should be viewed with suspicion.

The energy crisis has led to renewed interest in heat conservation. The underwriter should determine if additional insulation has been added to a structure. For example, if a roof and wall structure was designed and originally constructed in accordance with a standard fire rating, a problem might occur if additional combustible insulation was added. In addition, this insulation, if improperly installed, could have the adverse effect of holding the heat being generated by the fire within the structure, concentrating it on the building members and possibly weakening them to the point of early collapse.

Roofing

The exterior surface of a roof is used for two basic purposes. The first is as a weather seal. The quality of this weather seal can be important to an underwriter when "all-risks" coverage is being written. Secondly, the surface of a roof is a barrier against external fire. In its role as a protection barrier, it should be as noncombustible as possible.

Roofs are subject to attack from two sides: sparks and embers falling from outside fires, and heat from inside fires. Therefore, the combustibility of both sides is important. Untreated wooden shingles invite spread of exposure fires. Resistive coverings are classified as *A* (safest), *B*, and *C* (some fire resistance). Treated cedar shingles and zinc sheets over asphalt-saturated organic felt are *C*. Other metal roofs and various combinations of asphalt, felt, and gravel in layers range from *C* to *A*. Concrete, tile, and slate are *A*. But tile and slate are subject to other damage such as wind damage.

Asphalt shingles are probably the most common roof covering. While they are somewhat combustible, when properly constructed and installed they act as an excellent barrier from even severe fire exposures. Conversely, combustible materials such as wood shake shingles or tar paper afford almost no protection. Many underwriters look upon showers of fire brands as a thing of the past. However, even today they do occur, as in recent California brush fires. In the presence of high winds, a wood shake roof may send fire brands as much as a mile downwind.

Other Factors

Interior Decoration In the review of a structure the underwriter must be cognizant of features such as pictures, drapes, and wall hangings. Such items add not only significant values but also potential hazards. In occupancies such as restaurants, bowling alleys, bars, theaters, clubs, and funeral parlors, the interior decor should be carefully scrutinized. Otherwise, the underwriter may inadvertently judge that a risk is of low combustibility when, in fact, it is not.

Foyers of high-rise office buildings may have murals, fountains, pools, sculptures, and friezes. These are frequently introduced to obscure architectural faults or engineering features such as ductwork. They may constitute collapse or breakage hazards while at the same time attracting vandals.

Exterior Decoration Vermiculite and marble veneer panels are often found on the lower floors of office buildings. These are used to cover protected steel members or the residual form markings in poured concrete structures. They are subject to breakage and cracking from the effects of ice in loose joints. Older buildings may have glazed tiles capping parapets that can fall or be blown off in windstorms.

While not decoration, television, radio and microwave relay towers may be installed on tall buildings. They should be insured by means of a separate inland marine policy, but this intent can be made clear by means of a specific exclusion in the policy covering the building. Towers are subject to lightning, ice, and windstorm damage. In turn, their collapse may cause substantial damage to the building on which they are situated.

AGE

A key factor affecting the desirability of a risk is its age. The following are underwriting considerations with respect to older buildings (recognizing that all are not specifically "construction" related):

1. a different building code in force at the time of construction;
2. possible obsolescence of heating and electrical systems;
3. possible changes in occupancy relative to the originally intended use for the building;
4. potential indirect increases in losses imposed by current building codes; and
5. possible deterioration or erosion by dry rot, rust, termites, settling, or excessive wear.

While proper maintenance will mitigate the effects of age and deterioration, all buildings will eventually wear out. The degree of obsolescence or deterioration is directly related to the basic type of construction, the occupancy, physical abuse of the building, and the quality of the owner's maintenance.

A frame structure, for example, will normally show its age faster than a joisted masonry structure; a joisted masonry structure will show its age faster than a fire resistive structure. However, it must be noted that an office occupancy in a frame structure with good maintenance may well outlive a fire resistive building occupied by a drop forge operation with minimal maintenance.

The methodology of constructing buildings and the style of their construction materially changes with the passage of time. Building materials that were in use in the 1920s or 1930s have long been abandoned. Today's plumbing systems seldom use cast iron, galvanized iron, or brass piping. Iron is susceptible to corrosion and rusting. Brass pipes are susceptible to vibration and subsequently loose fittings. Electrical systems of forty, fifty, and sixty years ago were designed primarily for lighting while modern wiring systems are designed to accommodate space heating, computer systems, and heavy appliances.

A building that was designed for a dry-goods retailing occupancy fifty years ago might be wholly inadequate for a laundry, a printer, or a beverage distributor today. Weight loadings for machines and bottled goods may exceed the original specifications. Machine demands for electricity have increased greatly. In addition to these occupancy increases in hazard, the structural integrity of the building probably has deteriorated over time from its original strength.

Age and Perils

Fire The most desirable risk, given acceptable occupancy, is the newer structure. As the construction industry has moved forward, it has been able to build structures more appropriate for their occupancies which can be more easily replaced or repaired.

Modern technology has increased the use of noncombustible materials, introduced high capacity electrical systems, improved space heating and cooling systems, and changed the predominant fuels used on premises.

When examining a submission on a building more than twenty years old, some underwriters request that the owner obtain inspections by qualified electricians and heating contractors. The contractors' reports provide valuable information regarding the desirability of the risk.

Windstorm and Hail The elemental forces of wind, rain, and hail take their toll on the exterior of a building with the passage of time. Even a structure that is adequately maintained will begin to show its age in its exterior surfaces, particularly the roof. Without replacement of the shingles or the roof surfaces on a twenty- or thirty-year cycle, losses can be expected from hail or wind. The design of roof surfaces in the past did not include such things as self-sealing shingle tabs, commonplace today. Without such features, shingles can easily be detached and destroyed by gales or hurricanes.

Collapse Most "all-risks" forms normally will provide protection against collapse. This single peril has produced more extensive damage to structures, including total losses, than any other peril except fire and wind. All too often this peril is not underwritten but instead assumed by the underwriter to be inconsequential. Age weighs heavily on the overall desirability of a risk being insured for this peril, as it weakens structures through fatigue, misuse, or exposure to weather.

Hard Use. A structure that is heavily loaded with contents will begin to show its age or wear through such symptoms as depressed wooden floors or the scaling of concrete surfaces. Just as a metal spring will begin to lose its strength after it has been compressed numerous times, a building will begin to lose the ability to support its designed load criteria after continued excessive use. Hard use can greatly affect this loss potential. A risk that is well constructed but lightly occupied, such as an office or a condominium, will have a useful life of many years. A structure designed and used for heavy manufacturing will have a much shorter useful life. The occupancy literally will wear out the building, creating a potential catastrophic collapse situation.

Weather. The effects of weather, such as wind, rain, hail, or flood, will also have a material effect on useful life and the potential desirability of a structure. Wooden surfaces that are not adequately maintained will begin to rot and lose their structural strength. Concrete or brick surfaces also need protection against the effects of weather, although to a lesser degree than wood. As these surfaces and structural supports begin to weaken, they will no longer support the design load of the structure. Symptoms such as hairline cracks in columns or bearing walls are important keys to be recognized as potential loss causes. Water markings from floods or leaks also can be vital signals to potential loss causes.

Underwriters should remember that collapse can also occur in new structures. The collapse of the new Hartford Civic Auditorium, from heavy wet snow in the winter of 1977-78, may have been due to faulty design.

SOURCES OF CONSTRUCTION INFORMATION

There are many sources of construction information. In addition, underwriters should understand the types of basic construction that are to be found within their territories. They should know what construction types predominate and the current trends in construction.

General knowledge, however, is only a basis on which inferences may be drawn in the absence of more specific data. Specific data is available from:

1. applications,
2. rate cards and manuals,
3. bureau reports,
4. inspection reports and diagrams (usually accompanying the inspection report), and
5. local building codes.

Applications

The application provides the name of the insured, which frequently includes some generic phrase indicative of the occupancy in that structure. Furthermore, the application generally provides the address of the risk, its age, and possibly additional data regarding construction type, types and age of plumbing and heating systems, and the existence or absence of special protective devices such as automatic sprinkler systems. The application provides sufficient data for an underwriting decision only for the smaller and less sophisticated property risks.

Rate Cards and Manuals

Property insurance risks are either *class rated* or *specifically (schedule)* rated. A class rate applies to an entire category of similar risks. It does not vary based on the specialized features of any particular risk within the class. Rather, each class is delineated based on general construction type and occupancy. A specific rate, on the other hand, is developed for each structure. Its derivation is a result of an inspection during which the structural features are identified and graded according to published standards. These specific rating schedules are discussed in Chapter 9. Throughout most of the United States, class rates are found in manuals.

Specific rates were previously published on individually printed rate cards. However, ISO has moved away from this approach and now has the information stored on microfiche. (The term "rate card" is still used by many underwriters.) Companies can access this information in many ways including obtaining the microfiche themselves. For each address, an underwriter is able to obtain a number of pieces of objective information regarding the risk at that location. ISO has three numbers associated with each address (a file number, distribution area number, and risk number) which can be used to access a specific risk more quickly than looking up the town or township, the street, and the address.

In addition to the numbers above, the information contained for each location includes:

- Address
- Name of the occupancy(ies)
- Building and contents rates
- SCOH (Standard Classification of Occupancy Hazards) Code (almost obsolete)
- Class Code (a four digit numerical description of the occupancy)
- RCP Code (a four digit number denoting sprinkler versus nonsprinklered, construction classification, and protection classification)
- Extended Coverage Code
- An effective date of the information

After the underwriter has reviewed both the application and the "rate card" or manual, he or she has obtained some information with respect to construction, occupancy, protection, and exposure.

Additional information may be obtained from the producer. An inspection can also be used to obtain specific information on internal operations, private protection, housekeeping, and exposures.

Bureau Reports

On some risks there are highly detailed reports promulgated by the engineering department of the appropriate fire bureau. Normally these reports are developed on risks with sprinkler protection or risks of an unusual nature, such as large frame structures.

The report is a narrative which includes the class of the risk, the owner-occupant, construction, fire divisions, observed hazards, external exposures, private protection systems, and the history of the risk. A report will also reflect major problem areas and contain recommendations for necessary improvements.

Other types of bureau reports are also developed in areas of special concern. For example, reports are available from the San Francisco office of the ISO concerning special earthquake situations.

Inspection Reports and Diagrams

Diagrams Diagrams are provided in many bureau reports and company inspections. A well-drawn diagram is the next best thing to an on-site inspection by the underwriter. The ability to interpret a diagram properly is an essential property underwriting skill.

In the preparation of these diagrams, inspectors use a standard set of symbols to reflect the construction, occupancy, protection, and exposure characteristics of the structure. Exhibit 4-7 shows the symbols and Exhibit 4-8 the abbreviations currently in use. Until recently, color was used to indicate construction; at present, abbreviations are used.

Because color coding already exists in some current files and because some inspectors may continue to use colors in their drawings, the color interpretations for diagramed construction types are provided in Exhibit 4-9.

A complete building sketch is shown in Exhibit 4-10. This sketch includes not only information about the structure of the building, but also the fire protection and internal processes of the plant. A sketch of this type includes a great deal of valuable underwriting information.

The Use of Inspections The question of when an underwriter should order an inspection can be perplexing. For example, assume a submission of a light hazard occupancy with high values comes in from a producer who is relatively unknown to the underwriter. The application does not provide complete information. A rule of thumb is, when in doubt, inspect. While it is true that inspections cost money, poor risks, over the long run, cost even more money. The request for an inspection, in any event, should clearly state the information required.

Low-value submissions present a major problem because the average cost of a company loss control representative is at least $25 per hour. Therefore, a risk that might produce a premium of only $100 or $200 cannot support the cost of an inspection. In such cases the

Exhibit 4-7
Standard Plan Symbols*

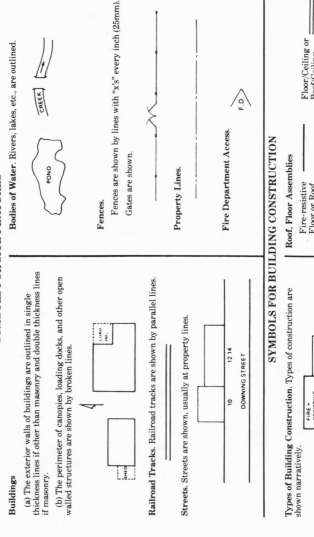

SYMBOLS FOR SITE FEATURES

Buildings

(a) The exterior walls of buildings are outlined in single thickness lines if other than masonry and double thickness lines if masonry.

(b) The perimeter of canopies, loading docks, and other open walled structures are shown by broken lines.

Railroad Tracks. Railroad tracks are shown by parallel lines.

Streets. Streets are shown, usually at property lines.

Bodies of Water. Rivers, lakes, etc., are outlined.

Fences.
Fences are shown by lines with "x's" every inch (25mm). Gates are shown.

Property Lines.

Fire Department Access.

SYMBOLS FOR BUILDING CONSTRUCTION

Types of Building Construction. Types of construction are shown narratively.

Height. Height is shown to indicate number of stories above ground, number of stories below ground, and height from grade to eaves.

Roof, Floor Assemblies

Fire-resistive Floor or Roof

Wood Joisted Floor or Roof

Other Floors or Roofs
(Sit deck on sit joists)
(Note Construction)

Floor/Ceiling or Roof/Ceiling Assembly
[Details indicated as necessary.]

Floor on Ground

Truss Roof

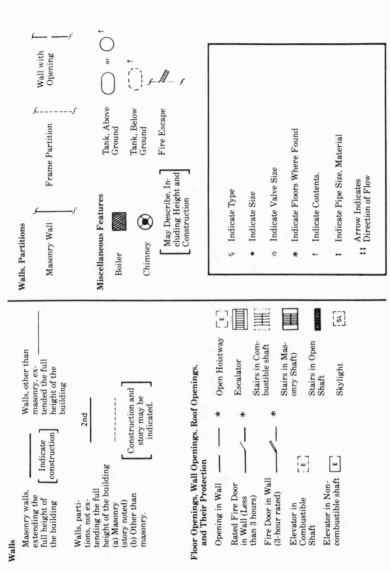

Walls

Masonry walls, extending the full height of the building [Indicate construction]

Walls, other than masonry, extended the full height of the building

Walls, partitions, not extending the full height of the building
(a) Masonry (story noted) — 2nd
(b) Other than masonry. [Construction and story may be indicated.]

Walls, Partitions

Masonry Wall

Frame Partition

Wall with Opening

Miscellaneous Features

Boiler

Chimney [May Describe, Including Height and Construction]

Tank, Above Ground — or

Tank, Below Ground

Fire Escape

ↄ Indicate Type

✶ Indicate Size

✫ Indicate Valve Size

✳ Indicate Floors Where Found

↑ Indicate Contents.

↕ Indicate Pipe Size, Material

↕ Arrow Indicates Direction of Flow

Floor Openings, Wall Openings, Roof Openings, and Their Protection

Opening in Wall — *

Rated Fire Door in Wall (Less than 3 hours) *

Fire Door in Wall (3-hour rated) *

Elevator in Combustible Shaft [E]

Elevator in Non-combustible shaft [E]

Open Hoistway [E]

Escalator

Stairs in Combustible shaft

Stairs in Masonry Shaft)

Stairs in Open Shaft

Skylight [SL]

continued on next page

SYMBOLS FOR WATER SUPPLY AND DISTRIBUTION

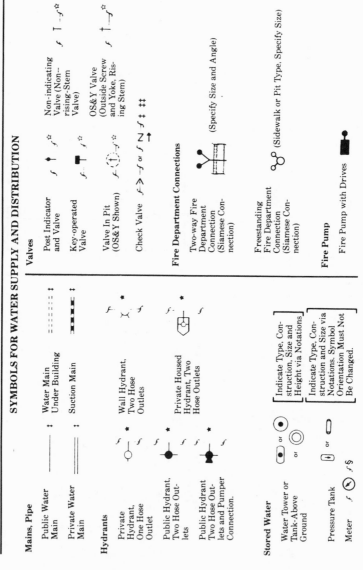

Mains, Pipe

Public Water Main

Private Water Main

Water Main Under Building

Suction Main

Hydrants

Private Hydrant, One Hose Outlet

Wall Hydrant, Two Hose Outlets

Public Hydrant, Two Hose Outlets

Private Housed Hydrant, Two Hose Outlets

Public Hydrant Two Hose Outlets and Pumper Connection.

Stored Water

Water Tower or Tank-Above Ground

Indicate Type, Construction, Size and Height via Notations.

Pressure Tank

Indicate Type, Construction and Size via Notations. Symbol Orientation Must Not Be Changed.

Meter

Valves

Post Indicator and Valve

Non-indicating Valve (Non–rising-Stem Valve)

Key-operated Valve

Valve In Pit (OS&Y Shown)

OS&Y Valve (Outside Screw and Yoke, Rising Stem)

Check Valve

Fire Department Connections

Two-way Fire Department Connection (Siamese Connection)

(Specify Size and Angle)

Freestanding Fire Department Connection (Siamese Connection)

(Sidewalk or Pit Type, Specify Size)

Fire Pump

Fire Pump with Drives

continued on next page

SYMBOLS FOR SPRINKLER SYSTEMS[1]

Piping, Valves, Control Devices

Sprinkler Riser

Check Valve, General

Alarm Check Valve

Dry Pipe Valve

Dry Pipe Valve with Quick Opening Device (Accelerator or Exhauster)

Deluge Valve

Alarm/Supervisory Devices

Flow Detector/Switch (Flow Alarm)

Pressure Detector/Switch (Water, Low Air, Hi Air, etc.)

Water Motor Alarm (Water Motor Gong)

(Shield Optional)

Electric Alarm Bell (Electric Alarm Gong)

SYMBOLS FOR EXTINGUISHING SYSTEMS

Wet (Charged) System

(a) Automatically Actuated   (b) Manually Actuated

Dry System

(a) Automatically Actuated   (b) Manually Actuated

Foam System

(a) Automatically Actuated   (b) Manually Actuated

For Liquid—, Gas—, and Electrical-type Fires

(a) Automatically Actuated   (b) Manually Actuated

For Fires of All Types, Except Metals

(a) Automatically Actuated   (b) Manually Actuated

Carbon Dioxide System

(a) Automatically Actuated   (b) Manually Actuated

Halon System

(a) Automatically Actuated   (b) Manually Actuated

Supplementary Symbols

Nonsprinklered Space   Partially Sprinklered Space

[1]These symbols are intended for use in identifying the type of installed system protecting an area within a building.

*Reprinted with permission from *Fire Protection Handbook*, 15th ed. (Quincy, MA; National Fire Protection Association, 1981), pp. 20-4, 20-5.

Exhibit 4-8
Legend of Common Abbreviations*

Term	Abbr.	Term	Abbr.
Above	ABV	Liquid	LIQ
Accelerator	ACC	Liquid Oxygen	LOX
Acetylene	ACET		
Aluminum	AL	Manufacture	MFR
Asbestos	ASB	Manufacturing	MFG
Asphalt Protected Metal	APM	Maximum Capacity	MAX CAP
Attic	A	Mean Sea Levels	MSL
Automatic	AUTO	Metal	MT
Automatic Fire Alarm	AFA	Mezzanine	MEZZ
Automatic, Sprinklers	AS	Mill Use	MU
Avenue	AVE		
		Normally Closed	NC
Basement	B	Normally Open	NO
Beam	BM	North	N
Board on Joist	BDOJ	Number	No
Brick	BR		
Building	BLDG	Open Sprinklers	OS
		Outside Screw & Yoke Valve	OS&Y
Cast Iron	CI		
Cement	CEM	Partition (Label Composition)	PTN (i.e., WD PTN)
Centrifugal Fire Pump	CFP	Plaster	PLAS
Cinder Block	CB	Plaster Board	PLAS BD
Composition Roof	COMPR	Platform	PLATF
Concrete	CONC	Pound (Unit of Force)	LB
Construction	CONST	Pressure	PRESS
Corrugated Iron	COR IR	Unit of Pressure (Pounds Per Square Inch)	PSI
Corrugated Steel	COR ST	Protected Steel	PROT ST
		Private	PRIVATE
Diameter	DIA	Public	PUB
Diesel-Engine	D ENG		
Domestic	DOM	Railroad	RR
Double Hydrant	DH	Reinforced Concrete	RC
Dry Pipe Valve	DPV	Reinforcing Steel	RST
		Reservoir	RES
East	E	Revolutions per Minute	RPM
Electric Motor Driven	EMD	Roof	RF
Elevator	ELEV	Room	RM
Engine	ENG		
Exhauster	EXH	Slate Shingle Roof	SSR
		Space	SP

Term	Abbr.		Term	Abbr.
Feet	FT		South	S
Fibre Board	FBR BD		Stainless Steel	SST
Fire Escape	FE		Steam Fire Pump	SFP
Fire Department Pumper Connection	FDPC		Steel	ST
Fire Detection Units	FDU		Steel Deck	ST DK
Products of Combustion	POC		Stone	STONE
Rate of Heat Rise	RHR		Story	STO
Fixed Temperature	FTEP		Street	STREET
Fire Pump	FP		Stucco	STUC
Floor	FL		Suspended Acoustical Plaster Ceiling	SAPL
Frame	FR		Suspended Acoustical Tile Ceiling	SATL
Fuel Oil (Label with Grade Number)	FO#_____		Suspended Plaster Ceiling	SPC
			Suspended Sprayed Acoustical Ceiling	SSAL
Gallon	GAL		Tank (Label Capacity in Gallons)	TK
Gallons Per Day	GPD		Tenant	TEN
Gallons Per Minute	GPM		Tile Block	TB
Galvanized Iron	GALVI		Timber	TMBR
Galvanized Steel	GALVS		Tin Clad	TIN CL
Gas, Natural	GAS		Triple Hydrant	TH
Gasoline	GASOLINE		Truss	TR
Gasoline Engine Driven	GED			
Generator	GEN		Under	UND
Glass	GL			
Glass Block	GLB		Vault	VLT
Gypsum	GYM		Veneer	VEN
Gypsum Board	GYM BD		Volts (Indicated Number Of)	450v
High Voltage	HV		Wall Board	WLBD
Hollow Tile	HT		Wall Hydrant	WLH
Hose Connection	HC		Water Pipe	WP
Hydrant	HYD		West	W
Inch, Inches	IN		Wire Glass	WGL
Iron	IR		Wire Net	WN
Iron Clad	IR CL		Wood	WD
Iron Pipe	IP		Wood Frame	WD FR
Joist, Joisted	J		Yard	YD

Some words that have a common abbreviation, e.g. "ST" for "street," are spelled out fully to avoid confusion with similar abbreviations used herein for other terms.

*Reprinted with permission from *Fire Protection Handbook*, 15th ed. (Quincy, MA: National Fire Protection Association, 1981), p. 20-6.

Exhibit 4-9
Color Code for Construction Materials for Walls*

Color	Interpretation
Brown	Fire resistive protected steel
Red	Brick, Hollow tile
Yellow	Frame, wood, stucco
Blue	Concrete, stone, or hollow concrete block
Gray	Noncombustible (sheet metal or metal lath and plaster) unprotected steel

*Reprinted with permission from *Fire Protection Handbook*, 15th ed. (Quincy, MA: National Fire Protection Association, 1981), p. 20-8.

underwriter might rely upon personal knowledge of the risk, and its locale. In addition, review of the "rate card" or manual or the bureau report may be sufficient. The underwriter might request the producer to provide a snapshot to supplement the application on low-value submissions.

The underwriter must make decisions based on knowledge in order to develop a successful book of business. Therefore, since underwriters cannot visit each premises, they must rely upon others to furnish them with adequate information. The cost of information is an important constraint. Underwriting management should provide written guidelines for the ordering of inspections either by company personnel or outside firms.

Local Building Codes

Local building codes can provide the underwriter with information regarding the construction of buildings erected under the provisions of that code. It is important to remember that older buildings may have been constructed according to the provisions of a different code from that which presently is in effect. Building codes are of two types:

1. *specification codes,* which set forth in detail the size, type and installation techniques for all structural members and other building components; or
2. *performance codes,* which set forth criteria which the structural members and other building components must meet.

The building code is one of the factors evaluated in the rating of public fire protection. This is covered in Chapter 6.

Exhibit 4-10
Building Sketch*

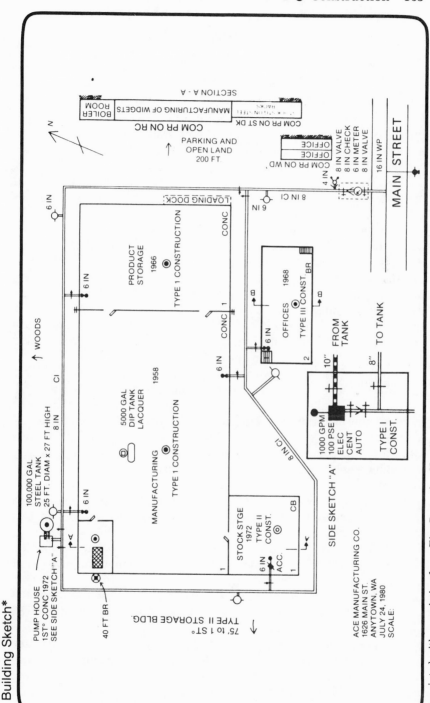

*Reprinted with permission from *Fire Protection Handbook*, 15th ed. (Quincy, MA: National Fire Protection Association, 1981), p. 20-7.

BUILDERS' RISK

Course of Construction Coverage

In addition to completed structures, assets are exposed to risks of loss or damage in buildings in the course of construction. This exposure during construction is known as *builders' risk*. The decision to accept or reject builders' risk submissions requires the same process as for a completed structure; that is, the COPE hazards must be analyzed. In addition, there are new hazards introduced that either are not present after structural completion or are intensified by the course of construction itself.

This policy is written on several different forms. Builders' risk may be written on a form attached to a standard fire policy, as an endorsement to an existing contract, or by a variety of printed or manuscript forms on an inland marine contract. As a matter of general practice, inland marine forms are the most commonly used. These range from simple installation floaters to elaborate manuscript contracts designed for large and complex projects. Since these are nonbureau forms, the underwriter has wide latitude in negotiating perils covered, conditions, and price.

Insurance to value, always an important consideration in property insurance, is something of a paradox in builders' risk. On the one hand, the completed value of a structure is fairly easy to determine—the value of the materials being used and the labor costs will be clearly known as expenses actually paid. On the other hand, the structure's value at any point in the course of construction can be precisely determined only if the contractor has precise specifications, a meticulous set of books for the project, and can specify definitively that purchased and delivered materials have or have not been installed or used. Unfortunately, the typical building project is not run in this fashion.

Consequently, most projects use the *completed value form* as the basis for policy format. This stipulates the estimated 100 percent building cost at completion as the limit of liability. It also assumes a fairly steady accrual of value from start to finish; as a consequence, the values used for premium purposes are arbitrarily set at either 50 or 55 percent of this amount.

When a building project is large enough and the contractor maintains accurate records, the contract is often written on a *reporting form* basis. Provisional amounts of insurance are set at the outset, and reports of added values are made changing this applicable limit. Premium is charged only for the values existing. This basis is especially attractive to an insured whose structure will have minimal values exposed throughout a lengthy building period with a heavy accrual of values just before completion. An example would be a factory where the superstructure is raised and only in the final stages are there introduced high-value items such as moving assembly lines and overhead cranes.

Perils Insured Against

The perils insured against in course of construction range from fire and extended coverage to "all-risks," with the "all-risks" versions becoming increasingly popular.

The occupancy of the completed structure has little effect on the course of construction exposure. During the course of construction, occupancy is by the contractors. They are soldering, welding, cutting, painting, using various electrical and gasoline driven machines and may also have volatile gases on the site. In addition, the nature of their work creates housekeeping problems, such as congestion, poor storage handling, high probabilities of spontaneous combustion, waste disposal—including bonfires, and accumulations of dusts, powders, and shavings.

Fire Fire can be additionally hazardous if water delivery systems are incomplete. Public water, for example, may be simultaneously under construction along with the building. In high-rise structures, standpipes must keep pace with each floor addition and be operable. (Often the water is not turned on until the building is completed.).

Wood or other combustible materials frequently are used. Even in fully fire resistive structures, temporary partitions, scaffolding, braces, and concrete forms may be used extensively. Plastic windbreaks and wood forms have resulted in some very large fires in slip-form poured concrete projects. Salamanders and tars in hot-roofing are also common hazards, whereas they are infrequent exposures in completed structures.

Windstorm Windstorms can be more dangerous because all buildings in course of construction are in a weakened state. Walls may not yet be bonded to one another and roofs are in various stages of completion or are still unanchored. Until windows and doors are installed and the entire structure enclosed, even a light storm can create unusual stresses and pressures which, in turn, can lead to failures.

Riot, Vandalism, and Malicious Mischief Strikes and riot exposures can be hazardous during builders' risk, especially in areas where jurisdictional strife and confrontations of union versus nonunion labor forces exist. Vandals are frequently attracted to building sites. Sites, in turn, are vacated almost every evening and during weekends.

Collapse As stated earlier, during course of construction every building of every construction type is significantly weaker than when in a completed state. Therefore, collapse becomes a serious hazard. Collapse primarily results from faulty design, faulty welds in steel superstructures, and improper bracing and curing in poured concrete and windstorm. The American Society of Civil Engineers (ASCE) has conducted or sponsored much research into the first three of these areas and meticulous standards have been promulgated. The underwriter must be assured that design and construction supervision meet ASCE standards. A letter from the architect or engineering firm stipulating the design qualification alleviates much worry and assists subrogation procedures where warranted. Day-to-day building supervision by the contractor should be supplemented, at the owner's expense, by a qualified *clerk of the works*. The clerk, usually a professional engineer, has as his or her sole responsibility the daily overseeing of each project component to see that materials, methodology, and quality of workmanship meet engineering specifications and ASCE standards. The clerk's authority includes the power to demand cessation of all work and to require the redoing of unacceptable portions.

There may be times when the clerk of the works and the contractor will have conflicts of interest. When projects are unduly delayed, the contractor may face contract penalties. The owner and therefore the clerk also may face substantial financial costs due to the delay. Thus, in concert, both parties may decide to cut corners. An especially vulnerable situation arises when the construction type is poured, reinforced concrete. In the course of construction it is vital that ASCE standards for forms and bracing be maintained to insure proper curing. Premature removal of supports can lead to collapse of a single floor and possibly the entire structure. The subsequent costs are incalculable and there is an invariable loss of human life. An example of this is the 1978 collapse of the scaffolding inside a cooling tower under construction in West Virginia. Fifty-one persons were killed. The failure to wait for the proper curing of the cement is suspected as the cause.

The underwriter can protect the insurance company's interest in such a project in two ways. First, he or she can insist that an independent engineer oversee all form and bracing removal timetables. Usually this can be done periodically by an insurance company engineer. Secondly, using an inland marine form, the underwriter can specify that a failure to meet accepted form and bracing standards will result in immediate cancellation of insurance.

Theft   Theft is frequently a requested coverage since losses have been significant from this peril. The underwriter should grant insurance against it only when minimum standards are met. The building site should have twenty-four hour guard service and, additionally, should be fenced wherever feasible.

Earthquake and Flood   Earthquake also presents a problem in that the structure may be susceptible to even a slight tremor. The hazard of flood may weaken the basic structural supports in the area of footings or foundations causing structural collapse prior to the completion of the building. These are perils that are infrequent but which cannot be overlooked.

Testing   Testing, as a peril, includes damage resulting from machinery malfunction immediately after its installation. The damage can be caused by improper installation or by a flaw in the machinery that was undetected upon leaving the factory. In either event, the underwriter providing such coverage is on dangerous ground—since the coverage depends on the skill, care, and operational expertise of a second party rather than against fortuitous, external events. Pricing for this peril must include proper provision for the large losses that are clearly possible.

Breakage of Structural Components   Breakage of structural components is usually an inexpensive event. Moreover, a reasonable deductible can usually reduce insured losses. However, when delicate and expensive machinery is involved, it can be very costly. For example, the placing on-stream of a large turbine for electrical generation involves cranes and the need for skilled riggers. A fall of only six inches can result in cracked casings. A cracked casing is essentially a total loss to the turbine. Since a turbine can cost in the hundreds of thousands of dollars, the potential loss severity is large. The exposure is increased when the underwriter is also providing business interruption insurance during course of construction for the same perils.

Builders' Risk and Probable Maximum Loss

The underwriter should recognize that in many structures, particularly noncombustible and fire resistive ones, the most dangerous time is during the course of construction.

When estimating the probable maximum loss, the following are major underwriting considerations:

1. Key structural members are exposed to an increase in hazard.
2. Sprinkler protection cannot be completed prior to the building being fully enclosed.

3. Fire walls will, in all likelihood, not have been fully closed off with approved fire doors; neither will vertical openings.
4. Duct work will not have required dampers.
5. Guards may not be fully trained nor visiting all areas of the premises.
6. Water for fighting fires may not be available at all or may not be available in sufficient quantity and pressure.
7. Fire department personnel may not be familiar with the building or the area, causing a delay in fighting a fire.
8. Construction equipment and materials on the grounds may hamper effective fire fighting efforts.

These items and the hazards mentioned earlier suggest that losses generally will be much greater than when the building is complete and occupied. Quite frequently the probable maximum loss for any type of construction will approach 100 percent. A major exception might be a housing development if there is sufficient distance between dwellings.

Builders' Risk Selection Decisions

Clearly, a building in the course of construction introduces additional hazards. But the underwriter has selection, coverage, risk improvement and pricing options with which to deal with these hazards. The expected value of small losses can be nullified with deductibles, the use of an inland marine unfiled form provides the requisite latitude for pricing each exposure to loss, and loss control services can minimize frequency and severity.

In addition, the underwriter can include warranties in the policy requiring:

1. periodic waste and debris disposal and site cleanup;
2. guard services;
3. adherence to accepted standards, such as ASCE specifications for poured concrete, building codes, and so on; and
4. adequate public water supply and adequate standpipes, extinguishers, and other private protection devices.

In the final analysis, as in almost every insurance transaction, the builders' risk underwriter must be satisfied that the people insured are qualified. If the contractor is experienced in a given type of construction, if he or she has a skilled and stable work force, if the project size is within the contractor's capability, and the contractor has adequate financial resources, the inherent risks are reduced.

SUMMARY

Commercial property underwriting begins with an analysis of the physical hazards. The acronym COPE, which stands for construction, occupancy, protection, and exposures, delineates the major categories of physical hazards.

Building construction is divided into six classes:

1. frame,
2. joisted masonry,
3. noncombustible,
4. masonry noncombustible,
5. modified fire resistive, and
6. fire resistive.

In addition to the type of construction, the design of the structure is of major importance. High-rise buildings and buildings with large horizontal spaces present unique underwriting problems. The combustibility of interior finishes and interior decorations must also be determined. The age of a building may also affect its acceptability. Older buildings are often constructed on the basis of outmoded building codes.

Data concerning a particular building may be obtained from the application, rate cards and manuals, bureau reports, inspection reports, diagrams drawn by inspectors, and local building codes. A particularly hazardous portion of commercial property underwriting deals with buildings in the course of construction. At this time, no matter what the designed occupancy, the building site is in effect occupied by the contractors who are soldering, welding, cutting, painting, and engaged in other hazardous processes. On an "all-risks" basis, collapse, testing, and breakage of structural components are perils which require careful underwriting.

Chapter Notes

1. Francis L. Brannigan, *Building Construction for the Fire Service* (Boston: National Fire Protection Association, 1971), p. 192.
2. *Building Construction for the Fire Service*, p. 192.
3. *Fire Protection Handbook*, 15th ed. (Quincy, MA: National Fire Protection Association, 1981), pp. 5-49, 5-50.
4. Insurance Services Office, *Commercial Fire Rating Schedule* (New York, 1977), pp. 3-4. Also in the ISO *Commercial Lines Manual*.
5. Insurance Services Office, *Commercial Fire Rating Schedule*, p. 4, Revision No. 4, 4-78.
6. *Fire Protection Handbook*, p. 5-33.

CHAPTER 5

Occupancy

INTRODUCTION

Occupancy or the use to which a structure is put is a prime consideration in commercial property underwriting. Just as construction, exposures, and protection are factors that have a bearing on loss potential, the operations and processes conducted within a structure introduce certain hazards influencing loss frequency and severity. The designed occupancy affects the characteristics of the structure itself in most cases as does the compatibility of the designed versus actual occupancy. The structures in a chemical refinery differ markedly from those in a steel mill, for example.

THE RATING OF OCCUPANCY HAZARDS

Commercial fire rating systems, such as that promulgated by ISO, provide an indication of the degree of occupancy hazard that is present in a particular classification. In the ISO system, each occupancy is assigned a Standard Classification of Occupancy Hazards (SCOH) code and a Commercial Statistical Plan (CSP) code. The ISO occupancy rating system includes four factors:

1. the basic occupancy charge;
2. the combustibility of contents, furniture, and fixtures;
3. the susceptibility of contents, furniture, and fixtures; and
4. additional occupancy hazards.

The Basic Occupancy Charge

This *basic occupancy charge*, which ranges from 10 percent to 1,000 percent (the percentages and to what they apply are explained in the pricing chapter), was designed for pricing purposes, although it also provides an indication of the relative hazard of the occupancy. There is clearly a great difference in the occupancy hazards between a parking garage with five or fewer spaces with a charge of 10 percent and a dry log sawmill sawing unbarked logs with a charge of 800 percent.[1]

While the essence of any rating system is to produce a premium that is commensurate with the hazard, the degree of hazard presented by a particular occupancy is still a major underwriting consideration for three reasons. First, the degree of hazard affects the size of the fire line that the underwriter is willing to accept. Second, occupancy is an important characteristic that must be evaluated when analyzing the composition of a book of business. A book of fire business made up entirely of saw mills would produce excellent average premium per unit but would also represent a high level of exposure to loss unlikely to win favor with reinsurers. Third, the basic hazard of the occupancy provides an insight into the importance of additional hazards which might be present in a particular risk. For example, while poor housekeeping is never desirable, the effect of poor housekeeping in an office building on the one hand and a sawmill on the other are different. If the basic occupancy hazard is high, the effect of any additional hazards is magnified.

Combustibility

Combustibility refers to the ability of something to ignite and burn. The combustibility of the contents usually found in a particular occupancy is a major determinant of the overall fire hazard. The ISO Commercial Fire Rating Schedule ranks the combustibility of contents according to five classes from noncombustible to rapid or flash burning, as described below.[2] Each class looks at the merchandise or materials, including furniture, stock, or equipment of the occupancy. This classification system is shown in Exhibit 5-1.

Noncombustible (C-1) This class includes "merchandise or materials, including furniture, stock or equipment which in permissible quantities do not in themselves constitute an active fuel for the spread of fire." An example of such an occupancy could be clay or glass products or metalworking (manufacturing). Since the basis of the combustibility grading system is the effect of the contents on the structure, this classification cannot be used in any case where the

Exhibit 5-1
Combustibility Classifications*

C-1	Noncombustible
C-2	Limited Combustibility
C-3	Combustible
C-4	Free burning
C-5	Rapid burning or flash burning

* Adapted with permission from Insurance Services Office, *Commercial Fire Rating Schedule* (New York: ISO, 1975), pp. 26.1 (Revision No. 7, 1-83) and 27 (Revision No. 7, 1-83).

occupancy contains sufficient combustible material to cause structural damage.

Limited Combustibility (C-2) This class includes occupancies which contain merchandise or materials of low combustibility and limited concentrations of combustible materials. Occupancies in this classification might include offices and banks, barber and beauty shops, habitational occupancies, and hospitals.

Combustible (C-3) This class includes occupancies with merchandise or materials of *moderate* combustibility. This includes mercantile occupancies such as food, hardware, and household appliance stores.

Free Burning (C-4) In this occupancy class, the merchandise or materials usually found burn freely and constitute an active fuel. These occupancies include baled cotton, furniture stock, and wood products.

Rapid or Flash Burning (C-5) This occupancy class contains merchandise or materials which represent an extreme fire hazard to the structure. The characteristics of the materials in these occupancies include contents which either:

1. burn with a great intensity,
2. spontaneously ignite and are difficult to extinguish,
3. give off flammable or explosive vapors at ordinary temperatures, or
4. as a result of an industrial process, produce large quantities of dust or other finely divided debris subject to flash fire or explosion.[3]

Examples of occupancies in this class might include ammunition, explosives, mattress manufacturing, and upholsterers.

Exhibit 5-2
Susceptibility Classifications*

Class	Description	Examples
S-1	Minimal damage	Pig iron, marble, heavy metals
S-2	Slight damage	Sheet metal, green hides or skins
S-3	Moderate damage	Boots, shoes, household appliances
S-4	Heavy damage	Books, clothing, furniture
S-5	Extreme loss (total loss possible)	Animals, birds, explosives, flowers, furs

*Adapted with permission from Insurance Services Office, *Commercial Fire Rating Schedule* (New York: ISO, 1975), p. 27.1 (Revision No. 7, 1-83).

Susceptibility

The severity of a particular fire loss is related not only to the combustibility of the materials within the structure, but also to the susceptibility of those materials to damage from fire, smoke, and water. A relatively small fire may produce a heavy monetary loss if the contents of the building are destroyed by smoke contamination. Contents, furniture, and fixtures of occupancies are classified by ISO ranging from occupancies which would likely suffer minimal damage to those that would suffer extreme loss. This is shown in Exhibit 5-2.

Additional Occupancy Hazards In addition to the basic occupancy charge and the determination of the combustibility and susceptibility of the materials found in the occupancy, surcharges may be made for extra hazards found in a particular risk. An example is the charge for cooking. Since restaurants have cooking included in their basic occupancy charge, this hazard is usual to that occupancy. On the other hand, a small industrial plant may have a complete employee cafeteria with a full commercial kitchen. This cooking hazard would be charged for in addition to the basic occupancy charge of the manufacturing classification. It is useful for the underwriter to keep these hazards in mind since their presence may have a major effect on the desirability of a particular risk. These additional occupancy hazards are shown in Exhibit 5-3.

Additional Classifications of Contents

ISO also classifies occupancies with regard to exposure to sprinkler

Exhibit 5-3
Additional Occupancy Hazards*

> Chemicals, acids or gases—storage and handling
> Combustible or flammable liquids—storage and handling
> Combustible or flammable liquids—painting or coating
> Highly combustible materials
> Cooking and cooking equipment
> Dust collection and refuse removal systems
> Heat producing or utilizing devices
> High piled stocks
> Smoking control (control of smoking in hazardous areas)
> Miscellaneous hazardous conditions:
>   a. Electrical equipment defects
>   b. Housekeeping
> Auxiliary or incidental operations or processes

*Adapted with permission from Insurance Services Office, *Commercial Fire Rating Schedule* (New York: ISO, 1975), pp. 96.1 (Revision No. 7,1-83) and 108 (Revision No. 6, 1-82).

leakage (slight, moderate, or high); vandalism or malicious mischief (a rating of one to four); earthquake (a rating of one to four); and the sprinkler protection occupancy class or SPOC (a rating of one to six used to determine the sprinkler system water supply requirements).

COMMON AND SPECIAL HAZARDS

Physical occupancy hazards may be separated into two categories, *common hazards* which are present in virtually every commercial occupancy, and *special hazards* which are found in a particular occupancy.

These are broad categories developed for convenience in analysis but they are not truly mutually exclusive. The circumstance in which a hazard occurs in a particular occupancy may take what is normally considered a common hazard and endow it with unique or special characteristics. An example is housekeeping which means the general cleanliness of the area, such as storage and disposal of trash or wastes, and the uncollected litter in the work area (e.g., waste, trash, packing materials, cigarette butts, paper, rags, and sawdust or woodchips). This is of concern for all occupancy classifications, but it can range from a minor concern in an office occupancy to a major consideration in the case of sawdust and woodchips in a furniture manufacturing occupancy. Other common hazards include housekeeping, including trash disposal, heating and air conditioning equipment, common electrical equipment and lighting, and smoking materials. (Cooking is usually considered a common hazard but in some cases such as a restaurant, it may also be a special hazard.) Each of these common hazards is described in Chapter 2. In that chapter, the term common hazard was not used since it is used primarily in conjunction with a discussion of occupancies when distinguishing common and special hazards.

Examples of special hazards include welding and the use of volatile chemicals in an industrial process. The list of occupancy classes is quite long and the list of special hazards is even longer. This chapter now looks first at broad industry classes together with some of their major characteristics. Following that, certain occupancy classes are examined indicating the type of hazards that are present. This represents only a small sample of the subject area. The analysis of occupancy hazards is a full-time task for the commercial property underwriter, because building materials and industrial processes do not remain static but represent a dynamic, changing environment.

OCCUPANCY HAZARDS
GROUPED BY MAJOR CATEGORIES

In the following section, occupancy hazards are considered for six broad categories. These are:

1. habitational,
2. office,
3. institutions,
4. mercantile,
5. service industries, and
6. manufacturing.

Any analysis of occupancy hazards by an underwriter should include the following:

1. ignition sources;
2. fire (fuel) load;
3. susceptibility and combustibility of contents, furniture, and fixtures;
4. interior finish of the structure; and
5. efficiency of management, encompassing:
   • control over housekeeping,
   • employee training and skills, and
   • loss programs.

Several of these will be addressed in this and the next section. The last item, however, is usually specific to an individual risk and can only be addressed when underwriting the risk. This section does not address each of these separately since some are not of major concern for a particular occupancy. This section tries to highlight the hazards of major concern, both common and special.

Habitational

This includes apartments, hotels, motels, and nursing homes. Habitational occupancies include the whole gamut of common hazards, with the addition of certain special hazards which are the result of the occupancy. Engineering a risk to reduce the loss potential from special hazards is very difficult for these classes.

The maintenance of the risk itself by the owners may be the most desirable situation, but supervising of the activities of the tenants cannot be accomplished in the same manner that an employer supervises its employees. The carelessness of one tenant is a source of potential loss and may undo the loss control efforts of both the owner and other tenants.

These occupancies range from modern high-rise structures to old buildings converted for the purpose. While new construction is built in accordance with modern building codes, the converted building may include much improvisation. Therefore the older building requires closer analysis of wiring, heating, and trash disposal systems than the newer structure.

The financial stability of the owner is an important underwriting consideration throughout the habitational class. In addition to the usual financial ratios, the vacancy rate is an important indicator of business success in this class. Hotel and motel vacancy rates are often heavily influenced by seasonal factors, but the vacancy rate of the particular risk under consideration can always be compared with that of successful operations of the same size and type within the same geographic area.

Fire Ignition NFPA statistics show that for hotels and apartments, three of the primary factors in ignition are smoking, electrical short or arc, and miscellaneous, open flames (not defined).[4] Many of these statistics are broken down by *source* of heat of ignition and *form* of heat of ignition. For example, a source might be an electrical appliance, but the form may be an electrical short in that appliance. Smoking materials are a factor in 21.5 percent of the hotel fires and 33.6 percent of the apartment fires. Given the nature of these occupancies, it is virtually impossible for the management to sufficiently control the incidence of smoking. Therefore, loss control efforts in these classes must focus on structural characteristics such as fire doors to contain the fires when they occur and private detection and suppression systems such as alarm systems and sprinklers to minimize the damage from the fires.

Combustibility and Susceptibility of Contents The existence of combustible contents in habitational occupancies contributes to fire severity. Mattress fires due to careless smoking in bed have resulted in extremely serious apartment, hotel, and nursing home fires. Such contents are not only subject to serious fire loss, but also are susceptible to loss from water damage, smoke, contamination, breakage, and other consequential damage.

Many hotels and motels have carpentry workshops where furniture is repaired, refinished, or reupholstered. The operation presents many of the hazards of a furniture factory or upholstering shop, such as the storage of paints, volatile solvents, and the use of combustible stuffing materials and fabrics. In addition there will be storage areas for surplus furniture, mattresses, and other items. To reduce the possibility of loss, these rooms should be sprinklered and cut off from the rest of the building in properly enclosed noncombustible rooms. Enclosed metal storage closets should be used for storing of paints and solvents and the room should be ventilated to carry off the fumes. Upholstering supplies should also be stored in metal storage bins.

Storage areas available to tenants of an apartment house present many hazards. Many types of personal property, flammable and often highly damageable, are found in these areas with often questionable housekeeping. Control of these hazards is difficult since often storage areas are accessible to both tenants and nontenants. Children frequently use them as play areas. The hazards of smoking or children playing with matches may exist. Prevention of fires in storage areas requires exceptional enforcement of security measures.

Hazards

Cooking. The cooking hazard exists in the majority of habitational occupancies and essentially becomes a special hazard. Every apartment dwelling has a kitchen or kitchenette with a domestic type of gas or electric stove. Hotel or motel eating facilities will range from the kitchenette in certain rooms, to the coffee shop, to the full restaurant facility. Nursing homes will have a similar hazard. Regardless of the type of cooking involved, the hazard exists and loss control measures must be taken. The previously cited NFPA statistics show cooking to be a factor in less than 10 percent of the fires.

Heating and Air Conditioning. Heating systems vary from the complex plant installed in a large metropolitan hotel to the wall heater in a seasonal hotel. The system may provide heat via a hot air duct system, steam radiators, hot water pipes, and electrical or gas space heaters. Regardless of the type of installation, it should be properly installed and properly maintained. The space heater which will be operated by the tenant should be so installed that combustibles cannot be stored near the open flame.

Today most units are air conditioned. Since air conditioning ducts are found throughout the building, they will, unless properly protected, transmit flames and smoke. Automatic dampers, which act as fire doors within the duct system to prevent the spread of smoke or fire, should be required. The dampers serve as cutoffs, particularly where a duct pierces a wall or goes through a floor. With the air being pushed through the ductwork by a motorized fan, automatic controls are provided to stop the fan in the event there is a fire within the equipment or in the building.

Plumbing. The amount of plumbing in habitational occupancies is quite extensive. Each apartment has a kitchen and bathrooms and there are usually bathrooms in each motel or hotel room. The kitchens and bathrooms of nursing homes are sizable. These units require a network of cold and hot water pipes and sanitation pipes running throughout the building. Tenants who permit water to overflow from sinks and toilets may cause severe water damage to their contents, warp wooden floors, and cause damage to lower floors.

In addition to the plumbing installed for sanitation and drinking purposes, a building heated by steam or hot water systems also requires a network of pipes. If the building is sprinklered, or has standpipes, the leakage hazard is increased. To avoid freezing during cold spells these systems should be insulated.

Panel heating or radiant heating systems with hot water pipes embedded in the walls, ceilings, or floors are subject to several hazards. Unless these are properly insulated, the pipes may freeze and break, requiring tearing up the concrete to repair the pipe. If there is subsidence, the piping is also subject to breakage. If the walls containing the pipes were torn from the building by severe winds, the damage to the heating system would be severe. Whatever the cause of the damage, repairs are extensive and costly.

Since plumbing must go through walls and floors, all openings should be fire stopped. For example, in one recent fire a fire-resistive apartment house sustained serious damage to two floors because of the lack of fire stopping around plumbing between floors. The fire spread through both floors and was so intense that the steel in the flooring buckled.

Offices

The office occupancy is a relatively low hazard classification. Materials found in offices are usually of limited combustibility and susceptible only to slight damage. Certain office buildings may include other features such as restaurants or heliports which represent special hazards. This occupancy ranges from the fire-resistive high rise on one end of the scale to the suite of offices located over a mercantile occupancy in a two-story frame building at the other end.

Fire Ignition The acts or omissions causing over half the fires in this occupancy were incendiary acts and mechanical failures. In 26.8 percent of the fires electrical arc or overload was a factor in ignition. Wiring systems are clearly a cause of concern with office occupancies. This is particularly true with respect to older buildings built to outmoded codes and in those buildings where substantial remodeling has taken place. Three other leading forms of heat of ignition are open flames or sparks, explosives or fireworks and exposure fires. Heating and electrical distribution equipment were the two leading ignition sources.[5]

Fuel Loads General design practice for office buildings assumes fuel loads of between twenty and thirty pounds per square foot in office buildings.[6] As noted in Chapter 2, materials employed in office furnishings and decorations have changed over the years. Older wooden desks and filing cabinets have given way to steel equipment, reducing the hazard from this source. Steel desks and filing cabinets can reduce the fuel load measurably because they do not contribute any fuel to the fire and can protect their contents from fire. Exhibit 5-4 indicates the effects of steel containers on fuel load.

The percentages in the body of Exhibit 5-4 indicate the level to which the fuel load has been reduced (i.e., the lower the number, the greater the reduction). This is attributed to the use of a particular type of steel office equipment. The base level is the case when all the contents are in the open.

There are three other trends in modern offices which tend to increase the fire hazard. One is the increased use of plastics in office machines, decor, and interior finish. Computer media are frequently combustible plastics, particularly tapes.

The second trend is the increased use of movable partitions and wall modules to provide more flexibility in office space utilization. These partitions are usually less than ceiling height and are used to provide more of an air of spaciousness, particularly when dividing a large room into numerous small offices and reception areas. Since these partitions stop far short of the ceiling, the result is a single open area which is one

Exhibit 5-4
Effects of Steel Containers on Fuel Load*

Effective Impact of Ordinary Combustible Materials in Steel Containers			
	Part of Combustibles in Containers		
Container	Less than ½	½ to ¾	More than ¾
Backed and partitioned shelving	75%	75%	75%
Shelving with doors and transfer cases	60%	50%	25%
Filing cabinets and desks	40%	20%	10%

*Reprinted with permission from Gordon P. McKinnon, ed., *Fire Protection Handbook*, 14th ed. (Boston: National Fire Protection Association, 1976), p. 8–40.

fire division. This makes prevention of ignition of paramount importance since a fire will quickly involve the entire room if flashover occurs.

The third trend is the increased use of elaborate decor in offices. Frequently heavy drapes, wall coverings, and other decorations are added to offices. Wall-to-wall carpeting is often found in executive offices. Much of this decor is both flammable and easily damaged. Recent data and fire experience has shown that massively higher levels of *fire intensity* (a measure of the level of energy produced by a fire) will be found in rooms or spaces that have combustible finish relative to those without combustible finish.[7]

Other factors affecting fire (fuel) load especially in offices include the following:

1. The larger the exposed surface area of combustible, the faster the rate of fire development.
2. The higher the percentage of space occupied by combustible material versus the total space available, the more likely and faster the development of fire.
3. The higher the surface flame spread rating of any material, the more rapid the development of fire.
4. Combustibles on a ceiling contribute to flame spread and fire development more than those on a wall.
5. Combustibles near a wall or ceiling contribute more to fire development than those away from the walls and ceiling.
6. The combination of combustible walls and ceilings and proximity of combustible materials, particularly in a corner arrangement, contribute more to the development and spread of fire than the same

materials in other positions in the room.

7. Various materials have various inherent rates of heat release when burning. The higher the rate of heat release of the material, the more rapid the development.[8]

Hazards Today most office occupancies have eating facilities for employees. These range from a simple coffee urn to a lounge with domestic cooking appliances, or a cafeteria which provides hot meals. In an office, the coffee urn or domestic cooking appliance must be kept clean. A frayed electrical cord on the coffee urn is an obvious source of potential loss. The careless office employee who permits the water to boil over, thereby extinguishing the flame in a gas burner, may be responsible for an explosion.

Solvents used for cleaning office machinery should be stored in secure containers in locked cabinets. A minimum quantity should be kept in the office with bulk storage in steel containers or cabinets.

Electronic computer systems range from the highly complex installation to the minicomputer used for recordkeeping in a relatively small office. A fire will result in a heavy loss since the equipment is susceptible to damage from heat, fire, corrosive fumes, gases, and smoke. It is also possible that water used to fight the fire will damage the equipment if not removed immediately. NFPA has established standards for computer installations and wiring.

A large computer is usually located in a separate room. This room should be kept immaculately clean, air conditioned, and under strict supervision. The furnishings should be noncombustible and necessary supplies of combustible materials such as paper and recording media should be kept in enclosed metal file cases or cabinets. Quantities in use at any one time should be kept at a minimum.

In metropolitan areas heliports are often located on the roofs of high-rise buildings. The ports serve as landing areas for passenger helicopters and some freight delivery. The buildings are subject to damage from the helicopter during landings and takeoffs. High octane fuel is present which could cause a fire or explosion. On the other hand, the presence of the heliport on top of a high-rise building has some distinct advantages when fighting a fire in the middle or upper floors of the structure. Fire department helicopters (if any) may be able to deliver men and equipment to the top of the building to fight the blaze from above.

Institutions

This category includes schools, churches, municipalities, and hospitals. This would also include special purpose facilities such as prisons and police and fire stations.

Fire Ignition   Due to the wide variety of occupancies found within this category it is difficult to generalize with respect to fire ignition sources and forms. Arson is clearly a major underwriting problem. NFPA statistics show that when the incendiary act and suspicious origin fires are combined, this represents 50.9 percent of the cases for churches.[9] The same statistics show that incendiary acts and suspicious fires account for 74.5 percent of the school and college fires. In virtually all of these cases this is arson against the insured, so moral hazard of the insured is not a major factor. Rather, these fires usually occur as a result of blighted neighborhoods and outbreaks of urban violence. Another factor is the trend of recent years which has found churches, schools, and colleges to be the focal point for social movements and unrest. Many of these social issues arouse deep emotional responses in the community leading to violence, property destruction, and arson.

Combustible, Explosive, or Susceptible Supplies   School, college, hospital, or municipal occupancies often contain hazardous supplies. These include chemicals used in science programs, cleaning solvents, and the hospital laboratory or pharmacy contents. These items should be stored in metal enclosed receptacles with a limited amount in use at any one time. Only that amount being used should be outside of the receptacles. Rooms where such supplies are used should have adequate ventilation to carry off fumes and gases which could explode. Bunsen burners should be set on a metal base and connected to the gas source with rubber tubing. The gas shutoff should be at the permanent pipe. The supervision of chemistry students and the security of laboratory supplies are items of concern at schools and colleges. Maintenance shops and storage rooms in schools and hospitals and similar institutions may contain high hazard wood and metal working operations and supplies of combustible materials. Craft shops in schools and hospitals may contain highly combustible supplies.

Some institutional contents may be highly susceptible. These include hospital technical equipment and church artifacts which are not only susceptible to a serious loss by fire or water, but also represent high values. Stained and leaded glass windows, vestments, and church fixtures are especially susceptible and are also subject to vandalism or theft.

Hazard Analysis

Cooking.   The cooking hazard may be less severe in an institutional risk than it would be in a restaurant. Food preparation is not continuous, being limited to the number of meals provided by the institution. A grade or high school as a rule would be limited to lunches, whereas a hospital would prepare three meals. Dietary considerations in many institutions limit the amount of deep-fried foods served. These cooking facilities nevertheless require proper maintenance with hoods and ducts being routinely cleaned. There should also be an automatic extinguishing system.

Cooking in a church is usually limited to "church suppers" and similar events. Appliances are usually of the household variety. Since the cooking will be done by the church group sponsoring the meal, it is left up to many individuals to keep the equipment clean. Housekeeping is not easily controlled and carelessness may be a hazard in such cases. Ignorance as to how to properly operate the equipment is also a concern.

Municipalities, depending on the services provided, could have a wide range of cooking hazards such as employee cafeterias and institutional cooking for prisons, orphanages, and nursing homes. A city commissary may exist for purchasing foodstuffs in quantity and bulk preparation of food. Fire preventive measures such as sprinkler systems, fire extinguishers, prompt removal of combustibles and trash, and careful housekeeping should be maintained.

Heating and Air Conditioning. The heating systems in an institutional occupancy are usually substantial. Large boiler and furnace systems may require employment of a full-time engineer. The use of most churches is not continuous and heat is often turned down or even off between services. Often the thermostat is turned very high at the time of the church service. This forcing of an excessive amount of heat could result in a boiler explosion or a fire. Due to its infrequent use, the church heating system may not be properly maintained and combustibles may be stored near the unit.

An institutional heating unit, because of its large size, should be in a separate enclosed room isolated from the rest of the building. The furnace room should never be used as a storage area.

Many institutions are housed in old buildings with air conditioning systems added during remodeling. The adequacy of all wiring, the protection of vertical and horizontal wall and floor openings, and the location of fire dampers should be evaluated by an inspection.

Heat Treatment. Engineering and vocational schools are likely to contain hazards which are comparable to those found in industrial plants, such as heat treating of metals. These metals are heated in an oven or furnace and then bathed in a coolant which may be fish oil, salts, or chemicals. The temperature of the coolant must be carefully controlled to prevent possible fire or explosion. The immersion tank itself must also be protected with a hood to prevent water coming in contact with the contents and causing an explosion.

Oxygen and Gas Hazards. The use of oxygen and gases, as in a hospital, is a serious hazard. (Fire problems of enriched environments were discussed in Chapter 2.) Oxygen and ether constitute an explosive mixture. Anesthetics are usually combustible and open flames or electric sparks should be avoided in areas where anesthetics are used and stored.

Welding in school craft shops or city garages involves use of acetylene gas. Welding produces sparks which unless shielded will fly several feet from where the work is performed. Welding should be done in well-ventilated areas or separate rooms and there should be an asbestos shield to prevent flying sparks. There should be no combustibles in the area. An attendant should be on hand with a fire extinguisher and a bucket of sand ready to extinguish a fire. If the welding takes place on a wooden floor, the floor should be wetted down during the process.

These gases, anesthetics, oxygen, and acetylene must be properly stored in approved metal cylinders which are sealed with a fusible metal link. Storage of these cylinders should be in a separate fire division from the main building. The area should be well ventilated. If electrical motors and fans are used in the storage area, they should be explosion proof with blades and bearings made of nonsparking materials.

Plumbing Systems. Plumbing systems in institutions are quite extensive due to the requirements of sanitation, cooking, laboratory, and other needs. In addition, piping frequently will be installed throughout the building to supply water for private fire protection consisting of sprinklers, standpipes, pumps, and gravity tanks. These should be properly maintained.

Routine flow and pressure tests should be made by trained personnel. The equipment should be protected from freezing in unheated areas such as entry ways, attics, and beneath floors and platforms.

Institutional occupancies, like habitational and office occupancies, are subject to abuse by the public. Toilet and sink overflow and plugged drains often result in water damage. Avoiding such contingencies is extremely difficult and requires constant monitoring and education of the institutional population. Plumbing systems in schools are especially subject to vandalism.

Financial. The problem of obtaining scarce operating funds often leads to overzealous campaigns to reduce expenses. Upkeep and maintenance of the premises frequently are the first to suffer in cost cutting programs. Everything else being equal, an insured strapped for operating funds is a poor risk.

Age of Buildings. Old buildings are common among institutional occupancies. Schools in changing or deteriorating areas are often willfully neglected. Church congregations dwindle and those remaining find it financially impossible to maintain old church buildings. Well-established hospitals in cities are often in old buildings; modernization and upkeep are very expensive. Older buildings frequently do not have necessary fire walls or cutoffs.

Mercantile Occupancies

This category includes retail stores such as department stores, clothing stores, hardware stores, and specialty shops and grocery stores. A rapidly growing segment of this category is shopping centers, particularly those with covered malls.

Fire Ignition Three forms of heat of ignition accounted for almost 75 percent of the fires in this category. These are electrical arcs or overload, heat from smoking materials, and open flames or sparks.[10] Clearly, control of smoking and the condition of electrical wiring are major underwriting concerns for this occupancy category.

Incendiary and suspicious fires constitute almost 25 percent of the frequency of fires in this category. Moral hazard is an important underwriting consideration. Analysis should include any past history of suspicious fire losses, the prosperity of the business, and the length of time in business. Other factors include the credit standing of the owner, the existence of labor problems, and the possible effects of technological or market changes on this particular store.

Cooking in a supermarket or department store restaurant and cooking demonstrations (e.g., warming samples of new foods) adds the hazards of a commercial restaurant in close proximity to highly susceptible merchandise.

Combustible or Susceptible Contents In mercantile occupancies the combustibility of the contents varies depending upon the merchandise being sold. Usually the entire inventory is susceptible to fire, smoke, and water damage.

Many mercantile operations carry highly combustible items in inventory or as operating supplies. A sporting goods store usually stocks ammunition, fuel for camping stoves, and portable lanterns. Hardware stores stock paints, varnishes, solvents, and other combustible liquids. A fast growing variation of the hardware store is the home center which, in addition to the items just enumerated, stocks lumber and building supplies. A furniture store has refinishing chemicals and polishes as operating supplies. The store may also provide upholstering service. Even the appliance and television retailer may operate a repair service using combustible liquids.

In a retail operation, shelving, showcases, displays on the selling floor, and adequate storage facilities off the selling floor must be provided. Unless proper care is taken, the operation can become congested with accumulations of cartons, excelsior, and other debris. Housekeeping is important since unpacking of merchandise can generate a high volume of combustible trash. This trash and other debris should be promptly removed from the premises. Proper containers and storage facilities should be provided for highly combustible items. The public should be prohibited from entering storage and service areas and smoking should not be permitted in these areas.

Most stocks of merchandise are subject to water damage and smoke. Women's clothing is especially subject to severe loss from smoke and water damage. The stock of a hardware store will rust from the water used in fighting a fire. Residual damage such as smoke and water, therefore, can turn a small fire into a large loss.

Food in the neighborhood store or supermarket usually will be destroyed by health authorities should there be a fire and smoke damage on the premises. In this class a small fire can result in a large loss.

Service Occupancies

This category includes dry cleaners, laundries, and automobile service stations. Another segment of this category includes upholstery shops and furniture and appliance repair shops.

Fire Ignition The service category includes such a diverse assortment of occupancies that it is not useful to generalize with respect to the fire ignition sequence. This does not mean that the underwriter should ignore this facet of the analysis of these occupancies. It does mean that data with respect to the usual fire causes for these classes must be developed from either company files or from statistics gathered by industry associations. One fire source that is common to many service industries is the ignition of flammable liquids such as gasoline in service stations and solvents in dry cleaners.

Flammable or Combustible Liquids Solvents, oils, paints, and grease are highly combustible. Due to the combustibility of solvents, dry cleaning operations should be done in a separate area. This area should be well ventilated, all equipment should be grounded, and lighting and other switches should be explosion proof. To reduce the possibility of fire or explosion, most cleaners use a Stoddard solvent with a flash point comparable to that of kerosene.

Repair shops use flammable paints, refinishing fluids, and cleaning solvents which should be used with care in a well ventilated area.

Hazards

Housekeeping. In both dry cleaners and laundries, lint escapes from drying units and settles on machinery, motors, and equipment. Lint accumulation presents both a fire and explosion hazard which is compounded in a dry cleaning operation by the accumulation of vapors from the solvents that permeate the premises. Therefore, housekeeping is of prime importance. Timely cleaning of the lint traps and the removal of lint from machinery is essential. Proper ventilation to remove lint and accumulated vapors from the air is required.

The quality of storage provides an indication of the overall quality of housekeeping. The inventory should be stored in a manner that is prescribed for the type of commodity. Flammable items such as solvents, fluids, and paints should be stored in metal enclosed lockers. Metal containers with self-closing lids should be used for trash, and trash and rubbish should be routinely removed to an outside storage area away from the building.

Welding and Painting. Service stations, in addition to gasoline, oil, and other flammable liquids, may have acetylene tanks to provide gas for welding and cutting. Welding and cutting in rooms where vapor from flammable gases exists is an extreme hazard. Spray painting is also hazardous unless the station is kept very clean, ventilated, and the hazard is properly controlled. The best control is to limit welding, cutting, and spray painting to an approved paint booth isolated from gasoline and vapors.

Heating Processes. Dry cleaners and laundries require a sizable boiler which should be in a separate room fully isolated from the rest of the premises. In addition, hand irons, dryers, mangles, and presses are all heat-generating equipment. Electrical equipment should have "on-off" warning lights, be adequately grounded, and have master cutoff switches. Steam pipes from the boiler should be insulated and combustibles should not be stored close to the pipes.

Soldering irons in television and appliance shops should have "on-off" lights and be used on a metal table with a metal resting stand.

Although the refrigeration unit may not be thought of in terms of a heating process, the motors will generate heat. Motor installations have a grill or screen permitting air circulation. Blockage of this ventilation will cause the motor to run hot, constituting an ignition source.

Other Hazards. Self-service operations represent a growing segment of this category. Self-service laundries, dry cleaners, and gas stations are very common. Although self-service equipment is designed to simplify its use, a trained attendant should be on hand. The attendant should be ready to react to an emergency if the equipment is misused or if a defect should develop. Self-service operations are subject to vandalism, particularly self-service laundries which may operate on a twenty-four-hour basis. Without an attendant, the underwriter generally will find such a risk unacceptable for *any* property coverage.

Gas stations are also subject to vehicle collision damage to the gas pumps, spillage of gasoline from overfilling, and gasoline leakage from underground storage tanks.

Manufacturing and Wholesale Distribution

The occupancies within this category vary according to the nature of the product being manufactured or distributed. Each occupancy must be considered on its own merits with the underwriter's evaluation based on the special hazards found in that occupancy.

A steel manufacturer has blast furnaces, rolling mills, and associated steel processing equipment. A macaroni manufacturer has an extensive drying process and a severe dust hazard. The physical layout of the manufacturing plant may be extensive with separate buildings for each phase of the manufacturing process; or, it may be a small one-product operation with a few employees concentrated in a small area of a multitenant loft building.

The wholesale distributor requires extensive warehousing facilities. Large undivided areas and high ceilings are common characteristics of a warehousing operation. The warehouse may contain a single product or a variety of commodities. Again, the underwriter must consider the wholesale distribution occupancy in terms of the commodities involved and the nature of that wholesaler's operations. Some wholesalers do a great deal of packing and crating which entails the hazards of highly combustible packing materials while other operations are limited to storage and shipping.

Fire Ignition   Again, it is difficult to generalize with respect to fire ignition sequence due to the diversity of the manufacturing and wholesale distribution category. However, within the industrial sector, there are certain characteristics of fire ignition which should be noted by the underwriter.

The first characteristic is the low incidence of incendiary and suspicious fires. According to NFPA statistics, these two categories together were involved in only 9.1 percent of the fires, based on frequency.[11] However, this type of fire has much greater than average severity, so that this hazard can by no means be ignored. The leading act or omission causing industrial fires is mechanical failure or malfunction which resulted in 52.1 percent of the fires.[12] Given the vast array of machinery and equipment found in the industrial category, the underwriter should stress the quality of maintenance as an underwriting variable. The desirable manufacturing risk not only has good housekeeping, but also has an ongoing program of equipment inspection and maintenance.

Inventory Combustibility and Susceptibility The combustibility and susceptibility of inventory varies widely within the manufacturing and wholesale distribution occupancies. The characteristics of not only the finished product or commodity but also stocks of raw materials and semifinished goods must be considered. In manufacturing, finished products of relatively low hazard may have highly combustible or susceptible components.

The food wholesaler sustaining a relatively small fire may have a total loss with respect to inventory due to governmental regulation prohibiting the sale of such items. Similarly, the manufacturer of jewelry or precision instruments will sustain a more serious loss than the manufacturer of a more durable type of stock which may be more readily refinished in the event of damage.

Paper products are not only subject to fire but are also severely susceptible to water damage. It is not uncommon to have extensive water damage to paper stocks where there is actually minimal fire loss. Technological development has produced many uses of plastic substitutes for metal as components of a variety of products. Most plastics are highly susceptible to fire and heat.

Clothing and cloth products are susceptible to severe damage from fire, smoke, and water. Salvaging part of the inventory permeated by the odor of smoke or reprocessing that which is water soaked is an expensive process.

Wood product inventories are highly combustible and susceptible. Such inventories are not limited to furniture, but also include recreational vehicles, mobile homes, musical instruments, and toys and novelties.

A metal fabricator working with magnesium, beryllium, and similar metals is subject to extreme fire and explosion hazards. The metal itself may be highly combustible. This hazard is increased by the manufacturing processes of grinding, burning, or welding.

Regardless of the commodity, physical arrangement of the inventory and housekeeping are factors which must be evaluated. A congested layout contributes to loss severity. Aisle space should be adequate, with stocks stored on steel shelving or on pallets. High piling of stock should be avoided, particularly when the risk is sprinklered and high piling could block the sprinkler system. Flammable commodities should be stored separately from nonflammable stock. The storage of flammable items should be in accordance with NFPA standards.

Combustibility of Materials and Supplies The type of supplies necessary to an occupancy may introduce hazards which may not be as obvious to the underwriter as those presented by the inventory. Most occupancies include some form of packing and shipping materials, together with materials and supplies necessary to the production or warehousing of the inventory. These supplies should be evaluated in terms of storage, combustibility, and handling.

Paper goods such as cardboard cartons are commonly used for packing and shipping of finished products. Packing such as shredded paper or excelsior is used particularly with fragile items such as glassware. Recent technology has resulted in increased use of plastic packing material which can be molded to fit the item being packed. Where the commodity requires crating, such as for export, wooden crates provide the needed strength.

The type of packing material used will dictate the necessary loss control techniques. The packing and shipping area should be isolated from the balance of the operation preferably in a separate fire division with no accumulation of debris. All packing materials are combustible and should not be stored near boilers or any source of heat. Storage of supplies in stacks or piles can present a problem of excessive weight. This is particularly true with respect to cardboard, which is water absorbent. If stacks of cardboard become wet during a fire, structural damage to the building could result if the weight exceeds the floor load capacity. To reduce the possibility of this occurring, such stocks should be palletized.

Plastics, depending upon their chemical content, may burn or melt and should be stored in separate metal bins. Excelsior burns rapidly since it is a loose packing material with much air space. If excelsior is damp it is also subject to spontaneous combustion. Because of its flammability it should be stored in a metal packing bin with a self-closing cover, with only a minimal amount of the material in use at any one time.

Rack storage provides a horizontal and vertical flue for a fire to spread. In addition, overloading of the rack facility will cause it to collapse. The racks found in a warehousing operation may be not only high but also quite long. Sometimes it is advisable to have sprinklers within the racks and not just at the ceiling.

When an extensive amount of wood is used for crating, the operation has many of the elements of a woodworking or carpentry occupancy. Rough wood used must be stored, cut to size, and trimmed.

This results in dust and shavings, requiring an exhaust system and careful housekeeping.

Janitorial supplies are common to every risk. As previously noted, cleaning solvents and polishes are usually flammable and should be stored on metal shelving or in metal lockers. It is ironic that while good housekeeping may exist in the overall occupancy, it may not extend to the area where volatile and flammable supplies are stored.

Hazards

Heat Sources. This includes special power sources such as steam pressure vessels and turbines. These power sources are either direct drive electric motors, steam power with belts and shafts, or internal combustion engines.

Electric motors should be of the proper size and type for this purpose. Constant operation of these motors will cause overheating to the point that insulation may burn and a short circuit could cause a fire. To prevent overheating, the equipment should be kept clean, well lubricated, and routinely inspected. A simple test is to place the palm of the hand on the motor casing. If it is too hot for comfort, the motor is overloaded.

With steam power, pressure is built up within the boiler and unless the pressure is controlled the boiler will explode. The safety pressure relief valve is an important component of any steam boiler and should be frequently inspected. Steam pipes should be fully insulated to avoid heat loss and to reduce the hazard of heat transfer to combustibles. Bearings may become overheated unless kept clean and well lubricated. Drive belts should be kept taut to prevent the possibility of slippage and friction.

Internal combustion engines present several fire hazards. The exhaust system should be arranged so that there is adequate clearance between the exhaust stack and combustibles. It is not uncommon for the exhaust system to be run underground outside of the building. In this case it should be kept free from weeds and trash which could be ignited from the hot exhaust gases and possible backfires. If the fuel tank is fastened to the engine, it should be secure and not permitted to vibrate and loosen the fuel lines. The area in which the engine is located should be properly vented to carry off accumulations of fumes.

Heat Treatment Processes. Oil baths, annealing, hardening and tempering, high frequency induction heating, and molten salt baths are heat treatment processes which operate at extreme temperatures. The process area must be kept free of combustible materials. Hot sparks or slag could splash on combustibles, or hot metal objects could be placed on combustibles, if they are present. Usually tempering vats containing oil for quenching or rapid cooling of metal objects are used. These vats should have temperature controls, self-closing covers, and overflow pits and drains. Hoods should cover the vats to prevent water from getting into the vat, particularly from sprinkler systems.[13]

Welding and Cutting. Here, as in other occupancies, welding and burning operations are a principal cause of fires primarily due to the sparks and hot slag deposited on combustibles. Hazardous welding and cutting operations are found quite frequently in a variety of plants, and their presence is a problem. Usually, no one individual is responsible for control of this hazard.

Finishing Processes. A finishing process usually will be hazardous either* because of the flammability of the material used or the inherent nature of the process. Painting and finishing operations involve the use of oils and solvents which are subject to flash fires and explosion. Rags become paint soaked and should be disposed of in containers with tightly fitting covers. The finishing method used may be by hand, spraying, or dipping. Spray painting is the most hazardous.

Spray painting should be done in a well-ventilated area cut off from the rest of the operation or at least in an approved effective booth which contains the paint spray. Electrical fixtures should be explosion-proof and the booth should be kept clean. Dip tanks should be sturdily constructed of metal and secured to prevent overturning. Chemical extinguishers should be kept at hand close to a dip tank or spray booth. All paints, oils, and solvents should be stored in metal lockers and only the amount needed for the operation should be out in the open.

Sanding and buffing operations produce wood dust that settles on all surfaces, including any exposed overhead structural members. Therefore, an explosion hazard exists and flash fires may occur. Disposing of the dust and chips which accumulate necessitates not only routine cleaning but also an adequate exhaust system to remove the dust from the air.

Spontaneous Heating. Spontaneous heating is "the process of increase in temperature of a material without drawing heat from its surroundings...."[14] If the material is heated to ignition, it is called *spontaneous ignition* or *spontaneous combustion.* Spontaneous heating is actually an oxidation process, and the result of the process depends upon the rate of heat generation or oxidation, air supply, and the insulation properties of the immediate surroundings.

Spontaneous combustion will result if oil mops are left in a poorly ventilated closet. Vegetable fibers which have been processed for their oil content, such as cottonseed and copra, and other fibers with a natural high oil content such as hemp and sisal, are extremely hazardous. Such material should be in low piles and moved frequently. High piles of coal, wet hay, and sawdust are subject to spontaneous heating and should be checked regularly with probes or should have thermocouples inserted to warn of heat buildup.

Spontaneous heating can also result from paint residue or oils which are not particularly dangerous at ordinary temperatures but can be adversely affected by the heat of industrial drying ovens.

Friction and Static Electricity. Any manufacturing operation using machinery is subject to possible fire from friction as heat is built up between a pulley and sheave and a fast-moving, rubberized fabric belt. If the belt is ignited, flaming pieces will be thrown over a wide area. Occupancies that involve grinding, milling, or crushing of non-combustible materials are subject to possible buildup of friction which might ignite nearby combustible materials.

In addition to actual ignition, friction also creates static electricity by throwing off stationary electric charges. Static electricity is dangerous in grinding, milling, or crushing operations where flammable vapors, gases, or dust are present, since it provides an ignition source for fire and explosion. Detection equipment indicating the presence of static electricity should be installed. A common device used for detection purposes is a neon tube tester which glows when it comes in contact with a body charged with static electricity. Since static electricity occurs when the atmosphere is clear and dry and static charges will be eliminated if the relative humidity is high, the relative humidity should be kept as high as possible. Electrical equipment should be well grounded to prevent electrical charges from accumulating in the machinery.

Numerous industrial fires can be attributed to friction and static electricity as well as mechanical breakdown, so machinery should be carefully inspected and maintained. Also combustible material should not be placed close to equipment, and the ventilation system should be adequate to carry off any flammable vapors, gases, and dust.

Industrial Materials Handling Equipment. Most manufacturing and wholesale warehousing occupancies use industrial lift trucks for materials handling within the plant or warehouse or on the loading dock. Industrial lift trucks may be electrically operated using storage batteries as a power source or equipped with gasoline, diesel, or LP Gas internal combustion engines. Internal combustion engine vehicles create exhaust fumes and have the potential for leakage or spillage of fuel. In addition, fuel must be stored for their operation. Often careless operation of a lift truck results in collision with the building structure or machinery and equipment. Frequently the vision of the operator is hindered by the size of the load being carried and sprinkler pipes, refrigerant pipes, or steam pipes are damaged.

Areas in which such equipment is used should be well ventilated to carry off the exhaust fumes. Operators should be trained and qualified to use the equipment. There should be adequate aisle space, and potential obstructions should be removed or protected to minimize damage from collision.

Fuel supplies for the equipment should be stored and refueling of equipment should be accomplished outside and away from the building. If there is bulk gasoline storage in underground tanks, the fittings should be tight to avoid leakage and the tanks should have vents for the discharge of vapors during filling. Dispensing hoses and nozzles should have automatic shutoff valves to stop the flow of gasoline when the tank of the lift truck is filled.

LP Gas may be stored under pressure either in bulk tanks or cylinders. In either situation the location of the installation should be outside and away from the building, protected from possible damage from collision or vandalism. Battery-powered vehicles require frequent charging. If overcharged, the batteries emit hydrogen gas, which is flammable and odorless. The charging of the batteries should be confined to a well-ventilated, detached building.

Flammable Liquids. The storage and use of flammable liquids, solvents, and paints is a hazard that exists in most manufacturing risks to one degree or another. The volatile material may be inherent to the operation as in a metal shop or chemical plant or it may be incidental to the occupancy and only used for cleaning and maintenance.

Careless handling of flammable liquids is perhaps the greatest single hazard in a metal working occupancy. Oily metal parts are commonly washed in solvents which may be highly volatile and flammable. Oil coolants are used in the turning and milling of hard metals. Hydraulic oil under extreme pressure is used to operate hydraulic presses. Finishing the product may involve spray painting. Throughout the entire fabricating process a hazard is present not only from the existence and use of the flammable commodity but also from flammable or explosive vapors.

Plastics Manufacturing. Plastic materials consist of a combination of various chemical elements which can produce a solid or liquid state and can be cast molded, heated, or melted into a raw product which is then processed to produce a finished product. Finishing processes include (1) extrusion, which consists of forcing the raw material through a die to produce a particular shape; (2) injection molding, where the plastic compound is melted, then injected through a heated nozzle into a cooled, sealed mold; (3) pressing of the plastic in a heated mold under pressure; and (4) rolling of the plastic into strips.

Fire and explosion are major hazards in the plastics industry. Burning plastics produce poisonous gases, result in intense heat, and generate heavy black smoke, making it extremely difficult to fight any fire. Most plastics present an explosion hazard when finely divided as a powder or dust.

The construction of a building in which there is plastics manufacturing should be noncombustible or fire-resistive and designed for the purpose with hazardous operations in a separate fire division from the nonhazardous operations. There should be a comprehensive training program for personnel to assure that they not only have a thorough knowledge of their job assignments but also know how to react in an emergency situation.

Chemical Hazards. Chemical hazards involve a wide variety of materials, processes, and products ranging from paint manufacture to pharmaceuticals. Inspectors must be trained to identify the chemical hazards and to determine the adequacy of the storage, handling, and processing operations.

Considerations include identifying chemicals which should be stored in a building isolated from the main manufacturing plant. Proper construction of storage buildings varies depending on the characteristics of the chemical. Some chemicals require a vented storage area because of the explosive instability of the material.

Much information is available to both the underwriter and the engineer in analyzing chemical hazards. NFPA publication number 49, *Hazardous Chemical Data,* lists many chemicals together with their characteristics and the appropriate precautions. If the process involves an unlisted chemical, it is necessary to make a thorough evaluation of the chemical and process.

Explosive Dusts. Most dust particles when mixed with air in the proper proportion may explode. Certain types of dust, such as grain or flour dust, are particularly volatile.

Dust accumulation on machinery bearings creates friction. The accumulation of dust on shelving and structural members may result in a flash fire. When dust is present, housekeeping is most important. Bakeries are subject to accumulations of flour dust; coal dust is also highly explosive.

Dust from grinding, milling, and polishing of metal is very hazardous particularly with respect to lighter metals such as aluminum or magnesium. Wood dust or flour from large scale wood sanding operations may settle on structural members. If this dust is jarred loose an explosion may occur.

These types of operations produce a large amount of dust in the air which must be removed. The installation of suction fans, hoods, and forced ventilation should be so arranged as to prevent a cloud of the dust from forming. Electrical motors and other electrical equipment should be dustproof, and well grounded to prevent static electricity. Electric lights should have explosion proof fixtures. Where metal grinding is involved, magnets may be used to keep the particles from escaping into the air.

HAZARDS OF REPRESENTATIVE OCCUPANCY CLASSES

The following classes represent a sample drawn to illustrate typical occupany hazards frequently encountered in commercial property underwriting. In this section each occupancy is considered in isolation as if it were the only occupancy class found in the submission or renewal under consideration. Very frequently a submission will include a building which has either multiple occupancies or a single occupancy which includes several distinct types of operations. A high-rise office building, for example, may include a restaurant on its top floor. In this case the basic hazards of a restaurant are present, even though the risk is primarily an office occupancy.

Restaurant

Fire Ignition   The source of heat of ignition that is the leading cause of restaurant fires is cooking equipment. In addition, incendiary acts are involved in over 20 percent of the fires in this occupancy class.[15]

The Occupancy Rating   The basic charge for restaurants is 100 percent of the basic building grade. The furniture, fixtures, and contents of restaurants are rated C-3, combustible, and S-4, susceptible to heavy damage.

Hazard Analysis   The most severe cooking hazard is grease. The existence of grease is inevitable, particularly when there is a considerable amount of deep frying coupled with a failure to keep the area and appliances free from accumulation of grease. A fire is then almost a certainty. Hoods over the cooking appliance, grease filters, ducts, and exhaust fans should be cleaned weekly to prevent a fire from spreading. Automatic extinguishing systems should be installed so that a fire on the appliance or in the hoods or ducts will be quickly extinguished. As a prerequisite for acceptance of all commercial cooking system hazards, the conservative approach would be to insist that the insured have a maintenance agreement including periodic inspections with a qualified professional servicing firm.

Other considerations in restaurants include the fact that they are often located in old or remodeled buildings. This may result in the presence of concealed spaces. Inadequate ventilation or exhaust systems present another hazard. The building service systems, such as the heating and air conditioning systems, may be a cause of loss. Another hazard is the presence of overloaded or frayed electrical circuits and the use of extension cords. Careless disposal of cigarettes and trash is particularly hazardous.

It is not infrequent that a fire occurs because of ashtrays not being emptied prior to the removal of the tablecloth after a meal has been served. As a matter of expediency, the ashtray is emptied onto the tablecloth which is placed in a container with other soiled linens. If there is a smoldering cigarette, the result could be a heavy loss.

A contributing factor in many restaurant fires is the presence of flammable decor such as drapes, rugs, and plastic veneers. Windstorm losses for this type of occupancy may be traced to overhanging eaves, lack of proper roof anchoring, and the proximity of large trees.

The extent of combustible or susceptible property in a restaurant will vary depending on the type of decor. Common to all restaurant operations is the inventory of food, tables and chairs, linens, and utensils. The decor will range from the modern chrome of the fast-food operation to the dinner house with expensive drapery, wall coverings, carpeting, and upholstered furniture—all of which are subject to severe loss. The S-4 rating also reflects the fact that in any restaurant, food commodities are subject to destruction by law in the event of a small fire, should there be any possibility of contamination.

Since incendiary fires are a major cause of loss in this category, underwriting of the restaurant's management is important. The financial condition of the owners is a major consideration. A deteriorating financial condition may also be found in a changing area where a former business district is becoming residential or where a new highway has changed traffic patterns.

Bowling Alleys

The Occupancy Rating The basic occupancy charge for bowling alleys is 125 percent of the basic building grade. The furniture, fixtures, and contents of this class are rated C-3, combustible, and S-3, susceptible to moderate damage.

Hazard Analysis A major hazard in bowling alleys is defective wiring. This may include malfunctioning automatic pinsetters or ungrounded transformers located outside the structure and vulnerable to damage by vehicles and lightning. The maintenance of electrical equipment, air conditioning, and refrigeration is important. The nature of the bowling alley creates large open spaces without fire divisions. In addition there may be concealed spaces in ceilings, floors, and ball return areas. Often soundproofing of the building has been accomplished with combustible materials.

Particularly hazardous is the refinishing of pins and alleys. This can result in the creation of an explosive dust or vapor which can form a fireball. Smoking and trash disposal hazards make housekeeping a prime concern. Some bowling alleys (like other entertainment establishments) are frequented by undesirable elements of the community. When the financial condition of the establishment is poor, arson is a consideration. Some bowling alleys contain restaurants and cocktail lounges and these hazards must also be considered.

Commercial Printing

The Occupancy Rating The basic occupancy charge of this class is 100 percent of the basic building grade. The furniture, fixtures, and contents of this class are rated C-3, combustible, and S-3, susceptible to moderate damage. Note that while the basic occupancy charge is the same as that of a restaurant and the combustibility and susceptibility ratings are the same as a bowling alley, this class contains hazards which are quite different from either of the others. Although the operation, materials, and hazards of this class differ markedly from the others, the net effect with respect to the peril of fire is the same.

Hazard Analysis Commercial printing concerns contain a great deal of electrical equipment. Hot dryers with temperatures ranging up to 2,500 degrees Fahrenheit are found. Additional hazards include the presence of open gas flames and the storage and use of chemicals. Some of these chemicals are used in combination with solvents.

These chemicals and solvents may result in flammable vapors collecting along the floor or in depressed areas. There may also be accumulations of dust. Splashing, dripping, and residues from inks, oils, and chemicals are quite flammable. One ignition source is the creation of static electricity by rapid movement of paper in the pressroom. The storage of paper stock, waste paper, and rubbish provides a heavy fuel load. Smoking may present still another ignition source and should be carefully controlled by management.

Grain Elevators

The Occupancy Rating The basic occupancy charge for this classification is a function of the size of the grain elevator. The charge ranges from 175 percent of the basic building grade for grain elevators with capacities of less than 250,000 bushels to 235 percent of the basic building grade for grain elevators with capacities of more than 1 million bushels. The combustibility charge for this category which is based almost entirely on the contents is C-2, limited combustibility. This class also has a rating of S-2, susceptible to slight damage.

Hazard Analysis Grain dust is a major hazard in this classification, and the control of grain dust is essential. Any evidence of poor housekeeping or accumulations of dust are a cause for concern. Grain elevators are subject to fires from spontaneous combustion and are also subject to grain dust explosions. An ignition source is static electricity from moving machinery. Improperly grounded machinery, open motors sparking in dusty areas, sparking of tramp metal not removed from grain, bare light bulbs, and lightning provide other ignition sources.

Other hazardous conditions include gasoline or LP Gas that is spilled or improperly stored, and flammable chemicals used in fumigation. Some elevators contain potbelly stoves, salamanders, and portable heaters. Malfunctioning or improperly maintained machinery or equipment may also result in losses. When coverage includes extended coverage or "all-risks" perils, the underwriter should be aware that the location of dryers outside of buildings may expose them to heavy winds or the possibility of collapse due to the weight of snow. Smoking is extremely hazardous in a grain elevator and should be carefully controlled by management.[16]

SUMMARY

Commercial occupancies are rated with regard to four factors. These are:

1. basic occupancy charge;
2. combustibility of contents, furniture, and fixtures;
3. susceptibility of contents, furniture, and fixtures; and
4. additional occupancy hazards.

There are five combustibility classes ranging from noncombustible to flash burning. There are five susceptibility classes ranging from minimal damage to extreme loss which includes the possibility of total loss.

Hazards fall into two categories: common hazards, which are found in virtually all occupancies; and special hazards, which are found in a particular occupancy. Common hazards include housekeeping, including trash disposal, heating and air conditioning equipment, common electrical equipment and lighting and smoking materials.

The fire ignition sequence that has been responsible for losses in the past in a particular occupancy category provides an insight into hazards that must be considered. Incendiary acts and suspicious fires account for 74.5 percent of the frequency in school and college fires, for example. In addition to the principal operation of a particular occupancy there are often ancillary operations such as an employee cafeteria or packing and shipping departments which contain additional hazards. The analysis of occupancy hazards requires analysis of all these factors, together with a determination of the manner in which the occupancy hazards are either reduced or amplified by the structure in which the occupancy is housed.

An analysis of occupancy factors by an underwriter should include:

1. ignition sources;
2. fuel load;
3. susceptibility and combustibility of contents and furniture and fixtures;
4. interior finish of structure;
5. efficiency of management encompassing:
    * housekeeping,
    * employee training and skills, and
    * loss control programs.

Chapter Notes

---

1. Insurance Services Office, *Commercial Rating Schedule* (New York, 1975), pp. 38 (Revision No. 6, 1-82) and 91 (Revision No. 6, 1-82).
2. *Commercial Fire Rating Schedule*, pp. 26.1 (Revision No. 7, 1-83) and 27 (Revision No. 7, 1-83).
3. Descriptions were obtained from *Commercial Fire Rating Schedule*, pp. 26.1 (Revision No. 7, 1-83) and 27 (Revision No. 7, 1-83).
4. *Fire Protecton Handbook*, 14th edition, eds. Gordon P. McKinnon and Keith Towers (Boston: National Fire Protection Association, 1976), pp. 1-30, 1-31. The reader may also wish to refer to *Fire in the United States* (Federal Emergency Management Agency, 1982) for additional breakdowns of causes of fires, fire losses, and fire injuries.
5. *Fire Protection Handbook*, p. 1-33.
6. *Fire Protection Handbook*, p. 8-37.
7. *Fire Protection Handbook*, p. 8-41.
8. *Fire Protection Handbook*, p. 8-40.
9. *Fire Protection Handbook*, p. 1-30.
10. *Fire Protection Handbook*, p. 1-33.
11. *Fire Protection Handbook*, p. 1-32.
12. *Fire Protection Handbook*, p. 1-32.
13. W.O. Lincoln and G.W. Tisdale, *Insurance Inspection and Underwriting*, 8th ed. (New York: The Spectator, 1965), pp. 288, 498, 985, 1044, and 1050. This is also an excellent source of occupancy hazard information.
14. *Fire Protection Handbook*, 15th ed. (Quincy, MA: National Fire Protection Association, 1981), p. 3-11.
15 *Fire Protection Handbook*, 14th ed., pp. 1-32, 1-33.
16. An excellent source of occupancy hazard information is *Best's Loss Control Engineering Manual* (Oldwick, NJ: A.M. Best Co., 1975).

CHAPTER 6

Protection

INTRODUCTION

Fire protection consists of public and private protection. *Public fire protection* is provided by municipalities to all properties within their jurisdiction. The term "municipality" refers to cities, towns, counties, villages, or fire protection districts. The fire fighting personnel of the municipality may be either paid or volunteer. In certain cases, properties located outside the boundary lines of a fire district may contract to have fire equipment respond in the event of an incident.

Private fire protection is provided by the property owner. This can range from a single extinguisher or water barrel up to sophisticated automatic sprinkler systems with central station supervision, fire brigades, and fire companies. Although there are exceptions, smaller commercial risks tend to lean more heavily on public protection while larger commercial risks are able to provide more private protection to supplement the public facilities. From an underwriting standpoint, the total fire protection, public and private, that is available to the particular commercial property being underwritten is of considerable importance in weighing the physical hazards of fire.

Elements of Fire Protection

Both public and private protection consist of the following three elements:

1. prevention,
2. detection, and
3. extinguishment.

Prevention Fire prevention activities include all measures taken to reduce fire frequency prior to the actual outbreak of fire. The goal of fire prevention is to safeguard lives and property. Fire prevention activities include improvement of housekeeping, inspection of premises for hazardous conditions, the passage and enforcement of laws, rules, or ordinances dealing with hazardous substances and conditions, and the passage and enforcement of fire and building code provisions relating to the incidence and spread of fire.

In the public sector, fire prevention activities are the responsibility of the fire department, the fire marshal's office, and the municipal organization with responsibility for the passage and enforcement of fire and building codes. Private fire prevention activities constitute a portion of the firm's loss control program. Improvement of housekeeping, enforcement of regulations concerning hazardous substances, controlling ignition sources, and frequent inspections serve to reduce loss frequency and severity.

Detection Fire detection activities include all measures and equipment utilized to detect the presence of fire and to notify fire fighting personnel of the outbreak of a fire. In the public sector, the fire service communications system serves the detection function. Fire alarms may be transmitted by means of alarm systems, telephone, or radio. Private detection systems include guard services and automatic fire sensing devices. Since virtually all fires not resulting from incendiarism or explosion start small, rapid detection is vital in the reduction of loss severity.

Extinguishment Fire extinguishment activities include all measures and equipment utilized to contain and extinguish a fire. Public fire extinguishment activities are those undertaken by the fire companies on the fire scene. Private fire extinguishment activities include the operation of automatic sprinkler systems, the use of fire extinguishers, and the action of fire brigades. Efficient extinguishment can greatly reduce severity. Inept or ineffective extinguishment can result in a total loss or in heavy losses from water damage which often exceed the loss from fire itself.

PUBLIC PROTECTION SYSTEMS

Rating of a Municipality's Fire Defense[1]

Grading Schedule for Municipal Fire Protection Cities and towns are graded from class 1 (most desirable) to class 10 (least desirable) according to their fire protection equipment and activities. Prior to 1980, the grading was performed in accordance with the

Grading Schedule for Municipal Fire Protection. The *Grading Schedule* was first developed by the National Board of Fire Underwriters (NBFU) in 1916. It was revised and modernized many times between 1916 and 1974 by the NBFU and its successor organization, Insurance Services Office (ISO).

In its final form, the *Grading Schedule* based the town class on the relative merits of the municipality's:

1. water supply,
2. fire department,
3. fire service communications,
4. fire safety control, and
5. climate (in some cases).

In addition, under the heading of *divergence,* an adjustment in the town class might have been made for a municipality with a good water supply but a poor fire department or a good fire department but a poor water supply. The *Grading Schedule* was replaced in 1980 by the *Fire Suppression Rating Schedule,* developed by ISO. Exhibit 6-1 briefly compares the two schedules.

Fire Suppression Rating Schedule The purpose of the *Fire Suppression Rating Schedule* (FSRS) is the same as that of the earlier schedule, to evaluate a municipality's fire defenses. However, the scope of the new schedule is quite different.

The FSRS is divided into two major sections. The first section, entitled *Public Fire Suppression,* is used to develop the town class rating, which applies to all class rated properties and to schedule (or specifically) rated properties that require a water flow of 3,500 gallons per minute (gpm) or less for fire suppression purposes. The second section, entitled *Individual Property Fire Suppression,* is used to develop a public protection classification for individual properties with a needed fire flow (NFF) of more than 3,500 gpm. A property might have an NFF of over 3,500 gpm because of its construction, occupancy, exposure, unprotected wall opening, or some combination of them.

Exhibit 6-2 shows the factors considered in the calculation of the public protection classification and the percentage attributable to each factor. In order for a municipality to qualify for a public protection classification of one through nine, it must have either (1) a piece of fire fighting equipment that has a water pump with a rated capacity of at least 250 gpm at pressure of 150 pounds per square inch (psi) *and* a water system capable of delivering 250 gpm at a fire site for a period of two hours during the period of highest consumption, or (2) at least one piece of fire fighting equipment that has a pump capacity of 50 gpm and

Exhibit 6-1
Comparison of Grading Schedule for Municipal Fire Protection (1974) and Fire Suppression Rating Schedule*

Comparison of Major Items Considered

1974 Schedule	Relative Weight
Water supply	39%
Fire Department	39%
Fire Alarm	9%
Building Laws	1.8%
Electrical Laws	.8%
Fire Prevention Laws	10.5%
Climate Conditions	(variable)
	100%

FSR Schedule	Relative Weight
Water Supply	40%
Fire Department	50%
Fire Alarm	10%
	100%

Building, Electrical and Fire Prevention Laws and Climatic Conditions are not included in the FSRS for the following reasons.

Comparison of Items Considered in the Review of Water Supply

1974 Schedule	Relative Weight
• Adequacy of Supply Work	6%
• Reliability of Source of Supply	6%
• Reliability of Pumping Capacity	3%
• Reliability of Power Supply	4%
• Condition, Arrangement, Operation and Reliability of System Components	4%
• Adequacy of Mains	16%
• Reliability of Mains	2%
• Installation of Mains	2%
• Arrangement of Distribution System	2%
• Additional Factors and Conditions Relating to Supply and Distribution	4%
• Distribution of Hydrants	5%
• Hydrants — Size, Type and Installation	2%
• Hydrants — Inspection and Condition	2%
• Miscellaneous Factors and Conditions	6%
	64%

(Max=39%)

1. Most communities have adopted one of the available model codes; therefore, we are not really measuring differences.

2. Evaluation of enforcement of codes and climatic conditions is subjective when trying to review on a citywide basis.

3. Results of the laws and enforcement manifest themselves in the actual conditions found in individual properties when surveyed for application of the Commercial Fire Rating Schedule.

FSR Schedule	Relative Weight
● Supply Works	
● Fire Flow Delivery	
● Distribution of Hydrants	35%
● Hydrants — Size, Type and Installation	2%
● Hydrants — Inspection and Condition	3%
	40%

The water supply items dealing with reliability in the 1974 Schedule are not included in the FSR Schedule because recent history has indicated that the dependability and replacement capability of water supply equipment is such that measurement of these features has little bearing on the water supply performance. The remaining items of the 1974 Schedule that are not included in the FSRS are omitted because they either require subjective review or are considered not significant enough to measure in the performance of the water system for fire insurance rating purposes.

The emphasis of the FSRS review of a water system is the consideration of the actual water supply that is available for fire suppression at representative locations throughout the city.

continued on next page

Comparison of Items Considered in the Review of the Fire Department

1974 Schedule

	Relative Weight
• Pumpers	4.8%
• Ladder Trucks	3.4%
• Distribution of Companies and Types of Apparatus	4%
• Pumper Capacity	4.4%
• Design, Maintenance, and Condition of Apparatus	3%
• Number of Officers	2%
• Department Manning	8%
• Engine and Ladder Company Unit Manning	6.4%
• Master and Special Stream Devices	1%
• Equipment for Pumpers and Ladders	2%
• Hose	2.8%
• Condition of Hose	1.6%
• Training	6%
• Response to Alarms	2%
• Fire Operations	8%
• Special Protection	6%
• Miscellaneous Factors and Conditions	6%
	71.4% (Max=39%)

Comparison of Items Considered in the Review of the Fire Alarm System

1974 Schedule

	Relative Weight
• Communication Center	0.8%
• Communication Center	2.8%
• Equipment and Current Supply Boxes	1.2%
• Alarm Circuits and Alarm Facilities, Including Current Supply at Fire Stations	2%
• Material, Construction, Condition and Protection of Circuit	1%
• Radio	0.8%
• Fire Department Telephone Service	1.7%
• Fire Alarm Operators	0.8%
• Conditions Adversely Affecting Use	1.3%
• Credit for Boxes Installed in Residential Districts	-.4%
	12.4% (Max=9%)

FSR Schedule

	Relative Weight
• Receipt of Fire Alarms	2%
• Operators	3%
• Alarm Dispatch Circuit Facilities	5%
	10%

FSR Schedule

	Relative Weight
• Engine Companies	11%
• Ladder Service Companies	6%
• Distribution of Companies	4%
• Pumper Capacity	5%
• Department Manning	15%
• Training	9%
	50%

As in the Water Supply feature, items that require subjective review, and items considering minor features are not included in the FSRS. The FSRS places emphasis on the review of first alarm response of the fire department because of the importance of initial attacks to minimize potential losses. Additionally, the entire Fire Department item has been given increased weight in the overall review to recognize the value of fire department operations in early stages of fire suppression and the fact that some operations are possible with less than needed water supplies.

As in the Water Supply and Fire Department, features that are subjective, and minor items dealing with the fire alarm system, are not included in the FSRS. The emphasis has been placed on the performance of handling and dispatching fire alarms rather than the method of notification.

* Adopted with permission from Insurance Services Office, New York, NY, 1980.

Exhibit 6-2

I.S.O. Suppression Rating Schedule

Factors Considered in Calculation of Public Protection Classification	
Factor	Percentage Weight
Water Supply	40%
Fire Department	50
Fire Alarm	10

at least a 300 gallon water tank. If the municipality does not have either (1) or (2) it is rated as class 10.

A municipality that has either (1) or (2) above will be rated from class 1 to class 9, depending on the characteristics of its fire department, water supply system and fire alarm system.

Some of the factors considered in evaluating the fire department are:

1. number of engine companies,
2. equipment of the engine companies,
3. number of ladder companies,
4. equipment of ladder companies,
5. geographic distribution of engine and ladder companies relative to the built-up areas of the municipality, and
6. personnel training.

Some factors considered in rating the water supply are:

1. part of the city protected by fire hydrants,
2. maximum daily water consumption,
3. fire flow and duration,
4. ability of the water system to deliver the needed fire flow at representative locations in the city, and
5. condition of fire hydrants.

The fire alarm rating is based on such things as the adequacy of the telephone system, the devices used to record calls to report fires, number of operators on duty to handle fire calls, fire radio communications facilities, emergency power equipment, and so forth.

The rating of each municipality begins at a basis of 100 points. Credits are given to reduce the points for each factor for which the municipality's fire suppression facilities exceed the minimum required by the schedule.

The public protection classification (PPC) is calculated by the formula:

$$PPC = \frac{100 - [(CFA + CFD + CWS) - 0.5 [(CWS) - 0.8 (CFD)]]}{10}$$

where

CFA = credit for receiving and handling fire alarms
CFD = credit for fire department
CWS = credit for water supply.

Thus, the numeric public protection classification decreases from class 10 for a city with minimal fire suppression facilities to class 1 for a city with excellent fire suppression facilities. Since credits for fire department, water supply, and fire alarm system are not weighted equally in the above formula, it is not possible to assign a specific number of credits to each public protection classification. The number of credits needed to achieve any specified classification depends on the respective proportions related to water system, fire department, and fire alarms.

The public protection classification for individual properties, calculated in Section II of the *Fire Suppression Rating Schedule,* is based on the fire fighting facilities and water supply available to the individual property. The public protection classification for an individual property cannot be superior to the public protection classification of the municipality in which it is located. It can be inferior to the municipality, but not worse than class 9 if the municipality is rated class 9 or better.

Other Public Protection Services

There are three other important public protection services which are provided by some fire departments:

1. pre-fire planning surveys,
2. salvage teams, and
3. arson squads.

Pre-Fire Planning Surveys Pre-fire planning surveys represent an important fire prevention activity from the standpoint of the commercial property risk. They consist of training runs of fire equipment to the commercial premises and walk-throughs of the premises by the fire department personnel. These surveys enable the fire department personnel to familiarize themselves with the location of major buildings and equipment, fire hydrants, standpipes, and sprinkler system *siamese connections.* The siamese connection, sometimes called the *fire department connection,* is a twin pipe connection with caps placed on the outside of a building to which the fire department may connect their hoses and provide water. This is the only source of water for a dry standpipe. As the size of the industrial plant or complex increases, these pre-fire planning surveys become more vital. Crucial minutes can be saved in the event of an outbreak of fire if the municipal fire fighting personnel are familiar enough with the premises to go to the affected building and hook up their pumpers and hose streams immediately. These inspections should also determine whether there are any nonstandard threads on the various fire department connections. Since fire departments use connectors with a standard thread, a nonstandard connection would be useless during a fire.

Particularly with large commercial risks, it is important from an underwriting standpoint to determine whether pre-fire planning surveys are conducted at the property under consideration. The frequency of these surveys and their adequacy are also important considerations. The pre-fire planning survey can serve as a starting point for the commercial firm's own private loss control plan.

Salvage Teams While the initial task of the fire department is extinguishment of the fire, water damage can cause heavy property loss. Some fire departments have specially trained salvage teams who utilize tarpaulins, drains, lifts, and similar equipment to minimize property damage due to the water used in extinguishment.[2] In those commercial occupancies where the contents are particularly susceptible to water damage, salvage teams might be able to reduce severity.

Arson Squads In recent years the incidence of arson has increased sharply. Arson for profit is particularly troublesome in commercial lines. This aspect of moral hazard is susceptible to some degree of control. In those communities where vigorous investigation and prosecution efforts have been instituted, arson incidence has declined. In Connecticut, two arson vans were credited with more than doubling arson arrests. These vans contain equipment which can quickly determine the cause and point of origin of a fire. The vans, purchased by insurance company members of Connecticut's FAIR Plan, are operated by the state police.[3]

In order for the arson detection efforts of the municipality to serve as a deterrent to arson for profit, the work of the arson squad must be coordinated with that of the police department and the district attorney or other prosecuting agency. Only through coordinated efforts will convictions for arson be obtained. A task force has been created in Seattle, Washington for this purpose.[4] Arson "hot lines," which offer rewards for turning in an arsonist, are used in many areas. The presence or absence of an arson squad is an indication of community awareness and concern toward this problem. While the resources of smaller municipalities usually do not permit the formation of specialized squads of this type, the arson problem is more severe primarily in larger communities, making some specific arson control program imperative.

PRIVATE FIRE PREVENTION SYSTEMS

Major Elements of Private Fire Prevention

The primary objective of private fire prevention efforts is the reduction of loss frequency. The three major elements of private fire prevention are:

1. control of housekeeping,
2. adherence to building codes and standards, and
3. fire protection planning.

Control of Housekeeping Housekeeping activities are primarily aimed at reduction of fire frequency, although good housekeeping may also have some effect on severity. Good housekeeping requires that some manager of the firm must be given the responsibility to establish and supervise good housekeeping procedures. In large organizations, this responsibility may be delegated to lower management levels, but controls should be established to assure that the activities are properly carried out.

Housekeeping activities fall into eight categories, not all of which are applicable to every commercial property risk:

1. smoking;
2. waste cans;
3. ash cans and refuse receptacles;
4. packing materials and sawdust;
5. old furniture and paper;
6. floor oils, polishes, and cleaners;
7. outdoor housekeeping; and
8. dumps.[5]

Recommended housekeeping procedures for each of these categories are set forth in the National Fire Protection Association *Inspection Manual.*[6] Frequent inspections of the premises are usually required to assure that good housekeeping standards are being met. Proper housekeeping standards, rigidly enforced, are the foundation of a private fire prevention program. Neither public fire department nor insurance company inspections are made frequently enough to fulfill this role.

Adherence to Building Codes and Standards Although the municipality has building inspectors to assure compliance with the applicable codes, a private fire prevention program must also consider this area. Often municipal inspections are perfunctory and infrequent. In addition, the municipal codes may not be up to the standards set by the NFPA.

Private fire prevention programs include the monitoring of all building construction and installation of new equipment to determine that the appropriate codes and standards are adhered to. NFPA standards must be considered at the initial stages of any plans. In this way, adherence to the standards is much more likely. Older buildings which do not comply with the code may present problems. In cases where the cost of bringing the structure up to the code is prohibitive, the fire prevention program can only note the deficiency and attempt to reduce the fire hazard as much as possible.

Where there are specialized manufacturing and industrial operations and processes, the applicable NFPA standards will determine the conditions which should be met. Another area requiring careful monitoring is the storage of raw materials or inventory, as described in Chapter 5.

Fire Protection Planning Just as the municipal fire department engages in pre-fire planning, this same activity is part of a complete private fire prevention program. In large industrial complexes, pre-fire planning is often a part of an overall disaster control plan.

A suggested fire control plan has five steps. These are as follows:

1. A plan of the grounds and buildings comprising the installation should be obtained.
2. The location of all main control valves (process equipment, water supply, fuel supply, and so on), check valves, pumps, hose houses, standpipes, and hydrants should be plainly marked, easily accessible, and identified on the plan.
3. A water supply plan should be prepared indicating all available water supply sources, both public and private, with their estimated capacities and available pressure. These sources include ponds, lakes, rivers, water mains, storage tanks, and any associated pumps.
4. All portable fire extinguishers should be located on the plan. It should be determined that this equipment is appropriate for the area where it is located, adequate in size and number, and properly located.
5. Information on detection and extinguishment systems should be obtained, even if they have not been installed. It should be determined if the protective and economic advantages of such equipment make its installation feasible. All operating features of existing systems should be noted on the plan.[7]

Fire control plans may vary in length from a single page in the case of a small commercial risk to book length in the instance of a large manufacturing plant. The plan provides a starting point for training the firm's personnel in fire response. The appropriate response may greatly reduce the severity of any fire which does occur.

If the firm is large enough to have a fire brigade, the location of extinguishing equipment and control valves should be known by all members of the brigade. In all cases where automatic sprinkler systems are installed, personnel should be trained not to turn off the sprinkler system until instructed to do so by fire department personnel. Too frequently an employee will shut off the sprinkler system to prevent further water damage, only to have the fire flare up and result in a total loss.

As part of the firm's private pre-fire planning, inspection of all automatic sprinkler systems and automatic fire detection systems should be undertaken on a regular basis. Standpipes and fire department siamese connections for automatic sprinkler systems should also be inspected.

Commercial Fire Loss Control Programs

Management Attitude A successful fire loss control program will have the active support of the firm's top management and the cooperation of all other levels of management, including the first line supervisors. If management does not actively support the program, it is not likely to be effective. Fire loss control requires almost daily monitoring of housekeeping activities, consistent adherence to relevant codes and standards, and effective pre-fire planning and training. Since this involves so many of the firm's personnel at so many different levels, management cooperation and coordination are essential.

Management attitude is difficult to evaluate from outside the firm. Most firms will at least attempt to appear interested in fire loss control while the insurance company inspector is on the premises. Since good housekeeping can only be maintained by consistent monitoring, the state of the firm's housekeeping is often an indication of the degree of commitment possessed by management. A firm may have an excellent fire loss control plan on paper, but if a walk through the plant discloses cigarette butts on the floor in the woodworking shop and oily rags stored in cardboard boxes in the machine shop, the extent of management's active support of the program is questionable.

Measuring Effectiveness The effectiveness of a commercial property loss control program may be measured by means of benefit-cost analysis. This technique takes the quantified benefits of any program or project and relates them to the costs incurred in that program. In the case where the costs or benefits occur over a time period greater than one year, the future benefits and/or costs are discounted back to the present, utilizing the interest rate reflecting the opportunity cost of the funds invested in the project. This discounting procedure is referred to as obtaining the *present value* of the cost and benefit streams.

A benefit-cost ratio then is:

$$\frac{\text{Present Value of Benefits}}{\text{Present Value of Costs}} = \text{Benefit} - \text{Cost Ratio}$$

In order for any project to be economically feasible, the benefit-cost ratio must exceed 1.0. The higher the value, the more desirable the project. In commercial property loss control programs some of the costs and benefits are relatively easy to quantify while others are more difficult. This concept is of importance to the underwriter since many insureds consider that loss control programs are only benefiting the insurance company and not the insured. Where the insured can be shown the economic value of such programs to the firm, the underwriter has an easier task obtaining the insured's cooperation to improve the risk by means of loss control techniques.

The costs and benefits of basic loss control efforts such as housekeeping and fire protection planning are difficult to measure since the costs are usually merged with other operating costs and the benefits are usually not reflected directly in the fire rate. There are a number of indirect costs associated with even minor fires, such as disruption of production and additional clean-up and maintenance expenses. While serious production shutdowns are covered by business interruption insurance, minor interruptions are usually not insured.

Given the size of the business and the type of occupancy, an estimate can be made of the expected minor fire frequency in the absence of a loss control program. The difference between this frequency and the actual experience would be the number of minor fires prevented. Next, the cost in terms of lost work effort and clean-up per minor fire could be estimated. The product of these two is the benefit of the housekeeping program. This can then be compared with those additional costs identified with the housekeeping effort.

When the loss control program includes the installation of automatic sprinklers and other fire detection and extinguishment systems which are reflected in the fire rates, the benefit-cost calculation is much more straightforward. The costs of the sprinkler system can be easily identified. The reduction in fire rate benefit can be accurately estimated.

Then a value can be assigned to those other benefits of the system which can be identified. These other benefits include:

1. prevention of costly downtime and production interruptions;
2. protection of workers' jobs, particularly where ordinary payroll is excluded from business interruption;
3. prevention of the loss of customers who might go to another source after a fire;
4. greater design freedom and building flexibility; and
5. water conservation.[8]

It should be noted that many of the costs or benefits used in computing the benefit-cost ratio may be estimates. Thus, the ratio will also be an estimate. The fact that most aspects of the firm which will be affected by the system in question have been quantified should not lead the safety manager or other responsible person in the firm to believe that the ratio is more accurate than it actually is. The people making the estimate of the customers who will go elsewhere were the firm to have a fire may grossly overestimate the loyalty of the firm's customers, causing the estimate of the benefits to be overstated. In such a case, a benefit-cost ratio of 1.05/1.00 may be more accurately stated at 0.95/1.00 when correctly estimating the loss of customers following a fire. The ratio is only an estimate and is only as accurate as its components. Perhaps using ranges would help. For example, below .50 would be rejected, above 1.50 would be accepted, and from .50 to 1.50 would be studied earlier.

When evaluating the fire rate savings on building construction, it is necessary to take into account the fact that the sprinklers will reduce the contents fire rate as well. A study undertaken for the federal government indicated that sprinkler system costs for government warehouses were approximatey 4.64 percent of the total building cost. When the value of the contents was included, the sprinkler system costs amounted to less than one percent of the total value. Some sprinkler system manufacturers estimate that if the value of the contents is at least three times the value of the building, the sprinkler system cost can be amortized in less than ten years.[9] Since the planning horizon for purposes of benefit-cost analysis is usually considerably longer than ten years, the benefit-cost ratio of such a project would be considerably greater than 1.0.

Available Services There are a number of outside resources that can be utilized in the commercial property loss control program. The insurance company inspection service provides important information and insights into areas where improvements can be made in the risk. The insurance company can provide helpful expertise in the loss control area and can also indicate the effect that proposed changes or system installations will make on fire rates. The local fire rating bureau can provide analysis of new construction at the blueprint stage and make suggested changes which would have the effect of lowering rates. Valuable advice may also be obtained from brokers and fire protection consultants.

Sprinkler system manufacturers are another source of information for analysis of the impact of sprinkler and other extinguishment and detection systems on fire rates. The local municipal fire department often provides inspection service and pre-fire planning information which is of assistance to the firm's loss control program.

PRIVATE FIRE DETECTION SYSTEMS

Control of Loss Severity

With the exception of incendiarism and explosions, most fires start small. If fire extinguishment efforts can be instituted immediately, the fire often can be confined to a small area and loss severity minimized. A great many fires occur at night, on weekends, or other periods when the commercial establishment is closed. Frequently these fires are first reported by passersby. In order for the fire to reach sufficient size to be noticed, the structure must be considerably involved. Even immediate response on the part of the municipal fire fighters will not prevent heavy property damage. A private detection system can greatly speed the response of both private and public extinguishment efforts and reduce the severity of a fire.

Watch Service Systems

A watch service system utilizes people to patrol the business premises during those periods when the firm is closed. In addition, large plants and warehouses use guard patrols to periodically inspect those areas and structures that are infrequently occupied by other employees. The effectiveness of the watch service system is dependent upon the personnel employed. A sleeping guard provides little protection for the commercial property. The task of wandering through a closed industrial plant or warehouse is neither challenging nor interesting, leading to few persons choosing this as a career. Frequently employers will transfer a long-time employee who can no longer fulfill a more arduous assignment to the position of night guard. Elderly guards may be prone to occasional naps, illness, or injury, preventing them from completing their rounds. This has led to the development of a number of systems for the supervision of guards.

Watch service systems include:

1. unsupervised watch services,
2. clock and tape systems,
3. central station systems,
4. tour systems, and
5. merchant police.

Unsupervised Watch Services The unsupervised watch service system consists of one or more guards who are on the premises during the hours that the business is closed. These private guards are often untrained in using portable fire extinguishers but usually can be relied upon to summon the appropriate fire brigade or municipal fire department as soon as they detect the fire. In a small premises, the detection of the fire by the guard will be delayed if the guard is asleep, ill, injured in a fall, or rendered helpless by burglars. Even without the occurrence of fire, the guard's illness or injury may not be discovered until morning when the premises are reopened.

There is a second defect of the unsupervised watch service system in all but the smallest commercial premises. The guard may be instructed to make regular rounds of the entire premises, checking all floors of all buildings to minimize the time between the outbreak of fire and its occurrence, but there is no way to ascertain performance. While there are many dedicated and conscientious guards, a guard may simply curl up in a corner and sleep, or if awake, sit in a corner and smoke, providing an additional ignition source. In most cases, however, the unsupervised guard is better than no detection system at all.

Clock and Tape Systems The basic clock and tape system consists of a portable time recorder and a key which must be inserted into devices located at various locations around the commercial premises. In some cases, the devices must be punched in sequence. The time clock contains a tape which can be checked after the premises are reopened to determine if the guard properly followed his or her route.

The clock and tape system is superior to those that provide no supervision since it can be determined if the guard performed satisfactorily. The obvious defect of this system is that it does not provide this information until after the fact, the next morning in most cases. Therefore if the guard is attacked by burglars, falls and is injured, suffers a heart attack, or simply falls asleep, that fact will not be known until the next morning. Meanwhile, the premises are unprotected. This shortcoming of the clock and tape system is particularly serious in the event of a burglary since the burglars may set fire to the premises in order to destroy any evidence they may have left behind.

When a clock and tape system is installed, the guard's tour should be designed so that every portion of the premises will be visited at appropriate intervals. The underwriter should determine how often each station is visited by the guard and ascertain that the number of stations is sufficient to assure proper coverage of the premises. If a large industrial plant with many buildings only employs a single guard, he or she may only visit each station once or twice during the night. This would permit a fire to burn for some time without detection. The diligence of the supervisor in checking the clock tapes should also be determined. If the tapes are checked infrequently, or not at all, the system is essentially unsupervised. Insurance company engineers and fire inspectors frequently review these clock records during their periodic loss prevention surveys.

Central Station Systems The major defect in the clock and tape system, which is the lagged notification of interruptions in the guard's rounds, is remedied by the installation of a central station system. This system utilizes similar stations and keys to those of the clock and tape system but rather than retaining the information locally on tape, it is sent electrically to a central station. At the central station, personnel monitor the systems of a number of commercial properties. If a guard does not signal in at the appointed time, either the guard is telephoned or someone is dispatched to the premises to determine the cause. The time that the property is unguarded by a detection system is determined by the amount of latitude given the guard relative to the appointed time of clocking in, and the length of time that it takes to reach the property from the central station. This second time lag could be lengthy in the case of commercial properties located some distance from the central station.

A major disadvantage of the central station system is the increased cost relative to the clock and tape system. This cost must be weighed against the advantages of this system, which is the best system available utilizing guards. When the central station system is employed for other purposes such as monitoring process temperatures, waterflow alarms, and burglary alarms, these systems become more cost effective. A combined surveillance system provides more protection for the money.

Tour Systems The tour system represents a compromise between the inherent time lags of the clock and tape system and the high costs of the full central station system. In the tour system, only certain stations are wired to the central monitoring station (e.g., every tenth station or stations in critical locations). This provides an opportunity for relatively rapid response to the interruption of the guard's rounds with some reduction in cost.

With both full central station and tour systems, the stations connected to the central monitor board may be wired to permit the sending of a fire alarm. This feature can reduce the response time for the municipal fire department and has the added advantage of providing a backup communication system in the event of a failure in the local telephone system.

Merchant Police All of the previous systems utilize guards employed by the particular business firm being protected. In the event that the firm, for reasons of size, cost, or other considerations does not use one of the preceding systems, merchant police guard service is an alternative.

The usual merchant police system utilizes guards who patrol a route covering a number of properties. They drive or walk up to the exterior of the property and check to ascertain that all exterior doors are secure and that there are no other visible problems. The merchant police approach has three major disadvantages:

1. The guards usually are limited to checking the exterior of the premises.
2. Since the guards are responsible for a number of properties, a considerable time lag may occur between visits.
3. The guards are employed and supervised by the merchant police company and are not under the control and supervision of the individual insured.

All types of watch service systems act to some degree as deterrents to and detection systems for burglary as well as fire. The merchant police system in particular is more geared to burglary detection than fire detection since the building may well be completely involved in fire before it is detected by the merchant police guard. If the commercial property is located in an area where there are few, if any, passersby at night and on weekends, the merchant police system does assure some surveillance during these periods.

Automatic Systems

Automatic fire detection systems consist of mechanical or electronic detectors which sense the presence of smoke or fire and sound an alarm. There are two major types of automatic fire detection systems:

1. local alarm systems, and
2. remote and central station systems.

Local Alarm   In a local alarm fire detection system the detector is wired to an alarm bell on the exterior of the premises. The local alarm may either be a gong or buzzer. The system is designed to alert passersby to the existence of a problem in the hope that they will turn in the alarm.

In commercial districts the local alarm frequently does not lead to the intended result. During nights and weekends there may not be many persons on the streets in the commercial district, and still fewer who are willing to get involved. Even those who would attempt to help may not know the appropriate response. They cannot distinguish between fire and burglar alarms and may call the police rather than the fire department, leading to further delay. If the only passersby are motorists, it is unlikely that they would hear the alarm and even less likely that they would stop and search for the source of the noise. The local alarm fire detection system relies upon the bystander to perform an important part of the detection function, summoning the municipal fire department. This reliance is frequently unwarranted. During business hours, the local alarm system does notify the employees of the fire, permitting them to take appropriate action.

Remote and Central Station   Remote and central station fire detection systems utilize mechanical and electronic detection devices similar to those found in local alarm systems. In these systems, the alarm is transmitted to a monitoring point in a remote or central station.

A remote station system connects the devices on the commercial premises with a local police or fire station where the system is continuously monitored. The alarm circuits in these systems usually consist of leased lines between the protected property and the remote station.

In a central station system, the detectors are wired to a central station which is a private concern providing this service. In some central station systems, municipal fire department notification is by radio while other systems utilize telephone. Usually the central station company will also dispatch a vehicle to respond to the alarm.

Types of Detectors   There are a variety of detectors which can be wired to local alarm, remote, or central station systems. The type of system appropriate for a particular commercial property risk depends upon the size of the property and the type of occupancy.[10] Automatic detectors include:

1. heat detectors,
2. smoke detectors,
3. flame detectors,

4. intrusion detectors,
5. sprinkler system supervisory devices, and
6. closed circuit television monitors.

Heat Detectors. Heat detectors are designed to sound an alarm in the event of abnormal heat conditions. The two major types of heat detectors are:

1. fixed temperature, and
2. rate of temperature rise.

FIXED TEMPERATURE. Fixed temperature heat detectors, also called *thermostats*, sound an alarm when the temperature at which they have been set is exceeded. These devices use a fusible link, bulb, or other device which reacts to the temperature. These are also known as *spot type* detectors.

RATE OF TEMPERATURE RISE. In certain occupancies where a rapid increase in temperature may be an indication of a major problem, *line type* detectors are used. These detectors utilize a thermostatic cable or pneumatic tube to register the rapid increase in temperature. Some spot-type detectors also react to a rapid increase in temperature.

Smoke Detectors. Smoke detectors sense the presence of visible or invisible particles of combustion. Since the smoke must be in the vicinity of the detector, locations such as air conditioning ducts may require that the detectors have auxiliary equipment to transport air samples to the detector. There are two major types of smoke detectors:

1. ionization, and
2. photoelectric cells.

IONIZATION. The ionization type of detector responds to smoke particles in the air. The air in the chamber is ionized and therefore conductive. Smoke in the chamber decreases the conductance of the air, sounding an alarm. Exhibit 6-3 shows a simple ionization smoke detector.

PHOTOELECTRIC CELLS. There are two types of photoelectric cell detectors. Both of these respond to the presence of smoke particles in the air. The first type (light scattering) sends a signal when light is reflected by smoke in the air onto a light-sensitive element. The second type (light obscuration) projects a beam of light across the space to a receiver. When the beam is interrupted by smoke, the alarm is sounded. Exhibit 6-4 shows a simple photoelectric cell smoke detector (light scattering type).

Recent price breakthroughs in ionization and photoelectric detectors have lead to increased use of this type of detector. These detectors have superior reaction times, making them very desirable.

Exhibit 6-3
Ionization Smoke Detector*

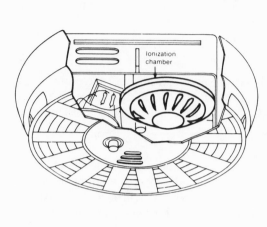 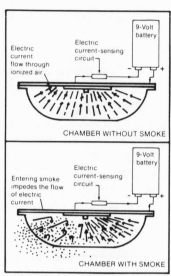

An ionization detector uses a tiny bit of americium 241 in its ionization chamber (above, left). In the absence of smoke (upper right), current flows unhindered within the chamber. But when smoke enters, the current is impeded; a special circuit senses the reduction and sounds the alarm. In general, ionization models respond very quickly to the wispy smoke of a fast fire—one feeding on paper, for example—but relatively slowly to the dense smoke of a slow, smoldering fire, as in a mattress.

*Reprinted with permission from *Consumer Reports* (Mount Vernon, NY: Consumers Union), August 1980, p. 475.

Flame Detectors. Flame detectors sound an alarm in the presence of radiant energy. This radiant energy may be either visible or outside the range of human vision.

Intrusion Detectors. The basic purpose of the intrusion detector is to register the presence of burglars or other tresspassers on the business property during hours that the enterprise is closed. Since burglars often set fires in order to eliminate evidence, these detectors have an effect upon the physical characteristics of the risk from a fire standpoint. There are three major categories of intrusion detectors (a more detailed breakdown is found in the crime chapter):

1. electric tapes,
2. photoelectric cells, and
3. sonic detectors.

Exhibit 6-4
Photoelectric Smoke Detector — Light Scattering Type*

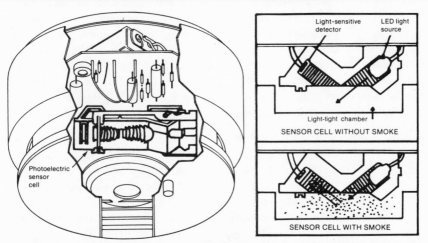

There's a light-sensitive sensor cell (above, left) in an interior chamber of a photoelectric unit. Without smoke (upper right), the light bypasses the cell. But smoke that enters scatters the beam so that the cell can "see" it. When enough light reaches the cell, an alarm is sounded. In general, photoelectric models respond best to slow, smoldering fires.

*Reprinted with permission from *Consumer Reports* (Mount Vernon, NY: Consumers Union), August 1980, p. 475.

ELECTRIC TAPES. In an electric tape system, all doors, windows, and other openings are bordered with tapes through which an electrical impulse is generated. An intruder, upon breaking and entering, will break the tape, sounding the alarm. In some cases, it is a magnetic field rather than a tape which is broken.

PHOTOELECTRIC CELLS. In a photoelectric cell system, a light beam is transmitted across the protected space to a receiver. An intruder, passing between the light source and the receiver will interrupt the beam, sounding the alarm. When this less visible type of detector is wired to a remote or central station, apprehension of the intruder is enhanced. The electric tape system, on the other hand, is easily seen and may be defeated by an experienced criminal.

SONIC DETECTORS. A sonic detector reacts to the presence of noise in the space being protected. Since most breaking and entering is accompanied by noise, this type of detector can be quite effective. However, it would also react to a stray cat knocking over materials, leading to false alarms in those buildings frequented by cats or rodents.

Sprinkler System Supervisory Devices. The most significant single cause of failure of automatic sprinkler systems is human error.[11] This results from either the closing of the sprinkler system water control valves prior to a fire, or the premature closing of the valves before a fire is under control. Sprinkler system components may be monitored by the use of electrical contact switches which relay the condition of the system components to a local, remote, or central station monitor. Many insurance organizations require locking of sprinkler valves in an open position to deter improperly closed valves.

Sprinkler system supervisory devices include:

1. Water flow alarms which sound when one or more sprinkler heads have opened. A small fire extinguished by one sprinkler head could result in heavy water damage if the water is allowed to flow until the next morning or the end of the weekend.
2. Gravity tank supervision including low and high water level alarms and alarms signaling the failure of water heating systems in tanks subjected to freezing temperatures.
3. Devices indicating loss of pressure in pressure tank systems.
4. Devices indicating the loss of electric or steam power to fire pumps.
5. Water supply valve monitors which indicate the condition of each valve in the system. When a valve is closed, this registers immediately on the monitor board.
6. Devices registering the air or gas pressure in dry pipe sprinkler systems.[12]

Closed Circuit Television Monitors. Some properties may be protected by closed circuit television systems which transmit pictures from cameras located throughout the premises. These systems are usually monitored in a local station on the industrial premises. The closed circuit system can detect intruders, visible smoke, and visible flame. The system may also be used in conjunction with other detectors to provide additional information on situations triggering alarms.

PRIVATE EXTINGUISHMENT SYSTEMS

Private extinguishment systems consist of equipment and personnel used by the commercial firm to extinguish fires prior to the arrival of the municipal fire department or to aid the efforts of the municipal department upon its arrival. In the case of isolated commercial properties, the private extinguishment system may operate entirely in lieu of a municipal fire department.

These systems fall into four major categories:

1. portable fire extinguishers,
2. standpipe and hose systems,
3. automatic sprinkler systems, and
4. fire brigades.

Portable Fire Extinguishers

Portable fire extinguishers are frequently referred to as "first aid" equipment. They are designed to permit the personnel of the commercial firm to attempt to extinguish the fire while awaiting the arrival of the municipal fire department. The personnel should be trained in the operation of the equipment and also should be trained to call the fire department, even if they think that they have the fire under control. Delay in summoning the municipal fire department may result in a total loss.

The extinguishers should be suitable in type, size, and number for the type of materials and degree of hazard. The extinguishers should be periodically inspected and tested and should have appropriate certification. Maintenance, including hydrostatic testing, should be performed on a regular basis and adequate records kept. The extinguishers should be properly distributed about the area to be protected, with appropriate types of extinguishers located near any special hazards. Finally, the extinguishers should be readily accessible. An extinguisher is useless if it cannot be easily reached.

Fires are placed in four categories:

1. Class A—fires in ordinary combustible materials such as wood, cloth, paper, rubber, and many plastics. For these, quenching and cooling effects of water or solutions containing a large percentage of water are of first importance.
2. Class B—fires in flammable liquids, gases, and greases. For these, a blanketing or smothering effect is essential. Fires in some materials reactive to water but which can be smothered are in this class.
3. Class C—fires involving energized electrical equipment. In these cases the extinguishing medium must be nonconductive or the extinguisher will become extremely hazardous to human life.
4. Class D—fires in combustible metals such as magnesium, titanium, zirconium, sodium, and potassium. These combustible metals are violently reactive with water. Most other extinguishing agents are ineffective.[13]

The characteristics of fire extinguishers are given in Exhibit 6-5

Exhibit 6-5
Characteristics of Extinguishers*

Extinguishing Agent	Method of Operation	Capacity	Horizontal Range of Stream	Approximate Time of Discharge
Water	Stored Pressure	2½ gal	30–40 ft	1 min
Water	Pump	1½ gal	30–40 ft	45 min
		2½ gal	30–40 ft	1 min
		4 gal	30–40 ft	2 min
		5 gal	30–40 ft	2–3 min
Water (Antifreeze Calcium Chloride)	Cartridge and Stored Pressure	1¼, 1½ gal	30–40 ft	30 sec
		2½ gal	30–40 ft	1 min
		33 gal (wheeled)	50 ft	3 min
Water (Wetting Agent)	Cartridge and Stored Pressure	25 gal (wheeled)	35 ft	1½ min
		45 gal (wheeled)	35 ft	2 min
Water (Soda Acid)	Chemically Generated Expellent	1¼, 1½ gal	30–40 ft	30 sec
		2½ gal	30–40 ft	1 min
		17 gal (wheeled)	50 ft	3 min
		33 gal (wheeled)	50 ft	3 min
Loaded Stream	Stored Pressure	2½ gal	30–40 ft	1 min
	Cartridge and Stored Pressure	33 gal (wheeled)	50 ft	3 min
Foam	Pressurized	approx. 1 lb	5–10 ft	30 sec
Foam	Chemically Generated Expellent	1¼, 1½ gal	30–40 ft	40 sec
		2½ gal	30–40 ft	1½ min
		5 gal	30–40 ft	2 min
		17 gal (wheeled)	50 ft	3 min
		33 gal (wheeled)	50 ft	3 min
Carbon Dioxide	Self Expellent	2½ to 5 lb	3–8 ft	8 to 30 sec
		10 to 15 lb	3–8 ft	8 to 30 sec
		20 lb	3–8 ft	10 to 30 sec
		50 to 100 lb (wheeled)	3–10 ft	10 to 30 sec
Dry Chemical (Sodium Bicarbonate)	Stored Pressure	1 lb	5–8 ft	8 to 10 sec
		1½ to 2½ lb	5–8 ft	8 to 12 sec
	Cartridge and Stored Pressure	2¾ to 5 lb	5–20 ft	8 to 20 sec
		10 to 30 lb	5–20 ft	10 to 25 sec
	Nitrogen Cylinder or Stored Pressure	75 to 350 lb (wheeled)	15–45 ft	20 to 105 sec

Extinguishing Agent	Method of Operation	Capacity	Horizontal Range of Stream	Approximate Time of Discharge
Dry Chemical (Potassium Bicarbonate)	Stored Pressure	1 to 2 lb	5–8 ft	8 to 10 sec
	Stored Pressure	2¼ to 5 lb	5–12 ft	8 to 10 sec
	Cartridge or Stored Pressure	5½ to 10 lb	5–20 ft	8 to 25 sec
		16 to 30 lb	15–45 ft	8 to 25 sec
	Nitrogen Cylinder or Stored Pressure	125 to 300 lb (wheeled)	15–45 ft	30 to 60 sec
Dry Chemical (Potassium Chloride)	Stored Pressure	2 to 2½ lb	5–8 ft	8 to 10 sec
	Cartridge or Stored Pressure	5 to 10 lb	5–20 ft	8 to 25 sec
		19½ to 30 lb	15–45 ft	8 to 25 sec
	Nitrogen Cylinder or Stored Pressure	50 to 160 lb (wheeled)	15–45 ft	30 to 60 sec
Dry Chemical (Ammonium Phosphate)	Stored Pressure	1 to 5 lb	5–12 ft	8 to 10 sec
Dry Chemical (Ammonium Phosphate)	Stored Pressure or Cartridge	4 to 8½ lb	5–12 ft	8 to 12 sec
		9 to 17 lb	5–20 ft	10 to 25 sec
		17 to 30 lb	5–20 ft	10 to 25 sec
	Nitrogen Cylinder or Stored Pressure	50 to 300 lb (wheeled)	15–45 ft	30 to 60 sec
Dry Chemical (Foam Compatible)	Cartridge and Stored Pressure	4¼ to 9 lb	5–20 ft	8 to 10 sec
		9 to 27 lb	5–20 ft	10 to 25 sec
		18 to 30 lb	5–20 lb	10 to 25 sec
	Nitrogen cylinder and Stored Pressure	150 to 350 lb (wheeled)	15–45 ft	20 to 150 sec
Dry Chemical (Foam Compatible) (Potassium Chloride)	Cartridge and Stored Pressure	2½ to 5 lb	5–12 ft	8 to 10 sec
		9½ to 20 lb	5–20 ft	8 to 25 sec
		19½ to 30 lb	5–20 ft	10 to 25 sec
	Nitrogen cylinder and Stored Pressure	50 lb (wheeled)	15–45 ft	30 sec
Dry Chemical (Foam Compatible) (Potassium Bicarbonate Urea Based)	Stored Pressure	5 to 11 lb	11–22 ft	13 to 18 sec
	Stored Pressure	17 to 19 lb	15–30 ft	26 to 30 sec
		175 lb (wheeled)	70 ft	62 sec
Bromotrifluoromethane	Self Expellent	2½ lb	4–6 ft	8 to 10 sec
Bromochlorodifluoromethane	Stored Pressure	2 to 4 lb	8–12 ft	8 to 12 sec
		9 lb	9–15 ft	8 to 15 sec

*Adapted with permission from Charles A. Tuck, Jr., ed., *NFPA Inspection Manual*, 4th ed. (Boston: National Fire Protection Association, 1976), pp. 280–283.

Standpipe and Hose Systems

Standpipe and hose systems are designed to facilitate the application of water to structure fires. They essentially reduce the need for fire fighters to drag hoses filled with water up many flights of stairs or over long distances. Buildings with large floor areas such as manufacturing buildings, shopping malls, and warehouses may have horizontal standpipe systems. Vertical standpipes are found in most buildings over four stories in height.

Standpipe and hose systems may be designed either for operation by the occupants of the building, by the municipal fire department or trained fire brigade, or by both. In cases where untrained personnel are to operate the hoses, the hose diameter is usually limited to one and one-half inches.

Types There are four types of standpipe systems defined by the NFPA:

1. Wet standpipe system having supply valve open and water pressure maintained at all times.
2. Standpipe system so arranged through the use of approved devices as to admit water to the system automatically by opening a hose valve.
3. Standpipe system arranged to admit water to the system through manual operation of approved remote control devices located at each hose station.
4. Dry standpipe having no permanent water supply.[14]

The National Fire Protection Association has issued standards for standpipe and hose systems. In these standards, those systems designed for use by trained personnel only are designated Class I systems, and those designed to be used by untrained personnel receive a Class II designation. Class III systems are dual purpose. A summary of the NFPA standards for various type systems and the intended use of the systems is given in Exhibit 6-6.

Inspection of Standpipe Systems The underwriter may not assume that the existence of a standpipe and hose system in a structure means that the system is functional. Inspection and testing on a periodic basis, not less than once a year, is required to determine that all of the components of the system are in proper operating condition. A very important part of the system are the siamese connections. These connections may have improper threads or may be stuffed with refuse, rendering them useless.

A survey of 125 buildings in Los Angeles produced the following results:

Exhibit 6-6
Summary of National Fire Protection Association Standpipe Standards*

Type	Intended Use	Size Hose and Distribution	Minimum Size Pipe	Minimum Water Supply
Class I	Heavy streams	2½-in. connections	4 in. up to 100 ft.	500 gpm 1st standpipe
	Fire department	All portions of each story or section within 30 ft. of nozzle with 100 ft. of hose	6 in. above 100 ft.	250 gpm each additional (2,500 gpm maximum)
	Trained personnel			
	Advanced stages of fire		(275 ft. maximum unless pressure regulated)	30 minute duration
				65 psi at top outlet with 500 gpm flow
Class II	Small streams	1½-in. connections (Distribution same as Class I)	2 in. up to 50 ft.	100 gpm per building
	Building occupants		2½ in. above 50 ft.	30 minute duration
	Incipient fire			65 psi at top outlet with 100 gpm flowing
Class III	Both of above	Same as Class I with added 1½-in. outlets or 1½-in. adapters and 1½-in. hose	Same as Class I	Same as Class I

*Reprinted with permission from *Standard for the Installation of Standpipe and Hose Systems* (Boston: National Fire Protection Association, 1974), p. 4.

1. In 25 percent of the buildings it was impossible to deliver water to the dry standpipes.
2. 45 percent of the buildings failed to pass the test requirements.
3. 70 percent of the buildings had "Pacific Coast Threads" (which do not conform to fire department standards).
4. 14 percent of the buildings had faulty pipes.
5. 12 percent of the clapper type valves leaked excessively.
6. 8 percent of the standpipes were never completely connected (either at the laterals to the outlets or at the top section of the standpipe).[15]

Combined Standpipe and Automatic Sprinkler Systems The NFPA in 1971 adopted provisions for the combination of standpipe and sprinkler systems. While automatic sprinklers are highly desirable in high-rise buildings, owners frequently fail to install them due to the increased cost. Since most structures over four floors in height must have at least a dry standpipe system, the use of standpipes as risers for automatic sprinkler systems greatly reduces the cost of providing automatic sprinkler protection.

The basic requirements for a combined standpipe and automatic sprinkler system include the following:

1. riser and hose valves located in fire resistive stair enclosures,
2. separate floor control valves for sprinklers located in the fire resistive stair enclosure,
3. risers at least six inches in size, and
4. adequate water supply for both sprinklers and standpipes.[16]

Automatic Sprinkler Systems

Automatic sprinkler systems are an important part of private extinguishment efforts. Since the sprinkler heads react automatically to fire, they can often control or extinguish the blaze unaided. There are also fire department connections which permit the fire department to hook up to the sprinkler system and greatly increase the pressure and water flow through the heads. These systems may produce other benefits for the insured since a lighter weight, less costly construction type may be adequate for a given occupancy if properly sprinklered.

Water Supply The most reliable water source results from the connection of the sprinkler system directly to a public or private water main. The reliability of the water supply is then dependent only upon the underlying water system. If it is public water, the FSRS rating for that municipality includes an analysis of the water supply. Any private water supply system can be evaluated using a similar technique. Where the reliability of the main water supply is questionable, a secondary source of supply can be provided.

Fire pumps can be provided and hooked up to suction tanks to provide a water source for the system. A pressure tank which forces water into the system under air pressure is another possible water source. A third source is a gravity tank which may be located on the roof of the structure or on a separate tower. The height of the gravity tank provides an acceptable head pressure for the water. These systems require periodic maintenance, and in some climates provision must be made to prevent the water in the tank and standpipe from freezing.

Exhibit 6-7 shows one example of an automatic sprinkler system with a gravity tank.

Wet Versus Dry Pipe Systems There are two major types of automatic sprinkler systems, wet and dry pipe. (The deluge and preaction systems are discussed separately, after the discussion of dry and wet systems, since they do not specifically fall under the dry or wet system classification.) The wet pipe system is the most effective and

Exhibit 6-7
Automatic Sprinkler System*

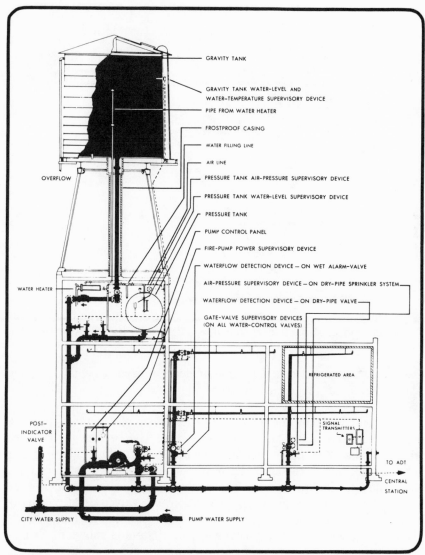

GRAVITY TANK

GRAVITY TANK WATER-LEVEL AND
WATER-TEMPERATURE SUPERVISORY DEVICE

PIPE FROM WATER HEATER

FROSTPROOF CASING

WATER FILLING LINE

AIR LINE

OVERFLOW

PRESSURE TANK AIR-PRESSURE SUPERVISORY DEVICE

PRESSURE TANK WATER-LEVEL SUPERVISORY DEVICE

PRESSURE TANK

PUMP CONTROL PANEL

FIRE-PUMP POWER SUPERVISORY DEVICE

WATERFLOW DETECTION DEVICE — ON WET ALARM-VALVE

AIR-PRESSURE SUPERVISORY DEVICE — ON DRY-PIPE SPRINKLER SYSTEM

WATERFLOW DETECTION DEVICE — ON DRY-PIPE VALVE

GATE-VALVE SUPERVISORY DEVICES
(ON ALL WATER-CONTROL VALVES)

WATER HEATER

REFRIGERATED AREA

POST-
INDICATOR
VALVE

SIGNAL
TRANSMITTERS

TO ADT

CENTRAL
STATION

CITY WATER SUPPLY

PUMP WATER SUPPLY

*Reprinted with permission of ADT Security Systems.

efficient of the two, primarily because there is no time delay. The dry pipe system also requires additional maintenance.

Wet Pipe Systems. The wet pipe system consists of water-filled pipes with various sprinkler heads installed at intervals along the pipes. The sprinkler heads are distributed across the area to be protected,

Exhibit 6-8
The Automatic Sprinkler System*

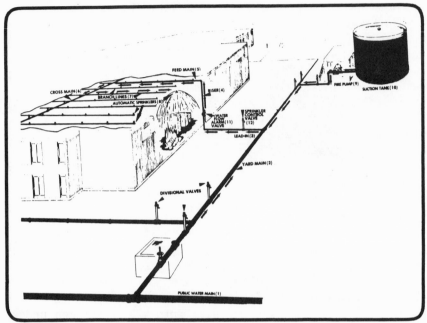

*Reprinted with permission from *The Handbook of Property Conservation* (Norwood, MA: Factory Mutual Engineering Corporation, 1973), p. 103.

usually in a grid pattern. The type of head utilized depends upon the requirements of the occupancy and the location of the head in the system.

The water supply for the system may be supplemented by the fire department connection, increasing pressure. The system is activated when the heat or flame of the fire melts a fusible link or other activating device on the sprinkler head. Since there is water in the pipe, water flow is instantaneous. The system also includes supervisory alarm devices to monitor the condition of valves, water supply components, and to sound an alarm when one or more sprinkler heads open. The schematic for a typical wet pipe system is shown in Exhibit 6-8.

The piping is filled with water under pressure that is immediately discharged when a sprinkler operates. The water continues to flow, controlling or extinguishing a fire, until it is shut off.

As shown in Exhibit 6-8, a fire has actuated one sprinkler. This sprinkler starts a small flow of water in the piping. The main water supply comes from the public water main (1). From the public main, water flows through a series of valves (which are always open except when shut down for maintenance) to the yard main (2), to the lead-in (3), through the riser (4), into the feed main (5), to the cross main (6), into the branch line (7), and out through the open sprinkler (8).

The fire pump (9), which starts automatically when a flow of water is detected, draws additional water from a stored supply in the suction tank (10) into the yard main. This additional water from the fire pump and suction tank provides a supplementary supply to assure that enough water at sufficient pressure will be made available to meet the demand of the sprinklers.

Any water flowing through the waterflow alarm valve (11) sounds a local alarm and may send a signal to a central station which notifies the public fire department. The sprinkler control valve (12) will be used to shut off water to the sprinkler system only after control has been gained over the fire and only when the person in charge of fire fighting efforts designates that the valve be shut.

Dry Pipe Systems. Since the wet pipe system has water in the riser, this system is subject to damage under freezing conditions. There are many warehouses and other occupancies where no heat is maintained part, or all, of the time during the winter. The dry pipe system can be used in this situation since it does not contain water in any of the pipes above the dry pipe control valve. The risers, mains, and branch lines in this system are filled with air or nitrogen under pressure. This air pressure forces the water to remain at the level of the control valve. When a sprinkler head opens, the air pressure is released, permitting water to enter the piping system. The water will only flow out those heads that have been activated by the fire. A dry pipe system is shown in the refrigerated area of Exhibit 6-7.

Relative Performance. The dry pipe system includes a lag factor which cannot be avoided. When a sprinkler head is opened in the dry pipe system, air or nitrogen is released immediately. The water must flow from the dry pipe control valve to the head, providing the fire with some time to grow or spread. Data in Exhibit 6-9 shows that with dry pipe systems more sprinkler heads are usually required to control a fire. For example, in 80.2 percent of the fires involving wet systems, extinguishment was accomplished with five or fewer sprinkler heads. On the other hand, 81 percent of the fires involving dry pipe systems required twenty or fewer sprinkler heads.

Deluge and Preaction Systems The *deluge system* utilizes sprinkler heads which are always open. There is a separate detection system which is connected to a deluge valve. When the deluge valve opens, water is discharged from every head in the system connected to that valve, creating a "deluge" of water. This system is employed in occupancies with a severe fuel hazard which could result in a fast

Exhibit 6-9
Cumulative Number of Sprinkler Heads Operating for Wet Pipe, Dry Pipe, and All Types of Sprinkler Systems—1925-1969*

Number of Automatic Sprinklers Operating	Wet Systems Percent	Dry Systems Percent	Unknown Systems Percent	Total Number of Fires	Percent of Total Number of Fires
1	42.6	20.1	33.1	29,733	37.4
2 or fewer	61.0	32.7	50.0	43,396	54.6
3 or fewer	70.2	41.5	59.8	50,769	63.8
4 or fewer	76.2	48.7	66.7	55,795	70.1
5 or fewer	80.2	53.7	70.9	59,156	73.4
6 or fewer	83.2	57.8	75.0	61,814	77.7
7 or fewer	85.2	61.3	77.7	63,724	80.1
8 or fewer	87.0	64.2	80.3	65,348	82.2
9 or fewer	88.3	66.4	82.0	66,571	83.7
10 or fewer	89.4	68.5	83.5	67,629	85.0
11 or fewer	90.4	70.3	84.5	68,533	86.2
12 or fewer	91.2	72.4	86.1	69,464	87.3
13 or fewer	91.7	73.8	87.0	69,990	88.0
14 or fewer	92.6	75.3	88.0	70,788	89.0
15 or fewer	93.1	76.2	89.9	71,313	89.7
20 or fewer	95.0	81.0	91.5	73,347	92.2
25 or fewer	96.0	84.3	92.9	74,464	93.6
30 or fewer	96.9	86.7	94.2	75,411	94.8
35 or fewer	97.3	88.6	95.0	75,976	95.5
40 or fewer	97.7	90.0	95.8	76,472	96.2
50 or fewer	98.1	91.9	96.7	77,079	96.9
75 or fewer	98.9	94.7	98.0	77,995	98.1
100 or fewer	99.4	96.3	98.5	78,533	98.7
200 or fewer	99.8	99.7	99.9	79,384	99.8
All fires	100.0	100.0	100.0	79,544	100.0
No data or no water				1,881	
Total Number of Fires	54,158	13,217	12,169	81,425	

*Reprinted with permission from *Automatic Sprinkler Performance Tables* (Boston: National Fire Protection Association, 1970).

spreading fire. Such occupancies include storage or use of flammable liquids, cooling towers, explosive or ordnance plants, and aircraft hangars. Since this system discharges large quantities of water, the water supply capacity must be correspondingly large.

Since the deluge system requires time for the water to flow from the deluge valve to the open heads, resulting in the same type of lag found in dry pipe systems, the *preprimed deluge system* has been devised. This system has water in the risers and horizontal pipes, right up to the sprinkler heads, with the head openings plugged with rubber stoppers. When the deluge valve opens, the resulting water pressure pushes out the stoppers.

In occupancies where accidental damage to sprinkler heads or piping and the resultant discharge could cause heavy damage to the contents, the *preaction system* is used. This system combines some of the elements of the dry and wet pipe systems. The sprinkler heads have fusible links and the pipes are filled with air or nitrogen under pressure. Rather than a standard dry pipe control valve, the water is held back by a deluge valve with a separate fire detection system. In the event that a sprinkler head is damaged, the release of the air or nitrogen pressure causes an alarm to sound. The separate fire detection system will prevent water from entering the system unless there is an actual fire. This is often used in occupancies such as computer centers where water damage is a severe hazard.

The preaction system can also provide time for the occupants to fight the fire with portable fire extinguishers. If they let the fire get out of control, the deluge valve will open, sending water to all sprinkler heads whose fusible links have opened.

Other Types of Automatic Sprinkler Systems Depending on the occupancy, there are a variety of specialized types of sprinkler systems using extinguishing agents other than streams of water. A detailed description of those systems is beyond the scope of this text. These include the following systems:

1. *Water spray or "fog" systems.* These systems discharge water with a predetermined pattern, particle size, velocity, and density. They are most commonly used to protect flammable liquid and gas tankage and certain types of electrical equipment.
2. *Air foam systems.* These include a wide variety of systems using both ordinary foam and high expansion foam. Fixed foam systems are often used for the protection of aircraft hangars, petrochemical areas, and various hazardous occupancies.
3. *Carbon dioxide systems.* There are two basic types of carbon dioxide systems, *total flooding* and *local application*. In the total flooding system, the room or enclosure in which the fire is located is flooded with sufficient carbon dioxide so that the air is diluted to a point which will not support combustion. Local application systems discharge carbon dioxide directly onto the surface of the burning material. Local application systems are

frequently used with flammable liquids such as in dip tanks, spray booths, and restaurant ranges, hoods, and ducts.

4. *Halogenated agent systems.* These agents include Halon 1301 and Halon 1211, which break the chain reaction and stop the fire. As is the case with carbon dioxide, both total flooding and local application systems may be used. Total flooding systems are used in computer rooms, magnetic-tape storage vaults, electronic controls rooms, and the storage areas on large cargo aircraft. Local application systems are used with printing presses, dip tanks, spray booths, and oil-filled electric transformers.

Supervision of Automatic Sprinkler Systems The operation of an automatic sprinkler system will only be effective if the maintenance and supervision of the system are properly carried out. The probability of failure of an automatic sprinkler system has been estimated at .004 for all fires and .006 for fires large enough to activate the system.[17] A detailed analysis of unsatisfactory sprinkler system performance is shown in Exhibit 6-10.

The use of automatic monitoring devices to supervise the system has previously been discussed under the heading of detection systems. It is important that these devices not only be installed but that the detection system be properly maintained and monitored twenty-four hours a day. A water flow alarm does not convey any information if there is no one around to react to it.

Automatic sprinkler control valves should be inspected weekly or monthly if locked in the open position. Fire pumps should also be inspected weekly and preferably operated. Weekly checks should also be made of gravity tanks, including their water level. This weekly check should also include the condition of sprinkler heads. Some of these heads can become covered with paint, dust, or other substances, effectively insulating the fusible link. A head in this condition will respond late, or not at all.[18]

Fire Department Procedures The performance of the automatic sprinkler system will be greatly enhanced if it is connected to the response of the municipal fire department or industrial fire brigade. The fire department connection on the sprinkler system should be checked to determine that it is operable, clean, and of the proper thread design. This can be checked as part of the fire department pre-fire planning survey. The response of a fire department will be much more efficient if such a survey has been conducted. The underwriter may determine whether such a survey has been conducted, the date of the last survey, and whether any significant changes have occurred in the risk since the most recent survey. A typical pre-fire survey diagram is shown in

Exhibit 6-10
Detailed Analysis of Unsatisfactory Sprinkler Performance*

	Residential	Assembly	Educational	Institutional	Office	Mercantile	Industrial	Storage	Miscellaneous Occupancies	Total
Water to sprinklers shut off										
Valve defective or leaky	—	—	—	—	—	—	3	—	1	4
Unsupervised valve closed for undetermined reason	2	9	—	1	—	16	176	36	7	247
Premature shutoff	2	4	1	—	—	13	193	23	7	243
Alterations or repairs to system	3	5	—	—	1	14	179	28	10	240
To prevent freezing	1	1	1	2	1	24	127	18	26	201
Cold-weather valve closed out of season	—	1	—	—	—	7	24	4	—	36
To abet arson	1	—	2	—	—	5	33	6	2	49
Fear of water damage	—	—	—	—	2	—	18	1	—	21
Miscellaneous other reasons	4	3	—	—	—	4	38	6	14	69
Partial protection										
Originated in unsprinklered area	7	10	8	3	2	10	180	23	1	244
Spread to unsprinklered area	2	—	—	—	—	1	7	—	—	10
Inadequate water supply										
Insufficient water or low water pressure from public supply	2	2	—	—	—	2	114	19	—	139
Insufficient water or low water pressure from private supply	1	—	1	1	—	—	26	6	—	35
Insufficient water for both sprinklers and hose streams	1	1	—	—	1	—	53	13	—	69
Gravity tank empty	1	—	—	—	—	1	22	3	—	27
Pump failure or pump not started	—	—	—	1	—	—	14	—	—	15

Continued on next page

										Total
Mains broken	—	—	—	—	—	1	11	1	—	13
Miscellaneous reasons	—	—	—	—	—	—	12	1	—	13
System frozen										
Pipes or valves frozen	1	—	—	—	—	4	32	5	2	44
Slow operation										
Excessive heads on dry-pipe valve	—	—	—	—	—	—	19	1	—	20
High-temperature sprinklers	—	—	1	—	—	—	9	—	—	10
Failure of quick-opening device	—	—	—	—	—	—	4	—	—	4
Heat-actuating devices inadequate or inoperative	—	—	—	—	—	—	3	—	—	3
Miscellaneous reasons	—	—	—	—	—	4	10	5	—	19
Defective dry-pipe valve										
Defective or improperly adjusted dry-pipe valve	—	—	—	—	1	5	38	9	—	53
Faulty building construction										
Concealed horizontal or vertical spaces lacking protection	11	9	4	1	2	34	94	5	1	161
Floor or roof collapse	—	—	1	—	—	1	12	6	1	21
Miscellaneous deficiencies	—	—	—	—	—	—	5	—	—	5
Obstruction to distribution										
Fires under benches, etc.	—	—	—	—	—	2	98	8	—	108
High piling of stock	—	—	—	—	—	3	60	41	—	104
Partitions erected	1	—	—	—	—	5	12	4	1	23
Miscellaneous reasons	2	1	—	—	—	1	13	4	—	21
Hazard of occupancy										
Hazard too severe for sprinkler equipment as installed	—	—	—	—	—	6	182	23	3	214
Explosion damaged system	1	—	—	—	1	6	161	13	2	184

										Total
Water overflowed containers of flammable liquids	—	—	—	—	—	1	15	—	—	16
Miscellaneous reasons	—	—	—	—	—	—	8	2	—	10
Exposure fire										
Exposure fire overpowered sprinkler system in exposed building	—	1	—	—	—	1	36	12	2	52
Inadequate maintenance										
Plugged sprinklers	—	2	—	—	—	1	39	8	—	50
Sprinklers dirty, corroded or coated	—	2	—	—	—	1	41	4	2	48
Obstructed piping	2	—	1	1	2	2	117	25	1	150
Defective check valve	—	—	—	—	—	—	2	2	—	4
Miscellaneous reasons	—	—	—	—	1	—	9	—	—	10
Antiquated system										
Pipe sizes, sprinkler spacing substandard or old standard	2	1	—	—	—	1	51	3	—	58
Valves substandard or old standard	—	—	—	—	—	—	1	—	—	1
Sprinklers substandard or old standard	—	—	—	—	1	—	3	—	1	5
Miscellaneous deficiencies due to age	—	—	—	—	—	—	1	—	—	1
Miscellaneous and unknown										
Causes of unsatisfactory sprinkler performance unknown or cannot be otherwise classified	1	—	2	—	1	1	46	7	3	60
Total	48	52	20	12	13	176	2,351	375	87	3,134

*Reprinted with permission from *Automatic Sprinkler Performance Tables* (Boston: National Fire Protection Association, 1970).

Exhibit 6-11. Note that it shows sprinklered and nonsprinklered areas, water supply points, and the location of the fire department connection. The information on this diagram can save the municipal fire department much valuable time.

Fire Brigades

For large industrial establishments, particularly those located in areas remote from municipal services, a fire brigade may be established. Since the personnel in the fire brigade often have other duties in the plant, the operation of the brigade may be considered similar to that of a volunteer fire department. In those plants where the fire brigade members have no other duties, they can be considered equivalent to full-time fire department members.

The fire brigade is a fire department and should be evaluated on the same basis. The fire brigade's efficiency depends on:

1. the training of the personnel,
2. the amount and type of fire fighting equipment, and
3. the size and reliability of the water supply.

Fire brigades may range from little more than an organized attempt to utilize portable fire extinguishers until the arrival of the municipal fire department, to fully organized engine and ladder companies, able to deal with first response fires on their own and only requiring help in the case of larger fires.

Extinguishment Systems as a Hazard

Both wet and dry pipe sprinkler systems present a hazard of water damage in the event of leakage or damage to the system. This hazard is increased in the case of occupancies with contents that are highly susceptible to water damage.

The sprinkler leakage hazard can be dealt with by careful maintenance of the sprinkler system and by assuring that sprinkler heads are of the appropriate design, located where they will not be easily damaged, and properly maintained. The preaction system discussed earlier is another method of reducing the chance of loss from this hazard.

Exhibit 6-11
A Typical Pre-Fire Survey Diagram*

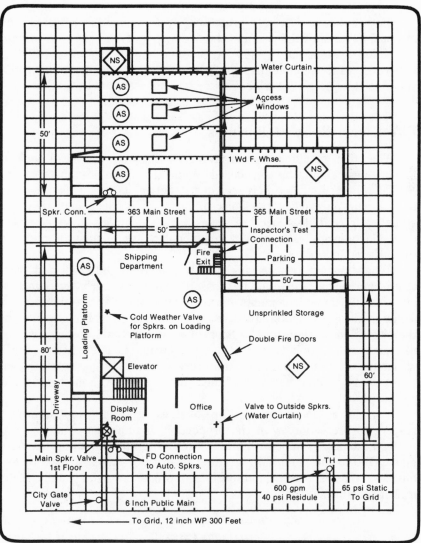

*Reprinted with permission from *Recommendations for Fire Department Operations in Properties Protected by Sprinkler and Standpipe Systems* (Boston: National Fire Protection Association, 1973).

PROTECTION AS A VARIABLE
IN UNDERWRITING DECISIONS

Effect on Premium

Both public and private protection systems have an effect on the physical hazards of the risk and the fire rate for that hazard. A private protection system has a very large effect upon the fire rate. It is important to determine that the system is properly maintained and supervised to justify the lower rate.

Effect on a Book of Business

The effect of differences in protection class on an overall book of fire business should be considered. While the differences in fire rates should account for the differences in risk between Class 2 and Class 10, this is true only when the book of business is large enough to be statistically credible. Since fire losses have a relatively low frequency, particularly large losses, a very large book of fire business is required for full credibility.

When moving from sprinklered to unsprinklered risks and from Class 1 municipal protection to Class 10, it is particularly the detection and extinguishment elements of fire protection that are deficient or lacking. These elements have their greatest effect on fire severity, or the size of loss. Therefore, a book of business made up primarily of unsprinklered risks in Classes 8, 9, and 10 would be likely to have more variability in loss results, and therefore more "risk" in the statistical sense than a book of business of the same premium volume made up of risks with better fire protection.

For this reason, a book of fire business is usually balanced with respect to protection, with the proportion of unprotected and poorly protected business kept within limits set by top underwriting management. Due to the potentially greater severity of losses, a book of fire business that is heavy in unprotected properties will usually incur higher reinsurance costs.

SUMMARY

Fire protection is of two types, public and private. Public fire protection is provided by municipalities to all properties within their jurisdiction. Private fire protection is provided by the property owner. Both public and private protection consist of three elements:

1. prevention,
2. detection, and
3. extinguishment.

Fire prevention activities include all measures designed to reduce fire frequency or severity prior to the actual outbreak of fire. Fire detection activities include all measures and equipment designed to notify fire fighting personnel of the fire. Fire extinguishment activities include all measures utilized to contain and extinguish a fire. Municipal fire departments are evaluated according to the ISO Fire Suppression Rating Schedule. This schedule evaluates three major aspects of the fire department, which are:

1. water supply,
2. fire department personnel and equipment, and
3. fire alarm.

Private fire prevention efforts fall into three major categories:

1. control of housekeeping,
2. adherence to building codes and standards, and
3. fire protection planning.

Private detection systems are designed to reduce loss severity by speeding the response of fire fighting personnel and equipment. These systems may be either manual or automatic. Manual systems include guards, either hired by the property owner or by a merchant police system. These guards may be supervised either by a central station system or by a clock and tape. Automatic detectors may be connected either to a local alarm or to a central or remote station. Private extinguishment systems include:

1. portable fire extinguishers,
2. standpipe and hose systems,
3. automatic sprinkler systems, and
4. fire brigades.

Protection is a variable in underwriting decisions. Both private and public protection have an effect on rates. Since unprotected risks are likely to have greater variability in loss results than protected risks, protection is a consideration in the composition of a book of business.

Chapter Notes

1. This section is based on Chapter 10 of Bernard L. Webb, J. J. Launie, Willis Park Rokes, and Norman A. Baglini, *Insurance Company Operations* (Malvern, PA: American Institute for Property and Liability Underwriters, 1984).
2. Robert B. Holtom, *Commercial Fire Underwriting* (Cincinnati: National Underwriter Company, 1969), p. 64.
3. "Insurer-Bought Vans Credited With Doubling Arson Arrests in Conn.," *National Underwriter* (Property-Casualty Edition), November 14, 1977, p. 46.
4. Hugh M. Maguire, "Eight-Agency Effort Fights Arson," *Fire Command!* December 1975.
5. *NFPA Inspection Manual*, 4th ed., National Fire Prevention Association, Boston, June 1976, pp. 33-38.
6. *NFPA Inspection Manual*, pp. 33-38.
7. J. V. Grimaldi and R. H. Simonds, *Safety Management*, 3rd ed. (Homewood, IL: Richard D. Irwin, 1975), p. 549.
8. Raymond J. Casey, "Convincing Consumers to Install Automatic Sprinklers," *Fire Journal*, March 1971, pp. 35-36, 41.
9. Carrol E. Burtner, "The Economics of a Fire Protection Program," *Fire Technology*, February 1966, pp. 5-14.
10. *NFPA Inspection Manual*, pp. 296-298.
11. See Exhibit 6-10.
12. John L. Bryan, *Automatic Sprinkler and Standpipe Systems*, National Fire Protection Association, Boston, 1976, pp. 362-370.
13. *NFPA Inspection Manual*, pp. 277-278.
14. National Fire Protection Association, *Standard for the Installation of Standpipe and Hose Systems*, 1974, NFPA, Boston, p. 4.
15. Paul R. Lyons, "Dry Standpipe Survey in Los Angeles," *Fire Journal*, May 1969, pp. 65-66.
16. James M. Hammack, "Combined Sprinkler System and Standpipes (Some Random Thoughts)," *Fire Journal*, September 1971, p. 68.
17. Bert M. Cohn, "The Validity of Trade-offs for Automatic Sprinkler Protection," *Fire Protection News*, Gage Babcock and Associates, Inc., August 1974, pp. 1-4.
18. Bryan, pp. 76-78, 205-207.

CHAPTER 7

External Exposures and Coverages

ANALYZING EXTERNAL EXPOSURES

Introduction

The previous chapters have covered construction, occupancy, and protection. Each of these three elements greatly affect the underwriting decision-making process. Another important underwriting consideration is *exposure*. Generally, *exposure* refers to any situation or condition that may cause a loss. In fire underwriting, the term has a more specific meaning and refers to causes of loss from *external* sources. A relatively unhazardous occupancy such as a real estate office could be considered unacceptable if it were located next to a dynamite factory. Although the underwriter has relatively little control over external exposures, there are means by which the risk from such exposures can be reduced.

Major Considerations

The biggest problem in evaluating external exposures is that information is not as readily available as it is with respect to construction, occupancy, and protection. Information regarding external exposures must be developed by the underwriter's asking specific questions of the producer or ordering a loss control pre-inspection. Exhibit 7-1 shows a portion of an inspection form which develops external exposure information. Basically, in evaluating an external exposure, all other fire underwriting factors must be considered for the *exposing* building (an adjacent building) as well as for the *exposed* building (the building to be insured). That is, the C, O, and P portion of the COPE factors must be considered. Additionally, climatic conditions such as low humidity and high winds can enhance the likelihood of an exposure fire.

Construction Consider this example in Exhibit 7-2 of a brick real estate office. Assume that on each side of the office is an empty lot and that on the far side of each lot is an additional building, one frame and one brick. It appears from the diagram that each of the neighboring buildings is the same distance from the real estate office. Which building creates the greater external exposure to the real estate office? From a construction standpoint, it is more likely that the exposing frame building will burn rather than the brick building and thus it should be concluded that the frame building presents a greater exposure to the real estate office.

The construction of the real estate office, however, cannot be disregarded. Is it likely that the brick office will catch fire if the frame building is burning? The answer to this question depends on the separation distance between the two buildings and the construction variations of the real estate office. The closer the burning frame building is, the more likely the brick building will ignite. Equally important are the construction variables such as windows, doors, and type of roof of the real estate office. A window or wooden door which faces the frame building would obviously reduce the resistiveness of the real estate office to an exposure fire from the frame building. A shingled roof or "A-frame" or gabled construction would make the real estate office more susceptible to exposure fires than if the roof were flat and/or constructed out of fire resistive material.

The relative heights of the exposing and exposed buildings are also important in evaluating external exposure. If the frame building were two stories high and the real estate office only one story, a flat roof on the office building would serve as a good receptacle for flaming embers from the burning frame building. If the frame building were several floors higher (and relatively closer to the brick building), its collapse would be an additional exposure to the real estate office.

Recognizing the effect of the construction of exposing buildings, guidelines have been developed stating the separation distances suggested for various types of construction. An example of such a guideline is shown in Exhibit 7-3. Using this guide for the real estate office example, if the frame building is thirty feet or more from the brick real estate office, the underwriter should probably not consider the frame building as an exposure unless, of course, there are

Exhibit 7-1
Loss Control Engineering—External Exposures

Attachments	Square Feet	Neighborhood and Locale	Public Protection	Private Protection
Number Type		☐ Average	**No. Hydrants**	☐ Sprinklers
☐ Porches	____	☐ Below Average	____ W/in 500 Feet	☐ Standpipe
☐ Garage	____	☐ Improving		☐ Extinguishers
☐ Fireplace	____	☐ Deteriorating	**Feet to**	☐ Fire Alarm
☐ Balconies	____	☐ Stable	____ Nearest Hydrant	☐ Detection System
☐ Car Ports	____	☐ Merc ☐ Suburb		☐ Watchman
☐ Out Bldgs	____	☐ Urban ☐ Factory/	**Distance to**	☐ Other
☐ Other	____	☐ Congested Warehouse	____ Fire Dept (miles)	☐ None
		☐ Outside ☐ Isolated		
		☐ Corp Limits		

Air Conditioning
☐ Central ☐ Window

Exposures	North	South	East	West
Height (Stories)				
Construction	☐ Masonry ☐ Frame ☐ Other	☐ Masonry ☐ Frame ☐ Other	☐ Masonry ☐ Frame ☐ Other	☐ Masonry ☐ Frame ☐ Other
Occupancy and Name				
Distance				
Condition	☐ Avg ☐ Below Avg	☐ Avg ☐ Below Avg	☐ Avg ☐ Below Avg	☐ Avg ☐ Below Avg

Interior Stair, Aisle and Floor Cond.: _____

Exterior Fire and Liability Hazards, Including Windstorm: _____

Exhibit 7-2
Diagram for Determination of Exposure to Insured Building

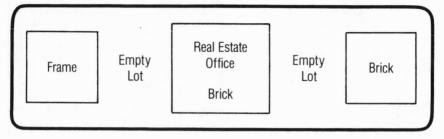

Exhibit 7-3
Separation Distances (Protection Classes 1–8)

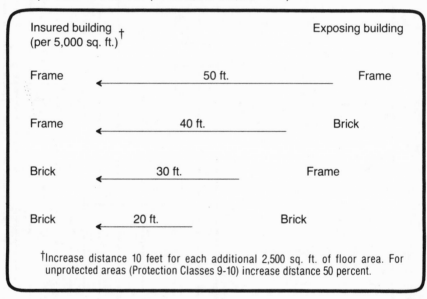

†Increase distance 10 feet for each additional 2,500 sq. ft. of floor area. For unprotected areas (Protection Classes 9-10) increase distance 50 percent.

construction deficiencies such as windows, doors, or a combustible roof on the real estate office.

The result would be different if the frame building were being submitted to the underwriter for fire coverage. In this case the exposing brick building would only be thirty feet from the exposed frame building. According to the guideline, this is an unsafe distance.

Emphasis should be placed on construction variables or deficiencies. A brick building with large windows, wooden doors, or a combustible roof may be considered to be no better than a frame building as far as its susceptibility to combustion is concerned. The underwriter must evaluate the effect of an external exposure in relation to the actual risk, including its construction deficiencies.

Before considering the occupancy of the exposing building, one other element of the above example should be considered—the empty lots. Lack of adjacent or surrounding buildings does not necessarily mean that a risk is free of external exposures. If an empty lot is filled with overgrown, dry grass, it is of itself a very hazardous exposure. Combustible materials or debris close to the building would also constitute an exposure hazard.

Occupancy If internal exposures (occupancy) affect the susceptibility to a fire loss, it follows that the occupancy of an exposing building can affect the exposed building. In the real estate office example, assume that the frame building is occupied by a restaurant. A high risk occupancy such as a restaurant may present an exposure hazard even if the distance between the structures is greater than that indicated in the guidelines.

The combustibility of the contents and the degree of heat which the contents will produce are also important in considering the occupancy of an exposing building. The radiation resulting from intense heat can also cause an exposure fire. The nature of the contents and operations, therefore, is a very important consideration in evaluating external exposures.

Protection Protection has a very important effect on exposure. The distance guidelines shown in Exhibit 7-3 are based not only on the construction of the buildings but also on the effectiveness of the fire department and water supply as categorized by the town grade. The average time it will take a fire department to respond in the various protection classifications is an important consideration. In unprotected areas (classes 9-10) the response from the fire department usually cannot be determined with any certainty; thus, the guide in Exhibit 7-3 indicates that the distances must be increased 50 percent in order to adequately reduce the exposure.

There are several forms of protection which can effectively reduce the chances of external exposure losses. The first, and perhaps most important, is *clear space.* Clear space not only eliminates fire exposure but also gives the fire department sufficient space in which to operate. Remember, however, that dry grass, high winds, or areas cluttered with combustible materials or debris defeat rather than enhance the effectiveness of clear space in protecting against exposure fires.

A second form of protection from an exposure fire is automatic sprinkler systems within the *exposed* building. A sprinkler system within an *exposing* building, if functioning, would probably eliminate the exposure totally by extinguishing the fire in the exposing building.

The wall and roof construction can have a decided effect in reducing exposure fires, but the effectiveness of even a noncombustible wall can be reduced or eliminated by unprotected openings such as glass windows or wooden doors. There are, however, ways of protecting such openings. Ordinary windows can be replaced with glass blocks or wired glass. Automatic steel shutters can be placed over ordinary windows. Wooden exterior doors could be replaced with automatic fire doors. Outside sprinklers could be placed over openings. A protective wall or fence could even be constructed between the exposing and exposed buildings.

The value of any of these methods of protection is dependent upon adequate response of the fire department. After half an hour the exposing building could be burning out of control and the effect of any protective device on the exposed building could not be relied upon.

Multiple Occupancies Thus far the analysis has concerned the exposure between separate buildings. Exposure also exists within one multi-sectioned building. An example will help clarify this. Exhibit 7-4 shows a typical one-story shopping center.

Assume that the building is owned by one person or corporation, but that each separate business is owned and operated independently and leased from the owner. If asked to insure the contents of the real estate office, the underwriter should definitely consider the exposures. In this case the real estate office is exposed by a supermarket and a restaurant. The exposure, in fact, is much more prominent than in the previous example since the real estate office shares common walls with two other occupancies. The same factors—construction, occupancy, and protection—must be considered in evaluating the exposures in a multi-sectioned building.

In a multi-occupancy building, distance is not really a factor since the occupancies are adjacent (except to the extent that one occupancy is adjacent and another is two occupancies away). Construction, however, is very important. Naturally a fire resistive building will be a less hazardous risk for fire insurance than a frame building, but this is only the first consideration. Assuming the building in Exhibit 7-4 is of fire resistive construction, the next factor the underwriter should consider is the nature of the walls between the real estate office and the adjacent businesses. Are the construction materials and thickness of the walls such that they will hold until the fire department arrives? In other words, do the walls meet the specifications of a true fire wall? Are the parapets high enough to keep the embers from blowing from one section of the building to another? Is the roof construction of a material that will resist combustion?

As in the first example, there is a restaurant which exposes the real

Exhibit 7-4
Diagram for Determination of Exposure to Insured Store in Shopping
Center

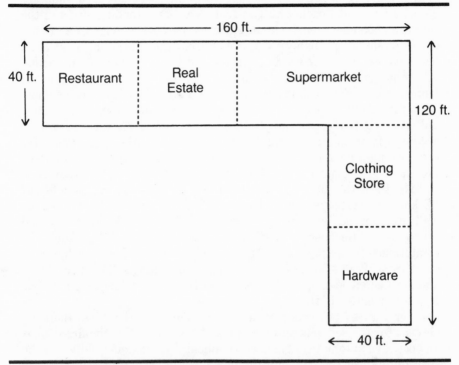

estate office, but in this case the restaurant shares a common wall with
the real estate office. The proximity of a hazardous occupancy in this
example makes the adequacy of the construction even more important.
It is therefore absolutely necessary that the real estate office be a
totally separate fire division from the restaurant in order to reduce the
exposure to an acceptable level. If this cannot be accomplished, the
underwriter, from a practical point of view, will be insuring a
restaurant at office occupancy rates.

Besides the protective items already discussed in conjunction with
the construction, the underwriter must also consider the water supply,
response of the fire department, and accessibility of the premises for
the fire fighters.

The subject of determining the probable maximum loss (PML) on a
building or its contents has been discussed in earlier chapters.
Construction, occupancy, and protection each can contribute to the
establishment of a PML less than 100 percent. In the example of the
multiple occupancy shopping center, the underwriter, by analysis of

each element of COPE, can determine if the probable maximum loss of this particular building will be less than 100 percent. If the construction of this building is fire resistive and the walls between each shop are genuine fire walls, each with two-foot parapets extending through the roof in a protected area, it can be surmised that in the event of a fire the entire building probably will not burn. The question, therefore, becomes how much of the building—or better, how much of the value of the building—is likely to be damaged in the event of a fire. It is the underwriter's responsibility to determine PML. Most insurance companies provide guidelines to their underwriters to enable them to establish uniform and fairly accurate PMLs. Exhibit 7-5 is an excerpt from a section of an underwriting manual indicating the guidelines for establishing a PML on a multi-sectional building based on the ability of the walls to contain the fire (or a twelve-inch thick wall is required).

No PML can be established for wall #1 because of insufficient thickness and construction and because it is not parapeted. No PML for wall #2 can be established because of insufficient thickness and construction. Because wall #3 is not parapeted, a PML cannot be established. The parapet of wall #4 is only twelve inches and therefore insufficient. Wall #5 is not sufficient for establishing a PML because of an unprotected opening in the wall. Wall #6 has an inadequate fire door for establishing a PML.

For wall #7 one can consider establishing a PML of less than 100 percent for the sections on both sides of the fire wall if the fire door is an operative automatic labeled class A door. The combustibility and the susceptibility of the contents to smoke, water, and heat radiation are the key determining factors. For example, a risk with contents of normal combustibility and susceptibility may result in the following PML: (1) building—100 percent of the values in one section plus 25 to 33 percent of the values in the section on the other side of the wall; (2) contents—100 percent of the values in one section plus 33 to 50 percent of the values in the section on the other side of the wall.

Under normal conditions one could consider wall #8 on each side of the fire wall for a separate PML if the fire doors are operative automatic labeled Class A doors. For wall #9, one could consider each side of the fire wall for a separate PML under normal conditions.

The same thought process shown in Exhibit 7-5 is used in determining the *key risk*. The key risk is the one building in a group of buildings which will produce the largest loss and expose the company's reinsurance treaties to the largest loss. In an apartment complex, for example, if the distances are great enough and the construction good enough, each building may be a separate fire division and thus the buildings are not exposed to one another. The building which will produce the greatest loss is, therefore, designated as the key risk and

Exhibit 7-5
Wall - Integrity

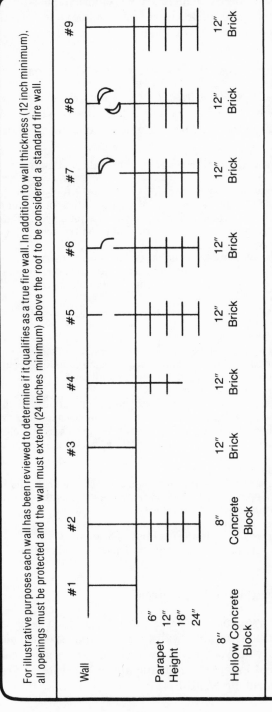

For illustrative purposes each wall has been reviewed to determine if it qualifies as a true fire wall. In addition to wall thickness (12 inch minimum), all openings must be protected and the wall must extend (24 inches minimum) above the roof to be considered a standard fire wall.

Wall	#1	#2	#3	#4	#5	#6	#7	#8	#9
Parapet Height	6" 12" 18" 24"								
	8" Hollow Concrete Block	8" Concrete Block	12" Brick	12" Brick	12" Brick	12" Brick	12" Brick	12" Brick	12" Brick

One-story brick with wood roof (not peaked, round, or mansard). Mercantile occupancies. No special hazards. Stock is of normal combustibility and susceptibility. Fire protection is Class 4.

the values of the other buildings are disregarded, possibly allowing the insurance company to insure the entire complex because the probable maximum loss is the key risk building.

Factors Influencing the Severity of Exposures

The *Fire Protection Handbook* summarizes the factors which influence the severity of an exposure fire on a building. In addition to the temperature and the duration of the exposing fire, these include:

1. Exposing fire
   (a) Type of construction of exterior walls and roofs.
   (b) Width of exposing fire.
   (c) Height of exposing fire.
   (d) Percent of openings in exposing wall area. Exterior walls that are combustible or which do not have sufficient resistance to contain the fire should be treated as having 100 percent openings.
   (e) Ventilation characteristics of the burning room.
   (f) The fuel dispersion, or surface-to-volume ratio of the fuel.
   (g) The size, geometry, and surface-to-volume ratio of the room involved.
   (h) The thermal properties, conductivity, specific heat, and density of the interior finish.
2. Exposed building
   (a) Type of construction of exterior walls and roofs.
   (b) Orientation and surface area of exposed exterior walls.
   (c) Percent of openings in exterior wall area.
   (d) Protection openings.
   (e) Exposure of interior finish and combustibles to the radiation, convection, and flying brands of the exposing fire.
   (f) Thermal properties, conductivity, specific heat, density, and fuel dispersion of the interior finish materials and the building contents.
3. Site and protection features
   (a) Separation distance between exposing and exposed building.
   (b) Shielding effect of intervening noncombustible construction.
   (c) Wind direction and velocity.
   (d) Air temperature and humidity.
   (e) Accessibility for fire fighting operation.
   (f) Extent and character of fire department operations.[1]

Control of External Exposures

Existing exposures can be controlled by good construction with modifications such as fire walls, fire doors, special barriers, and parapets. Good water supply, quick response from the fire department, and internal and external automatic sprinkler systems are additional methods of controlling exposure.

Although several protective devices are available, the underwriter really has relatively little control over external exposures. A good water supply and a quick response from the fire department will help, but the underwriter cannot be guaranteed regarding either. He or she cannot realistically ask the owner of an exposing building to rebuild it with better construction in order to reduce the exposure of the building being considered for fire insurance. It is also unrealistic to expect a business in a nearby building to change its operations because it presents a hazardous exposure to the building submitted. Nor will the insured move to a more suitable location with a better water supply and a quicker response from the fire department. A risk that is otherwise totally acceptable because of good construction, unhazardous occupancy, and excellent protection may be unacceptable for fire insurance due to uncontrollable external exposures.

The *Fire Protection Handbook* summarizes several methods by which the exposure hazard can be reduced, given two buildings. These include:

1. Clear space between buildings.
2. Total automatic sprinkler protection.
3. Blank walls of noncombustible materials.
4. Barrier walls (self-supporting) between building and exposure.
5. Extension of exterior masonry walls to form parapets or wings.
6. Automatic outside water curtains for combustible walls.
7. Elimination of opening by filling it with equivalent construction.
8. Glass block panels in openings.
9. Wired glass in steel sash (fixed or automatic closing) in openings.
10. Automatic or deluge sprinklers outside over openings.
11. Automatic (rolling steel) fire shutters on openings.
12. Automatic fire doors on door openings.
13. Automatic fire dampers on wall openings.[2]

ANALYZING INSURANCE CONTRACTS AS A VARIABLE IN UNDERWRITING DECISIONS

Modifying Coverage

As with most of the insurance contracts currently used, the fire policy has become a rather standard contract. At one time it was a more flexible coverage, often being designed for the needs of an individual risk. Standardization evolved, as in most other lines of insurance, due to regulation, legal considerations, and by mutual agreement among insurance companies. The owner of property has basic needs with regard to protection from financial loss from damaged property. The fire policy was created to fulfill that basic need and modified through the years to meet additional needs as they became significant.

The standard fire policy approved in most jurisdictions is basically the 1943 edition of a policy approved in the state of New York that year. Most property insurance policies currently in use are based on the standard wording of this policy. Since the policy has been approved in most states and has been tested in the courts with relatively consistent results, most insurers use the standard form as the basis for their property forms. Since regulatory authorities require that many forms be filed and approved before marketing, most insurers do not file separate forms or manuscript fire policies.

Rating bureaus have been most helpful in filing broadened coverage endorsements which have fulfilled the property insurance needs of most risks. There is a special reason for insurance companies to favor uniform fire policies. Since it is not uncommon for several insurers to share a portion of one large risk on their various policies, uniformity makes this sharing an easier task. It eliminates questions as to whether a loss is covered or which insurer is responsible for what portion of the loss. Without uniformity an underwriter might have difficulty in determining what losses he or she may be assuming alone because of additional exclusions in the other companies' forms.

Insurance companies have marketed modified and broader fire insurance contracts as a marketing tool to capture a desirable segment of the market. These modifications usually are in the form of an endorsement which broadens the basic contract rather than an entirely new fire policy. If successful in the marketplace, other insurers, usually by means of rating bureaus, follow the lead of the pioneer insurer, and the broadened coverage then becomes the new standard. This is basically how package policies evolved. The SMP is now standard except for certain modifications such as auto coverage for which some companies have made independent filings.

Warranties

A warranty is a condition of an insurance policy whereby the policyholder warrants the existence of certain facts or conditions whose truth is essential to the validity of the policy. The warranty therefore is an additional means of modifying coverage. There are several types of warranties utilized on fire insurance contracts. A number of contracts contain a *protective safeguards provision* which states that any endorsement making such safeguard part of the policy requires the insured to maintain such safeguard; otherwise, coverage is suspended. The most common examples are automatic sprinkler warranties and guard service warranties. If such safeguard endorsements are attached to the policy, the insured warrants that he or she will maintain the guard service or keep the sprinkler system in an operable condition. If it is not, coverage is suspended for the period the safeguard is not in effect. The insured agrees to such a warranty because of the rate credit for maintaining such protective safeguards. The underwriter is also protected since coverage is suspended if the exposure does not remain reduced by the warranty agreement.

The *vacancy and unoccupancy clause* of the standard fire policy is, in effect, a warranty. If the insured does not report these conditions and specifically insure them, coverage will be suspended.

Other types of protective safeguard endorsements that have been used occasionally are *cleaning fluid clauses* and *clear space warranties*. In the former the insured warrants that only specified (nonflammable) cleaning fluids will be used. The latter clause has been used for lumberyards wherein the owner warrants to keep specified distances open and free from lumber and other materials in order to lessen the spread of fire.

Although the types of warranties in fire insurance are limited, they still provide an effective way of modifying coverage on an individual basis and at the same time reduce the severity of loss. Many warranties have been tested in court and their validity has been upheld.

Insurable Interests

Fire insurance is a two-party contract; that is, the insurer pays the insured for his or her own property losses. Although it is loss to the property for which the insurer responds, there is a personal contract with the insured. It is therefore important that the insured's legal name be clearly stated in the policy declarations.

In commercial fire insurance, the named insured is frequently a corporation, although it can also be any other legal entity such as an individual or a partnership. Whatever the entity, it must be correctly and completely stated on the policy. Since the insured must have an insurable interest in the property at the time of loss in order to collect, it is important that the underwriter determine if the insured actually owns all or part of the property described on the policy.

In the case of multiple ownership of the property, such as a partnership, it is important for the full partnership name to appear as the insured in the policy declarations. The insuring agreement makes it quite clear that the policy will pay for loss, but not "in any event for more than the interest of the insured. . . ." Thus, if only one partner were named in the declarations, only his or her interest would be covered and only part of the loss would be paid. Adjusters normally confirm insurable interest when a loss occurs, especially if there are multiple owners. Major misunderstandings are avoided if the insureds are properly named on the policy.

Assignment

Several of the policy conditions depend on the proper identification of the insured. The policy cannot be assigned to another party without written permission from the insurer. Thus, if the property is sold, the new owner does not automatically become the new insured. This condition enables the underwriter to reevaluate the risk when ownership changes. There is no guarantee that the new owner will use the property for the same purpose as the previous owner. Although this condition seems reasonable, it has been tested in the courts, not always with results favorable to the insurance company.

Duties of the Insured

The "cancellation clause" and "requirements in case loss occurs clause" both specify duties the insured must fulfill in order for payment to be made under the fire policy. In the case of multiple owners, it is not feasible, nor necessary, for each insured to carry out these conditions. Generally the underwriter will issue an endorsement which specifies one insured as agent for all others. It becomes this person's responsibility to carry out these conditions.

Mortgagee Clause

The standard fire policy contains a clause spelling out the rights and duties of mortgagees. The mortgagee has an outstanding loan evidenced by a lien or mortgage for which the building is collateral, consequently providing an insurable interest. To protect their interest, mortgagees require owners to purchase a fire insurance policy and name the mortgagee on the policy. In this manner the mortgagee becomes a party to the policy. The furniture, fixtures, or contents could also be encumbered by a lien. In this case the loss payee endorsement may be used.

Except in those cases when the property is 100 percent owned by the insured, a mortgagee or lien holder is involved. It is important for the underwriter to notify the mortgagee of changes, losses, and especially cancellation—in other words, to fulfill the insurer's conditions in accordance with the policy provisions.

Term

Although fire policies can be written for periods of five, three, or one year, most underwriters avoid the five-year term. Some insurers still use three-year policies but retain the right to apply rate changes on an annual basis. Inadequate rates and inflation have encouraged underwriters to refrain from guaranteeing rates for three or five years. Amounts of insurance also need to be increased more frequently than every three years in periods of inflation. The effect of five-year policies on the unearned premium reserve is another reason for their discontinuation.

INSURANCE TO VALUE

Most fire insurance losses are partial losses. In fact, it is estimated that only about 2 percent of all fire losses are total losses. This fact has a great effect on the insured's and insurer's attitudes toward insurance to value. From the insured's standpoint there is a strong tendency to insure only up to the value of the expected loss. The underwriter is thus faced with the situation of not having sufficient premium to pay for total losses. If the rate were inflexible, there would also not be enough premium to pay for the numerous partial losses as well.

While overinsurance is less of a problem if the policy is not written on a valued amount basis, it may indicate moral hazard. The underwriter should be alert to overinsurance situations and attempt to determine why the situation exists. An insured who has not read the policy may think he or she will always collect the full value of the policy in the event of a total loss. This could result in a difficult loss adjustment. If the amount of insurance seems high in view of the description of the property, it is possible that the property has not been described correctly, or there may be additional property other than that which was indicated on the application. An ominous possibility is that the overinsurance is deliberate with fraudulent intent. Most of the arson-for-profit losses involve deliberate overinsurance. Underwriters should always investigate when they suspect an overinsurance situation.

Valuation Clauses

Coinsurance In order to reduce the adverse selection inherent in fire insurance underwriting, several provisions have been developed to help control this problem. The principal device used to assure proper insurance to value is *coinsurance.* A typical coinsurance clause is as follows:

Coinsurance Clause

This Company shall not be liable for a greater proportion of any loss to the property covered than the amount of insurance under this policy for such property bears to the amount produced by multiplying the actual cash value of such property at the time of the loss by the coinsurance percentage applicable (specified on the first page of this policy, or by endorsement). In the event that the aggregate claim for any loss is both less than $10,000 and less than 5 percent of the total amount of insurance applicable to the property involved at the time such loss occurs, no special inventory or appraisement of the undamaged property shall be required, providing that nothing herein shall be construed to waive the application of the first paragraph of this clause.

The value of property covered under Extensions of Coverage, and the cost of the removal of debris, shall not be considered in the determination of actual cash value when applying the Coinsurance Clause.

The purpose of this clause is to encourage the insured to carry insurance to value (by using the clause, the insured received a rate credit). Essentially the clause states that if the insured carries an amount of insurance equal to the actual cash value times the stated coinsurance percentage, all losses will be paid in full by the company (up to total amount of insurance). If the insured carries less than this amount, he or she will share proportionally in every loss. An example will show the importance of this provision.

Assume the insured owns a building which has an actual cash value of $100,000. If an 80 percent coinsurance clause is stated to apply in the policy, the insured must carry $100,000 × 80 percent, or $80,000 as the amount of insurance. The formula that is used to determine the amount of payment made when the insurance is written with a coinsurance clause applying is:

$$\frac{\text{Insurance carried}}{\text{Insurance required}} \times \text{Loss} = \frac{\text{Amount of payment by insurer}}{\text{(limited to policy amount)}}$$

Assume that the insured chose to carry only $60,000 of coverage. Using the formula and assuming a loss of $60,000, the payment would be:

$$\frac{\$60,000 \text{ (insurance carried)}}{\$100,000 \text{ (ACV)} \times 80\% \text{ coinsurance}} \times \$60,000 \text{ (loss)} = \$45,000$$

If the entire building burned, resulting in a loss of $100,000, the formula would indicate a payment of $75,000, but the maximum amount paid is the total amount of insurance. As a result, in this case the insured would only collect $60,000.

In periods of inflation, when property is grossly underinsured, the underwriter can lose the expected protection of the coinsurance clause. For example, assuming a value of $120,000:

$$\frac{\$60,000 \text{(insurance carried)}}{\$96,000 \text{ (insurance required)}} \times \$120,000 \text{ (total loss)}$$

$$= \$75,000, \text{ limited to policy amount of } \$60,000$$

Thus, the full insurance is consumed despite the insured's failure to comply with the coinsurance clause. The operation of the coinsurance clause, then, has no effect on the loss payment when the amount of loss exceeds the coinsurance percentage of value at the time of loss. In this case, insurance pays the entire loss not exceeding policy amount.

An 80 percent coinsurance clause has no effect when insurance is carried to an amount of 80 percent of value or more. In this case, insurance pays the entire loss not exceeding the policy amount.

Assuming a 90 percent coinsurance clause was applied to values of $100,000, the insured would be required to carry $90,000 of insurance to avoid the penalty of the coinsurance clause. Higher coinsurance percentages are adopted for two reasons: (1) as the coinsurance percentage increases, the rate decreases; and (2) if the coinsurance requirement is met, more of the total value of the property is covered. Therefore, in the case of a 100 percent coinsurance clause, the total value of the building would be covered if the insured carried the required amount of insurance. Coinsurance clauses are usually written at 80 percent, 90 percent, and 100 percent. Some property forms require 80 percent or 90 percent coinsurance as a minimum. Some insurance companies will not write fire insurance with less than 80 percent coinsurance.

Since most fire losses are less than total, if the coinsurance clause did not exist, the rate charged would not be equitable unless every insured carried adequate insurance to value. The coinsurance clause eliminates this possible discrimination and at the same time offers the underwriter a method of encouraging complete coverage.

It should be noted that the coinsurance clause applies separately to each type of property; that is, building or contents.

The major problem produced by the coinsurance clause is that it is often misunderstood by the insured. In periods of inflation the amount of insurance may become inadequate if it is not increased annually. Underwriters should always determine the value of the property before agreeing to an insurance amount or coinsurance percentage.

Flat Amount A fire insurance policy may be written on a flat amount basis, which means that the insurance is not subject to a coinsurance clause. Since there is no penalty for underinsurance, it would seem that such a basis would be quite advantageous for the insured. The rate used, however, is without any credit for coinsurance. Therefore, the insured would pay as much as 40 percent to 50 percent more. Underwriters generally are reluctant to write fire insurance on a flat basis. Potential moral hazard makes this a very unattractive method of writing fire insurance from an underwriting standpoint.

Agreed Amount Instead of basing valuation on the actual cash value of the property at the time of loss, certain property may be written on an agreed amount basis. The *agreed amount endorsement* in effect suspends the coinsurance clause, and claim adjustments are based on the amount stated in the endorsement. Generally insurers do not permit stock to be written on an agreed amount basis. This type of property is subject to large fluctuations in value and therefore an agreed amount of value is not appropriate. Buildings, machinery, equipment, certain types of furniture, fixtures, and improvements and betterments normally are not subject to such fluctuations, and therefore the underwriter and insured can come to an agreement as to the proper value and consequently the amount of insurance.

Since the underwriter is in effect waiving the coinsurance clause by providing agreed amount coverage, it is absolutely necessary for the agreed amount to equal at least the amount it would have been had a 90 percent coinsurance clause been used. Even if the policy is written for a three-year term, underwriters will usually require a new agreed amount endorsement to be issued annually. Often the agreed amount will be increased each annual period. Property which is subject to rapid depreciation should not be written on an agreed amount basis.

Although the agreed amount endorsement is attached to the policy, the underwriter may, in certain cases, require a coinsurance clause. The coinsurance clause would protect the underwriter if the annual agreed amount endorsement expired.

To prevent claims adjustment problems when there is more than one policy covering the same property, underwriters insist that all policies either be written on an agreed amount basis or none.

Valued Policy Laws Several states have enacted valued policy laws, most of which are still in effect. These laws require that the full amount of the policy must be paid if there is a total loss to the building. It is important to notice that the law generally applies only (1) to buildings and (2) to total losses. There are some exceptions where the law in some states applies to personal property and/or partial losses. The effect on fire insurance in a valued policy law state is that a total loss is settled on the basis of the amount of insurance stated on the policy rather than the actual cash value at the time of loss. In other words, the actual cash value of the property should be determined at the time the policy is written rather than at the time of loss.

Extensions of Coverage

The general property form, which is a basic fire and extended coverage form attached to the fire policy, contains an extensions of coverage section. The purpose of this section of the policy is to provide limited extensions of coverage beyond the scheduled property described in the declarations and covered in other sections of the general property form. These extensions are limited in two ways: (1) by the amount of insurance applicable, and (2) by the type of property covered.

Newly Acquired Property The newly acquired property provision extends coverage for newly acquired buildings and personal property at the insured location or elsewhere but for a limited time and for a limited amount. For example, if the policy insures a $200,000 building and the insured acquires a new building with a value of $100,000, the policy is extended to automatically cover the $100,000 building for thirty days, but only $20,000 coverage is granted for this period. In other words, the newly acquired building is subject to a sublimit—10 percent of the amount of insurance carried but not more than $25,000. The contents extension of coverage is limited to 10 percent also but only up to $10,000. Such coverage extension gives the insured sufficient time to arrange for specific coverage on the new property but is subject to a sublimit which may not be adequate for the value of the property. The insured therefore is encouraged to arrange for specific insurance and the underwriter is reasonably protected by the sublimit and the time limit.

The underwriter should alert the insured to these limits and encourage the insured to purchase specific insurance if these types of property exist. The underwriter should also make it clear that the value of the property included in these extensions constitutes part of the amount of insurance indicated on the policy and *not additional amounts of insurance.* If a fire destroys the $200,000 specifically insured building *and* the $100,000 newly acquired building, the insurance at the time of loss may be inadequate. For example, assume a 100 percent coinsurance clause and that the building meets the coinsurance requirement:

Extension of coverage = 10% of building value

$$\$200,000 \times 10\% = \$20,000$$

If the insured had a total loss of both buildings, he or she could collect a maximum of $200,000, the policy limit. If the insured chose to apply the 10 percent extension to the new building, only $180,000 of insurance would be left to pay for the loss of the insured building. The newly acquired property extension does not create an additional amount of insurance.

Other Extensions of Coverage Some of the other extensions of coverage include personal effects, valuable papers and records, and trees, shrubs, and plants. A typical set of such provisions is as follows:

Personal Effects: The named Insured may apply up to 5%, but not exceeding $500, of the amount of insurance for Coverage B—Personal Property of the Insured to cover direct loss by a peril insured against to personal effects while located on the described premises, belonging to the named Insured, officers, partners or employees thereof, and limited to $100 on personal effects owned by any one individual. This Extension of Coverage does not apply if the loss is covered by any other insurance, whether collectible or not, or which would have been covered by such other insurance in the absence of this policy. At the option of this Company, loss under this Extension of Coverage may be adjusted with and payable to the named Insured.

Valuable Papers and Records: The named Insured may apply up to 5%, but not exceeding $500, of the amount of insurance for Coverage B—Personal Property of the Insured at a described location to cover direct loss by a peril insured against under this policy to valuable papers and records. This Extension of Coverage covers only the cost of research and other expense necessarily incurred by the named Insured to reproduce, replace, or restore such valuable papers and records consisting of books of account, manuscripts, abstracts, drawings, card index systems, film, tape, disc, drum, cell and other magnetic recording or storage media for electronic data processing, and other records, all the property of the named Insured at such location(s).

Outdoor Trees, Shrubs and Plants: The named Insured may apply up to 5%, but not exceeding $1,000, of the sum of the amount(s) of insurance for Coverage A—Building(s) and Coverage B—Personal Property of the Insured to cover outdoor trees, shrubs and plants at the location(s) described in this policy against direct loss in any one occurrence by the perils of fire, lightning, explosion, riot, civil commotion or aircraft, but only to the extent such perils are insured against. This Company shall not be liable for more than $250 on any one tree, shrub or plant, including debris removal expense.

While intended to accommodate the insured's needs, these clauses contain limitations on the amount of insurance and type of property. The personal effects coverage is further stated to be excess insurance; the valuable papers extension is limited to expenses; the outdoor trees extension is further limited to loss by certain specified perils. Other forms of property insurance have been specifically designed to cover these types of property, and only a limited amount is granted by the extensions. The insured (or others) are thus encouraged to purchase specific forms such as homeowners, valuable papers, and standing timber to be properly protected for such losses.

Fluctuating Values at Risk

Certain risks, by the nature of their operations, have wide variations in values at different times or at different locations. Any business with seasonal operations such as a clothing store, Christmas decoration shop, or garden tool store will have large amounts of stock on hand during their respective peak seasons but relatively low values of stock at other times. It is not feasible for the underwriter or the insured to write the fire insurance on a specific or scheduled basis. Numerous endorsements would have to be executed during the policy period, which would be expensive and troublesome. As a result, various *reporting forms* have been designed to handle the special problems of risks with seasonal type businesses and/or fluctuating values.

The principal function of reporting forms is to provide adequate coverage at all times yet only charge premiums for the actual values at risk during the policy period. A provisional amount of insurance is determined which is generally the sum of the limits of liability or values for all locations. A deposit premium—usually 75 percent of the premium developed by multiplying the rate times the total limit of liability—is charged at the inception of the policy. A limit of liability is stated on the reporting form. This is the largest amount the insured can collect at any one location.

The *value reporting clause* requires the insured to report the values at each location each month no later than thirty days after the last day of each calendar month. The reporting form covers only up to the amount on the last monthly report and only the locations reported. In effect, this is a 100 percent coinsurance clause since the insurer will pay the loss in the same percentage as the last monthly value bears to the actual cash value at the time the report was made. If the insured fails to make the initial monthly report, another policy provision limits the payment to 75 percent to 90 percent (depending on the form used) of the limit of liability stated on the endorsement for that location.

The actual premium is determined at the expiration date of the policy and is based on an average of the total value throughout the policy period based on the monthly reports.

The effectiveness of the reporting form in providing adequate coverage at all times is dependent on the proper insurance to value at the outset and the timely filing of monthly statements. A severe penalty can result if monthly reports are delinquent. The value reporting clause stipulates that the amount of the last report is the maximum amount recoverable in the event of delinquency. It is necessary for the underwriter to ascertain that the producer and the insured understand the operation of the form and maintain their cooperation in receiving the monthly reports on a regular and timely basis. Reminders often must be utilized to accomplish this.

The underwriter must also review the monthly reports, being alert to significant increases and decreases in the reporting values. In the former case, the limits of liability may become inadequate at mid-term and an adjustment may be necessary. Sudden decreases in reported values may indicate improper reporting procedures or financial problems. The underwriter should be concerned about values which month by month remain consistent. This could mean that the insured does not understand the reporting form or is not taking proper inventories.

It is possible that specific insurance may be written on some of the locations. In this case, the reporting form would serve as an excess coverage over specific insurance to cover fluctuations in value. The reporting form would not pay for a loss until specific insurance is exhausted. It is therefore important that the underwriter providing excess coverage on a reporting form keep track of property for which there is specific insurance. If the specific insurance is terminated, the amount of insurance on the reporting form must be increased.

From this discussion it should be apparent that reporting forms cover only contents or personal property. The form is not intended to cover buildings. For multi-location risks it is possible to cover buildings on a blanket basis and contents on a reporting form.

Replacement Cost Coverage

Many of the provisions and restrictions which have been included in the replacement cost endorsements are methods of reducing moral hazard, encouraging insurance to value, and enabling the underwriter to collect sufficient premium to pay for losses.

Although most replacement cost forms permit the insured to collect the actual cash value initially with any additional amount available later when repairs commence, the coinsurance clause is still based on replacement cost. Therefore, if the insurance does not meet the required amount of the coinsurance clause, the insured can suffer a penalty even if he or she chooses to accept the actual cash value.

It would seem that 100 percent coinsurance would be required on replacement cost forms, and at one time this was the case. Today many underwriters will write replacement cost coverage with a 90 percent or 80 percent coinsurance clause. Although replacement cost coverage is available on buildings, improvements and betterments, furniture, and fixtures, it is generally not possible to write it on merchandise, materials, supplies, and most other contents. Since most types of personal property must be written on an actual cash value basis, it is necessary to consider what the proper value of such property is at the time of loss.

Certain types of personal property such as merchandise, raw materials, and stock do not depreciate; therefore, the actual cash value will usually be equal to the market value. Merchandise held for sale is valued at cost to the insured and not selling price to the customer.

Since successful fire underwriting is based on adequate insurance to value and the value is based on replacement cost, it becomes imperative for the underwriter to be able to determine, with reasonable accuracy, the replacement cost (and depreciated value) of property before he or she agrees to insure it. Several sources of information are available to assist in establishing the values. Building appraisal methods were discussed in Chapter 1.

SUMMARY

Besides analyzing the hazards arising from the construction, occupancy, and lack of protection, the fire underwriter must also evaluate the external exposures which may be a source of loss. Each of the underwriting factors must be reconsidered in the evaluation of the exposure hazard. An exposure hazard may necessitate limiting the amount of insurance which can be assumed on a specific property. Other exposures may preclude acceptance of the property for fire insurance at all. In most cases the underwriter has little control over reducing the effect of an external exposure and therefore the only alternative available would be declination of the insurance.

Although the basic fire policy is standardized, many endorsements are available to modify the coverage to meet the specific needs of a particular risk. Other aspects of the contract to be considered are insurable interest, assignment, duties of the insured, mortgagee clause, and the term of the contract. Each modification must be evaluated by the underwriter to determine the possible increase in potential loss created by the modification.

In all aspects of fire underwriting, proper insurance to value is a primary and necessary consideration. By use of proper insurance amounts, adequate rates, and special clauses, the underwriter tries to control the book of property business to assure that the premiums are adequate for the exposures assumed. Capacity, catastrophe, and insurability set the parameters for the underwriter's task. Any imbalance among exposure, price, and coverage could create a serious and very undesirable result in the property insurance experience.

Chapter Notes

1. *Fire Protection Handbook*, 15th ed. (Quincy, MA: National Fire Protection Association, 1981), pp. 5-18, 5-19.
2. *Fire Protection Handbook*, p. 5-20.

CHAPTER 8

Underwriting Commercial Indirect Property Losses

INTRODUCTION

Indirect Loss Exposures

The previous chapters have dealt primarily with the analysis of property losses which occur as a result of direct damage by an insured peril. A business firm which suffers a direct damage loss will usually also have a loss of income. In some cases a relatively minor direct damage loss can result in a substantial income loss. For example, a manufacturing plant producing intricate mechanical assemblies may have a certain machine which is essential to the manufacture of all their output. If this machine is destroyed in a relatively minor fire with a direct damage loss of $20,000, all further manufacturing would come to a halt until the machine is repaired or replaced. If the machine were unique in that no substitute could be found and replacement required custom manufacture taking three months, the business would be shut down for three months. The resulting loss of income could be substantial.

There are three major indirect loss exposures for business firms. These are:

1. loss of income due to property damage to buildings, equipment, or inventory;
2. extra expense due to extraordinary expenses incurred in continuing a business operation after damage to the operating facilities; and

3. contingent losses due to the interruption of production or sales occasioned by direct damage to the plant or facility of a subcontractor, supplier, or customer.

A business firm has two things at risk: the balance sheet and the income statement. Direct damage property losses destroy values recorded on the balance sheet. The indirect losses which occur as a consequence affect the income statement.

Indirect Loss Coverages

The major indirect property damage loss coverage categories are:

- business interruption,
- extra expense,
- contingent extra expense,
- consequential loss,
- rental income,
- leasehold interest,
- tuition insurance, and
- contingent liability from operation of building laws.

Business Interruption or Extra Expense?

Coverages such as rental income, leasehold interest, and tuition insurance apply to particular situations where the destruction of property leads to a unique type of income loss. The applicability of these coverages is usually readily apparent to insured, producer, and underwriter alike. The selection of coverage is not so self-evident in most manufacturing and service industries. *Business interruption* coverage is designed to replace the funds which would have been generated by the business if it had not been shut down by damage to its property. Were it not for the insured event, the business would be able to generate sufficient funds to cover all continuing expenses and (in most cases) produce a profit. As the term, "business interruption" implies, this coverage assumes that the operation of the business is partially or completely suspended.

There are those businesses or operating components of businesses which would not cease operations even in the event of a total loss to their operating plant or facility. These businesses would continue to operate utilizing temporary facilities, usually at a much higher cost. *Extra expense* insurance is designed to provide the necessary funds to defray the extra expenses required to continue operation after damage caused by an insured peril. Businesses customarily requiring extra expense coverage rather than business interruption include newspapers and retail dairies.

The first question that must be answered in the determination of the appropriate coverage is, will the operation shut down or remain open in the event of an insured loss? If the operation shuts down, business interruption is indicated. If the operation would remain open, extra expense may be needed. If it is impossible to determine exactly what action would be taken, as might be the case when operation might be possible after damage to some components but not possible after damage to others, the combined form including both business interruption and extra expense may be necessary.

BUSINESS INTERRUPTION

There are a number of forms which may be used to provide coverage for business interruption. These include:

1. gross earnings form,
2. earnings form,
3. valued or per diem form, and
4. contingent business interruption form.

Gross Earnings Form

Coverage The gross earnings form provides coverage for loss from interruption of business resulting from direct damage to real or personal property caused by an insured peril.

Form 3 is intended for mercantile and nonmanufacturing companies and form 4 for manufacturing and mining. The basic difference between these two forms is the manner in which gross earnings is defined.

In the mercantile form, gross earnings is defined as:

... the sum of: (a) Total net sales and (b) Other earnings derived from operations of the business, less the cost of: (c) Merchandise sold, including packaging material therefor, (d) Materials and supplies consumed directly in supplying the service(s) sold by the Insured, and (e) Service(s) purchased from outsiders (not employees of the Insured) for resale which do not continue under contract.

The manufacturing form defines gross earnings as:

... the sum of: (a) Total net sales value of production, (b) Total net sales of merchandise, and (c) Other earnings derived from operation of the business, less the cost of: (d) Raw stock from which such production is derived, (e) Supplies consisting of materials consumed directly in the conversion of such raw stock into finished stock or in supplying the service(s) sold by the Insured, (f) Merchandise sold, including packaging materials therefor, and (g) Service(s) purchased from outsiders (not employees of the Insured) for resale which do not continue under contract.

Perils. The business interruption policy provides coverage only for named perils. The only interruptions in the business operation that are covered are those arising out of the consequences of one of the named perils. "All-risks" coverage is written quite freely, however. This coverage may be written separately or as a separate item on a direct damage policy. When written as a separate item, the direct and indirect coverage amounts cannot be blanketed. The amount of insurance under the direct damage cannot be used to provide additional business interruption coverage for a loss or to meet a coinsurance requirement. The reverse is also true.

Insuring Agreement. The gross earnings form protects against loss resulting directly from the necessary interruption of business caused by damage to or destruction of real or personal property by the insured perils.

An interruption may be total or partial but it must be necessary, that is, beyond the insured's control, and the damage must occur on the premises occupied by the insured. If a fire damages a neighboring property and causes the insured to lose business, there is no protection afforded in the insuring agreement.

When an interruption occurs, the insurer is liable only for the *actual loss sustained,* not exceeding the reduction in gross earnings, less charges and expenses that do not necessarily continue. Actual loss sustained is analogous to actual cash value, and makes the contract one of indemnity. This requires a determination of the amount the insured would have earned if there had been no loss. In cases of partial suspension, the *reduced* earnings must be compared to what the insured would have earned if a loss had not occurred.

In determining the actual loss sustained the time element is measured by the length of time required, with the exercise of *due diligence and dispatch,* to rebuild, repair, or replace the damaged or destroyed property. If the property is not repaired or replaced, the form would still provide reimbursement for the time it *would have* taken to repair or replace the property.

The time element is not terminated when a damaged or destroyed building is repaired or rebuilt. Time is permitted for the insured to refurnish supplies and restock merchandise. For a manufacturer, time is allowed to bring the production process to the same place where it was before the loss.

Expenses to Reduce Loss. The contract provision permitting the insured to use extraordinary means and expenses to reduce the loss is closely coupled with the insured's duty to get back into business as soon as possible. The cost of these measures—if they effectively reduce the loss—will be met by the insurer.

The policy reads:

> This policy also covers such expenses as are necessarily incurred for the purpose of reducing loss under this policy (except expense incurred to extinguish a fire), but in no event shall the aggregate of such expenses exceed the amount by which the loss otherwise payable under this policy is reduced.

Thus, if the insured spends $15,000 over and above normal expenses to expedite recovery of operations and this expenditure reduces the loss by $15,000, the insured will be reimbursed for the expense. If the expenditure reduced the loss only by $12,000, the insured would collect all but $3,000 of the extra cost.

The business interruption loss can be reduced by expediting the restoration of damaged properties with overtime work or by adding extra personnel. Extra expenses incurred in operating at a temporary location would also be eligible for reimbursement under this clause subject to the limitations in the clause.

Interruption by Civil Authority. Frequently a fire or other peril will cause an interruption at a number of adjacent businesses. Police and fire fighters may deny access to an entire city block when a serious fire occurs. An insured's business, in such a situation, may be interrupted even though the fire occurred away from the insured's premises. This type of loss will be covered for a maximum of two consecutive weeks according to the "interruption by civil authority" clause.

This clause requires that access to the insured's business must be denied by the order of governmental authorities, due to damage or destruction of property from an insured peril. Riot, if an insured peril, could lead to reimbursement. The threat of a riot or a curfew imposed because of a possible riot would not be an insured peril. Furthermore, the insured peril must damage or destroy property that is adjacent to the insured's property. The word "adjacent" is interpreted to mean nearby; it does not necessarily mean adjoining.

EDP Media Limitation. If a business is interrupted by an insured peril that damages or destroys electronic data processing programming records, media, or equipment and no other property has been damaged, coverage is limited to a period of thirty days. This limitation may not apply if other property has been damaged along with the EDP equipment. In this case, the time element is the time required to repair or replace the other property, if longer than thirty days. In most territories the EDP limitation, for an additional premium, may be extended to 90 or 180 days or eliminated entirely.

Exclusions. In addition to the exclusions previously mentioned, the gross earnings form contains several special exclusions.

Losses caused by the *enforcement of a state or local building ordinance* are excluded. This exclusion corresponds to a similar exclusion in most fire, multi-peril, and other direct damage policies. This excludes any increase in the length of time required to repair or rebuild a building necessitated by the building code. This exclusion may be eliminated for an additional premium.

An insurer is not liable for a loss resulting from *interference at the described premises by strikers* or other persons with the rebuilding, repairing, or replacing the property or with the resumption or continuation of business. However, if there is a strike at other locations, such as at a supplier's location, increased time of interruption due to this off-premises strike would be covered.

The third special exclusion excludes losses caused by the *suspension, lapse, or cancellation of a lease, license, contract, or order.* However, if the suspension lapse or cancellation is a direct result of the interruption of the insured's business, it is covered. For example, a company has an order to manufacture parts for a new airplane. If the order is canceled and a shutdown results, there would be no coverage. If, on the other hand, a fire causes a shutdown and the order is canceled as a result, the earnings that the order would have generated during the period of interruption would be considered in determining the insured's actual loss sustained.

Determination of Values at Risk One of the difficulties of the gross earnings form of business interruption is that it is necessary to make two separate evaluations of the amount of insured exposure. The basic measure of potential loss to the insured is the reduction in gross earnings less charges and expenses which do not necessarily continue during the interruption.

Calculation of this exposure then involves three steps:

1. Projection of gross earnings, including any seasonal fluctuations.
2. Determination of the probable period of interruption. In most cases, this is the time to rebuild the damaged facility, or in the case of a manufacturing process, the time to return the goods in process to their pre-loss level, whichever is longer.
3. Identification of the charges and expenses which do not necessarily continue.

Each of these steps involves projections and estimates, usually prior to the policy year in question, and definitely prior to the loss. The range of possible error is quite wide.

On the other hand, in most cases, the policy language includes a *contribution* (coinsurance) *clause* of, depending on the territory and other clauses elected, between 50 and 100 percent of gross earnings as defined. The gross earnings referred to in the contribution clause are the *projected* gross earnings during the twelve-month period immediately following the loss. The gross earnings figure utilized for coinsurance purposes usually includes some expenses and charges which may not have to be necessarily continued. Also this definition makes no reference to the expected period of reconstruction (or the expected duration of interruption).

This leaves one with the challenging task of selecting a contribution clause in such a manner that the amount of insurance purchased to satisfy the contribution clause or other policy language will be sufficient to cover the expected loss.

Modification of Gross Earnings by Endorsement Three endorsements may be used to modify the definition of gross earnings. These are:

1. the ordinary payroll exclusion endorsement,
2. the ordinary payroll limited coverage endorsement, and
3. the power, heat, and refrigeration endorsement (manufacturing and mining risks only).

Ordinary Payroll Exclusion Endorsement. Gross earnings as defined in the policy includes all payroll. If the insured determines that most employees would not be retained on the payroll in the event of an interruption, then gross earnings can be redefined to exclude this expense. *Ordinary payroll* is defined as the entire payroll expense except for officers, executives, department managers, employees under contract, and other important employees. This endorsement is one technique for providing greater correspondence between the expected value at risk and the contribution clause requirement. However, the rules of most jurisdictions require that the contribution clause be at least 80 percent when this endorsement is used.

Ordinary Payroll Limited Coverage Endorsement. This endorsement permits the insured to include ordinary payroll for interruptions of a certain duration but to exclude it for longer shutdowns. In most jurisdictions ordinary payroll may be covered for 90, 120, 150, or 180 days. The effect of this endorsement is, once again, to modify the definition of gross earnings to more closely conform to the expected value at risk.

Power, Heat, and Refrigeration Endorsement. This endorsement, which is limited to manufacturing or mining risks, changes the definition of gross earnings in the contribution clause to exclude a portion of the heat, light, and refrigeration charges. Therefore a manufacturing risk with very large costs in heat, power, and refrigeration can deduct these amounts when making the twelve-month projection to determine the appropriate amount of insurance for coinsurance purposes. Any minimum or other charges which would continue under contract may not be excluded.

With this endorsement, as would be the case with the two ordinary payroll endorsements, the need for the endorsement would be determined in the course of calculating the insured's loss exposure. The loss exposure should be determined first, then the insurance contract modified to reflect this exposure.

Other Endorsements Affecting the Amount of Insurance
There are three other endorsements which may be utilized either to deal with problems created by the existence of the contribution clause or to change the definition of the period of indemnity. These are:

1. the agreed amount endorsement,
2. the premium adjustment endorsement, and
3. the endorsement extending the period of indemnity.

Agreed Amount Endorsement. One way to avoid contribution clause penalties is to add the agreed amount endorsement which suspends the contribution clause for a period of one year from the date of the endorsement or until policy expiration if that occurs sooner. A fixed amount of insurance is substituted for the contribution clause percentage. If the insured maintains the agreed amount of insurance, any loss will be paid in full up to that amount. In most jurisdictions, the insured must file a statement of business interruption values with the rating bureau at inception of the endorsement and annually thereafter. In many jurisdictions there is the equivalent of the full reporting clause used in direct damage reporting form policies. This provision *full amount clause* or honesty clause limits liability under the business interruption contract to that proportion of the loss which reported values bear to actual values. Therefore, if actual values were $1 million and reported values $750,000, only 75 percent of any loss would be covered. When this provision is in the agreed amount endorsement, the producer attempting to use this endorsement to "simplify" the contract may have exchanged one problem for another. Conversely, this provision provides important protection for the insurer in obtaining adequate insurance to value.

Premium Adjustment Endorsement. The premium adjustment endorsement represents another technique which can be utilized to mitigate contribution clause problems. This endorsement converts the gross earnings policy to a premium adjustment form. The insured selects a limit of liability designed to be sufficiently high to eliminate any possible contribution clause violation. The insured files showing the gross earnings as defined for the latest available fiscal year. Within 120 days of the end of each succeeding fiscal year, an updated report is required. This endorsement also contains a full amount clause similar to that in the agreed amount endorsement.

The practical effect of this endorsement is that it permits selection of a limit of liability high enough to avoid a contribution clause penalty, even if the values at risk increase at a rate somewhat higher than expected. The premium is related to the actual values at risk, which are determined after the fact. This can be especially useful for insureds whose business operations result in fluctuating values or where it is particularly difficult to accurately forecast future growth in gross earnings.

Endorsement Extending the Period of Indemnity. In many businesses, earnings would continue to be depressed after the business had been reopened and restored to the condition existing prior to the loss. For many businesses, former customers would take their business elsewhere during the period of the business interruption. Therefore it may be some time before business is restored to the level reached prior to the loss.

The endorsement extending the period of indemnity provides the insured with the opportunity to purchase, in thirty-day increments, additional coverage for the actual loss sustained for such length of time as would be required with due diligence and dispatch to restore the insured's business to the condition that would have existed had no loss occurred. In most jurisdictions, coverage can be purchased for up to one year. The coverage under this endorsement commences when the coverage under the basic business interruption contract ceases.

This endorsement is subject to all the provisions of the basic gross earnings form to which it is attached, including the contribution clause. Therefore, an additional amount of insurance should be purchased over and above that required to meet the contribution clause requirements of the basic contract. The amount of insurance required would be that for the maximum period needed to restore the insured's business to the former level of operation.

Calculation of Business Interruption Values The business interruption worksheet is designed to determine the amount of insurance required according to the language of the contract. It is *not* designed to determine the amount of the insured's exposure. That must be calculated following the three steps described above under "Determination of Values at Risk" prior to completion of the worksheet. For example, the decision regarding which, if any, payroll endorsement should be used must be based on analysis of the insured's operation.

A Nonmanufacturing Example. The ABC Merchandise Company consists of a retail store in a leased building of ordinary construction, located in a moderately congested business district. The income statement for the most recent year is shown in Exhibit 8-1.

This risk wishes to purchase business interruption insurance on the gross earnings form to be attached to the direct damage policy on the improvements and betterments, furniture and fixtures, and contents.

PROJECTION OF GROSS EARNINGS. The first step is the determination of gross earnings, including the effect of seasonal fluctuations, projected one year into the future. Since the insurance concept of gross earnings is not defined the same as the accounting term gross profits, the income statement must be restated to conform to the insurance gross earnings definition. This is shown in Exhibit 8-2.

Note that in the income statement shown in Exhibit 8-1 the gross profit on sales was $300,000. From this value bad debts of $1,000 and supplies and wrappings of $2,000, which were the packaging materials and materials and supplies consumed directly in supplying the merchandise, were deducted. (The business interruption worksheet in Exhibit 8-8 shows why these were selected.) The other income of $1,000 was added, yielding a gross earnings value of $298,000 for the previous twelve-month period. For this example it is assumed that the business has no significant seasonal fluctuations.

Since the policy covers gross earnings for the period following the loss, the insured's exposure and the coinsurance calculation will be based on the gross earnings in the twelve months following the loss. Therefore it is necessary to project future gross earnings, for two years since the loss might occur on the last day of the policy period, one year from now. The simplest method to follow in this calculation is the extrapolation of the trend in sales. Sales for the past five years, obtained from prior income statements, are shown in Exhibit 8-3.

The average rate of growth in sales is 6.75 percent per year. Since gross earnings tend to change proportionately with sales over the shortrun, sales projections can be used to forecast changes in gross earnings. The assumption may be made that future sales and gross earnings are going to increase at a rate equal to the recent average growth rate of 6.75 percent. This technique is known as *extrapolation of a trend.* The projected values for sales and gross earnings under this assumption are shown in Exhibit 8-4.

Exhibit 8-1
ABC Merchandise Company Income Statement—January 1 to
December 31, 19X7*

Sales			$910,000
Less			
Returns and allowances		$ 3,000	
Cash discounts		7,000	10,000
Net sales			$900,000
Cost of goods sold:			
Inventory, Jan. 1		$ 50,000	
Purchases	$600,000		
Freight inward	2,000		
	$602,000		
Returns	$2,000		
Discounts	5,000	7,000	595,000
Merchandise available for sale		$645,000	
Less inventory, Dec. 31		45,000	
Cost of goods sold			600,000
Gross profit on sales			$300,000
Expenses:			
Salaries		$160,000	
Payroll taxes		8,000	
Rent		50,000	
Supplies, wrappings, etc.		2,000	
Postage, etc.		1,000	
Telephone and telegraph		10,000	
Depreciation on furniture and fixtures		20,000	
Bad debts		1,000	
Advertising		19,000	
Delivery expense		6,000	
Taxes, licenses, etc.		1,000	
Insurance premiums		2,000	
Total expenses			280,000
			$ 20,000
Other income:			
Sublease (corner store)		$ 200	
Vending machines		800	1,000
Net income for the year			$ 21,000

*Reprinted with permission from P. I. Thomas and P. B. Reed, *Adjustment of Property Losses*, 4th ed. (New York: McGraw-Hill Book Co., 1977), p. 414.

Exhibit 8-2
ABC Merchandise Company Business-Interruption Value*

Sales			$910,000
Less:			
Returns and allowances		$ 3,000	
Cash discounts		7,000	
Bad debts		1,000	11,000
Net sales			$899,000
Cost of goods sold:			
Inventory, Jan. 1			$ 50,000
Purchases		$600,000	
Freight inward		2,000	
		$602,000	
Returns	$2,000		
Discounts	5,000	7,000	595,000
Merchandise available for sale			$645,000
Less inventory, Dec. 31			45,000
Cost of goods sold			600,000
Gross profit on sales			$299,000
Deduct: supplies, wrappings, etc.			2,000
			$297,000
Other income:			
Sublease (corner store)		$ 200	
Vending machines		800	1,000
Gross earnings and value			$298,000

Note: Bad debts are deducted from sales, as they are money never received. Supplies and wrappings are deductible by definition as consumable items. Transposition of these items does not change the "net income."

*Reprinted with permission from P. I. Thomas and P. B. Reed, *Adjustment of Property Losses*, 4th ed. (New York: McGraw-Hill Book Co., 1977), p. 415.

Large businesses usually have income statements and balance sheets prepared by the finance department for their own use in forecasting future sales and financing requirements. If these are available, they can provide excellent estimates of the values necessary to determine the business interruption exposure. In this case, as would be typical of a business this size, no such data are available.

DETERMINATION OF THE PROBABLE PERIOD OF INTERRUPTION. The business interruption exposure of the insured is directly related to the probable period of interrupted operations. In the case of a total loss, this would be the time to rebuild a structure of similar construction

Exhibit 8-3
ABC Merchandise Company Sales for
19X3-19X7

Year	Sales	Percentage of Growth
19X3	$700,000	
19X4	743,000	6.1%
19X5	805,000	8.3
19X6	860,000	6.8
19X7	910,000	5.8
		Average growth 6.75%

Exhibit 8-4
A Two-Year Forecast of Sales and Gross Earnings

Year	Sales	Gross Earnings[†]
19X7	$ 910,000	$298,000
19X8 (projected)	971,000	318,000
19X9 (projected)	1,037,000	339,000

[†]Rounded to the nearest hundred thousand.

type plus the time to install fixtures, restock, orient new employees, and prepare for reopening. The time to rebuild depends upon many factors, including the following:

- *Type of construction*, fire resistive through frame.
- *Size of building*, particularly the number of floors.
- *Grade of construction* and unusual features. An elaborate building with marble inlays, reflector pools, and intricate lighting fixtures will take longer to rebuild than a more spartan building of the same construction type, square footage, and number of floors.
- *Degree of congestion*. In the highly congested districts of large cities it is necessary to build barricades and a roof over sidewalks and to haul materials and debris through crowded streets. This increases the rebuilding time.
- *Time to obtain necessary permits*. In certain areas of the country, such as the area under the jurisdiction of the

California Coastal Commission, permits even to rebuild an existing building can take several months to obtain.

- *The weather.* In areas with severe winters, construction times during the winter may be greatly extended. Construction time may be increased 15 percent in climates where a nominal amount of inclement weather may be expected to 35 percent where rigorous winters occur.

Average construction time for various occupancies is shown in Exhibit 8-5. Information on the time to rebuild the particular structure under consideration may be determined by consulting a local building contractor or by obtaining the services of an appraisal company. In this case it is assumed that the insured will wish to continue to lease a similar type of building at the same location. The building will take five months to rebuild, given its type, size, grade of construction, location, and climatic zone. An additional month would be required to prepare for reopening, giving a total expected maximum period of interruption of six months.

IDENTIFICATION OF NONCONTINUING EXPENSES. The insuring agreement of the gross earnings form indemnifies the insured for the reduction in gross earnings less those charges and expenses which do not necessarily continue. The loss may be abated by the discontinuation of certain expenses. It is difficult to identify noncontinuing expenses prior to the incidence of the loss because the continuation of certain expenses is often a function of the length of the period of interruption. For example, if a business will be shut down for six months, most telephone and telegraph expenses can be eliminated for the first five months of the shutdown. During the start-up period they would probably be above normal and there may be some minimum charges during the balance of the period, but the reduction in expense would be substantial. On the other hand, a two-week shutdown might see telephone expenses actually increase as the business contacted customers and suppliers to coordinate the reopening.

Some attempt must be made to identify noncontinuing expenses for each individual risk, based upon certain assumptions. The first assumption should be that the expenses will be identified for the maximum likely period of interruption. This period will be the insured's maximum exposure.

The first expense to be examined for possible abatement is ordinary payroll. The ABC Merchandise Company has a payroll expense of $160,000. Assume that $40,000 of this consists of the manager's salary and $120,000 is ordinary payroll for workers who will not be retained in the event of an interruption of operations. In this case the ordinary payroll exclusion endorsement would be indicated for

Exhibit 8-5
Average Construction Time*

Designed Occupancy	Project Cost (in thousands of dollars)									
	50	100	500	1,000	2,500	5,000	10,000	25,000	50,000	100,000
Apartments and retirement homes, low-rise	90	105	195	240	315	375	—	—	—	—
Apartments and retirement homes, hi-rise	—	—	—	375	440	510	580	705	—	—
Auditoriums and clubhouses	80	100	210	265	365	450	550	735	980	—
Banks	100	120	235	300	410	505	—	—	—	—
Churches	120	160	325	415	555	680	825	—	—	—
Department stores and shopping malls	—	—	260	320	415	470	565	730	—	—
Dormitories	—	130	260	335	445	540	625	—	—	—
Garages and parking structures	65	90	195	260	355	440	530	—	—	—
Governmental buildings	95	150	315	410	550	670	795	995	1,155	1,330
Hotels and motels	100	140	275	355	485	605	730	910	1,055	1,205
Hospitals	—	—	425	495	615	725	850	1,040	1,190	1,350
Industrial buildings	85	105	185	230	295	355	415	500	—	—
Libraries	90	140	310	390	530	595	690	—	—	—
Medical office buildings	95	135	285	340	440	525	610	—	—	—
Nursing homes	—	225	335	400	510	605	710	880	—	—
Office buildings	85	125	260	330	440	525	620	760	865	980
Residences, single family and townhouses	90	115	215	270	—	—	—	—	—	—
Restaurants	95	135	265	330	430	505	—	—	—	—
Retail stores, markets, and discount stores	80	125	250	290	380	455	530	—	—	—
Schools and colleges	90	125	260	340	460	570	690	890	1,055	—
Warehouses	70	100	200	255	335	405	475	—	—	—

*Reprinted with permission from Marshall Valuation Service (Los Angeles: Marshall and Swift Publication Company, December 1976). This table of average periods of construction lists points on empirical curves, which have been developed from figures for actual construction jobs. The data was adjusted for time lost due to labor shutdowns and extreme cases were discarded. No adjustments were made for holidays, inspection delays, or other minor shutdowns. Figures are the number of contract days from ground breaking to completion.

this insured. In addition, the payroll taxes of $8,000 would be reduced proportionately to $2,000, a 75 percent reduction.

Whether or not the rent would be a continuing expense depends upon the terms of the lease and the plans of the insured. If the insured would like to remain at the same location after the occurrence of a total loss, then rent payments would continue. On the other hand, most leases permit cancellation of the lease in the event of damage to 50 percent or more of the leased structure. In this case, assume that the insured wishes to remain at this location and will continue to make the rent payments as a necessary expense.

Telephone and telegraph expenses would be greatly reduced during a six-month shutdown. Based upon the minimum charges and the expenses of the last month prior to reopening, this expense is estimated to be reduced by 75 percent to $2,500.

During a shutdown which might result without severe damage to the physical facilities, the depreciation on the furniture and fixtures would continue. On the other hand, if the furniture and fixtures were destroyed, there would be no depreciation during the five-month period during which the building was being replaced. Therefore, in this case since the depreciation item refers only to furniture and fixtures, an estimate of 75 percent abatement would be conservative. If the depreciation included the building, a 50 percent estimate might be more appropriate.

While the advertising expense might be reduced for much of the period of interruption, the need for heavy advertising to inform customers of the reopening makes it unlikely that advertising expense can be reduced.

Whether or not the delivery expense can be abated depends upon the type of delivery service utilized. If the insured owns his or her own trucks, the depreciation expense on this equipment would continue, assuming that the trucks were not destroyed in the loss. Wear and tear would not continue during the interruption. The use of delivery services might entail a minimum charge contained in the delivery service contract. In this case, assume that the insured utilizes an outside delivery service contract with no minimum charge; therefore the entire $6,000 delivery expense ceases.

Taxes and license fees must be examined on a case-by-case basis to determine the extent to which they can be abated. Certain property taxes, while usually levied as of a set date such as March first, can be reduced upon petition if the property is heavily damaged or destroyed. In this case, it is assumed that all of the taxes and fees would be continuing expenses.

Insurance premiums may or may not be reduced during an interruption depending on the type of insurance and the policy

Exhibit 8-6
Estimate of Abatable Expenses

	Actual for 19X7	Estimated Abatements	Estimated Continuing Expenses
Expenses			
Salaries	$160,000	$120,000	$ 40,000
Payroll taxes	8,000	6,000	2,000
Rent	50,000	0	50,000
Postage, etc.	1,000	0	1,000
Telephone and telegraph	10,000	7,500	2,500
Depreciation on furniture and fixtures	20,000	15,000	5,000
Advertising	19,000	0	19,000
Delivery expense	6,000	6,000	0
Taxes, licenses, etc.	1,000	0	1,000
Insurance premiums	2,000	1,000	1,000
Total expenses	$277,000	$155,500	$121,500

conditions. Workers' compensation premium based on payroll would be reduced to the extent that ordinary payroll is reduced. Legal liability insurance would most likely continue for a nonmanufacturing risk, since the premium is usually a fixed sum rather than being on an audit basis. Auto insurance would be reduced if the fleet were taken off the road during the time of interruption. Group life and health insurance premiums are also a function of payroll and would be reduced if ordinary payroll is excluded. Finally, direct damage property insurance would be reduced during the time period necessary to replace the building. If the building is owned, course of construction coverage would be required but the insurance on the furniture and fixtures would be eliminated until the completion of the building. In this case, based upon the exclusion of ordinary payroll and the reduction in the property insurance on the furniture and fixtures during the interruption, an estimate of a 50 percent reduction of the insurance premium would be reasonable.

Based on these assumptions, the estimated amount of noncontinuing expenses is $120,000 ordinary payroll and $35,500 other expenses for a one-year period, if the operation were to remain at the 19X7 level. This is shown in Exhibit 8-6. This must be adjusted to reflect the expected length of interruption and also the expected upward trend in sales.

In estimation of both the PML and the amount of insurance, the

Exhibit 8-7
Estimated Business Interruption PML

	19X7 Values	×	Trend Factor (one year)	=	Projected Values	×	Maximum Expected Interruption	=	PML
Gross Earnings	$298,000		1.0675		$318,000				
Less:									
Ordinary payroll	120,000		1.0675		128,100				
Abatable expenses	35,500		1.0675		37,900				
Exposure (annual basis)	$142,500		1.0675		$152,000		0.5 (6 months)		$76,000

trend factor reflecting the increase in sales is applied for one year. One of the difficulties in the estimation of business interruption values is that if the loss occurs late in the policy year, it could extend into the period two years in the future. One approach is to utilize a one-year trend factor and then review the business interruption values six months into the policy year and adjust the values upward at that time if necessary. The derivation of the PML based upon these assumptions is shown in Exhibit 8-7. The PML is $76,000. Next the business interruption worksheet is completed using this same information. Note that the ordinary payroll exclusion endorsement is utilized requiring the use of the 80 percent coinsurance clause. This is shown in Exhibit 8-8 and is based on the data in Exhibits 8-2, 8-3, and 8-4. The amount of insurance required is $151,920.

PML RELATED TO THE AMOUNT OF INSURANCE. Since the PML is $76,000 and the amount of insurance $151,920, it would appear that the amount of insurance required to comply with the contribution clause is excessive. This appearance is deceptive because the PML was arrived at based on certain assumptions which should now be reexamined.

The first assumption was that this insured had no seasonality in its operations. Actually most businesses exhibit some degree of seasonal fluctuation. Some classes of business have 45 percent of their sales concentrated in the peak three months and 60 to 80 percent in the peak six months. A business located at a summer resort would be an extreme example. In this case, 100 percent of the sales could be concentrated in the four month "season."

Changing the assumption in this case to 70 percent of the business being concentrated in the peak six consecutive months would increase the PML to $106,400.

Although six months is the expected length of maximum interruption, this figure is an expected value, which is an average. As is the case with any expected value, the actual length of interruption may vary considerably due to unexpected factors such as unusual weather, strikes which make materials unavailable, and similar occurrences. (The variability of actual results about an expected value is discussed in the AIU 61 text.) Therefore, even if the estimate of losses for a six-month period were exactly accurate, the gross earnings form in this case provides a cushion of protection for interruptions longer than the maximum expected loss.

A third factor is that the estimates of noncontinuing expenses are also subject to variations between the estimated value and the actual. Only after the loss can the determination be made as to exactly which expenses will continue and which can be abated.

The gross earnings form recognizes in its rating structure the difference between the amount of insurance and the probably maximum loss. Since compliance with the contribution clause provides full insurance to value for the possible, but unlikely total loss of unusually long duration, the rate is lower than would otherwise be the case.

THE EARNINGS FORM AS AN ALTERNATIVE. In the event that the producer and insured are convinced of the accuracy of their estimate of the PML, the earnings form, which has no contribution clause and utilizes a fixed dollar value per time period as the limit of indemnity, is available. In this case an insured with no seasonal fluctuations in sales might purchase an earnings form for $76,000 with one-sixth of that amount as a monthly limit.

This has two disadvantages.

1. The earnings form takes a higher rate, as is common in property insurance forms with no contribution clause due to the possibility of insurance to less than full value of the exposure.
2. The earnings form purchased only for the amount of the PML would provide no cushion for errors in the estimates of the degree of seasonality, length of maximum interruption, or amount of abatable expenses.

A Manufacturing Example. The SCR Manufacturing Company manufactures widgets in a frame building located in a heavily congested area of a major city. In the manufacturing example, the entire process of determining the values at risk will not be repeated since much of it is similar to the procedure outlined in the nonmanufacturing example. The difference occurs in the determination of gross earnings as defined in the policy form and the calculation of the amount of insurance.

The calculation of the amount of exposure and the PML would

Exhibit 8-8
Business Interruption Work Sheet for ABC Merchandise Company[†]

COMBINATION BUSINESS INTERRUPTION WORK SHEET (Form No. TE-15—Edition Date 3-70)

(For Use With Gross Earnings Form Nos. 3 and 4 for Mercantile, Non-Manufacturing or Manufacturing Risks)

Name of Insured .... ABC Merchandise Company ....

Location of Risk .... Anywhere, USA ....

Date ....

ALL ENTRIES TO BE ON AN ANNUAL BASIS	COLUMN 1 Actual Values for Year Ended 12/31/X7	COLUMN 2 *Estimated Values for Year Ending 12/31/X8 (Nearest Thousand)
A. Total annual net sales value of production from Manufacturing Operations; and total annual net sales from Merchandising or Non-Manufacturing Operations (Gross sales less discounts, returns, bad accounts and prepaid freight, if included in sales)	$ 899,000	$ 960,000
B. **Add** other earnings (if any) derived from operation of the business:		
1. Cash Discounts Received (not reflected in the amounts deducted under D)		
2. Commissions or Rents from Leased Departments		
3. Other Income	1,000	1,000
C. Total ("A" plus "B")	$ 900,000	$ 961,000
D. **Deduct only cost of:**		
1. Raw stock from which such production is derived	$	
2. Supplies consisting of materials consumed		

directly in the conversion of such raw stock into finished stock or in supplying the service(s) sold by the insured .... 2,000 | 2,000

3. Merchandise sold, including packaging materials therefor .... 600,000 | 641,000

4. Service(s) purchased from outsiders (not employees of the insured) for resale which do not continue under contract ....

Total Deductions .... $ 602,000 | $ 643,000

E. **GROSS EARNINGS ("C" Minus "D")** .... $ 298,000 | $ 318,000

IF INSURANCE IS TO BE WRITTEN WITHOUT PAYROLL ENDORSEMENTS:

F. Take 50, 60, 70 or 80% of "E.", Column 2, as amount of insurance required, depending upon percentage Contribution Clause to be used (_____%) .... $

IF INSURANCE IS TO BE WRITTEN WITH ORDINARY PAYROLL EXCLUSION ENDORSEMENT, Deduct From "E" Above:

G. All Ordinary Payroll Expense .... $ 120,000 | $ 128,100

H. Business Interruption Basis for Contribution ("E" minus "G") .... $ 178,000 | $ 189,900

I. Amount of Insurance—Take 80 or 90% of H, Column 2, depending upon percentage Contribution Clause to be used (80 %) .... 142,400 | 151,920

IF INSURANCE IS TO BE WRITTEN WITH ORDINARY PAYROLL-LIMITED COVERAGE ENDORSEMENT, Complete the Following:

J. Select the largest Ordinary Payroll Expense for 90† consecutive calendar days .... $

K. Business Interruption Basis for Contribution ("H" plus "J") .... $

L. Amount of Insurance—Take 80 or 90% of K, Column 2, depending upon percentage Contribution Clause to be used (___ %) .... $

†NOTE: The $1,000 and $2,000 figures were trended, but when rounded, the figure did not change.

Exhibit 8-9

SCR Manufacturing Company Income Statement—January 1 to December 31, 19X7*

Sales (less returns and allowances)		$650,000
Less cash discounts		5,000
Net sales		$645,000
Cost of goods sold		425,000
Gross profit on sales		$220,000
Selling expenses:		
Salespersons' salaries	$52,000	
Payroll taxes	2,150	
Sales office rent	5,000	
Depreciation, furniture and fixtures	350	
Advertising	9,500	
Miscellaneous expense	11,000	80,000
		$140,000
Administrative expenses:		
Office rent	$ 6,500	
Office salaries	30,000	
Payroll taxes—general	1,100	
Bad debts	500	
Telephone and telegraph	3,500	
Interest expense	500	
Heat, light	800	
Depreciation, furniture and fixtures	200	
Taxes	4,200	
Insurance	800	
Miscellaneous expense	16,900	65,000
Net income for the year		$ 75,000

*Reprinted with permission from P. I. Thomas and P. B. Reed, *Adjustment of Property Losses*, 4th ed. (New York: McGraw-Hill Book Co., 1977), p. 416.

include as a first step this same determination of gross earnings, as defined for a manufacturer. Then the gross earnings values would be projected into the future, as was the case in the nonmanufacturing example. The income statement for the most recent year is shown in Exhibit 8-9.

DETERMINATION OF GROSS EARNINGS. With a manufacturing risk, the initial task is the restatement of the income statement to determine the "net sales value of production." Business interruption coverage for a manufacturer is based on idemnifying the insured against the loss of production facilities due to an insured peril.

Exhibit 8-10
Determination of Sales Value of Production*

Sales (less returns and allowances)		$650,000
Less:		
Bad debts	$ 500	
Cash discounts	5,000	5,500
Net sales		$644,500
Less finished stock inventory, Jan. 1, at selling price (153% of $79,000)		120,870
		$523,630
Add finished stock inventory, Dec. 31, at selling price		
(153% of $45,000)		68,850
Sales value of production		$592,480

*Reprinted with permission from P. I. Thomas and P. B. Reed, *Adjustment of Property Losses*, 4th ed. (New York: McGraw-Hill Book Co., 1977), p. 417.

Therefore the exposure is related to the value of production which would be prevented during an interruption. The form excludes loss of earnings resulting from damage to or destruction of "finished stock" or for the time required to reproduce finished stock. This can be covered by a *selling price clause* attached to a direct damage policy. The rationale for this is that since this exposure may be covered by an endorsement to the direct damage policy, inclusion of the coverage under the business interruption form would permit double insurance.[1]

The *net sales value of production* is defined as net sales less finished stock inventory at the beginning of the period, valued at selling price, plus finished stock inventory at the end of the period, valued at selling price.

The conversion of the finished stock inventory value from a cost to a selling price basis is accomplished by applying the ratio of sales ($650,000) to the cost of goods sold ($425,000).

Therefore,

$$\frac{\$650,000}{\$425,000} = 1.53 \text{ or } 153 \text{ percent}$$

The determination of the net sales value of production is shown in Exhibit 8-10.

The next step is the determination of the cost of raw stock and materials, which is deducted from the net sales value of production. The data for this calculation is contained in the determination of the cost of goods sold for the income statement. These data are shown in Exhibit 8-11. The final step in the calculation of gross earnings is to deduct the raw materials and the supplies used in production and shipping from the net sales value of production. Since some raw materials may have been used to produce stock in process, the stock in process inventory at the beginning and end of the periods is compared. If there is an increase in the stock in process inventory during the year, the amount of this increase is also deducted from the net sales value of production to obtain gross earnings. This calculation is shown in Exhibit 8-12.

THE PROJECTION OF GROSS EARNINGS. In most businesses, over the short run if there is no major change in the operation, the relationship between income and costs can be assumed to be stable. Therefore, when forecasting the future trend of gross earnings, the past trend in sales can be used. In this example, it is assumed that there is no seasonality; therefore, annual data can be used as was the case in the nonmanufacturing example. If there were seasonality in the data, the procedure would remain essentially the same except that monthly data would be used to determine the future level of sales of production for each month. The sales for the past five years for the SCR Manufacturing Company are shown in Exhibit 8-13. The average rate of growth is 5.7 percent. In the completion of the business interruption worksheet, this trend factor of 5.7 percent will be used for all values. It is important to note that this is based on the assumption that all of the cost factors included in the determination of gross earnings vary proportionately with sales. If there is a major change in the operation, such as the start-up of a new process or product or the closing of an outmoded production facility, this assumption of proportionality may not be valid. If there is a change in the operation, each component of the gross earnings determination should be separately forecast utilizing whatever information is available.

DETERMINATION OF THE REQUIRED AMOUNT OF INSURANCE. The required amount of insurance is based on the projected gross earnings value. In this case it is assumed that the manufacturer plans to retain all workers for interruptions of 90 days or less. Therefore the ordinary payroll limited coverage endorsement is utilized. This requires at least an 80 percent contribution percentage. In this case it is assumed that 80 percent will be sufficient. The determination of the required amount of insurance, $216,985, is shown in Exhibit 8-14. Note that when utilizing the ordinary payroll limited coverage endorsement, all ordinary payroll is deducted. The ordinary payroll in this case is assumed to be $252,500, consisting of $52,000 salespersons' salaries, $30,000 office salaries, and $170,500 direct labor. Since the payroll is to be covered for 90 days or one-fourth of a year, 25 percent of this amount is then added back in to determine the basis for contribution clause purposes.

Exhibit 8-11
SCR Manufacturing Company Schedule of Cost of Goods Sold—
January 1 to December 31, 19X7*

Inventory of finished stock, Jan. 1			$ 79,000
Inventory of stock in process, Jan. 1		$ 4,000	
Materials:			
Inventory, raw materials, Jan. 1		$ 11,500	
Purchases		141,500	
Freight inward		1,200	
		$154,200	
Less returns	$1,200		
Cash discounts	1,000	2,200	
		$152,000	
Less inventory, Dec. 31		12,500	
Raw materials used		139,500	
Direct labor		170,500	
Manufacturing overhead:			
Indirect labor		$ 42,500	
Payroll taxes		4,100	
Insurance, factory		400	
Taxes, factory		4,500	
Heat, light, and power		4,800	
Repairs and maintenance		5,200	
Depreciation, building		4,500	
Depreciation, machinery		8,000	
Supplies used in production		5,000	
Supplies, shipping		6,000	
Total manufacturing expense		85,000	
		$399,000	
Less inventory of stock in process, Dec. 31		8,000	391,000
Cost of goods manufactured			$470,000
Less inventory of finished stock, Dec. 31			45,000
Cost of goods sold			$425,000

*Reprinted with permission from P.I. Thomas and P.B. Reed, *Adjustment of Property Losses*, 4th ed. (New York: McGraw-Hill Book Co., 1977), p. 417.

Underwriting Considerations Since a business interruption loss requires that there be direct damage to the insured premises by a covered peril, analysis of the physical and moral hazards of the risk begins with an analysis of the direct damage exposure. If the business interruption form is added to a direct damage policy, this analysis has presumably already been completed. In those instances when business

Exhibit 8-12

Determination of Gross Earnings*

Sales value of production		$592,480
Materials:		
Raw materials used (see Table 8-11)	$139,500	
Supplies used in production and shipping	11,000	
	$150,500	
Add stock-in-process inventory, Jan. 1	4,000	
	$154,500	
Less stock-in-process inventory, Dec. 31	8,000	146,500
Gross earnings		$445,980

*Reprinted with permission from P. I. Thomas and P. B. Reed, *Adjustment of Property Losses*, 4th ed. (New York: McGraw-Hill Book Co., 1977), p. 417.

Exhibit 8-13
SCR Manufacturing Company Sales for 19X3-19X7

Year	Sales	Percentage of Growth
19X3	$520,000	
19X4	550,000	5.8%
19X5	580,000	5.5
19X6	609,000	5.0
19X7	650,000	6.7
		Average growth 5.7%

interruption is written separately, analysis of the COPE factors is required to determine the direct damage loss exposure.

The nature of the business interruption coverage adds some other considerations. Time is the principal element in business interruption coverage. A relatively minor property loss destroying only 5 percent of the structure might result in a total business interruption loss up to the policy limit if the destroyed property included a machine vital to the manufacturing process that could not be replaced in less than one year.[2] The severity of a business interruption loss is not directly related to the severity of the underlying direct damage loss.

Seasonality and Rebuilding Time. As previously noted in the estimation of business interruption values, the degree of seasonality in

Exhibit 8-14
Business Interruption Work Sheet for SCR Manufacturing Company

COMBINATION BUSINESS INTERRUPTION WORK SHEET (Form No. TE-15—Edition Date 3-70)

(For Use With Gross Earnings Form Nos. 3 and 4 for Mercantile, Non-Manufacturing or Manufacturing Risks)

Name of Insured .... SCR Manufacturing Company ....

Location of Risk .... Anytown, USA ....

Date ....

ALL ENTRIES TO BE ON AN ANNUAL BASIS	COLUMN 1 Actual Values for Year Ended 12/31/X7	COLUMN 2 *Estimated Values for Year Ending 12/31/X8
A. Total annual net sales value of production from Manufacturing Operations; and total annual net sales from Merchandising or Non-Manufacturing Operations (Gross sales less discounts, returns, bad accounts and prepaid freight, if included in sales)	$ 592,480	(5.7% Trend Factor) $ 626,251
B. **Add** other earnings (if any) derived from operation of the business:		
1. Cash Discounts Received (not reflected in the amounts deducted under D)		
2. Commissions or Rents from Leased Departments		
3.		
C. Total ("A" plus "B")	$ 592,480	$ 626,251
D. **Deduct only cost of:**		
1. Raw stock from which such production is derived	$ 135,500*	$ 143,224

2. Supplies consisting of materials consumed directly in the conversion of such raw stock into finished stock or in supplying the service(s) sold by the insured .... 11,000 | 11,627

3. Merchandise sold, including packaging materials therefor ....

4. Service(s) purchased from outsiders (not employees of the insured) for resale which do not continue under contract ....

Total Deductions .... $146,500 | $154,851

E. GROSS EARNINGS ("C" Minus "D") .... $445,980 | $471,400

*$139,500 — $4,000 increase in stock in process inventory.

IF INSURANCE IS TO BE WRITTEN WITHOUT PAYROLL ENDORSEMENTS:

F. Take 50, 60, 70 or 80% of "E," Column 2, as amount of insurance required, depending upon percentage Contribution Clause to be used (_____%) ....

IF INSURANCE IS TO BE WRITTEN WITH ORDINARY PAYROLL EXCLUSION ENDORSEMENT, Deduct From "E" Above:

G. All Ordinary Payroll Expense 30,000+52,000+170,500 .... $252,500 | $266,892

H. Business Interruption Basis for Contribution ("E" minus "G") .... $193,480 | $204,508

I. Amount of Insurance—Take 80 or 90% of H, Column 2, depending upon percentage Contribution Clause to be used (_____%) .... $

IF INSURANCE IS TO BE WRITTEN WITH ORDINARY PAYROLL-LIMITED COVERAGE ENDORSEMENT, Complete the Following:

J. Select the largest Ordinary Payroll Expense for 90† consecutive calendar days $252,500 \times 0.25 =$ .... $63,125 | $66,723

$266,892 \times 0.25 =$

K. Business Interruption Basis for Contribution ("H" plus "J") .... $256,605 | $271,231

L. Amount of Insurance—Take 80 or 90% of K, Column 2, depending upon percentage Contribution Clause to be used (80 %) .... 205,284 | 216,985

Exhibit 8-15
Ratios† of Monthly Sales to Annual Sales of Fourteen Classes of Retail Business*

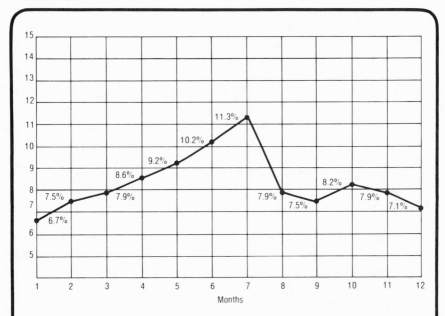

†These ratios are composites of fluctuation ratios of the following classes of business:
(1) department stores, including mail order; (2) draperies and lamps; (3) drugs; (4) floor coverings; (5) furniture and appliances; (6) general merchandise, including dry goods; (7) lumber and building materials; (8) liquor stores; (9) home furnishings; (10) shoe stores; (11) variety stores; (12) women's ready-to-wear; (13) grocery stores; and (14) men's and boys' wear, clothing and furnishings.

*Reprinted with permission from E.C. Bardwell, *New Profits—Business Interruption Insurance* (Indianapolis: The Rough Notes Co., 1976), p. 14.

the insured's operations is a major factor in determining potential exposure. This is an important underwriting consideration because a highly seasonal business with 80 percent or more of its business concentrated in a three-month peak season would suffer a severe business interruption loss from a relatively short shutdown. Exhibit 8-15 shows the seasonality of sales in the retail business area.

Similarly, the time period required to rebuild the insured premises is a major factor in the determination of exposure. Specialized structures requiring long construction periods, the possibility of lengthy delays in obtaining permits, severe climatic conditions inhibiting construction during certain times of the year, and congested urban locations are all factors increasing exposure to loss.

Bottlenecks. Manufacturing and mining risks are particularly susceptible to bottlenecks. This term is used to refer to a machine, process, or building which is essential to the continued operation of an entire facility or manufacturing plant. A relatively minor direct damage loss can lead to a severe business interruption loss in the case of a bottleneck. The existence of a potential bottleneck can be determined by use of a flow diagram of the production process. Exhibit 8-16 shows an example of such a bottleneck. It is process AB in the fifth stage of production. Since the entire manufacturing flow includes the AB process, the operation would be totally interrupted if that process were destroyed. This exposure would be heightened if the AB process depends on a machine made by elves in the Black Forest with no parts or substitute machines locally available. Some manufacturing processes utilize machines that must be custom manufactured with the re-installation process taking many months. If the process is vital but is duplicated on machines in separate fire divisions, the exposure is greatly reduced.

While bottlenecks usually are found in processing or manufacturing risks, a congested area or an unusual building configuration can result in a bottleneck during the reconstruction period.

An example of a bottleneck caused by the configuration of a building is the large institutional risk shown in Exhibit 8-17. This institution consists of seven major fire divisions. Division A, completely surrounded by the others, was the dormitory facility for faculty and students alike in a residential school for blind children. A fire severely damaged only this portion of the school, resulting in a constructive total loss to that section. While it was originally estimated that no division would require more than six months to completely reconstruct, debris removal alone took four months. Note that there is no access to Division A without damaging other portions, and cranes and large mechanical shovels could not be used. Debris removal required torch cutting of the fire-twisted steel beams into small pieces to be taken in wheelbarrows through small specially cut doors in the undamaged wings. This hand work was repeated during reconstruction. The interruption totalled eighteen months, three times the estimate.

Lengthy Production Processes. If the manufacturing or processing operation takes an unusually long time to complete, this could extend the business interruption exposure. If a product must be aged or seasoned, destruction of the facility could lead to a lengthy interruption since this time would be added to the length of time necessary to restore the structure and machinery to operating condition.

This also applies to stock in process. Since the business interruption gross earnings form covers actual loss sustained, the time period

Exhibit 8-16
A Manufacturing Bottleneck*

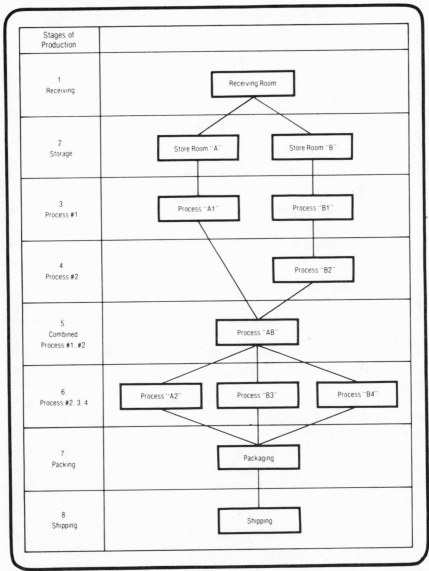

*Reprinted with permission from Matthew Lenz, Jr., *Risk Management Manual* (Santa Monica: The Merritt Company, 1976), p. 18

Exhibit 8-17

A Construction Bottleneck

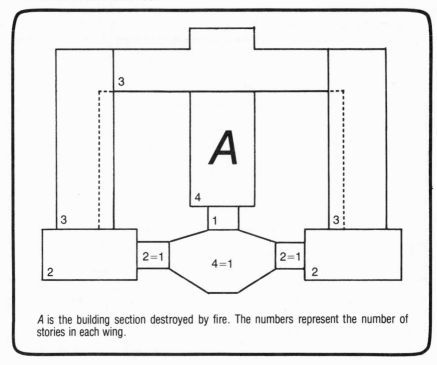

A is the building section destroyed by fire. The numbers represent the number of stories in each wing.

of coverage includes the time required to get the stock in process to the point it had been prior to the loss. If a risk manufactures large turbines which require two years to complete, a fire in the twenty-third month would mean that the business interruption loss would extend for twenty-three months after the damaged buildings, machinery, and raw stock had been restored.

Disaster Contingency Plans. On Thanksgiving Day, 1982, a fire destroyed much of the Northwestern National Bank Building in Minneapolis. In spite of the extensive damage, the bank was able to reopen Monday morning in new offices and with most of the services being performed. While the presence of a glut of office space in downtown Minneapolis allowed the bank to find additional temporary office space quickly, a major factor in the recovery was the presence of an up-to-date disaster contingency plan.

All of the financial records of the firm were kept four blocks away at the main office of the firm which handled the record keeping for the bank. These were not harmed. A duplicate set of all records was kept at a second office on the other side of the town. There was a transfer of the files daily between the two offices so that each would be up-to-date. Many records (such as wills, signature cards, and so on) were also on microfilm so that new hard copies could be made.

Perhaps more importantly, the plan instructed everyone as to what to do and where to report in case of a disaster such as the one the bank suffered. Telephone numbers, equipment needed by each department, space needed, order numbers, suppliers, and so on were an important part of the plan. New teller facilities were opened and the bank received permission to allow other banks owned by the same parent holding company to receive transactions. There were also six branch offices that were not destroyed.

There were still some problems such as personnel having to learn how to use different models of equipment, no terminals immediately hooked up for the tellers to check balances, and so on, but these were minor compared to those solved by having the disaster-recovery plan (as it was called). While not all insureds would need to go to such great lengths in devising a plan (the bank's plan was three inches thick), every insured should at least consider informally what would need to be done in the event of a disaster and preferably should make some written plans.[3]

While the business interruption form requires due diligence and dispatch in the restoration of the operation, proper planning can further reduce the length of interruption. A disaster contingency plan would include detailed written plans for the restoration of the operation in the event of destruction of part or all of the buildings and equipment. The disaster contingency plan should be tied in to the flow chart of the firm's operation indicating the actions that would be necessary in the event of the destruction of each component part of the process. This type of plan could also indicate if continuation of the operation would be feasible in the event of certain types of damage. If that were the case, extra expense insurance might be indicated, either in lieu of business interruption or on a combined form.

Valued or Per Diem Forms

Determination of the proper amount of insurance for the gross earnings form is a difficult task. This disadvantage of that form of coverage is accompanied by the fact that loss adjustment of business interruption losses under that type of form is more complex than direct damage loss adjustment.

Both of these disadvantages can be largely overcome by use of valued or per diem forms of business interruption. These have been used in the inland marine field for some time with respect to bridges and tunnels. In the valued or per diem form, a certain stated amount of coverage is available for each day, week, or month that operations are interrupted. The form also includes an aggregate limit for any one occurrence.

If on a per diem form coverage is set at $3,000, the loss adjustment simply consists of the total number of days of interruption. During partial suspension of operation, the percentage of reduction in operations is determined and applied to the per diem amount. Since the values have been agreed to in advance, the valued form does not include a contribution clause.

Valued or per diem forms create additional problems. This form of coverage has three major disadvantages:

1. higher rate,
2. possible underinsurance, and
3. possible overinsurance.

Higher Rate   The rate of this coverage is higher than the gross earnings rate. While the overall premium may be reduced, this reduction comes from selection of a lower amount of coverage.

Underinsurance   With the per diem form the insured will most likely select an amount of insurance equal to the expected maximum loss per time period. While it is difficult to identify exactly those expenses which will continue and the amount that can be abated, this estimation can be made with greater accuracy than forecasts of the maximum period of interruption. Since most losses are partial, the insured may be paid in full for the majority of the interruptions even with a clearly inadequate aggregate limit. Therefore the possibility of underinsurance is very high. A partial loss to the insured operation may result in a total loss under the policy.

The only way that the extent of insurance to value can be determined is to complete the worksheet and other analysis of the risk as if it were to be written on the gross earnings form. Only in this manner can the underwriter be assured of obtaining adequate premium for the exposure.

Overinsurance   Since the loss payment will consist of the agreed limit times the number of days, the form does not tie the payment to the actual loss sustained by the insured. Moral hazard is therefore inherent in this type of coverage. An insured whose operation has become unprofitable may be able to generate a positive cash flow by means of an intentionally caused loss. Completion of the gross earnings form worksheets would also indicate the existence of overinsurance. The financial and moral stability of the insured is a vital underwriting consideration with valued business interruption coverage.

Contingent Business Interruption

The insured's operations may be interrupted by damage or destruction of property at the premises of a supplier, customer, or neighboring business. This exposure can be insured through use of contingent business interruption. This coverage may be desirable in three situations:

1. when the insured's operation is dependent upon one or a few suppliers for raw materials, processing, or services,
2. when the insured has a single customer or a small number of customers that purchase the majority of the products, or
3. when the insured is dependent upon a neighboring business to generate the majority of the flow of customers. This may occur in a shopping center where the smaller businesses in the center are dependent upon one or two *leader* properties (usually major department stores) to generate the flow of shoppers into the center.

Properties that supply materials, supplies, or services to the insured are known as *contributing* properties. Properties of customers purchasing the insured's products are known as *recipient* properties.

Coverage The contingent business interruption form pays for interruption of the insured's operation as a result of damage caused by an insured peril at the contributing or recipient premises. If, for example, components destined for the insured's manufacturing operation are destroyed by fire at a contributing plant, the policy will pay for any interruption in the insured's operation, even if the contributing plant itself was not shut down.

The contribution clause requires maintenance of the amount of insurance based on the amount of business which is dependent on the operation of the other plant or customer.

Underwriting Considerations The contributing or recipient property should be underwritten in the same manner as any other property risk, considering the COPE factors and the moral and financial hazards of the risk. In addition, since the property is not under the control of the insured, the ability to obtain meaningful compliance with loss control recommendations is important.

The exposure is closely related to the relative degree of dependence of the insured on the supplier or customer. This dependence can often be determined by use of a flow chart of the entire chain of supply and distribution including the insured and the recipient and contributing properties. An example is shown in Exhibit 8-18. Note that all the output from factory #1 goes to subcontractor #1 and part of that output undergoes further processing at subcontractor #2. If these two subcontractors, particularly subcontractor #1, perform a service which is not available elsewhere, the insured would have a substantial contingent business interruption exposure.

EXTRA EXPENSE

Certain types of businesses may continue operation rather than shutting down after damage or destruction of their operating facilities. Newspapers, retail dairies, and dry cleaning establishments frequently will continue to operate utilizing temporary facilities. Continuation of the operation of the firm after a loss involves extraordinary extra expenses. Extra expense insurance will provide coverage for these extra expenses, while the business interruption policy will cover expenses only to the extent that they reduce the business interruption loss.

Coverage

The extra expense policy covers all necessary extra expense incurred during the *period of restoration*. The period of restoration is defined as the time period that is necessary with due diligence and dispatch to repair or replace the damaged property or facility. The loss must be the result of direct damage caused by an insured peril, as is the case with business interruption.

The extra expense policy does not have a contribution clause, as such. The form provides for stipulated limits of liability with the amount of extra expense recoverable related to the length of the period of recovery.

The basic policy sets forth the limits of liability as follows:

1. 40 percent of the policy limit when the period of restoration is not in excess of one month,
2. 80 percent of the policy limit when the period of restoration is in excess of one month but not in excess of two months, and
3. 100 percent when the period of restoration is in excess of two months.

A "month" is defined as thirty consecutive days. The recovery limits are cumulative. From an underwriting standpoint it is important to note that 80 percent of the policy limit will be available for an interruption of thirty-one days. This means that a relatively small physical damage loss can lead to a virtual total loss under the extra expense policy. While it is necessary for the insured to prove all extra

Exhibit 8-18
External Flow*

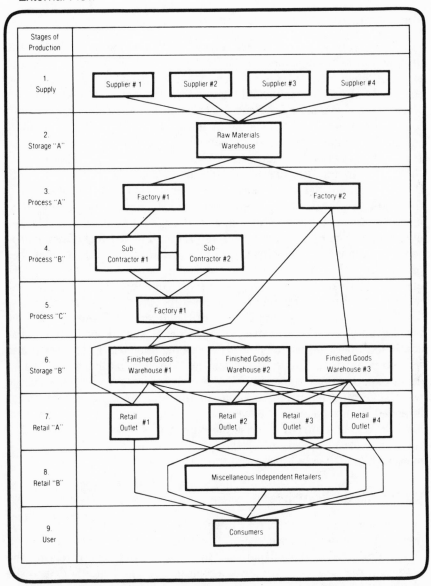

*Reprinted with permission from Matthew Lenz, Jr., *Risk Management Manual* (Santa Monica: The Merritt Company, 1976), p. 17.

expenses, most extra expenses of continuing an operation in temporary facilities are incurred at the outset in obtaining the temporary facility and resuming production or operation.

Determination of the Amount of Insurance

The extra expenses necessary to continue operation after the destruction of a major operating facility bear no direct relationship to sales. In each case these expenses must be estimated by determining the cost of each component necessary to continue operation. A worksheet which can be utilized for this estimation is shown in Exhibit 8-19. These cost estimates should be integrated with the firm's disaster contingency plan. Prior to the occurrence of a loss, it may be possible for the firm to make arrangements with other firms in the same area that have similar facilities for the temporary use of those facilities in the event of a disaster such as a fire or windstorm loss. For example, if there are two large asphalt batch plants in the area, the managements of these firms might agree on a mutual contingency plan. If the operation of one of the plants were interrupted by a direct damage loss, the other plant's excess capacity would be made available at an agreed price. Since this type of agreement is mutually beneficial, the price arrived at is likely to be lower than that which could be arranged the morning after one of the plants was destroyed by fire.

In addition to the determination of the amount of exposure and the proper amount of insurance, the insured should determine that continued operation is feasible. If it is not, business interruption and *not* extra expense should be purchased. One firm had been purchasing extra expense for its machine shop operation for several years. There were several other machine shops in the area and the risk manager intended to purchase their excess production capacity in the event of a loss. On taking a survey the risk manager was shocked to discover that the total excess capacity of all the available machine shops would have met less than 5 percent of his requirements.

Rating Extra Expense

The basic extra expense form with the limits of 40 percent the first month, 80 percent the second, and 100 percent after two months takes a rate that is twice the 80 percent coinsurance building rate (for the highest rated peril being insured against). This high rate is due to the likelihood of underinsurance with this form. With 40 percent of the limit available within the first thirty-day period, a relatively minor interruption could result in a substantial extra expense loss, as previously noted.

Exhibit 8-19

Extra Expense Work Sheet*

Expenses Necessary to Continue Business	First Month		Second Month		Third Month	
Rent of temporary premises						
Cleaning temporary premises						
Labor equipping temporary premises						
Rent of temporary machinery, equipment, etc.						
Net cost of equipment, etc., purchased						
Expense of moving equipment, etc.						
Light, power, and heat at temporary premises						
Labor at temporary premises						
Insurance expense at temporary premises						
Janitor and watchman at temporary premises						
Other expenses at or because of temporary premises (advertising, telephone, telegraph, legal, etc.)						
Total due to temporary premises						
Add payments to others for manufacturing or processing						
Add necessarily continuing expenses at original location after a loss						
Add bonuses for quick services, etc.						
Total expenses after a loss						
Deduct total of all expenses which would have been incurred at the original location for the corresponding period had no loss incurred						
Extra expense insurance to be carried						

*Reprinted with permission from Henry C. Klein, *Business Interruption Insurance* (Indianapolis: The Rough Notes Co., 1964), p. 253.

If the insured anticipates that extra expenses will continue at a fairly high level for an extended time period, the percentage limit specified for the first month can be changed. Utilizing the worksheet, the insured should estimate the extra expenses to be incurred the first month, and the amounts for each succeeding month up to the end of the anticipated recovery period. The percentage limits can then be modified

Exhibit 8-20
80 Percent Coinsurance Building Rate
Factors for Extra Expense Insurance*

Limits of Liability (by month)	Factor
100%	4.00
40-80-100%	2.00
35-70-100%	1.90
30-60-90-100%	1.80
25-50-75-100%	1.70
20-40-60-80-100%	1.60

*Adapted with permission from *Commercial Lines Manual*
(New York: Insurance Services Office, copyright 1980), p.
CF-25 (2nd Edition, 5-81).

accordingly. The rate is related to the percentage limit specified for the first month. The factors to use for some fairly standard percentages are shown in Exhibit 8-20. The factors are applied to the 80 percent coinsurance building rate.

Underwriting Considerations

Extra expense requires the same underwriting analysis as business interruption. Since the form essentially has no contribution clause, and since the expenses are likely to be heavy in even a brief interruption of normal operations, underinsurance is a major problem. The existence of a disaster contingency plan indicates that the insured has given some thought to the problems of the continuation of operations in the event of an insured loss. This will provide a means of evaluating the adequacy of the stipulated amount of insurance. The insured with no contingency plans and only vague estimates of anticipated costs should be carefully underwritten.

Contingent Extra Expense

Extra expense coverage can be purchased to indemnify the insured for extra expenses incurred due to direct loss or damage at contributing properties. If a substitute supplier could be utilized, the contingent extra expense coverage would cover the cost of materials or services in excess of those costs normally incurred.

The amount of insurance and percentages apportioned to the

various months should be determined based upon the anticipated exposure at the supplier's plant and the estimated costs. It is unlikely that this type of exposure would have the high initial costs of setting up business at an alternative location; therefore, a lower percentage limit allocated to the first month may be indicated.

The rate for contingent extra expense is determined in the same manner as direct extra expense. The rate is based on the building fire insurance rate of the contributing property. This contributing property should meet the same underwriting standards applied to other property insurance submissions.

Combined Business Interruption and Extra Expense

Some businesses whose major exposure is loss of earnings due to a shutdown found that recovery under the expense to reduce loss portion of the business interruption policy is not sufficient to cover the extra expenses incurred in rapid resumption of operations. The combined business interruption and extra expense form indemnifies the insured for those extra expenses necessarily incurred to resume operations over and above the amount which directly reduces the business interruption loss. The amount of extra expense coverage available is related to the amount of business interruption insurance and the duration of the recovery period. In most rating jurisdictions, the ordinary payroll exclusion and the ordinary payroll limited coverage endorsement may not be used with this form. Each portion of the combined form should be underwritten on the same basis as the coverage when provided separately.

OTHER INDIRECT LOSS COVERAGES

Consequential Loss

While it is true that any indirect loss arising out of direct loss from fire and allied perils is a consequential loss, the term "consequential" here refers only to changes in temperature or other physical condition due to failure of cooling or heating appliances following damage by an insured peril. The loss to a power generating station which causes refrigerated meat to rot is an example.

Direct damage policies in most jurisdictions provide consequential loss coverage resulting from direct damage occurring only on the insured's premises.

Losses resulting from off-premises power failures must be covered by specific endorsement to direct damage policies. In most jurisdictions this is done by charging 50 percent of the building rate in which the cooling or heating apparatus is located (for coverage on public utilities, rates are specified in the manual).

The major underwriting consideration with this coverage is capacity. This coverage does *not* increase the coverage limits but adds to the type of losses indemnified.

Rental Value

An apartment house owner or the owner of a large office building has a specialized type of time element loss exposure—loss of rental income. This can be covered by rental value insurance which may be written either on a coinsurance form or a monthly limitation form. (Tenants or lessees also have an exposure if obligated to continue rent payments even if the premises is destroyed.)

In determining the exposure for rental value coverage, the lease provisions governing the right of tenants to cancel leases after a major loss are an important consideration. The rents may be flat amounts or a percentage of the tenant's sales.

Often the rental value policy may be written for a lower premium than a similar business interruption policy covering the same exposure. The underwriting considerations for this coverage are the same as business interruption.

Leasehold Interest

A business firm with a favorable lease would suffer a loss if the lease were canceled due to a direct damage loss to the premises. Leasehold interest insurance covers the value of the lease relative to what would otherwise be available in the present market. The longer the time remaining on the lease, and the greater the difference between the lease terms and those currently available in the market, the greater the value. The underwriting considerations for leasehold interest are the same as for business interruption. The rules for this coverage are found in the direct damage section of the manual. Coverage is provided via an endorsement.

Tuition Fees Insurance

A private school, college, or university has a unique business interruption exposure. If a direct damage loss damaged or destroyed the school buildings or facilities, the entire tuition fees (excluding room, board, laboratory, and other income sources) from a semester or an entire school year could be lost, even if the loss occurred during the summer when the school was closed. The tuition fees form is designed to cover this exposure. The restoration period as defined in this form commences on the date of the direct damage or destruction by an insured peril and ends on the day preceding the beginning of the first school year following the date that the damaged property could be rebuilt, repaired, or replaced.

The underwriting of tuition fees insurance is similar to other business interruption coverage. As noted in Chapter 5, schools are particularly susceptible to incendiary fires. This hazard should be carefully underwritten.

Demolition Costs; Contingent Liability from Operation of Building Laws; and Increased Cost of Construction Forms

Most communities have building laws and zoning laws that may restrict the kind of structure that can be built or rebuilt in certain areas. If a building currently does not meet existing regulations and then suffers a loss, the code may require upgrading when the damage is repaired.

Such codes present the insured with the prospect of four distinct additional losses:

1. Direct physical damage can result in condemnation of the remaining portion. Thus, a 50 percent loss can become a 100 percent loss.
2. The cost to demolish and remove the debris from the undamaged portion.
3. The additional cost above and beyond the original loss to build a better grade of structure.
4. Loss arising out of the additional time required to destroy and/or rebuild to conform to building laws or codes.

All of these exposures can be covered. The first two are provided by extending the insurance to make the full amount of the policy available for the loss. Endorsements to provide this are variously titled within different fire rating jurisdictions. Most frequently these are known as: (1) *contingent liability from operation of building laws* and (2) *demolition cost insurance* respectively.

The third exposure, that is, the increased cost imposed by laws demanding a higher grade of construction, is called *increased cost of construction insurance.* This endorsement provides an additional amount of insurance which is determined by whatever upgrading may be required above and beyond the full replacement cost of the extant building. The final exposure is covered by a time element coverage endorsement called *contingent liability from operation of building laws endorsement—demolition and increased time to rebuild.*

The underwriter has two primary concerns when these exposures exist. First, on behalf of the insured, it is desirable to make sure that the insured is aware of these exposures. Second, providing the covers can increase the moral hazard. If the protection exists it may tempt an insured to upgrade at the expense of the insurer. These coverages may increase the probable severity of a loss; therefore, this must be taken into account when setting fire lines and determining the probable maximum loss.

SUMMARY

The previous chapters have covered direct property loss exposures. In addition, business firms are exposed to major indirect property losses. These include:

1. loss of income due to property damage to buildings, equipment, or inventory;
2. extra expense due to extraordinary expenses incurred in continuing a business operation after damage to the operating facilities; and
3. contingent losses due to the interruption of production or sales occasioned by direct damage to the plant or facility of a subcontractor, supplier, or customer.

The gross earnings form of business interruption covers the reduction in gross earnings during a shutdown occasioned by an insured peril. The reduction in gross earnings is reduced by the amount of charges and expenses which do not necessarily continue. This form requires estimation of the insured's exposure and then determination of the proper amount of insurance in order to comply with the contribution clause.

Calculation of the insured's exposure includes:

1. projection of gross earnings including any seasonal fluctuations,
2. determination of the probable period of interruption, and
3. identification of the charges and expenses which do not necessarily continue.

Gross earnings, which is defined differently for nonmanufacturing and manufacturing risks, may be modified by endorsement. These endorsements include the ordinary payroll exclusion endorsement, the ordinary payroll limited coverage endorsement, and the power, heat, and refrigeration endorsement for manufacturing risks.

The amount of insurance may also be affected by the agreed amount endorsement, the premium adjustment endorsement, and the endorsement extending the period of indemnity. Another form of business interruption coverage which does not include a contribution clause is the earnings form.

Business interruption must be underwritten utilizing the same COPE factors as direct damage coverage. Additional underwriting considerations include seasonality and rebuilding time, bottlenecks, lengthy production processes, and the existence or lack of disaster contingency plans. Business interruption may also be written on a valued or per diem basis.

Extra expense insurance provides coverage for the extraordinary expenses required to continue a business in operation after a direct damage loss caused by an insured peril. Determination of the appropriate amount of extra expense insurance is often difficult. Often a minor direct damage loss can result in a heavy loss under this coverage, particularly when written with 40 percent of the overall limit of liability available within the first thirty days of interruption.

Other indirect loss coverages include consequential loss, rental income, leasehold interest, tuition fees insurance, demolition cost contingent liability from operation of building laws, and increased cost of construction.

Chapter Notes

1. Clyde M. Kahler, "Business Interruption Insurance," doctoral dissertation, University of Pennsylvania, 1930, p. 149.
2. Robert B. Holtom, *Commercial Fire Underwriting* (Cincinnati: The National Underwriter Co., 1969), p. 144.
3. This description of the Northwestern National Bank fire is based on Lawrence Ingrassia, "Planning, Luck Help Big Bank Overcome Fire," *The Wall Street Journal*, 3 December 1982, pp. 33, 39.

CHAPTER 9

Pricing

INTRODUCTION

Pricing is a very important part of the underwriting process. The underwriter must determine if the premium generated is sufficient to cover the losses and expenses associated with a risk. It is important that the underwriter should know not only what the premium or price is, but also how it was developed.

Chapter 8 of the AIU 61 text discusses pricing in property and liability insurance. A brief review of the terms introduced in that chapter is necessary before discussing pricing in property and multiple-lines insurance. A *rate* is a price that is charged for insurance coverage on a "specific unit" called a *base of exposure*. Examples of a base include per $100 of coverage or per building. The product of the rate and the exposure unit is the *premium*. The actual process of applying the rate to the number of specific units or the selection of a rating plan is known as *rating* the risk. The technique of developing rates is known as *rate making*.

The insurance actuary works within an environment in which both micro- and macro-economic concepts must be taken into consideration. The micro-economic concept is generally termed *pricing*. Under the pricing concept, the actuary makes certain that the insurance company develops sufficient premiums to pay for the losses and expenses during a specified period of time plus allow the insurer a small profit.

In property as well as other lines of insurance, the underwriter most often uses rates established by someone else. While the underwriter may not directly establish the rates, he or she plays an important role in their development. Underwriters should know their role in the rate-making process and how their decisions and actions affect the rates that are developed. For example, the underwriter needs to understand the pooling concept and needs to know about the risks which are intended to make up the "group" or "class" for rate-making purposes.

FIRE INSURANCE RATES

The establishment of fire insurance rates is a highly specialized procedure which requires the skills of rating specialists to make inspections, collect and organize physical data as well as loss experience data, and analyze the many factors that measure the relative fire hazards of different risks. It would be prohibitively expensive and inefficient for each insurer to maintain its own organization to carry out this function. The preferred method of resolving this problem is for groups of insurers to establish a centralized organization to promulgate insurance rates.

In most states many insurers base their rates for dwellings and homeowners insurance primarily on their own experience. But for rate structures on commercial insureds, the Insurance Services Office (ISO), with regional and state branches, is the primary fire insurance rate promulgation organization. Nearly all fire insurance rates are one of two types: (1) *class rates*, and (2) *specific* or *schedule rates*.

Class Rating

It has been stated often in the texts in the Associate in Underwriting program that no two risks (especially commercial risks) present exactly the same hazards to an insurer. Two structures identical in construction features will usually have significant differences in their maintenance, their contents, the location of each in relation to external exposures, the number and nature of occupants, and so on. However, even though all risks are different in one way or another, it is not financially feasible to inspect each and every structure for the purpose of establishing a specific fire insurance rate. The cost of such service, even if the personnel were available to the insurance industry, would tend to make insurance costs prohibitive. Therefore, many risks which are very similar in nature although not identical are assigned a fire rate based on a *class rate* assigned to a broad category of risks.

Class rates are usually applied to private dwellings, small apartment houses, farms, schools, churches, clubs, and an increasing percentage of small mercantile and nonmanufacturing establishments. Such risks make up 80 percent or more of the total properties in the United States. Class rates, however, are used mostly for smaller insureds and therefore account for less than half the collected insurance premiums.

For risks that are class rated, the rates are based on a very brief list of major characteristics with all risks sharing those same characteristics being assigned the same insurance rate. Several class rating plans are used in various jurisdictions for various types of risks. For example, nearly all states utilize some type of dwelling program which is a class rating system for dwellings, farms, small apartments, and similar risks. In such dwelling plans, the insured's rate depends on the construction classification, the protection classification, and the amount of insurance. Many states also use a simplified mercantile rating plan, which is a class rating schedule utilized for small retailing risks. In such a program the specific mercantile occupancy of the risk helps determine the insurance rate.

ISO Fire Class Rate Plan   The most common fire class rating plan used for commercial or business risks is the ISO fire class rate plan, which, with some modifications, is used in almost every state. Consequently, this section will discuss in some detail the structure and operation of this plan.

The ISO fire class rate plan was developed to provide rates for mercantile, nonmanufacturing and warehouse buildings of certain commercial statistical plan (CSP) codes and of frame, joisted masonry, and noncombustible construction. These buildings should have 15,000 square feet or less of total floor area. Some hotels and motels (without restaurants) of all construction types and with less than 15,000 square feet of floor area are also eligible, as are habitational properties (of all construction types and with unlimited square footage) not eligible for the dwelling policy program, and certain special exposures (e.g., properties in the open). Among the ineligible properties not already mentioned are (1) buildings eligible for rating under the dwelling policy program or the farm section of the manual; (2) properties protected by automatic sprinklers, automatic fire detection systems, or watchman services (these are specific or schedule rated); or (3) properties with certain occupancies such as spray painting, restaurants, agricultural product storage, or most manufacturing operations. The ISO plan includes more commercial buildings in its eligibility list than earlier class rating schedules. There are a number of important reasons for class rating smaller commercial risks. Because the occupancy and area are limited in certain mercantile and service occupancies, these smaller risks do not have the frequency or variety of hazards found in larger buildings. The rate variations of specific (schedule) rates among these smaller buildings is relatively limited, and thus the average class rate approach is a feasible and efficient rate-making technique. Further, the expense of field inspection and subsequent rate promulgation requires a relatively large share of the small premium developed by the average small commercial building; thus, a class rating approach helps to lower insurance costs.

The ISO plan also applies the class rating approach to many more habitational risks (apartments, dwellings not occupied by the owner, etc.) than did previous class plans. For these habitational properties, the primary reasons for adopting the use of the class rate was the relatively low hazard level and the homogeneity of the units within each habitational class. Prior to this ISO plan, class rating methods were already being used in some regions of the country for rating certain classes of small habitational buildings such as apartments and motels and also for various types of property in the open such as fences and bridges. However, the ISO plan has expanded on the number of applicable classes as well as the number of states where the class rating is used for these classes.

Special rules are provided for multiple occupancy buildings and the "special property" mentioned. This group includes amusement equipment in the open, bridges, billboards, drive-in theaters, and so on. Rates in the manual are 80 percent coinsurance rates.

Specific (Schedule) Rating

Even with the advent of the ISO fire class rates, a significant number of risks, representing an even more significant fire insurance premium volume, will continue to be specifically (or schedule) rated.

Specific or *schedule rates*, in fire insurance, are established by rating experts (usually from the ISO) following an inspection of the individual risk for the purpose of applying a rating schedule. No matter what schedule is used, all use some type of charge (debit or credit) from a base rate for conditions which deviate from a standard or which increase or decrease the exposure to loss from fire.

Schedules are employed, following detailed risk inspections, because there is no practical method of determining, by statistical analysis of losses or loss causes, the exact value which should be placed on every hazard contributing to the fire exposure. The possible combinations of hazards in a given risk population are infinite in number. Consequently, the values assigned in any rate schedule can only be granted after a technical analysis and personal observation of the fire hazards. Schedule rating is not perfect, but it is certainly superior to the judgment method which preceded it. The principal advantages are:

1. It provides an incentive to improve the risk by offering reduced rates for improved construction and elimination of fire hazards.
2. It provides more equitable rates by elimination of the element of individual judgment and by systematic treatment of the features entering into a rate.
3. It provides a reason for more thorough inspections of risks.
4. It eliminates some criticism of the rates as all concerned can better understand how individual rates are made.

The ISO Commercial Fire Rating Schedule, developed in 1974, has replaced the Universal Mercantile and Dean Analytic Schedules in almost all states. The latter two are used only in a few areas or by regional rating organizations.

Universal Mercantile Schedule The first fire rating schedule to be widely used in this country was the Standard Universal Schedule for Rating Mercantile Risks (usually shortened to the Universal Mercantile Schedule). It was introduced toward the end of the nineteenth century and was, until the advent of the ISO Commercial Fire Rating Schedule, in use in modified form in about half of the states of the United States.

The starting point for this schedule is a "standard" (although desirable from an insurance standpoint) building in a "standard" city.

This standard building located in a standard city is assigned a *basis* or *key* rate which was deemed sufficient to produce premiums to cover fire loss costs (based on the last five years of experience), to cover the cost of carrying on business, and to generate an insurance profit of 5 percent. The basis rate is modified by deficiency charges to reflect deviations from the standard city definition and by credits to reflect unusually good features. To determine the specific rate charged an individual risk in that city, the key rate is then modified to reflect deficiencies or superior conditions found by an inspection of the individual risk.

The Universal Mercantile Schedule uses flat dollars and cents charges to compensate for deficiencies in the building being rated and percentage credits to compensate for especially good features. In that manner, positive features can help offset deficiency charges, although the probability of developing substantial credits from the key rate is very small. The credits are percentages due of the theory that as the exposure becomes more hazardous, favorable features will become relatively more advantageous. The final rate produced is an 80 percent coinsurance rate.

Dean Analytic Schedule Another fire rating schedule which was once widely used is called the Analytic System for the Measurement of Relative Fire Hazard, commonly referred to as the Dean

Schedule from the name of its author, A. F. Dean. It was introduced in the Midwest in the early 1900s and was used in about half the country prior to the introduction of the ISO Commercial Fire Rating Schedule.

Like the Universal Mercantile Schedule, the Dean Schedule begins with a basis rate for a standard building in a given city. In the Dean Schedule, however, the basis rate is determined by the ISO protection grading of the city being rated, the construction classification of the building being examined, the presence or absence of some dangerous occupancies, and in some cases the height of the building. To establish an individual rate, only the features of construction, occupancy, exposure, and private protection for that individual risk need be considered. Percentage debits are added for the poor features and percentage credits are allowed for the good features. By making these charges and credits in percentages rather than in flat amounts, a relativity is maintained so that a defect in a higher-rated or poor risk contributes more to the final rate than a similar defect in a lower-rated or good risk. The final rate produced is a flat rate—that is, without coinsurance.

ISO Commercial Fire Rating Schedule The Commercial Fire Rating Schedule represents a part of the ISO program of modernizing fire rating methods, insurance forms, and rules. One of the primary problems with some of the schedules being used is that different charges or credits are often provided for similar construction, hazard, or protection features from one schedule to the other. In addition, there have been significant changes in construction materials and processing hazards which have not been adequately recognized in the rating schedules. Changes in building codes and improvements in city fire protection in the past fifty years have greatly reduced the exposure hazard and consequently reduced the need for a complex exposure rating analysis in protected cities. As a result it became apparent that a number of minor rating items for construction and hazards in some schedules were of little or no significance and could be eliminated or consolidated with similar rating items.

Following the consolidation of the regional and state rating bureaus into the Insurance Services Office, the decision was made to develop a new rating schedule for nonsprinklered property, with a parallel development of a simplified class rating method for smaller buildings. This decision was made in order to increase rate-making efficiency and also to provide property owners and insureds with businesses in many different states with a uniform fire rating system. The basic development work for the new schedule was started in February of 1972 and continued until July of 1974. Additional changes and refinements were made in the schedule as a result of field testing and review during the period of July through December of 1974. The resulting schedule is now used in over forty states.

The ISO Commercial Fire Rating Schedule evaluates a building after analysis of the various fire factors and produces a building and contents grade in points. This point grading is then multiplied by a conversion factor applicable to the particular occupancy and construction classification in the state to produce an 80 percent coinsurance schedule rate.

The ISO Commercial Fire Rating Schedule does not apply to properties eligible for class rating. It additionally does not apply to sprinklered properties (except in states where conversion factors for sprinklered buildings have been provided; which in essence makes it applicable to sprinklered buildings since most states have such factors) or to properties that are to be rated under special schedules.

Content of the Schedule. The ISO Commercial Fire Rating Schedule consists of the following sections:

    I. General Rules
    II. Basic Construction
   III. Secondary Construction
   IV. Occupancy Rules
    V. Occupancy Classifications—Nonmanufacturing
   VI. Occupancy Classifications—Manufacturing and Special Hazards
  VII. Hazards of Occupancy
 VIII. Exposure
   IX. Protection Class Factors
    X. Internal Protection Credits
   XI. Building Conversion Factors (found on state rate pages)
  XII. Contents

General Rules. The general rules section provides the basic rules and definitions including those for the various kinds of construction materials, the classification of the six construction types, and rules for separate rating of fire divisions.

Calculating a Schedule Rate. The major steps in the schedule rating process under the ISO schedule are the determination of the:

- basic building grade
- unexposed building grade
- exposed building grade
- gross building grade
- final building grade
- gross contents grade
- final content grade

BASIC BUILDING GRADE. The schedule begins with a *schedule base* of fifty points. Even though this may appear to be a return to a single base, a final step in the rate calculation multiplies the accumulated points by one of over 500 building conversion factors (Section XI) which in essence creates that many bases.

In determining a schedule rate for a risk, the first evaluation is that of the primary construction elements such as the walls, floors, and roof. The schedule evaluates these on the basis of their damageability, recognizing the variation in relative combustibility and fire resistance of construction materials. Charges for the basic construction *(basic construction charges)* are made in points in proportion to the percentage that each construction material constitutes of the total material.

The divisions in the basic construction section include:

Exterior Wall Charges
- masonry walls—damageability and stability
- fire resistive wall supports—fire resistance and damageability
- panels in masonry or fire resistive walls
- noncombustible or slow burning walls on noncombustible or slow burning supports
- combustible walls

Floor and Roof Charges
- masonry and fire resistive floors and roof supports
- noncombustible and slow burning floors and roof
- combustible floors and roof

The charges for the basic construction vary quite widely. These charges are usually shown either (1) in a table based upon the relationship between two or more characteristics of the construction (e.g., wall type as related to wall material and thickness), or (2) in a list next to a verbal description of the basic construction. Exhibit 9-1 is the table of wall charges for bearing or nonbearing masonry walls. As shown in the table, wall types are divided into three categories:[1]

Type W-1: Brick, reinforced concrete, pre-cast or pre-stressed concrete. Also, where properly reinforced and listed with a fire resistance rating of not less than three hours: hollow concrete blocks or other masonry units.

Type W-2: Natural stone, non-reinforced concrete. Also, concrete wall sections with unprotected metal reinforcing, or with unprotected metal ties between the masonry sections. Also, hollow concrete blocks completely filled with concrete and properly reinforced. Also, hollow

Exhibit 9-1

Table of Wall Charges—Thickness and Damageability of Masonry Walls*

Wall Material and Thickness	Wall Types W-1	W-2	W-3
Reinforced Concrete (w-1 only)			
Less than 6 inches in thickness	20	—	—
6 inches or over in thickness	00	—	—
All Other Masonry Walls:			
Less than 8 inches in thickness	20	40	60
8 inches or over, but less than 12 inches in thickness	00	20	40
12 inches or over in thickness	00	00	30

*Reprinted with permission from *Commercial Fire Rating Schedule* (New York: Insurance Services Office, 1976), (Revision No. 4, 4-78).

concrete blocks or other masonry units which are reinforced and listed with a fire resistance rating of not less than two hours

Type W-3: Adobe, clay tile, gypsum blocks. Also, masonry materials, including hollow concrete blocks or other masonry units, not provided for in W-1 or W-2 above.

Note: Where materials in more than one classification above are combined in the same wall section (such as hollow block faced by brick), the appropriate classification shall be determined by the most inferior material in the wall section; however, the entire thickness of all material shall be considered.

The charges for noncombustible and slow burning floors and roof are shown as a list. The charges are as shown in Exhibit 9-2. The charges in Exhibit 9-2 contemplate that the lowest floor level in the building is concrete, earth, stone, or other noncombustible material. Where over 10 percent of this floor is combustible, a charge is added.[2]

The total of the schedule base and the sum of the basic construction charge is the *unmodified basic building grade*. This sum is then modified by a *contents combustibility factor* ranging from 0.2 to 1.2 based upon the combustibility class applied to the building, whether the building is sprinklered, and the total charges for combustible construction. Charges for combustible construction were a portion of the charges used in determining the basic construction charge and include charges for (1) combustible panels in masonry or fire resistive walls, (2) combustible walls, and (3) combustible floors and roof. The product of the unmodified basic building grade and the contents combustibility factor is the *basic building grade* which is a minimum of thirty-five points.

Exhibit 9-2
Charges for Floors and Roof*

	Points
(1) Noncombustible or slow burning floors or roof on metal supports (beams and columns) individually protected with a fire resistance rating of not less than one hour	80
(2) Masonry floor or roof slabs, 4 inches or over in thickness, on unprotected metal or slow burning supports	100
(3) Masonry floor or roof slabs (including pre-stressed concrete units with a fire resistance rating of less than one hour), less than 4 inches but not less than 2 in thickness, on unprotected metal or slow burning supports NOTE: Charges under items (1), (2), or (3) above include roofs with exterior combustible insulation.	120
(4) Noncombustible floors or roof (except roof decks provided for under listings below) on unprotected metal supports	200
(5) Noncombustible floors or roof (except roof decks provided for under listings below) on slow burning supports, or slow burning floor or roof materials (except roof decks provided for under listings below) on unprotected metal or slow burning supports	220
(6) Noncombustible or slow burning roof decks with exterior surfacing materials of felt, asphalt or tar (built-up roof cover), on unprotected metal or slow burning supports, but with no combustible insulation on the surface of the roof	235
(7) Noncombustible or slow burning roof decks with combustible insulation on the surface of the roof	290
(8) Noncombustible roofs with combustible insulation which have been tested for spread of fire on the underside and are listed as an acceptable roof deck construction—"Fire-Classified"	245

*Reprinted with permission from *Commercial Fire Rating Schedule* (New York: Insurance Services Office, 1975), p. 13 (Revision No. 6, 1-82).

UNEXPOSED BUILDING GRADE. Charges for secondary or non-structural construction are stated as percentages of the basic building grade. These are charges for vertical openings, area and height of the building, roof surface, combustible roof space, combustible interior construction, combustible or slow burning interior finish or insulation, combustible exterior finish or attachments, and building condition. Some charges are not applicable to all classes of building construction.

Charges for vertical openings apply only to buildings of fire resistive or modified fire resistive construction. The charge applies to floor openings for stairways, elevators, ramps, ventilating shafts, and similar openings. Protection for the openings is divided into four categories:

- V-1 Protection:

  Enclosures shall have walls of masonry or fire resistive construction grading one hour or over, except that in fire resistive buildings of four or more stories, the enclosure walls shall have two hours or over fire resistance.

  Doors for Type V-1 Protection shall be automatic or self-closing and be labeled for Class B opening protection (1 hour rating, except in fire resistive buildings of four or more stories where $1\frac{1}{2}$ hour doors are required).

- V-2 Protection:

  Enclosure walls shall be as in Type V-1. All doors shall be as in Type V-1, except that elevator doors shall be of metal or metal covered construction so arranged that the doors must be normally closed for operation of the elevator.

- V-3 Protection:

  Enclosure walls constructed of noncombustible materials which grade less than one hour (such as metal lath and plaster, gypsum board on metal studs, etc.).

  Openings for Type V-3 shall be protected by automatic or self-closing doors, either labeled for Class C situation ($\frac{3}{4}$ hour rating) or of metal or metal covered construction (wired glass permitted). Elevator doors (metal or metal covered) shall be so arranged that the doors must normally be closed for operation of the elevator.

  Also included in Type V-3 are enclosures or doors which grade one hour in fire resistive buildings of four or more stories, and which therefore do not qualify for Types V-1 or V-2 protection.

- V-4 Protection:

  Unprotected floor openings, Type V-4 also includes doors or enclosures not meeting minimum requirements for Types V-1, V-2 or V-3.

The following materials are acceptable for one-hour construction in enclosure walls: 4-inch brick, 4-inch reinforced concrete, 6-inch hollow block, 6-inch tile, or masonry or noncombustible materials listed with a fire resistance rating of not less than one hour.

The following materials are acceptable for two hours: 5-inch reinforced concrete, 6-inch brick, 8-inch hollow block, 8-inch tile, or masonry, or noncombustible materials listed with a fire resistance rating of not less than two hours.[3]

Exhibit 9-3 shows the charges for vertical openings in masonry and fire resistive floors.

The charge for area and height does not apply to buildings of CSP construction classes 3, 4, 5, or 6 with a combustibility class of C-1. The charge is based on the CSP construction class, combustibility class, height in stories, and effective (as defined in the manual) area. The charge may be modified by the presence of *division walls.* The schedule specifies that an acceptable division wall shall be constructed entirely of

Exhibit 9-3
Table of Vertical Opening Charges in Masonry or Fire Resistive Floors
(CSP Construction Classes 5 or 6 Only)*

Type of Vertical Opening Protection	Combustibility Class Applicable to the Building			
	C-1	C-2	C-3—C-4	C-5
V-1	0	0	0	0
V-2	0	0	10%	15%
V-3	0	10%	15%	20%
V-4	5%	15%	20%	30%

*Reprinted with permission from *Commercial Fire Rating Schedule* (New York: Insurance Services Office, 1982), p. 18 (Revision No. 6, 1-82).

noncombustible materials with a fire resistance rating of not less than one hour, or of masonry materials, and shall (1) extend from one exterior wall to another (or form an enclosed area within the building); (2) extend from one masonry or fire resistive floor to another masonry or fire resistive floor, or from a masonry or fire resistive floor to a roof of any construction; and (3) have all openings through the wall protected by an automatic or self-closing labeled Class B (one hour) fire door. Where division walls meet the above requirements, the maximum area on any floor used to determine the effective area shall be the largest undivided area plus 50 percent of the second largest undivided area on that floor.[4]

A charge not found in all fire schedules is that for building conditions. There are charges in the ISO schedule for substandard structural conditions according to the degree of deficiency, using Exhibit 9-4 as a guide. Exhibit 9-5 shows the portion of Section V giving the basic occupancy charges and the combustibility and susceptibility classifications for the photographics occupancy.

Section VII gives the charges for *hazards of occupancy* or additional occupancy hazards for each occupancy. These charges are stated as a percentage of the basic building grade and are to be added to the basic building grade. Hazards of occupancy are for special hazards which may be present in some occupancies. The hazards of occupancy charges are cumulative and can be as high as 200 percent (for heat producing devices) with the charge being subject to modification for various characteristics such as isolation and automatic

Exhibit 9-4
Charges for Substandard Structural Conditions*

a. Moderate Deficiencies: Appreciable areas of broken windows; interior finish in disrepair; exterior walls or roof in poor condition due to lack of maintenance, such as absence of sheathing or settling of foundation	50%
b. Major Deficiencies: Walls, floors or roof in serious disrepair, out of plumb due to failure of foundations or other structural supports; large cracks in walls, floors or roof; structure dilapidated due to lack of building repair and maintenance; building open to trespass or part of building abandoned and not maintained	400%
c. Extreme Deficiencies: Buildings abandoned or with severe dilapidation throughout; major areas of unrepaired fire damage	1000%

*Reprinted with permission from *Commercial Fire Rating Schedule* (New York: Insurance Services Office, 1978), p. 24 (Revision No. 4, 4-78).

Exhibit 9-5
Occupancy Classifications*

	Basic Occupancy Charge	Combustibility Classification	Susceptibility Classification
Photographics			
D1 Film Exchanges (Motion Pictures) SCOH = 057; CSP = 0570	80%	C-3	S-4

D2 E1 Film cutting rooms, E2 Developing,
  E3 Processing, E4 Printing
  CSP = 0921 SCOH = 057
	80%	C-3	S-4

D3 E1 Photographers studios,
  E2 Commercial Photographers
  SCOH = 057; CSP = 0921
  Photographic supplies, including
  cameras, films, etc. sales or storage—
  see General Mercantile
	25%	C-2	S-4

*Adapted with permission from *Commercial Fire Rating Schedule* (New York: Insurance Services Office, 1981), p. 61.1 (Revision No. 6, 1-82).

fire extinguishing devices. The modification for isolation is dependent upon the type enclosure and the automatic extinguishing system that are present. The schedule defines three enclosures depending upon the

Exhibit 9-6
Types of Auxiliary or Incidental Processes or Operations

D 1. Processes other than fumigating using flammable or combustible liquids and/or gases, such as cleaning, bleaching, dyeing, starching, bonding, laminating, finishing (other than painting or protective coating), and tempering
D 2. Food processing
D 3. Fumigating, using flammable or combustible liquids or gases
D 4. Glassworking
D 5. Metalworking
D 6. Plastics processing (other than coating or spraying)
D 7. Printing (other than printing or labeling operations which are part of an assembly line)
D 8. Textile work such as sewing, tailoring and silk screening
D 9. Upholstering
D10. Woodworking, hand or power work (if more than one major machine is involved and the area occupied by the woodworking operations exceeds 10% of the total area of the occupancy, consider as a separate occupancy and do not change hereunder)

*Reprinted with permission from *Commercial Fire Rating Schedule* (New York: Insurance Services Office, 1981), p. 108 (Revision No. 6, 1-82).

walls, floors, and roof, structural supports, and fire door protection for openings through walls. The modifications for these three enclosures are .50, .75, and .90 if there is no extinguishing system. If there are extinguishing systems, the modifications are .25, .375, and .45. No enclosure, but an extinguishing system, is .50. These modifications are applied to the hazards of occupancy charge otherwise calculated. The hazards of occupancy were enumerated in Chapter 5.

Another portion of Section VII includes charges for hazardous conditions not elsewhere charged for, such as major electrical equipment defects and poor housekeeping. The final division of the hazards of occupancy section presents the charges for auxiliary or incidental operations or processes which are not specifically contemplated by the basic occupancy charge for the primary occupancy or are not provided for under other hazards of occupancy. Exhibit 9-6 lists these incidental operations.

Hazards of occupancy charges consist primarily of those charges for each occupancy, but also include what are referred to as *hazards of occupancy applicable to the building*. These would include primarily deficiencies which are under the control of the building management and not of a specific occupant. These hazards are:

a. Building service heating deficiencies, where such heating equipment is under the control of the building management.

b. Deficiencies in the electrical service of the building.

c. Poor housekeeping in the building service areas, hallways common to several occupancies or common storage areas under the control of the building management.

d. Other deficiencies which are under the control of building management.[5]

The sum of the basic occupancy charge from Sections V or VI and the hazards of occupancy charge for each occupancy from Section VII is termed the *total occupancy charge* for each separate *occupancy*. Chapter 5 describes a number of various occupancies and gives their basic occupancy charge, combustibility and susceptibility classifications, and possible additional occupancy hazards charges.

In a sole occupancy building, the *net occupancy charge* applicable to the building is the sum of the total occupancy charge for the one occupancy plus the sum of all hazards of occupancy charges applicable to the building. Rules are also given for the determination of the net occupancy charge for multiple occupancy buildings.

Once the net occupancy charge applicable to the building is determined, it is modified by an *occupancy modification factor* based upon the total combustible charges (charges for combustible walls [including combustible panels], floors, and roofs made under Section II of the schedule), CSP construction class, and percentage of total square feet occupied by C-1 (noncombustible) and C-2 (limited combustibility) combustibility classification occupancies. The factors range from 0.2 to 1.

As with the secondary construction charges, the occupancy charge derived above as a percentage is multiplied by the basic building grade to arrive at the occupancy charges in points. The sum of the occupancy charges plus the secondary construction charges plus the basic building grade is called the *unexposed building grade* (in points).

EXPOSED BUILDING GRADE   The next step in the schedule rating process is the determination of charges for exposure to adjoining buildings. Charges under this section apply only to separately rated fire divisions as defined in Section I and are computed by multiplying the *exposure hazard charge* (in points) by the applicable factor for *exposure-conditions* plus a *communications charge*, if applicable. In protection classes 1 to 8 a charge is made for the single exposure producing the highest exposure charge. In protection classes 9 and 10, a charge is made for the two exposures producing the highest charges.

The following buildings are not to be charged as exposures:

● Buildings with automatic sprinkler systems rated and published as sprinklered buildings.

● Class rated habitational buildings and their appurtenant outbuildings.

- Buildings published as CSP Construction Classes 5 or 6.
- Buildings published as CSP Construction Classes 3 or 4 with C-1 or C-2 Contents Combustibility applicable to the building.
- Buildings with C-1 or C-2 Contents Combustibility applicable to the building, where the wall facing the building being rated is of masonry or noncombustible construction.[6]

The exposure hazard charge is obtained from a table based upon the relationships among several components which affect the exposure severity. These components include:

- Construction of facing wall of exposure—divided into masonry (66 ⅔ percent or more of facing wall is of masonry or fire resistive construction) and frame (all other walls).
- Occupancy hazard of the exposure—the categories used are (1) light hazard (C-1 or C-2 combustibility), (2) moderate hazard (C-3 or C-4 combustibility), and (3) high hazard (C-5 combustibility).
- Length-height of facing wall of exposure (multiply the length by the number of stories).
- Exposure distance—distance in feet from building being rated to exposure building.
- Protection class—of building being rated.[7]

The *exposure-condition factor* is intended to reflect the relative hazard of radiation and ignition from the wall or roof of the exposure to the wall or roof of the building being rated. The exposure condition factors range from zero to one depending upon (1) the construction of the facing wall of the exposure and the building being rated; (2) the CSP construction class of the building being rated; (3) the presence or absence of unprotected openings in the facing wall of the exposing building, the building being rated, or both; (4) the existence or lack of a noncombustible roof on either or both buildings; and, in some cases, (5) the combustibility of the contents.

In addition to the product (in points) of the exposure condition factor and the exposure hazard charge, there may be a charge (in points) for communications (openings) through party walls or passageways. This charge is added to the aformentioned product. The charges are stated as a factor to be applied to a specified point charge in the exposure hazard table described earlier. Special rules are provided for frame ranges, yard property, grain or seed tanks, flammable liquid or gas tanks, wharves, piers, and platforms, refuse burners and open fires, and yard property not elsewhere provided. The sum of the unexposed building grade plus the exposure charge (in points and including any communication charge) is referred to as the *exposed building grade.*

GROSS BUILDING GRADE. The exposed building grade is next modified by a *protection class factor* to determine the *gross building grade*. The protection class factor table gives the factor (ranging from .225 to 1.10) based upon the relationship among the protection class, the construction class, and the region and/or state where the risk is located.

FINAL BUILDING GRADE. The gross building grade is in turn modified by credits for internal protection (if any) to arrive at the *final building grade*. When credits are given under this section, a protection clause (warranty) is attached to the policy. Credits are given for:

- first aid equipment,
- watch service,
- automatic fire detection systems,
- partial or substandard automatic sprinkler systems,
- limited supply automatic fire protection systems (other than automatic sprinklers), and
- standard automatic sprinkler systems.

Internal protection credit for standpipes and hose is 5 percent and for portable fire extinguishers is 3 percent (if both meet the specified requirements found in the schedule). Credits for watch service range from 7 to 15 percent and credits for fire alarm systems can be as high as 25 percent. There is a wide variation on credits for protection systems.

Once the final building grade (in points) is determined, it is divided by 1,000 and this figure is then multiplied by a *building conversion factor* found in Section XI in the state rate pages. The building conversion factor reflects the relationship among the ISO construction class (1-6), the protection class (1-10), and the standard classification of occupancy hazards (SCOH) code applicable to the building, and the table varies by state. The product is the *final rate* which is an 80 percent coinsurance annual building rate in dollars and cents for fire and inherent explosion. Exhibit 9-7 gives a hypothetical building rate calculation as it might appear under the ISO Commercial Fire Rating Schedule.

GROSS CONTENTS GRADE. The determination of the contents rate is similar to that of the building rate. The first step is to determine the susceptibility classification applicable to the contents of each occupancy according to the occupancy listing in Sections V and VI. Chapter 5 of this text lists and describes these susceptibility classifications.

A *contents susceptibility charge* (in points) is determined from a Table of Contents Susceptibility Charges based on the CSP construction class, combustibility class, and protection class applicable to the

Exhibit 9-7

ISO Commercial Fire Rating Schedule—Illustrative Building Rate Calculation*

Schedule base		50 points
Basic construction charges:		
Six-inch clay tile walls		60 points
Combustible panels in walls		20 points
Combustible floor and roof		290 points
Unmodified basic building grade		420 points
Contents combustibility factor		x 1.1
Basic building grade		462 points
Secondary construction charges:		
Area-height	33%	
Combustible roof space	10%	
	43%	199 points
Occupancy charge	50%	231 points
Unexposed building grade		892 points
Exposure charge		70 points
Exposed building grade		962 points
Protection class factor		x 0.500
Gross building grade		481 points
Internal protection credits:		
Fire extinguishers	3%	−14 points
Watchman	7%	−34 points
Final building grade		433 points
Divide by 1,000		0.433
Building conversion factor		x 1.02
80% coinsurance building rate		$ 0.442

*Reprinted with permission from *Insurance Company Operations* (Malvern, PA: The American Institute for Property and Liability Underwriters, 1978), p. 79.

building, and the susceptibility class applicable to the contents. Charges range from 0 to 400. There may be an additional charge for buildings over ten stories.

The state rate pages contain a Table of Contents Conversion Factors. The *contents conversion factors* are based in each state upon the CSP occupancy code and the CSP construction class. The product of the contents susceptibility charge and the appropriate conversion factor is the *converted contents susceptibility charge* (in points).

To derive the *contents base* (in points), the gross building grade is multiplied by the appropriate building conversion factor. The *gross contents grade* is the sum of the contents base and the converted contents susceptibility charge. The gross contents grade is calculated for each separate occupancy.

FINAL CONTENTS GRADE. To the gross contents grade for each occupancy, credits (if any) for internal protection are given to derive the *final contents grade*. The final contents grade for each occupancy is divided by 1,000 to arrive at the 80 percent coinsurance annual rate for each occupancy.

Other Components of the Rate

The specific rating process is an attempt to analyze the individual exposures to loss by fire on a given risk. In so doing a fire insurance rate is calculated—a rate that would seem adequate to pay for fire insurance losses. However, loss costs are not the only component of fire insurance rates. No insurance company can survive for very long by simply collecting enough premiums to reimburse insureds for their fire losses under class and specific (schedule) rating. An insurer must also gain enough premium dollars to pay underwriting, policywriting, and acquisition expenses; to pay for loss settlement costs; to make a profit; and to build up a "cushion" to pay for unanticipated catastrophe losses.

Expenses The normal expenses incurred in writing fire insurance include service of the insurer (inspection, claims handling, etc.), acquisition costs (producer's salary or commission, advertising costs, etc.), underwriting and administrative expenses (salaries of underwriters, office overhead, etc.), and taxes. The AIU 61 text includes an in-depth discussion of these expenses in relation to all lines of insurance.

Profit and Contingencies The insurance organization, like other business firms, must obtain a net profit from its operations if it is to survive and grow. Additionally, policyholders in a mutual company and stockholders in a capital stock company have come to expect dividends. Dividends in the long run can result only from profitable operations. The success of an insurance operation is dependent on a reduction in uncertainty, which is achieved by the technique of pooling which attempts to take many diverse risks and combine them. Thus, pooling enhances loss predictability to such an extent that the result will be a rather small probability of unexpected losses.

However, while predictability is clearly improved by the pooling concept, an insurance company can still incur significant aggregate losses. Such aggregate losses can arise from greater than expected frequency of losses or from catastrophes. An example of unanticipated frequency is the rising number of claims due to arson. A prime example of a severe loss (catastrophe) in which significant insured losses occurred was the Texas grain elevator explosion and fire in December

1977. In order that insurance companies be able to meet loss situations in which unanticipated numbers of losses or catastrophes occur, a provision must be made in rates to reflect the possibility of these losses. Therefore, included in the rate calculations for each line of insurance in each company is a provision for profit and contingencies.

Since the premium generated is a part of the underwriter's consideration in reviewing a risk, the provision in the rate for profit and contingencies is also of concern to the underwriter. Property insurance rates contain a 1 percent provision for contingencies (unanticipated frequency of losses and catastrophe losses) and a 5 percent provision for profit for normal losses. These provisions are the result of a 1949 amendment to the profit formula of the National Association of Insurance Commissioners. (Some critics, however, suggest that there should not be a profit component.)

Even though there is a 1 percent contingency provision, the property underwriter must consider that this amount is not substantial, for example, in view of the tremendous wind and water losses in some coastal areas of the country. Although the 1 percent may be inadequate in these areas, it may be excessive in others, thus creating a reluctance on the part of regulators to raise the provision. There has also been a tendency for regulators not to include the entire effect of a catastrophe when evaluating the adequacy of the provision.

The underwriter must be cognizant of the fact that the contingency is there and that it should be adequate. The adequacy of the contingency clearly has an impact on the underwriting decision-making process. If it appears that the rates are inadequate (and thus profits are lacking), underwriting restraint is often implemented.

Deductibles

A deductible clause in a fire insurance contract provides that the insurer will pay a loss only when the loss is in excess of a specified amount or percentage of the amount of insurance. Deductibles written as part of property insurance contracts are sound in theory. Such deductibles eliminate many small "nuisance" claims and help to reduce a property insurer's total outlay, thus justifying a lower insurance premium for the individual risk.

Although some persons may argue that small losses and the small deductibles have no significant effect upon an insurer's loss ratios, it is important to remember that the settlement costs of small losses (including an insurer's overhead expenses) can multiply the dollar cost of small losses to the insurer. A small loss of $100 or $200 may often involve many times that amount in the salary expenses of underwriters, producers, and claims adjusters involved in the claim, and additional expenses in the completion of forms, record maintenance, and so on. Historical data demonstrates that payment of very small losses does have a significant effect on total insurance costs, primarily because most losses fall into the small size category. Elimination of such losses then obviously justifies some premium savings over the charge that would be necessary if such small losses were to be paid in full.

Underwriting Factors Not Included in the Rates

A number of factors are *not* taken into consideration in the fire insurance rating process. These factors could possibly affect the acceptability of the risk but are not included in the rating process for a number of reasons. For example, there are a number of factors which are not part of the rating process since they apply to a limited number of cases or perhaps to specific geographic locations. There are other factors which by their nature are too subjective to be included in a process which attempts to objectively analyze the relativity of exposure to loss by fire.

Some of the important factors not included in the fire rate-making process which affect the underwriting desirability of an individual risk are:

1. Specific risk location. A small gasoline service station which recently has been removed from the main line of traffic by the construction of a new highway bypass may become a poor risk if it is unable to replace tourist traffic with neighborhood customers. Location factors such as the deterioration of a neighborhood and the increase in vandalism and vacant buildings may also make a property risk less than desirable. These factors are not contemplated in most fire rate schedules.

2. Moral hazard. Current fire rate schedules or fire class rate programs give the same rate to a well established profitable merchant as to the underfinanced, unprofitable, newly established merchant located next door in the same shopping center. At the same time an insured with a history of questionable fires with unsatisfactory insurance settlements often receives the same fire rate as an otherwise identical insured who has a clean loss and insurance record for a number of years. Even though these facts may not positively prove the existence of a moral hazard, it is obvious that one risk is more desirable than another. Yet no fire rate schedule makes any attempt to recognize or evaluate the moral hazard or to reflect the financial condition of a risk in the rate promulgation process.

3. Electrical hazards. Although misuse of electrical equipment and systems is one of the major causes of building fires, the rating schedules and thus fire insurance rates do not adequately reflect exposure to loss from this source. While rate schedules do reflect deficiencies in the installation of electrical systems (e.g., the hazards of occupancy section of the ISO Commercial Fire Rating Schedule), the schedules overlook the misuse of such installations. The overuse of electrical extension cords, the overloading of outlets and circuits, the improper use of electrical motors, the use of inadequate electrical equipment— many of these deficiencies and more are ignored in the rating process. They are undesirable features of a risk which often are not adequately compensated for in the rate.

4. Maintenance. Class rates and most specific rates fail to distinguish between risks with excellent maintenance and those with poor maintenance. Thus, two risks with eight-inch masonry walls will receive the same rate, regardless of maintenance, in most cases. However, the ISO Commercial Fire Rating Schedule does attempt to use housekeeping as a factor. The secondary construction section includes a provision for charges for substandard structural conditions ranging from 50 to 1,000 percent. The latter charge is for abandoned buildings or those with severe dilapidation throughout, with major areas of unrepaired fire damage. The hazards of occupancy section, as mentioned, also contains charges for poor housekeeping. These charges are a step in the right direction since a well maintained risk is much more desirable than one which is poorly maintained. Although maintenance of equipment is not specifically mentioned, it is also a factor in the desirability of a risk. The property underwriter must be aware of which of the conditions are provided for in the rates and which are not. Additionally, the underwriter should be aware of the charge made for the deficiency since it may be that the charge is inadequate or excessive.

5. Management attitude and cooperation. Since the purpose of rate surveys in conformance with a schedule is to establish rates and not to make recommendations for risk improvement, the attitude of management toward making recommended modifications to a structure to correct deficiencies is not ascertained. To a property underwriter, however, the willingness of management to cooperate with the insurer in areas of risk improvement is an important determinant of risk acceptability and desirability.

Although not all inclusive, the above list includes some of the major variables affecting risk desirability which are not reflected in fire insurance rating schedules. Such items must be reflected elsewhere in the underwriting decision-making process, either in the underwriter's decision to accept or reject a risk or perhaps in his or her decision to include a judgment rate credit or debit in pricing the risk.

The lack of these items in the specific rating procedure has led to the existence of individual "schedule" rating plans used by many insurers to modify the published bureau fire rate to reflect deficiencies or attributes not properly reflected in the published rate. Exhibit 9-8 is an example of one table of credits and debits used to reflect such schedule inadequacies.

FIRE INSURANCE RATE REVIEW

The rating schedules discussed up to this point are used to apply established rates and percentages to different buildings to reflect the relative variation in hazards among them by the application of a schedule. The overall rates for schedule rating and class rates are determined through statistical analysis of loss and premium data. As described in the AIU 61 text, the loss ratio technique is used in most cases in fire insurance.

Data collection has been a problem in fire insurance rate review. Until several years ago, the rate plans in use did not call for the assimilation of data on loss exposures. Additionally, although the usual exposure unit is $100 of insurance, fire insurance on one risk is often spread among several insurers. Thus the coordination of data is a problem. Also, properties within a given class may vary significantly in value, and thus in loss exposure and actual losses.

In view of the preceding, the methods used to review fire insurance rates have been somewhat elementary when compared with those used in liability insurance. However, attempts are being made to remedy this situation (e.g., the collection of exposure unit data).

Experience Period

The experience period used in fire insurance rate review is generally five years, with the experience of each year weighted. The most recent years, which are presumably the more representative of current conditions, are given the greatest weight. The experience period is somewhat lengthy due to the need to smooth out the effect of any large fluctuations in experience.

Exhibit 9-8

Individual Risk Modification Table

	Range of Modifications	
	Credit	Debit
Management	15% to 20%	
1. Care and condition of equipment and premises, maintenance, arrangement, illumination, ventilation		
2. Cooperation of management with recommendations with respect to structural features, segregation and control of hazards and maintenance of protective equipment		
3. Employees: selection, training, supervision, experience, stability		
Location	10% to 20%	
1. Location, exterior environment, access, exposures, atmospheric abnormalities		
2. Dispersion or concentration of an individual risk		
General Factors	10% to 20%	
1. Miscellaneous hazards or protective features		
2. Financial condition		
Structural Features	10% to 20%	
1. Roof anchorage and other windstorm characteristics		
2. Superior or inferior structural features		
Obsolescence	0% to 10%	
Operations	10% to 10%	
1. Storage practice and hazardous processes		
2. Damageability, handling practices and controls		

Statistical Period

Experience has been traditionally reported on a calendar-year basis which is fairly accurate for fire insurance rate review due to the relatively prompt reporting and settlement of claims in this line of insurance. The new statistical plan used in many lines by ISO has begun to use the calendar-accident-year statistics which are intended to give a more accurate determination of incurred losses. Because the losses are reported and settled quickly, loss development factors are not used in fire insurance.

Expenses

The expense loading used in fire insurance rate review is fairly constant, but may vary among states due to the premium taxes and other provisions. Also included in the loading for expenses are provisions for profit and contingencies (as described earlier), general company expenses, FAIR plans (in some states), insolvency fund assessment (in some states), and the production cost allowance (i.e., acquisition costs).

Large Losses

Because large losses (over $100,000) are primarily a matter of chance, a procedure is used to spread these large losses over the experience for the entire country. The distribution by state depends upon the ratio of each state's volume of fire insurance premiums to the volume of fire insurance premiums countrywide. The limiting and spreading of the large losses helps prevent wide fluctuations in the fire insurance rates.

Credibility

Credibility is used in three places in the review of fire insurance rates. The first application is in the allocation of the large losses among states as described earlier. Second, credibility is used to determine the rate level change for the entire state, based upon the state's premium volume (statewide rate adjustment). The final application is the determination of the class relativities, once the statewide rate level change is calculated.

Trending

As with liability insurance, but not to as great a degree, trending is necessary in fire insurance rate review. Losses occurring in the experience period must be trended to reflect the amount that would be paid were the losses to occur in the future. The need to trend is primarily the result of inflation, and the trending technique used is based primarily on indexes of construction costs and wholesale prices.

As is shown in the workers' compensation rate review in Chapter 8 of the AIU 63 text, trending of losses involves two major steps:

1. adjustment of losses to current price levels (taking the increase in amounts of insurance into consideration), and

2. projection of losses to the point at the middle of the period during which losses will be incurred at the new rates.

After these two adjustments and the adjustment of premiums to current rate levels, the *pure loss ratios* (i.e., exclusive of loss adjustment expenses) are calculated for each year and then a *weighted pure loss ratio* is calculated (i.e., one loss ratio for all the years in the experience period based upon the weights assigned to each year). This loss ratio is then modified by a factor to reflect loss adjustment expenses. The result is the *experience period adjusted loss ratio* including loss adjustment expenses.

Statewide Rate Adjustment

The next step in the review process is that the expected loss ratio (1 — expense ratio) must also be trended to reflect inflation from the last rate change to the date of the current rate adjustment being calculated. The result is the *trended expected loss ratio*, which will be used in the determination of the actual loss ratio to be used in the rate adjustment formula.

A statewide *credibility-weighted loss ratio (CLR)* is then calculated as:

$$CLR = ALR(Z) + ELR(1-Z)$$

where Z = credibility factor, ALR = experience period adjusted loss ratio including loss adjustment expenses, and ELR = trended expected loss ratio. The credibility-weighted loss ratio is then used as the actual loss ratio (A) in the basic rate adjustment formula of:

$$\text{Rate Change} = \frac{A - ELR}{ELR}$$

where A = the actual loss ratio and E = the trended expected loss ratio.

Class Relativities

Once the rate change for the state is determined, the change must be applied to the various classes. Unlike some lines of insurance, there are not specific class relativities which can be used to apportion the state change among the classes. A somewhat lengthy procedure is used to determine the change in each class.

The first step is to determine the rate change among the five major industry groups:

1. habitational, excluding dwellings and farms
2. mercantile
3. nonmanufacturing
4. manufacturing
5. warehouses

Each group is assigned credibility factors by reference to one of three credibility tables based upon the hazards of the particular group (i.e., light, average, heavy). To the extent that a group is not fully credible, the experience of the region is used. Based upon this credibility, a credibility-weighted loss ratio for each group is calculated, the group relativities are determined, and then the indicated rate change for each group is determined.

Once the rate change indicators are determined for each group, the change for each class can now be calculated. Credibility factors are determined separately for (1) the state experience for the rating class, and (2) the regional experience for the rating class. The credibility-weighted loss ratio for each class is then computed as a weighted average of (1) the state and regional loss ratios for the rating class, and (2) the state loss ratio for the industry group according to a specified formula.

After the credibility-weighted loss ratio has been calculated for each rating class, the class relativities are determined (i.e., the relation of the indicated change in each class to the overall change). In this manner, the indicated rate change for each class is determined.

After the indicated rate change for each class is calculated, a recapitulation is made to make sure that the changes for each class actually combine to equal the overall indicated change. In addition, a rule by the ISO places a 25 percent limit on rate changes (upward or downward) by that organization in any class of fire insurance. If any rate change of a class is limited by the 25 percent cap, it is logical that the change in the other classes must be adjusted to be able to end up with an overall indicated rate change equal to that desired. This is accomplished through a relatively complex adjustment process.

The result of the rate review process is a new set of class rates as well as a set of rate adjustment factors. The rate adjustment factors are used to modify the rates used in specific or schedule rating (e.g., the ISO Commercial Fire Rating Schedule).

RATE MAKING FOR
EXTENDED COVERAGE PERILS

Extended coverage (EC) rates are normally class rates as opposed to the specific fire rates just discussed. The extended coverage rates originated as wind and hail rates with a small loading added to reflect the other perils of the EC endorsement. Extended coverage rates are classed according to the occupancy of the concerned risks, often with only very general class distinctions being made. In addition to the occupancy hazard, EC rates, especially in high wind areas, are often differentiated to distinguish between wind resistive and ordinary construction (in some states semi-wind resistive construction is also used).

Experience Period

Extended coverage rates are usually reviewed and adjusted on the basis of a ten-year experience period due to the greater variability in loss frequency of these type losses than fire losses. More will be said about this variability in the next section. The indicated rate level change factor is calculated as equal to the review period adjusted loss and loss adjustment expense ratio divided by the expected loss ratio. As in fire rate revision, the expected loss ratio is equal to 100 percent minus the expense, tax, and profit provisions. The review period adjusted loss ratio is the average of the latest ten years' ratios of adjusted *normal incurred losses* to adjusted earned premium. (This ratio is then multiplied by a factor to account for loss adjustment expense.)

The EC indicated rate change factor formula is:

$$\text{Rate Change Factor} = \frac{\text{Loss Ratio} + \text{Loss Adjustment Expense Ratio}}{\text{Expected Loss Ratio}}$$

The old rate would be multiplied by this factor to arrive at the new rate.

Catastrophe Evaluation

The definition of review period adjusted loss ratio includes the term *normal incurred losses.* This term is used to reflect the major problem with extended coverage rate adjustment, i.e., how to handle the catastrophe loss situation. Because windstorms, hurricanes, and tornadoes are all covered by the EC endorsement, the coverage is subject to rather frequent catastrophic losses.

Until recently, the EC rate adjustment process included an extra long experience period in an attempt to even out the results of such catastrophes. This process was modified and a new portion was added to reflect the catastrophe potential. Because of this, the primary EC rate level change described earlier uses only normal incurred losses for the ten-year adjustment period. *Normal losses* are defined as each year's EC losses up to but not exceeding 100 percent of the earned premium. Losses greater than 100 percent of the corresponding year's earned premium are called *excess* and are used to measure the long term (at least twenty years) loss potential for each state and to add a catastrophe adjustment to the EC rate review.

The current EC excess loss procedure develops state multipliers which, when combined with the states' normal review period loss ratios, should result in rate levels appropriate for both the normal and excess expected EC losses.

The *excess multiplier* for the state is made up of three components:

1. state excess component
2. regional excess component
3. countrywide excess component

The state's excess losses are limited to 400 percent of the corresponding earned premium. The losses in excess of the cap are then considered on a regional basis. Next, the regional excess component is derived as a weighted average of the contribution of each state in the region. The regional excess component is also limited and that portion in excess of the regional limit contributes to the countrywide excess component.

EFFECT OF RATE ON UNDERWRITING

A commercial property underwriter has two major responsibilities when dealing with property insurance rates other than using them to price a given risk. The underwriter must be able to (1) advise an insured concerning the rationale for the rate level being charged and explain the impact of risk modifications, and (2) determine the appropriateness of the rate for a given risk.

Understanding the Rate

An underwriter must be able to explain rate derivation including the calculation to an insured. If Adam Insured has a fire insurance rate of $.42 and Bonnie Insured, with a similar risk, has a fire insurance rate of $.20, Adam is at some point going to ask why his rate is so high. An underwriter who understands the rate schedule in use in his or her territory will be able to justify the rate to Adam, but more importantly will be able to make recommendations to correct deficiencies in the risk and possibly lower the rate. Obviously the underwriter will not have to explain the calculation to every insured, but he or she needs to be able to do so.

An insured with a high fire rate will be concerned with the possibility of eliminating chargeable deficiencies or installing protection devices in the insured building which will materially reduce the insurance premium. The underwriter who can demonstrate to the insured expected premium savings and future increased cash flow as the result of following the insurer's recommendations is more likely to continue to write the account than another underwriter who tells the insured to "take it or leave it" on a recommendation.

An insured will often ask the insurer for ways to reduce the insurance premium on a given risk. A thorough knowledge of the rate schedule will enable the underwriter to recommend more constructive premium reduction devices than carrying larger deductibles or reducing coverage. Rate credits for protective devices such as fire extinguishers, fire alarms, automatic sprinklers, and so on, are based on decreased loss expectancies as a result of such devices; the underwriter who can intelligently recommend such devices will in turn receive a more desirable risk. Indeed, the ability to make such recommendations and "sell" them to an insured partially on the basis of the expense savings through reduced rates will often provide an attractive alternative to declining a risk because of an unacceptably high hazard level.

Appropriateness of the Rate

No commercial property underwriter can make a proper decision to accept a risk without first examining the insured's rate and determining the appropriateness of the rate. As was explained earlier in this chapter, even though the insured's rate may have been derived from the application of a hazard schedule, it may not properly reflect all the hazards in the risk. As an illustration assume Adam Insured and Bonnie Insured have identical occupancies in identical buildings in (somehow) identical locations. The only difference is Adam's building has poor housekeeping, overuse of extension cords, overloading of electrical circuits, and the building has not been maintained for five years. Bonnie's building has excellent housekeeping, proper use of electrical devices, and the building is extremely well maintained. Because of deficiencies in many rating schedules, Adam and Bonnie might receive identical fire insurance rates. Obviously, the same rate cannot be exactly adequate for each of these insureds. The rate is probably too low to reflect the full loss exposures of Adam's deficient risk and too high to reflect the full loss exposures of Bonnie's excellent risk. The fire insurance rate can never be an absolute determinant of risk desirability from an underwriting perspective. The old adage "the rate contemplates the exposure" is not totally correct; the rate contemplates or reflects only those exposures which the rate schedule was designed to measure or reflects the exposure of the average risk in a given class. Indeed, if the rate always fully contemplated the exposures of a given risk, the underwriting function might be eliminated since all risks would be profitable (given a sufficient experience period).

Although the rate is not the ultimate or perfect measure of desirability it is an extremely important factor for the underwriter to consider. An underwriter may be presented with a newly constructed sprinklered fire resistive building in a well protected area and feel it is an excellent property insurance risk. However, after fully examining the submission, it may be found that the rate is only $.02 (a gross premium of only $200 per $1 million of insurance). In such an instance, the generated premium may not be enough to pay the expenses (producer's commission, inspection report, underwriting overhead, and so on) involved in writing the account, let alone produce any premium to pay the small losses and develop a profit. Although from a physical perspective the risk may be very desirable, from a rate perspective, it is an unattractive risk. An underwriter may prefer a poorer physical risk with a high rate to a superb physical risk with a severely depressed rate.

On the other hand, risks with rates that are abnormally high cannot be said to be desirable simply because the rate is high. A high rate should have some correlation to a high loss expectancy; a high rate in an occupancy with normally low rates should indicate to the underwriter that the rating process has uncovered some risk deficiencies not readily apparent from the risk submission. A thorough inspection or a check of the rate survey would be in order before determining the acceptability of the account. Some risks, such as restaurants, are expected to have high rates. These high rates, however, do not always indicate risk deficiencies; in the case of restaurants it indicates the relative loss expectancy of that occupancy as compared to, say, an office building.

Just as on an account with a low rate the underwriter should not let the physical nature of the risk overshadow the unacceptability of the price, on a risk with a high rate the underwriter must not let the size of the premium overshadow the undesirability of the physical nature of the risk. Many underwriters have been known to overlook severe deficiencies in a risk because of the thousands of dollars in premium it produces. When the loss occurs because of those overlooked deficiencies and costs the insurer tens of thousands of dollars, the underwriting decision will be quickly recognized for its shortcomings.

Property underwriters must develop a sense for rate levels for different occupancies in the underwriting territory concerned. Only through experience can an underwriter recognize whether a rate is too high or too low for the exposures presented for a given risk. Without that appreciation of rate levels, proper underwriting decisions cannot be made.

Rate levels and their adequacy are even more important for two groups of underwriters—those who are writing insurance at deviated or substandard rates and those who are underwriting in times of severe competition, particularly price competition. In such instances underwriters must be capable of ascertaining when a rate discount can be used and still produce an adequate premium for the involved exposures.

SUMMARY

Pricing is a very important part of the underwriting process, and the underwriter should know how the price is developed.

The establishment of fire insurance rates is a specialized procedure. The Insurance Services Office (ISO) is the primary fire insurance rate promulgation organization for commercial insureds.

Nearly all fire insurance rates are one of two types: (1) class rates, or (2) specific or schedule rates. Class rates are assigned to broad categories of risks and are used mostly for smaller insureds. The most common fire rating plan is the ISO Fire Class Rate Plan. Specific or schedule rates are developed by rate experts following an inspection of the risk. Schedules are then employed to assign values. The primary fire rate schedule is the ISO Commercial Fire Rating Schedule.

Other components of the fire insurance rate include expenses, profit and contingencies, and deductibles. Underwriting factors not included in the rate but which affect the desirability of a risk include location, moral hazard, electrical hazards, maintenance, and management attitudes.

The overall rates for schedule and class rating are determined through statistical analysis of loss and premium data. Experience period, statistical period, expenses, large losses, credibility, trending, statewide rate adjustment, and class relativities all enter into the determination of these overall rates. Extended coverage rates are normally class rates.

The underwriter should not only be able to determine the appropriateness of a rate; he or she should also be able to explain and justify the derivation of the rate to the insured.

Chapter Notes

1. These descriptions are from the *Commercial Fire Rating Schedule* (New York: Insurance Services Office, 1982), p. 7 (Revision No. 6, 1-82).
2. *Commercial Fire Rating Schedule*, p. 13 (Revision No. 6, 1-82).
3. *Commercial Fire Rating Schedule*, p. 17 (Revision No. 4, 4-78).
4. *Commercial Fire Rating Schedule*, p. 19 (Revision No. 5, 11-80).
5. *Commercial Fire Rating Schedule*, p. 95 (Revision No. 6, 1-82).
6. *Commercial Fire Rating Schedule*, p. 109 (Revision No. 4, 4-78).
7. *Commercial Fire Rating Schedule*, p. 109 (Revision No. 4, 4-78) and p. 110 (Revision No. 6, 1-82).

CHAPTER 10

Underwriting Commercial Inland Marine Insurance

THE DEFINITION OF MARINE INSURANCE

In 1929 the Interstate Underwriters Board promulgated rates and forms for fixed location coverages on chain store property to replace inland marine floaters which fire underwriters felt were encroaching upon their rightful domain. This was followed in 1930 by the Casualty-Marine Merchandise Agreement which attempted to curb the encroachment of inland marine underwriters into the casualty field. These efforts were only marginally successful.

On 2 June 1933, the National Association of Insurance Commissioners adopted "The Nation-Wide Definition and Interpretation of the Insuring Powers of Marine and Transportation Underwriters." The adoption by the NAIC served as a recommendation to state insurance regulators to officially give the document the force of department ruling. If adopted, the definition limited the insuring powers of marine insurers. At that time the NAIC set up the Committee on Interpretation of the Nation-Wide Marine Definition. This committee, as presently constituted, consists of five representatives each from the fire, marine, and casualty and surety sectors of the insurance industry. This committee has issued some 225 interpretations with respect to specific coverages.

The Nation-Wide Marine Definition was updated in 1953 to modernize the definition. Essentially, the definition, as a curb on insuring powers, was out-of-date due to the development of multiple-lines insurance. The 1953 definition also included a statement to the effect that it was not to be construed as a curb on the insuring powers.

It was thus more for classification and reporting purposes. While the 1953 definition was adopted by most of the states, each interpretative bulletin is separately evaluated by each of the several states with respect to adoption.

In December 1976 the NAIC adopted a proposed amended Nation-Wide Marine Definition which has been adopted by a majority of the states.

The Importance of the Nation-Wide Definition

Unlike fire or auto insurance, where the scope of the particular line of business is obvious, inland marine insurance includes a variety of subjects of insurance joined only by the common thread of custom and usage as ratified by the NAIC Definitions. The starting point for any analysis of marine insurance must therefore be the Definition. While the Definition makes no distinction between inland and ocean marine, custom and industry practice limits ocean marine to ocean cargo policies, commercial hulls, and larger yachts. Thus the Definition's primary impact is on inland marine insurance. Commercial ocean marine underwriting is described in Chapter 11.

As mentioned, the Nation-Wide Marine Definition does not limit the insuring powers of an underwriter. It is used for classification purposes such as to give insurers guidance as to how certain premiums and losses should be reported for statistical and annual statement purposes. In some states, the Definition may determine whether certain rates or forms have to be filed (many marine forms and rates are not filed). Thus, "marine" insurance is usually viewed as being more flexible than fire insurance. The entire area of inland marine insurance is subject to some different interpretations and thus the whole area is also "flexible," in that some borderline risks which may not technically fall within the Definition are written as inland marine and some small-premium inland marine exposures are written as part of a package policy and not as a separate inland marine policy.

NATIONAL ASSOCIATION OF INSURANCE COMMISSIONERS NATION-WIDE MARINE DEFINITION (1976)

The purpose of this instrument is to describe the kinds of risks and coverages which may be classified or identified under State Insurance Laws as Marine, Inland Marine or Transportation insurance, but does not include all of the kinds of risks and coverages which may be written, classified or identified under Marine, Inland Marine or Transportation insuring powers, nor shall it be construed to mean that the kinds of risks and coverages are solely Marine, Inland Marine or Transportation insurance in all instances.

This instrument shall not be construed to restrict or limit in any way the exercise of any insuring powers granted under charters and license whether used separately, in combination or otherwise.

I. **Marine and/or transportation policies may cover under the following conditions:**

A. IMPORTS

Imports may be covered wherever the property may be and without restrictions as to time, provided the coverage of the issuing companies includes hazards of transportation.

An import, as a proper subject of marine or transportation insurance, shall be deemed to maintain its character as such so long as the property remains segregated in such a way that it can be identified and has not become incorporated and mixed with the general mass of property in the United States, and shall be deemed to have been completed when such property has been:

(a) sold and delivered by the importer, factor or consignee; or

(b) removed from place of storage and placed on sale as part of importer's stock in trade at a point of sale-distribution; or

(c) delivered for manufacture, processing or change in form to premises of the importer or of another used for such purposes.

B. EXPORTS

Exports may be covered wherever the property may be without restriction as to time, provided the coverage of the issuing companies includes hazards of transportation.

An export, as a proper subject of marine or transportation insurance, shall be deemed to acquire its character as such when designated or while being prepared for export and retain that character unless diverted for domestic trade, and when so diverted, the provisions of this Ruling respecting domestic shipments shall apply, provided, however, that this provision shall not apply to long established methods of insuring certain commodities, e.g., cotton.

C. DOMESTIC SHIPMENTS

Domestic shipments on consignment, (provided the coverage of the issuing companies includes hazards of transportation) for sale or distribution, exhibit, or trial, or approval or action, while in transit, while in the custody of others and while being returned, provided that in no event shall the policy cover on premises owned, leased or operated by the consignor.

Domestic shipments not on consignment, provided the coverage of the issuing companies includes hazards of transportation, beginning and ending within the United States, provided that such shipments shall not be covered at manufacturing premises nor after arrival at premises owned, leased or operated by Assured or purchaser.

D. BRIDGES, TUNNELS and other instrumentalities of transportation and communication (excluding buildings, their improvements and betterments, furniture and furnishings, fixed contents and supplies held in storage).

The foregoing includes:

1. Bridges, tunnels, other similar instrumentalities, including auxiliary facilities and equipment attendant thereto.
2. Piers, wharves, docks, slips, dry docks and marine railways.
3. Pipelines, including on-line propulsion, regulating and other equipment appurtenant to such pipe-lines, but excluding all property at manufacturing, producing, refining, converting, treating or conditioning plants.
4. Power transmission and Telephone and Telegraph lines, excluding all property at generating, converting or transforming stations, substations and exchanges.
5. Radio and Television Communication Equipment in use as such including towers and antennae with auxiliary equipment, and appurtenant electrical operating and control apparatus.
6. Outdoor cranes, loading bridges and similar equipment used to load, unload and transport.

E. PERSONAL PROPERTY FLOATER RISKS covering individuals and/or generally

1. Personal effects floater polices.
2. The personal property floater.
3. Government service floaters.
4. Personal fur floaters.
5. Personal jewelry floaters.
6. Wedding present floaters for not exceeding 90 (ninety) days after the day of the wedding.
7. Silverware floaters.
8. Fine arts floaters covering paintings, etchings, pictures, tapestries, art glass windows, and other bona fide works of art of rarity, historical value or artistic merit.
9. Stamp and coin floaters.
10. Musical instrument floaters. Radios, televisions, record players and combinations thereof are not deemed musical instruments.
11. Mobile articles, machinery and equipment floaters (excluding motor vehicles designed for highway use and auto homes, trailers and semi-trailers except when hauled by tractors not designed for highway use) covering identified property of a mobile or floating nature pertaining to or usual to household. Such policies shall not cover furniture and fixtures not customarily used away from premises where such property is usually kept.
12. Installment sales and leased property policies covering property pertaining to a household and sold under conditional contract of sale, partial payment contract or installment sales contract or leased, but excluding motor vehicles designed for highway use. Such policies must cover in transit but shall not extend beyond the termination of the seller's or lessor's interest.
13. Live animal floaters.

F. COMMERCIAL PROPERTY FLOATER RISKS covering property pertaining to a business, profession or occupation
1. Radium floaters.
2. Physicians' and surgeons' instrument floaters. Such policies may include coverage of such furniture, fixtures and tenant Assured's interest in such improvements and betterments of buildings as are located in that portion of the premises occupied by the assured in the practice of his profession.
3. Pattern and die floaters.
4. Theatrical floaters, excluding buildings and their improvements and betterments, and furniture and fixtures that do not travel about with theatrical troupes.
5. Film floaters, including builders' risk during the production and coverage on completed negatives and positives and sound records.
6. Salesmen's samples floaters.
7. Exhibition policies on property while on exhibition and in transit to or from such exhibitions.
8. Live animal floaters.
9. Builders' risks and/or installation risks covering interest of owner, seller or contractor, against loss or damage to machinery, equipment, building materials or supplies, being used with and during the course of installation, testing, building, renovating or repairing. Such policies may cover at points or places where work is being performed, while in transit and during temporary storage or deposit, of property designated for and awaiting specific installation, building, renovating or repairing.

   Such coverage shall be limited to Builders' Risks or Installation Risks where Perils in addition to Fire and Extended Coverage are to be insured.

   If written for account of owner, the coverage shall cease upon completion and acceptance thereof; or if written for account of a seller or contractor the coverage shall terminate when the interest of the seller or contractor ceases.
10. Mobile Articles, Machinery and Equipment Floaters (excluding motor vehicles designed for highway use and auto homes, trailers and semi-trailers except when hauled by tractors not designed for highway use and snow plows constructed exclusively for highway use), covering identified property of a mobile or floating nature, not on sale or consignment, or in course of manufacture, which has come into custody or control of parties who intend to use such property for the purpose for which it was manufactured or created. Such policies shall not cover furniture and fixtures not customarily used away from premises where such property is usually kept.
11. Property in transit to or from and in the custody of bailees (not owned, controlled or operated by the bailor).

Such policies shall not cover bailee's property at his premises.

12. Installment Sales and Leased Property. Policies covering property sold under conditional contract of sale, partial payment contract, installment sales contract, or leased but excluding motor vehicles designed for highway use. Such policies must cover in transit but shall not extend beyond the termination of the seller's or lessor's interest. This section is not intended to include machinery and equipment under certain "lease-back" contracts.

13. Garment contractors floaters.

14. Furriers or fur storer's customer's policies (i.e., policies under which certificates or receipts are issued by furriers or fur storers) covering specified articles the property of customers.

15. Accounts receivable policies, valuable papers and records policies.

16. Floor plan policies, covering property for sale while in possession of dealers under a floor plan or any similar plan under which the dealer borrows money from a bank or lending institution with which to pay the manufacturer, provided:

    1. Such merchandise is specifically identifiable as encumbered to the bank or lending institution.

    2. The dealer's right to sell or otherwise dispose of such merchandise is conditioned upon its being released from encumbrance by the bank or lending institution.

    3. That such policies cover in transit and do not extend beyond the termination of the dealer's interest.

Provided that such policies shall not cover automobiles or motor vehicles; merchandise for which the dealer's collateral is the stock or inventory as distinguished from merchandise specifically identifiable as encumbered to the lending institution.

17. Sign and street clock policies, including neon signs, automatic or mechanical signs, street clocks, while in use as such.

18. Fine arts policies covering paintings, etchings, pictures, tapestries, art glass windows, and other bona fide works of art of rarity, historical value or artistic merit, for account of museums, galleries, universities, businesses, municipalities and other similar interests.

19. Policies covering personal property which, when sold to the ultimate purchaser, may be covered specifically, the the owner, under Inland Marine Policies including:

    (a) Musical instrument dealers policies, covering property consisting principally of musical instruments and their accessories. Radios, televisions, record players and combinations thereof are not deemed musical instruments.

  (b) Camera dealers policies, covering property consisting principally of cameras and their accessories.
  (c) Furrier's dealers policies, covering property consisting principally of furs and fur garments.
  (d) Equipment dealers policies, covering mobile equipment consisting of binders, reapers, tractors, harvesters, harrows, tedders and other similar agricultural equipment and accessories therefor; construction equipment consisting of bulldozers, road scrapers, tractors, compressors, pneumatic tools and similar equipment and accessories therefor; but excluding motor vehicles designed for highway use.
  (e) Stamp and coin dealers covering property of philatelic and numismatic nature.
  (f) Jewelers' block policies.
  (g) Fine arts dealers.
  Such policies may include coverage of money in locked safes or vaults on the Assured's premises. Such policies also may include coverage of furniture, fixtures, tools, machinery, patterns, molds, dies and tenant insureds interest in improvements of buildings.
  20. Wool growers floaters.
  21. Domestic bulk liquids policies, covering tanks and domestic bulk liquids stored therein.
  22. Difference in conditions coverage excluding fire and extended coverage perils.
  23. Electronic data processing policies.
II. **Unless otherwise permitted, nothing in the foregoing shall be construed to permit MARINE OR TRANSPORTATION POLICIES TO COVER:**
  A. Storage of Assured's merchandise, except as hereinbefore provided.
  B. Merchandise in course of manufacture, the property of and on the premises of the manufacturer.
  C. Furniture and fixtures and improvements and betterments to buildings.
  D. Monies and/or securities in safes, vaults, safety deposit vaults, bank or Assured's premises, except while in the course of transportation.

FILED AND NONFILED CLASSES

In terms of forms and rates, inland marine policies are divided into two categories—filed and nonfiled. Those classes in which the major rating bureaus have developed rates, rules, and forms for their member companies are defined as *filed.* *Nonfiled* classes are developed and rated in accordance with the underwriting practices of an individual insurance company. Most filed policies are relatively inflexible in terms of coverage or rates and are generally those for which there are a large number of similar exposures needing similar coverage.

Many loss exposures covered by inland marine insurance are handled on nonfiled forms. Insurers have forms they use for certain common classes of business, such as the contractors' equipment floater. Their use may vary substantially from one insurer to the next. Depending on company practice, any of these forms may be freely modified at the option of the underwriter. In many circumstances, it is necessary to design a "manuscript" policy to cover an unusual or one-of-a-kind exposure.

INLAND MARINE POLICY TERMS AND CONDITIONS

Valuation

The determination of property values after a loss has occurred may be substantially more difficult in the case of "floating" property or property in transit than for property at a fixed location. Ocean marine valuation problems are discussed in Chapter 11.

Valuation of Property in Transit Policies covering property in transit usually provide a method by which the value may be determined for loss adjustment purposes. A typical inland marine clause used for this purpose reads:

> The valuation of the property covered hereunder shall be the actual invoice cost, including prepaid freight, together with such costs and charges since shipment as may have accrued and become legally due thereon, and all premiums under this policy shall be paid on this basis. If there is no invoice, the valuation of the property insured hereunder shall be the actual cash market value of the property insured at point of destination on the date of the disaster.

This provision simplifies the determination of value if there is an invoice that sets forth the cost. This is frequently the case when goods are shipped to a purchaser of the property. The insured is obligated to prove the fact of the loss and also the valuation. The insured can do this by producing the invoice under which the goods were shipped, plus evidence of any other charges, such as prepaid freight, that might be added to the invoice cost to determine the value.

The determination of _cash market value_ of the property may be difficult in the absence of an invoice. Such difficulty would vary according to the nature of the property. It would be relatively easy to determine the value of grain, for example, because there is a constant market for the buying and selling of grain. The cash market value of shipment of grain could be determined on the basis of the prices quoted on the day of the loss at the grain markets, such as the Board of Trade in Chicago. An appropriate amount could be added or subtracted, depending upon the point of destination. It would be more difficult to determine the cash market value of a load of specially built furniture if the shipper had not determined an invoice value at the time of the shipment.

Actual Cash Value   An alternative valuation clause uses the same actual cash value language that would be found in a fire insurance policy. If the policy provides for transit coverage, this may not be appropriate, and loss adjustment would be more difficult.

Replacement Cost   Replacement cost clauses are not usually used in inland marine insurance policies. However, when new merchandise is involved, the actual cash value is often the same as the replacement cost, except for freight charges. In other cases, it is more appropriate to use a valued policy.

Valued Policies   There are many kinds of property for which the values would be particularly difficult or impossible to determine after a total loss. A large proportion of inland marine insurance is written to cover fine arts, antiques, valuable papers, and similar property which could easily be destroyed totally in a fire, and for which it would be impossible to determine values accurately after such destruction. The best answer to this problem has been to determine the value in advance and to provide that the agreed amount will be paid to the insured in case of a total loss. The valuable papers and records policy, for example, provides a blanket amount of coverage on such papers and records on an actual cash value basis, but it also provides for the scheduling of items with the provision that "the amount per article specified therein is the agreed value thereof for the purpose of this insurance."

In the event of a partial loss under most valued policies, the insurance will cover for the actual cash value of the damage, or for the cost to repair or replace the damaged property, not to exceed the agreed value.

Limitations on Partial Losses

There may be circumstances in connection with a loss in which the insured will claim that the resultant loss or damage exceeds the actual physical loss. For example, the loss of one part of a set may be alleged by the insured to constitute a loss of the full value of this set. Several clauses are used by insurers to clarify the intent of the policy or to specify how such possible controversies can be resolved.

Pairs and Sets Clause A pairs and sets clause is used in cases in which the insured property consists of a pair or set, such as a pawn from an antique chess set covered under a fine arts dealer's form. A typical clause used for this purpose reads:

> In the event of loss of or damage to any article or articles which are a part of a pair or set, the measure of loss of or damage to such article or articles shall be a reasonable and fair proportion of the total value of the pair or set, giving consideration to the importance of said article or articles, but in no event shall such loss or damage be construed to mean the total loss of the pair or set.

Obviously it becomes necessary for the adjuster and the insured to agree upon a reasonable and fair proportion of the total value in such a case, but the clause at least makes it clear that the insured does not have the privilege of claiming a total loss of the pair or set when only a part of it is lost.

Parts or Machinery Clause Many inland marine policies also contain a variation of this concept in what may be termed a parts or machinery clause which reads:

> In the event of loss of or damage to any part of property covered consisting, when complete for use, of several parts, the company shall only be liable for the value of the part lost or damaged.

This latter clause may be used when the insured property is part of a machine or a piece of equipment rather than clearly part of a pair or set, such as in the case of the chess set.

Labels Clause Losses of commercial property may involve damage to labels or wrappers of packaged goods without there being any actual damage to the contents. Here again, insureds may attempt to collect for the entire value of the property, contending that the loss of the labels completely destroys the value of the property. Companies frequently use what is called a "labels clause" when the property covered consists of cans, bottles, or similar containers from which the labels might be lost due to a peril. A typical clause for this purpose reads:

> In case of loss or damage affecting labels, capsules or wrappers, the loss shall be adjusted on the basis of an amount sufficient to pay the cost of new labels, capsules or wrappers, and the cost of reconditioning the goods.

Permissive and Restrictive Clauses Common to Inland Marine Policies

Sue and Labor Inland marine underwriters have taken from their ocean marine heritage the "sue and labor" clause. This goes beyond the mere obligation of the insured to protect property from further loss or damage. It provides that the insured shall (and in some cases the insurance company may) take action to preserve the property, that such expenses may be paid to prevent a loss, and that such action will not be considered a waiver of rights on the part of either the insured or the insurance company. These provisions are considered as necessary for property in transit by land as they always have been for property in transit by sea. Current versions of the sue and labor clause that are used in inland marine policies are somewhat modernized as compared to the ancient language which is still used in many ocean marine policies. One such clause referred to as a *protection of property clause* reads as follows:

> In case of loss, it shall be lawful and necessary for the insured, his or their factors, servants and assigns, to sue, labor, and travel for, in and about the defense, safeguard and recovery of the property insured hereunder, or any part thereof, without prejudice to this insurance, nor shall the acts of the Insured or the Company, in recovering, saving and preserving the property insured in case of loss be considered a waiver or an acceptance of abandonment. The expenses so incurred shall be borne by the Insured and the Company proportionately to the extent of their respective interests.

No Benefit to Bailee This provision of the insurance policy is a part of the insurer's attempts to preserve the right of subrogation against a carrier or bailee in cases where the carrier or bailee may have primary responsibility for the loss. The railroads in the United States during the early years of this century made strenuous efforts to reduce their losses to shippers from merchandise damaged or lost in transit. One of the devices that was established for this purpose by the railroads was a provision in the bill of lading that any insurance carried by the shipper will be for the benefit of the carrier or bailee. An application of this provision in the bill of lading would relieve the carrier of its obligation to make good any loss to the shipper or consignee. Insurance companies countered this move of the carriers with a provision in most inland marine policies that the insurance shall "in no wise inure directly or indirectly to the benefit of any carrier or other bailee."

There have been several court cases involving the conflict between the provision in the bill of lading that the carrier shall have the benefit of the shipper's insurance and this provision of the insurance policy that the coverage shall not inure to the benefit of the carrier. In general, the provision of the insurance policy has been upheld by the courts. Some bills of lading may be worded in such a way that any insurer payment of loss to the insured would wipe out the carrier's obligation. Underwriters must examine carefully the provisions of the bill of lading and of the insurance policy in such cases in order to determine whether payment of a loss should be made directly to the insured, or whether it should be made ostensibly as a loan, to be repaid if the insured does recover from a carrier.

A *loan receipt* is the device used to pay an insurance claim ostensibly as a loan. The pertinent part of the agreement reads as follows:

Received from _____ the sum of _____dollars not as a payment of any claim but as a loan and repayable (without interest) only to the extent of any net recovery the undersigned may make from any person or persons, corporation or corporations, or others, on account of loss by _____ to _____. on or about....[1]

With the use of the loan receipt, the insured would immediately receive the amount of the loss and then attempt recovery from the carrier. If recovery is successful, the insurer's loan is repaid.

Territorial Limits Insurance coverage on property at fixed locations usually specifies the location where the property is covered. There may be a certain amount of coverage away from the location named in the policy, but the intent is primarily to cover property at a place where hazards and other exposures to loss can be identified. Inland marine policies, in contrast, cover in transit or otherwise wherever the property happens to be, and many inland marine policies cover property anywhere in the world.

Many of the commercial inland marine policies cover only within territorial limits named in the policies. These territorial limitations are comparable to those imposed under the trading warranties that are used in ocean marine insurance. However, the limitations in inland marine policies are not expressed as warranties but as areas within which the coverage applies.

One of the typical limitations in inland marine policies applies to coverage within the "continental United States and Canada." The continental United States includes all of the contiguous forty-eight states, the District of Columbia, and Alaska. (Alaska, being on the North American continent, is a part of the continental United States.) Such a limitation would exclude Hawaii, any of the territories, and Puerto Rico. Inland marine underwriters customarily specifically include Hawaii, Puerto Rico, or any of the territories if it is the intent to cover property within those areas or property going to and from those areas from the continental United States. Another typical limitation is coverage only within the forty-eight contiguous states, the District of Columbia, and Canada. This wording would therefore exclude coverage in Alaska.

Commercial inland marine policies may specify coverage within a certain radius or distance from some fixed location. Such a "radius of operation" would ordinarily be the geometric radius "as the crow flies" rather than a distance by highway. The policy must specify that the radius is the distance by highway if that is the intent.

Deductibles Many inland marine policies have deductibles applying to any loss that may occur. In other cases, the deductibles apply only to the miscellaneous losses and not to specified perils such as fire and wind. Deductibles may reduce the frequency of small claims. There is a tendency to increase the size of deductibles because of inflation.

Inland marine policies covering commercial property and mechanical equipment of various kinds may contain a deductible applying to a specified peril. The collision coverage on a piece of contractor's equipment may include a $500 deductible, for example.

Warranties in Inland Marine Insurance Warranties are not used in inland marine insurance to the same extent they are in ocean marine insurance. Where used, their effect is much less severe than it is under an ocean marine policy. There are no implied warranties affecting inland marine insurance.

Inland marine insurance is under the same limitations as other insurance not subject to admiralty jurisdiction as far as the effect of warranties is concerned. Courts and legislatures in the United States tend to apply warranties lightly. For example, the courts generally take the position that a breach of warranty under an inland marine policy must have increased the chance of loss in order for it to affect the coverage. A breach of warranty under an ocean marine policy cancels the insurance from that point on even if the breach of warranty had no effect on the loss.

Abandonment The insured under an inland marine insurance policy does not have the privilege of offering abandonment to the insurance company in the way that is customary under an ocean marine insurance policy. Many inland marine policies contain a provision that specifically eliminates any privilege of abandonment. Other policies are silent regarding abandonment. One abandonment clause reads:

> There can be no abandonment to the company of any property. The circumstances in connection with inland marine losses are such that abandonment is not considered to be a necessary or desirable privilege for the insured.

Coinsurance Inland marine insurers generally follow ocean marine insurers in providing for some kind of a coinsurance on commercial policies. Inland marine policies frequently contain the equivalent of a 100 percent coinsurance clause, but this may not be labeled with the word "coinsurance." A typical clause that has the effect of a 100 percent coinsurance clause reads:

> In no event shall this company be liable for a greater proportion of any loss than the limit of liability under this policy bears to the total value of the property insured under this policy at the time such loss occurs.

Some insurers label such clauses specifically as coinsurance clauses in order to improve understanding on the part of policyholders.

The usual problems with coinsurance and the complications that it introduces into loss settlements are familiar to students of insurance. Coinsurance with inland marine policies has an additional problem. There are many situations involving inland marine coverage where the values exposed to loss are not under the control of the policyholder. The motor carrier, for example, may find at the time of a loss that he or she is carrying values far in excess of the policy limit of liability. It is impossible for a motor carrier to determine with any degree of accuracy the values of the loads being carried. The possibility of underinsurance must be taken into account in the negotiations between the insured and the insurer when the limits of liability are set. A similar situation may occur in connection with coverage for bailees. Laundries and dry cleaners, for example, do not ordinarily require any declaration of value when property is submitted for cleaning. A coinsurance clause in a policy might penalize the insured if a severe loss occurs during a peak period when the value of property on the bailee's premises far exceeds what is considered normal.

UNDERWRITING INLAND MARINE COVERAGES

As can be seen by the scope of the Nation-Wide Marine Definition, inland marine coverages include a wide variety of policies and types of exposures. It is not possible in a single chapter to properly analyze each of the many types of policies included in this area. The next section takes a typical coverage from each of the major areas of inland marine insurance and analyzes the underwriting of that coverage. These major areas include:

1. Property in transit
2. Instrumentalities of transportation and communication
3. Scheduled and blanket equipment floaters
4. Bailees' customers policies
5. Block policies
6. Miscellaneous inland marine coverages

Property in Transit

Classes of Carriers   There are three classes of carriers:

1. Common carriers
2. Contract carriers
3. Private carriers

Transportation insurance, particularly motor truck cargo, involves shipments by all three classes of carriers. When insuring cargo for the shipper's interest, the type of carrier to be employed is an important variable since it affects the shipper's right of recovery and therefore the insurer's right of subrogation.

Common and Contract Carriers.   A common carrier is an airline, railroad, or trucking company that undertakes to haul for all shippers seeking their services. In the United States, common carriers are regulated by both the federal and state governments with respect to routes, commodities hauled, and tariffs. A contract carrier hauls only for a specified shipper or shippers.

LIABILITY OF COMMON CARRIERS.   Common carriers are liable for the safe delivery of commodities entrusted to them for shipping. There are a number of limitations on the extent of this liability as a source of recovery for the shipper both from a standpoint of law and from the nature of industry practice.

The limitations from the standpoint of law are contained in certain exceptions to the common carrier's liability and in the provisions of the bills of lading. The common carrier is not liable for loss or damage to commodities as a result of:

1. acts of God
2. acts of the public enemy
3. exercise of public authority
4. neglect or fault on the part of the shipper
5. inherent vice

Therefore, a shipper's goods might be destroyed by lightning, which is deemed to be an act of God; the carrier thus would not be liable for the loss. If the goods were insured, this would also eliminate any possibility of subrogation for the insurer.

Even if the peril causing the loss falls within the province of the carrier's liability, the *bill of lading,* which is issued by the common carrier as a receipt from the carrier for the goods being transported, may contain important limitations on recovery. The bill of lading also serves as the contract of carriage between the shipper and the common carrier, setting forth the obligations and responsibilities of each party.

The "Uniform Straight Bill of Lading" contains a clause to the effect that "the agreed or declared value of the property is stated by the shipper not to exceed _____ per _____." This statement may be left blank (in which case there is no release of the carrier's liability) or it may be filled in (such as so many cents per pound), thereby releasing the carrier of part of its liability.

Over a period of time, the terminology used by underwriters has led to some confusion. Underwriters call a bill of lading in which there is no release of the carrier's liability a *straight bill of lading* or just a bill of lading. Those bills of lading in which there *is* a release of the carrier's liability have been called *released bills of lading.* The confusion arises from the fact that, in both cases, the underwriter is referring to a variation of the same document (a Uniform Straight Bill of Lading).

The term *straight* is technically (and properly) used to distinguish the straight bill of lading from an *order bill of lading*—the primary difference being that the straight bill of lading is non-negotiable and the order bill of lading is negotiable. The confusion regarding the terminology should not overshadow the underwriting significance of the distinction between these terms.

Under the "released" bills, the released value amounts are universally low. An underwriter providing a rate credit to a shipper due to the possibility of recovery from the carrier should check the bill of lading for the released values agreed to.

Another limitation on the carrier's liability occurs with large shippers who load their own freight cars. These shipments are made under a bill of lading which specifies *shipper's weight, load, and count.* In this case the carrier has no liability for a short load or count unless it can be proven that the carrying conveyance was broken into en route. This type of bill of lading is frequently used with railroad cars which are loaded at the shipper's siding and then sealed.

The limitations to recovery from industry practice stem from the fact that some carriers may resist all claims and may be slow to pay valid ones. Further, the carrier may not be solvent in the event of a large claim. Financially troubled trucking companies sometimes let small claims accumulate to the point where they are unable to pay them.

LIABILITY OF CONTRACT CARRIERS. The liability of a contract carrier is usually specified in the contract between the carrier and the shipper. The common law places a duty upon the carrier imposing liability for negligence. While it is against public policy in many states to permit anyone to contract away his or her entire responsibility for negligence, the terms of the contract can greatly raise the threshold or degree of negligence that must be proved for recovery.

Another limitation on recovery from a contract carrier is the solvency of the carrier. A contract carrier may not have sufficient financial strength to meet a judgment, if one is obtained.

Private Carriers. The Motor Carrier Act of 1935 defines a private carrier as one which carries its own goods or goods for which it is the lessee or bailee. Except in the bailment situation, which occurs relatively infrequently, there is no opportunity for recovery from a private carrier.

Transportation Insurance

Shipper's Interest. Commodities being shipped by land may be written either on an *annual transit form* or as a *trip transit form.* The annual transit form is designed for the insured who has a continuous or frequent transit exposure. The trip transit form is designed for the occasional shipment.

POLICY TERMS AND CONDITIONS. Shipper's interest policies may be written on either a named-perils or "all-risks" basis. This is a nonfiled class, and there is a great deal of flexibility in this coverage. The basic policy usually provides for coverage "in the ordinary course of transit," but this is often extended to cover storage incidental to transit.

The policy contains a limit of liability per shipment and usually an aggregate limit of liability in any one loss disaster or casualty. When there are several different modes of transportation used, such as trucks, rail, and air, there are usually separate limits of liability for each category.

This rating of this policy is based on the annual value shipped rather than the limits of liability. When different types of carriers are used, as would be the case when part of the shipments are by common carrier and the rest by contract carrier, different rates are usually employed. Different rates are also applied to the values shipped by each mode of transportation. If there is an incidental exposure of goods shipped on the shipper's own trucks, this may be added to the annual transit policy. When the exposure to the cargo on the shipper's own trucks is dominant, this should be written on an "owner's goods on owner's trucks" form.

UNDERWRITING CONSIDERATIONS. The major underwriting considerations for this coverage include:

1. the commodity and its susceptibility to loss or damage. Particularly troublesome are *target* commodities such as liquor and cigarettes which are attractive to thieves and hijackers.
2. the modes of transportation used and the type of carrier.
3. the type of bill of lading used and the terms of sale. The terms of sale, such as FOB destination, will indicate the portion of the trip that will be at the insured's risk.
4. loss experience of the shipper.
5. length of business of the shipper.
6. the type of packing and container used. Containerization reduces many handling and pilferage losses.
7. the limits of liability desired and the type of valuation clause to be employed.

When writing the owner's goods on owner's trucks form, there is no possibility of subrogation from a carrier. This would tend to justify a higher rate. On the other hand, shippers handling their own goods on their own trucks have more control over their own employees than over the employees of a common or contract carrier. Therefore, there may be a higher degree of care in handling, loading, and unloading. The hazards of misdelivery and shortage are also reduced. Each of these operations should be evaluated on its own merits, with the rate and the coverage tailored to the hazards and requirements of the particular risk.

Motor Truck Cargo Legal Liability. The motor truck cargo legal liability policy provides coverage for common or contract carriers to indemnify them for cargo losses for which the carrier is legally liable. This coverage is discussed in AIU 63.

Instrumentalities of Transportation and Communication

Bridges and Tunnels Insurance on bridges and tunnels is a "filed" classification rated by the bureaus on an individual risk basis. The program is designed to cover property damage to the bridge or tunnel itself, either completed or under construction, in addition to business interruption (or use and occupancy) coverage. This is a specialty coverage and should be written only by underwriters with some experience with this line. Most companies have neither the desire nor the experience to become involved in this potentially catastrophic class. Because of the high values, most risks are written on a *subscription,* or *participation,* basis with each company assuming a percentage of the total value. Often bridges are excluded from normal inland marine excess of loss reinsurance treaties and must either be fully retained or facultatively reinsured. The main requirement prior to authorization is a complete inspection outlining age, construction, condition, and protection. Blueprints and specifications may be necessary.

The major exposures are collision from vehicles or ships, ice, flood, hurricane, collapse, earthquakes, and landslides.

Piers, Wharves, Docks, Dry Docks, Marine Railways, Outdoor Cranes, and Loading Bridges Under the 1976 Definition, "all-risks" coverage is permitted for piers, wharves, and docks. The 1953 Definition required the exclusion of fire and extended coverage perils when insuring these risks under an inland marine policy. On the other hand, coverage on dry docks and marine railways has traditionally been written on an "all-risks" basis. Unlike bridges and tunnels coverage, these risks are "nonfiled," allowing greater latitude in developing the rates and forms. Local marinas with docks, piers, and small loading cranes are a rapidly increasing portion of this class. The marina operation may be seasonal or all year, depending on the location.

A thorough inspection placing special emphasis on age, construction, condition, and protection is required. Protection is important because breakwaters can reduce the hazards of wave wash. Ironically, the availability of water can be a concern. Public hydrant protection is not always adequate, making fire fighting from boats necessary— weather permitting.

In commercial docks and piers, fire is a major peril because of the possibility of combustible items being stored in adjacent warehouses or on the pier, wharf, or dock itself. Explosion can be an important peril if the risk is exposed by grain elevators, petrochemical storage tanks, or similar volatile risks. Marina risks are also susceptible to fire, particularly during the "lay-up" season when the marina may be unattended. Marinas with boat storage may represent a catastrophic fire risk at this time. Often the docks at a marina are exposed by frame storage buildings and sheds. Other perils to be considered are wave wash, ice, flood, windstorm, and collision from ships.

Radio and Television Communications Equipment Perhaps the most commonly written risks in the instrumentalities of the transportation and communication category are those covering radio and television communications equipment. While there are no standardized forms for this nonfiled class, individual company forms bear enough resemblance to one another that any one can be described as typical. Generally, the form covers tower(s) and antenna(e); equipment, controls, and wiring in the transmitter room, broadcast studio, mobile units, or the entire building; and tools used in the maintenance of equipment. In addition to the physical damage coverage provided, most companies offer business interruption, or use and occupancy, coverage.

Normally, each risk will require an inspection of three types of equipment—that is, the tower, the transmitter, and the studio. The tower is often at a different location from the transmitter and studio. Each type of equipment presents its own problems.

The tower with an antenna usually represents sizable values. A complete inspection report should be mandatory, and any deficiencies should be remedied before coverage is bound. The probable maximum loss *is* the amount subject. If a tower goes down, all that is left is the salvage. Towers and their antennae can be located on top of buildings or as a separate structure. There are two types of towers, guyed and freestanding. Either way they should be properly constructed to reduce the hazards of wind and ice storms. The ground surrounding separate towers should be fenced to discourage vandals, and the grass should be kept cut to reduce the possibility of brush fire damage to the guy wires or tower. The need for grounding against lightning is obvious. Sleet and ice storms, which build up both the weight and the surface of the tower exposed to wind, are a major hazard.

Other hazards include electrical malfunctions (although they are usually excluded, the resulting fire is covered); collapse caused by earth movement; and aircraft collision. The Federal Communications Commission has requirements concerning warning lights and other standards of protection. Tower exposures are compounded during construction. The experience of the contractor erecting the tower is of primary importance.

The transmitting equipment is usually located near the tower. It may be in a top floor if the tower is on a building, or at the base of a tower in a building that is a separate structure. The inspection should reveal housekeeping habits as well as disclose any unusual fire hazards.

The inspection of the studio should focus on fire hazards and the possibility of any "set" building or woodworking hazards. It should also show what security measures are provided for potential theft and vandalism perils.

Vans containing mobile equipment should be equipped with alarm systems. Mobile units, so-called minicams, and their related equipment should be carefully underwritten because of the extreme hazards they may be exposed to while on location.

Use and occupancy coverage provides for the revenue lost due to the interruption of transmission as a result of a physical loss to the covered property. The most important factor is the physical condition and protection of the property, especially the tower and antenna. The underwriter should be assured that provisions have been made for the use of alternate facilities in the event of a loss. The deductible for this coverage is usually stated in days. Since any time "off the air" can mean the loss of considerable revenues, a three- or four-day deductible provides the insured with the necessary incentive to expedite repairs.

An additional concern when writing any form of radio or television tower coverage is the provision for debris removal. The underwriter should see that the limit provided for this coverage accurately reflects the expected costs. This is particularly true for towers on top of tall buildings.

Other Instrumentalities of Transportation and Communication Other instrumentalities of transportation and communication include pipelines, power, and telephone and telegraph lines. These risks are infrequently written, and the forms and rates are "nonfiled." If such a risk is submitted to an underwriter, full details should be gathered for examination, with special emphasis placed on exposures to ice, windstorm, hail, earth movement or earthquake, lightning, and vandalism perils.

Scheduled and Blanket Equipment Floaters

Contractors' Equipment Floaters Contractors' equipment floaters represent the largest single inland marine classification in terms of premium volume. It is not unusual to find a company with 25 percent of its inland marine volume in this class. A company's inland marine results can be heavily influenced by its effectiveness in underwriting this class.

The name contractors' equipment is somewhat misleading since this class is not limited to contractors. Many other types of businesses employ mobile equipment eligible for this coverage. Trucking companies, lumberyards, and warehousing concerns employ forklift trucks. Heavy equipment manufacturers use forklift trucks, mobile cranes, and a variety of electric- and gasoline-powered carts. The class name is derived from the fact that this is equipment usually utilized by contractors.

Contractors' equipment includes many different types of handheld circular tools and machinery ranging from multimillion dollar power shovels to skill-saws. An earthmoving contractor would have bulldozers, scrapers, road patrols, off-highway trucks of massive dimensions, and other rollers and shovels. The use to which equipment is to be placed has a great deal of effect on the exposures. A bulldozer or scraper used by a paving contractor on level terrain is subject to relatively light hazards while the same piece of equipment would be subject to hazards of landslide, upset, and overturn if used for land clearance or overburden removal in mountainous terrain.

Mobile cranes is another category which can include units of high value. When cranes are written on an "all-risks" form, collapse of the crane boom is a major hazard. This is particularly true if the crane is used for lifting heavy loads or if it is used with a "headache ball" for building demolition.

A framing contractor would have a large schedule of hand tools including circular saws which are particularly susceptible to theft. This can be controlled with the use of deductibles, the exclusion of perils, or even the exclusion of a particular class of property that is unacceptably subject to loss.

The underwriter should become familiar with the particular type of contractor or business. The nature of the equipment, where it is used, and the manner in which the equipment is used are all important.

Coverage. This is a nonfiled class allowing the great degree of freedom necessary to tailor the forms and rates to fit the needs of the wide variety of insureds. Forms insuring "all-risks" and named perils are available.

"All-risks" forms usually exclude wear and tear, war and nuclear hazards, and infidelity of the insured or his or her employees. In addition to these exclusions, "all-risks" forms usually exclude loss or damage occasioned by the weight of a load in excess of the rated lifting capacity of the machine. Also, loss or damage to crane booms is often excluded unless caused by specified perils. These two exclusions are intended to eliminate claims as a result of the carelessness of the insured or his or her employees. The most commonly written policies are on a scheduled basis at actual cash value with a 100 percent coinsurance clause.

The underwriter should be careful that the limits of liability represent as closely as possible the true cash value. Depreciated book values carried on the insured's records for accounting purposes are not appropriate. Since most losses are partial, the company suffers by not receiving a fair premium for the risk if insurance to value is not carried. On the other hand, in the event of a large or total loss, the insured may find himself or herself a coinsurer for part of the loss. Schedules of equipment and values should be reviewed annually. Rather than applying "rule of thumb" depreciation, the underwriter should assure himself or herself that depreciation was applied against current replacement costs.

Some companies write blanket policies with or without maximum limits per item, and some companies offer replacement cost coverage. Most policies include a provision for automatic coverage on newly acquired equipment.

Percentage deductibles have become quite common for this class. The purpose of these deductibles is to reduce claim frequency caused by small losses. Since the limits of liability vary from the smallest tool to the largest bulldozer, a straight deductible is often not appropriate. A percentage deductible ranging from 1 to $2\frac{1}{2}$ percent will normally alleviate nuisance claims. Coverage on equipment leased by the insured, and extra expenses incurred by the insured renting replacements for items lost or damaged, is usually available.

Hazards and Exposures. Factors affecting the desirability and rating of these risks include:

- *Type of contractor and equipment.* Mining, tunneling, and quarrying operations require special treatment because of earth-movement and explosion hazards. Fire in subsurface mining operations is a major hazard. Equipment used on or near bridges, dams, or barges requires special handling because of the flood and other water hazards. Logging equipment has an unusual forest fire exposure. Gas and oil drilling rigs are subject to explosion hazards.
- *Financial standing of the insured.* This information may be readily available from the liability or bond department if the entire account is written in the same insurance company. If this is not the case, a detailed financial analysis of the contractor or other insured, including analysis of recent balance sheets, income statements, and work in progress, should be undertaken. Financially weak insureds often forgo maintenance and overload equipment, significantly increasing the probability of a major loss.
- *Concentration of values.* This could be a storage or repair location or the maximum liability at any job site.
- *Prior loss experience.*
- *Schedule of items and current realistically established values.*
- *Protection from V or MM and theft at the job site.*

The judgment rating is based on the underwriter's evaluation of the hazards. This could range anywhere from $5 per hundred for a small electrical contractor to rates of less than $0.50 per hundred for over a million dollars of road grading equipment.

The maximum amount subject is the total limit of liability or a lower limit if the policy contains a catastrophe limit. Normally, the probable maximum loss can be established based on the location of concentrated values, either the insured's storage and repair location or a large job site.

Miscellaneous Property Floaters In addition to contractors' equipment, a large number of mobile articles and equipment items are eligible for inland marine coverage. In some cases, the bureaus have filed programs outlining the rules, rates, and forms, such as for physicians' and surgeons' equipment. In other instances, for commonly written classes, forms are developed by individual companies, and their underwriting guides outline company philosophy regarding eligibility and rates. Examples of these classes might include pattern and die floaters, sales samples, and vending machine floaters.

In a great number of instances, there are no bureau or company forms designed to specifically cover the wide variety of items that may be written. Many companies develop forms to cover these less common risks. The forms are usually titled scheduled property floaters or miscellaneous property floaters. Most companies maintain both named perils and "all-risks" versions of these forms. The named perils form is usually quite limited, allowing the underwriter to add perils as needed. The "all-risks" forms contain a number of exclusions the underwriter can delete if broader coverage is desired.

Some commonly written articles insured under scheduled property floaters are caterers' equipment, church vestments, morticians' equipment, voting machines, and portable radio equipment. The list is restricted only by the Definition limitations concerning vehicles designed for highway use, property on sale or in the course of manufacture, and furniture and fixtures. (The Definition and its interpretation should be reviewed concerning the eligibility of a given type of property.)

The judgment rating of these risks is normally based on the fire contents rate, if there is a location exposure, plus a loading for whatever other perils are granted while on a premises or in transit. Factors that influence acceptance, underwriting, and pricing include:

- type, use, and value of property and its susceptibility to loss or damage by insured perils;
- location and transit exposures including territorial restrictions;
- loss protection while on location or in transit;
- deductible option;
- previous loss experience;
- financial standing of the insured.

The amount subject is the total limit of liability for all items covered. The probable maximum loss is usually represented by the maximum concentration of values at any given location or while in transit.

Bailees' Customers Policies

Bailment   Coverage of property in transit to or from or in the custody of bailees is specified as marine in the Definition. A *bailment* is defined as the legal relation that arises whenever one person delivers possession of personal property to another person under an agreement or contract by which the latter is under a duty to return the identical property to the former or to deliver or dispose of it as agreed. The person receiving the property is the *bailee*, the person turning over the property (usually the owner) is the *bailor*.

Liability of Bailees While there are several classes of bailments that affect the degree of care required of the bailee, commercial bailments are known as *mutual benefit bailments* and require the bailee to exercise ordinary care. This means that the bailee is liable for loss or damage only as the result of negligence. In many jurisdictions a presumption of negligence on the part of the bailee has been developed. This is due to the fact that in the event of a loss, the bailee is the only one with knowledge of the circumstances leading to the loss or damage. This places the burden of proof of the absence of negligence on the bailee. The bailee of valuable property, such as jewelry or furs, is held to a higher standard of care than is the case with property of lesser value.

The bailee may also assume additional liability by contract. The bailee may agree in the bailment contract to assume liability for loss or damage from certain specified perils or even to assume liability for any loss or damage to the bailed property. An advertisement stating that the bailee assumes all liability for loss or damage to the goods or that the bailee carries insurance for the benefit of the bailor may be construed by the courts as extending the bailee's liability just as if it had been in the contract of bailment.

Coverage The largest class of bailees' customers policies is the cleaners and dyers policy. Most of these policies are written as direct damage contracts rather than to cover the legal liability of the bailee. Courts have held that a bailee has an insurable interest in the bailed property due to the possible loss of goodwill in the event that the property is lost or destroyed by an insurable peril even in the absence of negligence.

These policies are written on both an "all-risks" and named perils basis. An unusual feature of the cleaners and dyers policy is that some of these contracts are written on the basis of gross receipts without a limit of liability. This lack of a limit of liability is due to the fact that in most cases the bailee does not know the value of the bailed property.

Where a limit of liability is inserted in the cleaners and dyers policy, it may be expressed as an aggregate limit of liability, a limit per item, or both. The limit per item is often tied into the cleaning charge such as a limit of ten times the cleaning charge for laundry and thirty times the cleaning charge for dry cleaning.

Important exclusions include misdelivery, mysterious disappearance, and loss or damage due to processing or work on the property. Goods held for storage are usually excluded, but this coverage may be added by endorsement.

Rating. The bailees' customers policy rating is usually based on the fire contents rate plus a judgment loading for other perils. The first step in developing the fire portion of the rate is to determine the average value at risk.

The average value at risk is determined as follows:

1. The average number of turnovers of customers' goods per year is ascertained by dividing the length of time for service into the number of working days per year.
2. The gross receipts are divided by the number of turnovers to determine the gross receipts per turnover period.
3. The gross receipts per turnover period are divided by the average charge per order to obtain the number of orders handled during each turnover period.
4. The number of orders is multiplied by the average value per order to obtain the average values at risk.

This average value at risk is then multiplied by the fire contents rate to obtain the fire premium. This nominal annual fire premium is then converted to a gross receipts basis by dividing the annual fire premium by the annual gross receipts.

As an example, assume a risk has annual gross receipts of $500,000, is open 360 days a year, and has an average service time of five days. The average service charge is $5, and the average value per order is $150. Note that garment charges and values are quoted per order and not per item. The fire contents rate is $1.20. Exhibit 10-1 shows a computation of gross receipts fire rate.

Underwriting Considerations. When setting lines and calculating retention limits for this type of risk, it is important to remember that these rate calculations are based on estimates of averages. The estimates might be low, in which case the actual values in the case of a total loss could be considerably greater. As with any average, each of these estimates is subject to variability. Ideally, a standard deviation should be calculated to determine how much the actual value might vary from the average. There is insufficient data to do this, so therefore the next best thing is to recognize that some variability is to be expected. (See AIU 61 for a discussion of this problem.)

Another factor that should be taken into account is that this procedure ignores seasonality or accumulations of values that might occur if there were a heavy influx of orders due to Christmas or Easter

Exhibit 10-1

Computation of Gross Receipts Fire Rate

$$\frac{360 \text{ working days}}{5 \text{ days' service time}} = 72 \text{ turnovers per year}$$

$$\frac{\$500{,}000 \text{ gross receipts}}{72 \text{ turnovers}} = \$6{,}944 \text{ receipts per turnover period}$$

$$\frac{\$6{,}944 \text{ receipts per turnover period}}{\$5.00 \text{ average service charge}} = 1{,}389 \text{ orders at one time}$$

$1{,}389 \text{ orders} \times \$150 \text{ per order} = \$208{,}350 \text{ average value at risk}$

$\$208{,}350 \times \$1.20 \text{ fire rate (per hundred)} = \$2{,}500$

$$\frac{\$2{,}500 \text{ annual fire premium}}{\$500{,}000 \text{ gross receipts}} = \$.50 \text{ gross receipts fire rate}^\dagger$$

† Note: In this case it was necessary to point off two places to the right in the answer since fire rates are quoted per $100 of value. The "other perils" rate would be added to this to obtain the final rate for the risk.

holidays. Extreme weather which retarded the rate at which customers claimed their garments might also result in a heavy accumulation of values. When estimating average values, the clientele of the bailee must be taken into account. It is unlikely that the average value per order of a dry cleaner in Beverly Hills, California, is $150, although in this case the service charge would also be higher than $5.

Other important underwriting considerations include the premises fire hazards, particularly the cleaning solutions and lint accumulations, both of which were covered in Chapter 5. Since crime coverages are included, the neighborhood, private protection, and building security should be analyzed. The transit exposures can be measured by the number and type of trucks, their protection systems, and the limits per vehicle required. Financial considerations are important, and the business experience and financial status of the owner should be ascertained. Prior loss experience is necessary, not only as an indication of the relative desirability of the risk but to provide information on the frequency and severity of losses from other perils for rating purposes.

Block Policies

Block Concept Shortly before the turn of the century, Cuthbert Heath, a towering figure in the history of Lloyd's of London, developed the first jewelers' block policy.[2] The origin of the term "block" is a bit cloudy, but most agree it is derived from the French "en bloc" meaning a combination. It was designed to cover the fire and burglary exposures usual to a jeweler while on his or her premises or in transit. The concept spread to the United States where, because state regulations governing fire company charters prohibited the combination of fire with burglary coverages, it was quickly adopted by marine underwriters.

The 1976 Definition lists seven types of dealers' policies covering the property of jewelers, furriers, and camera, musical instruments, equipment, fine arts, and stamp and coin dealers. This discussion will be limited to the first four classes. These four classes have many factors in common.

Coverage Rating bureaus file programs governing all four classes of coverage. However, furriers' block policies may be either filed or nonfiled depending on the operation of the furrier. Wholesale furriers are a nonfiled class. The policies cover stock of the insured and bailed property both on premises and in transit. The insuring agreement is "all-risks." The valuation clauses are similar in that they insure unsold stock at actual cash value not exceeding repair or replacement; undelivered sold property at the net selling price; and property of others at actual cash value, including the insured's labor performed and materials expended prior to the loss. Valuation clauses in individual policies should be reviewed for variations, for example, jewelers' and furriers' blocks further restrict unsold stock to the lowest value declared in the insured's inventory records, and camera dealers' policies limit the value of negatives and prints to the value of raw stock.

Jewelers' and furriers' block policies contain the unique feature of making the proposal, or application, a part of the policy. The signed proposal is the basis for the scheduled rate calculations, and as such, the insured warrants each and every statement to be true. The added protection granted to the the underwriter by using this procedure is felt necessary because of the valuable nature of the merchandise and the extreme sensitivity of the rating to the information contained therein.

Because of the tremendous values that may be represented by either a jeweler or furrier and the relatively remote possibility of a loss, other than by fire, causing a total loss, the policies contain no coinsurance provisions. This allows the insured to choose an amount of insurance that is affordable and yet representative of his or her expected maximum loss. The rate schedule provides for this with a formula relating the selected limit of liability to the actual values at risk based upon inventory and maximum exposure statements contained in the proposal.

Rating

Jewelers' and Furriers' Blocks. Factors that are contained in the proposal and affect the rate schedule calculations include:

1. *Type of insured*—such as, retailer, wholesaler, pawnbroker, and so on.
2. *Type of merchandise*—jewelers are given rate credits for nonjewelry stock.
3. *Premises protection*—
   a. *Vaults and safes* and the percent of property contained therein when the premises are closed.
   b. *Alarm systems.* The degree of burglar alarm system protection, i.e., local, central station, and/or holdup buttons, either on premises or safe or both.
   c. *Show windows* and their protection.
   d. *Private guard service.*
4. *Off-premises exposures*—
   a. *Property in transit* via registered mail, armored car service, or delivery service.
   b. *Property in the custody of salespersons.*
   c. *Property with banks* or other dealers or on exhibition.
   d. *Deductible provision.*
   e. *Previous loss experience.*

In addition, jewelers are allowed a rate credit for membership in the Jewelers' Security Alliance, a national trade organization that promotes loss prevention and crime security and detection within the jewelry industry.

Other Dealers' Block Policies. The rating for camera and musical instrument dealers is similar yet not as detailed. Equipment dealers' rates are greatly affected by the fact that, in many instances, the property is not contained within a building. This reduces the hazard of premises fire.

Policies covering cameras, musical instruments, and equipment also differ from their jewelry and fur counterparts in the incorporation of a coinsurance clause within the contract. Normally, the larger risks are written on a reporting basis, therefore providing the underwriter with premium commensurate with the true values at risk. Reporting, while possibly troublesome for the insured, removes to a great extent the chance of suffering a coinsurance penalty. Policies covering all five types of property contain provisions requiring the insured to keep and make available detailed inventory records.

Hazards and Exposures From the standpoint of the underwriter, policy conditions and rate schedules are similar for the properties insured, but the hazards and exposures differ widely based upon the stock covered. Strong emphasis is placed on the fire and crime perils; however, the relative importance of these perils and others shifts, depending on the type of property.

Jewelers' Block. The major peril is crime. High standards of protection and inventory controls should be required. An inspection may reveal any unusual fire hazards or exposures. Off-premises exposures and their protection should be thoroughly investigated and may provide the major exposure if values are high.

Furriers' Block. Furs are extremely susceptible to damage from fire, smoke, and water. Smoke detectors and CO_2 or Halon fire protection systems should be required. Risks located in older buildings with sprinkler systems in upper floors are hazardous. A sprinkler system is preferred to no protection, as water damage to furs is usually less than smoke damage from an uncontrolled fire. Air conditioning and humidity control equipment should be properly maintained, and a loss control survey should be ordered to reveal any repair operations. The furrier should also have the same crime protection as a comparable jeweler.

Camera and Musical Instrument Dealers. Reporting policies should be encouraged because of fluctuations in values caused by obsolescence or changes in currency exchange rates with foreign manufacturers in addition to the inventory's seasonal changes. High standards of burglary protection and a sound financial standing are important underwriting considerations.

Equipment or Implement Dealers. Repair operations increase the fire exposure, and property left in open yards outside the building increases the crime hazard. Risks should have clean, well-protected repair shops, and outside yards should be fenced and well lighted. Transit exposures should be carefully reviewed.

The limit of liability on the policy normally represents the amount subject. Reduction in the probable maximum loss can be allowed for separate fire divisions. Usually, a safe or vault meeting high standards can be thought of as a separate division. Distribution and arrangement of equipment in open yards may also allow for some reduction in the estimate of probable maximum loss.

Miscellaneous Inland Marine Coverages

The following lines of coverage are included to indicate the breadth of the inland marine field. These coverages do not fall completely into any of the five previous categories although some of them include many of the elements of floater or dealer policies. It is to be stressed that there are more inland marine coverages that have been left out than have been included in this section due to the limitations of the single chapter format.

This section covers the following:

1. Electronic Data Processing Policies
2. Accounts Receivable and Valuable Papers Coverage
3. Live Animals Coverage
4. Installment Sales Policies
5. Pattern and Die Floaters

Other important inland marine coverages are treated separately in the text with builders' risk discussed in Chapter 4 and difference in conditions in Chapter 13.

Electronic Data Processing [3] Recognizing the unique needs of data processing users and owners, inland marine underwriters have developed specialized forms of coverage. Companies currently offering this coverage usually package a combination of physical damage and time element forms. These may provide coverage:

1. on data processing equipment, "the hardware," either on an actual cash value or replacement cost basis;
2. on data processing media, "the software," either on an agreed value or actual reproduction cost basis;
3. for extra expense; and
4. for business interruption under a variety of forms and conditions—gross earnings and valued per diem, with and without actual loss sustained provisions.

The establishment of values and limits should be carefully calculated by the insured. Errors in the reproduction cost of the media could easily mean that a small loss may cause damage exceeding the policy limit.

A complete inspection is required of all submissions. It should highlight in addition to basic fire, crime, and vandalism hazards:

- how the computer room is separated from other occupancy hazards in the building.
- the storage and control of combustibles in the computer room.
- use and storage of cleaning solvents.
- protection of tapes and records.
- smoke detectors and other fire detection devices.
- presence of a sprinkler system anywhere in the building. The sprinkler leakage hazard should be weighed against the fact that it is better to have sprinkler protection against the peril of fire.

- condition of air conditioning and humidity control equipment.
- presence of any water damage, collapse, earthquake, or flood hazards.

In addition to the physical inspection, the financial condition of the insured should be determined.

When the insured is operating leased equipment, a copy of the lease agreement should be secured and reviewed to determine the extent of the insured's liability. On occasion, a lessor may require broader coverage than the company is willing to write. In such instances the gap in coverage should be brought to the attention of the producer.

Accounts Receivable and Valuable Papers

Accounts Receivable. Accounts receivable insurance was "borrowed" from casualty underwriters prior to the development of the Nation-Wide Definition. It was then included in the Definition as a recognized inland marine class and today is written in both departments. Accounts receivable is a consequential loss coverage providing for recovery of receivables uncollectible because of the destruction of records by an insured peril.

COVERAGE. Filings of the rates, rules, and forms for this coverage are made with the states by both marine rate bureaus. The form provides coverage against "all-risks" of loss or damage to the insured's records, subject to exclusions concerning the criminal or accidental tampering with records. The policy usually covers:

(a) all sums due from customers, when collections cannot be made as a direct result of loss or damage to accounts receivable records kept at the premises described in the policy;
(b) interest charges on any loans required to offset collections, pending repayment of the sums made uncollectible by the loss or damage;
(c) excess of normal collection expense made necessary by the loss or damage;
(d) other reasonably incurred expenses made by the insured to reestablish lost or damaged accounts receivable records.[4]

EXPOSURES AND HAZARDS. The process of adjusting a loss is in many cases the reverse of this sequence. Underwriters should review the form carefully concerning its provisions relating to the necessary reporting requirements prior and subsequent to any loss. The monthly figures given in the original application and subsequent monthly reports are extremely important in adjusting a claim.

The major cause of loss is fire, so the underwriter should analyze the risk to be sure that the risk meets the company's underwriting criteria from this standpoint. This is especially true since the base rate is only a fraction of the fire contents rate.

Other concerns of the underwriter are the insured's honesty and the financial condition of the business. Since the basic policy form contains monthly reporting requirements (a nonreporting endorsement is available, but only for risks with credit operations two or more years old and with limits of $100,000 or less), the underwriter has at hand a vehicle for monitoring any indications of declining revenues. Reports should also be watched for timeliness. Chronic late reporting may be an indication of either the insured's indifference or poor business procedures.

A completed application should be required for all submissions. It should contain a record of the accounts receivable for each of the latest available twenty-four months, the amount of bad debts normally incurred by the insured, and a description of any safes or vaults in which the records are kept.

RATING. The base rate is a fraction of the fire contents rate. The rating formula takes into consideration credits or debits for conditions that either reduce or increase the risk or loss. Credits are provided for:

- vaults, safes, or other receptacles bearing a fire label of either the Underwriters' Laboratories, Inc., or the Safe Manufacturers National Association.
- unlabeled metal safes of at least two-inch wall thickness.
- unlabeled vaults with inner and outer metal doors separated by twelve inches of air space.
- duplicate records kept at a separate location.
- wholesalers, manufacturers, and insurance agents if at least 51 percent of their business is so classed because of the greater ease in reestablishing their records after a loss.

A debit is applied if the records are not kept in a fully enclosed metal receptacle of any kind. The premium charged can also be affected by the request for transit coverage (the basic form provides transit coverage only in cases involving the protection of property from an imminent danger), the exclusion of designated accounts, or the utilization of a cycle billing procedure.

Valuable Papers and Records. Valuable papers and records coverage is frequently confused with accounts receivable coverage because they both appear to be providing coverage for printed records. However, valuable papers insurance is designed to cover the physical loss or damage to the papers or records themselves, while accounts receivable insurance is designed to cover the consequential loss of money due to the loss or damage to the records. Valuable papers insurance is not consequential coverage. Accounts receivable coverage reconstructs the physical records only in an effort to reduce the consequential loss of money.

Another possible reason for the confusion concerning these two classes is that valuable papers coverage was also "borrowed" by inland marine underwriters from burglary underwriters prior to the Definition. This is written in both departments, with some companies writing it as marine and others as burglary. Both bureaus file programs governing the rates, rules, and forms.

COVERAGE. The basic form provides "all-risks" coverage on all types of written, printed, or otherwise inscribed documents and records including books, maps, films, drawings, abstracts, deeds, mortgages, and manuscripts.

The form specifically excludes coverage on money and securities and property held as samples or for sale or delivery after sale. The valuation clause is unusual since it limits the actual cash value of the property to what it would cost to repair or replace the property with other of like kind and quality; and in fact, property that cannot be replaced is excluded unless scheduled. Specifically described items are valued on an agreed basis.

EXPOSURES AND HAZARDS. The major peril is fire, so the underwriter should review the risk in this light and, where practicable, require safe or vault protection. This is impossible when considering some risks like libraries. However, most risks with valuable papers are offices or institutions with light to moderate fire hazards. An exception would be an office of a manufacturer unprotected from possible manufacturing hazards.

Care should be taken in investigating the basis of the valuation of the property. Unlike most other inland marine policies, the valuable papers form contains *no* coinsurance clause. The form was developed this way since the valuation of some papers is subject to extreme value fluctuations. An example of this would be a manuscript of a book that, prior to publication, represents a substantial investment to both author and publisher. After publication the original manuscript's value is nominal unless someday the author becomes famous and the manuscript is in demand by collectors.

A safe procedure to follow is to have a clear understanding of what indemnification the insured expects from the company in the event of a loss. If, for example, a library expects replacement of its volumes with other volumes of like kind and quality, the blanket coverage on an actual cash value is acceptable. If, on the other hand, the insured expects replacement of a rare Shakespeare folio, the agreed value clause triggered by scheduling the item is in order. In any event, because of the peculiarities of the valuation clause and the absence of a coinsurance clause, the underwriter should be cautioned against possible adverse selection or misunderstandings of the coverage.

A transit exposure can present problems on some risks. The basic form contains a 10 percent transit limit subject to a $5,000 limit. Requests for higher limits should call for some investigation. Standards of burglary protection should be required proportionate to the value and attractiveness of the property.

Property contained in older buildings may be exposed to water damage hazards from deteriorating plumbing systems. At the very least, an underwriter may have to insist on file cabinets to protect papers from the damage a sprinkler system could cause. The policy also provides coverage for losses caused by flood or earthquake. Company policy concerning flood and earthquake should be examined before an underwriter accepts any risk with severe exposures from these catastrophic perils.

RATING. The rating of the policy is relatively straightforward. It is similar to the rating of accounts receivable policies providing for a base rate of the fire contents rate plus a loading, dependent on whether the coverage is blanket or scheduled. The credits available for risks having vaults, safes, cabinets, and other receptacles follow the accounts receivable policy approach. As with other filed inland marine classes, the underwriter should carefully review the rules and rates provided in the bureau manual in addition to the form.

Live Animals   There are two major categories of live animal coverage: livestock mortality policies and named perils livestock floaters. The livestock mortality policy is a specialty line written only by a few companies. Essentially this is life insurance for valuable animals such as prize bulls. The policy application must be accompanied by a veterinarian's examination of the animal.

Livestock Floater.   The livestock floater is a class that has been filed in most states. These policies cover cows, heifers, bulls, sheep, swine, and farm and riding horses. The filed forms usually exclude range animals such as beef cattle and range sheep; livery, show, and race horses; circus, carnival, or theatrical animals; and animals insured in connection with sales or auctions. These animals represent greater-than-average hazards.

COVERAGE AND RATES. The basic perils are death or destruction resulting from or made necessary by fire, lightning, collapse of bridges or culverts, flood, collision, derailment or overturn of transporting conveyances, windstorm, hail, explosion, riot, riot attending a strike, civil commotion, smoke, earthquake, aircraft, nonowned or operated vehicles, and marine perils during transit on ferries. Optional perils include artificial electricity, attack by dogs or wild animals, and accidental shooting and drowning. In most states the filed rates for this coverage are based on the fire insurance rate plus a loading for the other perils.

HAZARDS AND EXPOSURES. Financial stability and experience are two major characteristics that underwriters should look for in this class of business. Physical hazards include poor maintenance and upkeep of farm property, fences, barns, and stables. Livestock dealers must be carefully underwritten, particularly with respect to financial stability and prior loss experience. A surge in submissions for short-term coverage or short-term extensions of coverage to include optional perils may coincide with an outbreak of rabies in foxes, bats, or dogs in a certain area. This would result in serious adverse selection.

Other Live Animal Coverages. Other live animal coverages include horse and wagon floaters, race and show horse policies, dog floaters, veterinarian or kennel owner's forms, and poultry insurance. In certain parts of the country where range cattle and sheep are subject to severe winter weather, winter range policies are written. Poultry or feed company policies are frequently written on a reporting form.

Installment Sales Contracts

Coverage. These policies cover property sold under installment sales contracts or conditional sales agreements. These nonfiled forms are usually referred to as installment sales or deferred payment merchandise policies. They cover property, other than motor vehicles designed for highway use, while in transit and usually at other locations, until the termination of the seller's or vendor's interest in the property. Available forms include:

- *Vendor's single interest.* This is a single-interest form covering only the vendor's interest in the property—that is, the unpaid balances. The customer is released from paying the balance. This is often abbreviated as VSI.
- *Vendor's contingent interest.* This is a single-interest contract covering only the loss sustained, exclusive of profits. This differs from the vendor's single-interest form in that under this form only losses uncollectible from the customer are covered. The insured cannot release the customer from any responsibility, and subrogation rights are assigned to the company in the event of a claim settlement.
- *Vendor's and vendee's interest.* This is a dual interest contract covering the full value of the property until the vendor's interest terminates. This is an extremely popular method of

providing coverage, because in the event of a loss the customer's equity in the property is protected. Usually, the customer returns to the original vendor for replacement, providing an additional sale. Often this method involves the issuance of certificates to the insured as proof of coverage. Another technique is to record the customers' names, items, and amount of insurance on an *account* or *line sheet* which is submitted monthly.

The perils provided vary from company to company and are largely dependent upon the merchandise covered. Since virtually all property sold under installment plans is eligible, the rating is influenced by the type of property in relation to the perils granted and the exposures.

Exposures and Pricing. The desirability of this coverage and its pricing are affected by several key variables. First is the type of property and its susceptibility to loss or damage on location or in transit. Second is the intended use of the property. This could vary from contractors' equipment to computer equipment. Property intended specifically for high hazard risks or new businesses with high failure rates presents a severe exposure. Examples of this might include restaurant equipment or "faddish" operations like the trampoline courts which were once popular. Third is the financial stability of the insured and the credit screening procedures employed.

Usually the rate is based on an estimate of the average exposure of the combined location and transit hazards. If the property is of a mobile nature, the rate usually charged for the type of equipment is used as a base, with a loading for the lack of individual risk control and selection.

Under the dual interest form in which certificates of insurance are issued or insurance is provided on an account or line sheet basis, the vendor may not provide coverage for all credit customers. There is a possibility of adverse selection if the vendor uses this policy as a means of obtaining insurance for customers who would otherwise find insurance difficult to obtain. The underwriter should obtain records indicating the number of customers insured on this form as a percentage of total credit sales. The list of customers provided on the line sheet or the certificates should also be reviewed to determine if adverse selection is taking place.

Pattern and Die Floaters Many manufacturers who do not own their own foundry have dies or founding patterns that represent considerable values. These dies and patterns are sent out to various foundries for the production of castings. Usually the dies and patterns are retained at the foundry during a production run or for a series of runs over time. The patterns and dies are also in transit between foundries or between the manufacturer and the foundry.

Coverage. This is a nonfiled line, and therefore the coverage varies depending on the needs of the insured and the underwriting practices of the insurer. A typical form would provide named perils coverage, including fire, extended coverage, and burglary while at the foundries, and "all-risks" transit coverage.

Exposures and Pricing. The major exposures in this coverage are fire at the foundry locations and the transit hazards of moving the patterns between the owner's location and the foundry. The foundry exposure is underwritten and rated like any other fixed location risk in which fire is the major peril. The foundry in which the pattern is to be located should be specified, and the underwriter should determine that it meets the standards of acceptability for the insured perils. The fire rate for the foundry plus a loading for the additional perils is the basis of this portion of the rate.

The values shipped each year should be determined as the basis for the transit charge. The type of carrier used, whether common carrier, contract carrier, or the owner's trucks, has a major influence on the level of the transit charge.

Dies and patterns are usually not particularly susceptible to fire; nor are they normally attractive to thieves or burglars. If the die or pattern is either very large and heavy or fragile due to its configuration, it may be damaged in transit.

The insured should keep timely records of the value and location of each pattern or die. Obsolete patterns or dies should be identified and their value reduced to scrap. The obsolete pattern or die can result in overinsurance and an attendant moral hazard. The business experience, reputation, and financial standing of the insured should be investigated to avoid any potential moral hazard.

Manuscript Policies

The manuscript policy is almost the trademark of the marine underwriter. Drafting a manuscript policy is the fullest expression of the underwriting process. The underwriter has the greatest flexibility and is able to design the coverage and pricing of the form to fit the particular risk. Before picking up a pencil to write a manuscript form, the underwriter should reflect, for just a moment, on the fact that insurance policies are contracts of adhesion and any ambiguities will be resolved in favor of the insured.

On the other hand, the same ambiguities can be created when using a standard form to cover a risk for which it is not appropriate. In one case, an "all-risks" contractors' equipment form was used to cover a business machines rental operation. The court used the presence of the mechanical breakdown exclusion as evidence that the insurer contemplated covering other than normal office equipment. The loss involved some $70,000 worth of camera equipment rented to the government and fired into the stratosphere in a rocket nose cone. The parachute failed, as did the adaptation of an inappropriate form.

An existing manuscript drawn by someone else should be accepted only after review by higher underwriting management and by the company's legal department. The underwriter drawing up a manuscript form should have a clear understanding of what the risk entails and exactly what coverage is to be provided. The form will be attached to the basic policy jacket, and care should be exercised to determine that the form and jacket are consistent and create no ambiguities. Basically the format should be as follows:

- Property Covered | What property is covered?

- Limits of Liability, and Sublimits Including Territorial Limits | For how much is it covered? Where is it covered? On or off specific locations? In transit?

- Property Excluded | What property is not covered?

- Perils Covered | What risks and perils are covered?

- Perils Excluded | What risks and perils are excluded?

- Deductible | Is there a deductible? What size? Does it apply to all perils or only to specific perils?

- Valuation of the Property | How much is the property worth to the insured, or to others?

- Reporting or Coinsurance Provisions | Are these provisions present? What do they require?

- Special Conditions | Are there any special conditions included? What are they?

SUMMARY

Marine insurance is delineated in the Nation-Wide Marine Definition. This Definition was first adopted by the National Association of Insurance Commissioners in 1933, revised in 1953, and amended in 1976. The Definition does not limit the insuring powers of an insurer but is used for classification, rating, filing, and similar purposes.

While the Definition makes no distinction between ocean and inland marine, the scope of ocean marine is clearly defined. Inland marine coverages include the following major categories:

1. Property in transit
2. Instrumentalities of transportation and communication
3. Scheduled and blanket equipment floaters
4. Bailees' customers policies
5. Block policies
6. Miscellaneous inland marine coverages

For property in transit, the class of carrier is important. There are three classes of carriers: common, contract, and private. The federal and state governments set forth rules governing the liability of those classes of carriers that fall under their jurisdiction. The possibility of subrogation is affected by the type of bill of lading employed. The straight bill of lading does not limit the value of the commodity, but the released value bill of lading does.

Instrumentalities of transportation include bridges, tunnels, piers and wharves, and radio and television communications equipment. Each of these risks should be carefully evaluated for the exposures peculiar to their nature.

From a standpoint of premium volume, one of the largest classes of inland marine insurance is contractors' equipment. There is a considerable variety in the type of equipment and hazards to which the equipment is subject.

Bailees' customers policies provide direct loss coverage for the bailees' customers goods. The largest segment of this class is the cleaners and dyers policy.

Block policies are written for many types of dealers. These include: jewelers, furriers, and camera, musical instruments, equipment, fine arts, and stamp and coin dealers. An important aspect of all block policies is that they usually include a premises fire exposure not found in some other inland marine risks.

Other policies covered in the chapter include electronic data processing policies, accounts receivable and valuable papers, livestock floaters, installment sales floaters, floor plan merchandise, and pattern and die floaters.

Manuscript policies are almost a trademark of marine insurance. These provide the underwriter with the flexibility to custom design a contract to meet the requirements of a particular risk.

Chapter Notes

1. Ronald C. Horn, *Subrogation in Insurance Theory and Practice*, published for the S. S. Huebner Foundation for Insurance Education, University of Pennsylvania (Homewood, IL: Richard D. Irwin, 1964), p. 69.
2. D.E.W. Gibb, *Lloyd's of London: A Study in Individualism* (London: Macmillan & Co., 1957), pp. 165-166.
3. For a discussion of EDP insurance from the buyer's point of view, see H. A. Chadwick, "Insurance and Information Systems Management," *The Information Systems Handbook*, ed. by F. Warren McFarlan and Richard L. Nolan (Homewood, IL: Dow Jones-Irwin, 1975).
4. J.D. Youd, *A Practical Approach to Inland Marine Insurance* (Boston: Standard Publishing Co., 1974), p. 191.

CHAPTER 11

Underwriting Commercial Ocean Marine Insurance

INTRODUCTION[1]

Ocean marine is the oldest form of insurance, tracing its heritage back to the bottomry bonds and contracts of *respondia* of the ancient Mediterranean civilizations. The influence of ocean marine is seen in other forms of property and liability insurance, most notably in inland marine. Ocean marine contracts are usually written for broad named perils or "all-risks."[2]

There are three major segments of commercial ocean marine insurance:

1. Commercial hulls
2. Protection and indemnity
3. Cargo

There are certain characteristics of ocean marine insurance common to all segments of the business. The first of these is the fact that ocean marine contracts are conducted at a level of *uberrimae fidei* or on a level of utmost good faith. This stems from the early days of ocean marine insurance when the underwriter and the shipowner in London might have arranged insurance on a hull in New York on a "lost or not lost" basis. News traveled so slowly that a vessel might have already been on the bottom though this fact would not have been known in London. Ocean marine risks are still accepted "lost or not lost."

The marine underwriter is protected by certain agreements or conditions that are known as *implied warranties*. These are not actually part of the written policy but have just as much legal force as if they were included in the expressed terms of the contract. If it can be legally established that one or more of these warranties has been violated, the underwriter may declare the insurance agreement to be null and void.

All marine policies are subject to the implied warranty that the vessel concerned is *seaworthy* for the voyage. This means that it must be sound in all respects and able to cope successfully with the normal weather conditions it is expected to encounter. It must carry the necessary fuel, provisions, and other stores and must be manned by the proper number of qualified officers and crew. Cargo must be properly stowed and the vessel must not be overloaded. In writing hull insurance, underwriters customarily require evidence of seaworthiness through a survey (a technical examination) of the hull made by a qualified marine surveyor. A cargo owner cannot reasonably be expected to know whether or not the vessel that is to carry the goods is seaworthy. Therefore, so far as cargo insurance is concerned, the vessel's seaworthiness is admitted to exist. If, however, the shipment is lost or damaged by a peril insured against, and the vessel is found to have been unseaworthy, the cargo owner will be paid, and the underwriter will have a good subrogation case against the vessel owner. The admission of seaworthiness between the cargo owner and the insurance company does not carry through to exonerate the vessel owner.

Another implied warranty is that of *no deviation*, an agreement that there will be no departure from the voyage as it is contemplated. The risk accepted by the underwriter and the premium on the marine insurance written are based on a direct or specified voyage. Deviation is sometimes necessary or excusable, and it may well be that the *assured* (in ocean marine insurance, the insured is usually referred to as the "assured") will have no control over it or even any knowledge of it at the time it takes place. Consequently, it is common for the assured to be "held covered" by the policy with obligation to report the change in voyage when it becomes known. This is another example of the fact that marine insurance is based upon the good faith of the parties to the contract.

Multiple Perils Coverage

Multiple perils coverage has evolved gradually from the named perils form. The perils clause of the standard Lloyd's policy goes back well over 300 years and identifies the perils as "of the seas, men-of-war, fire, enemies, etc."

The old perils clause provided, in effect, coverage against three different risks—fire, war, and the perils of the seas. Inclusion of the war perils was essential in those days because voyages were long, and means of communication correspondingly slow. In those days war risk protection was essential to trade, and underwriters gave that protection in a most complete form.

By the time the twentieth century arrived, foreign trade had become so complex, and the values so large, that a more comprehensive form of cover was needed to meet the requirements of trade. For additional premium, underwriters met this need by extending their policies, where required, to cover such additional perils as contact with fresh water, breakage, leakage, theft and pilferage, contact with fuel oil or other cargo, ship's sweat, and many others. Not even all these perils were enough to completely protect some of the foreign traders, and the next step forward was an "all-risks" policy which is commonly written today. Common exclusions include inherent vice, such as spoilage of fresh fruit or vegetables shipped in an ordinary cargo vessel. Ordinary trade loss is similarly excluded as in the case of seepage of wine through the staves of a cask.

Valued Policy

The valued policy has long been a characteristic of ocean marine insurance. Under this arrangement the underwriter and the assured agree in advance on value so that, in the event of total loss, the assured will receive the full amount of insurance. Partial losses to cargo are usually paid as a percentage of the amount insured. Partial losses covered under hull insurance are usually paid on a "new for old" basis, that is, without depreciation.

In fire insurance one of the principal objections to the valued policy is that of moral hazard. Since the insured is in possession of and has control of his or her other property, there may be considerable inducement for the insured to have a loss and to collect the full amount of the insurance. Besides, after a loss, it is relatively easy to determine the actual cash value of the property destroyed or damaged and to adjust the loss on that basis.

In ocean marine insurance the circumstances are very different. The property, such as a cargo shipment, is completely out of the assured's control so that there is little, if any, possibility of fraud. In addition, if the shipment goes to the bottom, there is really no way for the assured to prove his or her loss—that is, to establish the value of the shipment. The valued policy presumes full insurance to value.

UNDERWRITING VARIABLES—
COMMERCIAL HULLS

Commercial hull insurance is divided into three major classifications:

1. Self-propelled, oceangoing hulls greater than 2,500 gross registered tons which are written by the American Hull Syndicate and independent American and overseas insurers.
2. Other commercial hulls, self-propelled and non-self-propelled.
3. Drilling rigs. (This specialized class will not be considered here.)

The American Hull Insurance Syndicate (AHIS)

This syndicate of insurers was formed in 1920 to promote the business of hull insurance among domestic American insurance companies and to provide a vehicle for competition in the world hull market. The American Hull Insurance Syndicate has its own underwriting staff which handles rating, policy issuance, premium collections, and loss settlements on behalf of all member companies. Producers deal directly with the syndicate. Due to the concentrated nature of the large hull business, most syndicate business is written by a few producers.

There are many American insurers who are not members of the American Hull Insurance Syndicate and who write this business separately. The AHIS almost never writes 100 percent of a fleet, leaving the remainder to be placed elsewhere.

The Water Quality Insurance Syndicate (WQIS)

Another syndicate that serves the vessel owner is WQIS. The federal government has passed several laws since 1970 making the shipowner liable for the spillage of oil and other hazardous substances. One of the most recent is the Clear Water Act of 1977. WQIS insures against liability to the federal government as well as the various states. In addition, it insures against liability to third parties for property damage caused by pollution. WQIS is headquartered in New York, and like the American Hull Insurance Syndicate, it issues its own policy, deals directly with agents and brokers, and maintains its own underwriting staff. It has jurisdiction over vessels of 100 GRT (gross registered tons) or more, and fleets in which one or more of the vessels are of 100 GRT or more.

Coverage

The American Institute of Marine Underwriters (AIMU) maintains a clause committee which drafts and publishes amendments to the American Institute hull policies as changes become necessary. Over a period of years AIMU has developed specialized forms for certain types of vessels, and forms that apply to a specific geographical area. There is a reasonable degree of language standardization in most of these policies, but the slight differences in coverage which may exist can be very important underwriting considerations. In view of this, it is absolutely essential that when quoting on a risk, the underwriter be very specific concerning the policy forms to be used. Certain large brokerage firms and companies have adopted their own forms which differ from the AIMU forms.

It is not possible, within this text, to include a detailed explanation of every major form and their standard endorsements. However, what follows is a description of the most commonly used form, the American Institute of Marine Underwriters Time Hull Form.

American Institute of Marine Underwriters Time Hull Form (Form 6-Z amended June 2, 1977)

The general provisions of this form include:

- *Interest Insured*—The policy covers the hull, machinery, including equipment, stores, provisions, furnishings, and boats; as well as equipment not owned by the assured but installed on the vessel for use provided the assured assumes responsibility for same. The amount covered on nonowned equipment does not increase the insured value of the vessel. Cargo containers, barges, and lighters that may belong to the vessel are not covered.
- *Valuation*—This is a valued policy. The amount of insurance and agreed valuation are stated in the policy.
- *Term*—Policies are customarily issued for one year, but it is permissible to issue short-term policies when the situation warrants it. If the vessel is at sea at expiration, coverage continues to port of destination provided prior notice is given to the company and an additional premium paid.
- *Deductible*—All policies contain a deductible that is determined at inception but which is not applicable in the event of total loss of the vessel.
- *Trading Warranty*—The vessel is restricted to a certain area that is agreed to in advance between the company and the assured. In the event the warranty is broken, a "held covered"

provision exists, provided the assured gives notice to the company and pays the additional premium as required.

- *Lay-Up Returns*—A vessel moored in a safe port is subject to fewer perils than while at sea. The policy provides a way to allow a return premium for the reduced exposure. Returns are allowed only if the vessel is laid up for at least thirty consecutive days. Returns are net at a rate named in the policy. No return is allowed if the vessel becomes a total loss during the policy term.
- *Cancellation*—According to the printed conditions, the policy *can be canceled only by mutual consent.* Cancellation for nonpayment of premium due gives the insurer the right to cancel with ten days' notice if the premium is not paid within thirty days of the due date. Termination due to ownership changes will be described later.
- *"Other Insurance"*—The policy specifically allows certain types of other insurance but warrants that no other insurance excepting that which is permitted shall be in force. Allowable other insurance includes:
  1. increased value for an amount not to exceed 25 percent of the *insured* value of the ship as additional insurance on disbursements, managers' commissions, profits, excess or increased value of hull and machinery, similar interests, and freight insured for time. Freight or hire, charter hire, insurance premiums, and similar amounts at risk may be covered under other insurance only for the percentages and amounts specified in the warranty. The warranty is called the *disbursements warranty* since many of the terms described with regard to additional amounts of insurance are related to disbursements made by the insured (e.g., insurance premiums).[3]
  2. war risks coverage.
- *Proportion of Losses Covered*—Total and constructive total losses are covered to the full amount insured. The vessel may not be considered a constructive total loss unless the expense of recovering and repairing the vessel exceeds the agreed upon value (which is not necessarily the insured value). The repaired value is stated as being the agreed value. The portion of partial losses in excess of the deductible is adjusted on a "new for old" basis, meaning no depreciation is taken.

Perils. The hull policy covers the vessel whether at sea, in port, or in drydock undergoing repairs. Coverage is not "all-risks," but is on a very broad named-perils basis.

- *Perils Clause*—The most important perils are:
  1. perils of the seas (such as heavy weather)
  2. fire, lightning, earthquake
  3. assailing thieves (theft by force)
  4. jettisons
  5. barratry of the master and mariners
  6. all other like perils and misfortunes unless excluded

- *Sue and Labor Clause*—The sue and labor clause requires the assured to take steps to protect and recover the vessel in the event of loss. The insurer can also take such steps and neither party's actions shall be considered a waiver or acceptance of abandonment. A proportionate share of reasonable sue and labor expenses are collectible even if a total loss is admitted under the policy.

- *Additional Perils (Inchmaree Clause)*—This covers certain additional perils, many of which are inherent to our modern technology, and includes:
  1. accidents in fueling and in loading, discharging, or handling cargo
  2. accidents in hauling, launching, and drydocking
  3. explosions on shipboard or elsewhere
  4. breakdown of machinery and bursting of boilers, or latent defects in the machinery and hull, but excluding the cost of replacing, repairing, or installing the defective part
  5. accidents to nuclear installations not on board the vessel
  6. contact with aircraft, rockets, and similar missiles
  7. negligence of master, officers, crew, or pilots
  8. negligence of charterers or repairers

- *General Average and Salvage Charges*—These are payable in full. A general average is a voluntary sacrifice or expense made by the vessel against the threat of a common peril in order to save the venture. The sacrifice must be successful in order for a general average to be declared. For example, if a fire occurs on the ship and a portion of the cargo must be jettisoned to prevent the spread of fire, the loss of such jettisoned cargo is considered a general average loss and the shipowner and owners of the undamaged cargo are responsible for a portion of the loss.

  Salvage means the rescue of a vessel and/or its cargo at sea. The person who saves the property of another from damage is entitled to a *salvage award*. While true salvage only pays if the action is voluntary and successful in saving the ship from endangerment by some hazard, the salvage clause in the hull policy refers to various documents or rules which in effect make the insurer liable for salvage charges if the *salvor* (the person doing the saving) is under contract and the mission is not successful.

- *Collision Liability Clause*—The collision liability clause is commonly referred to as the *running down clause* (RDC); this covers the liability of the vessel should it come into collision with another vessel, damaging the other vessel, its cargo, and freight, and be found at fault for the damage. Coverage is limited to the amount insured on the hull, but the amount is in addition to the hull insurance. The clause specifically excludes liability for loss or damage to piers, wharves, harbors, and other objects, removal of wreck, loss of life, personal injury, and illness (these are all recoverable under P&I policies).

Exclusions and Limitations.

- *War, Strikes, and Related Exclusions*—All consequences of hostilities or warlike actions, etc., are excluded as well as strikes, riots, malicious acts, or vandalism. These exclusions may, under certain circumstances, be waived or amended by the payment of an additional premium.
- *Change of Ownership*—Unless the company consents in writing, the policy is automatically terminated if a change in ownership occurs, a change is made in the flag of the vessel, or if the vessel is placed under new management (a transfer to a new firm or corporation and not internal management changes), or if "bare-boat" chartered (the charterer hires only the vessel itself, and provides the crew and all supplies necessary for operation).
- *Other Limitations*
  1. The policy will not pay claims for scraping or painting the vessel's bottom.
  2. Unrepaired damage is not covered if the vessel is subsequently a total loss. Otherwise, it is covered if it is demonstrated by the assured to have diminished the actual market value of the vessel at the end of the policy.
  3. If the contributory value (analogous to actual cash value) of the vessel determined, following a general average, is higher than the insured value, the policy will pay only in the proportion that the amount insured bears to the contributory value.

Deliberate Damage Pollution Hazard Clause. In August 1973 this clause was adopted and endorsed on all hull policies, usually at no additional premium. Briefly, this covers the physical loss of or destruction of the vessel ordered by governmental authorities to prevent or mitigate a pollution hazard or threat thereof resulting directly from damage to the vessel for which the insured is liable.

There are other sets of hull clauses used on certain types of vessels or risks, e.g., port risks, tugboats, builders' risks, and Great Lakes hulls.

Commercial Hull Hazards and Exposures

Hull underwriting focuses on three major areas:

1. The vessel
2. The ownership
3. The premium and loss experience

The Vessel Data should be gathered on the vessel including:

1. name (self-propelled or nonpropelled)
2. official registration number
3. type of vessel
4. year built
5. length
6. width
7. depth
8. tonnage—gross registered and net
9. material of hull
10. type of main engine
11. manufacturer of engine
12. age of engine
13. horsepower
14. trade (use) of vessel
15. navigation limits desired

Surveys. Most hulls are surveyed prior to acceptance to determine the soundness of the hull, the quality of the master and crew, the suitability of the vessel for the use intended and waters to be navigated, and the current value and replacement cost. An older vessel may be desirable from an underwriting standpoint, but this should be proven to the underwriter by a condition survey and a review of the vessel's past record. If not properly maintained, the hull and fittings will show serious deterioration. Of particular importance is the condition of the engines and other machinery. The broad coverage afforded by the Inchmaree clause has caused many underwriters to bear the expense of repairing worn-out machinery. When insuring vessels with obsolete machinery, the Inchmaree clause may be deleted or other coverage limitations made.

Navigation. Every vessel is designed and built to operate in a certain type of sea condition, ranging from the oceans of the world to quiet sheltered waters. A prudent vessel owner will not take unusual risks, but others take chances. Underwriters should know a vessel's limitations and provide in the policy only those navigation limits for which the vessel was designed. Surveyors can be very helpful here.

When a vessel trades far from the home port, the matter of adequate repair facilities and water and weather conditions along the route must be taken into consideration. For example, a large barge designed for ocean towing may not be manageable in the inland waterway.

Valuation, Undervaluation, Market Value, and Insured Value. In the hull insurance market, all losses are payable in full without depreciation for wear and tear but subject to a deductible. Insurers must therefore evaluate each hull, and charge premium commensurate with the exposure. Physical depreciation and obsolescence must also be considered.

It has always been difficult for underwriters and shipowners to arrive at a valuation of a vessel for insurance purposes. Reasonably high valuation is to be desired by underwriters so long as this is not so high as to seriously create any moral hazard in the risk.

When a wide discrepancy exists between insured value and replacement cost, one technique to assure adequate premium is to average the replacement cost and the insured value and base the premium on the average value, using the rate that would be used for a new vessel. Assume a 1960 sixty-five foot tug with a 750 horsepower engine:

Insured amount	$ 55,000
Replacement cost	225,000
Average	140,000

If the rate for new vessels costing $225,000 is 3 percent, this would produce a premium of $4,200 ($140,000 × .03).

Ownership and Vessel Management Data should be gathered on the ownership, including:

1. date vessel purchased
2. purchase price
3. cost of any improvements made in vessel
4. replacement cost (cost to build vessel today)

5. whether marine survey has been performed
6. whether vessel is subject to systematic inspection and overhaul; specify
7. how often vessel is drydocked
8. security arrangements during lay-up
9. assured's vessel management
   a. how long in business
   b. whether all of assured's vessels are insured
   c. experience and licenses of operators (captain, chief engineer, etc.)
10. financial strength of the owner

It has been estimated that as many as 80 percent of all hull losses can be directly attributed to human error. Consequently, ownership and vessel management are the most important underwriting factors.

The owner who is financially successful is likely to maintain his or her vessels in good repair, employ a competent and adequate crew, and be conscious of safety and loss control. On the other hand, the marginal owner, usually the one who does not have steady employment for a vessel, is likely to cut corners, take undue chances, and be a questionable risk.

A completed application supplemented by some authoritative information concerning the vessel owner's financial condition is required to assess the risk.

Premium and Loss Data The submission should include five years' premium and loss experience. The loss data should include the date, nature, and amount of all losses. Insured losses should also indicate the level of deductible that applied if any. The premium data should also indicate the form and amount of deductible.

It is particularly important that the loss data be sufficiently detailed to indicate the circumstances of each loss. In this manner, the effect of local conditions and the hazards of the assured's trading area can be properly evaluated.

Rating. Hull insurance is judgment rated. Most companies have average rate schedules that apply to certain types of hulls, local conditions, and trading areas. The physical characteristics of the vessel, the experience and business reputation of the owner, the ability and skill of the master and crew, and hazards of use and of the trading area have an effect on the rate. Local hazards are also important, including physical hazards such as strong currents, extraordinary tides, flooding, hurricanes, and ice. Other hazards include congestion, heavy occurrence of debris, floating logs, narrow channels, and bridge openings. Renewal rating is heavily dependent upon up-to-date premium and loss experience data.

Reinsurance. Virtually all types of reinsurance are used in hull insurance, protection and indemnity, and cargo insurance. Depending on the company and the size of the risk, the placement may be either on a treaty or facultative basis. Quota-share and excess-of-loss reinsurance are used to some degree.

UNDERWRITING VARIABLES—
PROTECTION AND INDEMNITY (P & I)

Protection and indemnity insurance covers the legal liability of the vessel owner for bodily injury, illness, death, and damage to property of others arising out of the ownership, use, and operation of the vessel. As in hull insurance, there are various types of P & I policies. These are marine contracts covering the liabilities of a vessel owner and maritime employer. Policies are specific in that they cover liabilities arising from named causes as opposed to "all causes."

Coverage

The major areas of coverage include the following:

- *Loss of Life and Bodily Injury.* This applies to persons injured aboard the vessel or elsewhere, including members of the crew if such injury is deemed to be the responsibility of the assured.
- *Property Damage.* This covers the owner's liability for loss of, or damage to, the property of others aboard the owner's vessel, fixed objects (such as piers, wharves, bridges, and other structures on the waterway), and other vessels and the property on board them (insofar as the collision clause in the hull policy does not apply).
- *Wreck Removal.* A vessel owner whose craft sinks in private waters or obstructs a channel or otherwise constitutes a menace to navigation may be faced with the legal responsibility of marking or removing the wreck, or of destroying the derelict. Insofar as the expense of this procedure constitutes a legal liability of the owner, it is covered by the P & I policy.
- *Sudden and Accidental Pollution.* Accidental discharge of fuel oil or other pollution-like substances into the water, or other violations that may be subject to fines or other penalties, unless as a result of the lack of due diligence on the owner's part, will be paid under the P & I policy.
- *Defense Costs.* The cost of litigation, including necessary bonds for release from court seizure, is covered whether against the vessel (*in rem*) or against the owner (*in personam*).

● *Fines.* The insured shipowner's or operator's liability for fines that may be imposed for violation of the law are also covered (sometimes subject to a deductible).

The major exclusions and limitations include the following:

1. Liability arising out of war risks.
2. Claims arising under any compensation act of a state or nation.
3. Liability which would be payable under the hull policy covering the vessel. This eliminates claims collectible under the collision liability section of the hull policy.
4. Loss or damage arising out of towage of another vessel, unless such towage is to assist a vessel in distress.

In underwriting hull business, a P & I limit equal to the hull value is referred to as the *primary coverage,* and for many years most vessel owners were content to insure only this limit on their hulls. More recently, this has proven inadequate, and often an owner will now require a liability limit well in excess of the value of the hull. This could range from $1 million on a small vessel to $100 million on large tonnage.

The amount over the hull value is often separately insured with another underwriter or underwriters as *excess P & I.* The placing of excess P & I is often done on a layered basis.

Analysis of Protection and Indemnity Hazards and Exposures

P & I Underwriting Information   When underwriting P & I the following data should be gathered:

Vessel
   ● Name of vessel
   ● Type of vessel
   ● Hull value of vessel
   ● Gross registered tonnage of vessel
   ● Latest survey of vessel

Operation
   ● Does vessel carry passengers? Maximum number carried?
   ● Does vessel carry cargo? What type carried?
   ● Is operation seasonal? If so, specify.
   ● Number of operating crew? Number of shifts.
   ● Area of navigation.
   ● Experience and capabilities of captains and crew.

Coverage

- Is pollution liability coverage desired?
- Is crew liability coverage desired?
- Is cargo liability coverage desired?
- Amount of P & I insurance desired?

Assured

- How many vessels owned by assured? Are all owned vessels insured?
- Subsidiary companies of assured.
- How long has assured been in business?
- How long has assured owned vessel?
- Financial condition of assured.

Premium and Loss Experience

- Gross premiums paid during last five years.
- Losses incurred during last five years.
- Claims paid during last five years.

Liability of the Shipowner An unacceptable hull risk will be an unacceptable P & I risk. The P & I policy agrees to pay for any liability imposed by law on the assured for death or personal injury. While liability to members of the public is a major exposure, there are additional responsibilities placed upon the assured for the crew, cargo aboard, and other property. The following is a brief outline of the shipowner's liability in these areas.

Seamen (Crew of the Vessel). There are three types of claims that can be made against the shipowner, each based on different grounds: wages, maintenance, and cure; unseaworthiness; the Jones Act.

- *Wages, Maintenance, and Cure*—A seaman who is injured or becomes ill while in the service of the ship is entitled to maintenance and cure, and to wages for the rest of the agreed-upon voyage or term of employment. Very briefly, the ship-owner is responsible for all costs due to injury or sickness during the seaman's employment, whether as a result of vessel duties or caused by willful misconduct such as intoxication, venereal disease, or deliberate disobedience of an order. Maintenance and cure must be furnished beyond the end of employment for a reasonable time thereafter, depending on the facts of the case. To collect something more, such as general damages for pain, suffering, and future disability, the seaman must establish fault (unseaworthiness of the vessel, or an unsafe place to work, etc.).
- *Unseaworthiness*—This is a general doctrine established by case law and not by statute. If unseaworthiness does cause an injury to a seaman, his or her right to recover general damages

is fixed, and it is not necessary to prove lack of due diligence or negligence. In effect, the law implies an absolute warranty of seaworthiness by the shipowner to the crew. Acceptance or recovery of maintenance and cure does not bar a suit for general damages on the ground of unseaworthiness, but items paid as wages, maintenance, and cure cannot be recovered again in the unseaworthiness action. In the event there is contributory negligence, the seaman is not barred from recovery, but contributory negligence may mitigate the damages otherwise allowable by prorating the total damage to the respective degree of fault.

- *Jones Act*—This gives seamen the right to recover general damages for injury or death caused by negligence of officers or crew of a ship in the course of employment. This may cover more than injuries on the ship as it could occur on ship's business ashore. As in unseaworthiness, contributory negligence and assumption of risk are not defenses but may be used to mitigate damages only. However, recovery for death, as well as personal injuries, is allowed.

Crew injuries generally make up the major portion of P & I losses. The record of crew claims and particularly outstanding claims should be examined carefully.

Stevedores, Longshoremen, and Harborworkers. The vessel owner's liability to stevedores, longshoremen, and harborworkers is confined to liability arising out of negligent acts. Those persons covered by the United States Longshoremen's and Harbor Workers' Compensation Act are persons temporarily employed aboard a vessel, and not part of the crew. Most P & I policies *exclude* this coverage, but it can be provided for an additional premium when necessary. This coverage is described in AIU 63.

Underwriting Other Marine Liabilities

Ship Repairer's Liability. Ship repair facilities of various sizes can be found at every port. It is a difficult class to underwrite, in many cases requiring extremely high limits of liability. As a result, coverage is often placed in several layers.

The policy covers the legal liability of the assured, as a ship repairer, for loss or damage to vessels and their equipment, while in the care, custody, or control of the assured. It also covers damage to other property caused by the vessel or the assured's employee while working on such vessel. The policy will respond only when liability has been determined by court judgments or by agreement between the parties with the written consent of the company.

Inasmuch as coverage is for legal liability, there are a number of important exclusions that help produce the true intent of the policy. These are:

- death or bodily injury
- liability asumed under contract
- liability arising out of work on any oil burning or oil tank vessel, or any vessel previously engaged in carrying explosive or flammable liquids, unless performed in accordance with NFPA or American Bureau of Shipping rules
- demurrage, loss of time, loss of freight, loss of charter, and/or similar expenses
- loss or damage recoverable under any other insurance
- loss or damage by collision, liability, tower's liability, or protection and indemnity liability arising out of the operation of any vessel owned or operated by the assured
- assured's own property
- vessels stored
- strikes, etc.
- loss or damage unless discovered within sixty days after delivery to the owners, or within sixty days after work is completed, whichever occurs first
- war risks

Underwriting should be extremely cautious. Financial reports, a physical inspection, and a fully completed application are recommended on any submission. Problems include substandard risks with high fire rates and yards using old or wooden drydocks.

Charterer's Liability. Even though the vessel owner provides captain and crew, the charterer assumes certain liabilities. A review of the charter agreement is essential to determine the extent of such liability. It will usually stipulate that the charterer will guarantee a safe berth during loading and unloading and that he or she will be liable for damage to the vessel sustained as a result of any loading or unloading operation. There are many different kinds of charter agreements, the basic forms of which are usually expanded by endorsement or addendum.

Terminal Operator's Liability. Operators of marine terminals require coverge for their legal liability to cargoes and vessels in their custody. A physical inspection of the premises and details of the principal commodities handled are essential underwriting prerequisites.

Stevedore's Liability. Stevedoring contractors must handle cargo in a businesslike manner, and they are liable for their own negligent acts and those of their employees. The larger operations usually have contracts with their employer (vessel owner), and this should be examined when assessing the exposure. Physical inspections are also desirable.

Wharfinger's Liability. Coverage is written on behalf of the owner of a pier, landing, or wharf, and insures his or her liability for loss or damage to vessels of others and their cargoes, while moored in his or her custody.

A physical inspection is desirable, and it is useful to know the type and average number of vessels handled in a year and at any one time. Policies are usually rated on either a gross receipts basis or on the number of vessels handled in a year.

UNDERWRITING VARIABLES—OCEAN CARGO

Insurable Interest

Ocean cargo insurance involves importing and exporting of goods or commodities. The first underwriting consideration is the extent of the assured's insurable interest in the goods during the ocean voyage. The answers to three questions will indicate the extent of insurable interest.

1. Are the exporters, as owners, responsible under contract for the goods during the ocean voyage?
2. Are the exporters responsible under contract for arranging the insurance even though they are not the owners during the ocean voyage?
3. If the buyers own the goods and bear the risk during the ocean voyage, do they collect their money on delivery of the goods or thereafter?

Terms of Sale The terms of sale indicate when, during a voyage, the title to the property passes from seller to buyer and therefore who has the insurable interest. They may also indicate who has the responsibility for the placing of marine insurance.

There are six major terms of sale. These six terms of sale illustrate the seller-buyer relationship in a continuum. Note that from ex point of origin through ex dock, the seller's responsibility increases while that of the buyer decreases. Also, the six terms progressively indicate the seller's increasing need for transportation insurance. For example, disregarding methods of payment, when the terms of sale are ex point of origin, the seller does not need transportation coverage since the buyer has the risk of ownership during the transportation of the goods. On the other hand, the seller risks financial loss up to the time goods are in the hands of the common carrier (e.g., steamship line) if the terms of sale are FAS; thus, as the terms of sale tend to lengthen the duration of the responsibility, the need for insurance coverage for the seller increases.

Ex Point of Origin (such as "Ex Factory," "Ex Warehouse," etc.) These terms require the seller to place the goods at the disposal of the buyer at the specified point of origin on the date or within a fixed period. The buyer must then take delivery at the agreed place and bear all future costs and risks. It should be emphasized that the goods are at the risk of the buyer from the time the buyer is obligated to take delivery, even though he or she may not actually take delivery at that time.

FOB (Free on Board) Here the seller is required to bear costs and charges and to assume risks until the goods are loaded on board a named carrier at a named point. This might be on board a railroad car at an inland point of departure or on board an ocean vessel at a port of shipment. Loss or damage to the shipment is borne by the seller until loaded at the point named and by the buyer after loading at that point. Insurance protection should be arranged accordingly. Actual transfer of interest is evidenced by the carrier furnishing a clean bill of lading or other transportation receipt.

In issuing bills of lading, notations are made of any defects in packaging or any apparent faults in the condition of the shipment. A bill of lading with such a notation is not "clean" and ordinarily will not meet the conditions required in a letter of credit used to finance overseas shipment.[4]

It should be noted that FOB sales terms, specifying named points beyond the seller's premises (for example, FOB vessel), place upon the seller the risks of transit until the title passes to the buyer at the point specified. He or she should obviously insure the cargo to the FOB point. In actual practice, however, FOB terms are often so loosely specified that it is not easily resolved whether the seller or the buyer should bear the risk of physical loss or damage. The seller is better advised in this case to provide his or her own insurance protection through the use of an FOB sales endorsement to the policy, rather than rely on the warehouse-to-warehouse coverage contained in the buyer's insurance policy. The FOB sales endorsement protects the seller from transit risks from the point of origin to the point at which title passes to the buyer.

When sales are made under letters of credit, payment thereunder normally cannot be made until an on-board bill of lading has been issued. If a loss or damage occurs before goods are loaded on board the ocean vessel, a clean on-board bill of lading will not be available and a letter of credit will not respond. This places a financial risk on the seller since he or she may not then be able to get the benefit of any insurance that the buyer may have arranged. Here again the seller should have his or her own insurance to provide full protection.

FAS (Free Along Side) (such as "FAS Vessel, Named Port of Shipment") These sales terms require the seller to place goods alongside the vessel or on the dock designated by the buyer and to be responsible for loss or damage up to that point. Insurance for the ocean voyage is ordinarily placed by the buyer, but the seller should protect himself or herself with an FOB sales endorsement, as already described, for risks prior to the transfer of title.

C&F (Cost & Freight), Named Point of Destination Under these terms the seller's price includes the cost of transportation to the named point but does not include the cost of insurance for the entire trip. Insurance under these terms is the responsibility of the buyer. The seller is responsible for loss or damage until the goods enter the custody of the ocean carrier or, if an on-board bill of lading is required, when the goods are actually delivered on board. Here again the seller needs insurance protection to that point at which his or her responsibility for loss or damage ceases.

CIF (Cost, Insurance and Freight), Named Point of Destination Under these terms the selling price includes the cost of the goods, marine insurance, and transportation charges to the named point of destination. The seller is responsible for loss or damage until the goods have been delivered to the point of destination, which may be a foreign country.

In CIF sales, the seller is obligated to provide and pay for marine insurance and to provide war risk insurance as obtainable in the market at the time of shipment, the cost of war risks insurance being borne by the buyer. The seller and buyer should be in clear agreement on this point since in time of war or crisis the cost of war risks insurance may change rapidly. It is desirable that the goods be insured against both marine and war risks with the same underwriter so that there can be the least possibility of dispute arising as to the cause of loss, as in the case of missing vessels and, to a lesser degree, wartime collisions.

Ex Dock, Named Port of Importation This term is more common to U.S. import practice than to export practice, where it is seldom used. The seller's price includes the cost of the goods and all additional charges necessary to put them on the dock at the named port of importation, with import duty paid. The seller is then obligated to provide and pay for marine insurance and, in the absence of specific agreement otherwise, war risks insurance. The seller is responsible for any loss or damage, or both, until the expiration of the free time allowed on the dock at named port of importation. Otherwise the comments under CIF terms apply here as well.

Methods of Payment

Methods of payment can vary in foreign trade. These include the following methods.

Cash in Advance   This is rather harsh and is generally required only when the prospective customer is not too well known to the manufacturer and when the order embraces the custom manufacture of a special type of goods not readily marketed. In a transaction of this kind on FOB terms, the American manufacturer, having been paid in advance, has no interest in the goods once they are shipped. Similarly, some goods are sold on terms that provide for cash payment against the shipping documents at time of shipment.

Open Account   Open account is the opposite of the cash-in-advance transaction. Sales in foreign trade on open account are usually made only to very old and reliable customers and, as a rule, only in connection with consumer goods that can readily be disposed of. It is a charge account, the buyer arranging settlement with the seller at regularly agreed intervals, monthly or quarterly. In such cases, when the terms of sale are FOB, the seller still has at least a financial interest in the goods that should be protected with insurance. If a large shipment is lost en route, the buyer may be unable to settle with the seller at the agreed time.

Draft   The draft, payable either on presentation *(sight draft)* or at some specified future date *(time draft)* such as 30, 60, or 90 days from the date of presentation, is widely used in peacetime. In a transaction of this kind, the seller gathers together the shipping documents, which usually consist of an invoice showing the kind and value of the goods making up the shipment, a bill of lading which is evidence of the fact that the goods are in the hands of a transportation company and have actually been shipped, and an insurance policy or certificate insuring the shipment. He or she then draws a draft on the customer for the amount of the transaction and takes all these documents, including the draft, to his or her bank, where he or she sells—or discounts—the draft. Therefore, in consideration of a discount charge, the bank uses its money to finance the shipment. The shipper is immediately paid and does not have working capital tied up awaiting payment from the consignee. However, the bank buys the draft with the stipulation that if the consignee refuses to pay, the American bank still has recourse against the seller. So, until the buyer pays the draft the seller has a risk that should be insured. Banks usually insist on the customer furnishing an insurance policy or certificate.

Letter of Credit   A letter of credit is a method widely used for both exports and imports. When a letter of credit is opened covering export shipments, the foreign purchaser goes to a bank and arranges with it to have that bank's correspondent bank in the United States open a credit in favor of the American seller. The so-called letter of credit that the seller receives in confirmation of the credit specifies what must be done to avail himself or herself of the credit. If the terms of sale are FOB, the seller is not obliged to furnish an insurance policy or certificate unless the credit specifically says so. If the letter of credit provides for an insurance certificate or policy, that insurance certificate or policy, insofar as the amount of insurance and risks insured are concerned, must be exactly as called for. Most letters of credit have a termination date, and some of them have lapsed before corrections could be made to improperly drawn insurance documents. At the time the exporter comes to use the credit, he or she goes through the same procedure as though drawing a sight draft on the consignee, and presents the documents to the American bank that has issued the credit. He or she immediately receives money from this bank and if the letter of credit is properly drawn, there is no recourse against him or her. Most American banks in handling letters of credit for their foreign correspondents prefer to see the credit provided for American insurance, particularly if the transaction is a large one.

Ocean Carrier's Liability

The liability of the ocean carrier is an important underwriting consideration since it indicates the amount of subrogation that may be available if the coverage is written. Producers should point out to insureds with goods involved in ocean carriage that although the Carriage of Goods by Sea Act of 1936 regulates the operations of carriers in numerous ways, it exempts the carrier and the ship from liability for loss due to specifically designated causes. Significant among these exemptions from liability are:

- act, neglect, or default of the master, mariners, pilot, or the servants of the carrier in the navigation or in the management of the ship.
- fire, unless caused by the actual fault or privity (private knowledge) of the carrier.
- perils, dangers, and accidents of the sea or other navigable waters.
- act of God.

- act of war.
- act of public enemies.
- strikes, riots, and civil commotions.

All of these are insurable perils; therefore, marine insurance on the goods is a way to protect the cargo owner against perils for which the carrier is not liable.

Types of Coverage

There are two general types of cargo policies, the *voyage policy* and the *open policy*. The voyage policy is used to arrange specific insurance as it is needed, and is purchased by individuals not regularly engaged in foreign trade. The greater volume of business is written under open policies. These are insurance contracts that remain in force until canceled and under which individual successive shipments are declared or reported. The open policy saves time and expense for all concerned, and the shipper gains many advantages from its use. The shipper has automatic protection (up to the maximum limits stated in the policy) from the time shipments leave the warehouse at the place named in the policy for the commencement of transit. The policyholder warrants that shipments will be declared as soon as practicable, but unintentional failure to report will not void the insurance, since the goods are "held covered," subject to policy conditions.

Under an open policy the shipper has prior knowledge of the rate of premium that will be charged and thus can be certain of the cost. Finally, the use of the open policy creates a business relationship that may exist over a long period of time. This permits the insurer to learn the special requirements of its assureds and to provide them with individualized protection, tailor made to fit the specific situation. This may be an important factor in loss adjustments at out-of-the-way ports around the world or in overcoming problems peculiar to a given commodity.

From the underwriter's standpoint, the use of open policies represents a means for the distribution of risk covering all shipments with no adverse selection.

There are three methods of reporting shipments under open policies: the *short form declaration*, the *bordereau form*, and the *special marine policy*. In reporting shipments under an open cargo policy, either the declaration or bordereau form is used (1) when the shipper is the only party with an insurable interest as might be the case if shipper "X" consigns the goods to himself or herself at the overseas branch; (2) when the consignee does not require evidence of insurance;

or (3) when insuring imports, for then no evidence of insurance is normally required.

In most cases, the exporter must furnish evidence of insurance to his or her customer, to banks, or to other third parties, in order to permit the collection of claims abroad. This calls for use of a *special marine policy* (or "certificate" as it is sometimes called) containing information similar to that shown on the declaration form. In addition, it calls for the marks and numbers of the shipment and the name of the party to whom loss shall be payable (usually the assured "or order," thus making the instrument negotiable upon endorsement by the assured). Some of these provisions are standard clauses and are incorporated by reference only, while others are specific and apply to the individual shipment in question.

It should be emphasized that the special marine policy, being negotiable, stands on its own feet without reference to the open policy. In most instances its terms and conditions will be identical with the provisions of the open policy under which it was issued, but if for any reason they are not, whether by intention or through error, the special policy will govern. It is necessary that this be so, for in the mechanics of foreign trade, the policy passes from hand to hand, and the party of title in the event of a loss would be the holder of an instrument that was not what it was purported to be. Usually, exporters who have open cargo policies have the privilege of issuing their own special marine policies. A copy of each policy issued is sent to the underwriter as a report of shipment.

It should be noted that a new cargo policy was devised by some groups in 1983. However, at the time of this writing, AIMU was still using the previous form and the descriptions in this book are based on that form.

Coverage Provisions of the Open Ocean Cargo Policy

Valuation This is a valued contract. It should reflect the "landed value" or value of the goods when delivered to the consignee. This is done by combining the invoice value, all known costs of handling and transportation, plus a percentage of this total to arrive at the insured value on which the premium is charged. The following is an example.

1. "Invoice value"—The price of the goods as shown on the invoice.
2. "Freight and all other charges"—This includes freight, handling, packing, storage, or any other charges specifically known before shipment. The approximate charge for insuring the shipment is also usually included.

3. "Plus percent advance"—This amount is determined by taking a percentage (usually 10 percent)) of the total of the first two items. The amount serves to provide a "cushion" to absorb expenses unknown at the time the shipment is declared. Examples are unexpected freight, storage or duty charges, or perhaps even an increase in the market price of the goods being shipped. If a shipment is underinsured (i.e., the amount insured does not at least equal the "landed value" of the goods), the shipper will have to bear part of the loss in case of a total loss, a partial loss, or a general average.

In declaring or reporting a shipment under the usual valuation clause which reads "valued premium included at invoice, plus freight and charges, plus 10 percent," the following method is usually used:

Invoice value	$5,000.00
Freight and all other charges (excluding insurance)	68.32
	$5,068.32
Premium on $5,068.32 at 0.625 (Marine and war rate)	31.68*
	$5,100.00
Plus 10% advance	510.00
Insured value—"Amount of Marine Insurance"	$5,610.00

*With the additional 10 percent value, the final premium will be $35.06 ($5,610 × 0.625 = $35.06).

A clause may sometimes be used to provide that if insurance is declared prior to shipment or prior to known or reported loss, the valuation shall be in the amount of the declaration. This clause assures maximum flexibility in meeting the needs of letters of credit or other financial requirements. Shipments not so declared are valued as provided by the formula contained in the valuation clause. At times of fluctuating values, importers dealing in such raw commodities as cotton, rubber, sugar, coffee, burlap, etc., may wish to be protected for an increase in value during the voyage. This can be accomplished by the use of an *increased value* clause. Under this clause, the premium is paid and losses are adjusted on the basis of peak value reached while the shipment is in transit. In certain trades, special valuation clauses may have become standardized by long usage and should be incorporated in the open policy accordingly.

Duration of Coverage—Marine Extension Clauses Many years ago the marine policy covered only from the time the goods were actually loaded on board the ocean vessel at the port of shipment until they were "discharged and safely landed" at the port of destination. This was later extended by adding the words "including transit by craft, raft and/or lighter to and from the vessel."

More recently, the *warehouse-to-warehouse* clause was instituted. Under this clause, the risks covered by the policy attach from the time goods leave the warehouse for commencement of transit, and continue to destination or until the expiration of fifteen days (thirty days if destination is outside the limits of the port), whichever shall occur first. In case of delay in excess of the time limit specified, and if the delay arises from circumstances beyond his or her control, the assured is "held covered" if prompt notice is given and additional premium is paid.

A growing demand for extensions of cover during World War II led underwriters to adopt the *marine extension clauses (MEC)* in 1942. This extension, which *supersedes* the aforementioned warehouse-to-warehouse clause, is now found in practically all open cargo policies.

In effect, the MEC adds no perils whatsoever. It covers without notice by the assured, or further additional premium, those situations in the warehouse-to-warehouse clause that otherwise require separate reports and premium. It broadens the warehouse-to-warehouse coverage by eliminating both the requirement that ordinary course of transit be maintained and the fifteen- or thirty-day time limit at destination. Moreover, continuation of coverage is provided when certain conditions necessitate discharge of goods from vessel at a port other than the original destination. It should be emphasized that the MEC covers only interruption or suspension of transit *beyond the control of the assured*.

The scope of insurance has thus been broadened from waterborne only to full warehouse-to-warehouse protection. Underwriters must be notified and additional coverage secured only if interruption of transit within the assured's control is contemplated. Such situations will occur at times, and shippers should fully inform their insurance agents or brokers of their needs in this respect in order that coverage may be extended as necessary.

Other Clauses

Attachment and Termination. The open policy covers all shipments made on or after the date of attachment until the policy is canceled. Cancellation may be made upon thirty days' notice by either the company or the assured. War risks and SR&CC (strikes, riots and civil commotions) coverage may be canceled by forty-eight hours' notice. Cancellation does not affect coverage on any shipment already in transit.

Geographical Limits. The description of voyages covered may vary from policy to policy according to the requirements of the assured. In many policies the statement will be so broad as to take in any voyage, as for example, a clause that reads "at and from Cleveland, Ohio, via ports and/or places in the United States to ports and/or places in the world." Today most insurance on cargo shipments is written with warehouse-to-warehouse coverage giving continuous protection in ordinary course of transit.

Conveyances. The policy covers shipments going by metal, self-propelled vessels and connecting conveyances, by air, and by mail, including parcel post. Barges or sailing vessels are excluded, except as connecting conveyances, because of their inherent hazards. So are mail shipments wholly within the continental U.S. and Canada since they are properly a subject for inland marine coverage.

Limits of Liability. The policy provides for a single overall limit of liability applying aboard any one vessel and connecting conveyance, or in any one place at any one time. Customarily there are lower sub-limits with respect to (1) shipments "on deck" of any one vessel subject to on deck bills of lading, (2) shipments in any one aircraft or connecting conveyance, and (3) any one mail or parcel post package. Limits should be high enough to provide a reasonable safety factor; but in no event should they be excessive, for this can result in the insurance company placing unneeded reinsurance.

Merchandise shipped "on deck" the ocean vessel in containers (intermodal, over the road, or similar type) are insured subject to the "under deck" limits and conditions. However, the merchandise involved must be subject to an under deck or an "optional" under deck/on deck bill of lading.

Accumulation Clause. This clause relates to the limits of liability and is designed to protect the assured against events he or she cannot reasonably be expected to foresee or control. An example would be the accumulation of two separate shipments in one pier warehouse whose combined value exceeds the applicable policy limit. In that event the assured is held covered for the full amount at risk, but in no event for more than *twice* the applicable limit.

Full Value Reporting Clause. Under the provisions of the full value reporting clause, the underwriter would receive premium on the full amount at risk even if it should exceed the applicable limit of liability. However, a loss would be paid only up to that stated limit in the policy.

The Rate Schedule Every open policy contains one or more rate pages. The rate schedule is usually drafted with separate rates for each country to which the assured has indicated that goods will be shipped. Some policies will have more than one column of rates applying to different insuring conditions, different types of commodity, or packaging, or different conveyances. When conditions in a certain quarter of the world are so uncertain and so hazardous that underwriters cannot set a rate until the time of shipment, the destination may be named; but instead of quoting a rate, the schedule will read "to be named" or "subject to special quotation."

The statements at the end of the schedule take care of situations not otherwise provided for, such as "shipments by other vessels and other voyages held covered at rates to be named at time of shipment." The schedule rates apply to shipments on board what are known as *approved* vessels. Goods on "other" vessels—that is, those that do not meet certain standards of age, size, etc.—will be subject to specially named rates. In practice, this means the application to the regular marine rate of a "steamer additional" or "vessel penalty" established for each such vessel. *Other voyages* are those to destinations not named in the schedule. There may also be statements providing that "on deck" shipments will be held covered at rates to be named, that there is a minimum premium per policy or per shipment, and that the rate schedule is subject to change on thirty days' notice. Cargo insurance is judgment rated, with the particular rate developed by considering the factors of the insured, commodity, packing, vessel, port, and prior experience.

Types of Losses Losses are of two types—total and partial. In marine insurance a total loss may be "actual" or "constructive." An *actual total loss* occurs when the goods are destroyed, when the assured is permanently deprived of their possession, or when they arrive so damaged as to cease to be a thing of the kind insured. Examples of this last item, which is spoken of as a "loss of specie," are cement arriving as rock, or textiles as rags. Disasters likely to give rise to total loss include fire, sinking, or stranding of the vessel, collision, and loss overboard in the course of loading or discharge. A *constructive total loss* occurs when the expense of recovering or repairing the goods would exceed their value after this expenditure has been incurred.

Partial losses in ocean marine insurance are termed *average*. Average is of two types, "particular" and "general." *Particular average* refers to a partial loss that falls upon a single interest, such as the owner of a specific cargo shipment. *General average* is a partial loss that affects all cargo interests on board a vessel, as well as the ship itself.

Most marine losses are actual total losses or particular average. General average often means the voluntary destruction by the shipmaster of part of the vessel or part or all of its cargo, or the deliberate expenditure of funds in time of grave peril. Examples are the expense of towing to port a ship that has lost its rudder, or the expense of cargo jettisoned to correct an increasing "list." This general average sacrifice, as it is known, *must be successful* in saving the venture. From the most ancient times, the maritime laws of all trading nations have held that such a sacrifice shall be borne by all for whose benefit the sacrifice was made and not alone by the interest sacrificed.

Perils Clause   A typical perils clause reads as follows:

> Touching the adventures and perils which this Company is contented to bear, and takes upon itself, they are of the seas, fires, assailing thieves, jettisons, barratry of the master and mariners, and all other like perils, losses and misfortunes (illicit or contraband trade excepted in all cases), that have or shall come to the hurt, detriment or damage of the said goods and merchandise, or any part thereof, except as may be otherwise provided for herein or endorsed hereon.

Total losses caused by these perils are covered in full. The extent of coverage in the event of *partial* loss is determined by the average terms.

Average Terms   The perils specified by the policy govern the *nature* of loss or damage recoverable whereas the average terms or insuring conditions govern the *extent* of coverage. In other words, the terms or conditions either restrict or broaden the coverage of the five basic perils previously discussed—perils of the seas, fire, assailing thieves, jettison, and barratry. If the average terms say, in effect, that partial losses will not be paid except under certain limited circumstances, then the coverage is restricted. If the insuring conditions say, in effect, that all losses will be paid in full, including those caused by additional perils named therein, then the coverage is broadened. It must be emphasized that average terms usually apply only to the perils clause; when a loss is caused by an "additional" peril, as appearing in one of the policy's standard clauses, the average terms are inapplicable. Examples of typical average terms are given in Exhibit 11-1.

Exhibit 11-2 provides a concise summary of the perils clause and average conditions.

Other Standard Policy Coverages   Although the perils clause and average terms have been discussed, there are still other coverages common to all open policies. Taking the form of specific clauses, the additional perils covered represent extensions to the basic protection of

Exhibit 11-1
Examples of Average Terms

TLO	This insurance is against the risk of total and constructive total loss only.
FPA (American Conditions)	Free of particular average unless caused by the vessel being stranded, sunk, burnt, on fire, or in collision.
FPA (English Conditions)	Free of particular average, unless the vessel be stranded, sunk, burnt, on fire, or in collision.
With Average (3 percent)	"To pay Particular Average if amounting to 3 percent unless General, or the vessel be stranded, sunk, burnt, on fire or in collision."
WA Irrespective of Percentage	"To pay average irrespective of percentage."
Additional Perils	"To pay average irrespective of percentage including breakage, fresh water damage, and loss by nondelivery of one or more entire shipping packages."
All Risks	"To cover against all risks of physical loss or damage from any external cause irrespective of percentage, but excluding, nevertheless, the risks of war, strikes, riots, seizure, detention and other risks excluded by the FC&S (free of capture and seizure) warranty and the SR&CC (strikes, riots and civil commotions) warranty in this policy, excepting to the extent that such risks are specifically covered by endorsement."

the perils clause. As a rule they are not affected by the average terms but rather stand on their own.

The Inchmaree Clause. The Inchmaree clause extends the policy to cover loss resulting from a latent defect of the carrying vessel's hull or machinery. Defined as a defect that is not discoverable by due diligence, latent defect is not by law recoverable from the vessel owner, and the Inchmaree clause thus plugs a gap that would otherwise exist in complete protection. Loss resulting from errors of navigation or management of the vessel by the master or the crew, and for which the vessel owner is likewise relieved of liability by law, is also covered by the Inchmaree clause.

Exhibit 11-2
A Summary of the Perils Clause and Average Conditions

A. The Perils Clause—Perils of the Seas, Fire, Assailing Thieves, Jettison, Barratry

B. Average Conditions:

	More Limited than Perils Clause				Equal to Perils Clause	Broader than Perils Clause	
	Total Loss Only (TLO)†	FPA American Conditions (FPAAC)	FPA English Conditions (FPAEC)	With Average 3 percent	Average Irrespective of Percentage	Average Irrespective plus Named Perils	All Risks
Coverage for Total Losses	Basic perils	Basic perils	Basic perils	Basic perils	Basic perils	Basic perils and others named	However caused except those excluded
Coverage for Partial Losses	No coverage	Caused by stranding, sinking, burning, on fire, in collision with another vessel	If the vessel be stranded, sunk, burnt, on fire, in collision with another vessel	Amounting to 3% Under 3% only if vessel be stranded, sunk, burnt, on fire, in collision with another vessel	Basic perils	Basic perils and others named	However caused except those excluded

† Rarely written on cargo.

Explosion and Fumigation. The *explosion* clause broadens the coverage to include explosion, however caused, except when caused by war perils. The *fumigation* clause provides for direct loss or damage to the insured goods caused by fumigation of the vessel.

Other Coverage Clauses. When the goods insured are on land in due course of overseas transit, the *shore* clause extends the basic perils to include the risks of collision, derailment, overturn, sprinkler leakage, windstorm, earthquake, flood, and collapse of docks or wharves. If the policy is written on an "all-risks" basis, the shore clause is superseded and essentially inapplicable. This is also true of the *packages lost in loading* clause which provides for total loss of a package during loading, transshipment, or discharge. Losses caused by governmental authorities acting to prevent pollution hazards are covered by the *deliberate damage—pollution hazard* clause, provided the property insured is on a waterborne conveyance and the accident creating the situation that required such action would have resulted in a recoverable claim under the policy.

Types of Losses Excluded Excluded from the basic marine cargo policy are war risks, strikes, riots, civil commotion, and radioactive contamination or nuclear incidents within the United States or its territories. Strikes and riots are usually added by endorsement or included with war risks and covered by a separate policy. Also excluded are losses arising from delay. Inherent vice is an implied exclusion. The underwriter is not liable for losses that arise as a result of the natural characteristics of the property insured. Usually, war risks, strikes, riots, and civil commotion are excluded from policy coverage. This is accomplished by the free of capture and seizure (FC&S) and the strikes, riots and civil commotions (SR&CC) clauses which are known as the *paramount warranties* because of the statement which precedes them:

> The following warranties shall be paramount and shall not be modified or superseded by any other provision included herein or stamped or endorsed hereon unless such other provision refers specifically to the risks excluded by these warranties and expressly assumes the said risks.

War Risks War risks are usually covered under a separate policy. The coverage is excluded from the basic open ocean cargo policy by the FC&S clause. The war risks policy covers risks of capture and seizure, destruction or damage by warlike operations in prosecution of hostilities, civil wars, insurrections, or in the application of sanctions under international agreements. Delay or loss of market is excluded. Also excluded is loss or expense arising from detainments, nationalization by the government to or from which the goods are insured, or seizure under quarantine or customs regulations.

War Risks Coverage. War risks insurance attaches as goods are first loaded on board an overseas vessel at the port of shipment, and it ceases to attach as goods are landed at the final port of discharge or on expiration of fifteen days from arrival of the overseas vessel, whichever occurs first. It includes transshipment and intermediate overland transit to an on-carrying overseas vessel, if any, but in no case for more than fifteen days counting from midnight of the day of arrival of the overseas vessel at the final port of discharge. If in transshipment, the fifteen-day period is exceeded, the insurance reattaches as the interest is loaded on the on-carrying vessel. If the voyage is terminated and the goods are discharged at other than the intended port, such port becomes the final port of discharge. The war risks policy is subject to forty-eight hours' cancellation by either party, but it cannot be canceled on shipments upon which insurance has already attached.

It is recommended that the war risks policy be placed with the same underwriter that has the open cargo policy. This prevents possible questions as to liability in the case of a missing vessel or where there may be doubt as to the real cause of loss.

War Risks Rates. Rates for the war risks policy include a factor for SR&CC coverage. Unlike the regular cargo marine rate, war risks rates are *not* attached as a schedule to the open policy; rather they are named only at time of shipment. Primarily this is done because of unstable world conditions, and the rates tend to fluctuate sometimes rather drastically and often with very short intervals.

War risks rates are published for underwriters by the American Cargo War Risk Reinsurance Exchange. The new rates come in a series of letters, and they designate only changes in rates for shipments to specific countries that are superseding previous letters. The rates for a particular country stand until superseded.

Underwriting Ocean Cargo Policies

Ocean Cargo Hazards and Exposures

Assured. Of utmost importance is the quality of the assured and his or her business reputation. He or she must have as a primary interest the safe arrival of the product at destination. An assured who cuts corners in packing and shipping practices cannot be profitably underwritten.

Commodity. Underwriters are asked to insure a wide variety of commodities. Commodities such as ingots of pig iron offer a very low susceptibility to loss or damage while others, such as fine glassware and china, are very easily damaged. Shipments of fishmeal or burlap can present extraordinary fire hazards. Auto parts and liquor are very attractive to thieves. Any bulk shipment or any shipment of raw materials will present its own unique problems. An unusual or sophisticated manufactured product will require a detailed explanation of the effects which its special characteristics will produce in the event of loss. There are chemicals which become worthless if they are exposed to air. There are electronic devices which require expensive recalibration in the event of the slightest damage. A few commodities and special hazards associated with them are shown in Exhibit 11-3.

In many cases common sense or past experience will indicate what could happen to a particular commodity, but when not familiar with the merchandise, it is always a good idea to have a survey made or at least discuss it with an expert.

Packing. Merchandise moving to a foreign destination is exposed to a multitude of hazards, including loading on and unloading from at least two land carriers and the overseas vessel, fresh water from rain and ship's sweat, salt water during heavy weather, and thieves who wait at every stop along the way. In order to withstand these perils, the merchandise must be well packed, braced and cushioned, protected against moisture, and difficult to pilfer. Blind markings should be used since a description of the contents only serves to label the package for the prospective thief. Shipments in domestic packing will not normally be sufficiently protected to withstand such hazards.

Excluding bulk shipments, much of today's cargo is shipped in large enclosed metal boxes known as *containers*. These are similar to the semi-trailers seen on the road every day without the chassis. They can be "stuffed" at the original point of shipment and unloaded at destination, thus eliminating extra handling at the port. Much of the most recent tonnage has been vessels constructed solely to transport containers.

Containerization may be an answer to pilferage and fresh water damage provided the container is watertight and carries the merchandise warehouse to warehouse. Since at least one-third of containers is shipped on deck, however, the risk of exposure to heavy weather and washing overboard is greatly increased. The threat of a hijack of an entire shipment and the danger of breakage due to shifting of cargo within the container are additional serious perils.

Still more recently there has been another module for transporting cargoes known as *LASH (lighter aboard ship), SEABEE, BACAT (Barge Aboard Catamaran)* and *FLASH (Feeder-LASH)* barges. These are all part of a group known as Barge-on-Board. (The FLASH is somewhat different in that it is used to feed the LASH vehicles.) As the

Exhibit 11-3
Some Commodity Characteristics

Automobiles	Marring, denting, and scratching
Auto parts	Pilferage and theft in certain areas of the world where new cars are not readily available
Canned goods	Rusting, denting, and theft
Chemicals in paper bags	Shortage and contamination from torn bags
Fishmeal	Highly susceptible to heating damage and fire
Fine arts	Handling damage and theft
Fresh fruit	Extremely sensitive to temperature change and difficult to keep from spoiling
Glass	Breakage and staining
Grain	Shortage and weevil damage
Household effects	Breakage, marring, chipping, scratching, shortage, and water damage
Liquids in bulk	Leakage, shortage, and contamination
Lumber (cut)	Shortage, staining, and handling damage
Machinery	Rust and breakage of parts
Paper in rolls	Chafing, cutting, and water damage
Rags	Fire and shortage
Refrigerators and stoves	Marring, scratching, chipping, and denting
Scrap metals	Alleged shortage due to difference in scale weights at origin and destination
Steel products	Rusting, bending, and twisting
Television sets	Breakage of tubes
Textiles	Hook damage, theft, and water damage

name implies, these are specially constructed barges that can be loaded at inland river ports, towed to a seaport, and loaded aboard vessels specially constructed for this trade. At an overseas port, they are off-loaded and towed or pushed to an inland destination. Meanwhile the "mother ship" is taking aboard other barges that have been previously loaded for the return trip. This method cuts the vessel's time in port from several days to several hours (ships do not make money in port). Theft and pilferage losses are reduced because of the heavy hatch covers. There is a chance of water damage, however. They also reduce congestion in many ports since the mother ship does not have to be berthed.

In order to underwrite a marine cargo risk, it is necessary that a complete description of the packing be received, along with complete details as to containers if shipments are containerized. Another type of vehicle used to speed loading and unloading is called the *Ro-Ro* (Roll on, Roll off). These are wheeled vehicles driven onto and off the specially designed vessels. They enable a shipper to load the cargo at its plant, move it to a pier, drive it onto a ship, and then drive it off at the destination. The reduction in cargo handling speeds up the loading process and reduces the theft and pilferage exposure. In addition, these can reduce port congestion, since special cargo handling equipment is not required. Because of the relative newness of the Ro-Ro, careful selection of a proper Ro-Ro carrier is requried.

Stowage Closely related to the packing and containerization is the stowage of the cargo. As mentioned, some cargo is usually shipped on the deck in addition to that under deck. Cargo shipped on deck should be carefully secured to avoid washing overboard and should be that which can withstand the "on deck" weathering. The underwriter should also get details of the methods of loading and unloading. Are surveys made during each to evaluate damage? The unloading survey is often called an *outturn survey.*

Vessel. If other than regular steamship lines are used, the full particulars of the type of vessel or craft and its ownership are of major importance. Vessels over twenty years of age or under 1,000 net tons are usually unattractive from an underwriting standpoint and require higher rates, along with scaled down limits of insurance. Many of the under-tonnage vessels of the world trade from southern U.S. ports throughout the Caribbean. Vessels such as these usually require *steamer additionals,* which are additional rates assessed against vessels that are over twenty years of age or under 1,000 net tons or do not meet certain other requirements. The experience of the ships owners is also an important consideration. Experience is quite impor-tant in shipping.

Season. If shipments are seasonal, the hazards may be increased. For example, winter shipments of steel sheet or canned goods from northern ports to tropical destinations can be expected to suffer from sweat damage. Certain areas of the world are subject to definite rainy seasons. Cargo moving through such ports during this season is likely to suffer some water damage.

Voyage. Navigation hazards vary from geographical trade to trade, as do port conditions which vary throughout the world. If the majority of the assured's shipments flow through ports in which lighters (described earlier) are employed, there is a far greater hazard than in ports where cargo is unloaded directly to the pier. Certain ports are extremely congested, with little protection against the elements and long delays in customs, where thievery is prevalent. Destinations in the interior of certain primitive areas present extremely difficult inland transit exposures. The quality of the connecting land transit also should be considered.

Past Experience. The prospective assured's past experience will be one of the prime factors in determining the desirability of a new cargo account and its rate level. It will attest to the adequacy of previous rates and show clearly the pattern of the assured's losses. Ideally, an exhibit of previous losses should be broken down to show the separation between PA (particular average) and FPA (free of particular average) losses. Basically PA losses are the preventable losses attributable directly to the nature of the assured's product, packing, shipping practices, etc. FPA losses are those caused by major perils over which the assured has no control.

It should be noted that poor experience does not necessarily lead to a declination of the risk. Analysis of the loss records may indicate that there are solutions to the assured's problems, such as better packing, change of carrier, or different average terms. In addition, the losses may be specific to a certain type of commodity and the underwriter could suggest measures to reduce losses to that commodity. It may also be that the commodity is no longer carried.

Experience for the Class. The underwriting data applicable to a particular risk can also be viewed in the light of the underwriter's own statistics and experience with like risks in similar trades under similar conditions. At this point it can often be determined if a new offering is better or worse than the average in its class.

Insurance. The perils insured against should be examined in the light of the commodities to be insured and their susceptibilities. Additionally, the capacity required by the shipper to insure the cargo might also be a consideration with some insureds and some commodities.

Ocean Cargo Rating Ocean cargo insurance rating is not regulated and is based upon an evaluation of underwriting information on the specific offering and the insuring conditions requested. There are certain factors that will affect the rate level.

Average Terms. The extent of coverage provided in the average terms will have a great bearing on the rate level of the policy. If coverage is confined to FPA perils, one rate level would apply. If coverage is against "all-risks," the rate will be sufficiently higher to compensate for the variety of additional perils to which the goods are exposed.

FPA Experience. Practically all shipments are exposed to the same basic perils. These include sinking, stranding, collision of vessels, and fire. Over a period of years statistics have enabled underwriters to accurately establish base FPA rates for all major trades.

PA Experience. In addition to the base FPA rate, each assured must also pay sufficient premium to cover those losses that are directly attributable to his or her own product. It is in the area of PA losses that experience rating is most important. The assured's rate level must be such that the FPA portion is not needed to pay for the assured's preventable losses.

Similar Commodities. Certain commodities such as wool, burlap, coffee, and similar items present the same exposures regardless of the buyer or seller. The experience of the commodity as a whole will dictate the rate level that will apply.

World Conditions. Political unrest and poor economic conditions can develop suddenly in certain areas of the world. Rates and insuring conditions must reflect these changes as they occur.

Ocean Cargo Loss Control

It has been estimated that almost 70 percent of ocean cargo losses are preventable. This places great importance upon proper loss control techniques. Packaging, packing, preparation, and marking can have considerable influence on losses. The type of container utilized can also minimize loss.

Loss control surveys include packing surveys, loading surveys, and outturn surveys. The significance of preventable losses can be seen in Exhibit 11-4, which is based on one company's experience. Note that about 70 percent of the losses are preventable.

Theft, Pilferage, and Nondelivery It has been estimated that one-third to one-half of preventable losses are attributable to theft,

Exhibit 11-4
Ocean Cargo Losses*

	Percent of all losses				
CAUSE OF LOSS	1961-65	1966-70	1971-75	1973-77	1975-79
Fortuitous Losses Sinking, Strandings, Fires, Collisions, Sea Water & Heavy Weather	26%	19%	26%	30%	30%
Preventable Losses	74%	81%	74%	70%	70%
PREVENTABLE LOSSES BY CATEGORY:					
Theft Group Theft, Pilferage and Non-Delivery	28%	32%	25%	21%	21%
Handling & Stowage Container Damage including Breakage, Leakage & Crushing, Contact with Oil & Other Cargo, Contamination	33%	40%	39%	39%	39%
Water Damage Group Fresh Water, Sweat, Salt Water	13%	9%	10%	10%	10%
Total Preventable Losses	74%	81%	74%	70%	70%

*Reprinted with permission from *Ports of the World*, 12th ed. (Philadelphia: Insurance Company of North America), p. 44.

pilferage, and nondelivery. Exhibit 11-4, however, shows this to be a decreasing percentage of losses.

Shippers should use only new, well-constructed packing. Early deterioration or collapse of flimsy or previously used cartons, boxes, or bags invites pilferage through exposure of the contents. Use of uniquely patterned gummed tapes will make possible quick detection of tampering. Corrugated fasteners will add to the security of wooden boxes. Shrink wrapping, strapping, and banding will further contribute to package security. Descriptive labeling, illustrations, or prominent display of trademarks and well-known company names on any type of cargo simplifies the pilferer's task.

Prompt pickup and delivery are important. The longer cargo rests on piers, in terminals, or in truck bodies, the more it is exposed to loss by theft and pilferage.

Minimizing Handling and Stowage Damage Cargo handling in the various air- and sea-ports of the world ranges from highly professional to totally unskilled handling. Rough seas, turbulent air, heavy traffic, and substandard roads subject cargo to every imaginable kind of motion and impact.

Minimizing Loss from Water Damage Rain, high humidity, condensation and seawater (separately or in combination) can reduce otherwise stable cargo into a ruin of soggy, stained, mildewed, rusty, or delabeled merchandise. Salt spray driving across the deck of an exposed lighter, a rain-swept customs compound, an open truck on an airport apron in a torrential downpour, the insidious dripping of condensation from the chilled interior of a ship's hold, or sweat forming on the cargo itself, are all common hazards. Each different commodity has its own unique characteristics which react differently when exposed to water.

Cargo should be protected from water damage from external sources such as rain, seawater, high humidity, and ship's sweat by adequate preparation and packing.

Crates and other large containers should have drain holes in the bottom to preclude collection of water within the packing. This is of particular importance when the cargo itself is subject to formation of condensation (cargo sweat).

Containerization does not guarantee protection against wetting. As containers age, "leakers" become more commonplace. Indeed, the increase in wetting damage is usually linked to an increase in reports of water damaged goods shipped in containers. Containerized cargo must be packed to the same degree of water protection as most general cargo.

Indelible inks, paint, and water repellent labels should be used to preclude obliteration of marks, shipping instructions, and handling symbols.

Containerization Placing cargo in containers will reduce certain types of loss. Handling is reduced and therefore breakage due to handling and theft and pilferage losses is reduced. If the shipper packs its own containers, handling by outsiders is eliminated except for customs inspection. The shipper can also pack to its own specifications and know they are followed. There is also a reduction in exposure to the elements. There are many types of containers—dry, ventilated, refrigerated, bulk (liquid and dry), automotive, insulated, flat rack, and livestock. There are independent firms which provide testing and inspection services of intermodal containers, both at initial delivery and periodically thereafter. An underwriter and the shipper should look for the certificate seals on the containers. While no guarantee of perfection, they are a first step in inspecting a container for quality and adequacy. Other things to look for include an interior free from splinters, snags, and bulges; cleanliness; watertight; fittings in good condition; no debts, bulges, or other damage to the exterior; doors that can securely lock; and hatch panels or covers in good condition. It is important that the container be appropriate for the commodity and that it be properly packed. Many containers are intermodal, which helps reduce the packing and unpacking exposure.

Container Hazards. Containers are subject to certain hazards. These include:

- Handling Hazards—rapid acceleration and deceleration during lifting and lowering; tilting during forklift operations; pushing and dragging in inadequately equipped ports; dropping when improper material handling equipment or inexperienced labor is used.
- Highway Hazards—impact against loading docks; coupling impact; braking and acceleration; sway on curves; vibration and road shocks.
- Railway Hazards—acceleration and deceleration; coupling impact (sometimes severe during humping operations); sway on curves; vibration.
- Ocean and Waterway Hazards—rolling, pitching, heaving, surging, swaying, and yaw motions; wave impact (green water impacting on deck-stowed containers during heavy weather).
- Water Damage Hazards—rainwater entry, leaking container; saltwater entry, leaking container; condensation (ship's sweat); condensation (cargo sweat); flooding (container stored on inadequately drained surface).
- Theft and Pilferage Hazards—exposure of cargo during transfer into or from container (other than door-to-door service); hijacking of entire container.
- Contamination Hazards—residual material or odors from previous cargoes; incompatible cargo stowed in the same container.
- Fire Hazards—ignition caused by friction; ignition caused by spontaneous combustion.[5]

Ocean Hazards. The hazards of rolling, pitching, surging, swaying and yaw motions are unique to ocean carriage. Packing and

Exhibit 11-5
Ship Movements at Sea*

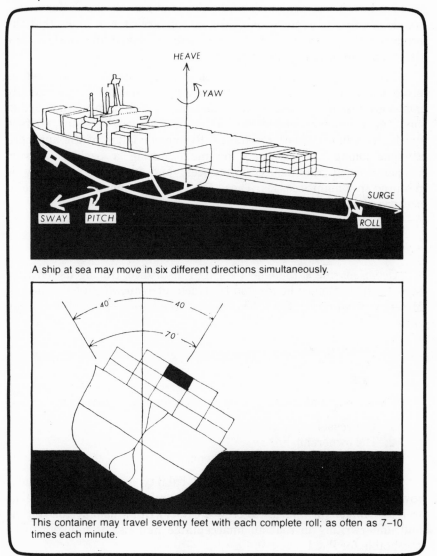

A ship at sea may move in six different directions simultaneously.

This container may travel seventy feet with each complete roll; as often as 7–10 times each minute.

*Reprinted with permission from *Ports of the World*, 12th ed. (Philadelphia: Insurance Company of North America), p. 58.

containerization adequate for land transit may fail here. This can be seen in Exhibit 11-5.

Packing

Wooden Boxes. The manner in which the commodity is packed will greatly affect losses. One of the best types of containers is the nailed wooden box. There are available lumber and nail standards for nailed wooden boxes. It is not enough for the underwriter to know that the product is being shipped in a wooden box; the type of box should be determined in the packing survey.

Cushioning. Fragile and brittle items must be suspended or protected against shock and vibration by a cushion that gradually increases resistance against item movement. Selection of the correct cushioning material depends on the item's size, weight, shape, surface finish, and built-in shock resistance. Recommendation of the appropriate cushioning material may be made during a packing survey. Cooperation of the insured, producer, and insurance company is required to minimize losses. These few examples indicate the scope of ocean cargo loss control.

SUMMARY

Ocean marine is the oldest form of insurance, tracing its heritage back to the bottomry bonds and contracts of *respondia* of the ancient Mediterranean civilizations. There are three major segments of ocean cargo:

1. Commercial hulls
2. Protection and indemnity
3. Cargo

Commercial hull underwriting focuses on three major areas:

1. The vessel
2. The ownership
3. The premium and loss experience

Protection and indemnity is legal liability insurance. It includes coverage for claims arising out of the ownership and use of a vessel as well as liability for injuries to crews. Underwriting usually follows the hull underwriting in that an unacceptable hull risk is unlikely to be acceptable for P & I.

Ocean cargo insurance involves the import and export of commodities. Therefore, the extent of insurable interest, the terms of sale, and the method of payment are important underwriting considerations.

Coverage on an open ocean cargo policy is determined by the wording of the perils clause and the average conditions. In addition, there are additional perils provided which do not depend on the average conditions such as the Inchmaree clause. War risks are usually written on a separate policy. Important underwriting considerations for ocean cargo include the assured, the commodity, packing, the vessel, the port or ports involved, and the season of the year. The loss experience of the commodity and of the particular assured is especially important. Since almost 70 percent of ocean cargo losses are preventable, loss control can have a sizable impact. Preventable losses fall into three major categories:

1. Theft, pilferage, and nondelivery
2. Handling and stowage damage
3. Water damage

Containerization and proper packing can help to minimize losses.

Chapter Notes

1. This chapter draws heavily on "Marine Insurance," dated December 1976, produced by Marine and Aviation—Marketing Operations, Insurance Company of North America and on *Ports of the World*, 12th Edition, also published by the Insurance Company of North America. The authors also wish to acknowledge the assistance of Homer O. White, Jr., CPCU, formerly with the Insurance Company of North America, and Jack Adee, of Fireman's Fund Insurance Companies.
2. William D. Winter, *Marine Insurance*, 3rd ed. (New York: McGraw-Hill Book Co., 1952), p. 94.
3. William H. Rodda, *Marine Insurance: Ocean and Inland*, (Englewood Cliffs, New Jersey: Prentice-Hall, Inc., 1970), p. 56.
4. William D. Winter, p. 57.
5. *Ports of the World*, 12th ed. (Philadelphia: Insurance Company of North America).

CHAPTER 12

Underwriting Commercial Crime Insurance

INTRODUCTION

It is a cardinal rule for publishers of academic prose that an author must avoid writing in a personal style at all costs. If nothing else, this guarantees that the textbook, in this case, will remain antiseptic, sleep-inducing, and dull. Since the last sentence has already violated another stricture (it contains multiple redundancies), there will follow an attempt to tell a personal anecdote. It is this writer's hope that his editor will be indulgent, because there is a chance that this particular anecdote has an appropriate point to it ... maybe even more than one appropriate point.

Not too long ago, perhaps when our average reader was just about to be weaned, your author was a young home office underwriter handling large property risks. My accomplice in this tale was an experienced, grizzled underwriting manager operating out of our branch office in Minneapolis. We shall call him Henry, for in fact, that was his name. On a given day, not too long ago you may remember, Henry called me. What follows is a fairly accurate recollection of our phone conversation. (It will also become clear how a conversation of so long ago can be so well remembered):

Henry: "How would you like to write fire insurance on a cave?"
Hout: (Home Office Underwriter Type): "Henry, I know you too well. There is no need for home office approval for fire insurance on a cave. But I will confess to curiosity. Where is this cave?"
Henry: "Kansas."

Hout: "You know I'm an eastern boy. But as I recall, Kansas is flat."

Henry: "Well, to tell the truth, it's not so much a cave as an underground cavern."

Hout: "A cavern?"

Henry: "Yeah, you know, something left over when the ocean receded a few billion years ago. It's about eight miles long, all told, and full of salt."

Hout: "Eight miles of salt! What's the valuation?"

Henry: "The owner values the cave contents at $20,000,000."

Hout: "That is a lot of salt."

Henry: "Well, you've been nice to hear me out so far, so I think you should know that the $20,000,000 is for the gas in the cavern, not the salt."

Hout: "Gas! The kind that burns and explodes and such?"

Henry: "The very same kind. Now I want to take a 25 percent line, at a 100 percent PML, and all with a nice fat $8.00 rate."

Hout: "An $8.00 fire rate sounds real nice."

Henry: "I just knew you'd like that part. But that's for a broad 'all-risks' cover. It's a manuscript form provided by the broker. O.K.?"

Hout: "O.K. Send in the PIDS, no doubt to be written in your own inimitable style."

A PIDS was a Property Insurance Data Sheet. For certain classes of risk it was then a required procedure; properly written it explained in a few terse sentences all the pertinent facts about a risk. The denouement of this tale is that Henry's PIDS included the phrase "Perils: All risks including theft and mysterious disappearance; approved by Hout on (date)."

The points to be made via this true story are, perhaps, obvious. But in the interests of clarity they will be examined more closely. However, for the curious and for those who insist on full closure there are these additional facts:

1. There were no losses during policy term.
2. The policy was not renewed. The Hout's superior also read the PIDS. He suggested firmly that one try for the brass ring was enough.
3. The two protagonists, or accomplices, of this tale were good friends. Indeed, the Hout had come to consider Henry a mentor, of sorts, and was gladly "taken to school" on more than one occasion.

Nevertheless, the points intended by all this are as follows:

● The Hout was seduced by the opening phrase about "... writing fire insurance on a cave." That established a very positive mental picture and he was easily led through the remainder of the scenario.

Researchers have found that underwriters are frequently the captives of their first impressions. In this case, the first impression was a positive one. The same research indicates that despite even very negative data that may follow, underwriters who are initially favorably impressed keep that impression and ignore or minimize data that tends to mitigate it.[1]

The moral is: Beware of smooth talking agents and brokers who appear to be offering a "sure thing" or "pig iron under water." Get, instead, all of the facts and weigh them objectively for what each is actually worth. The facts you learn last may well be more important than those you learned earlier.

● Perhaps you are aware of the old adage, "... the sweet fragrance of a large premium overcometh the bad smell of the risk." In our case in point, the Hout was overcome.

● Lastly, and to explain why this tale is part of a chapter on crime insurance, the Hout was skewered for underwriting against just one peril, i.e., fire. He never asked what was meant by a "broad all-risks cover." Indeed, on reflection, he probably did not care. Even after reading the PIDS comment on perils—i.e., "... all risks, including theft and mysterious disappearance"— he did not realize the significance of his decision.

Crime coverages, it is strongly suspected, are all too often poorly underwritten when included as perils in an "all-risks" policy, or when they are added to a package policy via endorsement as they so often are. Let us hope the reason for this is something that can be corrected, like ignorance. By reading the rest of this chapter, you may even begin to correct this situation.

Let us look again at our gas in the underground cavern. As a commodity, or kind of property, is it susceptible to theft? That is to say, is the nature of this gas such that it permits itself to be stolen? The answer must be "yes"; it can indeed be stolen. Perhaps not easily; perhaps not without specialized, expensive equipment; and perhaps not without a certain amount of rare expertise—but it can, nonetheless, be stolen.

Is gas *fungible?* In other words, as a specific kind of property, does it have value permitting it to satisfy an obligation? Can it be exchanged in trade as money or food? Again, the answer is "yes"; but the fungibility is awkward, to say the least. It compares very unfavorably, say, to cash, gems, narcotics, or even television sets as a fungible commodity.

Is there a viable market for gas? Of course there is. A thief in possession of gas would no doubt be able to find a buyer, with no questions asked. Yet, it should be pointed out, many commercial thefts are done "on order." That is, a market (e.g., a seller or user) seeks gas and hires thieves to "produce" it.

Finally, after satisfying these questions, the underwriter must sum up his answers in the larger question: How likely is it that this gas will be stolen? This is what makes underwriting challenging and fun. The challenge is that there is no master to whom we can look for the answer; we must decide for ourselves. There are no credible statistics for "theft of gas from underground caverns." And, because there is no master providing us "truth" in such a case, whatever we decide is probably as good a decision as the next person's—that's fun!

It seems reasonable to assume that the likelihood of theft of gas from the cavern is relatively low. (We shall examine just how that assumption was made later on in this chapter.) While it is not impossible, the likelihood is extremely low. Let us say, on a scale of one-to-ten, theft of this gas rates, at the worst, a "2." Who is to say we are wrong?

Now, we must look at the cavern gas exposed to "mysterious disappearance." What were the properties of the gas? For example, was it heavier or lighter than air? If heavier, it could drop "through the cracks," so to speak. If lighter, it could easily rise through cracks and fissures to be lost in the ambient air. But is such a loss "mysterious disappearance"?

This is an appropriate time to review the definitions for commercial crime insurance.

Definitions in Commercial Crime Insurance

Theft Theft is the unlawful taking of property. The manner in which the property is taken is not specified. Therefore it includes burglary, robbery, shoplifting and other acts of stealth, as well as conversion.

Burglary Burglary is the forceful entry or exit into or from premises, a building, a safe, or a vault, with the intent to commit theft. Burglary policies limit this definition by covering only when the premises are not open for business. The definition of "forceful entry *or exit*" includes thieves who may hide within a fenced area or in a building during business hours and only after the business is closed take property and force their way to the outside. There must be visible evidence of forced entry or exit.

The peril of burglary is a "premises only" exposure, and insurance coverage applies solely to the described premises although property taken from a safe or elsewhere in the premises is covered as long as the evidence of entry exists. The premises restriction applies since the underwriter needs to be assured that the physical protection and location are acceptable in relation to the type of property and its value.

Robbery Robbery is broadly defined to mean the illegal taking of property by violence or threat of violence inflicted on a messenger or custodian. It includes kidnapping.

Robbery policies include the theft of property from within a show window on the premises while regularly open for business if the thief has broken the window glass from the outside. The careful reader may discern that this is a burglary; i.e., it is a forceful entry. But robbery policies include this coverage while *regularly open for business;* it would be an excluded loss under a burglary policy.

Conversion Conversion is the unauthorized assumption of the rights of ownership to personal property. The illegal *taking* of property is theft. Keeping it or trying to sell it or use it is conversion. Crime insurance policies are invariably silent concerning "conversion," *per se.*

Inventory Shortage "All-risks" policies insuring against theft usually exclude "shortage of property on taking inventory." There is a subtle but substantive difference between that particular kind of exclusion and one that reads: "This policy excludes loss arising out of inventory shortage."

Presumably, in the former example, an actual physical act of performing inventory accounting must take place. The loss that surfaces therefrom is excluded.

But a loss that surfaces out of an "inventory shortage" may be simply one where the property was clearly in its accustomed place earlier this morning and was not there when its owner checked, say, an hour or so later.

Mysterious Disappearance Mysterious disappearance is the loss of property, the cause of which has no reasonable explanation.

Gas that disappears from a cavern where there are cracks in the floor and ceiling is no mystery. The gas presumably escapes because there is opportunity and its distinctive properties (i.e., it is either heavier or lighter than air) permit it.

However, suppose there were no cracks in the cavern. Suppose it was tight and secure and leakage could be ruled out. Further suppose that the cavern was full of gas yesterday; it is only half full today;

there is no evidence of burglary, robbery, or theft; there was, however, *opportunity* for theft during the night. Some may contend this constitutes mysterious disappearance. Others may contend that an opportunity for theft leads to a reasonable *presumption of theft*, especially in the absence of any information to the contrary.

THE CONSTRUCTION OF CRIME POLICIES

The purpose of the foregoing discussion is not to engage in some kind of insurance sophistry or verbal pedantry. Underwriters issue contracts to their insureds. These contracts, and the prices under-writers charge, are the two most important variables in their reaching a viable, meaningful commercial agreement. The meanings of the words used in those agreements are of vital significance. Underwriting towards some purpose is all too often defeated because a contract must be redefined and litigated in a court of law simply because the parties to that contract were imprecise in its execution. The burden of sound policy construction weighs heavier on the underwriter than on the insured.

Insurance against crime perils is increasingly accomplished by "all-risks" property policies. For example, the SMP special personal property form (MP-101A) is an "all-risks" form. The insuring agree-ments read, in pertinent part, as follows:

- This policy insures against all risks of direct physical loss . . .
- This policy does not insure under this form against loss caused by:
  . . .2. unexplained or mysterious disappearance of property, or shortage of property disclosed on taking inventory;
  . . .9. voluntary parting with title or possession of any property by the insured or others to whom the property may be entrusted if induced to do so by any fraudulent scheme, trick device, or false pretense;
  . . .10. any fraudulent, dishonest or criminal act done by or at the instigation of any insured, partner or joint adventurer in or of any insured, an officer, director or trustee of any insured; pilferage, appropriation or concealment of any property covered due to any fraudulent, dishonest or criminal act of any employee while working or otherwise, or agent of any insured, or any person to whom the property covered may be entrusted.

The perils insured against ("all-risks") and the cited exclusions make this a fairly broad theft policy. It clearly covers burglary and robbery except when these are performed by owners (insureds, etc.) and employees (see exclusion 10). It does not limit burglary to a time when the firm is not open for business. It also covers thefts of stealth, e.g., shoplifting.

But the policy, in at least one aspect, is less broad than a mercantile robbery or safe burglary policy. That form does not exclude loss arising from acts of employees. However, the "all-risks" SMP excludes them in exclusion 10.

What is the liability of an underwriter who tells a producer, "This all-risks SMP replaces the current mercantile robbery and safe burglary policy currently in force. It provides the same or broader theft coverage." ? The answer is that there will indeed be liability (of the underwriter) *if*, after the SMP is written replacing the current cover, an employee commits an act of safe burglary or robbery. By the same token, there will be liability of the producer should he or she repeat the underwriter's statement to the client.

The underwriters who created the SMP form MP101A probably did not intend to have their policy less broad than the mercantile robbery and safe burglary form. It probably was in their desire to exclude fidelity losses that they chose those particular words in exclusion 10.

Suppose the Insurance Institute of America contracted with an Edward P. Launie to print and distribute books on the Institute's behalf. Further suppose this contract was in the form of a joint venture. Edward Launie, for his own peculiar and bizarre reasons, believes he has been cheated by the Institute. Late one night he arrives at Malvern and commits arson resulting in the total loss of a building. The "all-risks" SMP excludes such a loss under exclusion 10. Launie is a "joint adventurer" and his committing arson was a "criminal act." A separate fire policy would respond for this loss.

The two situations cited here illustrate the difficulties in constructing broad, "all-risks" covers. The contradictions of intent that can result from manuscript forms and individual company forms (i.e., DICs) can multiply these cited situations many times over.

CONDITIONS AND TERMS OF COVERAGE

For the past decade, underwriting of property and liability insurance has been performed in the midst of widespread conditions of market chaos. Home office strategies regarding line of business market shares and investment portfolios have tended to offset and even ignore statutory underwriting profit considerations. Many readers of this text will have experienced only this kind of environment and, as a result thereof, never practiced seriously the disciplines of product line underwriting.

One of the unfortunate results of this chaos has been the carelessness to which coverages (i.e., the policies themselves) have been subjected. Crime coverages have been no exception. As stated earlier, for example, theft covers are increasingly included within broad, "all-risks" policies. The theft conditions are invariably merely "after-thoughts." Additionally, there has been a deterioration in conformity to filings. Filed forms and rules are frequently ignored and endorsements and other wording changes are being made in contravention of these filings as well as in contravention of disciplined underwriting practice. The flexibility an underwriter has in changing terms and conditions carries with it an obligation to use prudence and care in initiating and constructing such changes.

Variables of conditions and terms of the contract to which an underwriter may have access include:

- breadth of perils insured against,
- limits of liability,
- deductibles,
- warranties to representation and the maintenance of loss prevention systems and devices, and
- pricing and loss control.

Perils Insured Against

Underwriters are advised to use the prescribed and time-tested covers for robbery, burglary, and theft—e.g., the ISO forms or similar products. Basically, these are "named perils" forms. It is not the purpose of this text to review such contracts, but their proven capability to treat most crime exposures recommends their continued use. The doctrine of *concurrent causation* recently advanced by the California courts has merit and applicability to contemplated "all-risks" covers for theft. Some of the considerations impelled by this new doctrine were discussed briefly in the previous section.

Theft, as thus far used in this chapter, includes fidelity or employee dishonesty. Because of its special characteristics it will be treated more fully later on.

Limits of Liability

The amounts of insurance acceptable to the underwriter are dictated by:

- company policy regarding "net willing to lose,"
- reinsurance considerations, and
- probable maximum loss and amount subject considerations.

All three of these items are interrelated. The *net willing to lose* is a factor of policyholder reserves—i.e., the net capacity of the insurance company. It is also a function of the insurer's philosophy and attitude toward risk; e.g., is it "bullish," somewhat conservative, or even risk averse?

Reinsurance treaties will dictate the primary insurer's net retentions or shares of retentions. They may also dictate treatments for specific lines of crime coverages or specific types of risk within class.

Probable maximum loss, as in fire insurance, is primarily a function of moral hazard and loss control systems. But the property itself is also extremely important—e.g., its *susceptibility, fungibility,* and *marketability.*

Amount subject has some unique considerations in crime underwriting. Assuming amount subject to be the total amount exposed to loss, it can be reasonably calculated, just as for other property insurance perils. The problem, or unique consideration, is the high prevalence of underinsurance in crime insurance.

For most other types of insurance, the insured purchases an amount close to the value of the exposed property either because of realization of the possibility of serious or total loss (fire insurance) or because of lending institution requirements (auto physical damage insurance). The insured's assumption that only small crime losses will occur, coupled with the desire to reduce crime premiums, tends to minimize the amount of crime insurance purchased and maximize the problem of underinsurance. There is a dishonesty exposure factor with which the Surety Association computes a recommended amount of insurance. Also, the American Bank Association suggests a minimum range of coverage. In addition, stock exchanges have minimum amounts required. With respect to banks and other financial institutions, the Federal Deposit Insurance Corporation and the Federal Home Loan Bank Board suggest ranges of amount based on size.

Two other methods employed to encourage adequate amounts of insurance and reduce the problem of underinsurance are (1) the coinsurance requirement of the mercantile open stock burglary policy, and (2) a graduated scale which reduces the rate as higher limits are written.

In the final analysis, underinsurance tends to make small losses a higher percentage of the amount of insurance. At its extreme, this tendency causes small losses to be total losses to the policy. Insurance rating and pricing tend to contemplate partial losses. Therefore, underinsurance can lead to underpricing. In the face of underinsurance, the underwriter must increase the price.

Deductibles

When viewed as a percentage of policies written, deductibles are seldom used as underwriting tools in crime insurance. They are, however, used in policies for larger risks where frequency of loss provides some credibility for small loss prediction and where more sophisticated insurance buyers may seek cost reductions through retention that can be absorbed in the cash flow of the enterprise.

Deductibles in crime insurance serve the same purposes for underwriters as they do in other types of insurance: (1) they prevent erosion of the loss portion of the premium by eliminating small, more predictable losses; and (2) they tend to make insureds more conscious of loss prevention and the practical, direct returns they can receive by effecting and maintaining loss prevention systems and devices.

Warranties

A warranty is a policy condition in which the insured stipulates facts or circumstances whose truth is essential and precedent to valid coverage. Legally, the several states have viewed policy warranties variously; at the whim of the court, a warranty can be almost ignored or can be adhered to strictly. Generally, however, it can be assumed that a warranted condition that fails to exist at the time of loss *and* which is material to the loss negates coverage. But the intent of a warranty clearly is not to create a loophole through which an adjuster can deny liability; a warranty intends to impress heavily upon the insured the obligation to implement or maintain certain conditions— conditions that will substantively mitigate loss and enable an otherwise uninsurable risk to be acceptable to the underwriter.

Warranties currently are rarely found in crime policies. To insert them in a typically filed crime form may even be in violation of its filing. Yet their successful use in jewelers' block forms (a broad, primarily theft, cover) suggests their utility in all crime policies. Certainly the larger crime risks that have manuscript or tailored forms could well use them. They are a powerful tool of moral suasion. Warranties can be used to emphasize the maintenance of loss control systems and to obtain accurate and more reasonable levels of insurance to value.

Pricing and Loss Control

A published class rate normally is meant to represent a unit cost for the *average risk* within class. Where filed rating formulas permit rate adjustments, credits or debits can be used to reflect the consider- ations the underwriter weighs in reaching a final decision. The problem inevitably revolves around the single question of what is average within a class.

The *average* risk is a theoretical construct. The average crime risk within a class may or may not exist in reality. This fact, on the one hand, provides an underwriter great latitude; it demands a judgment. On the other hand, it poses a demand that the underwriter weigh each risk against this theoretical construct and make an *educated* or *knowledgeable* judgment and presupposes that an underwriter has looked at many similar risks. In the absence of this experience, the underwriters must use the published or suggested rate.

Pricing includes the act of judging individual risk rate adequacy. Invariably the adequacy revolves around loss control systems and devices. Underwriting manuals published by insurers provide minimum standards for many loss control systems. The underwriter, at his or her peril, provides rate credits when these standards are not met. However, pricing tradeoffs are available when loss control standards are exceeded. The underwriter also may quote two prices: one price based upon the insured's willingness to implement increased loss control and a higher price should the risk remain as submitted.

UNDERWRITING DECISION-MAKING
FOR CRIME INSURANCE

Assessing Crime Loss Potential

Characteristics of Property Subject to Crime Losses   As seen earlier in the story about gas in an underground cavern, it is necessary to review carefully the characteristics of the property that is to be covered by crime insurance. These extrinsic and intrinsic characteristics may be identifiable individually as phenomena but are frequently weighed collectively. These characteristics, you will recall, are determined by three questions:

- Is the property susceptible to crime?
- Is the property fungible?
- Is there a ready market for it as stolen property?

Susceptibility deals with the nature of the goods—size, weight, portability, visibility, and accessibility. The emphasis given each of these items is relative. Size or weight, by themselves, may or may not preclude an object's being stolen. For example, a forty-ton, steel truss bridge was stolen from a West Virginia creek in the late 1950s. Yet, despite this experience, bulky items like bridges and buildings are properly viewed as having low susceptibility. Jewelry, clothing, small electric appliances, precious metals, books, hand tools, and so forth, on the other hand, are highly susceptible.

Fungibility deals with a property's valuation as an item of

exchange. Money, securities, and other negotiable instruments are highly fungible. Bulk gas, bridges, and the like must, ultimately, be viewed as "essentially not fungible"—that is, they may meet a rare exchange demand but are not to be viewed as regularly traded goods. A semi-trailer load of name-brand golf balls has low fungibility. It is, however, susceptible.

There is also a high probability that a ready market exists for the semi-trailer load of golf balls. The marketability rests in its having a large, diverse distribution character, its difficulty in being traced, and its size and popular use. Marketability is also frequently a function of the economy. Economy, in turn, deals with supply and demand. Copper in the late 1960s was a target commodity due to world-wide scarcity and concomitant high prices. "All-risks" underwriters paid many losses arising out of stolen copper plumbing from vacant or unoccupied buildings. In more than one instance, a television tower had its antenna wire ripped from its extensively buried grounding.

As a last resort, thieves may turn to the original owner as their market. Several boxcars filled with automobile and truck engine blocks "disappeared" early in this decade. It was only after months had passed with no trace of them being found that the manufacturer was contacted. After price and delivery negotiations were completed, the engines ended up at their initially intended destination.

Additional Factors Determining Loss Potential Besides qualities of the property itself, these additional considerations will assist an underwriter in assessing probabilities of loss:

- territory
- public protection
- private protection
- the moral and morale hazards
- adverse selection

The last two will be described in a later section.

Territory. Territory includes considerations of such things as topography, neighborhood, climate, and especially the prevailing incidence of crime. Seasonal occupancy, as in a remote recreational resort, for example, increases probability of crime loss. It is the conventional wisdom that cities have a higher frequency of crime than rural areas.

Public Protection. Public protection is primarily the size, adequacy, efficiency, and professionalism of the local police force. Yet it also includes the quality of a locale's communications network.

Private Protection. Private protection deals with an insured's own devices or systems for preventing or minimizing loss. Devices include:

- safes or vaults for items of high value
- cages and specially constructed rooms or limited access areas
- indoor and outdoor lighting
- fences and walls
- adequate premises openings—e.g., gates, doors, windows, skylights, etc.
- watchmen and guard dog services
- intrusion and detection alarms
- electronic surveillance systems
- inventory and other management control activities

Loss control, or protection devices and systems, are generally thought to serve at least two important functions:

1. They are meant to preclude crime losses.
2. They are meant to deter crime.

Willie Sutton, a notorious bank robber of the 1940s and 1950s, was once asked by a reporter why he chose to rob and burglarize banks when there clearly were easier targets for his talents and skills. His answer was, "Because that's where the money is." Willie held banks and jails in contempt; his career was spent in breaking into the one and breaking out of the other.

Willie illustrates the fact that a dedicated thief, whether amateur or professional, invariably can crack the defenses. In other words, safes, vaults, fencing, and so on rarely preclude access to desired property when the thief is strongly motivated.

But protection devices and systems do make an invaluable contribution to deterrence. They frustrate, they confuse, they slow down criminal processes, and, finally, they frequently cause a thief to have second thoughts and send him off seeking an easier target.

The point to be made here for underwriters is that even the best protection systems merely reduce the probability of frequency and severity of loss—they do not eliminate it. Yet the value of this reduction in probability of loss cannot be over-emphasized. After moral hazard, protection, and private protection in particular, is the most important, pivotal consideration in crime insurance underwriting.

Types of Private Protection

Private protection devices can be grouped into two major categories: (1) barriers to criminal access and (2) detection devices. Barriers include physical properties of the premises, safes, and vaults. Detection devices are guards, alarms, and surveillance systems.

Physical Protection

Premise Protection. Physical protection devices for the premises include door and window locks, bars, and screens to reduce illegal entry. Any premises is susceptible to illegal entry through doors, windows, and skylights (if present). Fencing and walls protect buildings and yard storage.

Since doors present the main entry to the premises, they should be adequately secured and constructed to resist illegal entry. The location of the door is an important consideration. Generally back doors opening into alleys or yards are vulnerable since they are often shielded from public view. Door protection includes adequate locks, wire guards, angle iron cross bars, and sheet metal linings.

Separate rooms and heavily screened cages are frequently built into premises to house especially vulnerable operations. For example, shop floors usually have cages for storage and distribution of valuable tools and dies.

Safes and Vaults. A safe is a movable device; a vault is part of the premises. Safes may be built with inner as well as outer doors. There are two basic categories of safes: (1) fire-resistive and (2) burglar-resistive. Fire-resistive safes are for record storage; they are not satisfactory barriers to criminals. There are several classes of burglar-resistive safes based on construction specifications and burglar vulnerability. These are shown in Exhibit 12-1.

While a safe or vault offers additional crime security, the quality of this protection depends on the type and condition. Many unlabeled and obsolete safes are still in use. The underwriter should acquire full information on a declared safe before determining its significance as an adequate protection device.

Product-line underwriting managers often establish acceptability and limit of liability requirements based on safe or vault protection. Exhibit 12-2 is an example of such requirements.

Detection Systems

Alarms. Intrusion alarm systems consist of detection devices and alarms connected by a wiring network. These systems vary in sophistication, area of coverage, and number of protected openings. The value of an intrusion alarm system is dependent on proper maintenance and periodic testing as well as care that it is activated at all times when the premises are not open for business.

Alarm systems consist of local alarms, police station connection, and central alarm systems. These were covered in Chapter 6 with respect to fire alarms.

CLASSIFICATION. Alarm systems are rated by Underwriters' Laboratories, Inc. Since intrusion alarm systems should resist efforts to defeat them, this aspect is included in their rating. Local alarms are rated either A or B. An A-rated alarm will resist attempts to silence it for two minutes. This resistance is required for only ninety seconds with a B-rated alarm.

Central station protection is also certified by Underwriters' Laboratories, Inc., as follows:

- Grade AA protection requires a dedicated direct wire connection using leased telephone lines from the premises to the central station. (The term *dedicated* means the leased lines are not used for any other purpose.) The entire circuit must have both AC and DC line supervision. This will detect any attempt to defeat or compromise the security system by cutting, crossing, or disconnecting wires or substituting detectors. Grade AA certification also requires guard response within fifteen minutes.
- In Grade A protection the only difference is that line supervision is DC only.
- Grade B protection is also a direct wire connection, but it uses a shared circuit. The circuit may be shared by up to 15 security alarms and 250 fire alarms. Guard response within twenty minutes is required.
- Grade C protection also employs a shared circuit, but the guard response time is extended to thirty minutes.

The extent of intrusion protection is rated by Underwriters' Laboratories, Inc., based on three classifications:

- Class 1 requires hard wire protection of walls, partitions, floors, windows, doors, and ceilings.
- A Class 2 system has detectors on all windows, doors, nonconcrete floors, and ceilings.
- A Class 3 system has intrusion devices only on windows and doors.

These systems are summarized in Exhibit 12-3.

SELECTION CRITERIA. As with safes and vaults, underwriters often establish alarm protection requirements based on type of merchandise and amounts of insurance, with insurability contingent upon the adequacy of the installation.

Often an insured will be required to install a particular type of system in order to qualify for insurance coverage. If several types of installations meet the underwriting requirements, then considerations of cost effectiveness and relative efficiency become relevant. The premium discounts available for certain systems act as an incentive for

Exhibit 12-1
Safe Classifications*

Safe, Chest, Cabinet or Vault Classification	Construction		
	Doors	Walls	
		Safe, Chest or Cabinet	Vault
B (Fire resistive)	Steel less than 1" thick, or iron	Body of steel less than 1/2" thick, or iron	Brick, concrete, stone, tile, iron or steel
	Any iron or steel safe or chest having a slot through which money can be deposited		Not Applicable
C (Burglar-resistive)	Steel at least 1" thick	Body of steel at least 1/2" thick	Steel at least 1/2" thick; or reinforced concrete or stone at least 9" thick; or non-reinforced concrete or stone at least 12" thick
	Safe or chest bearing following label: "Underwriters' Laboratories, Inc. Inspected Keylocked Safe KL Burglary"		Not Applicable
E (Burglar-resistive)	Steel at least 1½" thick	Body of steel at least 1" thick	Same as for C
ER (Burglar-resistive)	Safe or chest bearing the following label: "Underwriters' Laboratories, Inc., Inspected Tool Resisting Safe TL-15 Burglary"		Not Applicable

Classification	Door / Safe Specification		Body or Walls
F (Burglar-resistive)	Safe or chest bearing one of the following labels: 1. "Underwriters' Laboratories, Inc. Inspected Tool Resisting Safe TL-30 Burglary" 2. "Underwriters' Laboratories, Inc. Inspected Torch Resisting Safe TR-30 Burglary" 3. "Underwriters' Laboratories, Inc. Inspected Explosive Resisting Safe with Relocking Device X-60 Burglary"		Not Applicable
G (Burglar-resistive)	One or more steel doors (one in front of the other) each at least 1½" thick and aggregating at least 3" thickness	Not Applicable	Steel at least ½" thick; or reinforced concrete or stone at least 12" thick; or non-reinforced concrete or stone at least 18" thick
H (Burglar-resistive)	Safe or chest bearing one of the following labels: 1. "Underwriters' Laboratories, Inc. Inspected Torch and Explosive Resisting Safe TX-60 Burglary" 2. "Underwriters' Laboratories, Inc. Inspected Torch Resisting Safe TR-60 Burglary" 3. "Underwriters' Laboratories, Inc. Inspected Torch and Tool Resisting Safe TRTL-30 Burglary"		Not Applicable
I (Burglar-resistive)	Safe or chest bearing one of the following labels: 1. "Underwriters' Laboratories, Inc. Inspected Torch and Tool Resisting Safe TRTL-60 Burglary" 2. "Underwriters' Laboratories, Inc. Inspected Torch, Explosive and Tool Resisting Safe TXTL-60 Burglary"		Not Applicable
MS insurance covering the contents of a vault meeting these specifications or better.	Steel at least 3½" thick		Steel at least 1" thick or 18" of reinforced concrete or 36" of non-reinforced concrete

*Reprinted with permission from *Commercial Lines Manual* (New York: Insurance Services Office, 1977), p. CR-21.

Exhibit 12-2

Table of Minimum Recommended Safe or Vault Protection*

ESTIMATED TARGET ATTRACTION VALUE (SEE EXPOSURE ANALYSIS)	(1) (2) SMNA LABEL		(1) (2) UND. LAB. LABEL	INSURANCE CLASS
	SPEC R-1 GROUP 8		NONE	NOT ACCEPTABLE
UP TO $200	SPEC M-1 GROUP 12 (ANY SAFE WITH DEPOSIT SLOT ACCESSIBLE FROM EXTERIOR		NONE	B
	SPEC R-1 (3) GROUP 9 or 10			
$201 TO $1,000	SPEC R-1 or GROUP 6 or 7	SPEC B-1 GROUP 6	KL	C
$1,001 TO $12,500	SPEC B-1 GROUP 5		UL LABEL FOR (4) RELOCKING DEVICE ONLY	E (SQUARE DOOR)
	SPEC UB-1 GROUP U6		TL15	ER
(5) $12,501 TO $25,000	SPEC B-1 GROUP 2, 3, or 4		UL LABEL FOR (4) RELOCKING DEVICE ONLY	E (ROUND DOOR)
(5) $25,001 TO $50,000	SPEC UB-1 or GROUP U5	SPEC B-1 GROUP 1	X60 TL 30 TR30	F
(5) $50,001 TO $100,000	SPEC UB-1 GROUP U1, U2, or U4		TXTL60 TX60 TRTL30X6 TRTL60 TR60	G,H,I,J

*Adapted with permission from *Travelers Commercial Lines Department Manual*, February 1982.

the insured. Generally, the only alarm systems deserving premium discounts are those with unexpired certificates from Underwriters' Laboratories, Inc.

Guards. Guards may be employed for three major functions: (1) during operating hours to protect against robbery, shoplifting, and employee dishonesty; (2) after business hours to control burglary losses; and (3) to accompany employees or messengers carrying money or merchandise off premises as a protection against robbery or violence. The types of guard systems employed after business hours to deter burglary often include fire detection responsibilities. These systems were covered in Chapter 6. Guards have become more prevalent during the past decade as overall crime rates and potential and actual losses have increased.

Guards and guard dogs conceivably could be categorized as barriers to criminal access. Certainly, in a sense, they do indeed serve that function. But for reasons of safety-to-life and the potential costs of liability suits arising out of guard actions, guards have a primary duty to detect crime and sound appropriate alarms.

Surveillance Cameras Video surveillance is an effective protective device. These systems either supplement or supplant guards. This type of installation ranges from the small camera attached to the wall in a prominent location within a convenience store to monitor customer activities to an elaborate, complete-area coverage system for a multistory office or business complex.

A system may select for video surveillance either key (vulnerable) crime hazard areas such as entrances, exits, and aisles or encompass the entire operating area. Normally surveillance cameras are visible and this sometimes acts as a crime deterrent. The recording mechanism of the device should be at another location so that it cannot be destroyed or put out of service by the criminal. While numerous types of equipment are available, the continually operating camera is preferable to those that must be activated by an employee. These systems are frequently used in banks. They are now also employed in retail stores as a deterrent to shoplifting.

Moral and Morale Hazard

The moral or morale hazard of a crime risk is sometimes difficult to assess adequately; however, the following characteristics can be of assistance:

- *Ownership and Management.* Experience, longevity, and the cooperation of ownership with producers, loss control personnel, and underwriters are key factors to assessing moral or morale hazard. Responsible management is willing to cooperate in the control and elimination of crime causes. When the need is demonstrated, management will be willing to incur reasonable expense in working with the underwriter and loss control representative to improve and update adequate private protection.
- *Financial and Moral Reputation.* Risks that are not well established or financially reputable are questionable and may be undesirable crime risks. In a few situations the underwriter may initially determine a general financial or moral reputation problem, but normally this type of information is secured through investigative data or reports. Financial ratings are an initial underwriting requirement and can be supplemented with outside inspection reports which stress the financial analysis. Financial success and reputation of the business are primary tools used to evaluate moral hazard.

Exhibit 12-3
Certificate Classification Chart*

Type of Alarm		Certification	Extent of Protection	Bell Required	Police	Listed Central Station	Guard Response[1]	Line Security Certificate Available
Local Mercantile (Outside Bell) Premises, Safe or Vault	1 Party Control	A,B	Premises 2,3 Safe and Vault Complete or Partial	Yes	Optional	Optional	No	No[2]
Local Mercantile (Inside Bell) Premises, Safe or Vault		A, B	Premises 2,3 Safe and Vault Complete or Partial	Yes	Either Police or Listed Central Station (Fire or Burglary)		No	No[2]
Police Connected Mercantile Premises, Safe or Vault		AA, A, B	Premises 2,3 Safe and Vault Complete or Partial	Yes	Either Police or Listed Central Station (Fire or Burglary)		No	AA
Local Bank Safe or Vault		A, B	Complete or Partial	Yes	Optional[4]	Optional[4]	No	No[2]
Police Connected Bank Safe or Vault		AA, A BB, B	Complete or Partial	Yes	Either Police or Listed Central Station (Fire or Burglary)		No	AA
Central Station Direct Wire Premises, Safe or Vault		AA, A BB, B CC, C	Premises 1,2,3 Safe and Vault Complete or Partial	No	No	Yes[6]	15 Min. (A, AA) 20 Min. (B, BB) 30 Min. (C, CC)	AA, BB, CC

		2 Party Control				
Transmitter Systems (Circuit Alarm) Premises, Safe or Vault	BB, B / CC, C	Premises 1,2,3 Safe and Vault Complete or Partial	No	No	Yes[6]	20 Min. (B, BB) / 30 Min. (C, CC)	BB, CC[3]
Combination Central Station and Local Alarm (Outside Bell) Premises, Safe or Vault	AA, A / BB, B / CC, C	Premises 1,2,3 Safe and Vault Complete or Partial	Yes	No	Yes[6]	20 Min. (A, AA) / 20 Min. (B, BB) / 30 Min. (C, CC)	AA, BB, CC[3]
Combination Central Station and Local Alarm (Inside Bell) Premises, Safe or Vault	BB, B / CC, C	Premises 1,2,3 Safe and Vault Complete or Partial	Yes	No	Yes[6]	20 Min. (B, BB) / 30 Min. (C, CC)	BB, CC[3]
Central Station Multiplex Alarms Premises, Safe or Vault	AA, A / BB, B / CC, C	Premises 1,2,3 Safe and Vault Complete or Partial	5	No	Yes[6]	15 Min. (A, AA) / 20 Min. (B, BB) / 30 Min. (C, CC)	AA, BB, CC
Central Station Digital Communication Premises, Safe or Vault	B, C	Premises 1,2,3 Safe and Vault Complete or Partial	No	No	Yes[6]	20 Min. (B) / 30 Min. (C)	No

1. Response times are maximum times under normal conditions.
2. Line security is an option but cannot be shown on the Certificate.
3. Line security is available but on a limited basis.
4. If bell is inside, remote connection required.
5. May or may not be required depending upon equipment used.
6. Recording of opening and closing signals is mandatory.

*Reprinted with permission from Commercial Lines Manual (New York: Insurance Services Office, 1977), p. CR-15.

- *Past Loss Experience.* The type, number, and circumstances of prior losses offer valuable underwriting input as to the moral or morale hazard of the risk. Any questionable losses should be carefully investigated.

Perhaps talk about moral and morale hazard has become tired, overworked "bromides" for underwriters. Yet, the fact remains: "The most primary and essential tenet of underwriting: insurers *insure people,* cover property, and insure against perils."

Adverse Selection

Another problem confronting the crime underwriter is adverse selection, that is, the tendency of those risks with the largest degree of exposure to purchase crime insurance. All forms of insurance present some degree of adverse selection, but there is probably none in which there is both so small a proportion of insured-to-total risks and so dramatic a difference in hazard between those insured and those noninsured. In other types of insurance—fire or workers' compensation—practically all risks are insured, but this is not yet the situation in crime insurance.

The tendency exists for the insured with good management, good location, financial success, adequate protective devices, and favorable past loss experience not to purchase crime insurance or, if so, only in a primary or nominal amount. Conversely, the poor crime risk is more likely to secure coverage to hedge against the crime loss. Adverse selection will never be totally eliminated from crime insurance, but its adverse effect can be controlled by sales efforts and pricing, thereby increasing the base of potential and actual insureds and achieving more desirable results.

Crime Underwriting Options

Having collected data and arranged it and digested it into information, the crime underwriter then decides what is to be done with a submission. As in all underwriting decisions, the alternative options are to:

- decline the risk, or
- accept the risk (with or without modification).

If the underwriter declines the risk, he or she must notify the producer or applicant of this decision. These parties deserve a considerate answer. Producers, especially, must have the reasons for the declination explained. By performing this task in the proper manner, the underwriter can avoid similar submissions which simply waste time. Also, well presented and explained declinations will increase the probability that subsequent submissions will meet acceptable criteria.

Accepting the risk provides, in turn, four major options:

- accept as submitted and price accordingly,
- change conditions and terms and price accordingly,
- demand loss control or loss prevention improvements as a condition of cover and price accordingly, or
- change conditions and terms, insist on loss control improvements, and price accordingly.

FIDELITY

Fidelity insurance covers theft by employees. Because of certain characteristics, it is unique among crime insurances and thus warrants the separate treatment given it here. Its unique character includes the following:

- *Property exposed is accessible.* The very nature of employee theft provides the employee opportunity to learn his firm's routines, schedules, habits, fellow employees, and the existence, absence, and/or relative effectiveness of management controls.
- *Losses can be hidden from discovery.* Unlike burglary and robbery, which by definition are visible crimes, employee theft is by stealth. And, just as with accessibility, the act of theft can be deliberately obscured or covered for varying lengths of time given a knowledge of routines, schedules, and so on, of the firm.
- *The probability of severe loss greatly exceeds other kinds of crime.* The thief's access to property continues until the crime is discoverd. The length of the time of access, in turn, contributes to the size of loss. Even the huge robberies that get the most notoriety are more often that not the result of "insiders."
- *Management control systems are the primary loss control devices.* Safes, vaults, alarm systems, and so on are secondary defenses against fidelity losses. Management's monitoring of revenue, merchandise, and raw material flows into and out of its possession is the first line of defense.
- *Management's reluctance to accept the fact that there may be thieves within the employee complement.* Employers are frequently unwilling to believe that their employees might steal from them; this of course, is an attitude that simply ignores

reality. The reluctance to accept the reality in turn leads to practices that contribute to opportunities for such thefts or at least exacerbate exposures to loss.

● *Management's reluctance to prosecute employee thefts.* It is a generally accepted fact that many employers will not sign complaints and freely testify at criminal proceedings against their employees. The reasons for this appear to be a wish to avoid damaging publicity; an acceptance of the culprit's "hard luck" story; and a desire to have the whole affair quickly over-and-done-with, especially when there is a promise of restitution.

These characteristics of fidelity crimes pose additional problems for underwriters:

1. There is seldom an account with a frequency problem. Losses, when reported, are already fairly large losses, and the final determination of amount of loss invariably greatly exceeds the initial report.
2. Because of the widespread reluctance to accept the reality that an employer may have dishonest employees, there exists an adverse selection problem. For example, the Insurance Information Institute has said, "Although most financial institutions are bonded, fewer than 25 percent of mercantile establishments protect themselves with fidelity bonds." Fidelity bond written premiums totaled only $360,041,000 with a 113.5 percent combined ratio in 1982 (a decline in premium volume from 1981).[2]

Fidelity Underwriting

A fidelity bond is usually written for an indefinite term; there is, however, an annual rating period. The relationship between the insurer and insured, because it is considered a long-term one, must be established on a sound basis at the outset. The underwriter must be satisfied that certain conditions exist prior to bonding:

1. The insured firm (proprietor, partners, or officers) exemplifies management of the highest moral character. The moral hazard, in other words, must be *nonexistent.*
2. The insured should be profitable. Profits are indicative of competence within market spheres, management planning and control systems that work, financial capability of responding to recommended loss control expenditures, and an employee culture that rewards positive performance.

A new firm may not be profitable due to heavy capitalization expenses and because markets are in developmental stages. At the very least, the underwriter must be assured that the founders have meaningful, sufficient experience in prior work.

3. Burglary and robbery loss control systems are in place and maintained. Appropriate defenses against external crime are a deterrence to employees, too.

4. Amounts of insurance are within the limits prescribed by the company.

5. Management controls exist and are maintained. Management controls are a *sine qua non* of fidelity underwriting. Their existence is evidence of management care and concern. Their absence is, with few exceptions, sufficient reason to decline the account.

Fidelity Loss Control[3]

Fidelity loss control is synonymous with "management controls." Listed below are controls applicable to essentially all kinds of firms; these may be considered minimal standards for acceptability. As limits of liability increase, these controls should increase in stringency.

Selection Practices Whether a small, sole proprietorship or a large, multi-national corporation:

- New hires must be screened and their references checked. Applicants with gaps in their employment history must have satisfactory explanations. Those with pertinent criminal convictions, if hired, must be placed in positions where employee theft is essentially impossible.
- Promotions of seasoned employees also require review, especially when the promotion or transfer is into a sensitive position.
- Management must remain sensitive to all employee behavior in order to detect unreasonable or unexplained dramatic changes in life-styles.

Periodic Audits Audits generally test accounts receivable, cash accounts, inventories, and disbursements (accounts payable, travel and entertainment expense accounts, and so on). The tests are samplings of these accounts and are measured against industry or company-wide norms. They provide early detection of malfeasance and they are a highly visible communication to interested employees that management is monitoring performance.

The frequency of audits is usually a management decision, yet the underwriter should feel free to require greater frequency if the amounts of insurance exposed to loss or the nature of the risk warrants. Generally, an audit should occur at least annually. Insurers often establish limit of liability thresholds at which audits must be conducted by Certified Public Accountants rather than by internal auditors.

For small accounts (e.g., firms with ten or fewer employees), internal auditors (company employees) may not exist and the expense of outside auditors may be deemed too great by the owners. In such cases, an underwriter may forgo audits if: (1) bookkeeping records are sound and up-to-date, and (2) there are reasonable grounds to believe that owners are exercising personal supervision on a daily basis and more thorough reviews at least monthly.

Monthly Bank Account Reconciliations Probably nothing is more tempting to employees with their own cash flow difficulties than to be given authority over a checking account where they know the superiors recklessly fail to reconcile the bank statements against revenues and disbursements to that account. It is essential that reconciliation be performed by a person in authority who does not prepare or make deposits or prepare or sign checks or drafts.

Divided Responsibilities Employees who regularly handle merchandise should not have responsibility for handling cash; conversely, those handling cash should not handle merchandise. For the small account, this may not be practical. In such cases an owner must make frequent spot checks.

Physical Inventories Physical inventories by persons other than those directly responsible for merchandise, parts, materials, or their control records should be conducted at least annually.

Annual Vacations All nonowner employees should take annual leaves of not less than five consecutive days. This permits reassignment of positions and opportunities for indiscretions to surface. The ever faithful, long-term employee who refuses to take vacations should be viewed by managers and owners as highly suspect.

COMPUTER CRIME

It is, no doubt, obvious that businesses in the United States are expanding rapidly their use of electronic data processing. What may not be as obvious is the fact that this expansion creates a vital dependency. The computer's ability to perform almost simultaneously a host of diverse functions, at unbelievably high speed and at nominal cost, has created whole new industries and fostered growth in still others that simply could not exist until its advent. This dependency, furthermore, must be considered by underwriters as a highly significant increase in hazard. The existence of expensive data processing networks and their intimate involvement in almost every facet of a firm's operations creates risk.

According to at least one authority, the six greatest computer loss exposures are (1) acts of God; (2) hardware or program failure; (3) human carelessness; (4) invasion of privacy; (5) malicious damage; and (6) theft losses.[4]

Malicious damage and theft are criminal acts that can be committed by outsiders or by employees. While the ultimate loss can be severe from either of these two sources, the opportunity for committing successful crime against the computer is greater for insiders. As an example, a disgruntled employee with the appropriate technical expertise can program data to "self-destruct" at some given time in the future. Because all large computer installations have built-in clocks and calendar systems, this employee can resign and be employed in another part of the country before the "accident" actually occurs. If very clever, this same employee can program a self-destruct program for the very program that causes the original "accident."[5]

Computer *downtime* (i.e., the period during which it is not operational) is expensive. Operational recovery after physical damage or data loss has a major enemy in time. Financial loss increases exponentially with recovery time (see Exhibit 12-4). Therefore downtime of several days may result in revenue drains exceeding the financial capacities of many firms.

Because of the large potential losses arising out of computers, data processing managers and risk managers are forced to view computer risks as possible disasters. Since insurance recoveries seldom make full restitution for actual damages because of extensive indirect costs and losses of customers, the prudent insured must look primarily to private protection and thorough management controls. Similarly, the crime underwriter must view loss controls as essential bases for risk acceptance. The degree to which a firm's management understands the magnitude of potential loss via its data processing system and the care that it takes in establishing and maintaining security cannot be overemphasized. Having established that management does indeed understand its exposure and has taken steps to secure EDP operations, the underwriter need only establish the proper price for the cover.

Exhibit 12-4
Loss Related to Computer Down Time

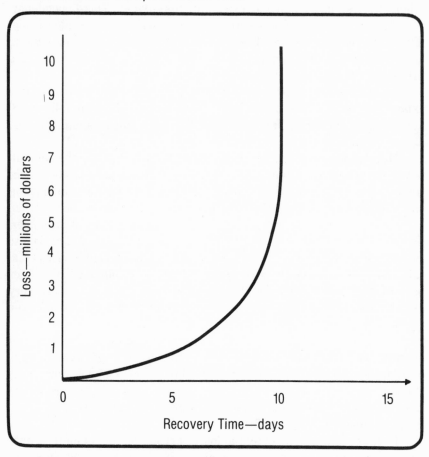

Computer Security Considerations[6]

The following are security recommendations applicable to the majority of data processing installations.

Personnel Requirements

1. Only highly competent data processing personnel, who have been investigated thoroughly, should be permitted use of or access to the computer operations area. Access should be screened by guards or limited to the few personnel provided keys, codes, or cards for entry.
2. Visitors should be required to wear security pass badges and should be escorted while on the premises.

3. The security department should be kept advised on a daily basis of authorized personnel who are permitted access to the computer. Access during "phase-out periods" should be severely limited for employees who have been discharged or who are resigning under questionable circumstances and may attempt to "get even."

4. At least two persons should be in the hardware room at all times.

Data Security

1. When terminals are located outside the main facility perimeter and access to the computer is by teletype, the computer should be programmed not to release information unless an identity code peculiar to that terminal is received on tape. Such codes should be kept secret, changed frequently, and used only by authorized personnel.

2. Computer tapes and storage discs should be controlled by a competent tape librarian.

3. All tapes, files, and other sources of information should be duplicated and stored in fire and theft-resistant storage areas, separate from the computer center.

4. Where confidential information is stored, electronic shielding may be required to prevent the "capture" of emissions. When a computer is in use, electronic emissions occur. These emissions can be "captured" by the use of special equipment and information going into or coming from the computer can be "read" by unauthorized persons.

5. Information that travels between the computer and terminals in remote areas should be coded. Data may be transmitted by wire or satellites; these can be intercepted by unauthorized parties. Codes minimize the probability that intercepted data can be used to damage the owner.

6. When financial transactions are made, such as payroll check preparation, or wire transfers of bank accounts, and so on, frequent internal and external audits should be made.

7. Frequent and thorough audit trails should be incorporated into computer programs. Programs dealing with money or sensitive data should have edits that require authorizations at the highest levels before accepting changes.

Access Security

1. Computer centers and terminals should be designated as exclusion areas with suitable access controls in effect.

2. Computer facilities, including power transformers, air conditioning equipment, and other important related installations should be located away from areas to which the public has access.
3. The computer center and terminals should have adequate perimeter protection, augmented by intrusion alarms and by frequent security patrols.
4. Access should be controlled physically by locks and alarms.

General Considerations

1. The location of the computer center and its use should be made as inconspicuous as possible. For example, no large signs identifying the location of the computer center should be displayed.
2. A safe security perimeter should consider possible fire bomb exposure to the computer room from off-premises locations. The exposure of computers to small arms fire should also be considered in designing the window and wall locations for the computer room.
3. Back-up facilities are important loss control techniques. A firm may have written contracts with nearby data processing facilities to which it can transfer operations in an emergency. The three most common arrangements are:
    a. Use of another firm's excess capacity.
    b. A *cold site* which is a commercial back-up venture consisting of an available, properly wired, alarmed, empty computer room in which substitute leased hardware can be quickly installed.
    c. A *hot site* where a third party keeps a compatible computer installed and running twenty-four hours a day for emergency users.

SUMMARY

Crime insurance covers losses intentionally caused by others. The major crime perils are theft, burglary, robbery, conversion, inventory shortage, and mysterious disappearance, all of which are precisely defined for purposes of insurance coverage. Insurance against crime perils is increasingly accomplished by "all-risks" property policies, such as the SMP special personal property form MP-101A.

Assessing crime loss potential involves examining both the characteristics of the property subject to loss and the characteristics of the risk itself. Territory, public protection, private protection, moral and morale hazard, and adverse selection must all be evaluated.

Types of private protection include premises protection, safes and vaults, and detection systems such as alarms, guards, and surveillance cameras.

Evaluating moral and morale hazards involves investigating the risk's ownership and management, financial and moral reputation, and past loss experience. The problem of adverse selection is a serious one for the crime underwriter; sales efforts and pricing are several of the means available to mitigate it.

Accepting a risk for crime insurance opens four major options to the underwriter: (1) accept as submitted and price accordingly; (2) change conditions and terms and price accordingly; (3) demand loss control or loss prevention improvements as conditions of cover and price accordingly; and (4) change conditions and terms, insist on loss control improvements, and price accordingly.

Fidelity insurance covers theft by employees. It is unique among crime insurances because the property exposed is accessible, losses can be hidden from discovery, the probability of severe loss is high, and management control systems are the primary loss control devices. In addition, management is often reluctant to accept the fact that employee theft is a possibility and often refuses to prosecute employees when thefts are discovered.

When writing a fidelity bond, the underwriter must be satisfied that certain conditions exist, including no moral hazard, sound profitability, adequate burglary and robbery loss control systems, and sufficient management controls. Fidelity loss control factors include selection practices, periodic audits, monthly bank account reconciliations, divided responsibilities, physical inventories, and annual vacations for all non-owner employees.

The burgeoning computer industry has given rise to diverse and potentially catastrophic crime potential. Security considerations for computer installations include personnel requirements, data security, access security, location of the facility, and back-up facilities.

Chapter Notes

---

1. John S. Hammond, III and E. P. Hollingsworth, "How Underwriters Think, Progress Report and Recommendations from the Underwriting Research Program," (May 1971). A research paper privately distributed.
2. *Insurance Facts*, 1983-84 Edition (New York: Insurance Information Institute, 1983), p. 31.
3. The section on fidelity loss control was heavily influenced by The Travelers *Commercial Lines Department Manual*.
4. Frank Lamieux, quoted in *Summary Paper*, 1983, published by *The Institutional Investor* from a seminar: International Risk Management Seminar, "The Emerging Risk of Computer Disaster."
5. This illustration is alleged to have occurred within the IRS, from an interview with Carlton E. Wade, Senior Vice President, Frank B. Hall & Co. Inc., November 1983.
6. Computer Security Considerations was adapted from two position papers: "Protection of Electronic Data Processing Facilities" by Wallace Merrell, Sr., Loss Control Engineer, Frank B. Hall & Co. Inc., June 1980; and "Electronic Data Processing Exposures and Preventive Measures" by Peter Rollinger, P.E., Frank B. Hall & Co. Inc., October 1980.

CHAPTER 13

Underwriting Other Property Lines and Package Policies

INTRODUCTION

This chapter combines several topics. The first part of the chapter briefly discusses some specialty property lines that have heretofore been omitted—boiler and machinery insurance, glass insurance, difference in conditions insurance (DIC), crop hail insurance, and rain insurance. Although the underwriting of these specialty lines is limited to a small number of underwriters, it is helpful for all property underwriters to be aware of the basic coverage provided and the key underwriting factors.

The second part of the chapter describes the major underwriting considerations in package policies. The combination of both property and liability coverages in one policy calls for a high degree of judgment in weighing the positive and negative aspects of the submission.

The third part of this chapter deals with the underwriting of "large" property risks. The definition of a large risk will vary greatly from one insurance company to another. The discussion here is limited to the distinctive features of large risk underwriting.

The final section of the chapter consists of a hypothetical case study, complete with the exhibits that would be in the underwriting file. The objective of the case study is to review and apply many of the skills and concepts presented in the previous twelve chapters. Although an underwriting decision is made, it is not the only correct decision that could be reached. Instead, it reflects the thinking of some experienced underwriters and its inclusion in this text is an invitation to the reader to analyze the case, evaluate the handling of it, and suggest alternative courses of action.

UNDERWRITING SPECIALTY PROPERTY LINES

Boiler and Machinery Insurance

It is likely that a majority of property insurance underwriters seldom become directly involved with underwriting boiler and machinery insurance. Many large and small insurers do not themselves underwrite this line of business. Some of these insurers forgo handling this line of insurance altogether, and leave the business to the few specialty insurers or multiple-line insurers who do issue boiler and machinery policies. Others reinsure 100 percent of their boiler and machinery book of business. Even though policies are issued bearing such insurers' names, with coverage ostensibly underwritten by such insurers, the underwriting and pricing is done entirely by a specialty company.

Of the companies that write boiler and machinery insurance, the underwriting is done by specialists who concentrate in that line of business. Boiler and machinery insurance has historically had a low loss ratio compared to other lines of insurance. The loss ratio alone, however, can be deceiving. Expenses in boiler and machinery insurance are relatively high, because a high proportion of the premiums collected are allocated to loss prevention and inspection services. It is important, therefore, to recognize that the permissible loss ratio in boiler and machinery insurance is fairly low, and that an apparently low loss ratio does not necessarily mean that the line of business has been profitable.

This section on boiler and machinery insurance underwriting is intended to introduce the basics of boiler and machinery insurance underwriting to those who have had little direct contact with that field.

Coverage A boiler and machinery policy affords coverage to four basic types of mechanical equipment (referred to as *objects*): boilers; fired and unfired pressure vessels; mechanical objects such as compressors, steam turbines, and internal combustion engines; and electrical items such as motors, transformers, and switchboards. The insuring agreement covers "accidents" to "objects" as defined in the policy.

The "object" is the boiler or item of machinery insured under the policy. Each object is specifically listed in the policy unless a blanket form is used. In the latter case, a class or group of objects is listed in the policy. Typical objects insured include high and low pressure boilers, steam boilers, hot water boilers, air conditioning compressors, deep well pumps, refrigeration and air conditioning systems, turbines, flywheels, expansion tools, auxiliary piping, and various types of electrical apparatus.

Under the broad form boiler and machinery policy, an "accident" is defined as:

> "Accident" shall mean a sudden and accidental breakdown of the Object or a part thereof, which manifests itself at the time of its occurrence by physical damage to the Object that necessitates repair or replacement of the Object or part thereof; but Accident shall *not* mean (a) depletion, deterioration, corrosion, or erosion of material; (b) wear and tear; (c) leakage at any valve, fitting, shaft seal, gland packing, joint, or connection; (d) the breakdown of any vacuum tube, gas tube, or brush; (e) the breakdown of any electronic computer or electronic data processing equipment; (f) the breakdown of any structure or foundation supporting the Object or any part thereof; (g) an explosion of gas or unconsumed fuel within the furnace of any Object or within the passages from the furnace of said Object to the atmosphere; nor (h) the functioning of any safety device or protective device.

The insuring agreement in a typical boiler and machinery policy includes six coverages:

1. property of the insured
2. expediting expenses
3. property damage liability
4. bodily injury liability
5. defense, settlement and supplementary payments
6. automatic coverage

At the time of this writing, bodily injury liability is optional in several states. It is less important now than in the past because most insureds carry general liability insurance that provides bodily injury liability coverage for most occurrences including boiler and machinery accidents.

Property of the Insured. Payment will be made for loss to the insured's property directly damaged by an accident to an insured object. Coverage is provided not only for the object itself, but also any other property belonging to the insured.

Expediting Expenses. Coverage is provided for the reasonable extra cost of temporary repair and for expediting the repair of the damaged property of the insured. Included are items such as overtime and the extra cost of express transportation of materials. There is a basic limit of $1,000 automatically provided for expediting expenses, which is a part of the policy limit. This amount can be increased by endorsement if additional coverage is desired.

Property Damage Liability. Payment is made for property of others directly damaged by an "accident," for which the insured is legally obligated to pay. Liability for loss of use of damaged property is also covered, as is property of others in the care, custody, and control of the insured. This coverage is excess over the insured's other liability coverages.

Bodily Injury Liability. Optional coverage is available to provide for the loss of services, bodily injury or death of a person as the result of an "accident," if the insured is legally obligated to pay. Payment will not be made for losses which come under workers' compensation, unemployment compensation, or other disability benefit laws. This coverage is also excess insurance, over the insured's other liability coverages.

Defense, Settlement, and Supplementary Payments. The insurer will defend the insured against any suits alleging property damage liability as the result of an "accident." The same costs will be paid for suits alleging bodily injury, if the optional bodily injury coverage is carried. These provisions are typical of those found in other general liability policies, and are paid regardless of the limit per "accident."

Automatic Coverage. This "coverage," which is really more of an extension of coverage, allows the insured ninety days of automatic coverage on equipment at newly acquired locations provided the objects are of the same general character as the ones already insured in the policy. The insured agrees to notify the insurer in writing within ninety days after property is acquired, and also agrees to pay the additional premium for insurance on the newly acquired property.[1]

A unique feature of boiler and machinery insurance is the application of the limits of liability. The single limit of liability applies per accident but if a loss includes payments under more than one of the six "coverages" listed above, the payments are made on a *priority basis.* For example, when a loss occurs, payment for property of the insured (item 1 above) is made first. Expediting expenses up to the $1,000 limit (item 2 above) are the next payments made. If property damage liability is involved, the remaining amount of insurance is available for payment for it. This continues through the six coverages provided. Consequently, underwriters must be acutely aware of the relationship between the insured's loss potential and the limit of liability requested. If a policy is issued with a $25,000 limit and a severe explosion occurs, the entire amount of insurance may be insufficient to pay for the damage to the property of the insured leaving nothing for expediting expenses, property damage liability, and the other coverages.

Indirect damage coverage is available on an optional basis, but direct damage coverage is required before the insured can purchase indirect coverage. The most common of these coverages are business interruption (formerly called "use and occupancy"), extra expense, and consequential damage.

Business interruption is designed to reimburse the insured for loss of income resulting from a covered accident. This is very similar to the business interruption insurance discussed in Chapter 8.

Extra expense coverage is intended to cover the additional cost (over and above the expediting expenses of $1,000) of continuing the business of the insured during the period of restoration. These extra expenses cover only the "extra expenses" beyond those normally incurred to conduct business during the same period had no loss occurred. This coverage is written on risks such as hospitals, newspapers, dairies, schools, and nursing homes.

Consequential damage coverage provides indemnity for loss on specified property of the insured when such loss is due to spoilage from lack of power, light, heat, steam, or refrigeration caused by an accident to an insured object. Dairies and other operations with cold storage facilities frequently purchase this coverage. A breakdown in the refrigeration system could cause substantial consequential losses in spoiled milk or other perishable commodities.

Inspections and Underwriting   There are several factors that should be considered initially when underwriting a boiler and machinery policy. They are:

1. The ability of the prospective insured's maintenance department to competently make repairs and perform preventive maintenance checks of the objects which are the subject of insurance.
2. The age of the objects. Older objects can be obsolete because replacement parts are not readily available. This can greatly increase the severity of business interruption or extra expense losses.
3. The location of the risk. Most states require boilers and pressure vessels to be inspected as much as two times yearly. The expense of traveling to outlying accounts to perform these inspections can equal the premium derived from the account.

These and many other factors can be evaluated only through a thorough physical inspection by an expert. Inspections are an integral part of boiler and machinery underwriting for two reasons. First, the underwriter's decision on acceptability and pricing is dependent upon a complete technical inspection to assure that all objects are correctly described and an appropriate premium charge is made. Second, many insureds purchase boiler and machinery insurance primarily for the inspection service to prevent losses and secondarily to reimburse for the losses that do occur.

Inspection services reduce not only the number of accidents but may also reduce the severity of accidents that cannot be prevented. This service, as expensive as it is, costs less than the losses that would have to be paid without it. In addition, the inspection services are usually required by state law for many businesses.

The inspection service may be described, in summary, as consisting of three principal functions, each of which has several features:[2]

1. *It represents the eye through which the underwriter sees the risk.*
   (a) It develops information regarding the physical condition of the object.
   (b) It investigates the hazards involved in the operation of the object.
   (c) It shows general plant conditions, particularly the relation of the insured object to surrounding property.
   (d) It develops underwriting and rating data.
   (e) It provides surveys and, for indirect damage risks, it provides particularly valuable underwriting information by pointing out the key equipment, the outside repair facilities, and the possibilities of securing outside power in the event of breakdowns.

2. *It is effective in the prevention of accidents.*
   (a) It reduces the frequency of accidents.
   (b) It often reduces the severity of accidents that it has been unable to prevent.
   (c) It helps the insured to maintain the objects in safe operating condition.
   (d) It promotes longer life of the objects.
   (e) It provides advice regarding more efficient operation of the objects.
   (f) It shows how objects should be repaired, when repairs are required.

3. *It affords an efficient engineering investigation of accidents.*
   (a) It assists the insured with advice in restoring plant production.
   (b) It assists the insured with advice in repairing damaged property.
   (c) It assists the insured in locating equipment to substitute for that which has been damaged.

(d) It determines the cause of the accident so as to prevent, if possible, other similar occurrences.

(e) It enables the companies to maintain statistics on causes of accidents for study in connection with the prevention of accidents.

Boiler and machinery inspection service can be the most valuable part of an insured's protection, and yet there is no guarantee to the insured that the service will be provided. It usually cannot be had without purchasing the insurance; nor will insurance generally be provided without the service. Although the expense of the service is borne by the policyholder, the cost of a policy would be greater if the service were dropped.

Glass Insurance

Coverage The comprehensive glass insurance policy may be written separately or as part of a package policy. In either case, the coverage and underwriting are similar.

Glass insurance covers all kinds of glass, whether structural or interior glass, of a building, including lettering and ornamentation. Generally, each specific piece of glass is scheduled in the policy with a description of its size and location in the building. For example, glass that is set in doors, in transoms, or showcases is described as such.

The policy covers damage to the glass (or lettering, etc.) caused by breakage of the glass or by chemicals accidentally or maliciously applied. The policy does not include the word "accidental" as applying to breakage. There is no coverage for scratching glass if there is no break in the glass. Likewise, the abrasion that results from sandstorms or wear and tear would not be covered. The three policy exclusions are (a) loss by fire, (b) loss due to war, whether declared or not, civil war, insurrection, rebellion, or revolution, or to any act or condition incident to the foregoing, and (c) loss from nuclear damage.

Coverage extensions of the plate glass policy include three items: (a) repairing or replacing frames immediately encasing and contiguous to the insured glass, (b) installation of temporary plates or boarding up openings because of an unavoidable delay in repairing or replacing damaged glass, and (c) removing and replacing any obstructions, such as signs or protective coverings, necessary to replace damaged glass. This extension is limited to $75 per occurrence at any one location. Additional dollar coverage may be purchased.

Glass is grouped into five classifications, identified as classes A, B, C, D, and E. Glass classified under classes A-D is insured for its replacement cost based on its dimensions. An amount of insurance is not required. The limit of the company's liability for damages does not exceed either (1) the actual cash value of the property at the time of loss, or (2) the cost to repair or replace the damaged property with other property of the "nearest obtainable kind and quality."

Glass that fits the definition of class E must be insured for a specific amount based on its replacement value. This includes memorial windows, stained glass windows, or other art glass.

Underwriting   The glass policy premium is relatively small since the policy provides for a complete replacement of the scheduled class. Any loss calls for a complete replacement of the glass. Because of these factors, little specific risk underwriting can be accomplished on glass policies. Loss control (especially prevention) is of great importance in glass insurance. Thus most underwriting programs consider high risk occupancies, types of glass, and high risk areas.

High Risk Occupancies.   These classes of risks normally have an attractive merchandise exposure, or a higher than average exposure to autos or human beings. Typical occupancies grouped under these categories are: auto showrooms, buildings in the course of construction, drive-in restaurants, greenhouses, laundromats, liquor stores, service stations, schools, supermarkets, taverns, and vacant buildings.

Types of Glass.   Certain types of glass or glass in certain conditions require special underwriting consideration. Examples are:

- A risk with a plate glass exceeding 100 square feet. Installation charges are high for this type of glass and, because of its size, it becomes more expensive. However, it should be noted that there is an endorsement called a *large plate endorsement* that could be added when insuring a plate of this size. The endorsement allows for the installation of two or more plates instead of one.
- Any glass that is broken or cracked—however, this type of glass, if desired, can be endorsed to allow coverage for new breaks only.
- Glass that is in an old building with deteriorated frames. Obviously with poor frames the exposure to wind or other causes increases substantially.
- Stained glass—the value to replace is increased because of the special techniques and craft required to replace stained glass. This is in addition to the fewer craftspeople available today to do this type of work.
- Neon signs—these are subject to temperature changes if on the exterior of a building.

- Glass that is now being produced on a limited basis or is extremely difficult to obtain. An example of this type of glass is vitrolite.

High Risk Areas or Locales.   Risks that are subject to a beach exposure or a hurricane and wave wash can present a catastrophic exposure. Also, some underwriters may restrict coverage in known earthquake areas or where there is a problem of earth subsidence. Other problem areas could come from locations subject to floods.

Pricing   The underwriter has several pricing techniques available. The premiums and the territorial multipliers are based on common exposures and usual charges for normal glass installation. Premiums are based on the size of the glass as well as class, use, and position in the building. If a particular type of glass is a problem because of high installation cost or high obstructions, additional charges may have to be applied to the manual rate. Glass with certain types of listed protection can receive discounts (actually called a multiplier).

Experience rating can also provide either a credit or debit based on the insured's loss experience and also a schedule debit or credit can be applied. Generally an account must produce at least $325 annual premium to be eligible for experience and schedule rating. Deductibles can be applied if a risk has a loss frequency situation. A deductible amount ranging from $50-$1,000 can be applied and it may apply separately to each building.

Loss Control   Underwriting can also be accomplished upon review of a loss file. If an insured has had vandalism losses to glass, he or she could install protective coverings such as screens, shutters, or metal bars over the glass at night or after business hours. Losses caused by burglary may be reduced with installation of a burglar alarm that includes foil around the window that will discourage burglars from breaking the windows. Removal of valuable property from a window will also reduce the temptation for someone to break the glass and steal the property.

In areas where a hurricane exposure may exist, shutters can be installed to protect the glass. Insureds whose premises are exposed to vehicles could install guard rails or curbs to protect the glass. Also if there have been windows broken by objects thrown from the wheels of vehicles, the glass could be protected with a screen.

The problem of the small premium size does not lend itself to an on-site inspection of any plate glass risks. Thus most companies will require that the plate glass coverage be written as part of the building coverage. Glass coverage is normally treated by most insurers as an accommodation type of business.

Difference in Conditions

Perhaps the broadest "all-risks" coverage is the difference in conditions (DIC) form. The form provides "all-risks" coverage including burglary, collapse, water damage, and, optionally, earthquake and flood coverage. Additional coverage such as transit and business interruption also can be purchased. An unusual aspect of the coverage is that it excludes the basic perils of fire and lightning, extended coverage, vandalism or malicious mischief, and sprinkler leakage. The general "all-risks" exclusions, such as war, nuclear perils, wear, tear, loss of use, loss of market, temperature changes, and mysterious disappearance, are applicable. Mechanical breakdown, steam boiler explosion, and electrical damage to electrical appliances are excluded under some DIC forms.

This is an attractive policy for many businesses since it "wraps around" the basic property coverages providing perils which are unavailable separately. The insured has the option of selecting the limit for each type of property to be covered. The limit does not necessarily need to be the value of the property at a particular location, or 80 or 90 percent of the value. In other words, the insured can purchase the amount of coverage deemed necessary for the perils covered on the DIC.

The underwriter must consider all the exposures to loss when reviewing any "all-risks" form. This is particularly true of underwriting the DIC. Special applications have been devised to develop specific underwriting information regarding the exposures to loss.

Since insurance to value is not required for the DIC perils, the underwriter is immediately placed in a position of being adversely selected against. Full evaluation of the loss potential is necessary, but it is not an adequate method of making DIC a profitable line. As a result, pricing is an important part of underwriting this line. Sufficient premium must be developed to pay for the losses and expenses within the limits selected by the insured. Being a nonfiled, open-rating type program, most insurers have created underwriting guides which help the underwriter properly price the coverage.

For example, a base rate per $100 of insurance with a $250 deductible may be $.03 for real property including improvements and betterments, $.045 for personal property, and $.025 for loss of income or rent. Loadings for transportation, flood, and earthquake, depending on the exposures of the particular risk, are added to this base rate of $.10.

Debits of up to 10 percent may be applied to any of these rates based on the underwriter's evaluation of the existing hazards, particularly the collapse and water damage hazards. Debits are also applied if the contents are relatively susceptible to damage. Separate loadings can be added if storage tanks are present, and a separate loading is included for the theft perils. Higher deductibles may be required. The resulting rate is then modified by a factor which is based on the relationship of the limit of liability to the total property values. This factor, of course, increases as the limit of liability (in relation to the total value) decreases, thus attempting to generate more premium in the cases where the adverse selection is greater.

Crop Hail Insurance

Crop hail insurance is designed to provide coverage against all direct loss or damage by hail to the crops described in the policy. The policy does not cover losses resulting from a beating rain or losses caused by wind.

Due to the potential for adverse selection when a severe storm is evident, applications must be in writing and payment may be required with the application. Coverage is not effective until a certain time period (usually twenty-four hours) after the signing of the application.

Most crop hail policies are written for the term of one growing season. This may range from August to November depending on the crop and the location.

The limits of liability range from $5 to $200 per acre depending on the crop and the expected return per acre.[3] It is customary to purchase several insurance policies from several insurers to secure the necessary amounts of coverage, each with a limitation per acre.

The policy specifies the particular crop that is covered and its location. The location is carefully specified by county, township, range number, and/or section or quarter section, depending upon the designation that is necessary to identify the exact location of the crop. There is another plan used by some companies called the *farm unit plan*. Insurance under this plan covers the entire farm unit.[4]

The Crop Hail Insurance Actuarial Association (CHIAA) does the statistical and the filing work for all subscribing companies and acts as an advisory body for crop hail policies and forms. It requires all of its members and subscribers to report all crop hail losses. It also requires a copy of all applications and each proof of loss that has been paid.

Another crop hail organization is the Hail Insurance Adjustment and Research Association (HIARA) which provides educational facilities and meetings to claims adjusters on the techniques of adjusting hail losses. The adjustment of hail losses is unique in that it is seasonal and it does require a specialty background of an individual who understands and recognizes the effect of hail damages to crops.

Hail losses must be handled quickly. Notice of loss must be given within forty-eight hours after loss or damage has occurred. Samples are taken to indicate the percentage of loss. These samples may include an actual count of stalks and the proportion of stalks damaged by the hail.

The underwriter will usually avoid crops that are subject to a large loss from an average hail storm, such as tree fruits, tomatoes, and some vegetables. Of course, the location in the country has an effect on this underwriting attitude as insurance coverage on these crops may be acceptable in the northeastern states as opposed to the midwestern states.

Another consideration is identifying areas with a consistent pattern of severe hail storms. These areas must be underwritten carefully to provide a spread of risks each year and also to be able to offer coverage over a span of years. The dollar limits of insurance on crops must be carefully reviewed and must be consistent with anticipated values of the harvested crops. This requires considerable experience and knowledge of growing grops as the farm market for growing crops is subject to significant market fluctuations.

Another concern is the total liability exposure in a particular locality or area. This possible accumulation of exposures requires a mapping or recording system of crop hail liability usually on the basis of sections, townships, or similar identifying areas. Since the spread of liability is important in underwriting this class of business, the amount of total liability must be watched closely. If the amount of insurance in the defined geographical area exceeds the predetermined limits, the underwriter may use reinsurance to reduce exposures.

Of course, rates are to be considered also. Through the pooling of statistics, rates are closely controlled and very detailed. The rates are generally adequate except in the high risk areas.

Crop hail insurance does appear to be increasing due to the changing methods of farming from the small producer to the large producers who have large financial debts and thus a large financial risk at stake for hail damage to growing crops. Hail is one of several cyclical perils and thus underwriting results must be evaluated on a long-term basis.

Rain Insurance

Rain insurance provides protection for loss of income or extra expense on a short-term money making event caused by rain, hail, snow, or sleet that occurs during a specified period of time. Generally this period of time (chosen by the insured) includes the hours during the event and a few hours before the insured event is to take place.

Normally, a rain policy is effective just prior to the commencement of the event and expires after the completion of the insured event.

Auto races, carnivals, excursions, exhibitions, fairs, golf matches, outdoor band concerts, rodeos, tennis matches, and track meets are typical insured events. Events extending over a longer period of time or series of events (such as a football season) are less exposed to severe losses by rain. Rain insurance is unique in that no direct damage is necessary before the insured consequential loss is covered.

The forms and rates for rain insurance are controlled by the Crop Hail Insurance Actuarial Association (CHIAA). There are two forms that are available for rain insurance—Form A, the basic form, and Form B, the optional form.

Form A, or the *basic form,* pays the difference between the amount of insurance and the actual income received, during the insured event provided it rains in excess of the amount of rainfall insured against. The rainfall must occur during the specified time period that is shown on the policy. The amount of rainfall is selected by the insured and may range from 5/100 up to 1 inch or more of rainfall.

Form B may be termed the *optional* or *valued form* as it pays the full amount of insurance when a loss occurs. It may be written to cover the total income of the event or may be written to cover extra expenses only. The latter arrangement is designed to provide protection if the event has a financial commitment it must pay, whether or not the income will exceed the expenses.

Rain insurance policies require that a rain gauge be read by either a U.S. Weather Bureau observer, a cooperative observer, or a reputable disinterested party. The rain gauge reader must be designated in advance of issuance of the policy and the rain gauge location must be specified prior to the issuance of the policy.

Most companies require that the premium payment and policy be issued at a minimum of seven days in advance of the date of the event to be insured. The rain gauge observer is critically important and the underwriter must be assured that the observer is not connected with the event. The most desirable situation is when personnel from the weather bureau are utilized.

In underwriting the basic form, the coverage should be limited to 100 percent of the gross income of the previous event. If there was no previous experience, the underwriter may limit the exposure to 100 percent of the total expenses. The optional or valued form has a choice of income or expenses. The underwriter probably would want to limit the income since it is a valued form up to 60 percent or 70 percent of the gross income from a previous event or, if there was no previous event, 100 percent of the projected expenses for the event. The optional form is the normally requested form. If the rain policy covers for a longer period of time, generally more than six or seven hours, the underwriter should request more rainfall be required for payment of a loss.

UNDERWRITING PACKAGE POLICIES

Kinds of Package Policies

The underwriting of package (or combination) policies depends to some degree on the kind of package policy. All package policies may be described as (a) simple collection or combination policies, (b) minimum requirement combination policies, (c) indivisible combination policies, and (d) nonstandard combination policies.[5]

A *simple combination policy* includes two or more standard coverages in a more convenient format for the insured. An example is the comprehensive 3-D policy that permits up to eighteen crime coverages to be packaged. There is no package discount and the underwriting of such packages is the same as if separate coverages were requested. This approach provides maximum flexibility to the underwriter who may choose not to issue the requested form but instead offer a more restricted form if necessary. Each coverage is priced separately and the package premium is simply a total of the premiums for the individual coverages.

In a *minimum requirement combination policy*, certain coverages are combined and the insured must purchase the minimum required coverages. An example is the SMP (special multi-peril) policy that requires fire and extended coverage on property (Section I) and some basic liability coverage (Section II). Additional coverages may be added on an optional basis.

Adverse selection is reduced by requiring certain minimum coverages. The policy writing, accounting, and billing expenses are less with one package policy rather than three or four separate single line (or monoline) policies. On an entire book of business this reduces expense costs. The benefits of reduction in expense costs and adverse selection are passed along to the insured in the form of a package discount, usually 15 to 20 percent.

Due to this package discount, most insurers limit the eligibility to "above average" risks. The underwriting guide or manual usually specifies what is "above average" in terms of type of business and physical hazards. One inspection may provide sufficient information for property, liability, and crime loss exposures. Since there is a minimum requirement of property and liability coverages, inspections are coordinated. This is unlike separate policies which could require separate inspections if ordered at different times.

Under the minimum requirement approach, the underwriter must not only analyze and evaluate each of the individual coverages, but must weigh the interrelationship of these diverse exposures. A single larger premium must reflect a combination of smaller premiums of varying levels of adequacy.

An *indivisible combination policy* provides a broad range of coverages on an all or nothing basis for a single indivisible premium. An example is the businessowners policy (BOP) developed by the Insurance Services Office. Unlike the minimum requirement policy, the premium is shown only in total and cannot be separated by coverage. Indivisible combination policies permit little coverage selection by the insured, thus reducing adverse selection. But such an arrangement permits almost no underwriting flexibility with regard to pricing and offering alternative coverages. The underwriter's challenge then is to evaluate the sum of the various exposures presented by a risk against the single premium to determine acceptability.

Nonstandard combination policies are usually manuscript contracts written to the insured's and the underwriter's specifications. Maximum flexibility is obtained by eliminating minimum coverages and pricing tends to be on an individual risk basis. This approach is limited to large insureds.

Underwriting Considerations

Underwriting decision making is simple on a submission with no adverse exposures. Likewise, the decision is clear if the submission has no redeeming values. The decision becomes difficult when part of the package is acceptable but the balance is not. Perhaps the property loss exposures of a small manufacturer are minimal due to loss control devices but the products liability exposure may be great due to the nature of the product. Or, the premises and operations liability exposures of a dry cleaner may be excellent as demonstrated in its loss-free history, but the property exposure may be questionable due to the use of a solvent with a low flash point.

In these cases, the underwriter must weigh the strengths against the weaknesses, identify any appropriate alternatives and choose the best one. To do this, an underwriter may ask questions such as:[6]

1. What are the respective *limits of liability* of each of the sections of the package policy?
2. What are the respective *premiums* for each policy section? (This question is inappropriate if the package policy has an indivisible premium, thus complicating the underwriter's decision.)

3. What are the respective *frequencies* of loss for each major policy section?
4. What are the respective *severities* of loss for each major policy section?

Interrelating and sometimes conflicting exposures are those in which a low hazard for one line of coverage increases the hazard of another coverage. This may be compounded by the fact that an underwriter may wish to offer suggestions to further lower the exposure in the first category which will increase the exposure in the second line of coverage. An example of this problem is a large building with only one entrance. This arrangement will reduce the hazards of burglary and theft since only one door opening must be monitored and secured. The lack of alternate openings, however, increases the fire hazard since it limits the access to the building. It also increases the hazard of third-party liability in preventing good egress from the building for personnel if a fire or other emergency were to occur.

The underwriter must therefore approach hazard control across all lines of coverage as well as consider the public. How does the underwriter decide in which direction to go? First, loss severity and frequency must be considered and, second, the desirability and cost of providing additional protection for one line of coverage to compensate for the reduction in hazard in another must be considered. Can the underwriter sell additional doors and windows in the blank walls of a building to allow fire department access and emergency egress with the burglary protection needed for these new openings in an occupancy vulnerable to a crime exposure? And if he or she can, is the increased access worth the additional cost to the insured, the resulting increased crime hazard, and the chance of losing the account to a competitor? The interrelation of hazards must be evaluated on an overall basis.

In addition, the underwriter must determine if the premium for the low hazard exposures compensates for the inadequate premiums of the higher hazard exposures. Most rating plans contain minimum rates and/or minimum premiums by coverage for low hazard risks. They have been developed to cover the expenses of underwriting and issuing a policy which may account for the majority of the cost in some instances. When a number of coverages are combined into a single package, the minimum rates, being primarily for expense purposes, may provide more than adequate premium when added to other line premiums.

In indivisible premium policies, the underwriter must use imagination to identify unusual exposures for which an indivisible "class rate" does not develop sufficient premium. For example, one such package provided "all-risks" coverage on liquor stores at a premium less than that for mercantile open stock alone.

Package underwriting also provides the opportunity to investigate the management abilities and techniques as they relate to the total loss control of the account. Management will influence all areas of loss potential to assure the continuing profitability of the operation and the development of programs for the recognition and control of loss exposures. The package policy analysis, because it has more expense dollars available from the larger premium enables the underwriter to look more closely at many aspects of management including their ability to make a profit. A profitable operation will have both the resources to invest in loss control as well as the desire to do so to remain in operation and continue to make money.

UNDERWRITING LARGE COMMERCIAL PROPERTY RISKS

Underwriting large commercial property accounts involves all of the considerations discussed previously in connection with smaller commercial property risks. But in addition, large multistate or multinational accounts pose the following problems not found in small or single location risks:

- The large loss potential which relates directly to the underwriter's authority to write the account.
- The complexity of operations and the equipment itself requiring more knowledge in underwriting and loss control.
- The interrelation and interdependency of plants and the resulting business interruption exposures.
- The geographical differences (natural and artificial) that occur due to widespread locations.
- The variation in age within locations making analysis of exposures more difficult.
- The varying hazard conditions due to differences in management style caused by a multi-management structure, the type of industry, or recent acquisitions.

All of these must be evaluated to estimate the loss potential of the entire account prior to risk acceptance.

The first major consideration is the sheer size of the exposure. Most underwriting guidelines contain net line limitations coupled with treaty and/or facultative reinsurance limit amounts that an underwriter must adhere to. For example, an underwriter may have the authority to write a line up to $500,000 at a single location placing this property exposure one-third for the company net, and two-thirds to an automatic reinsurance treaty. If the exposure exceeds $500,000, the underwriter may have to secure approval from a higher authority or may be prohibited from writing the line. The potential severity of a single loss is therefore a very definite first consideration.

A second consideration is the complexity of the exposures as an account increases in size. Machinery and equipment will tend to become more highly automated and more specialized. Operations hazards within plants and between plants will also magnify as the size of the risk increases. For example, assume that a stock storage hazard exposes a manufacturing operation hazard. The resulting hazard will be higher than the sum of the two individual risks. It will increase in an exponential fashion because the many fire sources of the manufacturing operation now have the additional fuel from the storage to cause a major loss. Either operation alone may be classed as a hazard of two or three. When they expose each other directly, the resulting hazard may range from eight to ten. (This is based on a scale of one to ten with one being minimal and ten being severe.) Loss control or inspection reports must therefore become much more detailed and be prepared by more experienced personnel to properly evaluate the larger and more complex exposures of a large property risk.

Third, the business interruption exposure between operating plants also becomes a more complex problem as the account size increases. The smaller risks tend to contain all operations at one location and may therefore be evaluated more easily and by one person. Larger companies may begin the manufacturing process in one part of the country, may ship labor intensive operations to more favorable labor markets, including overseas plants, and then ship the partly finished product to another plant for completion. Separate exposures in the warehousing and distribution operations may also be at different geographical locations. A loss at any point in the chain may interrupt or slow all other operations and must therefore be fully evaluated by the underwriter in developing the amount subject to a single loss as well as the probable frequency of loss. The possibility of duplication of operations and/or supplies from outside vendors must be evaluated to complete the business interruption underwriting process for the larger account.

Fourth, as property risks increase in size, they will tend to be located in many parts of the country or even in different countries. The underwriter's local knowledge that is so helpful in evaluating the small property exposure now may only suffice for a single plant in his or her area. The underwriter's knowledge of other parts of the country must therefore be increased if all exposures are to be evaluated properly. Other states may present loss exposures entirely unfamiliar to the underwriter in his or her local area. Exposures such as earthquake, flood, windstorm, or brush fire may pose severe hazards in certain areas and be unheard of in the underwriter's local sector. Conditions in fire protection may also not be as fully understood. Information from others must be secured on these hazards, whereas the information would be known by the underwriter if the risk were a local one.

Fifth, the larger property accounts will also contain buildings of varying age groups. Smaller exposures will most probably be constructed at one time whereas the larger risk may have many extensions or additions built at different times. This will make the evaluation of the condition of the buildings and the building equipment facilities more difficult.

Finally, the larger exposures will also contain varying conditions due to differences in management style at separate locations. Management attitudes toward loss control and plant arrangement will affect the degree of hazard of similar operations. Differences in management style will also occur within the various types of industries found in a large conglomerate. The approach to loss control, housekeeping, and plant security may vary markedly when directed by the management of a heavy manufacturing risk as opposed to a retail clothing outlet. The underwriter must evaluate these varying management attitudes before developing an overall judgment on the account.

In addition, recent acquisitions may also cause differences that must be evaluated individually in the large property risk as opposed to the single smaller property risk. A new acquisition, although in the same type of industry, may have markedly different safety or fire protection practices and may be an entirely different hazard level than the main portion of the account with the same general operations.

The final underwriting decision must therefore consider all of the above conditions with weights attached to each. The potential for change or improvement must also be evaluated with emphasis given to the interrelating business interruption exposures in the single line or vertically integrated manufacturing operation.

The large property risks develop a larger premium with which to balance high and low hazard exposures. In a case of very large accounts, a self-rated risk may be developed within a specified limit. For example: for an account with 100 or more locations, one may separate the gross rate into two parts—the high frequency, low severity part to cover losses up to a limit (usually in the $50,000 to $250,000 range) and the low frequency, high severity part for all losses over this limit. Premiums may be developed separately with a deposit established for the lower limit (frequent) losses to be adjusted annually to cover actual losses plus insurance company expenses. The severity part of the exposure may be insured at a fixed rate and pooled in the standard fashion of insurance. Smaller risks do not offer this alternative and all of the exposure must be pooled except for very small deductibles of usually $1,000 or less.

NARRAGANSETT MANUFACTURING CO., INC. CASE STUDY

The section which follows attempts to draw together and have the reader use, in an integrated fashion, much of the information presented throughout the earlier chapters of this book. The Narragansett Case demands that John Heath, the underwriter to whom it is presented, make a group of decisions not unlike those that underwriters must make when confronted with similarly sized property risks.

The presentation of this case allows the reader to watch John Heath at work. From time to time there are opportunities to anticipate John's behavior and reactions. Inevitably, readers also may play "Monday morning quarterback" (or Tuesday morning if it was the Monday night game) and disagree with some of the decisions he makes. It is one of the great fascinations of underwriting that two or more good underwriters can reach dissimilar conclusions from the same data.

The reader may wish to review Chapter 11, "Decision Making and Monitoring," from *Principles of Property and Liability Underwriting*, especially pages 455 through 479. The case begins with the letter and enclosures sent to John Heath by Herbert Wilson which appear in Exhibits 13-1, 13-2, 13-3, 13-4, 13-5 and 13-6.

Gathering Data and the Preliminary Commitment

Does John have enough data to make a preliminary commitment, i.e., can he respond positively to Herbert's request ". . . regarding your (John's) willingness to quote?"

Here is what John did:

- A quick visit with his commercial auto underwriting colleague confirmed his expectation that there was no adverse data from that end. Indeed, the colleague stated he was very happy with that line.

- A brief mental (almost unconscious) review of Herbert Wilson and his firm confirmed a positive reaction. Herbert is a professional producer with whom the IIA enjoys a good working relationship. The submission for this particular risk, while incomplete, was clearly above average.

Exhibit 13-1
Request for Quotation

WILSON AND SCOTT
. . . professional insurance brokerage

August 7, 19X8

John Heath, Sr. Underwriter
IIA Insurance Co.
Malvern, PA 19355

Dear John:

We have written the W.C., Liability and Auto Insurance for
Narragansett Mfg. Co., Inc. for seven years. The Commercial
Auto Line is currently with your company. The property
insurance, until recently was handled by Munsen & Hickock
who had it widely spread with good carriers. Although I
have competed hard over the years to win the opportunity to
place the property, Narragansett's E.C. Mullin always held
firm with Harry Munsen. As you know, Harry has recently
retired. In the past few days Mullin has decided we should
get the exclusive on the property business as well.

It is my thought that the bulk of the property be handled
via an all-risks package policy with appropriate endorsements
for the dry transit, the motor truck cargo, neon sign, and
the patterns. A separate ocean cargo policy probably should
be quoted for the international exposure.

John, will you please give me a written response regarding
your willingness to quote. I need this within five working
days. According to the information I have now, I will need
a firm quote within 45 days; I am assuming this is sufficient
time for inspections, etc. Enclosed find: (1) my description
of Narragansett's operations; (2) schedule of property; (3)
financial records; (4) coverage requested.

I trust you will think as highly of this account as I do.

Very truly yours,

Herbert Wilson

HERBERT WILSON

HW: al
Enclosures (4)

Exhibit 13-2

Narragansett Manufacturing Company, Inc.—Description of Operations

---

Enclosure No. 1   Narragansett Mfg. Co., Inc.

The firm was founded in 1883 by Israel Arnold, the great-
grandfather of the current chief executive. The orginal
plant was the small, square, two-story building now subordi-
nate to the two larger structures on Moses Brown Road. The
business was started as a small, quality foundry and, from
the beginning, produced items for electrical use--e.g.,
decorative street poles, bases for domestic floor lamps, etc.

The operations today include: (1) two manufacturing shops,
one in Pawtucket and the other in Palo Alto, California; (2)
a warehouse for storing raw materials and finished goods in
Pawtucket; and (3) a large, leased showroom in the Modern
Designs Building in New York.

The Pawtucket plant makes all the industrial and street
(outdoor) lighting equipment. In addition, it makes all the
castings of metal bases. Approximately 50 percent of the
domestic castings are, in turn, shipped to the Palo Alto
plant for assembly and distribution to West Coast buyers.
The Palo Alto plant makes approximately 85 percent of the
domestic socket switches, shipping some 40 percent of this
out-put to the Pawtucket plant. The Pawtucket plant purchases additional socket switches from an independent company
in Philadelphia, Pennsylvania. No metal castings are made
in California.

Approximately 50 percent of the production of both plants
are shipped to wholesalers and retailers via owned trucks--
two at each plant. Ten percent of the Pawtucket out-put is
shipped to a wholesaler in London, England; it goes via a
freight forwarder in Boston who heretofore has provided
marine insurance. The remainder of all shipments is via
common carrier.

Exhibit 13-3

Narragansett Manufacturing Company, Inc.—Schedule of Property

---

Enclosure No. 2   Narragansett Mfg. Co., Inc.

Schedule of Property

Address	Construction Type	Date	100% R/C Value	F. + EC Rate	Limit Liability
37 Moses Brown Road, Pawtucket, RI	(1)Masonry-- 4 stories	1938	$ 360,000	1.35	$ 288,000
	Machinery	various	400,000	0.96	200,000
	Contents	---	200,000	0.96	160,000
	(2)Masonry-- 2 stories	1969	220,000	0.77	176,000
	Contents- Office	---	165,000	0.58	132,000
	(3)Masonry-- 2 story foundry	1896	256,000	1.05	205,000
	Machinery incl.		---		
1253 Wheelwright Road, Pawtucket	Fire- resistive 3 story warehouse	1972	625,000	0.26	510,000
	Contents	---	2,000,000 to 3,400,000	0.30	4,000,000
1849 El Camino Real, Palo Alto, CA	Fire- resistive 1 story	1959	660,000	0.22	528,000
	Machinery	various	425,000	0.24	340,000
	Contents	---	1,650,000		1,320,000
549 E. 58th St., N.Y.C.	Fire- resistive 32 stories	1952	---	---	---
	Contents		200,000	0.19	160,000
			$5,161,000		$8,019,000

Exhibit 13-4
Narragansett Manufacturing Company, Inc.—
Comparative Balance Sheet

NARRAGANSETT MANUFACTURING CO., INC.

Enclosure No. 3 (A)

Comparative Balance Sheet
(000 omitted)

Assets

	12/31/X6	12/31/X7
Current Assets		
Cash	$ 65	$ 72
Securities	182	197
Net receivables	317	406
Inventories	486	645
Total current assets	1,050	1,320
Fixed Assets		
Gross plant and equipment	1,605	1,767
Less: depreciation	480	588
Net plant and equipment	2,085	2,355
Total Assets	$3,135	$3,675

Liabilities and Stockholders' Equity

	12/31/X6	12/31/X7
Current Liabilities		
Accounts payable	$ 66	$ 84
Notes payable	110	126
Accruals	8	9.5
Provision for federal tax	60	55.5
Total current liabilities	244	275
Long-Term Liabilities		
Mortgages payable	647	875
Total liabilities	891	1,150
Stockholders' Equity		
Capital stock (par value--$25)	2,000	2,250
Retained earnings	244	275
Total stockholders' equity	2,244	2,525
Total Liabilities and Stockholders' Equity	$3,125	$3,675

Exhibit 13-5
Narragansett Manufacturing Company, Inc.—
Comparative Statement of Income

NARRAGANSETT MANUFACTURING CO., INC.

Enclosure No. 3 (B)

Comparative Statement of Income
for the Years Ending 12/31/X6 and 12/31/X7

		12/31/X6		12/31/X7
Sales (net)		$7,875,000		$9,100,000
Cost of goods sold		5,197,500		5,915,000
Gross margin on sales		2,677,500		3,185,000
Other income		14,562		16,745
Gross income		2,692,062		3,201,745
Operating expenses				
Selling	605,626		768,379	
General and administrative	1,085,950		1,313,681	
Other	396,791		396,585	
Total operating expense		2,088,367		2,478,645
Operating income		603,695		723,100
Other expenses				
Interest		42,055		59,500
Net income before taxes		645,750		782,600
Tax (45%)		374,535		438,256
Net income after taxes		$ 271,215		$ 344,344
EPS		$2.71		$3.44

Exhibit 13-6

Narragansett Manufacturing Company, Inc.—Coverage Request

WILSON AND SCOTT

. . . professional insurance brokerage

Enclosure No. 4

Narragansett Application

1. Real Property -- limits as per schedule enclosed

    Replacement cost coverage -- 80% C/I
    No mortgagees

2. Personal Property -- no loss payees

    a. Contents as per schedule enclosed
    b. Cash and securities: $10,000 limit

3. Patterns, Molds, and Dies -- limit $200,000

4. Transportation

    a. Owned trucks -- limit $10,000 each
    b. Common carriers -- limit $50,000 each
    c. Ocean (below deck) -- limit $50,000 each

5. Neon Sign -- limit $25,000

6. Business Interruption -- blanket all locations
                            limit $600,000

7. Perils -- all-risks, including flood and quake

- The management hazard, in the absence of data to the contrary, looks very positive:
  1. Narragansett has a long history.
  2. Management, being a direct line with the founder, presumably knows the business. (John also makes a note to check this.)
  3. Several facts point to financial well-being: profitable past two years; improved performance of 19X7 over 19X6 (EPS and total bottom line); current ratio of 4.8 to 1 approaches highest quartile of industry group (see D&B, *Key Business Ratios*, Exhibit 13-7); current ratio of 19X7 (4.8) vs. 19X6 (4.3) indicates strengthened liquidity and ability to pay premiums, maintain premises, and comply with recommendations; debt to total assets ratio in 19X6 (.28) and 19X7 (.31); current debt to tangible net worth in 19X6 (.12) and 19X7 (.12), both of which are better than the highest quartile for the industry group (see *Key Business Ratios*).
- John next compared the property schedule with his *Line Authorization Guide* (Exhibit 13-8) to roughly estimate (1) whether there was a capacity problem and (2) whether treaties may be adversely affected.

Excerpts from John's IIA Insurance Company *Line Authorization Guide* are found in Exhibit 13-8. Each number found on the chart represents authorization to retain one line of insurance equaling $50,000. Therefore, a 2 allows a $100,000 retention, 3 allows a $150,000 retention, and so forth.

Line Authorization Guide Using the 100 percent values at risk in the Pawtucket warehouse on Wheelwright Road, John assumes the worst and selects the PML as the amount subject, or a value of $4,500,000. To determine the company's capacity for a risk of this type, John takes the following steps using the line authorization guide:

Step 1—Find the proper classification. John looks in the warehouse section and decides that an industrial warehouse is the most appropriate classification.

Step 2—Determine the number of lines authorized net of reinsurance. To do this, John must determine if this risk is located in a public protection class of one through five or six through ten. This information was not given to him directly, but he does find that the warehouse lies in a large metropolitan area of at least 80,000 persons, and the atlas indicates that it is contiguous to the city of Providence. Based on this, he assumes the risk is protected in class five or better. Exhibit 13-3 indicates that the structure is of fire-resistive construction. Looking at the guide for industrial warehouses with a protection class of one to

Exhibit 13-7
Key Business Ratios*

Line of Business	Current assets to current debt (Times)	Net profits on net sales (Percent)	Net profits on tangible net worth (Percent)	Net profits on net working capital (Percent)	Net sales to tangible net worth (Times)	Net sales to net working capital (Times)	Collection period (Days)	Net sales to inventory (Times)	Fixed assets to tangible net worth (Percent)	Current debt to tangible net worth (Percent)	Total debt to tangible net worth (Percent)	Inventory to net working capital (Percent)	Current debt to inventory (Percent)	Funded debts to net working capital (Percent)
Electric Lighting & Wiring Equipment	3.89	6.17	18.29	22.48	6.22	8.09	34	6.3	15.7	24.5	46.4	54.8	47.0	11.6
	2.59	3.33	11.79	14.60	3.18	4.59	45	4.5	34.0	47.3	76.3	74.1	73.0	31.1
	1.91	0.72	2.41	4.06	2.05	3.05	62	4.0	64.1	92.3	187.4	116.8	105.4	61.6
Elec. Trans. & Distribution Equipment	3.67	7.05	20.15	25.54	4.66	5.46	44	7.0	19.8	28.8	42.6	52.5	55.5	13.0
	2.48	4.29	15.02	17.74	3.58	4.28	59	5.4	31.5	48.7	113.1	74.7	82.9	27.2
	1.68	2.45	6.32	10.71	2.50	3.00	72	3.9	53.4	91.0	156.7	110.5	116.3	62.0
Electrical Industrial Apparatus	4.04	6.12	17.11	23.84	4.25	5.12	48	5.9	27.7	30.9	50.3	60.5	62.1	15.8
	2.67	4.03	11.89	14.22	2.96	3.78	59	4.6	41.2	49.5	76.5	78.2	82.7	31.3
	1.94	1.77	7.13	9.15	2.31	2.90	71	3.4	56.3	101.8	149.9	101.9	119.6	71.7
Electrical Work	3.38	4.10	19.02	23.07	6.89	8.54	—	—	9.7	35.1	58.6	—	—	8.4
	2.32	2.24	10.23	13.00	4.75	5.99	—	—	17.6	69.9	113.4	—	—	26.8
	1.68	0.79	1.63	2.20	3.15	4.17	—	—	38.4	121.2	186.1	—	—	63.8

*Adapted with permission from *Key Business Ratios* (New York: Dun & Bradstreet, 1978), p. 9.

Exhibit 13-8

IIA Insurance Company Line Authorization Guide

Number of Lines Net of Reinsurance by Construction Type[†]
(1 Line = $50,000)

Manufacturers	Classes 1–5				Classes 6–10			
	F	M	NC	FR	F	M	NC	FR
Electric light bulbs	2	4	5	7	1	2	4	5
Electric lighting	4	6	7	10	2	4	5	8
Electronic components	4	6	7	10	2	4	5	8
Engineering machinery	4	6	7	10	3	4	5	8

Warehouses	Classes 1–5				Classes 6–10			
	F	M	NC	FR	F	M	NC	FR
Industrial	3	4	6	8	2	2	3	3
Household furniture	2	4	5	6	1	2	3	4
Consumer goods	3	4	6	8	2	2	3	3
Food	2	4	5	6	1	2	3	4

[†]Construction type codes: F=frame, M=joisted masonry, NC=noncombustible and masonry noncombustible, FR=Modified fire resistive and fire resistive. When writing any business with protection classes 1–5, reinsurance treaty 403 may be used to cede ten times the "line" retained as shown in the table. When writing any business with protection classes 6–10, reinsurance treaty 403 may be used to cede five times the "line" retained as shown in the table.

five and of fire-resistive (FR) construction, John finds that eight lines are authorized net of reinsurance.

Step 3—Determine the net retention authorized. Because eight lines are authorized by the table, and the table indicates that each line authorized represents $50,000 of capacity, John figures the net retention as follows:

$$8 \text{ lines} \times \$50,000 = \$400,000 \text{ net retention}$$

Step 4—Determine reinsurance available. The bottom of the table indicates that when writing a risk in protection classes one to five, reinsurance treaty 403 allows ceding an amount ten times the "line" retained. In this case, with a $400,000 maximum retention, John figures reinsurance available as:

$$10 \times \$400,000 = \$4,000,000 \text{ of reinsurance available}$$

Step 5—Determine total authorization. John has determined net retention authorized to be $400,000 and reinsurance available as $4,000,000. Therefore, the *Line Authorization Guide* authorizes John to write $400,000 + $4,000,000 = $4,400,000. This amount is close enough to the limit of liability to allow John to write the entire amount without resorting to facultative reinsurance.

John next turns to the Palo Alto manufacturing plant. To determine total capacity, he again consults the atlas and finds that the plant is on a major thoroughfare through Palo Alto, so he assumes a protection class of five or better. To determine net retention, John finds the classification of manufacturers of electric lighting in protection classes one to five. Exhibit 13-3 indicates that the building is fire-resistive (FR), so the *Line Authorization Guide* shows ten lines available with $50,000 per line, or a net retention of $500,000. Reinsurance available with a protection class of five or better equals ten times $500,000 or $5,000,000. Thus, total capacity available equals $5,500,000, far in excess of the $2,700,000 needed.

Realizing that fire-resistive structures allow the highest authorization, John believes that the underwriting key location may be the plant in Pawtucket, which has masonry construction. Again, he assumes the worst, that all three buildings and their equipment are the amount subject and the PML. These values at 100 percent equal $1,601,000.

If the Pawtucket plant is class five protection or better, John figures net retention equals six lines times $50,000 per line or $300,000. Reinsurance available on the treaty would equal ten times that amount, or $3,000,000, for a total capacity of $3,300,000, which is clearly sufficient.

If the protection class is not five or better, John does not have sufficient authorization. For a manufacturer of lighting equipment in classes six through ten with masonry construction (M), four lines are available at $50,000 per line, or $200,000. With a protection class of six to ten, only five times the net retention is available under the reinsurance treaty, or $1,000,000. This results in a capacity of $200,000 + $1,000,000 or $1,200,000 which is clearly insufficient. John must be certain that the Pawtucket plant is well protected.

In summary, John has determined that under normal circumstances there is sufficient capacity to handle Narragansett. This is true as long as both the Pawtucket warehouse, where capacity was barely sufficient, and the Pawtucket plant are protection class five or better. If this is not the case, facultative reinsurance will be necessary. He is also aware that even if facultative reinsurance is not needed, he is using the company's full net and treaty capacity, which requires Narragansett to be a fine risk. John does not wish to stretch the company's resources for any but the most desirable risk.

Other Sources of Information To more fully understand and appreciate the operations and processes that electric lighting manufacturing and foundry work entail, John checks the sources from his deskside library, the IIA company underwriting manual and *Best's Underwriting Guide*. From *Best's Underwriting Guide* he also checks the section on machine shops since these are analogous hazards.

Although John did not find anything startling in these three items, it confirmed his experience that (1) the hazards can be coped with, given a prudent insured, and (2) they reminded him of some specific items to have an inspector check if he decided to have this prospect surveyed. A pertinent excerpt from the company underwriting manual is reproduced in Exhibit 13-9.

At this juncture, John summarizes his thinking. In the absence of contrary data, the risk appears to be writable—there is sound management, stable and flourishing financial situation, sufficient capacity, a risk of such size that the premium probably will warrant further inspections, and it comes from a trustworthy and professional producer. John then puts in a quick call to Herbert Wilson to let him know that a letter will be forthcoming confirming IIA's willingness to quote.

Inspections As stated above, John believed rather complete inspections by his company were economically feasible as well as prudent, given the magnitude of the Narragansett operations. In addition, the underwriting manual required them. However, he decided against an inspection of the New York City location. He reasoned that (1) the expense was unwarranted since values at risk were relatively minimal, the location would not impact on deriving the risk's PML, and prior experience with similar risks in that city proved them to be clean, neat, and well run, and (2) his company's inspectors in New York were over-loaded with work and this particular building would, in all likelihood, be on a sixty-day waiting list.

But John's experience also had taught him that the ordering of an inspection was a vital ingredient in the ultimate value of his decision; i.e., his decisions were only as good as his information and good information was obtainable only if he carefully directed the inspector's inquiry. John's memorandum to the Engineering Department appears in Exhibit 13-10.

Producer John expected it would be at least five weeks before the inspections were available. In the meantime, there was important additional information to be obtained from the producer.

John next wrote to Herbert confirming his willingness to quote within the allotted time. As was his custom, John inserted the following caveat regarding his commitment: "This commitment to quote is subject to withdrawal if the object-risk is, upon completion of inspec-

Exhibit 13-9
IIA Insurance Company Underwriting Manual

I I A
INSURANCE
COMPANY
Underwriting Manual

Electric Lamp Mfg.

Overall rating:

Generally, the property hazards are "average" to "slightly-above-average" in severity. Flash fires, explosions, spontaneous combustion, static electricity, and common hazards must be reviewed.

Note: Package underwriters should conduct an analysis of the products liability hazards emphasizing the required presence of U.L. standards for all sockets, wire gauge, insulation, and switches. The other public liability hazards for this class tend to be low.

Operations process(es):

1. Lamp bases are of (a) cast-metal, (b) plaster, and (c) wood.

    (a) Ingots melted, ladled/poured, cooled, then deburred by grinding and filing. Lathe turning may also be used. Finishing includes electroplating and spray lacquering.

    (b) Plaster mixed, poured, oven cured, sanded. Finishing via paint and lacquer.

    (c) Wood cut, glued, drilled, turned, sanded. Finishing via oils, stains, paint, lacquer.

2. Lamp shades are metal/wire frames with fabric or parchment covers. Seams and decorations glued or heat-sealed.

Raw materials:

Stock tubing and ingot metals; plaster; wood; screw machine parts; hardware; electric cords, sockets, switches; electroplating chemicals; lacquer, enamel, paint, stains, oils, thinner; cartons, excelsior, etc.

Equipment:

Saws, grinders, compressors, furnaces/ovens, sealers, drills, lathes, handtools, dip and electroplating tanks, molds.

Exhibit 13-10

Inspection Request

I. I. A.
INSURANCE
COMPANY
Malvern, Pennsylvania

INTER OFFICE
MEMO

Date:

To: Francis Muldowney, Mgr. Engin. Dept.

From: John Heath, Sr. Underwriter

Subject: NARRAGANSETT MFG. CO. -- INSPECTION REQUEST

Frank--I plan to make a firm quote on the captioned electric light manufacturer to our producer, Herb Wilson,
within 40 days. Quote to include real and personal property and U&O at schedule of locations attached. Coverage
all-risks via Flexipak with crime, transit, motor truck,
patterns/dies endorsed. As you know, our independent
filing permits deleting Flood and Quake exclusions via
subsidiary limits so I need comments re appropriateness
of these perils. Would greatly appreciate your assigning
Tom Brown from the Boston office to the Rhode Island locations, his work is always tops.

Need special attention on:

1. Definitive description operations, processes,
   special hazards--especially cutting oils, spray
   painting, electroplating acids, storage volatiles,
   garaging vehicles, packing-shipping area, etc. and
   U&O bottlenecks. U&O to be blanket. May be a
   contingent exposure from Philadelphia firm. Have
   Tom check this in interview with E.C. Mullin (his
   contact) at the Moses Brown address.

2. Distribution of values.

3. Estimates building values.

4. Check with Boston ISO re Fire, allied rates.

                                        J. Heath

   JH:

tions, deemed to be unsuitable for package policy treatment or otherwise deemed an unsatisfactory subject for insurance by this company. It is also understood and agreed that the insured will comply promptly with all reasonable risk improvement recommendations."

In addition, John asked for the following information from Herbert:

1. Transit:
    a. terms of sale for incoming and outgoing shipments?
    b. modes of carriage by percent of total values at risk?
    c. weigh bill terms?
    d. gross receipts shipped last 12 months? next 12 months?
    e. loss experience on owned trucks and common carrier?
    f. premium payment to be flat or reporting?
    g. deductible to apply?
2. Ocean: a, c, d, e, f, and g, above?
3. Are earthquake and flood coverages to apply at all locations? "The IIA Insurance Company will only provide subsidiary limits of $250,000 for earthquake in California and a maximum limit of $500,000 on flood anywhere in the United States."
4. Please clarify the values of machinery in building "C" at the Moses Brown address. Are the patterns and molds also stored in this building? If not where?
5. Please verify all building machinery items. ". . . These can often be severe obstacles at and after a loss. The terms of loss settlements are set forth in the policy but values are subject to disagreement in the absence of definitive statements at inception."
6. Please submit a gross earnings worksheet.
    • Statement of Palo Alto stoppage and effect on Pawtucket plant.
    • Does insured want a contingent U&O cover for the contributing property in Philadelphia?
    • If so, statement of effect at Pawtucket and address of Philadelphia Manufacturing.
7. Please submit statement regarding management tenure and experience.
8. Do warehouse values fluctuate? Reporting form basis? Can and will insured report values *accurately* and *on time*?

At this point, John could only await Herbert's response and the inspectors' reports. In the meantime, his time was spent reviewing other risks.

The inspections and Herbert's answer to John's questions arrived simultaneously. John groaned under what he initially felt was "information overload." Now, he had to wade through them and make notes wherever he thought he had sufficient cause—i.e., either *pro* or *con.*

The inspections and Herbert's response appear in Exhibits 13-11, 13-12, 13-13, 13-14, 13-15, 13-16, 13-17, 13-18, and 13-19.

Analyzing the Submission

To avoid getting indigestion from all the data at hand, John decided to tackle the risk as follows:

A. Direct damage at locations
B. Miscellaneous property—i.e., patterns, neon sign, burglary or money
C. Business interruption
D. Transportation
E. Ocean—actually, John was going to have a marine colleague underwrite and price this portion of the risk

Direct Damage John began reviewing the entire submission (Herbert's original letter, inspections, and diagrams, and Herbert's second letter) listing first the positive aspects of the risk's direct damage at the various locations:

Pros:

1. financially sound—better than average in class with respect to the balance sheet, income statement, and comparisons via D&B Key Ratios.
2. knowledgeable management—John responded very favorably to Herbert's comments about Mike Arnold and E. C. Mullin.
3. profitable and growing company.
4. good producer—record with IIA: excellent responses in second letter—i.e., answered *all* John's questions; really knows the account.
5. within IIA's capacity—i.e., initial line-setting exercise.
6. large premium size—John also made a mental reservation that this could be a "con," he was mindful of the underwriting caveat that "the sweet smell of premium often overcomes the stench of a risk . . . ."
7. fat building rates—the main plant rate promulgation was ". . . by the book," but according to Tom Brown the plant properly deserved a 7½ percent credit. The office building, of course, required reworking; Herbert must submit a broker of record letter to the ISO requesting a rate correction . . . this naturally would eliminate this "pro."

Exhibit 13-11
Inspection Report 1

Account Name ___Narragansett Mfg. Co., Inc.___ Location ___Pawtucket, R.I.*___

Person Contacted ___E.C. Mullin___ Surveyor ___T. Brown, P.E.___ Date _____ Hours ___6___

*3 bldgs., Moses Brown Rd.

Comment If other than "Good" condition. Attach photograph to reverse of Report Cover.

	Poor	Good	Excel	Comments
1.0 Management				
1.1 Housekeeping	☐	☒	☐	
1.2 Maintenance	☐	☐	☒	
1.3 Labor Relations	☐	☐	☒	

2.0 Construction - If mixed construction or more than one building, provide sketch in grid on reverse side of Report Cover.

	Poor	Good	Excel	Comments
2.1 Construction Quality	☐	☒	☒	
2.2 Suitability for this Occupancy	☐	☒	☐	
2.3 Electrical Installation	☐	☒	☐	
2.4 Heat/Air Conditioning	☐	☒	☐	
2.5 Area Divisions	☐	☒	☐	Largest Undivided Area: _3,000_ sq. ft. Bldg. "A"
2.6 Combustible Finish/Floor Covering	☐	☒	☐	
2.7 Combustible Concealed Spaces	☐	☐	☒	
2.8 Floor Openings Protection	☐	☐	☒	
2.9 Roof Covering/Condition	☐	☒	☐	
2.10 Foamed Plastic - If foamed plastics are used in walls, floors or roof, including prefab panels, give details on type, amount and protection afforded:				N/A

4="A"

5,000="C"
36,000="A"   TOTALS

2.11 No. of Floors 2="B"& "C" Basement? □ Yes ☒ No. Ground-Floor-Area 10,000="B" sq. ft. Total Area _____ sq. ft.

See Diagram

2.12 Estimate overall construction classification: _____ % Frame_____ % All-Metal_____ % Masonry_____ % Non-Combustible_____ % Fire Resistive.

2.13 Walls: □Frame (□Brick Veneer □Metal Clad) □All-Metal □Brick____in. □Hollow Block (□Brick Faced)____in. □Poured Concrete____in.

2.14 Roof: □Wood Joist □Heavy Timber □Metal   **2.15** Floors: □Wood Joist □Concrete □Heavy Timber □Metal

2.16 If Non-Combustible or Fire Resistive, complete the following:

LEVEL	FLOOR/ROOF CONSTRUCTION				FLOOR/ROOF SUPPORTS—HORIZONTAL				FLOOR/ROOF SUPPORTS—VERTICAL		
	Con-crete	Wood	Metal	Other	Con-crete	Heavy Steel	Light Steel	Type of Fireproofing	Con-crete	Steel	Type of Fireproofing
Basement	□	□	□	□	□	□	□	_____	□	□	_____
First Floor	□	□	□	□	□	□	□	_____	□	□	_____
Upper Floors	□	□	□	□	□	□	□	_____	□	□	_____
Roof	□	□	□	□	□	□	□	_____	□	□	_____

2.17 Additional Comments: Attached

. . . .

3.0 Age (years): □0-15 □16-35 □over 35.   Describe any remodeling or improvements which may alter chronological age:

"A"=1938   "B"=1969   "C"=1896   very well maintained

. . . .

4.0 Est. Replacement Cost $ see comments , **Est. Actual Cash Value $** _____ Calculated by □Costimator □Marshall □

5.0 Outside Exposures: Is risk exposed? ☒ Yes □ No.   If yes, provide a simple sketch in grid on reverse side of Report Cover indicating our risk, exposing structures (buildings, weeds, lumber yards, etc.), approximate distance between, construction, occupancy, and if exposure is sprinklered.

See Diagram

Continued on next page

6.0 Occupancy: If a MANUFACTURING, PROCESSING or WAREHOUSE risk, give details of operations, listing special hazards and the care and protection thereof (i.e. welding, woodworking, spray finishing, dip tanks, flammable liquids, hazardous chemicals, etc.) Also, note high piling of stock or unusual storage conditions.

If MERCANTILE or NON-MANUFACTURING (except WAREHOUSING), give details if operations include cooking, repairing, flammable liquids, high piling of stock, etc.

See Attached Comments

6.1 Combustibility of contents: ☐ Noncombustible ☒ Moderate ☐ High   **6.2** Adequacy and condition of equipment: ☐ Poor ☒ Good ☐ Excellent

6.3 Other Occupants (or vacancies)

	Yes	No	Comments (if not desirable)
Desirable?			
"C"--general office	☒	☐	50%--south side, both floors occupied by Harding
	☐	☐	Security Services
	☐	☐	
	☐	☐	

7.0 Economics: Neighborhood is ☒ Stable ☐ Deteriorating ☐ New ☐ Redeveloping

7.1 Location is ☐ Rural ☐ Residential ☐ Mercantile ☒ Industrial ☐ Mixed   **7.2** Is risk considered suitable for neighborhood? ☒ Yes ☐ No.

8.0 Protection:

8.1 Public Protection Class ___3___ Class at risk if poorer than town class _____ . Reason(s): ☐ Risk not accessible ☐ Inadequate hydrants ☐ Inadequate water supply ☐ Fire department over 3 miles ☐

8.2 Private protection: (Check if provided.) Comment if other than standard.

☒ Fire Extinguishers   Inadequate CO$_2$ at dip tanks

☒ Standpipe and Hose   Bldg. "A" only

☒ **Watchman** . 24 hours, employee of risk, no clock .
☐ Fire Detection/Alarm Systems (Describe) .
☐ Special Extinguishing System (Describe) .
☒ Sprinkler System (update Bureau Report or complete SRE-802) . "C" only, 100%

9.0 Other Perils: Describe any unusual exposures to windstorm, hail, wavewash, water damage, collapse, flood, vandalism or theft:

Good risk for all-risks.

10.0 Time Element: Machines used are ☒ domestic ☒ imported ☒ custom-made. **Goods sold/processed are** ☒ domestic ☐ imported.
10.1 Comments

2 Ingen-Stolle lathes (Sweden) . 1 Allianz-Krupp sheet press (Ger.).

All in "A"--estimate max. replacement time 9 months

11.0 Additional Comments: (include any significant losses):

See Attached

Exhibit 13-12
Diagram for Inspection Report 1

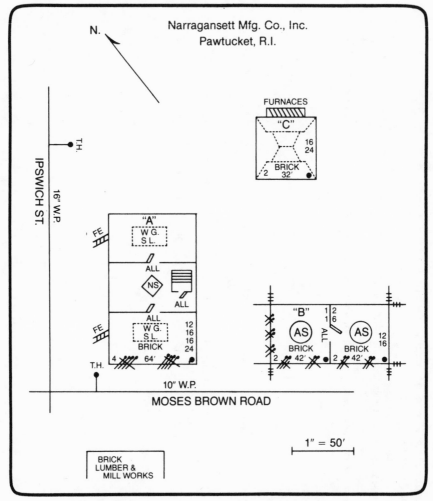

8. loss record—the V or MM exposure had been partially corrected via watch service and the 19X7 storm was one of the worst in recorded history. The absence of any others at least suggested an insured who was *not* claims conscious.

9. well-run plants and warehouse—John gave great weight to Brown's commentary, e.g., excellent maintenance, experienced skilled workers, "immaculate trucks," etc.

10. buildings—minimal depreciation; mill buildings that are rated as masonry but which, in fact, are justifiably also a sub-class of noncombustible or even fire-resistive.
11. special hazards—volatiles stored per NFPA 30 and ". . . all arrangements satisfactory"; these comments were high praise from an experienced engineer such as Tom Brown.
12. presence of 24-hour watch service.
13. very minor recommendations (except as noted under "cons").

John reviewed his "Pro" list and felt it was formidable. He then turned his attention to listing the "Cons."

Cons:
1. John was always uneasy about any risk he had not looked at personally. He found it especially unnerving given the hazardous occupancy.
2. the obsolete, inefficient foundry—this suggested a risk waiting for an insurance company to ". . . buy it."
3. the grossly undervalued building—the schedule gave a value for building "A" of $360,000 versus Tom Brown's work-up of: $47 per square foot = $1,692,000.
4. the lumber yard exposure—crowded piles, a high hazard class, a hazard that could throw literally a shower of firebrands . . . all only 75 feet from the main plant.
5. the historic flood level for the Pawtucket warehouse, potentially putting the first floor under water.
6. the California plant flood/rain water drainage problem.
7. the unacceptable structural deficiencies for quake at the California plant.
8. the new limited access highway which separated the Pawtucket warehouse from the hydrant—this meant a Public Protection of no better than class eight which in turn meant an inadequate rate.
9. wholly inadequate information on what to do about theft—did Herbert want fidelity coverage? broad form money and securities coverage? Did "all-risks" intend theft to be for all premises? and so on.

John felt his two lists were now about equal. The risk was clearly good and bad. If he simply accepted things as they were, that is, if he took all givens as immutable facts, he should simply decline. But John plowed on—believing that there probably were alternatives to each of the cons. Here are his decision trees and decisions:

1. Hazardous occupancy:
   a. decline

Exhibit 13-13
Inspection Report 2

Account Name ___Narragansett Mfg. Co., Inc.___ Location ___1253 Wheelwright, Pawtucket, R.I.___

Person Contacted ___E.C. Mullin___ Surveyor ___R. Brown, P.E.___ Date _____ Hours __3__

Comment if other than "Good" condition. Attach photograph to reverse of Report Cover.

1.0 Management	Poor	Good	Excel	Comments
1.1 Housekeeping	☐	☒	☐	
1.2 Maintenance	☐	☐	☒	
1.3 Labor Relations	☐	☐	☒	

2.0 Construction - If mixed construction or more than one building, provide sketch in grid on reverse side of Report Cover.

	Poor	Good	Excel	Comments
2.1 Construction Quality	☐	☒	☐	Suitable to use, "new," very good maintenance.
2.2 Suitability for this Occupancy	☐	☒	☐	
2.3 Electrical Installation	☐	☒	☐	
2.4 Heat/Air Conditioning	☐	☒	☐	
2.5 Area Divisions	☐	☒	☐	Largest Undivided Area: 4,800 _____ sq. ft.
2.6 Combustible Finish/Floor Covering	☐	☒	☐	
2.7 Combustible Concealed Spaces	☐	☒	☐	
2.8 Floor Openings Protection	☐	☒	☐	
2.9 Roof Covering/Condition	☐	☒	☐	
2.10 Foamed Plastic - If foamed plastics are used in walls, floors or roof, including prefab panels, give details on type, amount and protection afforded:

N/A

2.11 No. of Floors 3   **Basement?** ☒ Yes ☐ No.   **Ground Floor Area** 4,800   sq. ft.   **Total Area** 14,400   sq. ft.

2.12 Estimate overall construction classification: _____ % Frame. _____ % All-Metal. _____ % Masonry. _____ % Non-Combustible. 100 % Fire Resistive.

2.13 Walls: ☐ Frame (☐ Brick Veneer ☐ Metal Clad) ☐ All-Metal ☐ Brick _____ in. ☐ Hollow Block (☐ Brick-Faced) _____ in. ☒ Poured Concrete 18 in.

2.14 Roof: ☐ Wood Joist ☐ Heavy Timber ☒ Metal   Protected   **2.15 Floors:** ☐ Wood Joist ☒ Concrete ☐ Heavy Timber ☐ Metal

2.16 If Non-Combustible or Fire Resistive, complete the following:

LEVEL	FLOOR/ROOF CONSTRUCTION				FLOOR/ROOF SUPPORTS—HORIZONTAL			FLOOR/ROOF SUPPORTS—VERTICAL		
	Con-crete	Wood	Metal	Other	Con-crete / Heavy Steel	Light Steel	Type of Fireproofing	Con-crete / Steel		Type of Fireproofing
Basement	☒	☐	☐	☐	☒	☐	reinf. 4 hrs.	☒	☐	reinf. 4 hrs.
First Floor	☒	☐	☐	☐	☒	☐		☒	☐	
Upper Floors	☒	☐	☐	☐	☒	☐		☒	☐	
Roof	☐	☐	☐	☒	☒	☐		☒	☐	

2.17 Additional Comments: asbestos blown, approved.

....
....
....

3.0 Age (years): ☒ 0-15 ☐ 16-35 ☐ over 35.   Describe any remodeling or improvements which may alter chronological age:

1972   max. 5% deprec.   indexed cost new

4.0 Est. Replacement Cost $ 635,000   , **Est. Actual Cash Value $** 605,000   . Calculated by ☒ Costimator ☐ Marshall ☐.

5.0 Outside Exposures: Is risk exposed? ☐ Yes ☒ No.   If yes, provide a simple sketch in grid on reverse side of Report Cover indicating our risk, exposing structures (buildings, weeds, lumber yards, etc.), approximate distance between, construction, occupancy, and if exposure is sprinklered.

Continued on next page

6.0 Occupancy: If a MANUFACTURING, PROCESSING or WAREHOUSE risk, give details of operations, listing special hazards and the care and protection thereof (i.e. welding, woodworking, spray finishing, dip tanks, flammable liquids, hazardous chemicals, etc.) Also, note high piling of stock or unusual storage conditions.

If MERCANTILE or NON-MANUFACTURING (except WAREHOUSING), give details if operations include cooking, repairing, flammable liquids, high piling of stock, etc.

Metal tubing, fabrics, parchment, wire, sockets, packing cartons, wood,

plaster, etc. plus finished stock. No spec. Hazards. Common haz.

well handled.

6.1 Combustibility of contents: ☐ Noncombustible ☒ Moderate ☐ High   **6.2** Adequacy and condition of equipment: ☐ Poor ☐ Good ☒ Excellent

6.3 Other Occupants (or vacancies)

	Desirable?		
---	Yes	No	Comments (if not desirable)
	☐	☐	
	☐	☐	
	☐	☐	
	☐	☐	

7.0 Economics: Neighborhood is ☐ Stable ☐ Deteriorating ☐ New ☒ Redeveloping

7.1 Location is ☐ Rural ☐ Residential ☐ Mercantile ☐ Industrial ☐ Mixed   **7.2** Is risk considered suitable for neighborhood? ☒ Yes ☐ No.

8.0 Protection:

8.1 Public Protection Class __3__ Class at risk if poorer than town class __8__ ; Reason(s): ☐ Risk not accessible ☒ Inadequate hydrants ☐ Inadequate water supply ☐ Fire department over 3 miles ☐ See diagram; highway built 1976

8.2 Private protection: (Check if provided.) Comment if other than standard.   N/A – Standard

☐ Fire Extinguishers

☐ Standpipe and Hose

☐ Watchman

☐ Fire Detection/Alarm Systems (Describe)

☐ Special Extinguishing System (Describe)

☐ Sprinkler System (update Bureau Report or complete SRE-802)

9.0 Other Perils: Describe any unusual exposures to windstorm, hail, wavewash, water damage, collapse, flood, vandalism or theft:

Seekonk River 250 ft. due south; high water 1938.

Flood would breach 1/2 first floor.

10.0 Time Element: Machines used are ☒ domestic ☐ imported ☐ custom-made.   Goods sold/processed are ☐ domestic ☐ imported.

10.1 Comments

11.0 Additional Comments: (include any significant losses):

No losses. Other than noted: excel. risk in class.

Exhibit 13-14
Diagram for Inspection Report 2

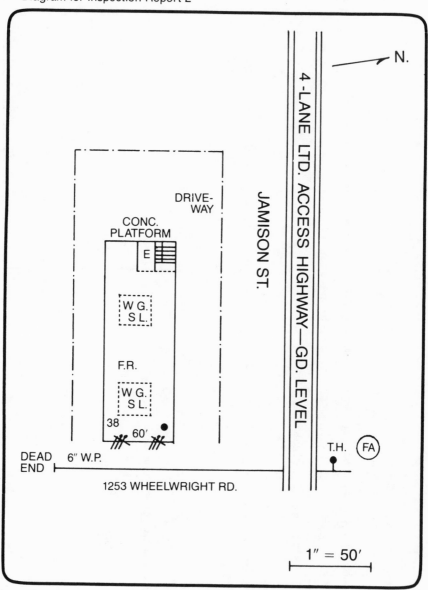

b. accept as is

c. improve

Decision—he reasoned that the occupancy class was indeed hazardous, but the published rates after all contemplated these hazards and the insured was "excellent." He reasoned that this "con" was therefore neutralized.

2. Obsolete foundry:

Decision—short of getting the insured to tear the foundry down or make substantial material improvements, John felt stymied. Besides, the insured was already wondering what to do; they too realized that it was inefficient. He therefore decided it would remain as a "con" but that even this was somewhat mitigated by an insured who, in all probability, was very unlikely to sell it to the insurance company.

3. Undervalued building:

Decision—insist that Narragansett accept Tom Brown's valuation and write the policy with a limit of at least $1,353,600 (i.e., 80 percent of $1,692,000). If the insured wanted to purchase an outside appraisal, the policy could be amended to another value if warranted.

4. Lumberyard exposure:

Decision—John reasoned that you cannot make a third party institute risk-improvement recommendations. Thus, this "con" was a fact with which he had to live. On the other hand, Tom Brown's recommendation regarding wired glass for the main plant was clearly intended to mitigate the exposure. He decided to make the recommendation a binding requirement for acceptance.

5. Warehouse flood:

Decision—the 1938 flood was a 200 year flood and thus the probability of an another occurrence soon was unlikely. Furthermore, the metal products primarily stored in the warehouse's first floor were relatively immune to water damage. Loss prevention via engineering was not feasible. Therefore, John decided that, given all the foregoing, he was willing to accept this "minimal" risk.

6. California flood:

Decision—the entire plant was susceptible to flash flooding. Therefore, as a prerequisite to providing a subsidiary flood limit for this location, John would insist upon a correction of the parking lot drainage problem either by a dike system of sufficient height or that the parking lot be regraded to slope away from the factory.

Exhibit 13-15
Inspection Report 3

Account Name Narragansett Mfg. Co., Inc. Location 1849 El Camino Real, Palo Alto, Ca.

Person Contacted S. Dreyfuss Surveyor R. Meany Date _____ Hours 2

Comment if other than "Good" condition. Attach photograph to reverse of Report Cover.

1.0 Management	Poor	Good	Excel	Comments
1.1 Housekeeping	☐	☐	☒	
1.2 Maintenance	☐	☐	☒	
1.3 Labor Relations	☐	☐	☒	

2.0 Construction - If mixed construction or more than one building, provide sketch in grid on reverse side of Report Cover.

	Poor	Good	Excel	Comments
2.1 Construction Quality	☐	☐	☒	
2.2 Suitability for this Occupancy	☐	☐	☒	NB: review of plans--does not meet ASCE standards for EQ.
2.3 Electrical Installation	☐	☒	☐	
2.4 Heat/Air Conditioning	☐	☐	☒	
2.5 Area Divisions	☐	☐	☒	Largest Undivided Area: 3,500 _____ sq. ft.
2.6 Combustible Finish/Floor Covering	☐	☒	☐	
2.7 Combustible Concealed Spaces	☐	☐	☒	
2.8 Floor Openings Protection	☐	☐	☒	
2.9 Roof Covering/Condition	☐	☒	☐	New 1975

2.10 Foamed Plastic - If foamed plastics are used in walls, floors or roof, including prefab panels. give details on type, amount and protection afforded:

N/A

2.11 No. of Floors One   Basement? ☐ Yes ☒ No.   Ground Floor Area 14,000   sq. ft.   Total Area same   sq. ft.

2.12 Estimate overall construction classification: % Frame.   % All-Metal.   % Masonry.   ∾ Non-Combustible. 100 % Fire Resistive.

2.13 Walls: ☐ Frame (☐ Brick Veneer ☐ Metal Clad) ☐ All-Metal ☒ Brick 16 in. ☐ Hollow Block (☐ Brick Faced)   in. ☐ Poured Concrete   in.

2.14 Roof: ☐ Wood Joist ☐ Heavy Timber ☐ Metal   **2.15** Floors: ☐ Wood Joist ☒ Concrete ☐ Heavy Timber ☐ Metal

2.16 If Non-Combustible or Fire Resistive, complete the following:

LEVEL	FLOOR/ROOF CONSTRUCTION				FLOOR/ROOF SUPPORTS—HORIZONTAL				Type of Fireproofing	FLOOR/ROOF SUPPORTS—VERTICAL		Type of Fireproofing
	Con-crete	Wood	Metal	Other	Con-crete	Heavy Steel	Light Steel			Con-crete	Steel	
Basement	☐	☐	☐	☐ N/A	☐	☐	☐	☐ N/A		☐	☐	
First Floor	☐	☐	☐	☐	☐	☐	☐	☐		☐	☐	
Upper Floors	☐	☐	☐	☐	☐	☐	☐	☐		☐	☐	
Roof	☒	☐	☐	☐ slab, pre-cast	☐	☐	☐	☐		☐	☐	

2.17 Additional Comments: ....

....

....

....

3.0 Age (years): ☐ 0-15 ☒ 16-35 ☐ over 35.   Describe any remodeling or improvements which may alter chronological age:

Bldg. purchased from competitor in 1962.

4.0 Est. Replacement Cost $ 660,000   , **Est. Actual Cash Value $** 595,000   . Calculated by ☐ Costimator ☐ Marshall ☐   indexed orig. cost

5.0 Outside Exposures: Is risk exposed? ☐ Yes ☒ No.   If yes, provide a simple sketch in grid on reverse side of Report Cover indicating our risk, exposing structures (buildings, weeds, lumber yards, etc.), approximate distance between, construction, occupancy, and if exposure is sprinklered.

Continued on next page

6.0 Occupancy: If a <u>MANUFACTURING, PROCESSING</u> or <u>WAREHOUSE</u> risk, give details of operations, listing special hazards and the care and protection thereof (i.e. welding, woodworking, spray finishing, dip tanks, flammable liquids, hazardous chemicals, etc.) Also, note high piling of stock or unusual storage conditions.

If MERCANTILE or NON-MANUFACTURING (except WAREHOUSING), give details if operations include cooking, repairing, flammable liquids, high piling of stock, etc.

Manufacturing domestic and commercial lighting fixtures: spot welding, soldering, spray painting, Bakelite extrusion, sheet pressing/cutting, lathing, grinding, assembly, packing, shipping -- all very well handled within class. Rates over-all as EXCELLENT!

6.1 Combustibility of contents: ☐ Noncombustible ☒ Moderate ☐ High

6.2 Adequacy and condition of equipment: ☐ Poor ☐ Good ☒ Excellent

6.3 Other Occupants (or vacancies)

Desirable? Yes No   Comments (if not desirable)

N/A

7.0 Economics: Neighborhood is ☒ Stable ☐ Deteriorating ☐ New ☐ Redeveloping

7.1 Location is ☐ Rural ☐ Residential ☐ Mercantile ☒ Industrial ☒ Mixed **7.2** Is risk considered suitable for neighborhood? ☒ Yes ☐ No.

8.0 Protection:

8.1 Public Protection Class ___4___ Class at risk if poorer than town class_____; Reason(s): ☐ Risk not accessible ☐ Inadequate hydrants ☐ Inadequate water supply ☐ Fire department over 3 miles ☐

8.2 Private protection: (Check if provided.) Comment if other than standard.   Standard!

☐ Fire Extinguishers

☐ Standpipe and Hose . . . .

☐ Watchman . . . .

☐ Fire Detection/Alarm Systems (Describe) . . . .

☐ Special Extinguishing System (Describe) . . . .

☐ Sprinkler System (update Bureau Report or complete SRE-802) . . . .

9.0 Other Perils: Describe any unusual exposures to windstorm, hail, wavewash, water damage, collapse, flood, vandalism or theft:

Large paved parking lot, rear slopes to building. Suspect inadequate

storm drainage; therefore, water damage possible to stock skidded less

than 6 inches.

10.0 Time Element: Machines used are ☒ domestic ☐ imported ☐ custom-made.   Goods sold/processed are ☒ domestic ☐ imported.

10.1 Comments . . . .

. . . .

. . . .

11.0 Additional Comments: (include any significant losses):

At any one time Dreyfuss states values in fire divisions may be over-

loaded -- i.e., as much as 75% except machinery, which is evenly split

in "C" and "B" areas.

Exhibit 13-16

Diagram for Inspection Report 3

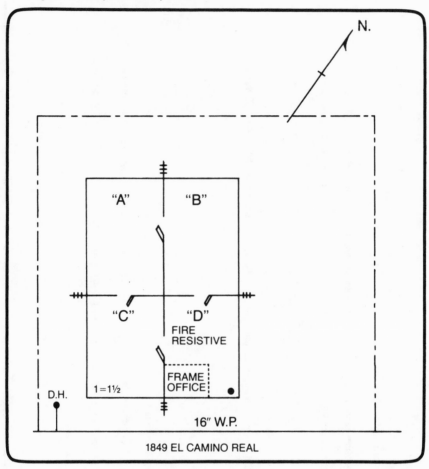

7. California quake:

    Decision—correcting basic building structural features was not feasible. But, providing a subsidiary limit also was unpalatable. John took the cowardly way out—he decided to proceed with all other work on this risk and then present his boss, the underwriting manager, with the earthquake dilemma. John felt fairly sure that his manager would approve the coverage.

8. Warehouse public water:

    Decision—John estimated that Narragansett Co. could reasonably ask the city to put in a new hydrant from the main in front of the warehouse. Alternatively, for an expenditure of approximately $1,000, the company could put a hydrant in itself. This cost would be quickly amortized against a much higher rate that would otherwise apply. John decided that either of these alternatives were acceptable but that at least one or the other was a prerequisite to acceptance.

9. Theft information:

Decision—rather than bother clarifying issues with Herbert, John arbitrarily decided to provide only broad form money and securities coverage. If Narragansett wanted fidelity coverage, he could ask for complete underwriting information plus a completed application and endorse it to the package after inception. In addition, it was impossible to provide theft of contents without more data, especially regarding the warehouse and Palo Alto locations. Finally, John believed that factory and warehouse theft of industrial products was high hazard business—the theft exposure is dependent on fluctuating metal markets; scarcities of metals encourage large burglaries where organized thieves steal by the truckload. He had once suffered a $75,000 theft loss of copper under such circumstances. He frankly wished to avoid the issue.

John tried to summarize his thinking up to this point. If the insured would accept the conditions John was prepared to offer on the direct damage, John felt that this particular risk would be somewhat above average in class. Some of the engineering recommendations, however, were absolutely necessary; i.e., the drainage problem in Palo Alto; the hydrant at the warehouse. In the absence of these, he would simply decline the risk. Even if the insured were willing to accept the flood/water damage exclusion for the California location, John believed the recommendation was still essential. He reasoned that water was realistically a source of electrical short circuiting which could cause a fire. The fire, in turn, would have to be fought under adverse circumstances.

The wired glass recommendation was very important. However, he was willing to live with it if *all other* recommendations (extinguishers, etc.) were complied with. In short, John thought of this particular measure as a possible "give up" in a negotiating situation, but it would be given up reluctantly and only at a fairly stiff price.

Miscellaneous Property John was uneasy about the patterns. He had great difficulty even picturing in his mind what they looked like. He was always reluctant to commit his company's resources under such circumstances. A loss would probably be large, approaching a total of

I. I. A.
INSURANCE
COMPANY
Malvern, Pennsylvania

INTER OFFICE
MEMO

Date:

To:

From:

Subject: NARRAGANSETT MFG. CO., INC.

INSPECTION COMMENTARY

Buildings -- Buildings "A" and "C" rate as true Heavy Mill Timber and
have horizontal and vertical members not less than 12
inches thick. Floor is 2 inched, grooved planking.
Walls as marked. Approved, well maintained roofs. See
diagram.

Three separate fire divisions in building "A." Building
"A" fusible link sliding fire doors at each floor are
home-made but due to quality of work have diagramed as
"approval." A check of ISO rate sheet indicates these
unapproved doors resulted in over-all 7-1/2 percent rate
debit. It is my opinion they should rate as two-hour
doors.

Machinery -- "A": Consist of lathes, planing machines, sheet presses,
grinders. Ages vary from 75 years to brand new. Schedule unavailable. Well maintained; where modified, work
via skilled craftsmen. Values appear heaviest on 3rd
floor, but difference is negligible.

Contents -- "A": Work in process varies, stock values fluctuate
floor to floor. E.C. Mullin estimates that concentration is in shipping department, rear first floor and
aggregates 40 percent of all stock in building.

Process -- "A" metal lamp bases forged in building "C," planed,
burred, polished in "A." Small parts turned. Whole
assembly is benchwork. Workers older, skilled. Cutting
oils with flash points well above 100°. Electroplating

NARRAGANSETT MFG. CO., INC.
Page 2

uses cyanide; tanks hooded and vented. Volatiles, including spraying, etc., stored per NFPA 30. All arrangements throughout satisfactory.

This is obviously a well-run shop. Pride in workmanship
and plant. Housekeeping excellent in class--i.e., it's
still messy. Packing area cleaned twice each day.

Valuation: Using model method ("Estimator") 1978 100 percent replacement cost, the square foot cost
is $47.00.

Depreciation: Estimate ACV at no less than 90 percent of
full replacement.

Building "C"--As stated, a true Mill structure. Large coal fire furnace system is obsolete and inefficient. Company strug-
gling to decide whether or not to replace. Alternative
is to give up all casting and have jobbed by another
local firm.

Furnaces operating during inspection--conditions dry;
sufficient available sand. Drop-forging with ladles.
Wood patterns removed to second·floor storage prior to
pouring.

Castings of light poles done in this building along with
all finishing, ex painting. Deburring, grinding of cast
iron via hand tools. This is four-man operation with
experienced skilled craftsmen.

Second floor pattern shop is typical wood-worker with
minimal dust due to well-arranged collectors. Patterns
stored in neat, metal racks; each well secured.

Building "C" also well maintained. Valuation difficult
because of furnaces; very rough estimate that R/C (via
"Estimator") is approximately $40-50 per sq. ft.

Building "B"--Office building is very plain, minimal interior finish,
but well built.

Valuation: R/C at $26 per sq. ft. (Values--equally dis-
tributed. Computer leased, insurance by
lessor.)

Miscellaneous:
1. Packing standard for commodity. Overseas cartons
satisfactory for stowage-stress via containerization.
Each package contains silica gel. Contents wrapped
in waxed paper. Cartons have plastic strapping,
testing at 75 pounds. All external markings coded.

Continued on next page

2. No garaging, per se, both 8-ton trucks parked equi-
distant buildings "C" and "B."

   Trucks immaculate. Non-union drivers, 14 and 23
   years service respectively.

3. Watchmen, salaried employees, on duty 24 hours; no
   clock or alarms.

4. Rates checked with ISO. All as listed. Rate for
   "building B" clearly in error; work sheet shows important computation mistake; rate s/be $.16. Sprin-
   kler on maintenance agreement with ADT; central station alarm plus outside gong.

5. Losses--no fire EC, or burglary claims in over 20
   years except as noted.

   (a) $3,000 V&MM to building "A" exterior only in 1968.
       Shortly thereafter hired watchmen.

   (b) 1978 winter storm: $5,000 neon sign wind loss.

6. Safe in "B," never more than $3,000 cash. U.L.
   labeled "TL-15." Only Mullin and Mike Arnold, president, have access.

7. Exposure--prosperous lumber yard, at inspection over-
   stocked with insufficient space between piles. Mill-
   work done 5-1/2 days per week. Risk average in class
   at best. Watchman service via patrol with central
   station ionization and photo-electric detectors in
   small, crowded building. Doberman in chain-linked
   yard. Owner claims building will be sprinklered within six months. No other external exposures within
   150 feet.

8. Neon sign atop building "A" well anchored to roof.
   Sign angled to face Moses Brown and Ipswich on southwest corner. Mullin states sign value is original
   cost new in 1969. Check with maker, Ludlum Sign; they
   state R/C roughly at $33,000.

   Warehouse at 1253 Wheelwright is poured, reinforced
   concrete with four-hour rating. Values evenly distributed with tubing and other metal, paints, lac-
   quers, solvents, first floor; flat packing cartons,
   paper, etc. primarily second floor; wiring, switches,
   etc. 3rd; basement for oil-fired hot water furnace
   only. All hands are full-time employees and good experience. Building very neat, excellent maintenance.
   Stock stored metal racks and shelves or pallet
   skidded. No external exposures.

NARRAGANSETT MFG. CO., INC.
Page 4

Recommendations:

Building "A"--

1. Need 4 CO_2 extinguishers second floor.

   Need 2 CO_2 extinguishers first floor.

2. Wired glass windows southside all four floors.

Building "B"--None.

Building "C"--None.

Warehouse --

1. Need exterior light for platform. Lamp needs wire screen for bulb protection.

2. Metal racks and shelves should be anchored or braced to avoid domino falling.

3. Stair fire door first floor wedged open with wood block; if necessary to keep open, suggest chain/spring with fusable link.

4. Owner should have city put new hydrant at 1253 or receive permission for private hydrant on city main.

Exhibit 13-18
Additional Information from Producer

WILSON AND SCOTT
. . . professional insurance brokerage

IIA Insurance Co.
Malvern, PA 19355

ATTENTION: John Heath, Sr. Underwriter

Narragansett Mfg. Co., Inc.

Dear John:

Here is the information you requested:

    I. a. All incoming and outgoing shipments are f.o.b. buyers premises.

       b. Modes of carriage:

19X7		Projected 19X9	
$4,500,000:	50% owned truck	$5,250,000:	same
4,000,000:	43% common	4,530,000:	same
600,000:	7% ocean carrier	700,000:	same

                Common Carriers: 25% rail 75% truck

       c. Ocean carriage weighbill: Full
          Truck and rail: Released value as per tariffs

       d. Gross receipts shipped: see above

       e. Loss experience

(1) Owned truck --	19X8(to date)	19X7	19X6
	nil	$ 300 -- breakage	nil
		5,000 -- theft	
		1,500 -- collision	

          (2) Rail   (6) = $2,000 O.S.D.   (3) = $4,500 O.S.D.   (7) = 3,800
                                                            O.S.D.
          (3) Truck (2) =   800 O.S.D.   (1) =   600 O.S.D.   (0) = nil
          (4) Ocean   nil   (2) = 4,000 theft & (3) = 6,000
                                      water damage   all thefts

       f. Premium payment: gross receipts monthly reporting with annual
          adjustment.

       g. Deductible: owned truck -- $500.
                   rail   -- 250.
                   public truck-- 250.
                   ocean   -- 500.

Narragansett Mfg. Co., Inc.
Page 2

II. Included above are answers to all ocean questions.

III. Please provide Quake at max. ($250K) for California plant only.
Flood at all locations for full $500,000.

IV. The foundry machinery is included under values for same in the
main factory. These items are primarily hand tools kept in main
building tool room and checked out to personnel as needed. Each
item returned to tool room at end of shift. Patterns are stored
second floor foundry. All dies are kept in main factory and values for same are included in machinery schedule. Patterns are
turned wood and sculpted-wood for sand and plaster castings.

V. Michael Arnold (pres.) and E.C. Mullin (exec. V.P.) state emphat-
ically that scheduled machinery values are as accurate as they
can list them. In 1972 they did itemized inventory of same. This
schedule updated and current values estimated by insured as of
10/31/X7. Valuations include current catalog values where applicable; where co. made modifications, the values are educated estimates. Frankly, John, I believe more accurate valuations are
not possible and presuming a loss the IIA claims adjuster will be
dealing with very honorable men who are reasonable and most
knowledgeable re their property.

VI. See G. E. figures attached. A total shutdown lasting in excess of
ten working days at Palo Alto would cause max. 20 percent reduction in Pawtucket plant for like time. Anything less at Palo Alto
would be negligible because of supplies on hand at warehouse. Contingent U&O from Phila. unnecessary since at least three other
suppliers of equal quality and similar pricing can be found in New
England area.

Narragansett's business is relatively stable throughout year. I
reviewed sales/production patterns 1972 to present with Arnold and
Mullin. There is hint of cyclicality in March through June when
perhaps 50 percent of production value is manufactured. Actually
this "hint" reached 50 percent in only two years and had low of
35 percent in 1975.

VII. Mike Arnold has run company since 1968. B.A. Haverford College
1954, MBA Amos Tuck (Dartmouth) 1956. Has been raised in the Company working all jobs. Is considered master die-maker. Is shirt-
sleeve owner who is very much admired and respected by entire work
force.

E.C. Mullin, age 60, started as apprentice in 1938. Has B.A.
Providence Coll. via night school. Has done every job in Company
including temporary CEO for 1-1/2 years 1950-1952.

VIII. Warehouse values fluctuate as per schedule. Books current on LIFO
basis and monthly reports to me will be accurate and on time.
Limit as scheduled. Un-named location limit $10,000.

John, please call if anything further is needed.

HW: Herb Wilson

Exhibit 13-19
Narragansett Manufacturing Company, Inc.—Business Interruption Work Sheet

COMBINATION BUSINESS INTERRUPTION WORK SHEET (Form No. TE-15—Edition Date 3-70)

(For Use With Gross Earnings Form Nos. 3 and 4 for Mercantile, Non-Manufacturing or Manufacturing Risks)

Name of Insured ____Narragansett Mfg. Co., Inc.____

Location of Risk ____Pawtucket, RI____

Date ____

ALL ENTRIES TO BE ON AN ANNUAL BASIS	COLUMN 1 Actual Values for Year Ended 12/31/X7 (000 omitted)	COLUMN 2 *Estimated Values for Year Ending 12/31/X9 (000 omitted)
A. Total annual net sales value of production from Manufacturing Operations; and total annual net sales from Merchandising or Non-Manufacturing Operations (Gross sales less discounts, returns, bad accounts and prepaid freight, if included in sales)	$ 9,100	$ 10,465
B. **Add** other earnings (if any) derived from operation of the business:		
1. Cash Discounts Received (not reflected in the amounts deducted under D)		
2. Commissions or Rents from Leased Departments		
3.	17	19
C. Total ("A" plus "B")	$ 9,117	$ 10,484
D. **Deduct** only cost of:		
1. Raw stock from which such production is derived	$ 2,855	$ 3,198
2. Supplies consisting of materials consumed directly in the conversion of such raw stock into finished stock or in supplying the service(s) sold by the insured	incl.	

3. Merchandise sold, including packaging materials therefor

4. Service(s) purchased from outsiders (not employees of the insured) for resale which do not continue under contract

Total Deductions .... $ 2,855 .... $ 3,198

E. GROSS EARNINGS ("C" Minus "D") .... $ 6,262 .... $ 7,286

IF INSURANCE IS TO BE WRITTEN WITHOUT PAYROLL ENDORSEMENTS:

F. Take 50, 60, 70 or 80% of "E.", Column 2, as amount of insurance required depending upon percentage Contribution Clause to be used (.70..%) .... 4,383.4 .... 5,100.2

IF INSURANCE IS TO BE WRITTEN WITH ORDINARY PAYROLL EXCLUSION ENDORSEMENT, Deduct From "E" Above:

G. All Ordinary Payroll Expense .... $ NA .... $ NA

H. Business Interruption Basis for Contribution ("E" minus "G") .... $ NA .... $ NA

I. Amount of Insurance—Take 80 or 90% of H, Column 2, depending upon percentage Contribution Clause to be used (......%)

IF INSURANCE IS TO BE WRITTEN WITH ORDINARY PAYROLL-LIMITED COVERAGE ENDORSEMENT, Complete the Following:

J. Select the largest Ordinary Payroll Expense for 90† consecutive calendar days .... $ NA .... $ NA

K. Business Interruption Basis for Contribution ("H" plus "J") ....

L. Amount of Insurance—Take 80 or 90% of K, Column 2, depending upon percentage Contribution Clause to be used (......%)

$200,000. On the other hand, the values were fairly small in proportion to the entire amount at risk and Narragansett was a prudent concern that recognized the importance of the patterns and hence would not treat them carelessly. He therefore decided they constituted no major problem in his over-all decision, and he therefore would quote them with a rate of $1.50. This charge was based on the fire and extended coverage rate ($1.05) plus an "all-risks" load that John pushed a little higher than usual to cover his "worry factor."

The neon sign was much more of a cut-and-dried issue for John. Tom Brown had said it was well anchored. Its height practically precluded V or MM losses. And the manual rate was very adequate; John's company had a rather large book of this business that for the past five years had a loss ratio hovering around 25 percent.

Business Interruption In reviewing the business interruption exposure, John reasoned as follows:

a. The total physical plant is a better-than-average risk.
b. The insured could suffer severely, beyond any possible insurance recovery, from any interruption and, therefore, is not apt to malinger, given any physical damage to real or personal property.
c. While blanket insurance increases the probability for loss, the interdependence is offset by the two plants being capable of turning out the bulk of the company's product line. Thus, a loss at one could be compensated for via extra shifts to increase production at the other. In short, then, frequency was counterbalanced by low severity. Finally, frequency was, in fact, a relatively low probability in itself.

John therefore believed that this exposure was insurable with adequate pricing and proper insurance to value. The rates were simply percentages of the building rates, and John accepted these as givens.

His review of the worksheet submitted by Herbert gave him a start: (1) the figure was at extreme odds with the amount of insurance requested on the application ($5,100,200 vs. $600,100); (2) both these figures were vastly different from the profit and loss statement provided by Herbert; (3) he wondered why a 70 percent coinsurance clause had been requested.

While puzzling over these items, it suddenly occurred to John that 70 percent coinsurance was probably the minimum required in the applicable rating jurisdiction. A check of the manual confirmed this. Then John decided to talk with the bond underwriter in his office; he had used him as a valuable resource in the past whenever he had trouble with financial statements. He prepared a comparison sheet for him. The

Exhibit 13-20
Underwriter's Comparison Sheet

	Business Interruption Worksheet	
Income Statement 19X7	Column 1	Column 2
Sales (net) $9,100,000	Line A = $9,100,000	$10,465,000
Other income 16,745	Line B-3 = 17,000	19,000
9,116,745	Line C = 9,117,000	10,484,000
Cost goods −5,915,000	Line D = −2,855,000	−3,198,000
$3,201,745	Line E = $6,262,000	$ 7,286,000

discrepancy was in the "cost of goods sold." The bond underwriter was given the figures shown in Exhibit 13-20.

After only a brief examination, John got his answer. The income statement's cost of goods sold figure *included* wages and salaries of employees as well as all other costs directly related to production. This is accepted and understood practice in accounting. The cost of goods sold on the business interruption worksheet was exclusive of employee wages and salaries. Therefore, the 19X7 income statement appeared to include $3,060,000 in payroll costs (i.e., $5,915,000 less $3,060,000 equals $2,855,000, Line D Column 1.)

John then called Herbert about the discrepancy in the application limit of liability requested versus the worksheet amount. Herbert was somewhat embarrassed by his mistake and agreed with John that the gross earnings figure via the worksheet was the amount to be quoted.

It occurred to John at this juncture that a limit of $5,100,200 added to the values already present at risk might cause capacity problems. He decided to postpone these considerations until everything else had been completed.

But with his problems about information discrepancies cleared, John believed the business interruption exposure was acceptable. Two "unconscious" thinking processes were latent considerations in John's conclusions about business interruption—one was that business interruption was a very profitable line for his company, over many, many years; the second was, that given a good physical risk, business interruption invariably was also good. (These two thoughts are common property underwriting clichés. They have become clichés because of their basic validity. However, two of the largest single fire losses within the past ten years were severely compounded by such simplistic thinking—a telephone exchange in New York City and an automobile factory in Europe. The business interruption exposures, in both instances, were clearly very key issues, in underwriting and in the ultimate loss settlements.)

Transportation In reviewing the transportation exposure, John reasoned as follows:

A. Terms of sale meant only outgoing shipments were to be covered.

B. Released value bills of lading issued by common carriers meant that IIA's policy was exposed for all covered losses and subrogation proceedings would mean only partial recoveries when the carrier was liable. The rates for these exposures must contemplate this.

C. The loss data was too sketchy. "Overages, shortages, and damages" were inconclusive. In addition, John would have preferred to have each loss specifically itemized. It made valuation of deductible effect almost impossible.

Losses *appeared* to be:

	Average Loss	Average Insured Loss with Deductible
Owned truck	$2,267	$2,750

(And the $500 deductible would wholly eliminate only the $300 breakage loss.)

Common truck	$ 467	$ 217

(The $250 deductible would appear to wholly eliminate none of the three losses.)

Rail	$ 644	$ 394

(The $250 deductible again would appear to wholly eliminate none of the 16 losses. The rail frequency problem was typical for Northeast U.S. railroads.)

John decided that any further thinking required pricing these exposures. His initial computations follow:

Owned truck	$5,250,000 @ .12 rate (no subrogation)	=	$6,300
Common truck	$3,397,500 @ .09 rate (with subrogation)	=	3,058
Rail	$1,132,500 @ .20 rate (with subrogation)	=	2,265
	Total		$11,623

At first, John thought that his rate (all rates were judgment rates) for rail carriage was light—three years' experience showed total losses of $10,300 (16 losses). With a total net deductible of $4,000 (16 × $250) the net loss was apparently $6,300 (assuming all losses exceeded the deductible). This compared to a three-year rail premium of $6,795, which left little for expenses. But, then, John realized that *all* public transit losses were subject to subrogation and therefore the true net losses would be eliminated except for subrogation expenses. He thus decided to go ahead and quote this total premium for Narragansett.

Calculation of Exposure

John decided, at this point, to calculate his exposure for line setting. But before proceeding directly with that, he reviewed the perils he was underwriting against:

- Fire was his greatest concern. The lumberyard exposure also had to be considered in this context.
- The extended coverage perils were primarily windstorm and explosion via the foundry coal-fired furnaces and the use of volatile flammables in the factories.
- Water damage, except for the two flood possibilities, gave him little concern since the buildings were well maintained and the main plant had a watch service to spot internal plumbing leaks.
- V or MM was a minor concern except for the Palo Alto plant— John now realized he had no data about this. Also, the warehouse was an isolated exposure. Again, it occurred to John for the first time that he did not know whether the watch service was applicable at this site.
- Collapse was a possibility but improbable given the building construction and maintenance.
- All other contingencies seemed unworthy of deliberate consideration.

John then looked at his risk for probable maximum losses. He was first forced to make an assumption, since he had no direct data at hand—the Palo Alto plant contributed something less than 50 percent of Narragansett's income. Furthermore, John reasoned that although a loss at the warehouse would affect income, its impact would be considerably less than at either factory—that is, both factories conceivably could maintain operations given a large loss at the warehouse, albeit the main factory would slow down its operations. From all this, John decided the Moses Brown address constituted his key underwriting location.

Here is John's calculation of PML:

1. The main factory was sufficiently separated from the other two buildings to equal, by itself, the amount subject.
2. Having four floors with three equal fire divisions, a fire in the center division would likely consume all four floors of that division. In addition, the residual damage (smoke, heat, fire extinguishment, etc.) could affect the two divisions on either side. Being somewhat conservative in setting PML's, John decided that values equal to an entire additional division could be thus affected. And since 40 percent of all contents values could aggregate in the rear division packing/shipping area, he used the center and rear divisions as his PML point of reference:

Building value $1,692,000 (100%) × $2/3$	=	$1,128,564
Contents (40% + 30%) × $200,000	=	140,000
Machinery $400,000 × $2/3$	=	266,800
Business interruption (see explanation following)	=	1,442,628
Total PML:		$2,977,992

The business interruption PML was figured by John as follows:

100% gross earnings—all locations	=	$7,286,000
100% gross earnings—main plant (60% of all locations as an assumption)	=	4,371,600
PML—33% of main plant gross earnings (John estimates a loss would last four months)	=	1,442,628

Referring back once again to his *Line Guide*, John can now take the risk to a rater for all manual rating. He then will take it to his supervisor for a decision on the California earthquake problem. A quote letter can then be written to Herbert. The only loose end is the ocean quotation from the marine underwriter.

SUMMARY

The discussion of underwriting specialty property lines concentrates on the basic coverage provided by and the key factors for underwriting some specialty lines —boiler and machinery insurance, glass insurance, difference in conditions (DIC) insurance, crop hail insurance, and rain insurance.

Boiler and machinery policies provide coverage for four basic types of mechanical equipment or "objects": boilers; fired and unfired pressure vessels; mechanical objects such as compressors, steam turbines, and internal combustion engines; and electrical items such as motors, transformers, and switchboards. The insuring agreement covers "accidents" to "objects" as defined in the policy. Some key underwriting factors for boiler and machinery insurance are the ability of the prospective insured's maintenance department to competently make repairs and perform preventive maintenance checks of the objects which are subject to insurance, the age of the objects, and the location of the risk. These and other factors require physical inspections to be an integral and important part of boiler and machinery underwriting.

Glass insurance covers all kinds of glass, whether structural or interior, including lettering and ornamentation. The policy covers damage caused by breakage of the glass or by chemicals accidentally or maliciously applied. Key underwriting factors include high risk occupancies, types of glass, and high risk areas.

The difference in conditions (DIC) policy is perhaps the broadest of "all-risks" coverages. The form provides coverage against burglary, collapse, water damage and, optionally, earthquake and flood. Such additional coverages as transit and business interruption can also be purchased. One unusual feature of the coverage is that it excludes the basic perils of fire and lightning, extended coverage, vandalism or malicious mischief, and sprinkler leakage. Underwriters must take care to consider all exposures to loss when handling this coverage. Special applications have been devised to aid in the development of specific underwriting information on the exposures to loss.

Crop hail insurance is designed to provide coverage against all direct loss or damage by hail to the crops described in the policy, not losses resulting from a beating rain or losses caused by wind.

Rain insurance provides protection for loss of income or extra expense caused by rain, hail, snow, or sleet, that occurs during a specified period of time at a short-term money-making event.

Package policies can be classified as (a) simple collection or combination policies, (b) minimum requirement combination policies, (c) indivisible combination policies, and (d) nonstandard combination policies. Underwriting decisions on package policies are most difficult when part of the package is acceptable but the balance is not. Some of the questions the underwriter should raise are: What are the respective limits of liability of each of the sections of the package policy? What are the respective premiums for each policy section? What are the respective frequencies of loss? What are the respective severities of loss for each major section?

Underwriting large commercial property risks poses some special problems. These problems include: the large loss potential; the complexity of operations and equipment; the increased complexity of business interruption exposures; geographical differences; and varying hazard conditions. A final underwriting decision should be based on the consideration and weighting of these and other factors.

The Narragansett Manufacturing Company case study presents some of the documents and problems which must be dealt with when underwriting large commercial property risks.

Chapter Notes

1. William H. Rodda, James S. Trieschmann, and Bob A. Hedges, *Commercial Property Risk Management and Insurance* (Malvern, PA: American Institute for Property and Liability Underwriters, 1978), Vol. 2, pp. 211-212.
2. Information supplied by the Hartford Steam Boiler Inspection and Insurance Company.
3. Rodda, Trieschmann, and Hedges, p. 228.
4. Rodda, Trieschmann, and Hedges, p. 228.
5. Rodda, Trieschmann, and Hedges, pp. 248-249.
6. G. William Glendenning and Robert B. Holtom, *Personal Lines Underwriting*, 2nd ed. (Malvern, PA: Insurance Institute of America, 1982), p. 539.

Bibliography

Best, Richard. "Fire Walls That Failed: The K Mart Corporation Distribution Center Fire." *Fire Journal*, May 1983, pp. 74, 83, and 86.

Best's Loss Control Engineering Manual. Oldwick, NJ: A.M. Best Co.

Brannigan, Francis L. *Building Construction for the Fire Service.* Boston: National Fire Protection Association, 1971.

Bryan, John L. *Automatic Sprinkler and Standpipe Systems.* Boston: National Fire Protection Association, 1976.

Burns, Robert T. "Windowless Buildings." *Firehouse*, September 1983, pp. 56, 58, and 160.

Burtner, Carrol E. "The Economics of a Fire Protection Program." *Fire Technology*, February 1966, pp. 5-14.

Casey, Raymond J. "Convincing Consumers to Install Automatic Sprinklers." *Fire Journal*, March 1971, pp. 35-36, 41.

Chadwick, H.A. "Insurance and Information Systems Management." *The Information Systems Handbook.* Eds. F. Warren McFarlan and Richard L. Nolan. Homewood, IL: Dow Jones-Irwin, 1975.

Cohn, Bert M. "The Validity of Trade-Offs for Automatic Sprinkler Protection." *Fire Protection News*, August 1974, pp. 1-4.

Commercial Fire Rating Schedule. New York: Insurance Services Office, 1975, 1976, 1978, 1980, 1981, 1982, 1983.

Considine, Robert. *Man Against Fire.* New York: Doubleday and Co., 1955.

Current Arson Issues. Chicago: Insurance Committee for Arson Control, 1981.

"Fire Loss Study with Respect to Credit Ratings." New York: Dun & Bradstreet, 1970.

Fire Protection Handbook. 15th ed. Quincy, MA: National Fire Protection Association, 1981.

—————————, 14th ed. Eds. Gordon P. McKinnon and Keith Towers. Boston: National Fire Protection Association, 1976.

Fire Suppression Rating Schedule. New York: Insurance Services Office, 1980.

Gibb, D.E.W. *Lloyd's of London: A Study in Individualism.* London: Macmillan & Co., 1957.

Glendenning, G. William and Holtom, Robert B. *Personal Lines Underwriting.* 2nd ed. Malvern, PA: Insurance Institute of America, 1982.

Grading Schedule for Municipal Fire Protection. New York: Insurance Services Office, 1974.

Grimaldi, J.V. and Simonds, R.H. *Safety Managment.* 3rd ed. Homewood, IL: Richard D. Irwin, 1975.

Hammack, James M. "Combined Sprinkler System and Standpipes (Some Random Thoughts)." *Fire Journal*, September 1971, p. 68.

Hammond, John S. III and Hollingsworth, E.P. "How Underwriters Think, Progress Report and Recommendations from the Underwriting Research Program." Privately distributed, 1971.

Holtom, Robert B. *Commercial Fire Underwriting*. Cincinnati: The National Underwriter Co., 1969.

Horn, Ronald C. *Subrogation in Insurance Theory and Practice*. Homewood, IL: Richard D. Irwin, 1964.

Ingrassia, Lawrence. "Planning, Luck Help Big Bank Overcome Fire." *The Wall Street Journal*, 3 December 1982, pp. 33, 39.

"Insurer-Bought Vans Credited with Doubling Arson Arrests in Conn." *The National Underwriter* (Property-Casualty Edition), 14 November 1977, p. 46.

Insurance Facts, 1983-84 Edition. New York: Insurance Information Institute, 1983.

Judging the Fire Risk. 4th ed. Chicago: Alliance of American Insurers, 1981.

Kahler, Clyde M. "Business Interruption Insurance." Ph.D. dissertation, University of Pennsylvania, 1930.

Lamieux, Frank. International Risk Management Seminar, "The Emerging Risk of Computer Disaster."

Launie, J.J.; Lee, J.F.; and Baglini, N.A. *Principles of Property and Liability Underwriting*. Rev. ed. Malvern, PA: Insurance Institute of America, 1977.

Lincoln, W.O. and Tisdale, G.W. *Insurance Inspection and Underwriting*. 8th ed. New York: The Spectator.

Lyons, Paul R. "Dry Standpipe Survey in Los Angeles." *Fire Journal*, May 1969, pp. 65-66.

Maguire, Hugh M. "Eight-Agency Effort Fights Arson." *Fire Command!* December 1975.

Marine Insurance. Philadelphia: Insurance Company of North America.

Morris, John V. *Fires and Firefighters*. Boston: Little, Brown & Co., 1955.

NFPA Inspection Manual. 4th ed. Boston: National Fire Protection Association, June 1976, pp. 33-38.

Ports of the World. 12th ed. Philadelphia: Insurance Company of North America.

Reed, P.B. and Thomas, P.I. *Adjustment of Property Losses*. New York: McGraw-Hill Book Co., 1969.

Rodda, William H. *Marine Insurance: Ocean and Inland*. Englewood Cliffs, NJ: Prentice-Hall, 1970.

_____; Trieschmann, James S.; and Hedges, Bob A. *Commercial Property Risk Management and Insurance*. Vol. II. Malvern, PA: American Institute for Property and Liability Underwriters, 1978.

Standard for the Installation of Standpipe and Hose Systems. Boston: National Fire Protection Association, 1974.

Studies of Floods and Flood Damage 1952-1955. New York: American Insurance Association.

Webb, Bernard L.; Launie, J.J.; Rokes, Willis Park; and Baglini, Norman A. *Insurance Company Operations*. 3rd ed. Malvern, PA: American Institute for Property and Liability Underwriters, 1984.

Weisman, Herman M. "The National Anti-Arson Strategy: Its Progress and Status." *Fire Journal*, May 1983, pp. 48, 49, and 145.

Winter, William D. *Marine Insurance*. 3rd ed. New York: McGraw-Hill Book Co., 1952.

Youd, J.D. *A Practical Approach to Inland Marine Insurance*. Boston: Standard Publishing Co., 1974.

Index

A

A-rated local alarm, *453*
Abandonment, *363*
Accidental floods, *108*
Accounts receivable and valuable papers policies, *382*
Accumulation clause, *418*
Actual cash value (ACV), *12, 359*
Actual loss sustained, *274*
Actual total loss, *419*
Additional classifications of contents, *174*
Adequate fire resistance, *61*
Adverse selection, crime, *458*
Age, fire risk and, *150*
and perils, *151*
Agreed amount basis, *264*
Agreed amount endorsement, *278*
Airflow in fires, *55*
Air foam systems, *237*
Alarms, *450*
classification of, *450*
American Cargo War Risk Reinsurance Exchange, *424*
American Hull Insurance Syndicate (AHIS), *396*
American Institute of Marine Underwriters (AIMU), *397*
American Institute of Marine Underwriters Time Hull Form, *397*
Amount subject, *8, 445*

Analytic System for the Measurement of Relative Fire Hazard (Dean Analytic Schedule), *321*
Annual transit form, *367*
Applications, *153*
Appraisals, *20*
rules of thumb for, *17*
Appraising values exposed to loss, *15*
Approved fire door, *147*
Arson, *67*
solutions for, *70*
Arson squads, *212*
Assets, fixed, *76*
Assignment, *260*
Atmospheric oxygen, *54*
Attachment and termination clause, *417*
Automatic sprinkler systems, *232*
supervision of, *238*
Automatic systems, *221*
Average risk, *446*
Average terms, *420*

B

B-rated local alarm, *453*
BACAT (Barge Aboard Catamaran), *425*
Bailee, *375*
liability of, *375*

543

Bailees' customers policies, *374*
Bailment, *374*
Bailor, *375*
Barge-on-Board, *424*
Base of exposure, *317*
Basic building grade, *324*, *325*
Basic construction charges, *324*
Basic occupancy charge, *172*
Basic occupancy rating, *171*
Basis rate, *321*
Beaufort Scale, *112*
Betterment, *14*
Bill of lading, *365*
  order, *366*
  straight, *366*
BLEVE, *87*
Block concept, *377*
Block policies, *377*
  coverage of, *378*
Boiler and machinery insurance, *470*
  inspections and underwriting for, *473*
Boiling liquid, *87*
Bordereau form, *414*
Bottlenecks, *300*
Bowling alley hazards, *198*
Brick veneer, *137*
Bridges and tunnels, *368*
Builders' risk, *164*
  and probable maximum loss, *167*
  selection decisions for, *168*
Building codes, local, *162*
  and standards, adherence to, *213*
Building construction classifications, *135*
Building conversion factor, *333*
Building design, earthquake and, *102*
Building openings, *146*
Buildings as fuel, *51*
Bureau reports, *154*
Burglary, *440*
Business interruption, *273*
Business interruption insurance, *272*
Business interruption values, calculation of, *279*

C

Calorific or fuel value, *51*, *66*
Camera and musical instrument dealers, *380*
Cancellation clause, *260*
Carbon dioxide systems, *237*
Cargo packing, *425*
Carriage of Goods by Sea Act of 1936, *413*
Carrier, common, *365*
  contract, *365*
  private, *367*
Case study, Narragansett Manufacturing Co., Inc., *488*
Cash in advance, *412*
Cash flow, *77*
Cash market value, *358*
Catastrophe control plan, development of a sample, *126*
Catastrophe evaluation, *344*
Catastrophe underwriting, *124*
Central station protection, *453*
Central station systems, *220*, *222*
C & F (Cost & Freight), *411*
  named point of destination, *411*
Charterer's liability, *408*
Chemical hazards, *196*
Chemical reactions, *45*
CIF (Cost, Insurance and Freight), named point of destination, *411*
Circulating medium, *59*
Civil authority, interruption by, *275*
Civil commotion, *91*
  definition of, *92*
Claims settlement, *7*
Class rate, *153*, *318*
Class rating, *11*, *318*
Class relativities, *342*
Classifications, building construction, *135*
Cleaning fluid clauses, *259*
Clear space, *251*
Clear space warranty, *259*
Clear Water Act of 1977, *396*
Clerk of the works, *166*

Clock and tape systems, *219*
Closed circuit television monitors, *226*
Coinsurance, *261*
  inland marine, *363*
Collapse, *122*
  age and, *152*
  builders' risk coverage and, *166*
Collapse coverage, *123*
Collapse loss, principal causes of, *123*
Collision liability clause, *400*
Combined business interruption and extra expense, *311*
Combined standpipe and automatic sprinkler systems, *231*
Combustibility, *172*
  and susceptibility of contents, *178*
Combustible, *48*
Combustible (C-3), *173*
Combustible, explosive, or susceptible supplies, *183*
Combustible or susceptible contents, *186*
Combustion, *39*
  products of, *51*
Commercial crime insurance, definitions in, *440*
Commercial fire loss control programs, *215*
Commercial hull hazards and exposures, *401*
Commercial hulls, *396*
Commercial printing hazards, *199*
Commercial property and commercial liability underwriting compared, *6*
Commercial property underwriting, historical development of, *2*
  introduction to, *1*
Commercial statistical plan (CSP), *319*
Common carrier, *365*
  liability of, *365*
Common hazards, *175*
Communications charge, *331*
Completed value form, *164*
Component method, *20*

Computer crime, *462*
Computer Science Corporation, *106*
Computer security considerations, *464*
Concrete, earthquake and, *103*
Concrete block, *137*
Concurrent causation, *444*
  doctrine of, *97*
Conduction, *58*
Confined spaces other than pressure vessels, *82*
Conflagrations, *2*
Consequential loss, *311*
Consolidated soil, *102*
Construction, *131*
  earthquake and, *103*
  exposure and, *248*
  mill, *138*
  mixed, *143*
  ordinary, *138*
  slow burning, *141*
Construction classifications, *135*
Construction considerations, hurricane, *116*
Construction coverage, course of, *164*
Construction design, *143*
Construction information, sources of, *153*
Construction materials, *148*
Constructive total loss, *419*
Contained fire, *61*
Container hazards, *432*
Containerization, *431*
Containers, *425*
Contents, additional classifications of, *174*
  combustibility and susceptibility of, *178*
Contents base, *334*
Contents combustibility factor, *325*
Contents conversion factors, *334*
Contents susceptibility charge, *333*
Contingent business interruption, *305*
Contingent extra expense, *310*
Contingent liability from operation of building laws, *313*

Contract carrier, *365*
  liability of, *366*
Contractors' equipment floaters, *371*
Contributing properties, *305*
Contribution (coinsurance) clause, *277*
Convection, *59*
Conversion, *441*
Cooking, *178*
Cooking equipment, *41*
COPE (construction, occupancy, protection, and exposures), *11, 131*
Course of construction coverage, *164*
Coverage, extensions of, *265*
Credibility, *341*
Credibility-weighted loss ratio (CLR), *342*
Crime, computer, *462*
Crime coverage, conditions and terms of, *443*
Crime coverages, underwriting, *437*
Crime deductibles, *445*
Crime insurance, underwriting decision-making for, *447*
Crime limits of liability, *444*
Crime loss potential, assessing, *447*
Crime losses, characteristics of property subject to, *447*
Crime perils insured against, *444*
Crime policies, construction of, *441*
Crime pricing and loss control, *446*
Crime underwriting options, *458*
Crime warranties, *446*
Crop hail insurance, *479*
Crop Hail Insurance Actuarial Association (CHIAA), *479*
Curtain boards, *146*
Cutting, welding and, *43*

D

Damage, likely, *65*
Damage control, *85*
  pressure vessel, *87*

Data security, *465*
Dealers' block policies, *379*
Dean Analytic Schedule, *321*
Debris floods, *109*
Decoration, interior and exterior, *150*
Deductibles, *336*
  crime, *445*
  inland marine, *363*
Deflagration, *82*
Deliberate damage pollution hazard clause, *401, 423*
Deluge system, *235*
Demolition costs, *313*
Depreciation, *14*
Depreciation grading chart, *22*
  use of, *23*
Depreciation and replacement, *77*
Designed openings, *65*
Detection systems, *450*
Detectors, types of, *222*
Deterioration, *76*
Determination of the amount of insurance, for extra expense coverage, *208*
Determination of value, *12*
Detonation, *82*
Diagrams, *155*
Difference in conditions (DIC) form, *478*
Disaster contingency plans, *302*
Disbursements warranty, *398*
Disposal, *53*
Dividends, *79*
Division, fire, *9*
Division walls, *327*
Docks, *369*
Draft, *412*
Dry docks, *369*
Dry pipe system, *230, 235*
Ductwork, *63*
Due diligence and dispatch, *274*
Dun & Bradstreet, *18*
Duration of coverage—marine extension clauses, *417*
Duties of the insured, *260*

E

Earth movement, *105*
Earthquake activity in the United States, areas of, *98*
Earthquake causes, *97*
Earthquake and other earth movement, *96*
Earthquake measurement, *98*
EDP Federal Corporation, *106*
EDP media limitation, *275*
Electric tapes, *225*
Electrical and equipment lines, *63*
Electrical wiring and equipment, *44*
Electricity, static, *45*
Electronic data processing policy, *381*
Endorsement extending the period of indemnity, *279*
Epicenter, *101*
Equipment floaters, scheduled and blanket, *371*
Equipment or implement dealers, *380*
Excess multiplier, *345*
Excess P & I coverage, *405*
Exclusions, gross earnings, *276*
Ex dock, named port of importation, *411*
Expediting expenses, *471*
Expenses, *341*
  as components of the rate, *335*
  to reduce loss, *275*
Experience period, *339, 344*
Experience period adjusted loss ratio, *342*
Explosion, *82*
  incidence of, in pressure vessels, *87*
  sources of, *83*
    pressure vessels, *86*
Explosion clause, *423*
Explosion prevention, *84*
  pressure vessel, *87*
Explosion vent, *85*
Explosive dusts, *196*
Explosive range, *55*

Ex point of origin, *410*
Exposed building, *248*
Exposed building grade, *331, 332*
Exposing building, *248*
Exposure, *247*
  base of, *317*
Exposure fires, *46*
Exposure hazard charge, *331*
Exposure-condition, *331*
Exposure-condition factor, *332*
Exposures, factors influencing the severity of, *256*
  major considerations in, *247*
Extended coverage periods, rate making for, *343*
Extensions of coverage, *265*
Exterior decoration, *150*
External exposures, control of, *256*
  and coverages, *247*
Extinguishment systems as a hazard, *242*
Extra expense, *306*
Extra expense insurance, *272*
Extrapolation of a trend, *280*

F

Fair Access to Insurance Requirements (FAIR) Plans, *94*
Fair market value, *12*
FAIR Plans, *94*
Farm unit plan, *479*
FAS (Free Along Side), *411*
FC&S clause, *423*
Federal Arson Task force, *70*
Federal Emergency Management Agency (FEMA), *70*
Fidelity, *459*
Fidelity bond, *460*
Fidelity loss control, *461*
Fidelity underwriting, *460*
Filed classification, *368*
Filed and nonfiled classes, *357*
Final building grade, *333*
Final contents grade, *335*
Final rate, *333*

Financial analysis for hazard
   evaluation, *74*
Fire, *39*
   age and, *151*
   analyzing loss potential from, *39*
   builders' risk coverage and, *165*
   contained, *61*
   duration of, and damage, *67*
   friendly, *40*
   hostile, *40*
   triangle of, *39*
Fire brigades, *242*
Fire department connection, *211*
Fire department procedures, *238*
Fire detection activities, *204*
Fire division, *9*, *145*
Fire door, approved, *147*
Fire extinguishers, portable, *227*
Fire extinguishment activities, *204*
Fire ignition, *177*
Fire ignition sequence, *42*
Fire insurance rate review, *339*
Fire insurance rates, *318*
Fire intensity, *181*
Fire load, *46*
Fire loss control programs,
   commercial, *215*
Fire partitions, *64*
Fire prevention activities, *204*
Fire prevention systems, private,
   213
Fire protection, elements of, *203*
   private, *203*
   public, *203*
Fire Protection Handbook, *256*
Fire protection planning, *214*
Fire resistance, *133*
   adequate, *61*
Fire resistive, *142*
   modified, *141*
Fire spread and extent, *58*
   horizontal, to another area, *62*
   uncontrolled, in an undivided
      area, *60*
   up and around, *63*
Fire-stop, *136*
Fire storm, *55*

Fire Suppression Rating Schedule,
   (FSRS), *205*
Fire tetrahedron, *39*
Fire walls, *63*, *145*
Fires, airflow in, *55*
   exposure, *46*
   oxygen for, *54*
First party versus third party, *6*
Fixed assets, *76*
Fixed ignition source, *41*
Fixed temperature, *223*
Flame detectors, *224*
Flame spread, *46*, *49*, *133*
Flammability, limits of, *83*
Flammable, *48*
Flammable or combustible liquids,
   187, *195*
Flammable range, *55*
Flaming, flash, *60*
FLASH (Feeder-LASH), *425*
Flash flaming, *60*
Flash points, *49*
Flashover, *60*
Flat amount basis, *264*
Floaters, contractors' equipment,
   371
   equipment, *371*
Flood, *106*
Flood causes, *108*
Flood exposures, determining, *109*
Flood hazard boundary map, *110*
Flood incidence, *109*
Flood insurance rate map (FIRM),
   110
Flood and the private sector, *106*
Flood problem, scope of, *107*
Flood protection, *110*
Floor separations, *65*
Fluctuating values at risk, *267*
FOB (Free on Board), *410*
FOB sales endorsement, *410*
Focus, *101*
FPA (free of particular average),
   428
Frame construction, earthquake
   and, *103*
Frame and metal partitions, *62*
Free burning (C-4), *173*

Free of capture and seizure (FC&S), *423*
Friction, *44*
  and static electricity, *194*
Friendly fire, *40*
Fuel, *66*
  buildings as, *51*
Fuel load, *46, 180*
Fuels, *48*
  for heat and power, common, *53*
Full amount clause, *278*
Full value reporting clause, *418*
Fumigation clause, *423*
Furniture, fixtures, and equipment, *34*
Furriers' block, *380*

G

Gas, inert, *84*
Gases and smoke, *51*
General average, *399, 419*
General class rates, *319*
General estimate method, *21*
General rules, *323*
Geographical limits clause, *418*
Glass, types of, *476*
Glass insurance, *475*
  underwriting, *476*
Glass windows, *63*
Grading Schedule for Municipal Fire Protection, 204
Grain elevator hazards, *199*
Graupel hail, *120*
Great Chicago Fire, *2*
Great Fire of London, *2*
Gross building grade, *333*
Gross contents grade, *333, 334*
Gross earnings, projection of, *280*
Gross earnings (form 3), *273*
Gross earnings (form 4), *273*
Gross earnings form, *273*
  coverage of, *273*
GRT (gross registered tons), *396*
Guards, *454*

H

Habitational class rates, *319*
Habitational occupancies, *177*
Hail, *120*
  incidence of, *122*
  windstorm and, *110*
Hail damage, *122*
Hail Insurance Adjustment and Research Association (HIARA), *479*
Halogenated agent systems, *238*
Hard use, *152*
Hazard analysis, for institutional occupancies, *183*
Hazard evaluation, financial analysis for, *74*
Hazards, common, *175*
  container, *432*
  fire, *178*
  ocean, *432*
  special, *175*
Hazards of occupancy, *328*
Hazards of representative occupancy classes, *197*
Heat, products of combustion and, *51*
Heat detectors, *223*
Heat generators, mobile, *43*
Heat and power, common fuels for, *53*
Heat spread, *58*
Heat treatment, *184*
Heath, Cuthbert, *377*
Heating, space, *41*
Heating and air conditioning, *178, 184*
Heating devices, *41*
High-rise buildings, *143*
High-rise construction, earthquake and, *103*
Horizontal spread to another area, *62*
Hostile fire, *40*
Hot liquids, *44*
"Hot work," *43*
Housekeeping, control of, *213*

fire and, *52*
Housing and Urban Development
    Act of 1968, *93*
Hughes Panel, *93*
Hull coverage, *397*
Hulls, commercial, *396*
Hurricane paths, *114*
Hurricanes, *111*
    characteristics of, *112*
    incidence of, *114*
    measurement of, *112*

I

Ignition, sources of, *41*
    spontaneous, *45*
Implied warranties, *393*
Incendiarism, *47*
Inchmaree clause, *399*, *421*
Incidence of explosion, pressure
    vessel, *87*
Increased cost of construction, *313*
Increased value clause, *416*
Indemnity, principle of, *7*
Indexes, national, *18*
Indirect loss coverages, *272*
Indirect loss exposures, *271*
Indirect property losses,
    commercial, underwriting, *271*
*Individual Property Fire
    Suppression*, *205*
Indivisible combination policy, *483*
Industrial materials handling
    equipment, *194*
Inert gas, *84*
Inflation, *32*
Inflation guard endorsement, *32*
Inland marine coverages,
    miscellaneous, *380*
    underwriting, *364*
Inland marine insurance,
    underwriting, *351*
Inland marine policies, permissive
    and restrictive clauses common
    to, *360*

Inland marine policy terms and
    conditions, *358*
Inspection, use of, *155*
Inspection Manual, *213*
Inspection reports and diagrams,
    155
Installment sales contracts, *386*
Institutional occupancies, *182*
Instrumentalities of transportation
    and communication, *368*
Insulation, *149*
Insurable interest, *7*, *259*
Insurance Committee for Arson
    Control, *70*
Insurance contracts, analyzing, as a
    variable in underwriting
    decisions, *257*
Insurance Model Arson Reporting
    Immunity Law, *70*
Insurance Services Office (ISO), *11*
Insurance to value, *261*
Insuring agreement, gross earnings,
    274
Insurrection, *92*
Interior decoration, *150*
Intrusion detectors, *224*
Inventory, *74*
Inventory shortage, *441*
Invoice value, *415*
Ionization detectors, *223*
ISO Commercial Fire Rating
    Schedule, *322*
    content of, *323*
ISO fire class rate plan, *319*

J

Jefferson case, *12*
Jewelers' block, *380*
Jewelers' and furriers' blocks, *379*
Joisted masonry, *138*
Jones Act, *407*

K

Key rate, *321*
Key risk, *254*

L

Labels clause, *360*
Landed value, *415*
Landslide, *105*
Large commercial property risks,
  underwriting, *485*
Large losses, *341*
Large plate endorsement, *476*
LASH barges (lighter aboard ship),
  425
Laws, valued policy, *264*
Lay-up returns, *398*
Leader properties, *305*
Lean limit, *83*
Leasehold interest insurance, *312*
Letter of credit, *413*
Liability, limit of, *10*
Likely damage, *65*
Limit of liability, *10*
Limited combustibility (C-2), *173*
Limits, territorial, *362*
Limits of flammability, *83*
Liquefaction, *102*
Liquefied petroleum gas (LP gas or
  LPG), *54*
Liquids, vaporization of, *49*
Litter, uncollected, *52*
Live animal coverage, *385*
Livestock floater, *385*
Loading bridges, *369*
Loan receipt, *362*
Local alarm system, *222*
Local application, *237*
Local building codes, *162*
Location multiplier, *29*
Loss, maximum possible, *8*
Loss control, fidelity, *461*
  ocean cargo, *429*
Loss exposures, indirect, *271*

Loss potential from fire, analyzing,
  39
Loss potential from other major
  perils, analyzing, *81*
Loss severity, control of, *218*
  measures of, *8*
Low level of oxygen, *55*
Lower flammability limit, *55*

M

Management attitude, towards fire
  loss control, *215*
Manufacturing and wholesale
  distribution occupancies, *189*
Manuscript policies, *388*
Marine extension clauses, *417*
Marine insurance, definition of, *351*
Marine liabilities, underwriting, *407*
Marine railways, *369*
Masonry, joisted, *138*
Masonry construction, earthquake
  and, *103*
Masonry noncombustible, *141*
Material, shape of, heating and, *50*
Maximum possible loss, *8*
Measures of loss severity, *8*
Mercantile occupancies, *186*
Merchant police, *221*
Mill construction, *138*
Minimum requirement combination
  policy, *482*
Mixed construction, *143*
Mobile heat generators, *43*
Mobile ignition source, *41*
Model method, *20*
Modified fire resistive, *141*
Modified Mercalli Scale of 1931, *98*
Modifying coverage, *257*
Moral and morale hazard, in crime
  risks, *457*
Mortgagee clause, *260*
Motor Carrier Act of 1935, *367*
Motor truck cargo legal liability,
  368
Mud slides, *105*

Multiple occupancies, exposure and, *252*

Multiple perils coverage, *394*

Mutual benefit bailments, *375*

Mysterious disappearance, *441*

N

Nation-Wide Marine Definition, *351*
importance of, *352*

National Advisory Commission on Civil Disorders, *93*

National Advisory Panel on Insurance in Riot-Affected Areas, *93*

National Flood Insurance Act of 1968, *106*

National Flood Insurance Association, *106*

National indexes, *18*

Natural causes, of fire, *45*

Net occupancy charge, *331*

Net sales value of production, *293*

Net willing to lose, *444*

Newly acquired property, *265*

No benefit to bailee clause, *361*

No deviation, *394*

Noncombustible, *141*

Noncombustible (C-1), *172*

Noncontinuing expenses, identification of, *284*

Nonfiled classes, *357*

Nonstandard combination policies, *483*

Normal incurred losses, *344*

Normal losses, *345*

O

Objects (boiler and machinery insurance), *470*

Obsolescence, *13, 76*

Occupancy, *171*
exposure and, *251*
hazards of, *328*

grouped by major categories, *176*
rating of, *171*

Occupancy, protection, and exposures, *133*

Occupancy modification factor, *331*

Occupancy rating, basic, *171*

Ocean cargo, underwriting variables for, *409*

Ocean cargo hazards and exposures, *424*

Ocean cargo loss control, *429*

Ocean cargo policies, underwriting, *424*

Ocean cargo rating, *429*

Ocean carrier's liability, *413*

Ocean hazards, *432*

Ocean marine insurance, underwriting, *393*

Office occupancies, *180*

Open account, *412*

Open ocean cargo policy, coverage provisions of, *415*

Open policy, *414*

Order bill of lading, *366*

Ordinary construction, *138*

Ordinary payroll, *277*

Ordinary payroll exclusion endorsement, *277*

Ordinary payroll limited coverage endorsement, *277*

Outdoor cranes, *369*

Outturn survey, *427*

Ownership and management, analysis of, (fire), *73*

Oxidants, *57*

Oxygen, atmospheric, *54*
for fires, *54*
and gas hazards, *185*
low level of, *55*

Oxygen rich atmospheres, *56*

P

PA (particular average), *428*

Package policies, kinds of, *482*

underwriting, *369*, *482*

Packages lost in loading clause, *423*

Packing, cargo, *425*

Pairs and sets clause, *360*

Paramount warranties, *423*

Parapets, *145*

Partial losses, limitations on, *359*

Particular average, *419*

Partitions, fire, *64*
 frame and metal, *62*

Parts or machinery clause, *360*

Pattern and die floaters, *387*

Payables, *78*

Penetrating storm, *114*

Performance building codes, *162*

Perils, additional, *4*
 gross earnings, *274*

Perils clause, hull, *399*

Perils of the seas, *394*

Period of restoration, *306*

Permissive and restrictive clauses
 common to inland marine
 policies, *360*

Photoelectric cells, *223*, *225*

Physical protection, *450*

P & I underwriting information,
 405

Piers, *369*

Plastics manufacturing, *195*

Plumbing, *179*

Plumbing systems, *185*

PML (probable maximum loss), *9*

PML related to the amount of
 insurance, *288*

Policies, valued, *15*, *359*

Ponding, *123*

Portable fire extinguishers, *227*

Power, heat, and refrigeration
 endorsement, *278*

Preaction systems, *235*

Pre-fire planning surveys, *211*

Premise protection, *450*

Premium, *317*

Premium adjustment endorsement,
 279

Present value, *216*

Pressure vessels, *86*

Pricing, *317*

Pricing comparisons, *11*

Pricing and loss control, crime, *446*

Primary P & I coverage, *405*

Principle of indemnity, *7*

Private carrier, *367*

Private extinguishment systems,
 226

Private fire detection systems, *218*

Private fire prevention, major
 elements of, *213*

Private fire prevention systems, *213*

Private fire protection, *203*

Private protection, *448*
 types of, *449*

Probable maximum loss (PML), *9*,
 132
 builders' risk and, *167*
 in crime, *445*

Profit and contingencies, rates and,
 335

Projected gross earnings, *277*

Properties, contributing, *305*
 leader, *305*
 recipient, *305*

Property, *1*
 financial analysis of, *74*
 newly acquired, *265*

Property floaters, miscellaneous,
 373

Property risks, large commercial,
 underwriting, *485*

Property in transit, *365*
 valuation of, *358*

Property underwriting, commercial,
 introduction to, *1*

Protection, *203*
 exposure and, *251*

Protection class factor, *333*

Protection and indemnity (P & I)
 insurance, *404*

Protection of property clause, *361*

Protection as a variable in
 underwriting decisions, *244*

Protective safeguards provision, *258*

Public fire protection, *203*

Public protection, *448*

Public protection systems, *204*

Pure loss ratio, *342*

R

Radiation, *59*
Radio and television
    communications equipment, *369*
Rain insurance, *480*
Raking storm, *114*
Rapid or flash burning (C-5), *173*
Rate, *317*
    appropriateness of, *346*
    effect of, on underwriting, *345*
    other components of, *335*
    understanding, *345*
Rate cards, *154*
    and manuals, *153*
Rate making, *317*
    for extended coverage perils, *343*
Rate of temperature rise, *223*
Rates, fire insurance, *318*
    specific or schedule, *318*, *320*
Rating, *317*
    class, *318*
Rating extra expense, *308*
Rating of a municipality's fire
    defense, *204*
Receivables, *78*
Recipient properties, *305*
Reinsurance considerations,
    catastrophe, *125*
Released value bill of lading, *366*
Remote station system, *222*
Rent insurance, *312*
Rental value, *312*
Replacement cost, *359*
Replacement cost coverage, *268*
Replacement cost valuation, *14*
Reporting form, *164*, *267*
Requirements in case loss occurs
    clause, *260*
Restaurant hazards, *197*
Rich limit, *83*
Richter scale, *98*
Riot, definition of, *92*

vandalism, and malicious
    mischief, builders' risk
    coverage and, *165*
Riot and civil commotion, *91*
    incidence of, *92*
Riots, urban, and their influence on
    insurance, *93*
Risers, *88*
Risk, key, *254*
Robbery, *441*
Roofing, *149*
Rules of thumb for appraisal, *17*
Running down clause (RDC), *400*

S

Safes and vaults, *450*
Saffir/Simpson Scale, *114*
Salamanders, *43*
Salvage award, *399*
Salvage charges, *399*
Salvage teams, *212*
San Francisco disaster, *3*
Schedule base, *324*
Schedule rate, calculating, *323*
Schedule (specific) rating, *11*
SEABEE, *425*
Seamen, *406*
Seasonality and rebuilding time,
    296
Seaworthiness, *394*
Selling price clause, *293*
Service occupancies, *187*
Settlement, claims, *7*
Ship repairer's liability, *407*
Shipowner, liability of, *406*
Shipper's interest, *367*
Shipper's weight, load, and count,
    366
Shore clause, *423*
Short form declaration, *414*
Siamese connections, *211*
Sight draft, *412*
Simple combination policy, *482*
Simple floods, *108*
Slow burning construction, *141*

Small hail, *120*

Smoke detectors, *223*

Smoking and matches, *45*

Smoldering, *55*

Snow-melt floods, *109*

Soft hail, *120*

Soil, consolidated, *102*

Soil conditions, earth movement and, *102*

Solids and gases, vaporization of, *49*

Sonic detectors, *225*

Sources of explosion, other than pressure vessels, *83*
   pressure vessels, *86*

Space heating, *41*

Special class rates, *320*

Special hazards, *175*

Special marine policy, *414*

Specific or schedule rates, *153*, *318*, *320*

Specific (schedule) rating, *11*, *320*

Specification building codes, *162*

Spontaneous heating, *193*

Spontaneous ignition, *45*

Spread, fire, *58*
   flame, *59*
   heat, *58*

Sprinkler leakage, causes of, *88*
   and water damage, *88*
   losses, factors affecting, *90*

Sprinkler system, *88*

Sprinkler system supervisory devices, *226*

Sprinkler systems, automatic, *232*

SR&CC clause, *423*

Stack effect, *61*

"Standard" building, *321*

"Standard" city, *321*

Standard fire policy, *258*

Standard Methods of Fire Tests of Building Construction and Materials, *133*

Standard & Poor's, *18*

Standpipe and hose systems, *230*
   inspection of, *230*

Statewide rate adjustment, *342*

Static electricity, *45*, *194*

Statistical period, *340*

Steamer additionals, *427*

Steiner Tunnel Test, *134*

Stevedore's liability, *408*

Stevedores, longshoremen, and harborworkers, *407*

Storage, fire and, *52*

Storm, penetrating, *114*
   raking, *114*

Storm surge and heavy rainfall, *117*

Stowage, *427*

Straight bill of lading, *366*

Strikes, riots and civil commotions (SR&CC) clause, *423*

Stucco, *137*

Subscription (participation) basis, *368*

Subsidence, *105*

Sue and labor clause, *360*, *399*

Surveillance cameras, *457*

Surveys, pre-fire planning, *211*

Susceptibility, *132*, *174*

T

Tectonic plate theory, *97*

Term, fire policy, *261*

Terminal operator's liability, *408*

Terms of sale, ocean cargo, *409*

Territorial limits, *362*

Tetrahedron, fire, *39*

Theft, *440*

Tidal floods, *108*

Tilt-up construction, *103*

Time draft, *412*

Tornadoes, *118*
   characteristics of, *119*
   damage caused by, *119*
   incidence of, *119*

Total fire in a single area, *61*

Total flooding, *237*

Total occupancy charge, *331*

Tour systems, *220*

Trading warranty, *397*

Transit, property in, *365*

Transportation and communication, instrumentalities of, *368*
Transportation insurance, *367*
Trending, *341*
Triangle of fire, *39*
Trip transit form, *367*
True hail, *120*
Tuition fees insurance, *312*
Tunnels, *368*

U

Uberrimae fidei, *393*
Uncollected litter, *52*
Underwriting, catastrophe, *124*
  commercial property, and commercial liability underwriting compared, *6*
  effect of rate on, *345*
  fidelity, *460*
Underwriting commercial inland marine insurance, *351*
Underwriting commercial ocean marine insurance, *393*
Underwriting considerations, gross earnings, *295*
Underwriting factors not included in the rates, *337*
Underwriting inland marine coverages, *364*
Underwriting package policies, *469*
Unexposed building grade, *326*, *331*
Uniform Straight Bill of Lading, *366*
United States Longshoremen's and Harbor Workers' Compensation Act, *407*
Universal Mercantile Schedule, *321*
Unmodified basic building grade, *325*
Upper flammability limit, *55*
Urban Property Protection and Reinsurance Act of 1968, *93*
Urban riots and their influence on insurance, *93*

V

Vacancy and unoccupancy clause, *259*
Valuation, inland marine, *358*
  replacement cost, *14*
Valuation clauses, *261*
Valuation problems, special, *31*
Valuation of property in transit, *358*
Value, calorific, *51*
  determination of, *12*
  landed, *415*
Value reporting clause, *267*
Valued or per diem forms, *303*
Valued policies, *15*, *264*, *359*
  ocean marine, *395*
Valued policy laws, *264*
Values at risk, determination of, for gross earnings forms, *276*
Values exposed to loss, appraising, *15*
Vandalism, incidence of, *95*
Vandalism exposure, dealing with, *96*
Vandalism or malicious mischief, *94*
Vaporization, *49*
Vendor's contingent interest, *386*
Vendor's single interest, *386*
Vendor's and vendee's interest, *386*
Veneer, brick, *137*
Vent, explosion, *85*
Venting, *56*
Vertical spread to another floor, *64*
Vessel, *401*
  pressure, *86*
Volcanoes, *106*
Vortex, *119*
Voyage policy, *414*

W

Wall charges, exterior, *324*
Walls, division, *327*
  fire, *145*

War risks, *423*

Warehouse-to-warehouse clause, *417*

Warfinger's liability, *409*

Warranties, *258*
  clear space, *259*
  crime, *446*
  implied, *393*
  inland marine, *363*

Watch service systems, *218*

Watch services, unsupervised, *219*

Water damage, *89*
  sprinkler leakage and, *88*

Water damage loss, causes of, *90*

Water Quality Insurance Syndicate (WQIS), *396*

Water spray or "fog" systems, *237*

Water supply, *232*

Waves, radiation, *59*

Weather, *152*

Weighted pure loss ratio, *342*

Welding and cutting, *43, 193*

Wet pipe system, *230, 233*
  versus dry pipe systems, *232*

Wharves, *369*

Wind floods, *108*

Windows, glass, *63*

Windstorm, builders' risk coverage and, *165*

Windstorm and hail, *110*
  age and, *152*

Write Your Own (WYO) Program, *106*